Joseph Smith

Joseph Smith

History, Methods, and Memory

Ronald O. Barney

The University of Utah Press
Salt Lake City

The Defiance House Man colophon is a registered trademark of The University of Utah Press. It is based on a four-foot-tall Ancient Puebloan pictograph (late PIII) near Glen Canyon, Utah.

LIBRARY OF CONGRESS CATALOGING-IN-PUBLICATION DATA

Names: Barney, Ronald O., 1949– author.
Title: Joseph Smith : history, methods, and memory / Ronald O. Barney.
Description: Salt Lake City : The University of Utah Press, [2020] | Includes bibliographical references and index. |
Identifiers: LCCN 2019049563 (print) | LCCN 2019049564 (ebook) | ISBN 9781607817550 (paperback) | ISBN 9781607817567 (ebook)
Subjects: LCSH: Smith, Joseph, Jr., 1805–1844. | Smith, Joseph, Jr., 1805–1844—Study and teaching. | Mormon Church—Presidents—Biography. | LCGFT: Biographies.
Classification: LCC BX8695.S6 B375 2020 (print) | LCC BX8695.S6 (ebook) | DDC 289.3092 [B]—dc23
LC record available at https://lccn.loc.gov/2019049563
LC ebook record available at https://lccn.loc.gov/2019049564

Errata and further information on this and other titles available online at UofUpress.com

Printed and bound in the United States of America.

This book is dedicated to
Steven R. Sorensen (1949–2009) and
Larry H. Miller (1944–2009)

Contents

Acknowledgments ix
Abbreviations and Editorial Method xiii
Introduction 1

Part I: Methodology

1. A New Era of Joseph Smith Study: Preparing the Ground 17
2. The Modern Study of Joseph Smith 32
3. History and Its Methods 50
4. Memory as History 65

Part II: Contextual Background

5. The Religious Times of Joseph Smith 87
6. Joseph Smith among His Contemporaries 105

Part III: Foundational Experiences

7. Joseph Smith's Declaration: His 1832 History 133
8. Order of the Priesthood: Restoration 161
9. Order of the Priesthood: Expansion 191
10. Order of the Priesthood: Organization 223

Part IV: Joseph Smith as a Man and Prophet

11. Underlying the Personality of Joseph Smith: Its Influence on His History 271
12. Underlying the Character of Joseph Smith 292
13. Underlying What Joseph Smith Thought and Taught 322
14. A Course of Revelation: Line upon Line, Precept upon Precept 348
15. Prophet, Seer, and Revelator 364

Epilogue 385
Select Bibliography 387
Index 413

Acknowledgments

It gives me pleasure to acknowledge the contributions of so many who have influenced me during my sojourn with Joseph Smith. Most of all, I am without words to express my appreciation to my wife, Marilyn Stafford Barney. She has endured for years my interests in discovering and then writing about the Mormon prophet, especially in the most recent five years as this project matured to completion. I am also grateful to my children and their spouses for their encouragement in my work: Josh and Colette Barney, Alison and Sean Pickett, and Chris and Julianna Barney.

The institutional support of the Church of Jesus Christ of Latter-day Saints, though not sponsoring or endorsing this work, has benefitted me during and after my career beyond my capacity to express appreciation. My friends and colleagues in the LDS Church History Department for a third of a century created and nurtured the kindly environment that not only spurred my interest in Joseph Smith but also provided a collegial and amicable setting in which to spend my career. These archivists, historians, and librarians have—often behind the scenes—helped create the informational basis and technological apparatus for what is now known as the modern study of Mormon history by preparing the LDS Church's vast holdings for public access. I will always be grateful to them. They include: Grant Anderson, Jeffery L. Anderson, Mary Teresa Anderson, Melvin L. Bashore, Christy L. Best, Karen S. Bolzendahl, Rachael Bowen, Jay G. Burrup, Anya Bybee, Kathy Cardon, Clint Christensen, Scott R. Christensen, Christine Cox, JoLynn Curtis, Richard H. Davis, W. Randall Dixon, Larry W. Draper, Patrick C. Dunshee, Terrence Durham, Donald L. Enders, Marie Erickson, Chad O. Foulger, Mary K. Gifford, Linda Haslam, Dale Heaps, Matthew K. Heiss, Duffy F. Hurtado, Gordon I. Irving, Alan Johnson, Jeffery O. Johnson, James L. Kimball Jr., Michael N. Landon, Jennifer L. Lund, Laurice Lundberg, Chris McAfee, Christine Marin, Andrea H. Maxfield, Brandon J. Metcalf, Blake Miller, Pauline K. Musig, Veneese Nelson, Steven L. Olsen, Kiersten Olson, Chad M. Orton, Brian D. Reeves, Glenn N. Rowe, William W. Slaughter, Steven R. Sorensen, Mark L. Staker, Brent G. Thompson, F. Annette Tucker-Matkin,

Richard E. Turley Jr., Ronald G. Watt, Vivian D. Wellman, and April Williamson. John K. Carmack and Marlin K. Jensen, who for years directed the Church History Department, not only fostered an enthusiastic setting for the study of LDS Church History, they also extended me many kindnesses and support. More recently, I have benefitted from the assistance of Keith A. Erekson, Matthew J. Grow, and Matthew S. McBride.

Having formerly been a team participant in the Joseph Smith Papers, my connections with the project's scholars from the beginning of this endeavor helped shape my thinking about the Mormon prophet in significant ways. I am grateful to Mark Ashurst-McGee, Kathryn Burnside, Jeffrey G. Cannon, Lee Ann Clanton, Gerrit J. Dirkmaat, Joseph F. Darowski, Kay Darowski, Jill M. Derr, Ronald K. Esplin, Matthew C. Godfrey, Andrew H. Hedges, Sharalyn D. Howcroft, Robin Scott Jensen, Richard L. Jensen, Dean C. Jessee, Riley M. Lorimer, Gordon A. Madsen, Larry E. Morris, Sharon E. Nielsen, Rachel Osborne, Alison Palmer, Alex D. Smith, Michael H. MacKay, R. Eric Smith, Jeffrey N. Walker, and Nathan N. Waite. For this volume I am particularly appreciative to the following project scholars for reviewing chapters of the manuscript: Matthew C. Godfrey, David W. Grua, Steven C. Harper, Robin Scott Jensen, Chase Kirkham, Elizabeth A. Kuehn, Spencer W. McBride, and Brent M. Rogers. Their generosity and scholarship provided corrections that steered me away from numerous errors and faulty interpretations. They also led me toward source documentation of which I was not aware. Val and Kathy Edwards, Doug and Janice Hill, and Jim and Angela O'Rullian also read early book chapters and provided help and insight.

Larry H. and Gail S. Miller, from their personal friendship and support of the Joseph Smith Papers Project, have been indispensable in the inauguration of the new era of Joseph Smith studies. Their influence for good in so many ways is indelible.

Others have contributed to my study of Joseph Smith and Mormon history. They are Maureen Ursenbach Beecher, Gary James Bergera, LaJean Purcell Carruth, Carol Jones, Dennis Lyman, Lachlan Mackay, D. Michael Quinn, Glenn Rawson, Ronald E. Romig, William D. Russell, William Shepherd, and Ronald W. Walker. I am also grateful to Scott Crapo, Val Edwards, J. P. Hughes, Hugh Matheson, and Jonathan Neville for sharing with me their enthusiasm about Joseph Smith.

Besides those in the LDS Church History Library, I have greatly benefited from individuals in other repositories. These include J. Michael Hunter and Ryan Lee at Brigham Young University's Harold B. Lee Library, Madison Donnelly and Liz Rogers at the University of Utah's J. Willard Marriott Library, and librarians at the Merrill-Cazier Library at Utah State University.

I am particularly indebted to my friends Curt Bench, Darius Gray, Stuart Hinckley, Brent Reber, Brian Romriell, and Dan Wotherspoon. All well read and having made their own contributions to Mormon studies, for years we have had adventurous weekly luncheon discussions about Joseph Smith and other Mormon issues. These sessions have been augmented by informed guests providing recent scholarship and diverse thinking about many aspects of the Church of Jesus Christ of Latter-day Saints. I cannot overstate the importance of having had these good people to criticize my thinking about the Mormon prophet.

Lastly, I am grateful to Tom Krause, Patrick Hadley, and Jessica Booth of the University of Utah Press for their assistance in bringing this book to fruition. I am especially appreciative to Beth O. Anderson for her careful and comprehensive edit of the manuscript.

Abbreviations and Editorial Method

Abbreviations

Scriptural references—including the Bible and the Mormon textual authorities of the Book of Mormon, Doctrine and Covenants, and the Pearl of Great Price—are abbreviated according to convention, such as Gen. for Genesis; Deut. for Deuteronomy; Matt. for Matthew; Rev. for Revelation; 2 Ne. for 2 Nephi; Abr. for Abraham; D&C for Doctrine and Covenants.

Joseph Smith Papers (Full Citations appear in Bibliography)

JSP, A1 *The Joseph Smith Papers, Administrative Records, Council of Fifty Minutes, March 1844–January 1846.*

JSP, D1 *The Joseph Smith Papers, Documents, Volume 1: July 1828–June 1831.*

JSP, D2 *The Joseph Smith Papers, Documents, Volume 2: July 1831–January 1833.*

JSP, D3 *The Joseph Smith Papers, Documents, Volume 3: February 1833–March 1834.*

JSP, D4 *The Joseph Smith Papers, Documents, Volume 4: April 1834–September 1835.*

JSP, D5 *The Joseph Smith Papers, Documents, Volume 5, October 1835–January 1838.*

JSP, D6 *The Joseph Smith Papers, Documents, Volume 6, February 1838–August 1839.*

JSP, D7 *The Joseph Smith Papers, Documents, Volume 7, September 1839–January 1841.*

JSP, H1 *The Joseph Smith Papers, Histories, Volume 1: Joseph Smith Histories, 1832–1844.*

JSP, H2 *The Joseph Smith Papers, Histories, Volume 2: Assigned Histories, 1831–1847.*

JSP, J1 *The Joseph Smith Papers, Journals, Volume 1: 1832–1839.*

JSP, J2 *The Joseph Smith Papers, Journals, Volume 2: December 1841–April 1843.*

JSP, J3 *The Joseph Smith Papers, Journals, Volume 3: May 1843–June 1844.*

JSP, R1 *The Joseph Smith Papers, Revelations and Translations, Volume 1: Manuscript Revelation Books.*

JSP, R2 *The Joseph Smith Papers, Revelations and Translations, Volume 2: Published Revelations.*

JSP, R3 *The Joseph Smith Papers, Revelations and Translations, Volume 3: Part 1 and Part 2, Printer's Manuscript of the Book of Mormon.*

JSP, R4 *The Joseph Smith Papers, Revelations and Translation, Volume 4: Book of Abraham and Related Manuscripts.*

Editorial Method

The primacy of the historical record as it is rendered is accentuated in this work. That is, what is represented is prepared by transcription, as best as possible, to convey the intent of those who produced the original materials. Given the frequency of use of material from *The Joseph Smith Papers*, which has been informed by the recommendations of the Association of Documentary Editing, their reasoned editorial conventions are applied in this work.[1] *The Joseph Smith Papers* and all in the documentary editing world have been influenced by the work of Mary-Jo Kline.[2]

Because of the frequency of entries from *The Joseph Smith Papers*, transcription of documentary material from that work generally follows the model used by their editors:

> The approach to transcription employed in *The Joseph Smith Papers* is a conservative style of what is known as "expanded transcription." The transcripts render most words letter by letter as accurately as possible, preserving the exact spelling of the originals. This includes incomplete words, variant spellings of personal names, repeated words, and idiosyncratic grammatical constructions.... Canceled words are typographically rendered with the strikethrough bar, while inserted words are enclosed within angle brackets.[3]

Thus, when quoting from *The Joseph Smith Papers* there are no uses of [*sic*] to indicate original rendering. Spelling is uncorrected, unless clarified for understanding.

[Brackets] generally represent this author's insertions, unless otherwise noted.

<Angle brackets> indicate insertions by the original author in the original text.

1. See "Editorial Method" in the introduction to *JSP, J1*: lvix–lxvi.
2. See Mary–Jo Kline and Susan Holbrook Perdue, "Editorial Texts Requiring Symbols or Textual Annotation," in *A Guide to Documentary Editing*, 3rd edition (Charlottesville, VA: University of Virginia Press, 2008).
3. *JSP, D3*:xxxiv.

~~Strikeouts~~ or ~~cancelled words~~ in the original text are thus rendered.

Underlined words in the original text are thus rendered.

Superscript words or numbers in the original text are thus rendered.

Some text, cumbersome as represented in *The Joseph Smith Papers'* standard transcription symbols, is presented in modern format called clear text, or transformed into modernized prose. When used, clear text is noted in the footnote.

Introduction

"Have we not had a prophet among us?"[1] The apparently earnest query of a Philadelphia editor to his readers in May 1861 at a moment of American horror had implications even for those roughing it out in the Great Basin. A month after Confederate artillery fired upon the military citadel at Fort Sumter, South Carolina, on April 12, 1861, a protracted and eviscerating uncivil war had commenced between the Southern and Northern states of America. The event also fired the imaginations of the Mormons in Utah who remembered the prophetic words of their martyred prophet, Joseph Smith,[2] given on Christmas day in 1832 that predicted such a clash.[3] JS, at the age of twenty-seven, puzzled and contemplating the mounting crisis of sectionalism currently occupying the country's government leaders and Americans at large, inquired of God to settle his mind. The "Nullification Crisis" that dominated for months the news and the hearts of those on the eastern seaboard also troubled JS's thinking as he contemplated

1. "A Mormon Prophecy," *Philadelphia Sunday Mercury*, May 5, 1861, facsimile in Robert J. Woodford, "The Historical Development of the Doctrine and Covenants" (PhD diss., Brigham Young University, 1974), 1110.
2. Because of the frequency of reference to Joseph Smith throughout this study, he will be referred to hereafter as the abbreviated JS. This is also the nomenclature of referral to Joseph Smith employed by the editors of the Joseph Smith Papers. The convention, explained in the *Chicago Manual of Style* (16th ed.), replaces the repeated use of the personal designations—Joseph, Smith, Joseph Smith—which are potentially loaded with categorization of either reverence or caution. Acronyms have been widely used in biographical works about others, such as FDR, JFK, and MLK. The use of the JS abbreviation should not be construed as diminishing in any way the warranted respect due to the founding father of Mormonism.
3. The Civil War prophecy, as it came to be known, first appeared in print in 1851 in Liverpool when Franklin D. Richards, who led the Mormons' British Mission, published it as part of the Pearl of Great Price. The revelation circulated prior to the war among the Saints by way of copies being made by missionaries and others, as well as through sermons of church leaders. See Woodford, "The Historical Development of the Doctrine and Covenants," 1104–9.

how the divide might affect the timeline of Jesus's Second Coming and the restoration of the gospel that the young prophet initiated a dozen years earlier. Dictating to his clerk, he articulated a revelation from Jesus Christ: "Verily thus saith the Lord concerning the wars that will shortly come to pass begining at the rebellion of South Carolina which will eventually terminate in the death & misery of many Souls[,] & the days will <come> that war will be poured out upon all nations begining at this place."[4] The divine insight was unlike most others that he uttered. Usually directed with church purposes as instructions for the church laity in their particular journeys of faith and struggle, JS's revelations were generally idiosyncratic to members of The Church of Jesus Christ of Latter-day Saints, hereafter also called the LDS Church. But the revelation from Jesus this time foretold an ominous outcome for a much larger sector of God's children. The "inhabitants of the earth" were to soon "feel the wrath & indignation & chastning hand of an Almighty God."[5] Though the conflict outlived the prophet, the Mormons never forgot the impending forecast of gloom or the evidence of JS's divine appointment.

The rise of their young prophet after 1830 with his attendant claims caught the attention of enough of the population that many of the reading public were at least generally aware of the outline and perceived downfall of Mormonism. Notwithstanding the numerous failures of the Saints to acquire sustainable status in America, as Mormonism gained strength from abroad and became a federal issue, Mormon-watching entered the public square. A month after Sumter, the *Philadelphia Sunday Mercury*'s editor, with the religion's 1851 Pearl of Great Price in hand—containing JS's Christmas 1832 prophecy—speculated: "In view of our present troubles, the prediction seems to be in progress of fulfilment, whether Joe Smith was a humbug or not." The editor then printed the text of what is now known within the faith as Doctrine and Covenants 87, one of JS's published revelations. Recognizing the particulars of JS's prophetic utterance, the editor concluded: "The war began in South Carolina. Insurrections of slavery are already dreaded. Famine will certainly afflict some Southern communities. The interference of Great Britain, on account of the want of cotton, is not improbable, if the war is protracted. In the meantime, a general war in Europe appears to be imminent. Have we not had a prophet among us?"[6] Though nothing of im-

4. Joseph Smith, Revelations and Translations, December 25, 1832, Manuscript Revelations Books, *JSP, R1*:224 [D&C 87:1–2 (1981)]. JS publicly reiterated the prophecy at other times, see Journal, April 2, 1843, *JSP, J2*:324–25. (Hereafter, reference to the *Joseph Smith Papers* volumes will appear in shortened form, as shown in the front matter "Abbreviations" section. See the bibliography for full citations.)

5. Joseph Smith, Revelations and Translations, December 25, 1832, Manuscript Revelations Books, *JSP, R1*:225 [D&C 87:6 (1981)].

6. "A Mormon Prophecy," *Philadelphia Sunday Mercury*. See the full background of the revelation, including a list of the earliest written and printed copies of the revelation, in

port happened to Mormonism due to the recognition, the revelation continues to buttress JS's credibility among his followers who still ask the same question. And while JS has never been America's prophet, he and the modern presence of his followers and their influence forces attention to his antebellum life.

Objective of *Joseph Smith: History, Methods, and Memory*

JS's relevance to American religious history has generally been little more than a footnote. But recent availability of the bulk of the historical documentation associated with his life, along with significant research into his ministry in the past half century or so, has stimulated enthusiasm for JS studies. The objective of this work is to present a source-driven portrait of important aspects of JS's life based on extant primary records, a significant portion of which have only been readily available since publication of the *Joseph Smith Papers*. As will be emphasized throughout the study, the documentary record serves as both an enabler and constrictor framing the breadth and limitations of what can and, to a degree, what cannot be said about the Mormon prophet. The early chapters are designed to emphasize the rudiments of historiographical application that are necessary in appraising his life. This is due, in part, to past abuse of historical methodology by some writers in evaluating JS, even professionals, evidenced by laxity in qualifying sources upon which they based their assertions. This is true among both defenders and detractors. Other factors complicate how Mormon history has been disseminated. Matters of adherence and conformity to church culture, surface-level understanding of its sacred texts, and advocacy of Christian living has previously characterized church curriculum; all designed to maintain the status quo by fostering an environment of spirituality and orthodoxy without tackling the difficult matters affecting faith. The sector of Mormon adherents and others who demand more open discussions about Mormon origins require reminders of historiography and explanations of JS that until of late have been hard to come by.

This work is an attempt to reemphasize the techniques refined for generations by the historical community that may help readers of the Mormon past to better negotiate the conflicted historical record. Thus, the means of staging the story in this volume has a scholarly tone and methodology presented in modern academic garb to qualify its credibility. However, the issues addressed are so fundamental that despite the use from time to time of academic dialogue, all interested in JS should recognize the necessity of treating the primary themes in a manner other than simply devotional or critical formulations. The reader will find portions of the book that evaluate at length and depth matters central to JS

Woodford, "Historical Development of the Doctrine and Covenants," 1104–26. Orson Pratt also sent a copy of the prophecy to the *New York Times*, which they duly published on July 2, 1861.

and the foundations of the faith. Some of the interpretations herein are unique, while some material is augmented from the work of others. The composite is meant to serve as just one attempt to show JS in the light of more recently accessible historical records that have, in some ways, previously lain in the shadows.

The Man Joseph Smith

The woodlands of the American Northeast in the first decade of the nineteenth century, where men and women of the soil had to rely on God to temper the elements and the landscape for their survival, was the ubiquitous backdrop for JS in his youth. Both sides of his family had cyclically relocated northward from their Massachusetts and Connecticut origins in the previous century. Born in Topsfield, Massachusetts in 1771, Joseph Smith Sr. became part of the pattern as he arrived at the age of majority. In 1796, after removal to Tunbridge, Vermont, he married Lucy Mack, born in 1775 in Gilsum, New Hampshire. They had eleven children. Their first, born about 1797, died without being identified in civil records. Ten children—seven boys and three girls—followed, with the youngest named Lucy after her mother, born in 1821. JS Jr. was the third child, born in Sharon, Vermont, in 1805. Only a generation past the American revolutionary period, the frontier lowborn had to manipulate the environment by hope and hard work. The attendance of one of their boys, eleven-year-old Hyrum, in the Moor's Charity School (connected with Dartmouth College) in Lebanon, New Hampshire, indicated a progressive determination in the family. However, the Smiths found themselves less than their circumstances and relocated from eastern Vermont/western New Hampshire to western New York where they landed in 1816. They settled in a region that had been opened by land speculators in the previous decade, offering opportunity for those with a familial workforce to clear and plant the land. Coincidentally, the village of Palmyra, New York, just north of their farm, witnessed a rush of civilization as American novice entrepreneurs and engineers plotted a mighty canal through the town to connect the Hudson River to Lake Erie, and consequently America's interior. The year after the Smiths arrived, work began on the canal, completed eight years later in 1825. Thereafter, the trappings of cultural advancement lured the Smiths and they looked for better things.

JS's parents, though of different devotions, were religious people and well aware of the appeals of religious contenders at the time. The King James Bible was a family staple.[7] JS, himself, was clearly a spiritually minded boy and, as he later stated, when he was about twelve "my mind became seriously imprest with regard to the all importent concerns ~~of~~ for the wellfare of my immortal Soul."

7. Because JS used the King James Version of the Bible throughout his life, despite some misgivings he held about its accuracy, citations throughout this book reference the KJV.

Plying the scriptures with which he was apparently familiar, he then began comparison of what he read with his "intimate acquaintance with those of different denominations" and by the age of about fourteen had determined none of the local churches measured up to his expectations. The dissonance and his own weak disposition drove him, as he recounted in 1832, to cry "unto the Lord for mercy for there was none else to whom I could go." In response, "a piller of ~~fire~~ light above the brightness of the sun at noon day come down from above and rested upon me and I was filled with the spirit of god and the <Lord> opened the heavens upon me and I saw the Lord and he spake unto me saying Joseph <my son> thy sins are forgiven thee."[8] Though nothing presently known came of the incident at the time, in three years another heavenly manifestation enveloped JS with the appearance of a messenger who told him that nearby lay a centuries-old artifact that contained a religious record describing the ancient inhabitants of the Western Hemisphere. Four years later he acquired what he described as gold plates. The story he later told of his acquisition of the plates and their subsequent "translation" into English from "reformed Egyptian" glyphs became the predominant story of early Mormonism. The volume he produced in 1830, the Book of Mormon, proved to be the catalyst that pulled thousands into his growing fold of followers. Just weeks later, with several dozen who believed him, he organized the Church of Christ on April 6 in Fayette Township, New York.

What happened thereafter became one of the notable, if controversial, religious enterprises in nineteenth-century America. JS directed the fledgling church by way of initiating his own slant to the religious establishment that surrounded him. He boldly stated that those innovations came from revelations he received from Jesus Christ. Besides the Book of Mormon, he accumulated the texts of the subsequent revelations he received that together signified the role he understood to be his unique province in preparation of the Lord's Second Advent: creating and preparing a people to receive Christ through the process of revelation. Though hundreds and then thousands gathered to JS's call, due to the vigorous and determined missionary force of Mormon elders, the movement met resistance from the outset. Opposition turned to persecution and the Mormons, as they came to be called, were forced from western New York to the Ohio Western Reserve where they built a city and a temple. They even attempted to create a satellite in western Missouri in 1831. Branches sprouted elsewhere in many locales where the missionaries labored. While much progress prevailed, outside pressures and internal dissension eventually pushed JS and the Mormons from Ohio and western Missouri to northwestern Missouri. But they were again rousted from any tranquility they might have had and were

8. Joseph Smith, Histories, circa summer 1832, *JSP, H1*:12–13. A discussion of the 1832 History and its account of the First Vision is addressed in Chapter 7.

driven eastward across the Mississippi River to Hancock County, Illinois. There Mormonism expanded according to JS's design, with establishment of the significant municipality—Nauvoo—and its grand temple. But he could never elude the hatred from without and within by those threatened by everything he did and represented. Local machinations conspired to eliminate him, which materialized on the afternoon of June 27, 1844, when a vigilante force stormed the jail that held him in Carthage, Illinois, and shot him to death, along with his brother Hyrum.

Early Portrayal of Joseph Smith's Life: *History of the Church*

Much has been written thereafter to describe the phenomenon of JS and his church. He has been characterized as prophet-hero by his people and imposter-villain by those who loathe him and his followers. That polemical world, however, casts the entire story in conflict with too much sympathy here or too much condemnation there. Because of the things that JS claimed, that polar atmosphere will never fade. However, we are now in position, from the perch of the present and all that has been learned about him in the past two generations, to reevaluate where the story of JS fits into what is now known about his environment and what became of Mormonism. The cumulative information gathered allows those today a window into his life that has matured in the twenty-first century. A reexamination is not only now plausible, it is necessary. It is a case of defining what has been with what now is.

In the 175 years since JS's death in 1844, the substance of what became the general profile of JS was, for most interested parties, primarily B.H. Roberts's edit of the six-volume *History of the Church of Jesus Christ of Latter-day Saints*, printed 1902–1912.[9] Roberts, an English convert as a boy who rose to become an assistant LDS Church historian and member of the church's First Council of Seventy—a church general authority—recognized the void among the Saints in their then current understanding of the prophet.

The historical antecedents for the *History of the Church* stemmed from a significant endeavor by JS and his clerks that began six years before the prophet's death. After an aborted attempt in 1832 to craft an account of his experiences with the divine, by 1838 JS recognized the necessity of preparing an account of Mormonism that included his life. On April 9, 1838, JS and Sidney Rigdon appealed to John Whitmer, former church historian who had separated from Mormon-

9. Joseph Smith, *History of the Church of Jesus Christ of Latter-day Saints, Period I. History of Joseph Smith, the Prophet, by Himself*, ed. Brigham H. Roberts, 2nd ed., rev., 7 vols. (Salt Lake City: The Church of Jesus Christ of Latter-day Saints, 1932–1951). A seventh volume, the "Apostolic Interregnum" between JS and Brigham Young's administrations was published in 1932. See Dean Jessee's overview of Roberts's work on the *History*, Dean C. Jessee, "The Reliability of Joseph Smith's History," *Journal of Mormon History* 3 (1976): 41–45.

ism the previous year, for the return of the history he had written to that time. Whitmer ignored their request. Recognizing then that what had been prepared previously with a design to portray Mormonism was inadequate, JS mounted an alternative. Using Sidney Rigdon and George W. Robinson as scribes, he initiated a new historical saga.[10] In what turned out to be a JS/Rigdon endeavor, their effort produced text that, unfortunately, does not survive. With significant interruptions to JS's intent to create a narrative, which included his incarceration over the winter of 1838–1839 in the jail at Liberty, Missouri, JS finally returned to the story in 1839.[11] (Because of the writing initiatives introduced in 1838 and 1839 to begin the history, for ease of reference the whole will be designated in this work as JS's 1838/39 history, though it was not completed until 1856.) First known in publication as the "History of Joseph Smith," the chronicle appeared serially 1842–1858 in the LDS Church's periodicals, the *Times and Seasons* and *Deseret News*.[12] Mormon leaders in Great Britain republished the serialization 1842–1863 in their *Latter Day Saints' Millennial Star*.

Even though the endeavor does not measure up to modern historiographical standards, the nearly twenty-year effort to prepare JS's history is one of the most remarkable Mormon achievements of the nineteenth-century church. Besides detailing JS's ministry, restoring life to a memory then held by only a handful who still remembered him, Roberts's *History of the Church* thereafter provided an overview of the church's foundational theology, doctrines, polity, character, and means of sustainability as created by the prophet. An enduring tradition had been created. Despite its obscurity in non-Mormon academic circles, its mid-century production ranks as a major historiographical presentation of religious expression in antebellum America. While modern critics have identified historical conventions used by the *History of the Church*'s nineteenth-century compilers that do not pass muster via academic standards today, those who prepared the record created for its time a monumental religious chronicle. And given how much of modern Mormonism was derived from Roberts's *History of the Church*,

10. Smith, Histories, Historical Introduction to "Whitmer, History, 1831–circa 1847," *JSP, H2*:9–10. For a general introduction to the creation of JS's history, which he initiated in 1838, through its eventual serialized publication in the *Times and Seasons* and *Deseret News*, see Dan Vogel's edit of the *History of Joseph Smith and the Church of Jesus Christ of Latter-day Saints: A Source- and Text-Critical Edition*, 8 vols. (Salt Lake City: Smith-Pettit Foundation, 2015), 1:x–xxv.

11. *See Joseph Smith Papers* editors' Historical Introduction to "History Drafts, 1838–circa 1841," in Smith, Histories, *JSP, H1*:192–202.

12. See the publications' history in Vogel, *History of Joseph Smith*, 1:cix–cxx. See also Dean C. Jessee, "The Writing of Joseph Smith's History" *BYU Studies* 11, no. 4 (Summer 1971): 439–74; and Jessee, "Reliability of Joseph Smith's History," 23–46. As the serialization of the "History of Joseph Smith" continued in the *Deseret News* from its origin in the *Times and Seasons*, the title of the series was changed to the "Life of Joseph Smith."

his compilation may, besides the LDS Church's sacred texts both ancient and modern, be the most important publication of twentieth-century Mormonism.[13]

That said, the *History of the Church* and its written and published antecedents, limit in many ways proper understanding of what has often been supposed to be JS's thinking and means of conveying his own perceptions. Most modern observers do not recognize that, while initiated by JS, the *History of the Church* was in its origin the enterprise of JS's clerks. As Dean C. Jessee—who has done more than any individual to represent JS in his historical context—revealed, "Joseph Smith did little of the actual writing himself." Thus, modern readers must understand that "a substantial number of Joseph's writings, including almost the entire content of his journals after 1836, were the product of other men's minds."[14] JS simply never had time to attend to the chronicle given the significant complications of his life. Thus, the collaborative effort of his well-meaning clerks became the primary mechanism for the content and nature of what was presented. Without experience at producing history and with no precedent upon which to assemble the historical materials, JS's clerks settled upon a strategy where, as Jessee stated, JS's life was presented in a "daily narrative based upon diaries kept by himself and his clerks, with the insertion of pertinent information from church periodicals, minute and record books of church and civic organizations, letters and documents kept on file, and news of current world happenings."[15] The materials were formatted to read as if they were prepared by JS himself, in the first person. While what he did is represented in the narrative, the account suggests his direct imprimatur as the author of the text, which

13. Brigham Young University professor Arnold K. Garr, published in 2002 a survey gleaned from 303 Mormon "scholars who teach, research, and write in the field of Mormonism." They were asked, "Excluding the scriptures, which would you consider the three most important books written by Latter-day Saint authors about Mormonism" in the categories of fiction, inspiration, devotion, biography, history, and doctrine. See Arnold K. Garr, "Which Are the Most Important Mormon Books" *BYU Studies* 41, no. 3 (2002): 35–47. Dominated by responses from LDS Church Education System employees, Roberts's *History of the Church* earned top place by the vast majority of respondents in the category of history. Further emphasizing its dominant influence, "By an overwhelming margin they selected *Teachings of the Prophet Joseph Smith* as the most important non-scriptural volume" ever published in Mormondom. That publication, printed in 1938 by Joseph Fielding Smith, primarily consisted of excerpts from Roberts's *History of the Church*, some considerably redacted. Joseph Fielding Smith, comp., *Teachings of the Prophet Joseph Smith* (1938; repr., Salt Lake City: Deseret Book, 1977. It should be noted that other surveys regarding Mormon history of scholarly respondents do not give such credence to Roberts's *History of the Church*.

14. Jessee, "Writing of Joseph Smith's History," 440; Dean C. Jessee, "Sources for the Study of Joseph Smith," in *Mormon Americana: A Guide to Sources and Collections in the United States*, ed. David J. Whittaker (Provo, UT: BYU Studies, 1995), 16.

15. Jessee, "Reliability of Joseph Smith's History," 34.

is misleading and has led to assumptions about him that are not warranted.[16] Indeed, even in such consequential matters as JS's First Vision and the story behind the coming forth of the Book of Mormon, the evidence suggests his clerks may have affected the narrative more than has been previously allowed.[17]

During the twentieth century, the *History of the Church* apparently satisfied interest in JS for most LDS Church purposes. But in the last half of the twentieth century, along with a heightened interest in JS and Mormon beginnings, the rise of the information age provided unprecedented access to materials not included in the *History* that provoked a reinvestigation of the Mormon past. Interest in Mormon beginnings coincided with development of the internet and all that it offered informationally, providing access to material about Mormon origins previously unavailable. One of the results of the advance of accessible data is recognition that the mid-nineteenth-century portrayal of JS's life, noteworthy as it was for its time, cannot continue as the primary means to understand and appreciate his life. This is anathema to many traditionalists. But as will be exhibited in what follows, the recent surge of academic preparation by church scholars and others of the most salient documentary materials regarding JS, and contextualization of the same, will inevitably supplant the limited resources previously available.

A New Era of the Study of Joseph Smith

Historical endeavors among Mormon scholars in the past generation or so have generally not been well received by LDS Church leaders or the laity. The spirit of revisionism has aroused suspicion that there may be an underlying intent in what some *believing* scholars have written to diminish the time-honored traditions held regarding Mormonism's first prophet. The wariness, ironically, is born of information increasingly made available from access to JS materials by the LDS Church itself. Interpretations of the information, also used by detractors to continue their criticisms of JS, has been unsettling to some of those raised before and in the information age. The stories about JS that the traditionalists heard in Sunday School and LDS seminary—based upon church curriculum, dependent on and derived mostly from the *History of the Church*—do not measure up to newly uncovered documentation on public display in the digital environment. For some today, the encounter with the origins of Mormonism that varies from conventions on which they were raised, along with certain prominent societal and cultural stances exhibited by the modern LDS Church, has

16. See Ibid. for Jessee's description of how the methodology influenced the finished product.
17. See the larger discussion of how JS's clerks/historians influenced the writing of his history in Chapter 4 of this work.

shattered worldviews born in the calm of standardized belief and behavior. A natural consequence of the situation has been the rise of a generation that has been exposed to documentation and interpretation of information that, frankly, have made the LDS Church, its leaders, and teachers look culpable in how it previously delivered its past. Those familiar with modern trends within the faith recognize that as the windows of history have further been opened there has been a concurrent rise in concerns by sectors within Mormonism about how JS has historically been made public by church advocates.[18]

Those troubled, who base their angst on their belief that they have been misled by the church, generally fail to recognize that newly presented materials that differ from what they heard during their upbringing have been available in *church-produced publications* for generations! While it is true that the matters provoking the discontent today were not presented in Mormon Primary, Sunday School, or seminary classwork, they have generally been known by those who have taken the trouble to keep pace with what was known of Mormon origins. Those dismayed in 1945, for example, when Fawn M. Brodie's critical biography of *No Man Knows My History* rocked their world,[19] may not have felt threatened had they read the extensive and credible work of Dr. Francis W. Kirkham in his *New Witness for Christ in America*, published by a church press three years earlier in 1942.[20] (A companion volume was published in 1951.) Many of the issues raised by Brodie at the time that challenged Mormon tradition had already been addressed and treated in Kirkham's work.

Some of the discord stems from what appear to be contradictions to previous Mormon portrayals of history uncovered or revised in the past generation. For instance, evidence that JS was, for sustenance and financial gain, a "money digger" and that he used a "seerstone," one of his scrying tools, in translating the Book of Mormon and in the reception of some of his revelations, were once generally considered anti-Mormon allegations. Acknowledgment of these features of JS's life by the LDS Church in its twenty-first-century publications has been difficult for some believers to reconcile. Once appreciation for JS's incremental growth and maturation has been thoroughly explained in its proper milieu, where he "outgrew" to some degree the culture in which he had been raised, the course of his life with which we are now better prepared to portray becomes

18. See, for example, LDS Church historian Marlin K. Jensen's appraisal of circumstances in 2012 in: https://www.reuters.com/article/us-mormonchurch/special-report-mormonism-besieged-by-the-modern-age-idUSTRE80T1CM20120131. Jensen shepherded production of the *Joseph Smith Papers* and many other advances in the study of Mormon history during his tenure as church historian, 2005–2012, to better contextualize the origins of the faith for church members.

19. Fawn M. Brodie, *No Man Knows My History: The Life of Joseph Smith*, 2nd ed. (New York: Alfred A. Knopf, 1979).

20. Francis W. Kirkham, *A New Witness for Christ in America: The Book of Mormon* (Independence, MO: Zion's Printing and Publishing, 1942).

more understandable.[21] Consequently, much of the fear of some Mormons regarding church origins has been supplanted with more informed perspectives that mitigate, for some, former concerns. The interpretations are also more suitable for interested non-Mormons desiring to comprehend the faith. There is no quick resolution to many of the disputes originating from the nineteenth-century historical record, but we are in a better situation at present than were our forebears to grasp Mormon beginnings and how the religion has been delivered through the years.

My "Cards on the Table"

It should be clear at the outset that in attempting to identify and reappraise salient matters needed to understand JS, I am compliant with the noted historian Arnold Toynbee's first requirement of historians, putting my "cards on the table."[22] Besides being a practicing Mormon, I was for thirty-four years employed by the LDS Church in its Church History Department as an archivist/historian and documentary editor. It is there that I became acquainted with the documents and issues surrounding JS's life. Numerous other serious and competent investigators of Mormonism had already seeded the field, indeed having already done the bulk of the preparatory pick and shovel work, creating an environment for discovery impossible to ignore. Critics have also fostered the study of JS by their intense scrutiny of aspects of the prophet's life, ultimately resulting in enlarged perspectives. The result of those scholarly believers' and detractors' work has been the rise and expansion of an engaging culture of openness and exploration that has not waned.

The work presented here results from my own evolving perspectives on JS and Mormon history. As credible, and some not so credible, information became more widely available in the past half century, the worldviews of many informed readers were altered. Many have written about their circumstances and challenges in discovering previously suppressed and unavailable documentation. Some have been reinforced by what they have learned. Others have been put off by the reluctance of the LDS Church to confront its past and the attendant historical record. In my own experience, the early 1980s—affected in part by Mark Hofmann's notorious forgeries—forced my reevaluation of JS and Mormon beginnings. Despite the temporary challenge to Mormonism by Hofmann's deception, the resulting surge in scholarly work on matters that Hofmann raised has benefitted endeavors to understand the faith and better equipped the scholarly community to handle the challenges of the past.

21. Richard L. Bushman, *Joseph Smith and the Beginnings of Mormonism* (Urbana, IL: University of Illinois Press, 1984), 7.

22. Arnold J. Toynbee, *Toynbee on Toynbee: A Conversation between Arnold J. Toynbee and G. R. Urban* (New York: Oxford University Press, 1974), 12.

It is difficult to properly scrutinize the multiple viewpoints that influence not only how the historical record was created but also how it is best represented. That varies widely depending on the intention of the interpreter. From a sympathetic angle, the writer who at least attempts to be somewhat objective, after having become aware of controversial matters in the extant documentation, always has difficulty in presenting it satisfactorily to the several audiences who have interest in what is being argued. Richard L. Bushman, whose narratives of JS's life are to date among the most well informed and best presented, described his own determination to handle the inevitable disparity between what the historical record demands and what the reader expects. After writing two biographies of JS, Bushman explained how he viewed the range of his readers' anticipations when discussing controversial matters of fact and belief: "The questions and doubts of the critics are in the minds of the believers too, right along with their faith." Both groups "know how the story looks to the faithful, and they also know how it looks to the skeptics." For the historian to properly represent the circumstance, he stated, requires emphasis on what the documentary record demands and allows.[23] The reader then becomes the arbiter of how successful the writer has been in organizing and displaying the history. That ideal, limited as it is to resolve all controversies, has prompted my approach.

Another required acknowledgment at the beginning of this review of JS's lifetime is necessary. Despite decades of serious investigation into JS's ministry I admit to being wholly unfit to prepare an actual *biography*—a life study—of JS. Besides the incomplete documentary record, his massive persona and accomplishment transcends the capacity of most individuals to comprehend and then explicate. JS operated in a realm that it is difficult for me even to imagine. When he said at the end of his life "no man knows my hist[ory],"[24] my view is that he must be taken as representing the reality of how his style and manner of communication limit what can be known about him. The reality exists that JS never desired to be completely known, even if he tried to explain himself and what he knew from time to time. As noted poet, novelist, and cultural critic Wendell Berry reminded us, "even the most inspired are limited in what they can tell of what they know."[25] Along with appreciating the enlarged scope of who JS was and what he did, given his disposition to keep much that he thought

23. Richard Lyman Bushman, *Believing History: Latter-day Saint Essays*, ed. Reid L. Neilson and Jed Woodworth (New York: Columbia University Press, 2007), 280, 281.
24. Smith, Sermon, April 7, 1844, Thomas Bullock, scribe, Historian's Office General Church Minutes, 1839–1877, CR 100 318, box 1, folder 20, item 4, 22, Church History Library, The Church of Jesus Christ of Latter-day Saints, Salt Lake City, Utah (hereafter CHL). A copy is available online in digital form accessed from the CHL catalog.
25. Wendell Berry, "The Burden of the Gospels: An Unconfident Reader," *Christian Century*, September 20, 2005, 26–27.

and experienced to himself, it is especially daunting when attempting to convey something substantive checked by the surviving though incomplete historical sources.

Yale literary scholar Harold Bloom lauded JS's facility with what he called the prophet's "religion-making imagination."[26] That view, however, is not widely shared. JS's antagonists have made it difficult to consider him without their dampening shroud overlaying the faith. I argue, however, it is the body of his teachings, his charismatic persona, capacity to inspire his followers, his religious credentials, and remarkable durability that best expose his capacities and gifts. The stance of empirical scrutiny insisted by many, i.e., staying aloof from devotional interpretations, has side effects in the pursuit of understanding. The inability to explain religious sensibilities that continue to move Mormons and other adherents of JS to occupy the pews on Sunday disallows a major feature of how the prophet's enduring message and religious innovations capture a growing segment of the population. By their own confessions, the faithful are stirred by emotion and feelings—the influences of the "Spirit"—that do not have much cachet in skeptical and scholarly circles these days. The well informed of that faith-driven minority segment of the population has produced a body of literature steeped in the primacy of JS's revelations that must be appreciated for how it continues to feed and nurture those committed to the church/es JS founded. Their writings have elaborated on the nuances and practicality of religious application derived from his teachings that capture, at least in their minds, the religious mystery upon which the perpetuation of the faith is based. And though there is abundant evidence of exaggeration and speculation through the years by some of JS's followers who have tried to make him more than the documentation allows, their failings are probably proportional to those who deprive him of the divine that he claimed and evidenced.

Lastly, everyone who has or once had an interest in JS, has informed themselves about him to the degree that they have taken a position about him. I recognize that my attempt to inform will be received in a number of ways by a diverse audience that has already made decisions about his character, personality, credibility, and authenticity. Truly, this is a fool's errand with no hope of solving JS's "Prophet Puzzle," as described by scholar of Mormonism Jan Shipps in 1974.[27] But it represents an attempt to reconcile a number of the disparities that cloud an understanding of features of his life at present.

26. Harold Bloom, *The American Religion: The Emergence of the Post-Christian Nation* (New York: Simon and Schuster, 1992), 109.
27. Jan Shipps, "The Prophet Puzzle: Suggestions Leading toward a More Comprehensive Interpretation of Joseph Smith," *Journal of Mormon History* 1 (1974).

PART I

Methodology

CHAPTER 1

A New Era of Joseph Smith Study

Preparing the Ground

Daryl Chase, director of the LDS Church Institute of Religion adjacent to the Utah State Agricultural College (later Utah State University) in Logan, Utah, prepared a brief biography of JS in 1944 to commemorate the one hundredth anniversary of the prophet's death. Given the vague status at the time of JS studies, he wrote that he hoped for a day when a well-equipped scholar with designs to write a substantive biography of JS would have "access to *all* the manuscript materials which are now gathered in American libraries and archives dealing with Joseph Smith and the rise of Mormonism." Further, that scholar needed to "search patiently for the old letters and journals which are still to be found in private homes and out-of-the-way places" that portray the Mormon prophet.[1] It took a generation, but by the time I joined the staff of the LDS Church Historical (now History) Department in Salt Lake City in late 1977, a register for their Joseph Smith Collection and the gathering of materials it represented had been available for scholarly research for four years. A multitude of complementary records in other repositories and collections regarding JS had been identified, augmenting the endeavor, making available *most* of the essential records about the man that presently survive.

The published register of the Joseph Smith Collection, produced in 1973 by one of the LDS Church's first professional archivists, Jeffery O. Johnson, with the "scope and content" of the collection prepared by Ronald K. Esplin (then a budding scholar who would leave a significant imprint on the study of JS), explained how the papers associated with JS's life were organized. The register included several series categorizing JS's papers: diaries (journals), correspondence, addresses, legal and financial papers, and a number of ephemeral records. Housed

1. Daryl Chase, *Joseph the Prophet: As He Lives in the Hearts of His People* (Salt Lake City: Deseret Book, 1944), 8. Chase later served as president of Utah State University for fourteen years.

in seven Hollinger boxes—five-inch-wide boxes made of cardboard-like material, acid and lignin free, and buffered with calcium carbonate to protect the documents from deterioration—the original documents were kept then in the second-floor vault in the east wing of the twenty-eight-story LDS Church Office Building completed in 1972.[2] Successor to the Church Historian's Office in the nearby Church Administration Building since 1917, the department professionalized concurrent to its new location.

The Joseph Smith Collection, a digital copy of which is now available online in the LDS Church History catalog,[3] exceeded in importance its comparatively small linear footage on the archival shelf. With several other seminal documents of the restoration, including nearly 30 percent of the surviving text of the original Book of Mormon manuscript and the handwritten texts of the revelations received by JS that composed the Doctrine and Covenants, JS's papers were arguably the most important gathering of foundational materials held by the church.[4] The collection is supplemented by a significant assemblage of related materials created by the recordkeeping mentality of the Saints in the first generation of Mormonism.[5]

In 1972, the LDS Church, coincident to completion of its new Church Office Building in downtown Salt Lake City, reorganized several of its administrative departments. In the move, it refashioned its historical agency, the Church Historian's Office—operating since the mid-nineteenth century—into the Church Historical Department. The newly created department had four divisions. Archival and library functions were established along with an Arts and Sites Division that cared for the museum-type collections of the church. The most visible entity of the new organization, however, was the History Division led by Leonard J. Arrington, the newly appointed church historian and first professional in the role. Arrington, who taught economics and history at Utah State University,

2. The LDS Church's History Department and its collections in Salt Lake City moved north across the street in 2009 to the new Church History Library. See also Jessee, "Sources for the Study of Joseph Smith," 8–9.

3. Joseph Smith Collection, 1827–1844, MS 155, CHL.

4. Other records pertinent to JS acquired in the last generation have augmented those materials, including the acquisition in 2017 by the LDS Church of the "printer's copy" of the Book of Mormon from the Community of Christ Church (previously known as the Reorganized Church of Jesus Christ of Latter Day Saints {RLDS} until the year 2000). "Church Buys Printer's Manuscript of Book of Mormon from Community of Christ," September 20, 2017, https://www.lds.org/church/news/church-buys-printers-manuscript-of-book-of-mormon-from-community-of-christ?lang=eng. The Joseph Smith Papers included the printer's copy in their publications as Joseph Smith, Revelations, "Book of Mormon," *JSP, R3*: Parts 1 and 2, in 2015.

5. A search of the LDS Church History Library online catalog for the name "Joseph Smith" identifies thousands of archival records (manuscript collections) and printed materials (books, etc.) that reference JS.

had emerged in the 1960s as the most important figure in Mormon academic circles. His own groundbreaking work in Mormon and Utah studies foreshadowed generations of work through his nurture of a generation of young scholars.[6] Arrington, whose vision was large, instituted with others the latent objective of creating a scholarly history of Mormonism. After he became church historian, he marshalled church support for this groundbreaking portrayal of the Mormon past.[7] High on the agenda was a strategy to explicate JS by preparing scholarly articles that described and analyzed the surviving historical record. Dean Jessee, who had worked in the Church Historian's Office since 1964, received the charge to survey the documentary record for a better understanding of JS's life. Jessee distributed his careful, groundbreaking work by way of articles in church-oriented periodicals beginning in the late 1960s. His *Personal Writings of Joseph Smith*, a gathering of the holographic material attributed to JS, appeared in 1984 with a revised and updated edition in 2002.[8] Following those important compositions, he then initiated a publication series titled *The Papers of Joseph Smith*, the first two volumes appearing in 1989 and 1992.[9] Jessee's careful work portended the expansion of JS studies in the twenty-first century.[10]

6. See Leonard J. Arrington, "The Founding of the LDS Church Historical Department" in *Adventures of a Church Historian* (Urbana, IL: University of Illinois Press, 1998), 74–91. See also Ronald W. Walker, David J. Whittaker, and James B. Allen, *Mormon History* (Urbana: University of Illinois Press, 2001), 60–68.

7. For the exhibit of Leonard Arrington's life, see his own *Adventures of a Church Historian*; Reid L. Neilson and Ronald W. Walker, eds., *Reflections of a Mormon Historian: Leonard J. Arrington on the New Mormon History* (Norman, OK: Arthur H. Clark, 2006); Gary Topping, *Leonard J. Arrington: A Historian's Life* (Norman, OK: Arthur H. Clark, 2008); and Arrington, *Confessions of a Mormon Historian: The Diaries of Leonard J. Arrington, 1971–1999*, ed. Gary James Bergera (Salt Lake City: Signature Books, 2018). A comprehensive biography can be found in Gregory A. Prince, *Leonard Arrington and the Writing of Mormon History* (Salt Lake City: University of Utah Press, and the Tanner Trust Fund, 2016). See also the perspectives of Davis Bitton and James B. Allen, Arrington's assistant church historians, in Bitton, "Ten Years in Camelot: A Personal Memoir," *Dialogue: A Journal of Mormon Thought* (hereafter *Dialogue*) 16, no. 3 (Autumn 1983): 9–19; and Allen's review of Prince's *Leonard Arrington*, found in *BYU Studies Quarterly* 57, no. 2 (2018): 176–84.

8. Dean C. Jessee, comp. and ed., *Personal Writings of Joseph Smith* (1984; rev. ed., Salt Lake City: Deseret Book and Brigham Young University Press, 2002).

9. Dean C. Jessee, ed., *The Papers of Joseph Smith: Autobiographical and Historical Writings, Volume 1* (Salt Lake City: Deseret Book, 1989); Dean C. Jessee, ed., *The Papers of Joseph Smith: Journal, 1832–1842, Volume 2* (Salt Lake City: Deseret Book, 1992), not to be confused with the *Joseph Smith Papers*, 2008–.

10. Dean Jessee's career and consequential intersection with Mormon history, including his creation of a documentary platform upon which JS studies could be conducted, is described in Robin Scott Jensen's interview of Jessee in "Joseph Smith's Chronicler: An Interview with Dean C. Jessee," *Mormon Historical Studies* 13, nos. 1–2 (Spring/Fall 2012): 99–124.

Another feature of Arrington's designation as LDS Church historian was the collaborative effort to produce what was billed as the "Sesquicentennial History" of the church (1830–1980), projected to include sixteen volumes covering the 150-year history of Mormonism and other attendant features of the faith. The period describing early Mormonism and its founding prophet in the study became the province of established scholar Richard L. Bushman, who had worked with Arrington on the project since the 1960s. While unforeseen complications thwarted completion of the sesquicentennial series, Bushman's work reached publication in 1984 as *Joseph Smith and the Beginnings of Mormonism.*[11] The book marked Bushman as one of the most significant scholars of JS at the time, fully expanded and enhanced twenty years later in his acclaimed *Joseph Smith, Rough Stone Rolling.*[12] His interpretive narrative, benefitting from the previous generation of scholarly work on the Mormon prophet, moved public knowledge and understanding of JS to a new level.

At the same time, the Reorganized Church of Jesus Christ of Latter Day Saints (RLDS Church), which diverged from what became Utah Mormonism—the LDS Church—in the 1850s, also had an investment in JS and accordingly preserved and studied the pertinent records by and about him that they had gathered since their origin. Because JS's family affiliated with the RLDS Church after the prophet's death, a number of the important documentary records created during his lifetime were given by them to the Reorganized Saints, which the RLDS Church maintained as they grew and gained momentum. They eventually established their headquarters in Independence, Jackson County, in western Missouri, on the site where JS first designated the location of latter-day Zion. There they built a substantial edifice—the Auditorium—that housed not only church offices and a large conference center but also a historical repository that preserved their religious heritage. In 1994 RLDS headquarters operations were transferred nearby to their newly constructed Temple.[13] At the turn of the millennium, the church changed its name to the Community of Christ, empha-

11. Richard L. Bushman, *Joseph Smith and the Beginnings of Mormonism* (Urbana, IL: University of Illinois Press, 1984). It received several awards upon publication. See a description of the genesis and demise of the Sesquicentennial History in Prince, *Leonard J. Arrington*, 168–73. Thomas G. Alexander, a sesquicentennial volume author himself, provided the view that: "The major failing in the sixteen-volume history was with the authors who failed to complete their writing. Had those authors completed their writing, those volumes would have most likely seen the light of day." Review by Thomas G. Alexander of Gary Topping's *Leonard J. Arrington* in *BYU Studies* 48, no. 3 (2009): 164–65.

12. Richard Lyman Bushman, *Joseph Smith: Rough Stone Rolling; A Cultural Biography of Mormonism's Founder* (New York: Alfred A. Knopf, 2005). *Rough Stone Rolling* also received several awards for its compelling presentation.

13. For a brief overview of the history of the archival and library collections of the Community of Christ, see https://www.cofchrist.org/about-the-library.

sizing their commitment to Jesus as mankind's savior and Christian principles and living.[14]

For a number of reasons, in the LDS Church the rise of scholarly interest in the study of JS provoked negative reaction from a number of its leaders. After a decade, the church transferred Arrington's History Division to Brigham Young University in the early 1980s, recasting the cadre of historians as the Joseph Fielding Smith Institute for Latter-day Saint History. BYU was viewed as a better fit for academic Mormon history than an institutional historical agency. Under direction of Ronald Esplin, who succeeded Arrington as the institute's director, Esplin, Jessee, and other BYU scholars developed a strategy to bring to fruition Jessee's original work regarding JS. By the middle of the first decade of the new century a team of scholars had been assembled by the Smith Institute at BYU to revive and enlarge Jessee's project. But variant views among church leaders and school administrators about the role of the Smith Institute at BYU moved leaders to disband the group and reassign its staff again to the church's history department in Salt Lake City. The move greatly benefitted the fledgling Joseph Smith Papers with resources and the church's historical materials readily at hand. As the plan developed, cooperation from the Community of Christ also amplified the project by making their JS materials available to the endeavor.

Fortuitously, along with church endorsement and resources, the Joseph Smith Papers project acquired added resources and momentum when Larry H. Miller—automobile dealer magnate, philanthropist, and owner of the Utah Jazz basketball team—joined forces financially propelling the project into reality. After Miller's untimely death in 2009, his wife Gail and her family continued to underwrite the work. With several dozen scholars and editorial associates' painstakingly preparing transcriptions and annotations of the surviving records tied to JS, the first printed segment of the Joseph Smith Papers, published by the church's new Church Historian's Press, appeared in 2008. Subsequent print volumes appeared at a rate of two per year. About two dozen were planned. Reviews

14. The RLDS Church/Community of Christ took a decidedly different approach to JS than did their LDS cousins. Along with other divergences, for example, the view of the role of JS's First Vision in the Community of Christ is clearly subordinate in importance to their members than it was to their LDS counterparts. See Richard P. Howard, "Joseph Smith's First Vision: The RLDS Tradition," *Journal of Mormon History* 7 (1980): 23–30. Still, the First Vision in historical context is advanced by the Community of Christ. See Mark A. Scherer, *The Journey of a People: The Era of Restoration, 1820–1844* (Independence, MO: Community of Christ, Seminary Press, 2013), 51–67. (This latter volume is the first of a three-part portrayal of the Community of Christ that covers their history to the present.)

In sharp contrast to the primacy of JS to the LDS Church in the twenty-first century, the centrality of JS to the Community of Christ has diminished for some of their members in the last generation. See Roger D. Launius, "Is Joseph Smith Relevant to the Community of Christ," *Dialogue* 39, no. 4 (Winter 2006): 58–67.

of the project have been laudatory. As one non-Mormon scholar extolled: "The project's high standards for documentary editing are complemented by maps, biographies, thorough historical introductions to the transcribed manuscripts, and stunningly detailed notes. This project remains the gold standard in the field of historical documentary editing."[15] As important and useful as the print volumes are, perhaps the most far-reaching feature of the project is a state-of-the-art website where the full range of JS documents and transcriptions will be found with annotation and other scholarly adornments, including materials associated with JS that will not be published in book form. The website, http://www.josephsmithpapers.org, was soon available with material being regularly added.

The bibliography of material written about JS since he first aroused the attention of the world, largely informed by the historical collection of the LDS Church, is vast and continues to grow. Arriving at a point where archivists and historians could apply professional standards to the administration of the church's records took many years to realize. BYU religion professor Robert L. Millet, who specialized in the doctrine and theology of the faith, affirmed: "We have witnessed in recent years a marvelous work in itself in the production of the Joseph Smith Papers, and the results are continually being made available to Latter-day Saints and other interested parties in published form as well as online. It is a deeply significant work."[16] The nineteenth-century prophet was transformed by the advance of information and interest, something that lay dormant for decades.

New Views of Joseph Smith

The rise of the modern consciousness about JS and Mormon origins followed analytical antecedents that had been advanced since the nineteenth century. But in 1945 when Fawn M. Brodie's *No Man Knows My History: The Life of Joseph Smith* burst the complacent culture of Mormonism with a significant challenge to JS and his claims, an arguably new era of interest in JS arose. Brodie's book gained wide praise in the American scholarly community making it unfeasible for the LDS and RLDS churches to ignore it. Thereafter, Latter-day Saint history gained interest and gravity that was significantly different than what had formerly been satisfactorily consumed through church-produced devotional publications.[17] While a number of other critical books had been written about

15. Thomas P. Slaughter, on dust jacket of *JSP, D3*.

16. Robert L. Millet, *Precept upon Precept: Joseph Smith and the Restoration of Doctrine* (Salt Lake City: Deseret Book, 2016), xi.

17. As might be imagined, a number of critiques of Brodie's work followed publication of her book. Among the Mormon historical community see: Newell G. Bringhurst, *Reconsidering No Man Knows My History* (Logan, UT: Utah State University Press, 1996);

JS previously, Brodie's work—in many ways a sympathetic though dismissive and skeptical portrait—applied to a degree the techniques of scholarly historiography to JS's life.

Brodie, a Mormon by birth but never among the devout, initiated interest in explaining JS in 1938, moving her to anxiously investigate Mormon origins. Rumors via critical publications had circulated for years about JS's youthful involvement in magic and treasure seeking, provoking speculation that the LDS Church held "secret" collections containing counter explanations of Mormon beginnings. As her manuscript matured, in 1943 she visited Salt Lake City. She had been told that the church held a document that cast JS's later explanations of Mormon foundations in question. Brodie later said: "I had been told that there was a diary of Joseph Smith in his own handwriting, written when he was in his early twenties [JS's 1832 History]. I knew one man at the Brigham Young University [M. Wilford Poulson], who is now dead, who had seen it and read it. But when I asked to see it, I was told I could not see it." In a "very long, and very difficult interview" with her uncle, David O. McKay, a Mormon apostle, she persuaded him to allow her access to the item. However, upon considering the tension in her family over the matter, she determined not to pursue the matter. "I felt that I would rather not take advantage of my uncle's name to use this material," she explained. Consequently, she then wrote to Apostle McKay declining his acquiescence and "never went back to the church library."[18] Thereafter, she completed her book, without consulting much of the most important archival information pertaining to her subject. Still, she secured a contract with a major American publisher that printed her book in 1945. While her work was not a knock-out punch, it staggered the tranquil setting of JS veneration.

It cannot be sustained that Brodie's book was *the* catalyst for the rise of modern Mormon historiography, but her determination to humanize JS's profile had a lasting effect on how he and early Mormonism merited consideration for the next generations. Undoubtedly, stimulated by the quandary established by Brodie and a few others, a group of young Mormon scholars applied their academic training to investigate their own religious roots. A generation earlier

---

Marvin S. Hill, "Brodie Revisited: A Reappraisal," *Dialogue* 7, no. 4 (Winter 1972): 72–85; and Hill, "Secular or Sectarian History? A Critique of No Man Knows My History," *Church History* 43, no. 1 (March 1974): 78–96, which also appears in the Bringhurst compilation. See also Charles L. Cohen, "No Man Knows My Psychology: Fawn Brodie, Joseph Smith, and Psychoanalysis," *BYU Studies* 44, no. 1 (2005): 55–78.

18. Fawn M. Brodie, Interview by Shirley E. Stephenson, November 30, 1975, "Fawn McKay Brodie: An Oral History Interview," *Dialogue* 14, no.2 (Summer 1981): 103. The larger Brodie episode with her uncle David O. McKay and also A. Will Lund, a keeper of the Church Historian's Office, is found in Newell G. Bringhurst, *Fawn McKay Brodie: A Biographer's Life* (Norman: University of Oklahoma Press, 1999), 84–85, 284n38, though there are discrepancies about the matter between the Brodie interview and the biography.

the church had sponsored a number of its religious educators, who ventured into the academic world, with the expectation that the teachers would acquire scholarly tools to better educate the church's youth. However, a number of those dispatched to high-profile universities for advanced training returned less orthodox, giving church leaders pause and uneasiness in how best to deliver the religion to its youth.[19] Still, in subsequent years a definable, well-educated Mormon academic community emerged, generally supportive of church objectives.

Most prominent in the rise of Mormon studies was the establishment of the Mormon History Association (MHA) in 1965. Printing the *Journal of Mormon History*, MHA and other forums with their publications of Mormon-related periodicals presented to an informed readership materials exploring matters never before raised in print. An "underground," where little-known or surreptitiously obtained documents from the LDS Church archives and other records also circulated among the intelligentsia, adding to the intrigue of the age. The "new Mormon history," as it came to be called, pointed to a distinct demarcation of professional from devotional history that proved both helpful and upsetting. Any rethinking by the new scholarship about entrenched "truths" was met with resistance by many of the faithful as destructive to the faith, though the purpose of much that was produced by church scholars was to enlarge and bolster not only "understanding"—but also ultimately faith.[20] The religion's detractors reveled that Mormons had to confront the fact that their foundations as previously presented were not as sure as earlier claimed. The significant effort of Mormon academics, many from Brigham Young University, the LDS Church History Department, and elsewhere, has since, for the most part, moved the skirmish regarding Mormon beginnings to a level rising above partisan frictions.

Coupled with the increased attention to Mormon foundational premises that the LDS community of scholars affected, a similar venture was mounted by scholars of the RLDS Church. While a rivalry had existed between leaders of the two organizations for generations, the scholarly community dropped the dogmatic scrapping and crossed lines engendering a common and mutually supportive enterprise to discover Mormon origins. Non-church sponsored academic societies, such as MHA, rose in both institutions fostering annual conferences along with academic periodicals. Many of the presentations in both

19. See Russel B. Swenson, "Mormons at the University of Chicago Divinity School: A Personal Reminiscence," *Dialogue* 7, no. 2 (Summer 1972): 45; Richard Sherlock, "Faith and History: The Snell Controversy," *Dialogue* 12, no. 1 (Spring 1979): 27–42; Casey Paul Griffiths, "The Chicago Experiment": Finding the Voice and Charting the Course of Religious Education in the Church," *BYU Studies* 49, no. 4 (2010): 91–130.
20. See examples of the endeavor in D. Michael Quinn, ed., *The New Mormon History* (Salt Lake City: Signature Books, 1992).

conferences and periodicals focused on JS. The collective work provoked another benefit from the historical kinship. A collaborative venture between the historical entities of both churches resulted in the conservation and sharing of a number of the foundational documents of the restoration pertinent to the founding prophet. Roused by generous personalities from both establishments, the undertaking promoted the high-spirited enterprise resulting in an ongoing cooperation between the two historical communities.

At the same time, disparaging studies of JS rose to offer alternate interpretations of Mormon origins. Often exhibiting more fervor by the number of their publications than the institutional scholars, the critics applied sophisticated investigations into the seminal events of Mormonism. The hard questions they asked served to significantly benefit what had before been dismissal of anything that confronted traditional interpretations of the faith. Perhaps ironically and unwittingly, the questions also urged Mormon scholars to better explore their own truth claims, significantly benefitting the overall study of the prophet and his church. The malaise that preceded academic Mormonism was displaced, at least in the scholarly community, by an appetite for answers to many historical issues. To be sure, there was resistance from the faithful sector who for the most part had previously enjoyed an uncontested devotional field to themselves. The scholars, however, insisted on a less polemic discourse determined to understand rather than prove. Though polarity continued, headway gained over the next half century went some distance in changing the discourse about Mormon origins.

An apt example of the somewhat surprising situation is the matter of JS's journals. Preparation of JS's personal records appeared in stages. He began writing a journal in 1832,[21] the same year he first produced an account of his early experiences as a prophet (the 1832 History that will be described in Chapter 7). While logic might suggest the LDS Church's interest in publishing his journals, the first to print them were Mormon critics Jerald and Sandra Tanner who distributed typescripts of the journals in 1979 (1832–36) and 1982 (1838–39) from their Utah Lighthouse Ministry in Salt Lake City, Utah.[22] In 1987 Signature Books, also in Salt Lake City, published their own transcription of JS's journals—the first time the collection had been distributed by a substantial press.[23]

21. The JS journals that he initiated in 1832 were thereafter prepared by his clerks and scribes and, with several breaks, continued to the end of his life in 1844.
22. H. Michael Marquardt, trans., *Joseph Smith's 1832–34 Diary: Also Joseph Smith's 1832 Account of His Early Life* (Salt Lake City: Modern Microfilm, 1979); H. Michael Marquardt, trans., *Joseph Smith's 1835–36 Diary* (Salt Lake City: Modern Microfilm, 1979); H. Michael Marquardt, trans., *Joseph Smith's 1838–39 Diaries* (Salt Lake City: Modern Microfilm, 1982).
23. Scott H. Faulring, ed., *An American Prophet's Record: The Diaries and Journals of Joseph Smith* (Salt Lake City: Signature Books, 1987).

Five years after the Signature Book publication, Dean C. Jessee, the first and most well-informed documentary specialist of JS material, published the initial ten years of JS's journal in 1992 as volume two in his *Papers of Joseph Smith* series. Plans to complete Jessee's undertaking, not of his own making, stalled completion of his designs. But in the first decade of the twenty-first century, as mentioned, the Joseph Fielding Smith Institute for Latter-day Saint History pushed for revival of Jessee's project.[24] With the LDS Church History Department cooperating, the creation of the Joseph Smith Papers Project resulted in a formidable transcription and contextual explanation behind JS's journals in three volumes covering his life, 1832–1844. The three volumes were published in the *Joseph Smith Papers* between 2008 and 2015, thirty years after the Tanners' publication of the journals.[25]

The Joseph Smith Papers and Other Projects

It was appropriation of JS materials by non-church entities that, in part, moved the historical agency of the LDS Church to take greater control of its resources, and with the tools of historiography prepare the Joseph Smith Collection for publication. Besides the journals, five other series of early church and complementary records constitute the Joseph Smith Papers. The largest series—the documents—include a chronological rendering of the records created, associated, and related to JS's life. The history series consists of the materials JS initiated to describe the founding events of Mormonism. The revelations and translations series comprises sacred texts in manuscript form—including the Book of Mormon, and the texts that became the Doctrine and Covenants and the Book of Abraham. The administrative records series contains minutes of council and conference meetings, which also enhance the project. A separate series of legal and business documentation is also being prepared by a private entity. With publication of the Joseph Smith Papers, the field of JS studies has never been better furbished than what it is at present. The LDS Church's remarkable twenty-first century delivery of its foundational collections for public access, a reversal of its previous posture, has reseeded the blotchy field of historical inquiry, providing source material never before approachable. The endeavor represents a significant advance in conveying its historical past. Another example: in 2002, anticipating change in U.S. copyright provisions, the church secured copyright control of thirty-one of its most significant manuscript collections, including the Joseph Smith Collection, by publishing them in digital form. The *Selected Collections from the Archives of the Church of Jesus Christ of Latter-day Saints*, edited by Richard E. Turley Jr., director of the church's historical enter-

24. Jessee, "Joseph Smith's Chronicler," 118.
25. *JSP, J1–3*.

prise at the time, utilized colored photographs of documents and transcriptions of many of the same—amounting to hundreds of thousands of images that were published on seventy-four DVD discs.[26] The collections in the project are now available in digital form in the LDS Church History Library catalog, along with numerous other manuscripts.

Another twenty-first-century effort of the LDS Church to popularize and portray its founder and his teachings among the Latter-day Saints was publication of the widely distributed *Teachings of Presidents of the Church: Joseph Smith* in 2008 for study in local congregations. While the series, which included all Latter-day Saint presidents, was not a scholarly publication and rather was intended for study by adult church classes, a significant endeavor was applied to prepare the JS materials for evaluation. The effort involved appraising what JS wrote and taught using academic standards to define from the existing documentary record what could and could not be attributed to JS. A committee from the church's history department used for a model the work of Don E. and Virginia Fehrenbacher, whose *Recollected Words of Abraham Lincoln* attempted to verify and categorize the words attributed to U.S. president Abraham Lincoln. The history department committee prepared criteria for judgment about the authenticity of words attributed to JS similar to what the Fehrenbachers did for the words of President Lincoln. In their classification, they designated an A to represent "a quotation cast in direct discourse and recorded contemporaneously—that is within a few days after the words were spoken." The letter B identified "an indirect quotation recorded contemporaneously"; a C, "a quotation recorded non-contemporaneously"; a D, "a quotation about whose authenticity there is more than average doubt"; and an E, "a quotation that is probably not authentic."[27] In the same spirit and with somewhat of a comparable method of classification, a lengthy review process of JS's life and teachings by the Church History Department provided a body of material providing a better grasp of what JS is reported to have said during his lifetime. From this collection of records the church prepared a curriculum manual of forty-eight chapters and 586 pages by theme for its adult members.[28]

26. Richard E. Turley Jr., ed., *Selected Collections from the Archives of The Church of Jesus Christ of Latter-day Saints*, 2 vols. (Provo, UT: Brigham Young University Press, 2002), DVD.

27. Don and Virginia Fehrenbacher, *Recollected Words of Abraham Lincoln* (Palo Alto, CA: Stanford University Press, 1996), lii–liii.

28. *Teachings of Presidents of the Church: Joseph Smith* (Salt Lake City: The Church of Jesus Christ of Latter-day Saints, 2007). As it turned out, the writing committee ultimately relied upon presentation of JS's teachings as documented in Roberts's *History of the Church*, with the thinking that many of the documents had already been edited and prepared for public consumption making for ease in republication.

A complementary endeavor to make known early Mormon publications was the work of the LDS Church's Brigham Young University's L. Tom Perry Special Collections.[29] By making available not only numerous manuscript collections of historical materials pertinent to nineteenth-century Mormonism, the special collections also included a significant number of digitized collections of early Mormon periodicals in PDF (Portable Document Format), such as images of the early church organs the *Evening and the Mormon Star*, the *Latter Day Saints' Messenger and Advocate*, etc. Other historical materials including significant compilations of extracted transcripts from many obscure but important documents represent a portion of the repository's holdings.[30]

The significant effort expended by Latter-day Saint scholars to give clarity to JS and other aspects of the Mormon past, as noted, has not always been well received by the Saints. Many church members remain happily imbedded in their historical traditions. Modern anecdotal reports are numerous, indicating the unsettling effect of current scholarship revising and clarifying early Mormonism.[31] But the pattern has now been established in projects like the church's recent analysis and explanation of the 1857 Mountain Meadows Massacre where over a hundred California-bound immigrants were killed by Mormon militiamen. For generations the church had deflected involvement. But comprehensive research conducted by personnel in the church's history and genealogy departments reflected in *Massacre at Mountain Meadows*, *Mountain Meadows Massacre: The Andrew Jenson and David H. Morris Collections*, and *Mountain Meadows Massacre: Collected Legal Papers* shows church interest in setting the record straight.[32] Similarly, the recent release by the church in the *Joseph Smith Papers* of its once secretive Council of Fifty minutes demonstrates the trend. Toward the end of JS's life, he created a body of fifty men to strategize

29. https://lib.byu.edu/special-collections.

30. https://lib.byu.edu/collections/?q=tag:digital.

31. Evidence of the disconnection of some over historical issues is ample in social media in the form of essays, podcasts, and blogs. It should be noted that Jana Riess, in her recent analysis of modern Mormonism based on extensive surveys of a wide range of those attached to Mormonism, did not find historical matters as aggravating to her respondents as were other social issues in the LDS Church. See Jana Riess, *The Next Mormons: How Millennials are Changing the LDS Church* (New York: Oxford University Press, 2019), 217, 219, 223–25.

32. Ronald W. Walker, Richard E. Turley Jr., and Glen M. Leonard, *Massacre at Mountain Meadows: An American Tragedy* (New York: Oxford University Press, 2008); Richard E. Turley Jr. and Ronald W. Walker, eds., *Mountain Meadows Massacre: The Andrew Jenson and David H. Morris Collections* (Provo and Salt Lake City: Brigham Young University Press and University of Utah Press, 2009); Richard E. Turley Jr., Janiece L. Johnson, and LaJean Purcell Carruth, eds., *Mountain Meadows Massacre: Collected Legal Papers*, 2 vols. (Norman: University of Oklahoma Press, 2017).

the church's future given their tenuous circumstances in Nauvoo at the time. The organization's controversial objectives in Nauvoo and afterward caused some church leaders thereafter to suppress the documents—apparently believing they would arouse public sentiment against JS and the early Saints. Release of the volume in 2018, after all that had previously been prepared by scholars to explain from other sources the Council of Fifty's purpose, generally renders their fears passé.[33] Also exhibiting the shift in portrayal of the Mormon past, are recent representations of Latter-day Saint women's roles in advancing the faith. Some of the most important church records relating to its women in the first generation, never previously contextualized in such a scholarly manner, have been prepared in *The First Fifty Years of Relief Society*.[34] Women's issues in the church have never been more vital, nor have efforts to make documentation about them in the early church been more urgent. Church members have recently witnessed a watershed regarding presentation of their past as never before. The most misunderstood or historically aggravating features of the Mormon past, can, it has been shown with responsible scholarship, be presented in both an honest and understandable manner.[35]

Almost lost upon the public in the surge of church historical initiatives has been the Church History Department's recent circulation online of its extensive print and manuscript catalog. For serious scholars of the Mormon past, easy access to the catalog has clearly accelerated opportunities to investigate the scope of Mormonism. The catalog includes an increasing number of digitized records of manuscript materials regarding the early church for easy review. Another innovation by the Church History Department was transcription of a significant

33. *JSP, A1*. See also Jedediah S. Rogers, ed., *The Council of Fifty: A Documentary History* (Salt Lake City: Signature Books, 2014).

34. Jill Mulvay Derr et al., *The First Fifty Years of Relief Society: Key Documents in Latter-day Saint Women's History* (Salt Lake City: Church Historian's Press, 2016). Of late, rectifying the disparity between the importance of women and their influence in early Mormonism by way of ensuring the records reflect their significance has become a priority of the LDS Church History enterprise. See Janiece Johnson and Jennifer Reeder, *The Witness of Women: Firsthand Experiences and Testimonies from the Restoration* (Salt Lake City: Deseret Book, 2017); Richard E. Turley Jr. and Brittany A. Chapman, eds., *Women of Faith in the Latter Days*, 4 vols., 1775–1870 (Salt Lake City: Deseret Book, 2011–2017); and Jennifer Reeder and Kate Holbrook, eds., *At the Pulpit: 185 Years of Discourses by Latter-day Saint Women* (Salt Lake City: Church Historian's Press, 2017).

35. See an overview of the Church History Department's transition over the past fifty years in Matthew J. Grow, "The Role of the Church History Department in Mormon Scholarship: A Reflection on the Leonard J. Arrington Era and the Present," in *To Be Learned is Good: Essays on Faith and Scholarship in Honor of Richard Lyman Bushman*, ed. J. Spencer Fluhman, Kathleen Flake, and Jed Woodworth (Provo, UT: Neal A. Maxwell Institute for Religious Scholarship, Brigham Young University, 2017), 167–78.

body of documents in the church's collection of nineteenth-century materials that had been created in Pitman shorthand, the writing method used to capture much of what was publicly delivered to the Saints after their settlement in the West. Sitting untouched for decades, church resources have been applied to transliterate the records by a scholar proficient in Pitman shorthand.[36] More recently, publication on the church's primary website—churchofjesuschrist.org, nee lds.org—of what are described as "Gospel Topics" has shown church confidence in not only responsible presentation of the past's sticky issues but also recognition by many that reliance on dated interpretations of history works against church interests. The "Topics" provide substantial summaries of controversial features associated with JS's life and other features of Mormon belief and practice.[37] And, at present, after several years of scholarly preparation, the LDS Church History Department has now published for general audiences the first of four volumes of what is described as a "new comprehensive history of the church": *Saints: The Story of the Church of Jesus Christ in the Latter Days*, the first volume appearing in 2018.[38] The objective is rooted in the prospect of presenting anew an accessible, updated, and credible portrait of the church's past.

The twenty-first-century sea change for the study of JS represented in publication of the *Joseph Smith Papers* comes with caveats aplenty. For the purposes of this volume, perhaps the most significant caution focuses on explaining to modern students that they must lay aside traditional satisfactions that "all is well" regarding how Mormon history has previously been conveyed. This requires recognition that much more is necessary to be known to appreciate the full scope—to the degree possible—of JS and his ministry. Frankly, we don't know as much as we think we know. As suggested, the recent efforts surrounding the advance in understanding the prophet will require overhauling what has been rendered as a somewhat seamless and polished encapsulation of his life. The Joseph Smith Papers and attendant information show him in his pristine and sometimes raw form. This, however, is unsettling for many, especially be-

36. LDS Church History Department scholar LaJean Carruth, besides mastering Brigham Young's unique "Deseret Alphabet," also became proficient in 1830s Pitman shorthand, enabling her to provide transcriptions in Pitman of church records for a significant amount of nineteenth-century documentation. See for example, Gerrit Dirkmaat and LaJean Purcell Carruth, "The Prophets Have Spoken, but What Did They Say," *BYU Studies Quarterly* 54, no. 4 (2015): 25–118.

37. https://www.lds.org/topics. The initial article addressing "Race and the Priesthood" appeared in December 2013. Other treatises followed, such as those qualifying translations of the Book of Mormon and Book of Abraham, and the church's practice of plural marriage.

38. *Saints: The Story of the Church of Jesus Christ in the Latter Days, Volume 1: The Standard of Truth, 1815–1846* (Salt Lake City: The Church of Jesus Christ of Latter-day Saints, 2018); https://history.lds.org/saints?lang=eng. See also the "Roundtable" discussion of *Saints* in *Journal of Mormon History* 45, no. 2 (April 2019): 49–67.

lievers who have relied upon those who have tended his legacy by accentuating only his massive achievements.

It is probably safe to say that most Latter-day Saints don't want to read about the sometimes crooked though progressive course of the faith with its warts and all. Yet it is in the course correction, the stumbling while climbing, along with the remarkable successes portrayed in the historical record that JS in his unsanitized appearance is best understood. Varnish, air brushing, and touch-ups have their place in communicating generalities. But when pressed to defend the authenticity of JS's life, the polished, whitewashed image becomes easy prey for some who delight in picking at the blemishes that exist. This is especially so when they can show that the church has not been forthright in the past in dealing with features of its history. One of the most important utilities of the Joseph Smith Papers is presentation by the editors of the uncooked materials in their contextual surroundings. Still, it is expected that some will ignore the *Joseph Smith Papers*, though the credibility of such works will be compromised; something like refraining from using the *Papers of Thomas Jefferson* to present a reliable rendering of the third American president.[39] Undoubtedly some will continue isolating irregularities from JS's life, attempting to assert that they are the norm. But students of the future will have the data to readily detect when someone has taken a less than comprehensive approach in interpreting the Mormon prophet.

39. Julian P. Boyd et al., eds., *The Papers of Thomas Jefferson*, 43 vols. (Princeton: Princeton University Press, 1950–).

CHAPTER 2

The Modern Study of Joseph Smith

A Baptist publication, the *Christian Reflector* (first printed in 1838 in Worcester, Massachusetts), prepared a backhanded summary of Joseph Smith in the aftermath of his death at the end of June 1844. By the time of the Carthage murders, JS had become notorious to Americans through the media of the day, meriting, under the circumstances, a response. Among all the country's mid-nineteenth-century cities, Nauvoo, Illinois, was the only one where charitable expressions about JS and his brother, killed at the hands of an infuriated mob, were uttered. "Good riddance" was the sentiment felt by most who had crossed Mormon paths. Even-tempered as most Americans were, the best that could be conceded at the time of JS's murder was that he cut an unusual figure reflected in his "coarse and vulgar deportment." His church fared no better. The *Christian Reflector* continued, "They were notorious for breach of contracts and the repudiation of their honest debts. All of them were addicted to vice. They obtained their living not by honorable labor, but by deceiving their neighbors with their marvellous tales of money digging." But of JS specifically, "[W]hatever may be the views of any in reference to his principles, objects, or moral character, all must admit that he was one of the most remarkable men of the age."[1] Few would have ever said as much about him while he was alive. But when he was safely dead, not from admiration but from perplexed wonder, he warranted explanation.

> Joe Smith arose from the very lowest grade of society, to the head of this large body, without any of those aids, by which most other men have ascended to their high stations. He is represented by those acquainted with him, as uneducated, uncouth in his manners, dissipated in his habits, and disgusting in his personal appearance; and yet unaided by the influence of literature, or the patronage of the great, he induced thousands to obey his mandates, and to rally around his standard. He fought his way through all these adverse circumstances, and left the impress of his de-

1. Gamma, "The Mormon Prophet," *Christian Reflector*, January 2, 1845, 1.

> praved genius upon his age, and his name will not be forgotten when that of many a statesman has long been buried in oblivion.... Reasoning from effect to cause, we must conclude that the Mormon prophet was of no common genius; few are able to commence and carry out an imposition like his, so long, and to such an extent.[2]

JS's death did not end controversy about his life or mission. Because Mormonism did not collapse and disappear, momentum regarding the apparent necessity of discrediting any accomplishment he may have begrudgingly earned from outsiders continued unabated. The survival and progress of his church created an environment thereafter that has obviously been contentious. Renunciation of him, particularly by those who were once Mormons, is now entrenched as a movement itself. This work is born in that conflicted setting.

Joseph Smith's Effect upon His Religion

Because all that might be known about JS is limited by the absence of what theoretically might exist concerning a complete documentary record, our frame of reference about him is limited by what does survive. That is especially true regarding JS's own perspectives. Had a full complement of records been created in the first place, and if they had been preserved, this would likely be a rather different story. JS's bold statement to the church's Twelve Apostles after they were first called in February 1835, presented his own consciousness of the difficulty: "If I now had in my possession, every decision which has been had, upon important items of doctrine and duties, which have been given since the commencement of this work, I would not part with it for any sum of money, but we have neglected to take minutes of such things, thinking, perhaps, that they would never benefit us afterward." Otherwise, they could "decide almost any point of doctrine, which might be agitated, but, this has been neglected."[3] LDS Church historian George A. Smith, a couple of years after finally unpacking in 1853 the early church records transported across the plains to Utah in 1847, wrote: "Many records are nearly obliterated by time damp & dirt[.] Others lost[.] Some half worked into mouse nests, & many Important events were never written except in the hearts of those who were concerned."[4] Recognizing the limitations that exist in ascertaining early Mormonism, then, becomes important. As it is, JS lives on the cusp of what *could* be known about him. For example, had he endured beyond 1844 another layer of measurement—photography—may have captured him in his time. As it was, JS died just five years after word spread of Frenchman Louis

2. Ibid.
3. Smith, Documents, February 27, 1835, Minute Book 1, *JSP, D4*:253.
4. George A. Smith to John C.L. Smith, February 28, 1855, Historian's Office, Letterpress Copybooks, vol. 1, 1854–1861, 106, CR 100 38, CHL.

Daguerre's famous invention of the "daguerreotype," one of the founding steps of modern photography. Had Daguerre's magic been widely available a decade earlier, it could have significantly benefitted modern students by visually exhibiting not only JS himself but also the world in which he lived.[5] The *Christian Reflector's* portrait of JS would have been augmented by our ability to *see* his visible persona and its accoutrements to satisfy at least one aspect of interest in knowing him. The uncertainty of just who and what JS was in such observations represents the dilemma confronting modern students. In the absence of visual documentation about JS, his family, and his church this book is reduced to being about the words written by and about JS; what we learn about him from the historical record.

The description of JS made in the *Christian Reflector* reflects the contradictory, disputed, and enigmatic portrait of the prophet.[6] As JS became controversial in his youth, he could not outgrow the stigma of his notoriety. Never in his thirty-eight years did he enjoy a moment of satisfaction that what he advanced and what he tried to accomplish was accepted by his countrymen. "Latter-day Saints, however much their Church may have had to stray from his paths, have been almost alone in apprehending the greatness of Joseph Smith," according to Harold Bloom.[7]

Two fundamentals necessary to understand by anyone in the modern world embarking on the study of JS are first, those who loved and wrote about him

5. Jeffrey G. Cannon, "The Image as Text and Context in Early Mormon History," in *Foundational Texts of Mormonism: Examining Major Early Sources*, ed. Mark Ashurst-McGee, Robin Scott Jensen, and Sharalyn D. Howcroft (New York: Oxford University Press, 2018), 336–350.

There is a continuing debate about the possibility that JS was photographed toward the end of his life. Besides a daguerreian photographer known to have been in Nauvoo prior to JS's death, JS's trip to the East in 1839–1840 took him to locales, such as Washington, D.C., and Philadelphia, where the enchantment of daguerreotypes increasingly captured a visual world previously available only through sketching or paint on canvas. See the range of debate on the matter in Shannon M. Tracy, *In Search of Joseph* (Orem, UT: KenningHouse, 1995); Ephraim Hatch, *Joseph Smith Portraits: A Search for the Prophet's Likeness* (Provo, UT: Religious Studies Center, Brigham Young University, 1998); S. Michael Tracy, *Millions Shall Know Brother Joseph Again: The Joseph Smith Photograph* (Salt Lake City: Eborn Publishing, 2008); Curtis G. Weber, "Skulls and Crossed Bones?: A Forensic Study of the Remains of Hyrum and Joseph Smith," http://mormonhistoricsites.org/wp-content/uploads/2013/04/Skulls-and-Crossed-Bones-A-Forensic-Study-of-the-Remains-of-Hyrum-and-Joseph-Smith.pdf; and Jared Tamez, review of S. Michael Tracy, *Millions Shall Know Brother Joseph Again*, *Journal of Mormon History* 35, no. 3 (Summer 2009): 249–55.

6. See Marvin S. Hill's brief but useful essay portraying the contradictory descriptions of JS reflecting the perspectives of defenders, detractors, and the uncommitted. "Foreword" in *The Essential Joseph Smith* (Salt Lake City: Signature Books, 1995), xv–xxviii.

7. Bloom, *American Religion*, 11.

when he was alive are just like those who loved and wrote about him after he died. And, they have modern counterparts. They are his defenders. Second, those who hated and wrote about him when he was alive are just like those who hated and wrote about him after he died. And, they have modern counterparts. They are his detractors. The majority of what has been written about JS in nearly two hundred years comes from one or the other of these categorizations. Each of the groupings are laden with significant baggage that inevitably shapes how the images they portray are consumed. Despite the inconsistencies, inequities, and misappropriations the designations may evoke, they are the markers and signage on the roadside that students of JS inevitably must consider as they travel the course of their study.

Given the declarations of JS and his followers' contentions, and the adversarial zeal funneled against them for that posture, the study of JS often dissolves to being an either/or argument. But binary thinking predictably frames issues of this sort far too narrowly. Still, the quest for middle ground in the case of JS's authenticity does not appear to be feasible, if middle ground means the defenders conceding that JS's veracity cannot be relied upon or his detractors yielding that he may very well have been what he claimed to be. This work is a slant, a methodology, of negotiating the historical record upon which all of us must rely; an exercise in perspective. It will be apparent throughout that this study is one of sympathy toward JS and what he tried to accomplish. Nevertheless, the approach is different than some of the faithful scholarly defenses of JS prepared in the form of amicus briefs that attempt to *prove* his veracity. While all that JS did to advance his objectives falls within the nondemonstrable realm of religious conviction and certainty, the methods of historical inquiry—where the credibility of the documentary artifacts are central to the discussion—best represents how the landscape of JS and Mormonism must be evaluated from all sectors of those interested in his life.

It is reasonable to conclude that many within the faith today who become bewildered with Mormonism simply cannot negotiate the arguably complex swirl of influences upon JS's religion that peaked at the conclusion to his life. There is no bullet-point summary from JS categorically describing how he viewed his progressive prophetic tenure or to explain his matured thinking once in Nauvoo, for example. Thus, modern observers who do not include the entire scope of the documentary record in appraising him are often forced into reliance on explanations that often dote on the esoteric superfluity of Mormonism. Many modern students are befuddled by JS's innovative appendices that reshaped 1830s Mormonism into what became a "new religious tradition."[8] Moderns are left to

8. Jan Shipps, *Mormonism: The Story of a New Religious Tradition* (Urbana: University of Illinois Press, 1985).

make sense of what was created by men who generally had no intent of being understood, except to the initiated. To JS and his devotees, the abstruse aspects of the faith layered into Mormonism actually became greater evidence of JS's prophetic mantle. To historically seasoned believers today, the last four years of JS's life are among the most compelling and progressive scenes in the JS drama. But recognition that even the best informed have had trouble understanding how the constituent parts fit into the whole is important in encountering the ambiguous nature of the fragmented record.

Underlying any argument made by a writer discussing JS, wherein he/she imposes their judgment upon a matter, is the question of impartiality and how that condition was shaped. Like the ingredients of a recipe that are forced into a grinder, rendering a product limited to the fixings inserted, selective and biased source material often decide the contenders' argument. The breadth of the record is not supportive of a man who transcended the mortal condition or perfected himself in all the virtues, though he often managed the vicissitudes of life with skill. As Brigham Young said in 1859 of his spiritual mentor, "when the vision was not upon him he was just like any other man and it would have taken him years and years longer in the flesh to become a Moses in all things."[9] In an analogy proffered by JS himself, he stated it was clearly the intent of the New Testament apostle James to blunt the notion of mortal perfection when he announced to believers that the biblical figure Elias [Elijah] was subject to the "like passions" of all men.[10] To disregard the reality that biblical prophets had to contend with the frailties of humanity, makes JS especially vulnerable to those who delight in noting instances of his displays of humanness.

Though scholarly investigations into the lives of significant American political and cultural figures far outweigh in number those applied to JS, nevertheless appraisals of him and the founding of his church are plentiful. Most treatments of JS are in the form of articles, chapters, essays, speeches, critiques, and other compositions. Some are affirmative, but many of them are critical and skeptical. Those who revered the Mormon prophet qualified their intent with laudatory statements such as JS biographer John Henry Evans's 1933 précis, "he created a new religion, founded a university, planned and built cities, organized and trained militias, covered the earth with missionaries, started a wide stream of immigration to Western America, and, most of all, put into men's hearts something of idealism and faith, of which they had not believed themselves capable."[11] Or another JS explicator, BYU's Truman Madsen's 1989 complimentary summation: "In Joseph Smith we have a man who physically, intellectually, emotion-

9. Brigham Young, Sermon, September 1, 1859, *Journal of Discourses*, 26 vols. (London and Liverpool: LDS Booksellers Depot, 1855–1886), 7:243 (hereafter *JD*).
10. Jas. 5:17.
11. John Henry Evans, *Joseph Smith, an American Prophet* (New York: Macmillan, 1933), 6.

ally, and spiritually was a living human multitude. He was many men in one, as it were. Many of his gifts were balanced with others, and all in all he was a superb instrument with whom the Lord could and did work in the dispensation of the fulness of times."[12] Conversely, others have argued of him that: "When a charismatic person assumes a position of leadership and fails to recognize the limitations of his power, convinced he can 'transform his…fantasies into reality for his followers,' he may develop what psychologists refer to as megalomaniacal fantasies, including paranoid delusions."[13] Or: "Despite its success and respectability…a crisis looms before Joseph Smith's church—and the crux of the predicament is Smith himself. Today's Mormonism is being forced into an uncomfortable confrontation with its early nineteenth-century origins—an inevitable encounter given the importance of the founding prophet to his religion."[14]

Two weeks after JS's assassination, two counties away from Nauvoo in Lewiston, Illinois, a correspondent to Horace Greeley's *New York Tribune*, wrote: "Joe Smith is dead and gone. He was one of the most remarkable men of the age. The time for writing his history has not arrived. Men who have known him long and well, differ in their estimate of his character; the future historian alone can reconcile the contradictory statements of his friends and enemies [in a way that will] place him in his true position."[15] One might think that after nearly two centuries the world might have figured out how to explain him in a manner to get nods from everyone. To do so misunderstands the very nature of who he was and what he claimed and did.

Hasn't There Already Been Enough Written about Joseph Smith?

While George A. Marsden worked on his Bancroft Prize-winning biography of the great eighteenth-century American religious figure Jonathan Edwards, he noted that "A number of people of common sense have asked me something like, 'Isn't there a good bit written on Jonathan Edwards already?' or 'Aren't there quite a few other biographies of Edwards?' Their implication, I believe—since they are people of common sense—has been, 'Why would anyone spend years working on a subject that has been so well covered.'"[16] As Marsden suggests,

12. Truman G. Madsen, *Joseph Smith, the Prophet* (1989; repr., Salt Lake City: Bookcraft, 1993), 33.
13. Gary James Bergera, "Joseph Smith and the Hazards of Charismatic Leadership," in *The Prophet Puzzle: Interpretive Essays on Joseph Smith*, ed. Bryan Waterman (Salt Lake City: Signature Books, 1999), 239.
14. Lance S. Owens, "Joseph Smith: America's Hermetic Prophet" in Waterman, *The Prophet Puzzle*, 155–56.
15. H. M., "Joe Smith, the Mormon Prophet," *New York Tribune*, July 20, 1844.
16. George A. Marsden, *Jonathan Edwards: A Life* (New Haven: Yale University Press, 2003), xvii.

those who do not know the scope of Edwards's life, the literature already produced about him, or the work necessary to recover him given the inevitable discovery of more information, may believe that what already exists is sufficient. Some personalities are so significant, however, that they seem never to exhaust the public's appetite for explanation. The supply of portraits of men like Martin Luther, who apparently warrants several literary treatments per year, or Mohandas K. Gandhi, whose international following cannot get enough of him, will likely continue unabated. Closer to home, America's immense figures like Thomas Jefferson, Abraham Lincoln, Franklin D. Roosevelt, and John F. Kennedy retain the attention of scholars who keep bookstore shelves stocked with their interpretations. The study of JS, though on a more limited scale, has parallels regarding its already extensive coverage. Defenders and detractors alike continue to add to the extensive bibliography about him.

In the aftermath of JS's ministry, once his immediate impact subsided, characterizations about him were expressed from surprising sources. John Reynolds, for example, the former Illinois governor and then United States congressman who introduced JS to President Martin Van Buren in November 1839, stated in his 1855 autobiography that, "No one can foretell the destiny of this sect [Mormonism]; and it would be blasphemy at this day to compare its founder to the Saviour; but, nevertheless, it may become veritable history in a thousand years that the standing and character of Joseph Smith, as a Prophet, may rank equal to any of the prophets who have preceded him."[17] Along with Josiah Quincy's familiar 1883 epithet of JS, the Mormon prophet cannot easily be dismissed: "It is by no means improbable that some future text-book, for the use of generations yet unborn, will contain a question something like this: What historical American of the nineteenth century has exerted the most powerful influence upon the destinies of his countrymen? And it is by no means impossible that the answer to that interrogatory may be thus written: *Joseph Smith, the Mormon prophet.* And the reply, absurd as it doubtless seems to most men now living, may be an obvious commonplace to their descendants."[18] Those statements alone, from reputable and seasoned men who had met and over time evaluated JS, demands he be taken seriously.

Among some believers there prevails a common thought that JS was plucked out of the countryside and, despite his natural limitations, became the recipient of a divine download that extraordinarily equipped him from the start to set up the "restored gospel." After all, he claimed that God and Jesus appeared to him,

17. John Reynolds, *My Own Times Embracing also, the History of My Life* (n.p.: n.p., 1855), 564.

18. Josiah Quincy, *Figures of the Past: From the Leaves of Old Journals* (Boston: Roberts Brothers, 1883), 376–77.

and that an angel named Moroni, with others, tutored him for his future ministry. Succinctly, what his followers view as his premortal foreordination included not only the blueprint necessary to accomplish his prophetic destiny, but also all the information required to do it. The evidence from the historical record demands a contrary conclusion. He could be surprised as well as disenchanted. Much of what he envisioned came to pass; but there were times when what he conceived fizzled. For example, the immense expectation he had for the short-lived United Firm (later called the United Order) in Kirtland and Zion proved disappointing. The revelation he delivered establishing the enterprise stated it would be "an everlasting Firm for the benefit of my Church, and for the salvation of men until I come."[19] What he witnessed in his ministry was the aftereffects of the faith he exuded, believing that his divine commission was just that, and that the promises he had been given would eventually find manifestation. However, he was not fated. Some things did not work out. Some prophetic statements never bore fruit. Thus, there existed in his thinking anticipation and caution at the same time. Speaking several months after the calling of the Twelve Apostles in early 1835, he spoke to them in a training session of sorts, "I supposed I had established this church on a permanent foundation when I went to Missourie and indeed I did so, for if I had been taken away it would have been enough, but I yet live, and therefore God requires more at my hands."[20] JS bared before his associates his limited foresight and suggested his mortal condition by the acknowledgment. It is debatable regarding when JS reached his apex of insight and inspiration. Many of the theological and cosmological advances he taught in his famous King Follett discourse near the end of his life, for instance, actually were expressed by him earlier. But it is demonstrable that his perspectives about his then current and future church expanded significantly until his death. The prospects of changes to doctrine and polity remained open ended for JS. The historical record also suggests that he never plateaued in his acquisition of insight and inspiration.

Recognition that the documentary record is incomplete regarding JS's life is especially important when considering not only many of the mundane events but also the most consequential features of his life. While we occasionally get to see JS on JS, it is rare. Indeed, as will be shown, personal reflections about much of his innermost thoughts and motivations in matters most desired by modern students were generally never committed by him to paper and therefore

19. Smith, Revelations, April 23, 1834, *JSP, R1*:274 [D&C 104:1 (1981)]. For a thorough description of the United Firm, see Max H. Parkin, "Joseph Smith and the United Firm: The Growth and Decline of the Church's First Master Plan of Business and Finance, Ohio and Missouri, 1832–1834," *BYU Studies* 46, no. 3 (2007).

20. Joseph Smith, Journals, November 12, 1835, *JSP, J1*:97.

do not exist, leaving us inevitably disappointed in our expectations for full disclosure and subject to making judgments about him that may actually misrepresent what he thought. Besides appreciating the fact that he did not obsess about having his thinking and personal life recorded, is the necessity of grasping that JS declined to disclose much for public consumption of what happened to him. His general inherent disposition proved that he kept his private experiences to himself until provoked by external circumstances to disclose them, a characteristic that will be discussed in Chapter 11. This is unsettling for those who expect him to have divulged his sacred experiences, thereby explaining and proving God's work with him. We will see, however, that there is a significant calendar of events of the divine sort that he only briefly mentioned in what little he wrote. And of those things, we have little information and clarification. It is also the case that he did not personally keep journals; chronicling his life was the duty of his clerks, leaving something to be desired regarding JS's personal insights. Because he turned his chronicle over to his clerks we are left without that which we most desire: "The absence of Joseph Smith's own expressions from a key historical record bearing his name means that the one voice central to historical understanding is unavailable," stated Dean Jessee.[21] Similarly, letters to friends and acquaintances were usually penned by clerks. JS's correspondence is generally conversational or instructional, absent personal disclosure about his feelings and emotions. There are a few exceptions to the pattern, including how he expressed himself in the sixteen surviving letters written over twelve years to his wife, Emma, and some communications to men such as W. W. Phelps.[22] Still, there are far too few expressions that reveal the inner JS.

There are other sides to the study of JS. It is demonstrable that, for the most part, those of the believer type who have invested in discovering JS and his church have tended to inform themselves with primarily devotional literature. To expect otherwise is to ignore the reality that most members affiliate with the church to live faith-based, productive Christian lives founded upon Jesus's teachings and biblical/Book of Mormon principles. The millions who weekly join in local worship services, enriched and fed by modern Mormonism, generally do not rely upon empirical explication of the faith to drive their dedication and commitment. No one joins JS's church believing it necessary to obtain a

21. Jessee, "Sources for the Study of Joseph Smith," 19.

22. See the insightful July 31, 1832, letter of JS to Phelps that portrays an exasperated JS who in Kirtland, Ohio, had little communication from those nine hundred miles away in Independence, Missouri. The communication in Frederick G. Williams's hand, besides illustrating the issues on his mind at the time, also expressed JS's disappointment that those in Zion, specifically Phelps, were seemingly indifferent to the weighty matters JS had to bear. This is one of the rare personal disclosures of the prophet, never meant to be made public. JS to W. W. Phelps, July 31, 1832, *JSP, D*2:257–72.

history degree to negotiate the past. However, the strategy to disregard most everything but devotional explanations to describe JS has created a version of belief that many now find hard to defend because of easily accessible contrary data. Access to information via the internet and social media now precludes all attempts to skirt consideration of the broad range of historical documentation that fixes JS on the stage of the early American republic and its powerful, defining culture. Only by viewing him through the wide-angle lens of full disclosure, limited though it inherently is, do we have a chance of reasonably appraising the profiles previously written about him.

The subsequent analyses, even by sympathetic scholars, have not always been flattering to the prophet. Brian Hauglid—professor at BYU's Maxwell Institute—attempting to describe the confusing contextual setting of JS's production and understanding of what became the Book of Abraham, stated "we must be willing to allow his (fallible) humanness to be a necessary part of his prophetic gifts." Regarding the modern attempt to either ignore or vainly elucidate the many unknowables of his life, Hauglid reminds JS students of the importance of allowing faith in JS as a prophet to be understood and appreciated in an atmosphere of abstruseness. Preparing his readers for what is to date Mormonism's most definitive analysis of JS's Book of Abraham and how it was created,[23] he cautioned readers to reserve their demand for conclusive declarations: "This point should be foremost in our minds when we encounter ambiguities concerning how, for example, the Abraham and Egyptian papers, and the papyri, related to the translation of the Book of Abraham" were prepared.[24]

Other confusing aspects of JS's efforts must also be considered. For instance, Mormon scholars Don Bradley and Joseph Smith Papers editor Mark Ashurst-McGee tried to explain JS's murky involvement with the so-called "Kinderhook plates." Hucksters in 1843 in Kinderhook, Illinois, seventy miles south of Nauvoo, apparently manufactured the half-dozen, brass, bell-shaped pieces of metal with purported etchings of antiquity with the intent to humiliate JS. Offering them to him to translate, they expected him to produce a translation that they could then show to be a fraud. Evidence from JS's scribe, William Clayton, indicates JS attempted to identify the etchings and render a text from them.[25] In the absence of demonstrable explanation regarding what JS thought about and did with the plates, Bradley and Ashurst-McGee postulate that JS "mistakenly accepted the Kinderhook plates as authentic artifacts; he mistakenly identified

23. Smith, Revelations, *Book of Abraham and Related Manuscripts, JSP, R4.*

24. Brian M. Hauglid, "The Book of Abraham and Translating the Sacred," *BYU Religious Education* (Winter 2017): 14.

25. William Clayton, *An Intimate Chronicle: The Journals of William Clayton*, ed. George D. Smith (Salt Lake City: Signature Books, 1995), 100 (May 1, 1843).

their characters as Egyptian; and he mistakenly thought that he had translated one or more of these characters."[26] Discovering that JS in his zeal sometimes exceeded his gifts, compromising the models of prophetic infallibility, is difficult to understand for those unfamiliar with the range of JS's experiences. Unrealistic outlines of his mantle leave out-of-sorts those who revere JS as just short of divine. It is little wonder that some in the church are fearful that a Mormonism with which they are not familiar threatens their faith and practice.

The Consideration of Faith as a Necessity to Appraise Joseph Smith

As mentioned, in JS studies it is trendy among some recent biographers to dismiss the divine in appraising him and his circumstances. Empiricism and its experiential demands have increasingly held sway in the modern world. New Testament scholar N. T. Wright argued there was an underlying dismissal of the supernatural in human affairs as early as the third century BCE. by way of Greek philosopher Epicurus. That perspective, later emphasized by eighteenth-century Enlightenment assertions, created an exercise for believers in the providence and intervention of God that can be described as a swim against the current. The effect on those subscribing to the Epicurean premise, as Wright stated, accepted "that the gods did not concern themselves with our world, whether to intervene in it or to judge its inhabitants after death."[27] The skeptical posture was

26. Don Bradley and Mark Ashurst-McGee, "Joseph Smith and the Kinderhook Plates," in *A Reason for Faith: Navigating LDS Doctrine & Church History*, ed. Laura Harris Hales (Provo, UT: Religious Studies Center, Brigham Young University; Salt Lake City: Deseret Book, 2016), 110. The *Nauvoo Neighbor* published bimonthly advertisements for a facsimile of the plates from the end of 1843 through the early months of 1844.

Some have pushed back on taking Clayton's notes at face value. See James B. Allen, "William Clayton and the Records of Church History," in *Preserving the History of the Latter-day Saints*, ed. Richard E. Turley Jr. and Steven C. Harper (Provo, UT: Religious Studies Center, Brigham Young University, 2010), 95–97, whose conclusion plays off Stanley B. Kimball, "Kinderhook Plates Brought to Joseph Smith Appear to Be a Nineteenth-Century Hoax," *Ensign*, August 1981, 66–74.

Something to also consider in light of JS's interest in translating ancient texts is clergyman Henry Caswell's critical allegation in April 1842 that he showed JS a "Greek Psalter" that he owned, with "its covers of worm-eaten oak, its discolored parchments, and its mysterious characters." Upon inspecting the manuscript, Caswell stated that JS told him: "[It] ain't Greek at all; except, perhaps a few words. What ain't Greek, is Egyptian; and what ain't Egyptian, is Greek. This book is very valuable. *It is a dictionary of Egyptian Hieroglyphics*," though there is no corroborating documentation about Caswell's published statement. Henry Caswell, *The City of the Mormons; Or, Three Days at Nauvoo, in 1842* (London: J. G. F. and J. Rivington, 1842), 5, 19–21, 35–36, 43, esp. 20–21, and 35.

27. N. T. Wright, *Surprised by Scripture: Engaging Contemporary Issues* (New York: HarperOne, 2014), 7.

popularly advanced in 1748 by Scottish polymath David Hume, whose method of philosophy encroached upon the prevailing perception of religious belief in his time. Hume's assertion that empirical verification must prevail in all matters where truth had to be verified had a profound effect on the western world: "*Does [the proposition] contain any experimental reasoning concerning matter of fact, and existence?* No. Commit it, then, to the flames: For it can contain nothing but sophistry and illusion."[28] Hume's standard of skepticism, which became widely accepted, had a chilling effect on religious faith and belief thereafter. It powerfully influenced the European and American elite, reinforcing cynicism as a rival to the status of Christianity. But, while the empirical premise is pervasive, it is not all bad for religionists. As has been widely shown, applying reason and scrutiny to religious belief has proven a great utility in sorting through the construction of faith and spirituality.

The notion of *fideism*, literally in Latin "faith-ism," as a means of explaining the otherwise unexplainables of the mortal experience is well grounded. It is at least as old as the patristic writers. The fact that later, noted philosophers such as Blaise Pascal, Søren Kierkegaard, and William James not only accommodate the premise of faith but advocate its usage in considering human professions of connections with God, suggests its viability in appraising JS. Not only is faith not superfluous, they argue, it is essential. James, who wrote at the beginning of the last century and who is acknowledged as the father of American psychological study, confronted cynicism by insisting upon faith's utility in explaining the impossible-to-measure spiritual influences that move the race. James agreed that "the existence of mystical states [religious faith and experience] absolutely overthrows the pretension of non-mystical states to be the sole and ultimate dictators of what we may believe."[29] In the tangled world of thought, James argued for "a defence of our right to adopt a believing attitude in religious matters."[30] And in his famous *Varieties of Religious Experience*, he concluded the volume with this affirmation: "If supernaturalism and inner union with the divine are true, you think, then not so much permission, as compulsion to believe, ought to be found."[31] Disqualifying everything about the divine professed by JS that cannot be proven, or rendering it in snide ridicule, eviscerates the entire premise of his declarations. Former LDS Church assistant church historian, Davis Bitton,

28. David Hume, *An Inquiry Concerning Human Understanding and Other Writings*, ed. Stephen Buckle (New York: Cambridge University Press, 2007), 144 (emphasis in original).
29. Robert D. Richardson, *William James: In the Maelstrom of American Modernism* (Boston: Houghton Mifflin, 2007), 414.
30. William James, "The Will to Believe" in *The World Treasury of Modern Religious Thought*, ed. Jaroslav Pelikan (Boston: Little, Brown, 1990), 95.
31. William James, *The Varieties of Religious Experience* (1902; repr., New York: Vintage Books, The Library of America, 1990), 386.

recognized the essential components of faith and belief as something more than sensory perception, concluding in his *Images of the Prophet Joseph Smith*: "Back in the days before the corruption of our language, before the flattening of our reality into a stark, naturalistic, horizontal plane, there used to be a name for the leap, the signing onto something magnificently demanding and all encompassing, the living out of something as if it were true, the growing conviction of the reality of things hoped for, things unseen. It used to be called *faith*."[32] To discard the hypothesis of nonverifiable belief in appreciating the divine within JS forces him into an arena where he cannot be known for who he was.

The Tradition of the Fathers

As suggested above, another important hazard that must be negotiated while considering the past is how the former and prevailing historical traditions have been handled regarding early Mormonism. The mid-nineteenth-century rendering of JS's life that became the *History of the Church* still strongly influences modern interpretations. This is especially difficult for defenders who, because of the widened boundaries provoked by newly accessible documentation and fresh interpretations—some by the LDS Church itself—must revise long-held viewpoints while also maintaining allegiance to Mormon truth claims. "Telling the complete story," analyst of biographical techniques William Zinsser concedes, "often means dismantling the one that already exists."[33] Discomfiting as the process is, there is nothing inherently noxious in revision, clarification, and greater understanding based on new information and a careful study of the documentary record rendered it in its proper context. "Truth," or *historical truth* as the case may be, "can be very inconvenient at times," said the noted Mormon essayist and past member of the LDS Church's Quorum of the Twelve, Richard L. Evans. "And so," Evans continued, "we sometimes try to talk ourselves into what we wish were true, or out of what we wish weren't true, by admitting all the evidence that would take us where we want to go, and excluding all the evidence that would take us where we don't want to go. In other words, we sometimes decide what we would like the answers to be, and then work back to make them seem to be what we would like."[34] Misunderstanding this premise can, it is arguable, be hazardous to the search for truth, or at least what one thinks may be the truth. But for those whose objective is to gather around them the most authentic forces of influence upon their thinking, applying the methods and caveats of

32. Davis Bitton, *Images of the Prophet Joseph Smith* (Salt Lake City: Aspen Books, 1996), 169–70 (emphasis in original).
33. William Zinsser, *Extraordinary Lives: The Art and Craft of American Biography* (Boston: Houghton Mifflin, 1986), 19.
34. Richard L. Evans, *At This Same Hour* (New York: Harper and Brothers, 1945–1949), 96.

historical inquiry opens the prospect that—to the degree possible—one has at least done the best with what one has to work with.

After an individual has measured and platted the landscape, established the boundaries, and tested the extent of current understanding, there remains the possibility that newly discovered information can alter previously determined judgments. It is an ongoing factor in every category of learning. In the biblical and early Christian world, for example, discovery of the Dead Sea Scrolls in 1947 and the Nag Hammadi texts in 1953 caused readjustments, even by experts, to perspectives about the periods the documents inform. Inevitably, in this generations' access to material regarding JS and early Mormonism discussed in this work, a transformation of thinking will be required due to traditions previously based on limited understanding. And, it is probably the case that in the future new insights, if not new documentation, will amend the scope of what we presently think we know about the prophet.

"History of Joseph Smith"

Traditions are established by societal acceptance of the components instrumental in shaping a viewpoint or a common concern. They are often decades, if not generations, in the making. Traditions, while providing anchors, stability, and unity can also be obstacles when a new lens is required to properly scrutinize the past. Were it not for JS's own prepared "History of Joseph Smith" described above and the legacy of the Smiths, dictated by his mother Lucy Mack Smith, our knowledge about JS and his heritage would be severely limited.[35] After those initial and subsequent historical enterprises surrounding JS's life were created,[36] few Mormon institutional endeavors were executed or even contemplated to ensure his life and works were perpetuated until the last quarter of the nineteenth century. And, for the most part, the ability at the time by church members to purchase or collect the few things that were written about JS remained an urban luxury. Though several projects to keep his memory alive were produced toward the century's end, once those who knew him passed on, it took a new generation

35. Lucy [Mack] Smith, *Biographical Sketches of Joseph Smith the Prophet and His Progenitors for Many Generations* (Liverpool: S.W. Richards, 1853). See the Lucy Mack Smith, History, 1845, on the Joseph Smith Papers website: http://www.josephsmithpapers.org/paper-summary/lucy-mack-smith-history-1845/354. The very useful *Lucy's Book: A Critical Edition of Lucy Mack Smith's Family Memoir*, edited by Lavina Fielding Anderson (Salt Lake City: Signature Books, 2001), compares the dictated manuscript(s) of Lucy's memoir to Martha Jane Knowlton Coray in 1844–45 with Orson Pratt's publication of the account in 1853. See also Sharalyn D. Howcroft, "A Textual and Archival Reexamination of Lucy Mack Smith's History" in Ashurst-McGee, Jensen, and Howcroft, *Foundational Texts of Mormonism*, 298–335.

36. See Jessee, "Reliability of Joseph Smith's History," 27–46.

of believers in the twentieth century to revive a memory of the prophet for public consumption. Publication of B. H. Roberts's monumental publication beginning in 1902, the *History of the Church* described above, filled for most followers every nook and cranny necessary to create and perpetuate customs and tradition. It cannot be overstated how important the production was for a new Mormon tradition of JS, based as it was on that lionized portrait of the prophet.

Modern Mormons' late nineteenth-century forebears knew JS primarily by reputation, though several publications had been produced to fill the void.[37] Roberts's twentieth-century edit of the history—emphasizing the early documentary record—introduced generations of Latter-day Saints to an otherwise vague and boundaryless memory of antebellum Mormonism. In the advent of recent efforts to properly place JS in the environment of Jacksonian America, principally through works like the Joseph Smith Papers, some earlier traditions have been punctured while others have been augmented by new information requiring new perspectives and interpretation. The twentieth-century generations raised on the *History of the Church*, to use an analogy, saw JS as a locomotive erupting from a mountain tunnel under full throttle, belching steam and smoke, blowing cinders, its penetrating whistle bellowing, all surrounded by its overall deafening persona as it burst into the open. The "History of Joseph Smith" that became the *History of the Church* portrayed JS as a massive presence: founder of the religion, producer of modern scripture, prophetic voice, healer, arbiter of God, builder of cities and temples, militia general, mayor and judge, even candidate for the presidency of the United States. All exhibits of JS under full steam. However, by modern studies of JS, observers have a better prospect of understanding him and what he did by joining him in his venture at the entrance to the tunnel, allowing the enlarged perspective from a generation of new research to take them on the journey through the mountain. Though there may be a feature of the precarious in the strategy, that is the opportunity that twenty-first-century scholarship offers.

While adjusting to what is seemingly new information is uncomfortable for many of the believing sort, the fallout from ignoring current issues confronting

37. See Edward W. Tullidge, *Life of Joseph the Prophet* (New York: Tullidge and Crandall, 1878); Andrew Jenson, "Joseph Smith, the Prophet," *Historical Record* 7, nos. 1–3 (January 1888): 353–576; George Q. Cannon, *The Life of Joseph Smith, the Prophet* (Salt Lake City: Juvenile Instructor Office, 1888). There were also thirty-nine sketches from individuals with their "Recollections of the Prophet Joseph Smith" that appeared in the *Juvenile Instructor*, January 15, 1892, to January 1, 1893. See also the report of the reminiscences of sixteen others who gathered in December 1894 for a celebration of JS's birth, *The Salt Lake Herald, Church and Farm Supplement*, January 12, 1895. Twenty-nine memories of JS by elderly members were also later published in the church's *The Young Woman's Journal* in the December 1905 and December 1906 issues. In all, the results remained a detachment from the JS evidenced in his documentary record.

JS followers leaves vulnerable those who for one reason or another are not privy to efforts by church scholars and leaders to better equip its members with an understanding of the past. For many, the problem has been ignorance due to indifference or antagonism to what the Mormon scholarly community has to offer. Mormons are no different than any other people who, confronted by fresh information regarding core beliefs, must come to terms with their past. But, for a people who have been shaped—and have been content for generations—by a history mostly fashioned in the nineteenth century this is especially difficult.

One of the reasons a sympathetic hand is necessary in this study of JS is to tackle the formidable demands necessary to create a contextual understanding of the prophet, while also allowing expression of JS's perspective and worldview in the description of his life. The tone herein presented also accommodates JS's limited capacity to describe himself, despite his substantive effort to do so in his "History of Joseph Smith." I have taken the approach of Paul Nagel, a recognized authority on the famous Adams and Lee families in American history, who suggests in describing a personality: "The story should be complete, but it should also be told with affection rather than with ruthlessness, encouraging the readers to peer for themselves into the darkened corner of a life." "Writing about another person's life," Nagel continued, "is an awesome task, so one must proceed with a gentleness born from knowing that the subject and the author share the frailties of human mortality."[38] Nagel's position recognizes that besides an author's limitations to fully explicate the subject, all humans fall short of unrealistic expectations of faultlessness.

One of the primary limitations to understand the increasing awareness of JS's humanness and the attendant ambiguities surrounding his existence, is derived from generations of effort by his defenders to relieve him from the kind of dissection forensic history offers. Affirmative declarations about his life, without critical review, have always been de facto among believing Latter-day Saints. Indeed, to state or speculate on any matter of JS's life outside the footprint of divine imprimatur has generally been unthinkable from devotees who wrote about him. Absent adherence to that model, those who deviated from the strategy sometimes became disenfranchised thereafter in one way or another. Hence, there has been a concerned and cautious atmosphere for those who have written about the prophet.

Where to from Here?

Given the swirling inconsistencies claimed and polar devices that often characterize claims about the prophet, JS has gotten away from us. Or so it seems. The several biographical portraits written about JS in the previous generation illustrate that despite modern respect for broad interpretations of historical figures,

38. Paul C. Nagel, "The Adams Women" in Zinsser, *Extraordinary Lives*, 114–15.

JS remains subject to the pull of polemical interpretations. A few have refrained from the tendency. Premier among them is *Rough Stone Rolling*. Richard Bushman's study of JS, which includes attention to a significant agenda addressing the panoramic landscape of his life, represents a landmark achievement in Mormon historiography. LDS church-owned *Deseret News* described Bushman as accomplishing "what no historian had before, a balanced, interesting, perhaps even definitive look at the life of the founder of The Church of Jesus Christ of Latter-day Saints—'warts and all.'"[39] Other recent studies made about JS are sophisticated, in most cases elaborately researched and well defended, but unmistakably critical. It leaves the uninformed wondering where to go for clarity. And then there is the factor of the LDS Church itself. How can one ignore or set aside the huge presence of the LDS Church and its influence in how JS is presented before the world? Indeed, the formidable existence of Mormonism is likely one of the primary motivations driving critics to skewer JS. Compromising him diminishes the influence of the faith. That factor must be understood in considering any modern appraisals of the prophet.

While JS will never supersede criticism and attendant commentaries by iconoclasts, dilettantes, and ax-grinders or the deifying accolades of some Mormon enthusiasts, recognizing from where and how the binary constructions were derived is central to the study of the prophet in light of the documentary record. An effect of ignoring the polarities that drive those who have written about JS and unfamiliarity of the terrain where the contest is played, is conceding the ground to the prolific and determined. Many are like those described by distinguished historian Jacques Barzun, "the glib popularizers" who sway the reader and seemingly win the day by persistence.[40]

Given the cautions, caveats, and other warnings that will be discussed in this volume, a question can reasonably be asked as to whether or not the study of JS is feasible to any but those with a scholarly bent augmented by an inordinate amount of time to scour the landscape for insight? It is significant for the reader to understand that there are many gaps in the historical record, along with JS's own reticence to reveal himself, precluding grasp of a comprehensive portrayal of his life. The objective of full disclosure is tempered by the reality that much of what we most want to know about JS was likely not created in the first place. Still, enough cumulative documentation survives that much about his devotions, ambitions, and character can be demonstrated. The future holds great promise that with the renewed surge of interest in early Mormonism and increasing public

39. "Author Bushman's Diary of 'Rough Stone Rolling' Tour is a Page Turner," *Deseret News*, January 7, 2007.

40. Jacques Barzun, *From Dawn to Decadence: 500 Years of Western Cultural Life, 1500 to the Present* (New York: HarperCollins, 2000), 570.

accessibility to the historical record, the plausibility of better understanding JS in his milieu certainly exceeds what was previously possible. And it may be that twenty-first-century info-savvy and techno-satiated students, informed by the new era of Mormon documentation and tools, can sidle up to the prospect that enough exists to beckon even those not historically oriented to engage in the endeavor. In any case, it requires a great deal of work to look into the Mormon past. Understanding the methodologies required to arrive at plausible understanding remains central to the endeavor.

CHAPTER 3

History and Its Methods

The study of the Mormon past, or any historical time for that matter, is not an issue of simply assembling the available documents, books, and other contributing sources into an order that makes sense to the investigator before rendering a judgment about what they represent. The historical profession was built upon the premise that there are numerous interpretive factors that one must apply to the spread of information assembled before there can be a reasonable expectation of understanding the object of study. Given access to the advances of Mormon studies in the past fifty years,[1] to obtain some semblance of understanding requires the pursuant to apply to the study what is termed the "historical method." In employing this way of trying to ascertain the past, a logician's deductive reasoning plays a role in this procedure. But discovering JS is not a scientific exercise. Nor is the enterprise based simply upon the tools employed by the scientific method, though the means of investigation has parallels. "The process of critically examining and analyzing the records and survivals of the past," the historical method, is, according to historian Louis Gottschalk, understood as "*historiography* (the writing of history.)"[2] As proven in other historical ventures, the strategy works in the study of Mormonism as well. The combination of unprecedented access to the historical record and enlarged understanding of Mormon origins finally provides a setting necessary to expand the search for JS to a status where scholars and laymen alike can ascertain what we can or we cannot say about him.

The title of this book suggests an exercise in the basics of looking at JS. In the study of any field, basics are required to be known before the observer can have confidence that how he/she is viewing the objective satisfies the requirements for success. Established by generations of those who have mastered the discipline's

1. See Newell G. Bringhurst and Lavina Fielding Anderson, eds., *Excavating Mormon Pasts: The New Historiography of the Last Half Century* (Salt Lake City: Greg Kofford Books, 2004).

2. Louis Gottschalk, *Understanding History: A Primer of Historical Method*, 2nd. ed. (New York: Alfred A. Knopf, 1969), 48.

methodology, it goes without saying that training is necessary to tackle such subjects as mathematics, chemistry, or physics. The hard sciences are demanding and require years of education and experience to acquire competency. Yet many suppose that they may enter the historical arena without a studied background in the period in question or the methodologies necessary to properly appraise their objectives. Instead they assume their inherent common sense fully equips them to make reasoned judgments in evaluating people and previous times long since gone because things cannot be that much different today than they once were. Those schooled in history, however, know that the methodologies that have developed and matured since the nineteenth century are imperative to help the student prepare themselves to properly investigate their object of interest. It is not necessary that one become proficient in all aspects of the discipline of history to consider days gone by. But there are fundamentals that must be understood in considering how to qualify and appreciate the components that inform the study. The essentials of investigation here identified are fundamental for the laymen and others to employ whose objective it is to responsibly consider JS.

As much as we would like to have the layout of history intact before us—events and conversations available today in the same measure as they were when they occurred—it is simply not possible to recreate and then fully ascertain the circumstances that have already slipped away. "Most human affairs happen without leaving vestiges or records of any kind behind them," Gottschalk stated. "The past having happened, has perished forever with only occasional traces." Driving the point, he asserted:

> To begin with, although the absolute number of historical writings is staggering, only a small part of what happened in the past was ever observed.... Only a part of what was observed in the past was remembered by those who observed it; only a part of what was remembered was recorded; only a part of what was recorded has survived; only a part of what has survived has come to the historians' attention; only a part of what has come to their attention is credible; only a part of what is credible has been grasped; only a part of what has been grasped can be expounded or narrated by the historian.[3]

Gottschalk implied that the investigator must recognize that essentials deemed imperative to modern students may never have been captured in the first place. It is imperative that students of JS recognize this truth, which has relevant application to the Mormon past. In 1974, Jan Shipps, long-time historian of Mormonism, indicated that the state of historical affairs regarding JS presented the enigma of what she called the "Prophet Puzzle." Acknowledging the uneven and conflicted nature of what was known about him, Shipps suggested much

3. Gottschalk, *Understanding History*, 45.

remained to be done in pursuing him. She suggested that inserting a higher-powered lens into the historical apparatus "might allow us to reconcile enough of the inconsistency to reveal ... [the] *whole* man."[4] But a more powerful scope cannot supply missing puzzle pieces. Thus, we are left to make sense of what remains of the documentary record and what it allows us to consider, incomplete though it is.

Absence of a Complete Documentary Record

It is difficult to overstate the fact that the life of JS suffers from not being able to be told in full because of the inadequate surviving historical record. Yet, most modern observers, especially those professing belief in Mormonism, based their perceptions of the man upon that reality. Neither the LDS Church nor most of those who have analyzed JS acknowledged that significant factor. As previously noted, the present palpable dissonance within Mormonism over its past is born of the contrast between a previously undernourished curriculum and the challenging documentation made accessible in the information age. What we don't have, vis-à-vis what we do, can sometimes distort just as easily as it can inform. It is necessary that the investigator recognize the limits of what is possible. For instance, Dean Jessee's careful study of JS informed us that: "Of the 1,587 manuscript pages comprising the Smith journal, 31 contain holograph writing, where he is known to have put his own thoughts on the paper. Another 250 were evidently dictated to scribes."[5] That is 2 percent and 16 percent respectively, indicating that the remainder of JS's journals were prepared for the most part without his imprimatur, though there is evidence he occasionally reviewed texts. While the amount of material composing the JS journal—almost 1,600 pages—suggests extensive information having been captured, in reality the journals are disappointing in revealing JS's thoughts, motives, and behaviors because they were actually created by others. Much of what has been dubbed as JS's thinking, Jessee indicates, was "the product of other men's minds."[6]

The truth is that there is such a void of necessary historical material that the overwhelming majority of life's players can never be authentically illuminated, no matter their importance. Recordkeeping in the past two centuries is spotty at best regarding the paper trail necessary to adequately describe those who have lived. Those who know what is required for a biography are more than aware of the dilemma. After distinguished biographer David McCullough's publisher had shepherded his National Book Award-winning portrayal of the early life of U.S. President Theodore Roosevelt, *Mornings on Horseback* (1981), he suggested to

4. Shipps, "Prophet Puzzle," 20 (emphasis in original).
5. Jessee, *Papers of Joseph Smith*, 2:xxii–xxiii.
6. Jessee, "Sources for the Study of Joseph Smith," 16.

McCullough that he tackle Teddy's famous distant cousin, U.S. President Franklin D. Roosevelt. McCullough declined the invitation. One would think that the most oft-elected executive official in American history would have created more than enough of the required material to satisfy a biographer's needs. "There are many reasons why I didn't do Franklin," McCullough explained, "but one is that Franklin Roosevelt never put his heart on paper. He never expressed what he really felt or really thought about anything, on paper. You have to resort to conjecture, again and again, with Franklin Roosevelt. That's simply the kind of person he was." Instead, McCullough applied his substantial talent to the latter Roosevelt's successor, Harry Truman, and produced a Pulitzer Prize winner. Why? "Truman, by contrast [to FDR], poured himself out [on paper], year after year for years."[7] In JS's case, besides the disappointing content of his journals in regards to revealing the man, the rest of the surviving documentary record also leaves much to be desired.

This premise must be recognized regarding what can be known about JS. *Life once lived* cannot be reestablished, no matter the scope of what remains of his life. If society's modern structural and cultural template was the same as it was in the period in which JS lived perhaps much of our dilemma would be solved. That, however, is not the case. The culture has significantly changed. *We must face the reality that information about the most important features of JS's life may never have been created in the first place; what may be most useful to us today eluded pen and paper altogether.* We may have an outline of the times in which he lived, but we are left to piece together the remaining fragments of the documentary record hoping that we can seize upon something that will give us the penetrating observation for which we yearn. Thus, we are in trouble if our objective is to recreate the past as it was. We are fated to suffer inevitable disappointment from the outset in the quest. Not a very cheery prospect, but it represents the reality of what lies before us. While much about JS survives, there are numerous parcels of JS's life that we wish to know and understand that are simply unavailable. Facing this reality, aggravating though it may be, is not illusory. But don't close the book yet; there is still a lot about JS to discuss.

Presentism/Historical Sense

Perhaps the most important mindset to employ in discovering the past is being careful that those who are subjects of the investigation are considered in their own light, the one that illuminated the circumstances in which they lived. Being sympathetic, compassionate, and curious is not enough. One must become sufficiently acquainted with the foreignness of the past to give ample allowance

7. David McCullough, in Zinsser, *Extraordinary Lives*, 35–36; David McCullough, *Truman* (New York: Simon and Schuster, 1992).

to the recognition that the historical terrain is difficult to both understand and negotiate. Judging from the present is a precarious initiative that may produce results ranging from reasonable to who are you kidding? Some in the historical community call the problem "presentism." The antidote to presentism, to the degree possible, is called "historical sense."[8] It is not just common sense, which is the resolution so many believe is sufficient to encounter a former day. Mormon historian James B. Allen called the phenomenon a "barrier to understanding history." He described it as a "tendency many of us have to superimpose upon past generations our own patterns of thought and perceptions of reality."[9] Historical mindedness requires effort on the part of the investigator, through study and research, to capture as best as possible the contextual circumstances surrounding the event or subject being pursued. The temptation is great to bypass the work necessary to resurrect even a portion of a former time and to rely upon what others have written about the period, though they may have shortcut the cumbersome process themselves. The result is the perpetuation of abbreviated understanding and premature conclusions.

Though modern observers want to genuinely approach the past, we inevitably impose upon our forebears our own world and thinking. "To judge earlier societies by more advanced code of ethics," Gottschalk reminded us, "to expect balanced judgments and normal conduct in time of war, revolution, or upheaval" informed by our own enlightened circumstances, or "to condemn an individual's act without attempting to comprehend his norms or environment" can seriously compromise our objectives. These and "other failures to place persons and events in their own historical setting would often lead to failure to understand the surviving documents and nearly always to misjudgments of the personalities and *mores* of that setting."[10] The pursuit of JS requires the same.

Pulitzer Prize-winning biographer Richard Rhodes related the contemporary circumstances surrounding the world of John James Audubon in his biography of America's most famous ornithologist and wildlife painter. It was a period in American history when natural science was less refined and structured; the time of JS's upbringing. Audubon "engaged birds with the intensity (and sometimes the ferocity) of a hunter because hunting was the cultural frame out of which his encounter with birds emerged." The early nineteenth century was a time "when wild game was still extensively harvested for food, observation for hunting had not yet disconnected from observation for scientific knowledge."

8. Gordon S. Wood, *The Purpose of the Past: Reflections on the Uses of History* (New York: Penguin Press, 2008), 11.
9. James B. Allen, "Emergence of a Fundamental: The Expanding Role of Joseph Smith's First Vision in Mormon Religious Thought," *Journal of Mormon History* 7 (1980): 43.
10. Gottschalk, *Understanding History*, 136–37 (emphasis in original).

Audubon's penchant for "killing birds for food and for sport, sometimes in great numbers" puzzles the modern observer. But as Rhodes explained, "To argue that he should have known better is anachronistic and nostalgic."[11] For many today it is enough to identify commonalities that we share with our forebears. Yet the temptation is great to indict those of a previous age with ethical laxity when encountering disparity between the course of the past and the present. "Latter-day moral judgments," historian Joseph J. Ellis has stated, "are notoriously easy to render from the comfortable perch that hindsight always provides."[12]

It is common today to impose the values of a world that has morphed over two centuries, in the case of Mormonism, on our historical benefactors. But "the present should not be the criterion for what we find in the past. Our perceptions and explanations of the past should not be directly shaped by the issues and problems of our own time."[13] Being quick to condemn without proper perspective is a common mistake. For example, JS has been charged with deceptively manipulating the original texts of his revelations, especially the Doctrine and Covenants, without explaining his actions to later readers. Today we expect transparency when such important matters are altered. Holding him accountable for the redactions is informed by modern academic standards that insist that when changes are made in texts, the reader must be notified of the adjustment. Because JS did not foresee editing conventions presently used, by silently adding to or detracting from the revelations based upon his growing perspectives without notifying the reader, he has been condemned as devious and fraudulent.[14]

It should be starkly evident that we of the twenty-first century are significantly different than those of JS's era. The five "revolutions" that have shaped the modern era—industry, transportation, technology, communication, and information—have supplanted the four environmental seasons around which everything affecting those in JS's agrarian culture grew. Moderns are mostly prohibited from empathizing with JS's world. Delving into that sphere must be approached with not only recognition of the inherent boundaries of the quest, but also with the good sense, sympathy, and understanding for those under investigation. While today's student can never time travel, even intellectually, to recover the past, having sensibilities and consideration toward those in a former

11. Richard Rhodes, *John James Audubon: The Making of an American* (New York: Alfred A. Knopf, 2004), 74–75.
12. Joseph J. Ellis, *American Sphinx: The Character of Thomas Jefferson* (New York: Vintage Books, 1998), 176.
13. Wood, *Purpose of the Past*, 10.
14. See Jerald and Sandra Tanner, *Mormonism Shadow or Reality*, enl. and rev., 4th ed. (Salt Lake City: Utah Lighthouse Ministry, 1982), 14–31D.

day and place provides a greater opportunity to hit upon the rhythms and cadences to which those in the past marched. Slinging mud in judgment about thinking or practices that do not suit our taste smacks of arrogance generally born of ignorance. "To be able to see the participants of the past," wrote historian Gordon S. Wood, "in the context of their own time, to describe their blindness and folly with sympathy, to recognize the extent to which they were caught up in changing circumstances over which they had little control, and to realize the degree to which they created results they never intended—to know all this about the past and to be able to relate it without anachronistic distortion to our present is what is meant by having a historical sense." And since "we can never completely escape, even imaginatively, from our present, some degree of anachronism is inevitable in all history writing."[15] Readers must recognize that inherent weakness in what the historian produces. As social commentator and historian Garry Wills reminds us, "We must fight off our knowledge of the goal to which in fact men's efforts were tending if we are to judge their own hopes and fears as they made those efforts."[16] This is particularly imperative in evaluating JS in context.

Judging the Credibility of the Documentary Record

Among the most difficult tasks shared by historians and students alike is to measure the degree of credibility to give to the sources and documentation created about a person such as JS. How does "an historian run his fact-detector over [the] debris of time?" G. R. Urban queried.[17] Using a linear continuum to illustrate the scope of viewpoints about JS, where along the spectrum of opinion does one apply a statement from a contemporary devotee who has embraced Mormonism without restraint? Likewise, where along the line does the statement fall of one who by his plea was betrayed by JS for one reason or another? In between there are a multitude of variations that the historian must consider. How much weight can be given to a testimonial, a "half-truth," or even a lie with a "nugget" of truth? Not unlike a courtroom where evidence is delivered by adversaries in a legal case, the jury must weigh the contentions of interested parties before making their judgment. Which ones evoke sympathy; which ones have the ring of credibility; which ones are palpably biased or polemic; or which ones must be taken with a grain of salt? "Having found the documents," Gottschalk maintained, "he [the researcher] will have to establish two things about them: first, are they authentic, or which parts of them are, if only some of them or sec-

15. Wood, *Purpose of the Past*, 11, 29.

16. Garry Wills, *Inventing America: Jefferson's Declaration of Independence* (New York: Vintage Books, 1979), 58.

17. Toynbee, *Toynbee on Toynbee*, 4.

tions of some of them are authentic? Second, how much of the authentic parts are credible, and to what an extent?"[18] While that may sound straightforward, in matters concerning the documentary record of JS, it is more complicated.

Given the ubiquitous place of the miraculous within Mormon discourse, with the concession that the supernatural is not measurable by empirical means, how *some* unusual stories from the Mormon past are presented becomes an issue. Proclamations by church members about incidents surrounding the "gifts of the spirit" and the intercession of God are legion. They are so central in understanding the mindset of early Mormons that to discard their importance factors out one of the defining classifications of the faith. Healings, speaking in tongues, visions, discernment of spirits, and God's intervention through miracles are fixtures within the corpus of Mormon belief. Because the incidents fit biblical models and parallel manifestations in other denominations that harbor belief in the supernatural, the gifts of the spirit claimed by the Latter-day Saints were not held among the Saints to be impossible or too far outside the boundary of credulity. The miraculous is not a problem for many due to the mostly accepted premise that extrasensory experiences are prevalent, though hard to define. But what about "extreme supernaturalism," as it has been called, the type of phenomenon that exceeds utilitarian necessity?

Brigham Young and Heber C. Kimball, for instance, publicly described circumstances where JS with Oliver Cowdery—upon returning the gold plates to the angel Moroni after their translation in 1829—were taken into a "cave" within the Hill Cumorah where vast quantities of Nephite and Lamanite plates were held. Kimball in 1856 indicated the incident was a "vision" to JS and Oliver.[19] Brigham Young on the other hand, while implying the story came from Cowdery himself, described in December 1869 according to Wilford Woodruff a distinctly material event. JS, according to Young, returned the gold plates after their translation not directly to the angel Moroni but to a "Cave in the Hill Comoro [Cumorah] with Oliver Cowdry" depositing "those plates upon a table or shelf." The room held "a large amount of gold plates Containing sacred records," indeed "tons of Choice treasures & records," as well as the Sword of Laban, a Book of Mormon artifact.[20] Eight years later, shortly before his death, Young related the story again, describing "a large table that stood in the room. Under this table there was a pile of plates as much as two feet high, and there were altogether in this room more plates than probably many wagon loads; they were piled up in

18. Gottschalk, *Understanding History*, 27.

19. Heber C. Kimball, on September 28, 1856, described the occurrence as a "vision" by JS "and others" as reported in *JD*, 4:105.

20. Wilford Woodruff, Journal, December 11, 1869, *Wilford Woodruff's Journal, 1833–1898*, trans. and ed. Scott G. Kenney, 9 vols. (Salt Lake City: Signature Books, 1983–1985), 6:508.

the corners and along the walls."[21] In the "cave in the Hill Cumorah" incident, is Kimball's "vision" the better description of the event than Young's later apparent objectification? Is this the miraculous or the extreme supermiraculous? What does a modern investigator make of such claims? These are questions that remain open ended but play into how today's researchers must evaluate records from the past.

There are other required considerations to qualify the credibility of a historical record: how close was the source to the person or event in question? Was the source an eyewitness, or was it a secondhand report? Though it must be allowed that the secondary supplier may have been more insightful than a primary observer, weighing the qualification and intent of the sources is a necessity. The factor of the timing and proximity of the historical artifact to the occurrence also greatly matters; was the account created at the time of the event, soon after, or several or many years after the fact? And, as is often the case, what does one do when there is competing documentation, i.e., qualified sources portraying different viewpoints? George Bernard Shaw is reported to have said "that when an historian had to rely on one document he was safe, but if there were two to be consulted he was in difficulty, and if three were available his position was hopeless."[22] Careful scrutiny of the intent of the document's creator is the burden of the student, an issue also spilling over to the validity of memory, a matter discussed later. These issues are central in evaluating the credibility of a record.

In surveying the literature created during JS's life, the investigator will inevitably encounter critics and what they wrote about him—like Alexander Campbell, E. D. Howe, and John C. Bennett. Despite their challenges to Mormonism, what they produced contained important contemporary perspectives about JS and his religion that cannot be dismissed out of hand.[23] Then there was Joseph H. Jackson, an acquaintance who later became an enemy of JS, who

21. Brigham Young, June 17, 1877, *JD*, 19:38. Orson Pratt also once described an enormous, tangible repository where other plates were created and kept by the ancients. *Latter Day Saints' Millennial Star*, July 7, 1866, 417. Another viewpoint to be considered is the statement of David Whitmer in response to a query by P. W. Poulson as reported by the latter in the August 13, 1878, *Deseret News*, 2. Poulson: "Where are the plates now?" Whitmer: "In a cave, where the angel has hidden them up . . ." Poulson: "Where is that cave?" Whitmer: "In the state of New York." Poulson: "In the Hill Cumorah?" Whitmer: "No, but not far from that place." See other accounts in Cameron J. Packer, "Cumorah's Cave," *Journal of Book of Mormon Studies* 13, nos. 1–2 (2004): 50–57.
22. Irving L. Janis, *Victims of Groupthink: A Psychological Study of Foreign-Policy Decisions and Fiascoes* (Boston: Houghton Mifflin, 1972), v.
23. A[lexander] Campbell, "Delusions," *The Millennial Harbinger*, February 7, 1831; Eber D. Howe, *Mormonism Unvailed: Or, A Faithful Account of that Singular Imposition and Delusion, From Its Rise to the Present Time* (Painesville, OH: self-published, 1834); John C. Bennett, *The History of the Saints: Or, an Exposé of Joe Smith and Mormonism*, 3rd ed. (1842; repr. Urbana, IL: University of Illinois Press, 2000).

lashed out at the prophet coincident to his death the summer of 1844. Illustrating the care that must be taken in evaluating what was being said about JS, some of Jackson's statements are historically defendable while others are so outlandish that they cannot stand against the mountain of contrary evidence. In one instance after softening up JS, Jackson claimed: "[JS] gave in, and acknowledged to me his proper character and principles. He admitted himself an atheist, and the Book of Mormon a humbug;—and that the original was written by Lyman [Solomon] Spalding, whose heirs now have it in their possession."[24] The statement is so preposterous that not even JS's most ardent detractors would accept Jackson's appraisal today. Because the opposition to JS then and now is vigorous, students of early Mormonism must understand that the publications identified above, and others of the same stripe, are not just another point of view. Their intent was to wholly discredit. It is granted that an impartial review of the sources may result in a critical determination about JS. But such an outcome is generally an altogether different type of scrutiny than that of evisceration, abhorrence, and disgust. On the other hand, the reader need not look too far down the library shelf to find comparably one-sided portraits of JS by his contemporary followers characterized as devotional and driven by similar selectivity in claims and affirmations used to influence the reader.

Another concern is what does one do when the evidence is thin or sketchy, and in what manner should a writer who draws conclusions based on flimsy data explain what he/she has done? Due to the inevitable liabilities without a complete documentary record, writers often resort to supposition to create their narrative. In commenting on issues not supported by the surviving sources, twentieth-century commentator Sydney J. Harris argued that, "The difference between a good historian and a bad historian is not that one knows more than the other, though that is important; it is that the good historian will tell you when he is guessing, which is much of the time."[25] Speculation is not against the historical rulebook. "I have nothing against conjecture," concluded William Zinsser, "as long as the biographer makes clear that it *is* conjecture." It is when speculation surpasses the record without notifying the reader that the author has crossed the line of nonfiction and fiction. "The temptation is to fictionalize—to impute motives that can't be documented, to dress up a scene or a character or an episode with details that might work in a novel but have no basis in fact."[26] Richard Bushman reminded us that writers about early Mormonism have often used the tactic to characterize JS and what he did: "Joseph 'may' have done this

24. Joseph H. Jackson, "Startling Disclosures," *Warsaw Signal*, June 5, 1844. See also Joseph H. Jackson, *A Narrative of the Adventures and Experience of Joseph H. Jackson in Nauvoo, Disclosing the Depths of Mormon Villainy* (Warsaw, IL: n.p., August 1844).
25. Sydney J. Harris, *Strictly Speaking* (Chicago: Henry Regnery, 1953), 240.
26. Zinsser, *Extraordinary Lives*, 88 (emphasis in original).

and 'probably' did that," intending that the "series of surmises [would replace] a documented narrative."[27] The student of JS, if not careful, can walk away from the historical process with distorted perspectives that are reliant upon conclusions that both ignore some evidence and surpass the constrictions imposed by the limits of the documentary record.

Other Methods That Attempt to Explain Joseph Smith

Another controversial tactic, touted as a bridge between history and psychology/psychiatry, is what has been called psychohistory or psychobiography. The prospect of uncovering the palpably unknown and unavailable psyche nudges practitioners to add their insights into the conversation. The quest is alluring to investigate "the mental aberrations of significant personalities in relation to their works."[28] Consequently, some from the psychology/psychiatric community have entered into the realm of history to submit JS to scrutiny generally not applied by historians. The practice is rooted in the premise that uncovering the organic influences of mind and biology plays a significant impetus for distinguishing characteristics of one's physiognomy. Though never embraced fully by the historical community, the strategy has, nevertheless, been employed for many years, even in JS's case. It should go without saying that the psychology/psychiatry professions offer insight into how people respond to external and internal stimuli. However, many historians are reluctant to accept the application of psychological techniques to ascertain the thinking and motivations of dead people from distant and culturally foreign time periods, especially when the historical record to support such contentions is scant.

Provoked by the prospect that a human's emotional and intellectual interior reveals much about an individual's behavior, it is claimed that the origins of unexplainable or subtle conduct of some are repressed or magnified by the subject's pathological maladies. Psychological designs are sometimes imposed despite the absence of the fundamental components that comprise the checklist of historical necessaries. And, none are immune from analysis. Used early in the twentieth century by Dr. Albert Schweitzer, even the person of Jesus of Nazareth found himself subject to the methodology. "The suspicion that the mind of Jesus might somehow have morbid characteristics" was to Schweitzer within the limits of exploration. Schweitzer ascertained that Jesus flaunted the "quixotic idea that he was destined to appear in the near future in a blaze of supernatural glory, surrounded by angels, on the clouds of heaven, to judge the world as the expected Messiah and to establish the Kingdom which was to follow."[29] With little consideration of why, when, and by whom the biblical gospels were crafted

27. Bushman, *Rough Stone Rolling*, 58.
28. Albert Schweitzer, *The Psychiatric Study of Jesus: Exposition and Criticism* (Boston: Beacon Press, 1963), 33.
29. Ibid., 34.

in the first place—explained by source and text criticism, the very records upon which reasonable conclusions must be derived—Schweitzer professed that in the "great drama of the public ministry of Christ stretching over three years, the megalomania, which mounted ceaselessly and immeasurably, formed the center around which everything else turned."[30] As one might imagine, Schweitzer's position was not well received or taken seriously by the Christian community, including much of its scholarly division. One of the reasons Christian scholars push back from Schweitzer's notions is that his analysis was prepared outside the historical arena that informs most of what we know about Jesus in the first place. Scholars of the early Christian era know that questions about the origins of the gospels, and the Pauline texts for that matter, precede in every way a psychological analysis based upon modern assumptions about how Jesus thought and why he did what he did.[31]

The environment of psychological investigation informed the initial study of that ilk about the Mormon prophet. I. Woodbridge Riley's significant turn-of-the-last-century "psychological study of Joseph Smith, Jr.," raised questions about JS and his behavior not previously addressed. Riley, at the time a University of New Brunswick professor, published his doctoral thesis as *The Founder of Mormonism* (1903) arguing that others who had tried to ascertain JS's mystifying influence and durability had done so without success. "Sectarians and phrenologists, spiritualists and mesmerists" had their say previously and "it now remains for the psychologist to have a try" to explain the Mormon prophet. Riley, having concluded that the Smith family exhibited characteristics of mental and biological disease, suggested that the genetic defect was inherent in the family: "These are causally connected with the seizures which afflicted [Lucy Mack Smith family] descendant[s] sixty years later. The case reads like epilepsy," which symptoms "go far to explain the 'visions and revelations' and other abnormalities of grandfather and grandson [JS Jr.] alike."[32] Riley's analysis of JS's thinking and motives opened the door for others to force JS into their psychological models to cull from him behavioral manifestations that explained his uniqueness.[33] Numerous other speculators have weighed in with their own postulations designed

30. Ibid., 41.

31. See John Shelby Spong, *Re-claiming the Bible for a Non-Religious World* (New York: HarperOne, 2011), 203–409.

32. I. Woodbridge Riley, *The Founder of Mormonism: A Psychological Study of Joseph Smith, Jr.* (London: William Heinemann, 1903), 15.

33. See Harry M. Beardsley, *Joseph Smith and His Mormon Empire* (Boston: Houghton Mifflin, 1931), 67, 81, 82–84, 126, 396–98. Others, such as Bernard DeVoto, who grew up around Mormons and became part of the famous early twentieth-century American literati, also pushed pathological explanations to account for JS's motivations. DeVoto settled on paranoia as the stimulus for JS's behavior and visions. Dale Morgan, *Dale Morgan on Early Mormonism: Correspondence & a New History*, ed. John Philip Walker (Salt Lake City: Signature Books, 1986), 92, 95.

to explain JS. But it was not until Fawn Brodie's dissection of his brain that "psychobiography" became increasingly accepted as fair game to explain the JS enigma.

More recently others applying psychiatric mockups to the generalities known about JS have attempted to evaluate him, though it is clear that in their narratives the demands of the overall documentary record are subordinate to their methods. The psychiatric approach necessarily employs speculative apparatus where explicit information does not exist to construct a plausible structure by which to judge JS. Concerning fundamental features of JS's early life, psychiatrist Jess Groesbeck suggested that the "apparent discrepancies between the different accounts of the First Vision *may reflect* Joseph's changing psychological state," a posture that is not beyond reason. But he also pushed the notion that a pathological strain afflicted the Smiths, explaining that Alvin, JS's older brother "*may have been* burdened with his parents' depression, particularly that of his father." Thereafter, "*one might postulate* that depression, struggle and loss, spiritually, emotionally and otherwise, plagued the Smith and Mack families for several generations." Other contentions applied by Groesbeck resulted in JS Jr. utilizing "a displacement mechanism at an unconscious level," which colored all that he did, including provoking Smith family dynamics that influenced in no small way his construction of the Book of Mormon text.[34] That the Smiths may have been subject to the afflictions that beset the rest of humanity is, obviously, entirely plausible. But it is evident that the psychiatric postulations were conceived from *evidence* gleaned from surveying but a small segment of the historical record such as Lucy Mack Smith's autobiographical account and the little that shows up about the family in JS's "History of Joseph Smith." Others with the same intent of tempering his declarations and questioning his wherewithal have applied psychological scrutiny to JS, in particular elaborating upon the prospect that he was bound by a dissociative personality.[35]

Recognizing Bias

In an ideal world, the historical enterprise of discovery is hopefully presented by those who enter the historian's arena as free from bias and prejudice as possible. In JS's case, he never managed to create an environment where those interested enough to attempt to explain him could do anything but pick sides. The defenders, though there are notable exceptions, have generally presented him in

34. C. Jess Groesbeck, "The Smiths and Their Dreams and Visions: A Psycho-Historical Study of the First Mormon Family," *Sunstone* 12 (March 1988): 22–29 (emphasis added).
35. William D. Morain, *The Sword of Laban: Joseph Smith, Jr. and the Dissociated Mind* (Washington: American Psychiatric Press, 1998); and Robert D. Anderson, *Inside the Mind of Joseph Smith: Psychobiography and the Book of Mormon* (Salt Lake City: Signature Books, 1999).

narratives that accentuate the features of his life that awakened and continue to provoke a segment of the population to seize Mormon essentials and truth claims. Those who disparage the prophet, on the other hand, by the very nature of what they are trying to accomplish, tend to present their portrayals as counters to Mormon traditions. Robert Remini explained one effect and general outcome of the latter's methods. The foremost Jacksonian-period scholar of his time, Remini wrote an evenhanded, though all-too-brief profile of JS in 2002 as part of a biographical series about significant personalities.[36] Alerting students about how they must apply care when reading secondary materials that had been written about JS, he stated, "if a historian does not believe Joseph Smith's claims and sets out to prove that the Prophet was a fake, intent on deceiving the gullible for his own selfish purposes, as some have said, then the work is polemical and valueless as history."[37] The same may be said about those whose designs are specifically designed to glorify and lionize JS.

Another subtle tool used by some writers to influence their readers can be found in the form of how the narrative is presented. Some disputatious writers, by the arrangement of their documentation, signal that they have done their duty to the historical record, thereby positioning their presentation to accentuate or diminish evidence to sway their readers toward their point of view. Historian Herbert Butterfield warned against the ploy: a serious sin in "historical composition is the organization of the story in such a way that bias cannot be recognized."[38] Here again the reader is called upon to perform analysis that exceeds the content of what they are reading, requiring them to investigate the issue beyond the presentation. Thus, the intent and tone of authors who have shaped the field of JS studies, devotional or antagonistic, must carefully be evaluated.

The Authenticity and Thoroughness of the Records

Yet another feature left to the student is the matter of judging the veracity of the documentary record, as well as the secondary literature derived from the sources. The question of authenticity of the record used to shape historical conclusions cannot be treated lightly. Is the purported evidence an authentic historical document? Until the mid-1980s the issue of forgery merited examination only occasionally regarding early Mormonism.[39] Contesting Mormon

36. Robert V. Remini, *Joseph Smith* (New York: Viking Penguin, 2002).

37. Robert V. Remini, "Biographical Reflections on the American Joseph Smith," in *The Worlds of Joseph Smith: A Bicentennial Conference at the Library of Congress*, ed. John W. Welch (Provo, UT: Brigham Young University Press), 23.

38. Herbert Butterfield, quoted in *An Urchin in the Storm: Essays about Books and Ideas*, ed. Stephen Jay Gould (New York: W. W. Norton, 1987), 150.

39. Two well-known attempts at the beginning of the twentieth century to foist upon the public counters to Mormon traditions were claims concerning Oliver Cowdery's post-Mormon career, specifically that he denied his testimony of the Book of Mormon and

historiography and tradition, a young college student, Mark Hofmann, in 1980 began to subtly leak to the Mormon community historical documents he had skillfully created to challenge Mormon truth claims.[40] The attention provoked by Hofmann's iconoclastic documents in the early 1980s, raised initially by the local and then national media, compounded after Hofmann committed two murders while trying to control and cover his unraveling scheme. His most significant documents he advanced for both monetary gain and to deflate Mormon traditions. They, along with his numerous other literary deceptions, were later found to be well-crafted forgeries. Since then, the matter of the authenticity of a historical document pertinent to early Mormonism is inevitably and routinely scrutinized.[41] Questioning the origin or provenance (chain of custody) of historical documents is an essential function of historians; it should also be on the minds of those who use the historical method to inform their worldview.

The many variables of historical inquiry discussed above may appear to the layman to be excessive and superfluous. They are significant, however, as many today are moved to examine Mormon origins due to the recent accessibility of documentation exhibiting the early church and the ministry of JS. Given the early returns regarding how the new information is received, it appears that some when presented with new historical insights in a context of faith are adaptive to accommodating the added data. Others, it is evident, are challenged in how the new generation of Mormon historiography reflects upon the modern LDS Church and the manner it has delivered church history in the past. It will undoubtedly require time for modern Mormon history to congeal into a transportable and defendable tradition for future students.

---

allegiance to JS: "A Confession of Oliver Overstreet," and *Defense in a Rehearsal of My Grounds for Separating Myself from the Latter Day Saints*. Background of the forgeries is presented by Mormon critics Jerald and Sandra Tanner. See their "Mormon and Anti-Mormon Forgeries" in *Salt Lake City Messenger*, October 1989, http://www.utlm.org/newsletters/no73.htm. See also BYU professor Richard L. Anderson's argument against the forgeries in "Did Oliver Cowdery, One of the Three Special Book of Mormon Witnesses, Express Doubt about His Testimony?," *Ensign*, April 1987, 23–25; and Richard E. Turley Jr., *Victims: The LDS Church and the Mark Hofmann Case* (Urbana, IL: University of Illinois Press, 1992), 14–16, who characterized both the "Confession of Oliver Overstreet" and *Defense* as forgeries meant to obfuscate Cowdery's later witness regarding early Mormonism.

40. For extensive portrayals of the Hofmann affair see Turley, *Victims*, and Linda Sillitoe and Allen Roberts, *Salamander: The Story of the Mormon Forgery Murders*, 2nd ed. (Salt Lake City: Signature Books, 1989).

41. See Jeremy Talmage, "Forging a Dream: The Fabrication of Mosiah Hancock's Premortal Vision," *Mormon Historical Studies* 18, no. 2 (Fall 2017): 71–91. See also a related example in Don L. Penrod, "Edwin Rushton as the Source of the White Horse Prophecy," *BYU Studies* 49, no. 3 (2010): 75–131.

CHAPTER 4

Memory as History

Preparing the day-by-day account of his 1835 missionary journey, George A. Smith—cousin of JS and church apostle who in 1853 became LDS Church historian—wrote circa 1857: "I was not able to write sufficiently well to keep a journal and my traveling companion Lyman Smith kept a very brief one, which was lost.... I write from memory, most of the dates, names and distances being forgotten, but the principal facts are fresh in my mind."[1] The methodology of producing history by George A. Smith represented how a large portion of nineteenth-century Mormonism found its way into memoirs as well as the printed page of institutional history. Folks at that time thought differently about how information was packaged and transported than do their descendants generations later. People today have a hierarchy for acceptance of historical material, a method generally not entertained before the twentieth century, at least not in Mormon circles. Because of the abundance of memory-stimulated documentation, what credence do we apply to memory as a source for history? While, when properly understood, all history is memory, the perception—whether immediate or dated—must be considered in the search for veracity.

George A. Smith's explanation of how he produced his story over twenty years after the fact, illustrates an oft-repeated exercise in describing the first decades of Mormonism. And what about matters that were simply forgotten? Oliver Cowdery, a handful of years after his involvement in Mormonism's foundational events, acknowledged in his rehearsal of early events pertinent to his involvement with JS that "in the history of a work of this magnitude, many items which would be interesting to those who follow, are forgotten."[2] Enthusiasts of

1. George A. Smith, Memoir, draft 2 for June 5, 1835, 62, George A. Smith Papers, ca. 1857, MS 1322, box 1, folder 2, CHL (available online in digital form accessed from the CHL catalog).

2. Oliver Cowdery to W. W. Phelps, "Letter IV," *Messenger and Advocate*, February 1835, 78.

history yearn for reliable, written-at-the-time records upon which to build their interpretations. But in the absence of primary documentation, memory is often called upon to fill the gaps left by those who, for a myriad of reasons, failed to create contemporaneous records. It is conceded that, after seasoning and experience, sometimes the view from hindsight can get closer to what happened than a contemporary snapshot. BYU professor Donald Q. Cannon noted the symbiosis when both the eyewitness and recollection combine to give perspective: "The reminiscence recalls the essential core issues, but also adds detail and color which probably were not part of the original experience. The diary entry, on the other hand, refines and sharpens the image produced by the reminiscence.... Both kinds of sources are important in helping us understand the past."[3] Thus, the factor of memory, the weight it carries, and how it influenced creation of the materials now pertinent to JS's life and time is crucial. But caution must be applied in ascertaining the distribution of credibility assigned to the accounts, whether produced early or late.

As is well known, there are positive uses of memory in giving perspective to history that can be established in no other way. Some significant studies about particular incidents in history that rely exclusively on the documentary record created at or near the time of the event often lack the view of a wide-angled lens informed by time. It is no surprise that a contemporary record created *on the spot* excludes peripheral particulars that may impact the circumstance of the event. While immediate documentation may be lengthier, containing minutia, details, and descriptions that may be forgotten over time, the vista from hindsight given via memory may provide outlook multiplied by later experience—thereby giving richer insight into the event in question, despite its limitations for accuracy. Thus, memories, immediate and delayed, can be of great importance to the historian in trying to understand the past.

Moderns must remember that the creation of Mormonism occurred in a number of ways, two of which are here significant. First, there is the experiential circumstances that gave early members personal knowledge and emotion; and then, as it trickled out, the production of written portrayal of what they had witnessed. In both cases, as those who verbally or literarily generated accounts, their reflections upon what happened thereafter shaped how those who came later thought about the faith and those who lived it. All of it, in one way or another, was based on memory. Even what we know of and from JS fits the condition. Though it is impossible to properly gauge, recognizing JS's memory as a dynamic in the historical material eventually produced is important in itself. As will be discussed in Chapter 7, the initial attempt by JS to create a historical nar-

3. Donald Q. Cannon, "Angus M. Cannon and David Whitmer: A Comment on History and Historical Method," *BYU Studies* 20, no. 3 (Spring 1980): 299.

rative in the summer of 1832 was an exercise in memory. The differences therein with the history he inaugurated six years later—the 1838/39 history known as "The History of Joseph Smith," later fashioned as the *History of the Church*—may be attributed to how his subsequent experience informed his memory and perspectives. As JS biographer Richard Bushman stated, "With Joseph's realization of himself as a prophet, the rearrangement of memory began."[4]

Generally, Louis Gottschalk reminded us, "a witness's reliability is, in general, inversely proportional to the *time-lapse* between the observation of the event and the witness' recollection, the closer the time of making a document was to the event it records, the better it is likely to be for historical purposes."[5] Numerous memory studies in recent years have noted the strengths and weaknesses of recollections based upon bias, circumstances, and the factor of elapsed time. And, while recording devices since the twentieth century have made retrieval of the "memory" more immediate and precise, in all cases the final morsel of information gleaned from the observation came through the human filter that remembered the matter. The burden of modern investigators of JS is to appraise the recollections for bias and the veracity of the declarant before making judgment as to whether or not the account fits within the established boundaries of historical evidence. Timing of the recorded occurrence affects the weight of the observation. But dated accounts do not necessarily disqualify the remembrance. Indeed, an expression written thirty years after an episode, informed by experience and other factors, may actually be the best representation of the moment. Nevertheless, the length of time dividing the memory from the episode will always require qualification of the account, as well as its accuracy.

Today we are fortunate that some of JS's contemporaries who listened to him or observed him in public or private chose to write on paper what they thought they heard him say or saw him do.[6] While much of that information is available today, qualifications regarding what the surviving texts reveal must be considered. For example, in his ministerial role JS apparently never read from a prepared text in his sermons or speeches, leaving us mostly ignorant of the precise manner of his verbal expression. Moreover, neither were there verbatim reports of what he said, where phonographers proficient in shorthand rendered complete reports of his sermons. As it was, a number of individuals penned notes of what they thought they heard JS say in his orations, including summaries kept

4. Bushman, *Rough Stone Rolling*, 69.

5. Gottschalk, *Understanding History*, 90.

6. See the very useful compilation and annotation of JS's Nauvoo-era sermons in Andrew F. Ehat and Lyndon W. Cook, eds., *Word of Joseph Smith: The Contemporary Accounts of the Nauvoo Discourses of the Prophet Joseph* (Provo, UT: Religious Studies Center, Brigham Young University, 1980).

by several of his clerks.[7] These, however, are not exact representations of what JS said, but rather are summations taken in longhand. Others favored us with dated recollections of what they observed in JS's deportment and behavior or what they believe they heard him say in conversation. Much of this was put to paper many years after the fact.[8] Some of these recollections were digested and held in the minds of the observers for decades before being prepared for consumption.

To state the obvious, in the absence of verbatim reports, much of what is known or believed to have been said by JS is based on someone else's memory, whether it was immediate, recent, or distant. The moment an incident is experienced or witnessed, a thought is triggered in the individual that we call a memory. Those impressions that deepen or fade over time, or usually something in between, are also generally influenced by sensory perceptions as well as later experiences that shape the thought.

The notion of memory as applied here is a common one, based on the premise that the human brain through a cognitive act processes information in the hippocampus that eventually resides in the cerebral cortex. The variability about how that information is retained is determined by the individual, consciously or not. But, as biblical scholar Bart Ehrman affirmed: "The past is not a fixed entity back there in time. It is always being transformed in our minds, depending on what our minds are occupied with in the here and now."[9] And as with every cognitive construction created in our brains, the mind accepts, dismisses, sorts, and aligns according to its experience and frame of reference. For some, an individual's experience or witness can seemingly be seared into one's mind at a moment. However, over time that memory and its importance or lack thereof is generally shaped by an individual's subsequent experience. Thus, as Abraham Lincoln scholar Douglas L. Wilson noted: "Reminiscent testimony is admittedly problematical. Not only is it often vague and ambiguous, it is notoriously subject

7. Consideration of JS's choice not to have his exact words preserved is found in Chapter 11. See also the discussion of JS's preaching by William V. Smith, "Joseph Smith's Sermons and the Early Mormon Documentary Record" in Ashurst-McGee, Jensen, and Howcroft, *Foundational Texts of Mormonism*, 190–230.

For texts of JS's sermons, see Ehat and Cook, *The Words of Joseph Smith*. Other compilations, less informational than Ehat and Cook, include Alma P. Burton, comp., *The Discourses of Joseph Smith* (Salt Lake City: Deseret Book, 1967); and Larry E. Dahl and Donald Q. Cannon, ed., *Encyclopedia of Joseph Smith's Teachings* (Salt Lake City: Deseret Book, 1997). See also *The Essential Joseph Smith* (Salt Lake City: Signature Books, 1995).

8. Compilation of those recollections were included in such works as Hyrum and Helen Mae Andrus, comps., *They Knew the Prophet* (Salt Lake City: Bookcraft, 1974); and Mark L. McConkie, *Remembering Joseph: Personal Recollections of Those Who Knew the Prophet Joseph Smith* (Salt Lake City: Deseret Book, 2003).

9. Bart D. Ehrman, *Jesus before the Gospels: How the Earliest Christians Remembered, Changed, and Invented Their Stories of the Savior* (New York: HarperOne, 2016), 7.

to the aberrations of memory, the prejudices of the informant, the selective character of the reporting, and the subtle transformations that occur when a story is either resurrected from the depths of the past or recalled repeatedly over time."[10] Without a formula to evaluate a memory fading and being reprocessed by the moment, and because JS is the subject of so much recollected documentation, the investigator must negotiate the applicability and usefulness of recollections in appraising the documentary record of early Mormonism.

Remembering Joseph and Joseph Remembering: "History of Joseph Smith" That Became the *History of the Church*

A utilitarian purpose of reminiscing about JS, resulting in a proliferation of memories of him, arose from the elderly generation in the last quarter of the nineteenth century attempting to influence those who *knew not Joseph.* A number of factors precipitated the assembly of a historical legacy upon which to base Mormon devotion to the founder. Toward the end of the nineteenth century, after many of those who had embraced Mormonism in its formative years had died, some of those remaining who had personally rubbed shoulders with JS recognized the necessity of creating a transportable faith and culture. In addition, there were purposes to address perceptions of the early faith that were raised by rivals to Utah Mormonism. The effort to familiarize the new generation with their founder gained momentum in the 1880s and 1890s before culminating with B. H. Roberts's production of JS's *History of the Church.*

As mentioned in the Introduction, Roberts, one of the most important twentieth-century explicators of early Mormonism, finally revived after its antebellum creation the presentation of the serialized "History of Joseph Smith" in a consumable form: books on a shelf. The afterglow of Brigham Young's significant impact upon the church still lingered. But with publication of the *History of the Church*, thereafter, JS—the mastermind of Mormonism—became more accessible and valued by subsequent generations of modern Latter-day Saints. In present appreciation of Roberts's compilation, it is also important to recognize how it has subsequently influenced perceptions of JS. Also previously noted, a problem exists because of the prevailing assumption among those unfamiliar with the origins of the *History of the Church* that JS authored that narrative. Modern publications often contain expressions quoting from the *History* stating that JS said this or that, when they do not understand that their attributions to JS were actually text prepared by a clerk. Those who understand JS's style of doing business know that his history was, like other documentation relating to the foundation of the church, compiled by his clerks and scribes under his direction.

10. Douglas L. Wilson, *Honor's Voice: The Transformation of Abraham Lincoln* (New York: Alfred A. Knopf, 1998), 6.

While it is unmistakable that JS and his experiences dominantly influenced how the history was prepared—with evidence of JS's sincere interest in having his story written and published—modern investigators must balance his intentions with the factor of his scribes and their memories upon the text.

The Role and Influence of Joseph Smith's Clerks/Historians

JS's persistent use of clerks/historians ensured the probability that errors were introduced into both the preparation of the revelations he received and the history he initiated. Despite the care applied to the work, misunderstandings, scribal errors, and faulty memory affected what JS intended to be written. Scribal irregularities could not be avoided. Minutes from a small gathering of eight church leaders on November 8, 1831, in Hiram, Ohio, for example, illustrates the point. Among the eight attending the "special Conference" were JS, Oliver Cowdery, and Sidney Rigdon. As they prepared for publication of JS's revelations, Rigdon addressed the matter of "errors or mistakes which are in commandments and revelations, made either by the ~~scribe~~ translation in consequence of the slow way of the scribe at the time of receiving or by the scribes themselves." Having JS on hand helped to remedy the problem: they all agreed that "Br Joseph Smith Jr correct those errors or mistakes which he m[a]y discover by the holy Spirit while ~~receiving the revelations wing~~ reviewing the revelations & commandments."[11] But that did not solve the ubiquitous problem in transferring thoughts, conversations, and events on to paper.[12]

The difficulty applied also to JS's history. The initial creation of his life by his clerks/historians was a cumbersome and protracted endeavor. As is well known, JS's 1838/39 "History of Joseph Smith" was successor to JS's earlier attempts to have his and the church's story told. The evidence suggests, given the human resources JS then applied to the project, that by the end of the 1830s it was one of his high priorities. As will be discussed later, circumstances surrounding him and Mormonism demanded a public accounting; and, he could not satisfy the need himself. It, therefore, became the province of close associates in the roles of clerks/historians to tackle the endeavor. Because it is not clearly evident in the "History of Joseph Smith" what is demonstrably JS and what came from his scribes there will always remain a feature of debate about the origins of who actually informed the text. There are examples where it is evident that he influenced what was prepared. When inserting the account of the lesser priesthood

11. Smith, November 8, 1831, Minute Book 2, https://www.josephsmithpapers.org/paper-summary/minute-book-2/1#full-transcript.

12. *Joseph Smith Papers* editors note the disparity of memory by compilers and leaders about dating JS's introduction of what became D&C 3 (1835), D&C 107 (1981) in spring 1835. Historical Introduction, "Instruction on Priesthood, between circa 1 March and circa 4 May 1835," *JSP, D4*:309–10 [D&C 107].

restoration into the narrative, for instance, James Mulholland, who clerked for JS at the time, undoubtedly applied to him for clarification about the particulars of the event. It is apparent that Mulholland used Cowdery's September 1834 eyewitness declaration of the event upon which to base his rendering. Cowdery had written to W. W. Phelps witnessing his encounter with JS of the New Testament's John the Baptist on May 15, 1829, near the Smith home in Harmony, Pennsylvania. The intent of Cowdery's letter published in the *Latter Day Saints' Messenger and Advocate* in October 1834 was to describe their acquisition of the priesthood from the Baptist. A comparative of Cowdery's September 1834 rendering of the angel's language with what finally appeared in JS's "History" shows JS's adjustments to Cowdery's text.[13] Besides such demonstrable instances of JS having a hand in crafting the account, it is also clear that JS from time to time reviewed the history.[14] It is apparent, though, that such intervention was infrequent.

In all, it is important in evaluating the production to remember it was a collaborative effort to explain JS and Mormonism to an audience unfamiliar with many of the particulars exhibited within the documentation. But the use of others to write JS's history had side effects. Because of other demands on the prophet's time, his clerks/historians were mostly left to create the text on their own, which shaped how JS would thereafter be known. The clerks/historians *manufactured*, in some ways, manageable narrative that represented complex and expansive circumstances that in reality had more than one point of view, the whole of which would have been impossible to capture. Though they included contemporary records to buttress what they wrote, in their endeavor to write an authentic account they also often wrote from their own memories to characterize a situation. The process inevitably transformed the nature of what had happened. As Joseph Smith Papers scholar Robin Jensen stated, the clerks/historian's work represented "another separation from the original manuscripts."[15] Additionally, it is a given that the original manuscripts were themselves the product of someone's perception of an event or thing that had occurred.

Misperceptions compounded the difficulty of precise historical reports. In the circumstance, for instance, where Mulholland prepared the story of JS's initial encounter with the Book of Mormon angel as presented in the "History of

13. Compare the language in O[liver]. Cowdery to [W. W. Phelps], September 7, 1834, *Latter Day Saints' Messenger and Advocate*, October 1834, 16, with "History of Joseph Smith," *Times and Seasons*, August 1, 1842, 865–66; and Drafts 2 (1838/39) and 3 (ca. 1841) of JS's history in Smith, Histories, "History Drafts, 1838–circa 1841," *JSP, H1*:292–93.

14. William Clayton, *Manchester Mormons: The Journal of William Clayton, 1840–1842*, ed. James B. Allen and Thomas G. Alexander (Santa Barbara, CA: Peregrine Smith, 1974), 219 (February 18, 1842).

15. Robin Scott Jensen, "Postscript to Dean C. Jessee's Reprint of 'The Reliability of Joseph Smith's History,'" *Journal of Mormon History* 43, no. 4 (October 2017): 34.

Joseph Smith," misinformation apparently influenced Mulholland's account. In modern popular portrayal, Moroni was the individual who directed JS in his eventual acquisition of the gold plates and its subsequent translation as the Book of Mormon. In several instances before Mulholland's 1839 account was written, Moroni had been identified as the Book of Mormon angel.[16] However, Mulholland's draft text identified the angel as "Nephi," another of the Book of Mormon characters. The statement about Nephi, rendered as Mulholland apparently understood it, then appeared without correction in the serialized "History of Joseph Smith" in the *Times and Seasons'* April 15, 1842, issue.[17] Though later Mormon publications declared that Moroni was the angel associated with the plates and the Hill Cumorah, no nineteenth-century clarification of the Nephi/Moroni discrepancy in the "History of Joseph Smith" was made after the *Times and Seasons'* publication.[18]

The inconsistency and confusion became apparent to later readers. In March 1876, an inquiring church member wrote to LDS Church historian Orson Pratt requesting clarification of the Nephi/Moroni dispute. Acknowledging the disparity created by the clerk/historian, but also demonstrating the cumulative perspective on Moroni's role over time and its impact upon how Mormon history was rendered, Pratt replied:

> As Moroni holds the keys of the Stick or Record of Ephraim, (See B. of Cov. pp. 201, 322,) we have reason to believe that Moroni was that angel. The discrepancy in the history to which you refer may have occurred through the ignorance or carelessness of the historian or transcriber. It is true, that the history reads as though the Prophet himself was writing: but the Prophet was a slow and awkward writer; and many events re-

16. Oliver Cowdery to W. W. Phelps, circa March 1835, "Letter VI," *Latter Day Saints' Messenger and Advocate*, April 1835, 112; D&C 50:2 (1835); [No author], *Elders' Journal of the Church of Jesus Christ of Latter Day Saints*, July 1838, 42–43 (JS was the *Elders' Journal* editor); *JSP, H1*:223n56.

17. Smith, Histories, "History Drafts, 1838–circa 1841," Drafts 2 and 3, *JSP, H1*:222–23; "History of Joseph Smith," *Times and Seasons*, April 15, 1842, 753.

18. See for example, Parley P. Pratt, *Mormonism Unveiled: Zion's Watchman Unmasked, and its Editor, Mr. L. R. Sunderland Exposed* (New York: O. Pratt and E. Fordham, 1838), 38; Parley P. Pratt, *Letter to Queen Victoria* (Manchester, England: n.p., 1841), 12; Parley P. Pratt, *Proclamation to the People of the Coasts and Islands of the Pacific; of Every Nation, Kindred, and Tongue by an Apostle of Jesus Christ* ([Sydney, New South Wales]: C. W. Wandell, [1851]), 9; Orson Pratt, *Divine Authority, or the Question, was Joseph Smith Sent of God?* (Liverpool: R. James, 1848), 4; Orson Pratt, *Reply to a Pamphlet Printed at Glasgow, with the "Approbation of Clergymen of Different Denominations"* (Liverpool: R. James, 1849), 2, 3, 16. Paul R. Cheesman attempted to reconcile the Nephi/Moroni disparity in his masters' thesis, "An Analysis of the Accounts Relating Joseph Smith's Early Visions" (master's thesis, Brigham Young University, 1965), 43–61.

corded were written by his scribes who undoubtedly trusted too much to their memories, and the items probably were not sufficiently scanned by Bro. Joseph, before they got into print.[19]

Noting the several angelic messengers who appeared to JS, Pratt continued, "In giving the instructions which these angels imparted to him in a verbal manner, it would not be surprising that some of the hearers should in<n>ocently confound and intermix the names of the Angels."[20] In fairness to James Mulholland, he may have been working from a no longer existing text or from other information that included the statement about Nephi. Questions about JS's review of what was published in his name are also provoked. The circumstance illustrates the backdrop that modern readers must apply to how JS's "History of Joseph Smith" was prepared.

The clerks/historians influenced other foundational information about early Mormonism. In either late 1841 or early 1842 a Boston lawyer, George Barstow, requested from JS an overview of Mormonism for a book he was writing on the history of his home state, New Hampshire. (LDS missionaries had in the previous two years created quite a stir in southern New Hampshire with many baptisms and creation of several church congregations.)[21] Though the response

19. Orson Pratt to John Christensen, March 11, 1876, Historian's Office Correspondence Files, 1856–1926, CR 100 394, Letters, B–L, 1876, CHL (available online in digital form accessed from the CHL catalog).

20. Ibid.

21. What is known as the Wentworth Letter, so identified because JS apparently supplied the text to John Wentworth, editor of the *Chicago Democrat*, should have been more properly known as the Barstow-Wentworth letter. Barstow, the Boston attorney, had asked his Dartmouth College friend, Wentworth, to write to JS to ask for a report on the status of Mormonism at the time. Barstow, born in New Hampshire, was at the time writing a history of his home state. He designed a portion of his book to cover the religious history within the Granite State. Because Mormonism flourished in southern New Hampshire at the time, establishing congregations and unprecedented momentum in several communities, Barstow applied to Wentworth, whom he apparently knew had previously made entreaties to the Mormons in Nauvoo, to inquire of JS for an account of the faith. JS's reply, "Church History," appeared only in the *Times and Seasons* in March 1842. It is not known if Wentworth ever received the account JS evidently sent to him, given that his papers were later destroyed. Barstow finally pared his volume to cover New Hampshire's history to only 1819, the date the state disestablished support of religious bodies with state monies. (*The History of New Hampshire From Its Discovery, in 1614, to the Passage of the Toleration Act, in 1819.*) This precluded inclusion of anything about Mormonism and leaves the reader ignorant of whether Barstow obtained JS's reply to his query. For an overview of the origin of the Wentworth letter and how Eli P. Maginn's missionary success in New Hampshire likely provoked its creation, see Ronald O. Barney, "'There is the Greatest Excitement in This Country That I Ever Beheld': Mormonism's New England Ministry of the Forgotten Eli P. Maginn," *Mormon Historical Studies* 15, no. 2 (Fall 2014): 157–272, esp. 222–32.

titled "Church History" (thereafter known as the Wentworth letter) was attributed to JS when it was printed in the *Times and Seasons* in March 1842, one of his scribes, probably W. W. Phelps, wrote the piece. In it the writer stated the church was organized on April 6, 1830, in "the town of Manchester, Ontario co., state of New York," where the Smith's resided at the time of the organization.[22] However, seven months later—again in the *Times and Seasons*—the site where the church first formalized was identified by JS's clerk James Mulholland (no doubt with JS's influence), as being twenty-five miles away in Fayette Township, New York, at the home of Peter Whitmer Sr.[23] Despite the clarification, two years later, JS allowed the "Church History" account, where Manchester was given as the place of organization, to satisfy in July 1843 another request for an account of the rise of Mormonism. Phelps drafted the reply by expanding the "Church History" piece that appeared as "Latter Day Saints" in I. Daniel Rupp's *He Pasa Ekklesia* [The Whole Church] in 1844.[24] Again, Phelps identified Manchester, New York, as the place where Mormonism originated.[25] Though there has been speculation, it is not known why JS allowed the disparity to continue. In some circles, the contradictory designations continue to muddle discussion of church beginnings.[26]

The issue of scribal influence in reporting Mormon history continued to affect later interpretations of the religion. George Q. Cannon, as a counselor in the LDS Church's First Presidency in 1891 and editor of its *Juvenile Instructor*, addressed what in his mind had to be clerical error in reporting a statement by Brigham Young concerning by which authority JS organized the church in 1830. A correspondent wrote to Cannon inquiring about Young's June 4, 1864, statement printed in the *Journal of Discourses* where Young was reported to have said that "the Lord had revealed to him [JS] the Aaronic Priesthood upon which the Church was first organized: after that he received the Melchisedec Priest-

22. "Church History," *Times and Seasons* 3, March 1, 1842, 708. Also printed in "Church History," *JSP, H1*:496.

23. "History of Joseph Smith," *Times and Seasons*, October 15, 1842, 944.

24. I. Daniel Rupp, ed., *He Pasa Ekklesia* [The Whole Church]. *An Original History of the Religious Denominations at Present Existing in the United States* (Philadelphia: James Y. Humphreys, 1844). See overview and text of Rupp's publication "'Latter Day Saints,' 1844," in *JSP, H1*:502–16.

25. "'Latter Day Saints,' 1844," *JSP, H1*:510. See Bruce A. Van Orden, *We'll Sing and We'll Shout: The Life and Times of W. W. Phelps* (Provo and Salt Lake City: Religious Studies Center, Brigham Young University and Deseret Book, 2018), 317.

26. The debate over the organizational site for the church can be reviewed in H. Michael Marquardt and Wesley P. Walters, *Inventing Mormonism: Tradition and the Historical Record* (Salt Lake City: Smith Research Associates, 1994), 153–72; and a counter perspective in Michael Hubbard MacKay, *Sacred Space: Exploring the Birthplace of Mormonism* (Provo, UT: Religious Studies Center, Brigham Young University, 2016).

hood, when the Church was more fully organized."[27] The sequence countered what Brigham had previously stated in 1853 about the authority to organize the church: "I know that Joseph received his Apostleship from Peter, James, and John, before a revelation on the subject was printed, and he never had a right to organize a Church before he was an apostle."[28] Cannon confirmed Young's report stating that the inconsistency could "only be explained as an incorrect report of the discourse on the part of the short-hand reporter, and an oversight on the part of the person who prepared the discourse for print."[29]

Recounting someone else's story without the benefit of that person's own written rehearsal of their experience inevitably introduced errors into the narrative being produced. Oliver Cowdery represented the difficulty in his own attempt to relate a number of the significant features of early Mormonism in his series of letters to W. W. Phelps while Cowdery served as editor of the church's *Messenger and Advocate*. Cowdery noted to his readers, in one instance, "You will recollect that I mentioned the time of a religious excitement, in Palmyra and vicinity to have been in the 15th year of our brother J. Smith Jr's, age—that was an error in the type—it should have been in the 17th."[30] While he attributed the discrepancy to a problem in setting the type, giving the conflation of events that he and a number of others applied to JS's initial experiences,[31] it may have been that Cowdery misunderstood the circumstances of JS's initial experiences and the sequence of events JS witnessed.

JS's initial use of clerks/historians to chronicle his life undoubtedly proved frustrating to him. Regrettably, both of the young men he first employed in the work of preparing his history—James Mulholland and Robert B. Thompson—died prematurely: Mulholland, age thirty-five, in November 1839, and Thompson, age twenty-nine, in August 1841. After their deaths, W. W. Phelps, with publishing experience, became involved helping to craft the first 157 pages of the manuscript taking the timeline of JS's life to November 1831. Of his involvement, Phelps wrote to Parley P. Pratt in Liverpool in June 1842 stating: "I am now on the largest amount of business that I have ever undertaken, since

27. Brigham Young, Sermon, June 4, 1864, *JD*, 10:303–4.
28. Brigham Young, Sermon, April 6, 1853, *JD*, 1:134–35, 137. I am grateful to LaJean Carruth, who compared George D. Watt's shorthand text of April 6, 1853, with the published report and found it consistent with Watt's report.
29. George Q. Cannon, "The Melchisedec Priesthood and the Organization of the Church," *Juvenile Instructor* 26, April 15, 1891, 237–38.
30. Cowdery to Phelps, "Letter IV," *Messenger and Advocate*, February 1835, 78.
31. See also William Smith's later report that combined the circumstances of JS's First Vision with Moroni's appearance and the coming forth of the Book of Mormon. William Smith, *William Smith on Mormonism* (Lamoni, IA: Herald Steam Book and Job Office, 1883), 6–10.

I have been in the church: It is to write and compile the History of br Joseph, embracing the entire history of the church." The dimension of JS's intention was so great, he wrote, that "it will occupy <my> ~~time~~ and talents for a long time, should <nothing> intervene."[32] As it turned out, however, Phelps's endeavor proved short-lived. Willard Richards, one of the Twelve Apostles, who had been keeping JS's journal since December 1841, then took over as JS's chronicler. Richards received the official appointment of JS's "private secretary & historian" on December 21, 1842.[33] With assistance from others, Richards gathered, compiled, and wrote the next 655 pages of historical text, carrying the prophet's story by the time of JS's death to August 1838.[34] Richards's procedure in preparing text was to take primary source documentation, such as JS's journals, minutes of meetings, correspondence, legal documents, newspaper articles, etc., while at the same time adding his own recollections and viewpoint—based upon memory—to bulk up the skeletal condition of the surviving notes to create narrative history. As the endeavor continued, he "transposed material from other writers and sources into the first person of Joseph Smith,"[35] which thereafter created the incorrect perception that JS authored everything that had been written. Besides serving as compiler and narrator, Richards also applied an interpretive angle to the manuscript that, according to Howard Searle, LDS educator and specialist in early Mormon historiography, "clearly belongs to the Judeo-Christian tradition of providential history." Richards's perspective "had much in common with the judgments of the Old Testament, the Greek formula of nemesis, and the Calvinist doctrine of divine retribution" that then prevailed in the Christian world, thereby crafting the tone and character of JS's story. Still, as Searle argued, the "result has been a history that is remarkably accurate in its factual content."[36]

Richards also fleshed out events for which there was little documentation. In an example of the methodology used to reconstruct what he believed he once heard JS say, Richards augmented scant notations with expanded constructions. Thus, his brief note from a portion of JS's May 21, 1843, sermon famously stated that JS said he was a "rough stone roling down hill."[37] However, as Dean Jessee explained, the passage once in Richards's hands was enlarged by 129 words with

32. W. W. Phelps to Parley P. Pratt, June 16, 1842, Parley P. Pratt, Correspondence, 1842–1855, MS 897, CHL.

33. Dean C. Jessee, "Priceless Words and Fallible Memories: Joseph Smith as Seen in the Effort to Preserve His Discourses," *BYU Studies* 31, no. 2 (Spring 1991): 27; Jessee, "Writing of Joseph Smith's History," 454.

34. Jessee, "Writing of Joseph Smith's History," 441.

35. Howard C. Searle, "Willard Richards as Historian," *BYU Studies* 31, no. 2 (Spring 1991): 48.

36. Ibid., 56, 57, 58.

37. Smith, Journals, May 21, 1843, *JSP, J*3:20.

what may have been Richards's memory of the sermon to read as it appears in the "History of Joseph Smith."[38]

As Richards's work progressed as JS's historian, JS initiated the serial publication of the 1838/39 history beginning in March 1842 in the church's *Times and Seasons* when the prophet became editor. The writing and publication of the "History" continued simultaneously until January 1846 when the majority of the Saints prepared to leave for the exodus to the West. Once established in the Great Basin, the church clerks/historians continued preparation of the "History [later Life] of Joseph Smith" through the end of 1856, which appeared sequentially from 1851–1858 in the church-owned *Deseret News*.[39] Upon completion of the enormous project, a quarter century after JS initiated the endeavor, George A. Smith and Wilford Woodruff—who as historians saw it through to the end—summarized it as "a history more correct in its details" than anything previously written. All because the "historians and clerks engaged in the work" were "eye and ear witnesses to nearly all the transactions recorded in this history." Underscoring its reliability they stated, "the history has been carefully revised under the strict inspection of President Brigham Young, and approved by him," rendering it "one of the most authentic histories ever written."[40] By the time the history was published in the 1840s and 1850s, JS's life had been influenced by not only his clerks/historians but also his successor.

British Mormons also had access to the "History of Joseph Smith" compilation through the *Latter Day Saints' Millennial Star* published in Liverpool (June 1842–May 1845, April 1852–May 1863). The *Millennial Star's* publication of the history then became the basis for the narrative's republication in the twentieth century. Dan Vogel, who analyzed the creation of and publication of JS's "History," described B.H. Roberts's role in preparing the "History" for a new audience. While "serving as editor of the *Millennial Star* in Liverpool, England, from 1887–1888," Vogel noted, "Roberts gathered and bound in three volumes the entire 'History of Joseph,' which had been printed in the *Millennial Star* volumes 14–25 (1852–1863)." But Roberts's work was not limited to just assembling the serialized history. Dean Jessee, reminded readers, "A comparison of the

38. Jessee, "Reliability of Joseph Smith's History," 40–41. See Vogel's treatment of "Reconstructing Joseph Smith's Sermons" by his clerks in Vogel, *History of Joseph Smith… A Source- and Text-Critical Edition*, 1:xvii–xviii.

39. Jessee, "Writing of Joseph Smith's History," 441; Vogel, *History of Joseph Smith… A Source- and Text-Critical Edition*, 1:xv.

See also Robin Scott Jensen's portrayal of how church leaders in the aftermath of JS's death attempted to bring the history of his life to completion for publication in 1845. Robin Scott Jensen, "'Archives of the Better World': The Nineteenth-Century Historian's Office and Mormonism's Archival Flexibility," (PhD diss., University of Utah, 2019), 63–81.

40. Smith and Woodruff quoted in Jessee, "Reliability of Joseph Smith's History," 36.

History edited by Brigham H. Roberts and published by the church beginning in 1902 with previous printings in the *Times and Seasons*, the *Millennial Star*, and the *Deseret News*, reveals numerous textual alterations and changes that are clearly the effort of a later generation to cope with textual problems of the *History*." Roberts, Jessee continued, "deleted other items that were regarded by the standards of his time as insignificant, outdated, in poor taste, or undignified."[41] Thus, modern students must understand that not only was the "History of Joseph Smith" that became the *History of the Church* created primarily by JS's clerks/historians and reviewed and edited by Brigham Young, but that B. H. Roberts's late nineteenth-century eye also tempered the text and shaped JS's image and ministry for the twentieth century.[42]

Recognition of the importance of the underlying circumstances of the creation and publication of JS's history is difficult to overstate. "By the end of 1840," Vogel wrote, "Smith's involvement with the project was more as an overseer and reviewer than an author."[43] Indeed, as Howard Searle noted, "It is apparent that the Prophet entrusted a great deal of the responsibility for his history to his scribes and the Church historian, for he had reviewed and checked the history" of only a small fraction of what became the history by the time of his demise.[44] The several clerks (which included Mulholland, Thompson, Phelps, Coray, and Richards before JS's death; and Thomas Bullock, George A. Smith, Wilford Woodruff, Leo Hawkins, Robert Campbell, and Jonathan Grimshaw after his death)[45] by their selection, compilation, and narration—with Roberts's involvement—created a JS for the twentieth-century church. One might expect that a product written by regular folk in distressed times, a lengthy process overall, would be rendered in homespun. However, even though it was prepared in the middle of the nineteenth century before historical methodology had developed in the later 1800s,[46] the preparation and quality of the "History of Joseph Smith" exceeds the environments in which it was prepared.

To be sure, the work of JS's clerks and reviewers has been censured by later critics. This comes in part because JS was exhibited in generally laudatory terms, with his intentions and actions demonstrable as representative of his divine calling. Biased, one-sided propaganda, and a whitewash of early Mormonism are

41. Jessee, "Reliability of Joseph Smith's History," 41, 43.

42. Vogel, *History of Joseph Smith . . . A Source and Text-Critical Edition*, 1:xxii.

43. Ibid., 1:ix

44. Searle, "Willard Richards as Historian," 51.

45. Jessee, "Writing Joseph Smith's History," 441.

46. Searle, "Willard Richards as Historian," 54–56; Jessee, "Reliability of Joseph Smith's History," 24–27.

the charges.[47] However, Vogel credited the clerks under their circumstances: "One should be cautious not to view their efforts through the lens of current standards, or to assign malicious intent where none was intended. If not entirely acceptable, ghost writing, changing third person to first, and incorporating source material without quotation marks were nevertheless typical practices in the nineteenth century.... The vast majority of alterations were for readability."[48] Even though the methodology does not pass historiographical muster today, and while it rings with "historical apologia,"[49] for its time it was an effort to authentically portray the atmosphere surrounding the rise and growth of the church and the prophet who commenced the work. The nearly four thousand pages of finished text that eventually became the *History of the Church* represent one of the most important endeavors of the first generation of Mormonism. The JS tradition, along with its theology, doctrine, and polity, fashioned by the clerks/historians, however, has been very difficult to surmount subsequently. All of that has changed in the information age of accessibility to the expanded documentary record.

Other Saints and Their Memories

As noted, concern in the later part of the nineteenth century arose among Mormons who had known JS regarding how he would be remembered—resulting in several initiatives to gather memories of the prophet.[50] But not all of the recollections struck true to some invested in preserving his memory. A particularly important illustration of the circumstances came from LDS Church First Presidency member Joseph F. Smith, a nephew of JS. In 1898, in what became the church's primary periodical for most of the twentieth century, the *Improvement Era*, President Smith portrayed the uneasiness of leaders about some of what had been published in the recent past. While applauding the concept of collecting the "aged brethren's" memories of JS, he warned of the problems of tainted

47. See, for example, Tanner and Tanner, *Mormonism: Shadow or Reality*, 126–142D; and Richard S. Van Wagoner's criticism in "The Making of a Mormon Myth: The 1844 Transfiguration of Brigham Young," *Dialogue* 28, no. 4 (Winter 1995): 160–61.

48. Vogel, *History of Joseph Smith... A Source- and Text-Critical Edition*, 1:xxiii.

49. Searle, "Willard Richards as Historian," 59.

50. See, for example, the "Recollections of the Prophet Joseph Smith" series printed in the church's *Juvenile Instructor*, vol. 27, nos. 2–8, 10–13, 15–16, 20 in 1892; and vol. 28, nos. 1 and 10 in 1893. The *Young Women's Journal* published a similar gathering of recollections in its December issues for vol. 16, no. 12, 1905; and vol. 17, no. 12, 1906. Sixteen persons who had known JS recounted their memories of him during a ninetieth anniversary gathering to commemorate his birth, as reported in *The Salt Lake Herald, Church and Farm Supplement*, January 12, 1895.

memory by some Saints who had been populating Mormon periodicals in the late nineteenth century with remembrances of JS and his times, some that he apparently thought questionable. "We fear that many things that are reported as coming from the Prophet Joseph Smith, and other early elders in the church, by not being carefully recorded or told with strict regard for accuracy, have lost something of their value as historical data, and unwarranted additions have sometimes been made to the original facts, until it is difficult to determine just how far some of the traditions which have come to us may be accepted as reliable representations of what was said or what was done."[51] The acknowledgment that some reminiscent accounts included embellishment and sensationalism, if not outright distortion, was a significant concession from not only the church leaders but also one of the Smith family.

A generation earlier, an 1862 column in the LDS Church's *Deseret News* reminded readers about the distortions of memory: "Who knows not how imperfect a thing memory is? It not merely forgets; it misleads. Things in memory do not merely fade away...they change their aspect; they change their place; they turn to something quite different from the fact."[52] The result, according to B. H. Roberts who played such an important role in the formulation of Mormon history, was that: "As in all narratives of events, by different witnesses, even by eye witnesses, and especially when given from memory and many years after the events took place, there are certain discrepancies."[53] The arguments are so self-evident that they hardly seem necessary to underscore the point. The significance of understanding and acknowledging this concept in Latter-day Saint history cannot be overstated.

Traditions from Memories Are Established or Disestablished

An illustration of how modern students are confronted with discordant memories from the nineteenth century, and those who interpret the same, involves the immediate aftermath of JS's death. Richard Van Wagoner, a Utah historian, published a challenging analysis of one of the most famous and consequential events in Mormon history: the August 8, 1844, "transfiguration" where Brigham Young before the assembled Saints was said to have assumed the visage and voice of JS in the aftermath of the latter's murder a month and a half earlier.[54] Though, according to Van Wagoner, the event was a legend "unsurpassed in Mormon lore, second only to Joseph Smith's own account of angelic ministrations and his 'first

51. Joseph F. Smith, "Shall We Record Testimony," *Improvement Era*, March 1898, 372.
52. "Keeping a Diary," *Deseret News*, July 18, 1862 (taken from the *London Magazine*).
53. B. H. Roberts, *A Comprehensive History of the Church of Jesus Christ of Latter-day Saints, Century I*, 6 vols. (Provo, UT: Brigham Young University Press, 1965), 1:96–98.
54. Van Wagoner, "Making of a Mormon Myth," 159–82.

vision,'" he claimed it never happened.[55] Because the stories relating the experience were presented as recollections, with no immediately written contemporary reports of the transfiguration in the form of diary, correspondence, or other records, Van Wagoner demanded that Mormons somehow accommodated the event into their thinking to justify their acceptance of Brigham Young as JS's successor. Someone hatched the story, he suggested, and with snowball effect the story turned into an avalanche of artificial memories. Lynne Watkins Jorgensen, an LDS Church family history professional, countered Van Wagoner's claims about the faulty collective recollection. She presented evidence that many, over a hundred, of those who testified in writing about the transfiguration event had demonstrable qualifications as explicators of their own real experiences diluting the premise of Van Wagoner's argument.[56] How then, does the modern observer handle the incongruity of the contradictory conclusions?

Then there is the popular story of the "angel" of the Lord appearing to JS, threatening him with destruction by a raised sword if he did not embrace God's command to instigate plural marriage. Given the generally accepted notion that JS had first entertained the idea while revising the Bible in the early 1830s, because he had not institutionally introduced the premise by the Nauvoo period, as the claims go, God sent an angel to coerce him into acting. The story is complicated by the fact that there is no contemporary account of the event or events, in particular from the prophet himself. The stories that do exist began circulating in Utah in the 1850s after the Mormons publicly announced the practice. Modern students are left to comprehend the claims. Did the reports actually represent what JS said? And what are the implications of God using such a menacing tactic to remind JS of the earlier inspiration he had received while revising the Bible? If such a confrontation actually occurred, there is also the question of the nature of event: Was it a vision, a dream, or something more concrete and objective?[57]

55. Van Wagoner, "Making of a Mormon Myth," 159. See also the effect of memory during Zion's Camp in Matthew C. Godfrey, "'We Believe the Hand of the Lord Is in It': Memories of Divine Intervention in the Zion's Camp Expedition," *BYU Studies Quarterly* 56, no. 4 (2017): 99–132.

56. Lynne Watkins Jorgensen, "The Mantle of the Prophet Joseph Passes to Brother Brigham: A Collective Spiritual Witness," *BYU Studies* 36, no. 4 (1996–97): 125–204. Reports of the event and its effect were created as early as three months after the moment. See the correspondence of Henry and Catharine Brooke with Leonard and Mary Pickel on November 15, 1844, which stated that Brigham Young, "favours Br Joseph, both in person, & manner of speaking more than any person you ever saw, looks like another," quoted in D. Michael Quinn, "The Mormon Succession Crisis of 1844," *BYU Studies* 16, no. 2 (Winter 1976): 212.

57. See an outline of the "angel with a drawn sword" accounts in Brian D. Hales, *Joseph Smith's Polygamy: History*, 3 vols. (Salt Lake City: Greg Kofford Books, 2013), 1:186–98.

There is an alternative explanation for JS's prompt to initiate plural marriage found in what LDS Church president John Taylor later stated was his eyewitness of JS's explanation of the occurrence. Taylor, the most emphatic defender of plural marriage's continuation by the Mormons in the 1880s, related the circumstance personally described to him by JS that moved the prophet to act upon the principle. On June 28, 1881, in Salt Lake City, Taylor's clerk, L. John Nuttall, wrote that Taylor, "related a circumstance of having met the Prophet Joseph at one time when the principle of revelation on celestial marriage was revealed, and had been talked about some." Upon seeing JS, who was riding toward Nauvoo on horseback, Taylor stated, "On meeting we passed the complement of the day" before entering conversation about plural marriage. Taylor stated, "the Prophet said, 'These things must be accepted and entered into, for they cannot be trifled with and the keys will <soon> be turned unless they are accepted.'"[58] The motive to act on JS's earlier impressions was much less ominous than an angel with a drawn sword. Thus, modern students must weigh the claims and disparities regarding an angel with a drawn sword and Taylor's witness, which are not congruent, but were all based upon the memories of those who claimed to have interaction with JS himself.

JS's plural marriages became a public issue when two of his sons found their way to Utah in 1869 to proselytize the Mormons in the West. The sons, Alexander and David, echoed their mother's declarations that JS had always been a monogamist. Their claims were a cardinal tenet of the RLDS Church, which had earned the Smith family's allegiance.[59] To refute JS's family's contentions, JS's nephew Joseph F. Smith, who had been ordained an LDS apostle in 1867, searched church records for contemporary documentation that he thought would establish the premise. He later explained to Orson Pratt, "I was astonished at the scarcity of evidence, I might say almost total absence of strict evidence upon the subject." To create verification of the practice, Joseph F. solicited testimonials from the women reputed to have been JS's plural wives, as there was "nothing written [and] but [a] few living who were personally knowing to

58. L. John Nuttall, *In the President's Office: The Diaries of L. John Nuttall, 1879–1892*, ed. Jedediah S. Rogers (Salt Lake City: Signature Books, Smith-Pettit Foundation, 2007), 58 (June 28, 1881). Two months later, at a meeting in Kamas, Utah, Nuttall again reported Taylor's emphasis on what he heard from the prophet: "The Prophet Jos Smith said to me at Nauvoo <in regard to celestial marriage,> These things of which I have told you have got to be entered into or the Keys will be turned. He had previously said the Kingdom could not go any further unless this law was observed" (66 {August 13, 1881}).

59. See Valeen Avery's explanation for Joseph F. Smith gathering affidavits in 1869 to confirm JS's introduction and practice of polygamy to counter the missionizing attempts in Utah by JS's sons, Alexander and David. Their design was to sway "Brighamite" Mormons from their position. Valeen Tippetts Avery, *From Mission to Madness: Last Son of the Mormon Prophet* (Urbana: University of Illinois Press, 1998), 103–4.

the fact that Joseph Taught the principle." From JS himself, Joseph F. lamented, there was "not a word, except the Revelation itself Showing that The Prophet was the Author—under God."[60] Without corroboration from the actual participants, as Joseph F. Smith rightly feared, the secrets would remain shrouded in mystery and intrigue. Today's investigator must sift through the memories and the purpose for which they were created to determine their contextual relevance and verity.

The complexities of the Mormon past are many. Those attempting to grasp early Mormonism must learn to navigate through later presentations of the faith derived from memory as a basis. Appreciating the fact that the documentation was created from someone's memory, whether immediate or otherwise, is one of the most important requisites for appreciating and evaluating the early faith. Along with the imperative of discovering the intent of the creator of the memory, today's readers must also employ an air of caution and qualification of those sources along with equal care in evaluating how later defenders and detractors have used the documentation/memories to formulate their assertive postures.

60. Joseph F. Smith to Orson Pratt Sr., July 19, 1875, quoted in Hales, *Joseph Smith's Polygamy*, 2:345. The numerous affidavits may be seen in two collections in the CHL, "Collected by the Historian's Office": Plural Marriage Affidavits, circa 1870 (MS 2673), and Affidavits about Celestial Marriage, 1869–1915 (MS 3423), both collections available online in digital form accessed from the CHL catalog.

PART II

Contextual Background

CHAPTER 5

The Religious Times of Joseph Smith

Applying even the most carefully prepared transcription of what JS created or had produced allows the modern reader only partial entrance into the Mormon prophet's realm. Accessible documentation is essential but serves only to illuminate what JS felt necessary to expound or have explained, along with peripheral additions to the record. Moderns are left to discover the landscape and scenery that was not explicitly included in the cumulative creation of his documentary record. Few would argue against the ideal of replicating to the degree possible the world in which he lived in the attempt to measure the myriad of influences that shaped his thinking and his life. The prospect of restoring that environment, however, is not only daunting but actually impossible for today's students to even contemplate. Still, the necessity of digging into history's recesses is required to hope for any understanding and perspective. Without a well-developed backdrop of JS's cultural milieu, showing as best as possible the characteristics giving color and definition to his life, he stands to moderns as little more than a stick figure or mythic icon. Yet it must be understood that applying the microscope to his life from the surviving historical record often raises as many questions as it provides answers.

Well known is the eruption of religion in America after decades of emigration from Europe to the young country. The "Second Great Awakening" of the late eighteenth and early nineteenth century licensed numerous players to engage their countrymen in an unprecedented focus on religious devotion.[1] Several complicated paths with European origins defined those manning most every pulpit in the land. Rebellion against orthodoxies fostered a growing roster of contenders for the hearts of American believers. The Reformed movement,

1. See Daniel Walker Howe, *What Hath God Wrought: The Transformation of America, 1815–1848* (New York: Oxford University Press, 2007), 164–202.

emanating from central Europe in the first decades of the sixteenth century, proved for many years to be the most substantive ideology pervading the land. In the aftermath of Martin Luther's dissent from Rome after 1517, several other personalities offered differing perspectives transforming the religious cultures they influenced. Men such as Huldreich Zwingli in Zurich, John Calvin the French pastor who operated from Geneva, and the Scottish minister John Knox formulated pivotal revisionist interpretations of scripture that had not only religious but political implications. In America, Reformed Protestantism primarily represented by way of Calvinist Congregationalists—Puritans—provided the agenda for most of those who filled the pews during much of the colonial period.[2] Though only a minority of America's colonists adhered to Calvinistic conformity—beliefs also found among the Presbyterians and Baptists—its influence upon the mores of society was disproportional to its numbers. As one might imagine, as the colonies grew, coupled with attendant diversity, challenges erupted. "People nursed at least four related complaints against Reformed orthodoxy," according to religion historian Nathan Hatch. These included its "implicit endorsement of the status quo, its tyranny over personal religious experience, its preoccupation with complicated and arcane dogma, and its clerical pretension and quest for control."[3] Increasingly, counters to the decades of Reformed influence focused on Christian renewal. There were "Any number of denominations, sects, movements, and individuals between 1780 and 1830 claim[ing] to be restoring a pristine biblical Christianity free from all human devices."[4] The restoration movement had great appeal.

The Joseph Smith Sr. family emerged during the post-American Revolutionary and Second Great Awakening periods. As previously stated, in order for modern observers to properly equip themselves with an understanding of the early American republic template, they must recognize that that world was the nursing mother to those who lived in it. Though the culture was multifaceted in impact, a diverse religious strain teemed within it, though not as pervasive as some today believe. Most of the "Revolutionary leaders were the least emotionally religious of any generation of leaders in our history," according to historian Gordon Wood. Indeed, at "best the Founding Fathers only passively believed in organized Christianity and at worst they scorned and ridiculed it." But by "the early decades of the nineteenth century American society appeared to be much more religious than it had been in the final decades of the eighteenth

2. Sydney E. Ahlstrom, *A Religious History of the American People*, 2 vols. (Garden City, NY: Image Books, 1975), 1:116–20.
3. Nathan O. Hatch, *The Democratization of American Christianity* (New Haven: Yale University Press, 1990), 171.
4. Hatch, *Democratization of American Christianity*, 179.

century."[5] The Second Great Awakening nurtured an invigoration of religion not previously known in the colonies. The societal transformation moved the populace to new perceptions about themselves, including personal impact upon the practice of faith and notions of human destiny. "Traditional structures of authority crumbled under the momentum of the Revolution, and common people increasingly discovered that they no longer had to accept the old distinctions that had separated them from the upper ranks of the gentry. Ordinary farmers, tradesmen, and artisans began to think they were as good as any gentleman and that they were actually counted for something in the movement of events," Wood asserted.[6] The American Revolution, according to Nathan Hatch, "dramatically expanded the circle of people who considered themselves capable of thinking for themselves about issues of freedom, equality, sovereignty, and representation."[7] As religious energy fragmented into a myriad of manifestations, various factors affected the several categories of belief that emerged. Influences such as urban or rural settings, whether or not the form of religion was "high" or "low," or if the slant was evangelical or Reformed, defined how the faith was practiced. Religion in the adolescent country, besides carrying over colonial traditions, had taken new forms.

Besides the dominant channels of belief, in the aftermath of the American Revolution "religious outsiders" became somewhat of a distinct subculture, a designation into which JS and his religion have been inserted.[8] That status significantly influenced how they were received as they witnessed through the countryside. When the Mormon missionaries disembarked after the Kirtland (1831) and Amherst (1832) conferences, those they encountered already knew about the biblical Jesus and the Old Testament prophets.[9] Besides the Reformed biblical standards of colonial America, the numerous post-Revolutionary era "isms" that included various expressions of Calvinism, trinitarianism, antinomianism, Universalism, and Catholicism presented formidable foils to the Mormon message. At the same time, the diversity ensured opportunities and options never before available. Specific issues pervading the culture like infant baptism,

5. Wood, *Purpose of the Past*, 46; Gordon S. Wood, *Empire of Liberty: A History of the Early Republic, 1789–1815* (New York: Oxford University Press, 2009), 576; Gordon S. Wood, "Evangelical America and Early Mormonism," *New York History* 61, no. 4 (October 1980): 359.

6. Wood, "Evangelical America and Early Mormonism," 366.

7. Hatch, *Democratization of American Christianity*, 6.

8. R. Laurence Moore, *Religious Outsiders and the Making of Americans* (New York: Oxford University Press, 1986), 25–47.

9. See discussions of the June 1831 and January 1832 conferences in Mark Staker's *Hearken, O Ye People: The Historical Setting of Joseph Smith's Ohio Revelations* (Salt Lake City: Greg Kofford Books, 2009), 155–62; and Smith, Documents, *JSP, D1*:317–32, and *JSP, D2*:157–63.

Freemasonry, Anti-Masonry, visions, dreams, temperance leagues, camp meetings, revivals, the influences of Lyman Beecher and Dwight Timothy, etc., show that Mormonism was a little fish in a very large pond. JS's church emerged amidst the contested Christian world. The multiplicity of social persuasions that colored the already diverse Christian pallet inevitably impacted those who embraced early Mormonism, including their prophet. While JS may have outgrown his culture as Richard Bushman argues, he could not escape it.[10] There was just too much vividly evident that potentially influenced him.[11]

After two hundred years, there is still a level of uncertainty in the minds of many about just who JS was and where he obtained the wherewithal to build the sustaining components of his religion. What was the source of his inspiration? "The American history of Joseph Smith looks for causes; what led Joseph Smith to think as he did?"[12] Most modern believers in Mormonism come from a tradition that has saluted the premise that, from the start, JS moved in all things by the direction and inspiration of Jesus, independent of his environment. Yet, as Daniel Wells later recounted as a counselor in Brigham Young's First Presidency: "Many of the principles which he [JS] taught were in the world—they were not new, yet it seemed as though they had never been thought of, comprehended, or understood by the children of men; at least, they had not been by me."[13] Because Mormons have been reluctant to acknowledge cultural influences upon JS, some critics have combed the countryside searching for components of Mormonism that show up in the environment, primarily to diminish Mormon claims of singularity. Because the questions from the periphery have fermented under the more obvious and accessible documentary record concerning early Mormonism, this methodology has become a threat to many believers who have built a substantial belief system without the necessity of historiographical augmentation. Because of the illumination of little-known features of JS's culture that present new interpretations, segments of the believing Mormon population will undoubtedly view this process as something less than faith promoting.

Mario DePillis, noted Catholic scholar of Mormonism, claimed in 1966 that devoted and believing "students of Mormonism have assumed for over a hundred and thirty years that the religion sprang full-blown from the brain

10. Bushman, *Joseph Smith and the Beginnings of Mormonism*, 7.

11. A critique of Bushman and the role or lack thereof of American culture affecting Mormonism is presented by Grant Underwood, "Attempting to Situate Joseph Smith," in Welch, *The Worlds of Joseph Smith*, 41–52.

12. Richard L. Bushman, "Joseph Smith's Many Histories," in Welch, *The Worlds of Joseph Smith*, 11.

13. Daniel H. Wells, Sermon, June 30, 1867, *JD*, 12:71. Wells knew JS well during the latter's Nauvoo tenure but did not become a Mormon himself until after JS's death.

of Joseph Smith in the form of the Book of Mormon."[14] Had they been better acquainted with the setting of the early American republic, he implied, they would have recognized that JS reflected much within his culture that became part of the religious thinking he espoused. The element of ignorance about JS's circumstances afflicting most modern Mormon students has proven to be an obstacle that generally undermines straightforward explanations of JS's strategy and means in establishing his church. Before one can understand JS in his times, he/she must hurdle the environmental factors that influenced his thinking and behavior. The ignorance about early America that pervades mainstream Mormonism makes recognition by scholars of atmospheric influence upon JS appear sinister, when in reality it may offer greater insight into the prophet and how he adeptly negotiated the world around him.

Some gospel defenders have juxtaposed Mormonism and the surrounding world with the intent of *proving* the uniqueness of JS's religion while ignoring influences upon him that may have been culled from the culture. Admittedly, most efforts to reveal and explain "parallels" between JS and his surroundings that have been published are controversial and generally negative in intent and explanation.[15] The off-putting charges have steered believers from considering the plausibility that another avenue for understanding the prophet's aptitude and gifts may exist in the culture in which he lived. "Too many detractors from Mormonism have suggested," explained Rick Grunder, "that Joseph Smith literally copied doctrine or Book of Mormon history from specific contemporary printed and manuscript sources." Grunder, an antiquarian bookseller and expert on the background of early American religion and Mormonism, continued that that view "runs far with too little, ready to grasp at the simplest or most superficial similarities, sometimes ignoring real content, or postulating explicit, labored connections to Mormonism's founder." Conversely, he concluded, "Apologetic response can then descend to picayune details or obtuse shades of

14. Mario S. DePillis, "The Quest for Religious Authority and the Rise of Mormonism," *Dialogue* 1, no. 1 (Spring 1966): 79.

15. The debate has bounced between detraction and defense for generations. See, for example, the charge by Fawn Brodie that some of JS's cosmological notions came from "reading Thomas Dick's *Philosophy of a Future State*." Brodie, *No Man Knows My History*, 171. On the other hand, acknowledging that "Joseph Smith's cosmology has an affinity with the views of Thomas Dick," Orson Pratt's biographer Breck England, argued that "Joseph Smith never mentioned Dick or his writings, and rejected most of Dick's ideas." Breck England, *The Life and Thought of Orson Pratt* (Salt Lake City: University of Utah Press, 1985), 102–5. See also Edward T. Jones, "The Theology of Thomas Dick and Its Possible Relation to Joseph Smith" (master's thesis, Brigham Young University, 1969), who concluded that there is "insufficient similarity in the two theologies to justify the assertions Mrs. Brodie makes" (95).

meaning that equally obscure the real phenomena at hand.... Both perspectives tend to miss the forest for the trees."[16]

Some, naturally, are threatened with information that calls into question traditional perceptions. Specific to the LDS Church, believers' concerns may stem from what is likely a misunderstanding about what the implications are of discovering that JS likely *was* influenced by the world around him. But rather than considering these matters as threats, the preponderant evidence is that JS used, perhaps unwittingly, the setting surrounding him to measure, weigh, infuse, discard, and otherwise evaluate the atmosphere that influenced circumstances in the locales where he lived. Clearly, in the beginning he compared what he was feeling inside with what he had heard from his associates, at camp meetings, religious services, and at his family's hearth. Evidence shows that though he had only a rudimentary education, he was literate and perceptive. While JS's accessibility to contemporary and traditional literature was limited, it has been shown that he was in a position to appraise his surroundings.[17] But given the paucity

16. Rick Grunder, *Mormon Parallels: A Bibliographic Source*, 2nd ed. (LaFayette, NY: Rick Grunder Books, 2014), 23, CD.

See examples of research directed at ascertaining the sources of JS's thinking. JS may have used a post-1769 KJV of the Bible to prepare Book of Mormon text according to Stan Larson, "The Historicity of the Matthean Sermon on the Mount in 3 Nephi" in *New Approaches to the Book of Mormon*, ed. Brent Lee Metcalfe (Salt Lake City: Signature Books, 1993), 115–63. Others besides Grunder have noted similarities in JS's work with literature that circulated in America at the time, such as Adam Clarke's 1811 *The Holy Bible...With a Commentary and Critical Notes*, 6 vols. (New York: Ezra Sargent, 1811), which may have influenced language that JS used in producing his revision of the Bible, 1830–1833. See also Thomas A. Wayment and Haley Wilson-Lemmon, "A Recovered Resource: The Use of Adam Clarke's Bible Commentary in Joseph Smith's Bible Translation," chap. 11 in *Producing Ancient Scripture: Joseph Smith's Translation Projects in the Development of Mormon Christianity*, eds. Michael Hubbard MacKay, Mark Ashurst-McGee, and Brian M. Hauglid (Salt Lake City: University of Utah Press, forthcoming 2020).

See also Jonathan Neville's review of Jonathan Edwards's 1736 "Men Naturally are God's Enemies" that had language common with JS's Book of Mormon. Jonathan Neville, "Joseph Smith, Jonathan Edwards, and the Book of Mormon," 18–30, unpublished. In addition, see the essays by David Paulsen, Roger Launius, Stephen Le Seuer, and Glen Leonard that describe modern appraisals of what has been written about JS during early Mormonism in Bringhurst and Anderson, *Excavating Mormon Pasts.*

17. Some have argued that to be informed as he was, JS had to have accessed the literary options around him. Descriptions of some of those possibilities can be found in Kenneth W. Godfrey, "A Note on the Nauvoo Library and Literary Society," *BYU Studies* 14, no. 3 (Spring 1974); Robert Paul, "Joseph Smith and the Manchester (New York) Library," *BYU Studies* 22, no. 3 (Summer 1982); and Christopher C. Jones, "The Complete Record of the Nauvoo Library and Literary Institute," *Mormon Historical Studies* 10, no. 1 (Spring 2009). See also Noel A. Carmack's conjecture about JS's survey of literature from which he may have "appropriated place names that appear in the Book of Mormon and pre-1830 maps, atlases, and geographical texts." Noel A. Carmack, "Joseph Smith, Captain Kidd Lore, and Treasure Seeking in New York and New England during the Early Republic," *Dialogue* 46, no. 3 (Fall 2013): 78, also 105, 107.

of direct information about particulars that influenced him, we are left, mostly, to conjecture about what stirred his mind and imagination. Still, the inquiry is required.

An important question to ask in the process of discovery is, if it is acknowledged that JS reflected his times, what were the aspects of his environment that he accepted and rejected in the composition of his church? Exhibited in the inspiration he received and the revelations he produced, it is clear that he accepted New Testament examples of prayer, Sabbath worship, water baptism, monetary offerings, communitarian consecration, temperance, music and hymns, the "body and blood of Christ" as sacramental emblems, preaching the gospel, Christian holidays, the resurrection, and the millennium. On the other hand, he rejected other Christian practices such infant baptism, a closed canon, and the holy kiss. That revivals and camp meetings did not find place in the practice of his religion may seem odd given their apparent significance in his time. JS even modified the dominating notions of a bisected afterlife, where heaven and hell were the only alternatives, by remapping the postmortal world. And, once JS established his church, he discarded most of the folk activities related to religion that he had entertained, like those characterized as fitting within the realm of magic. (It must be noted, though, that it has been successfully argued that JS never entirely rejected the magical world view.)[18] JS appeared determined to alter the status quo with which he had been familiar.

Cultural Coincidences?

It is recognized by biblical scholars that the peoples that surrounded the children of Israel influenced them in numerous ways. From a legal system found in the Babylonian Code of Hammurabi, which itself had precedence from the Sumerians and Akkadians, to the embrace by the Israelites of the universal flood story predating them in the epics of Atrahasis and Gilgamesh,[19] it should be no surprise that environments enveloping an individual and a people often served as the premise from which they constructed their own belief systems. Mormonism and JS, arguably, have been no different. Exhibiting the culture surrounding the Smiths, Rick Grunder prepared a significant assembly of documentation exhibiting features of the décor of JS's religious world. *Mormon Parallels*, Grunder's formidable compilation (more than two thousand pages), reveals in part the backdrop—or scenery, if you will—of Mormonism, features of which may have influenced JS's life. "The thesis of my thirty-year study," Grunder stated, "is that a very large part of what many of us have thought comprised the essence of

18. D. Michael Quinn, *Early Mormonism and the Magic World View*, 2nd ed. (Salt Lake City: Signature Books, 1998).
19. John Bright, *A History of Israel*, 3rd ed. (Philadelphia: Westminster Press, 1981), 50; Nahum M. Sarna, *Understanding Genesis: The Heritage of Biblical Israel* (New York: Schocken Books, 1972), 37.

Mormonism actually appeared in Joseph Smith's immediate world before it became part of Mormon language or thought." And regarding the components found within the scriptural texts JS produced, "Most of the seeds of Joseph Smith's texts and prophecies enjoyed popular cultural dissemination in forms familiar to non-Mormons before they grew into scripture of the latter day." The familiarities with those attachments to the culture did not scare off those pulled into the Mormon fold. For, "In surprising depth and degree, much of what Mormonism presents as if it were its own, actually flourished at various levels of society before Joseph Smith declared it."[20] Thus, to ignore what was before JS's eyes on a daily basis by insisting his religious career operated in a revelatory vacuum discounts much of the genius that has been attributed to him.[21] The influences from his cultural setting may have actually provoked his thinking and direction by stimulating initiatives later assumed to be exclusive features of his inspiration.

Charges of Cultural Larceny

There is in the Mormon understanding of God's schedule, acknowledgment that there existed a fertile preparatory period populated by "reformers" that coincided with the demise of the "Great Apostasy." The period traditionally allotted to the reformers ended, in many Latter-day Saints' minds, upon the birth of JS in 1805. Thereafter most assert he operated entirely under God's wing. However, the evidence is stark that the cumulative expansion of religious culture in the early American republic was the embryonic sac from which JS was born, though, as stated, he filtered from that atmosphere what he accepted. Further, recognizing that the "restoration" was ongoing throughout his life, it becomes evident that numerous stimulants—along with revelation—shaped his thinking, edging us closer to an understanding of his prophetic role. With the assumption that everything consequential in JS's life began after 1820, God's hand in shaping the prophet's thinking is constricted from what may be a much larger offering of influential factors moving him. His absorption of salient cultural stimuli may have opened a window of understanding to see the larger contributions of his surroundings ultimately influencing his thinking.

Among those whose religious zeal enlivened America's religious landscape was Alexander Campbell. The forty-three-year-old Scottish immigrant to America who significantly influenced his new country's restorationist thinking, prepared in his significant periodical, the *Millennial Harbinger*, a challenging critique and appraisal of JS's Book of Mormon in February 1831. Campbell was one of a foursome (including his father Thomas) who proved instrumental

20. Grunder, *Mormon Parallels*, 15–16.

21. Wayne Hudson, "The Prophethood of Joseph Smith" in *Joseph Smith Jr.: Reappraisals after Two Centuries*, ed. Reid L. Neilson and Terryl L. Givens (New York: Oxford University Press, 2009), 204; Bloom, *American Religion*, 95, 106.

in organizing what became the Disciples of Christ in the United States. Upon reading the Book of Mormon, he argued in "Delusions" (February 1831) that JS simply incorporated the hot topics of rural religion into the creation of his book. To Campbell, a religious leader as directly a competitor to JS as any other, the Book of Mormon decided "all the great controversies" of the time by inserting the contested religious environment into the Book of Mormon.[22] JS's spin on "infant baptism, ordination, the trinity, regeneration, repentance, justification, the fall of man, the atonement, transubstantiation, fasting, penance, church government, religious experience, the call to the ministry, the general resurrection, eternal punishment, who may baptize, and even the question of free masonary, republican government and the rights of man" amply illustrated JS's deceit.[23] He charged that "Smithisms" pervaded the book and summarized JS "as ignorant and impudent a knave as ever wrote a book," asserting JS to be

22. Campbell, "Delusions," 91, 93–94. See also the critique of Mormonism by Thomas Campbell, Alexander Campbell's father, "The Mormon Challenge," published in (Painesville, OH) *Telegraph* on February 15, 1831, the week after Alexander Campbell's castigation of JS and the Book of Mormon. The elder Campbell's article also includes a substantive letter to Sidney Rigdon, who had defected from Campbellism, dated February 4, 1831. Another Book of Mormon critique at the time, making many of the same arguments as the Campbells, was Jason Whitman's review in *The Unitarian* (Cambridge and Boston: James Munroe, 1834), excerpts of which are in Grunder, *Mormon Parallels*, no. 448 (1805–7).

23. Campbell, "Delusions," 93. See also Mark Staker's discussion of the influences on Campbell's thinking about priesthood and its similarities to conceptions of authority that emerged in Mormonism, including the premise that the Campbellites were "the harbinger to Mormonism." Staker, *Hearken, O Ye People*, 148–67; "Methodist Candor and Consistency," *Millennial Harbinger*, December 1843, 554, quoted in Staker, *Hearken, O Ye People*, 331.

Campbell's "Delusions" was also published the following year in Boston: Alexander Campbell, *Delusions, An Analysis of the Book of Mormon; With an Examination of Its Internal and External Evidences, and a Refutation of Its Pretences to Divine Authority* (Boston: Benjamin H. Greene, 1832). Campbell, with his father Thomas, had pulled separatist Baptists together to join with Barton Stone's comparable movement, and in early 1832 formed what became denominated the Disciples of Christ, but who were also known as Christians. From Campbell's early restorationist organization came several significant converts to Mormonism, including Sidney Rigdon, Parley P. Pratt, and Isaac Morley, adding to the rivalry.

JS finally replied personally to Campbell's attack in the last issue of his church's *Evening and the Morning Star* in September 1834, noting that Campbell was "lavish of his expositions of the falsity and incorrectness of the book of Mormon," but that he, JS, had taken higher ground by turning the other cheek "to obey the commandment of our Savior." And lest Campbell think he had demolished Mormonism, JS scorned: "Perhaps, he is of the opinion that he so completely overthrew the foundation on which it was based, that all that is now wanting to effect an utter downfall of those who have embraced its principles is, to continue to *bark* and howl, and cry, *Joe Smith!* False prophet!" Clearly JS meant his letter to convey, "but here we are!" Joseph Smith to Oliver Cowdery, September 24, 1834, *Evening and the Morning Star*, September 1834, 192.

the volume's "real author." He sneered at him as a "wonder of the world" in audaciously foisting upon the public his fraudulent ruse. With the primary intent of debunking JS's book as disingenuously mimicking contemporary culture, he characterized "Gulliver's travels" as "a heroic poem" compared to the Book of Mormon.[24] Moved in part by Mormon missionaries purging his flock of "Disciples" on Ohio's Western Reserve and his sister's marriage to the brother of Julie Clapp Murdock, a Mormon,[25] Campbell's critique became a mainstay thereafter for JS's opponents.

Claims against JS's proprietary commission from Jesus, couched within the premise that he gleaned his thinking from the texture of the times are long standing. John Henry Evans, however, a noted defender of Mormonism best known for his *One Hundred Years of Mormonism* (1905) and *Joseph Smith: An American Prophet* (1933),[26] recognized the ingenuity of what JS had done. Upon the centennial of JS's birth in 1905, Evans juxtaposed the charges with insight into JS's proficiency that argued for appreciation of the prophet's religious wherewithal. "It is a common belief in the world that the 'Mormon' prophet was a plagiarist; in other words, that the Church he founded is not an original contribution to religion. The *American Encyclopedia*, for example, asserts that, 'to make up the religion of the 'Mormons,' Hebraism, Persian dualism, Brahminism, Buddhistic apotheosis of saints; Christianity, both in its orthodoxy and heterodoxy; Mohammedanism, Druidism, Mesmerism, and Spirit-rapping have all contributed something.'" Acknowledging, however, that JS *did* utilize his surroundings in his seeric role, Evans suggested that JS's "genius" augmented the process. "The fact of the matter is, pressed to its ultimate analysis, this power of organizing and recasting material at hand is itself a species of creation, since the product is something that did not exist before." Further, "If it were possible to say that this principle was taken from this source, and that doctrine from that source, the fact would still remain that the result of this combination is something entirely new in the world—it did not exist in its present form before. The separate elements would have lost their former identity, and taken on a new shape; Joseph Smith's organizing genius would have wrought upon these constituent parts till he had produced a distinctly new religion."[27] Thus, recognizing JS's transformative capabilities in his environmental encounters may be one of the most affirmative characteristics of his personality and ministry.

Other monographs have addressed defined themes reflecting aspects of the early American republic's culture and beyond that may have influenced JS.

24. Campbell, "Delusions," 95.

25. Julie Clapp Murdock was the mother who died in childbirth bearing the Murdock twins immediately adopted by JS and Emma Smith.

26. John Henry Evans, *One Hundred Years of Mormonism* (Salt Lake City: Deseret News, 1905); and *Joseph Smith: An American Prophet* (New York: Macmillan, 1933).

27. John Henry Evans, "Genius or Seer?," *Improvement Era*, December 1905, 170, 173.

Dan Vogel's *Indian Origins and the Book of Mormon* and *Religious Seekers and the Advent of Mormonism* both discussed particulars of the prevailing climate of post-Revolutionary America that directly applied to Mormonism.[28] John Brooke's speculative *The Refiner's Fire* discussed Mormonism's purported seventeenth-century hermetic foundations.[29] Terryl Givens' *When Souls Had Wings* explained the antiquity and relevance to western culture regarding traditions about man's premortal existence, a theme that JS later amplified.[30] And Michael Homer's elaboration of Freemasonry's connection to Mormonism in *Joseph's Temples*,[31] shows several of the directions taken by scholars in the recent generation to explain and understand JS in his setting.

There is another aspect of JS's contemporary life illustrated by modern studies like those above that is imperative to note. Though largely ignored by observers of Mormonism until the past couple of generations, is the contentious matter of the Smiths' involvement in the strain of folk religion that advanced treasure seeking as a means of demonstrating God's bestowal of special gifts upon his children. Rumors and folk beliefs about buried treasure hidden by pirates, the Spanish, and others entertained the imaginations of many in the American Northeast. The prospects of the recovery of buried treasure intersected with religious mindsets. With prosperity and polite society elusive, as historian of the period Alan Taylor explained, to curry God's favor many "seekers" adhered "to a strict moral code and unqualified faith as indispensable to success." The Smiths in their money-digging ventures, like many other "rural folk," lived by the expectation that "God would signify his favor by bestowing material good fortune on the deserving" in the retrieval of treasure to relieve them from their pecuniary fate.[32] Mormon historian Michael Quinn has described that perception of religion and the supernatural as the embrace of the "magic world view," a feature of the divine unmistakably influencing the Smiths.[33] But rather

28. Dan Vogel, *Indian Origins and the Book of Mormon* (Salt Lake City: Signature Books, 1986); and *Religious Seekers and the Advent of Mormonism* (Salt Lake City: Signature Books, 1988).

29. John L. Brooke, *The Refiner's Fire: The Making of Mormon Cosmology, 1644–1844* (Cambridge: Cambridge University Press, 1994).

30. Terryl L. Givens, *When Souls Had Wings: Pre-Mortal Existence in Western Thought* (New York: Oxford University Press, 2010).

31. Michael W. Homer, *Joseph's Temples: The Dynamic Relationship between Freemasonry and Mormonism* (Salt Lake City: University of Utah Press, 2014).

32. Alan Taylor, "The Early Republic's Supernatural Economy: Treasure Seeking in the American Northeast, 1780–1830," *American Quarterly* 38, no. 1 (Spring 1986): 22. See also Whitney R. Cross, *The Burned-Over District: The Social and Intellectual History of Enthusiastic Religion in Western New York, 1800–1850* (1950; repr. Ithaca, NY: Cornell University Press, 1982), 79–82.

33. Quinn, *Early Mormonism and the Magic World View*. Quinn's significant study shows how the "magic world view" drove those who accepted it in most every aspect of their lives.

than the Smiths' acceptance of the notions disqualifying them as responsible and rational people, as anti-Mormons claimed, Taylor clarified that "belief in an alternative, supernatural economy helped psychologically to bridge the gap between their real conditions and what their competitive society taught them to aspire to; recovering a treasure would redress the unjust variance between the seeker's condition and his self-image."[34] Mormons today who accept the premise accommodate the proposition that the background of treasure seeking prepared JS for his encounter with the angel who introduced him to another kind of treasure buried in a hill.

Implicit in the effort to ascertain the sources of JS's enlightenment is the attempt of his critics to show that Mormonism was the sum of what he gathered from his environment, negating otherworldly inspirations. The task, however, to assign influence from JS's circumstances as the direct sources for his thinking is fraught with so many postulations that little is conclusive. As Gordon Wood stated: "In most cases tracing the sources of broadly shared ideas is a fool's errand. Many ideas are so much a part of the general culture that specifying a particular textual influence is impossible."[35] While it is clear that the culture in which JS lived impacted his thinking, the effort to establish a one to one ratio with an idea and JS's entertainment of the notion is to date not possible. Joseph Ellis, noted authority on early America and biographer of Thomas Jefferson, answering the question regarding the sources of Jefferson's inspiration stated: "The temptation to make an implicit connection between his [Jefferson's] ideas and his books is irresistible. Then once the connection is made with, say, Locke or Hutcheson, one can conveniently talk about particular texts as if one were talking about Jefferson's mind." This exercise has also been specifically applied to JS, though, like Jefferson, it is not conclusively demonstrable. Still, JS cannot shake the determination of some to connect him to the posture that "what one thinks is largely or entirely a product of what one reads."[36]

Contemporaries Who Espoused Their Own Visionary Experiences

JS's youth, where so many personality traits are set, was the period of the early American republic.[37] Perspectives of that time, though, transformed again with the emergence of Jacksonian democracy in the 1820s, adding yet another dimen-

34. Taylor, "Early Republic's Supernatural Economy," 19.

35. Wood, *Purpose of the Past*, 29.

36. Ellis, *American Sphinx*, 68.

37. Paul E. Johnson's *The Early American Republic, 1789–1829* (New York: Oxford University Press, 2006), and Gordon Woods's *Empire of Liberty*, outline the period.

sion to JS's perceptions and experience. Many of the outward expressions such as temperance and equality that developed within Mormonism were cast in light of the world of Jackson. Of similar impact upon early nineteenth-century America was the religious upheaval that flourished during that time. Nathan Hatch described what happened at that time as a "fragmentation that beset American religion in the period." It was later recognized as the "Second Great Awakening," which Hatch wrote has too often been viewed as "a conservative response to rapid social change." Instead, he wrote, it "was a religious environment that brought into question traditional authorities and exalted the right of the people to think for themselves. The result, quite simply, was a bewildering world of clashing opinion."[38] Little wonder that from his youth JS was open to and searching for alternatives given the volatile nature of his own surroundings.

As many have declared, had he lived in some other part of the globe at the beginning of the nineteenth century, it is unlikely the foreign environments would have allowed, stimulated, and provoked him as did America's emerging political and religious itinerary. "Only the culture of early nineteenth-century evangelical America could have produced" JS's Mormonism.[39] The Bible prevailed across the land and many became reliant on its display of heavenly intervention to not only organizations but also to individuals desirous of coming to the Lord. Exhibited among the masses within the Second Great Awakening, the consciousness of God and access to him proved ubiquitous in American homes, rural and urban. For those with designs on influencing others religiously, a standard to demonstrate one's call to the ministry or illustrate a profession of salvific grace emerged from the commotion: "An identifiable conversion experience, accompanied by a once-and-for-all decision for Christ, was the central event in the spiritual life of Christians," according to historian Daniel Walker Howe.[40] Another historical commentator of the period, Alice Felt Tyler, described the evangelical expectation: "Before conversion man's soul is shackled by sin; acceptance of religion means freedom from bondage; salvation must come through conversion consciously experienced at a definite time and place."[41] The anticipation and prospect of a transformative experience for those who received salvation or who declared their personal call to the ministry became pervasive.

Others, to illustrate JS's fit into common patterns of those professing special connections to God in early America, have rehearsed examples of religious

38. Hatch, *Democratization of American Christianity*, 81.

39. Wood, "Evangelical America and Early Mormonism," 386.

40. Howe, *What Hath God Wrought*, 171.

41. Alice Felt Tyler, *Freedom's Ferment: Phases of American Social History from the Colonial Period to the Outbreak of the Civil War* (New York: Harper Torchbooks, 1962), 35.

conversions and testimonials from the period preceding JS, some with characteristics common with JS.[42] As Richard Bushman explained, JS appeared in the midst of a "visionary world" where spiritual manifestations invoked religious conversion confirmed by sanctifying and experiential salvation. Detractors have used those stories that portray vivid religiosity to argue that JS's expressions about his numinous experiences were modified from his countrymen's accounts, some of which may have been familiar to him. Those who do not understand larger contextual Mormonism may fail to recognize the distortion of the characterization. Still, the question remains in the minds of many: Was JS moved to inquire of God by what he found in his religious environment? Was it the distribution of parallel spiritual accounts that gave him confidence to finally tell his tale, as represented in his 1832 and 1838/39 histories? The present historical record is not sufficient to be conclusive about any of these issues.

A Multitude of Influences

Besides the spiritually fertile ground described above, what about the other fixtures of JS's environment that may have sparked his thinking and his inspirations? Beyond the influences of the religious world and its variations is the multiplicity of secular and societal matters that play into probing deeper into the environment. Scholars and popular writers of the colonial and early American republic periods have produced interpretive volumes reflecting the abundance of information found in the documentary records of early America as found in county courthouses, libraries, and attics. Numerous monographs, doctoral dissertations, and articles have been written in the past century that describe the societal motions that moved the population from the frontier to hamlets and from the villages to cities. Those volumes address the complexities that faced individuals and families who built their lives around producing food, building shelters, and tending and improving their property and material investments. Issues such as domestic life, religion, employment/vocations, education, recreation, the economy, gender roles, military service, rural and urban life, music and art, among others, are to modern observers, particularly relevant.

42. See Neal E. Lambert and Richard H. Cracroft, "Literary Form and Historical Understanding: Joseph's First Vision," *Journal of Mormon History* 7 (1980); Richard L. Bushman, "The Visionary World of Joseph Smith," *BYU Studies* 37, no. 1 (1997–1998); Richard L. Bushman, "Joseph Smith and His Visions," in *The Oxford Handbook of Mormonism*, ed. Terryl L. Givens and Philip L. Barlow (New York: Oxford University Press, 2015); Elden J. Watson, "The 'Prognostication' of Asa Wild," *BYU Studies* 37, no. 3 (1997–98); Christopher C. Jones, "The Power and Form of Godliness: Methodist Conversion Narratives and Joseph Smith's First Vision," *Journal of Mormon History* 37, no. 2 (Spring 2011); and Gregory A. Prince, "Joseph Smith's First Vision in Historical Context: How a Historical Narrative Became Theological," *Journal of Mormon History* 41, no. 4 (October 2015).

Naturally, the spiritual and religious manifestations in JS's life arouse the most attention. Grasping his sacral and theological achievements and what influenced their inclusion in his life seems particularly relevant. But limiting the more comprehensive study of his life to just his religious motivations cheats us from appreciating his negotiation of the culture and society around him. Consider, for example, what became known as the Mormons' "word of wisdom."[43] For some believers it has been popular to say that JS received the revelation about the harmful effects of alcohol and tobacco "far in advance of anything suggested by scientists."[44] Though the point can be corroborated in the long run, the implication that JS discovered a health code through revelation before anyone else knew about it is misleading. Another LDS tradition beyond the evidence is that the Word of Wisdom primarily stemmed from an incident in Newel K. Whitney's Kirtland, Ohio, store related in the well-known 1868 anecdote recounted by Brigham Young. At a gathering of church elders in an upper room of the store in February 1833 the brethren would "light their pipes" and soon the room was filled with a "cloud of tobacco smoke" only to be followed by them biting off "a large chew of tobacco," which they then spit on the floor. The behavior resulted in "complaints of his [JS's] wife at having to clean so filthy a floor."[45] While details in Young's story may certainly have been a factor in the

43. Smith, Revelations, February 27, 1833, *JSP, R1*:238–40.

44. Hyrum M. Smith and Janne M. Sjodahl, *The Doctrine and Covenants, Containing Revelations Given to Joseph Smith, Jr., the Prophet* (Salt Lake City: Deseret Book, 1973), 571, first published in America in 1923. (Hyrum Mack Smith initially published the volume in 1919 in England.)

45. Brigham Young, Sermon, February 8, 1868, *JD*, 157–58. See also David Whitmer, Interview with David Cameron Dunbar, Richmond, MO, *Omaha Herald*, October 10, 1886, reprinted in *Salt Lake Tribune*, October 17, 1886, from "Uncle Dale's Readings in Early Mormon History, Newspapers of Utah," http://www.sidneyrigdon.com/dbroadhu/UT/tribune2.htm#101786. Dale Broadhurst's "Uncle Dale's Readings in Early Mormon History," is a significant collection of national newspapers, periodicals, and other publications that reported on Mormonism in its first generation. See the index at http://www.sidneyrigdon.com/dbroadhu/artindex.htm#NE.

See how the Brigham Young story served as justification for the revelation in John A. Widtsoe and Leah D. Widtsoe, *The Word of Wisdom: A Modern Interpretation* ([Salt Lake City]: Deseret News Press, 1938), 24–25; and Sidney B. Sperry, *Doctrine and Covenants Compendium* (Salt Lake City: Bookcraft, 1965), 445–46, where Sperry stated, "There are those who claim that the Word of Wisdom was an outgrowth of the temperance movement which was in vogue in the days of the Prophet Joseph Smith." Sperry's statement was a refutation of the argument made by Leonard Arrington's "An Economic Interpretation of the 'Word of Wisdom,'" *BYU Studies* 1, no. 1 (Winter 1959): 39–40. JS, according to Sperry, "was doubtless aware of this movement, but it is more probable that the Word of Wisdom came into being, as President Young explained, and as a direct result of the Prophet's concern with his and his wife's disgust at a filthy habit" (446).

revelation, ignoring what his countrymen were doing in matters of temperance at that time distorts the backdrop of JS's inspiration. The evangelical Christian-inspired "temperance movement" within the United States was in full motion in early 1833 where February 26 was declared a national temperance day specifically directed at curtailing consumption of alcoholic beverages. JS's revelation, a "word of wisdom," appeared the following day, February 27, 1833.[46] Given the other health reform efforts then prevalent in the country, it should not be surprising that JS weighed in on the consequential issues at the same time.

Similarly, the November 24, 1832, vote by South Carolina's Nullification Convention precipitated by their "states' rights" rejection of the federal tariffs of 1828 and 1832 that had shackled their economy yielded a "crisis" with an ultimatum of secession that threated national sovereignty.[47] A month later JS delivered his noted revelation on December 25, 1832, mentioned in the Introduction, portending the "rebellion of South Carolina" and the subsequent division of the "southern States" from "the northern States."[48] Uncharacteristic of the pattern of his divine communications that generally related to providing church members with the blended purpose of calling for improvement and submission along with reprimand and censure, the Christmas 1832 revelation addressed a different genre of warning and foreboding. Unless understood in the states-rights environment afflicting the country at the time, with the subsequent eruption of civil war in 1861, the student may make assumptions about JS's prescience that misleads and confuses.[49]

46. *American Quarterly Temperance Magazine*, May 1833, as published in Albany, New York, by the New York State Temperance Society; and *The American Temperance Almanac, For the Year of our Lord and Savior Jesus Christ* (New York: L. D. Dewey, and C. C. P. Crosby, 1833), quoted in Grunder, *Mormon Parallels*, nos. 12 and 13 (84–85).

Because there is no contemporary documentation, it is impossible to know if there was direct correlation between the national temperance movement and JS's embrace of the principle. Grunder stated, however, that, "A lengthy notice... announces that the American Temperance Society has designated Tuesday, February 26, 1833 as a national temperance day set aside for simultaneous meetings 'in all the cities, towns and villages throughout the United States.' On February 27, Joseph Smith dictated the Word of Wisdom (D&C 89)." Grunder, *Mormon Parallels*, 84–85. This could be construed as evidence that JS was aware of what surrounded him and that the revelation he received was designed to confirm what was stirring in American society.

47. Walker, *What God Hath Wrought*, 395–410.

48. Smith, Revelations, October 25, 1832, *JSP, R1*:224–25 [D&C 87 (1981)].

49. The broad impact of the prophecy on JS's followers at the time is not known, as he did not include it in the church's Book of Commandments (1833), the D&C (1835), or early church periodicals. It was finally added to a new edition of the D&C in 1876, after its first appearance in the Pearl of Great Price in England in 1851. Despite the late addition of the revelation to the Mormon canon, it was well known among the Saints. See Woodford, "Historical Development of the Doctrine and Covenants," 1104–9.

The Parallels?

As indicated earlier, Rick Grunder's *Mormon Parallels* is an extensive collection of annotated references to the literature of post-Revolutionary America showing parallels in the culture to JS's innovations; the literary antecedents that flourished before and during his lifetime. By referencing essays, pamphlets, orations, reports, sermons, minutes of meetings, newspaper articles, books, etc., that circulated, Grunder showed in part the religious atmosphere of the time, as well as many of the contemporary discussions about God and man. Much of the documentation had origins in the American Northeast and was mostly dated from the last half of the eighteenth to the mid-nineteenth centuries.[50] The argument is

50. As stated previously, parallelisms cannot on a one-to-one basis be tied to Mormon thought and teaching in JS's time. But, illustrated by several topical themes, it is clear that the environment held strains of what became Mormonism. See the following examples from Grunder: Book of Mormon, similarities to claims in: no. 101 (400); no. 167 (622); no. 193 (724); no. 256 (967); no. 338 (1297); no. 430 (1776); no. 448 (1805–7); no. 453 (1817); no. 491 (2008). Cosmology: no. 90 (371); no. 114 (464); no. 115 (472); no. 126 (520); no. 166 (618); no. 203 (796); no. 223 (831); no. 292 (1099); no. 316 (1163); no. 426 (1742); no. 429 (1752); no. 472 (1889). Egyptian, things: no. 169 (628); no. 193 (724); no. 256 (967). Eternal Marriage: no. 121 (495). Eternal Progression: no. 116 (477). Godhead: no. 37 (163); no. 98 (389); no. 223 (832); no. 235 (935); no. 325 (1265); no. 397 (1613); no. 469 (1877); no. 481 (1925); no. 482 (1963); no. 487 (1993); no. 492 (2011); no. 493 (2017). God's plan for America: no. 76 (312); no. 337 (1296); no. 406 (1667); no. 440 (1781). Jesus's Atonement: no. 90 (371); no. 148 (575). Masonry/Anti-Masonry: no. 9 (73); no. 51 (217); no. 103 (412); no. 105 (417); no. 202 (795); no. 254 (951); no. 255 (965); no. 259 (987); no. 261 (993); no. 262 (998); no. 263 (1004); no. 264 (1012); no. 265 (1018); no. 309 (1139); no. 313 (1155); no. 336 (1295); no. 349 (1338); no. 408 (1678); no. 413 (1698); no. 416 (1708); no. 417 (1719); no. 444 (1794); no. 455 (1837); no. 459 (1853); no. 461 (1858). Money Digging/Stone in Hat: no. 413 (1698); no. 438 (1779); no. 439 (1760); no. 460 (1856). Nullification Crisis: no. 244 (924); no. 267 (1021). Plan of Salvation/Three Degrees of Glory: no. 430 (1760); no. 475 (1897); no. 479 (1913). See also Mark Lyman Staker's discussion of Walter Scott/Campbellite teaching in 1828 on the "three kingdoms," *Hearken, O Ye People*, 322–23. Premortal Existence: no. 37 (163); no. 98 (389); no. 223 (832); no. 235 (935); no. 325 (1265); no. 397 (1613); no. 469 (1877). Priesthood/Aaronic and Melchizedek: no. 73 (285); no. 92 (381); no. 158 (610); no. 180 (644); no. 232 (890); no. 339 (1338); no. 382 (1569); no. 416 (1708); no. 455 (1837); no. 469 (1877). Prophets/Prophecy: no. 73 (285); no. 191 (700); no. 342 (1324); no. 420 (1723). Salvation and Baptism for the Dead: no. 65 (269); no. 76 (312); no. 77 (331); no. 158 (601); no. 376 (1547). Scriptural Style, writing in: no. 348 (1335); no. 406 (1667). Shaker Beliefs: no. 376 (1547). Temperance and the "Word of Wisdom": no. 7 (65); no. 12 (84); no. 13 (85); no. 14 (90); no. 104 (413); no. 204 (798); no. 331 (1280); no. 333 (1283); no. 409 (1691); no. 422 (1733); no. 433 (1767); no. 434 (1774); no. 435 (1775); no. 446 (1804); no. 499 (2041). Temple Ritual: no. 9 (73); no. 416 (1708). Urim and Thummim: no. 232 (890); no. 414 (1702); no. 430 (1760). Visionary Experiences: no. 102 (405); no. 180 (644); no. 181 (656); no. 247 (928); no. 258 (984); no. 311 (1152); no. 390 (1591); no. 412 (1697); no. 437 (1778). See also Mark Staker on Alexander Campbell and the influences upon him regarding notions of priesthood, as well as similarities and divergences between Campbell and Mormon priesthood nomenclature and function, *Hearken, O Ye People*, 148–67.

compelling that there were in JS's doctrine and theology both stark and subtle nuances to the religious ideas of the period, as well as remarkable productions of what he said were translations of ancient texts and Jesus's inspirations. These comparatives are not necessarily threats to Mormon traditions of unique dispensation, but rather acknowledge JS as an engaging and imaginative prophet who drew from not only Deity and his instincts but also the world in which he lived. This better fits the biblical model of ancient Israel's prophetic figures and shows his prescient instincts of "religion making."

The rhetoric of exceptionalism prevalent in Mormon culture has created a tradition of distinctiveness that is difficult to surmount; though, as suggested, the evidence is compelling to the contrary. It is imperative that JS be understood, or at least considered, in his culture and environment to show the range of his prophetic capacities. For those who recognize the magnitude of JS's life and what he did in his environment, the parallels are demonstrable evidence of his ability to grasp and act upon his circumstances, punctuated by the inspiration he stated he received, creating something that was unique for his time.

CHAPTER 6

Joseph Smith among His Contemporaries

As modern students attempt to assemble the criteria necessary to appraise JS by the observations of his contemporaries, it is important to see the full range of attitudes toward him portrayed in the historical record. This chapter is assembled to illustrate that range. Within the portrayals, the reader will see the emotions he generated in those who both disdained him and those who adored him. Because of who he was and what he then advanced, he begged characterization. And once he became germane, the observer usually took sides. Certainly, some were indifferent. But everyone who wrote about the prophet generally had a point in defining him. What follows are portraits from the world of those who intersected with JS. Once he and his people were encountered, they generally could not be ignored. How then can modern students weigh those opinions to ascertain the man? The polemical stage where he has been examined is confusing, making the study complicated; especially given that, like everyone else, he changed as he matured. His maturation did not make him immune from life's struggles nor did it thrust him to transcendent status; rather, he contended with human frailty all his days. The surviving documentary record, however, suggests that in matters of following the impressions given to him by God and his own visionary instincts he followed a course consistent with both his limitations and his strengths. The premise from which this is displayed is underlain with recognition that once he and his church became of concern among his contemporaries the nature of public opinion about him was generally cast from peoples' first impressions. Some were implacable opponents. Some who may have initially been suspicious came around. But some of those then reversed course and turned on him. The cases shown below exhibit the range of acceptance or rejection applied to JS, generally organized by categorization.

The Trend of Criticism of Joseph Smith

By the time of JS's advent as a religious figure, the country's religious atmosphere had already been shaped by the resistance of *normative* American Christianity to alternatives that sprung from the underbrush. Some contenders were benign but others showed the potential for serious disruption to the status quo. The diversity resulting from the country's Second Great Awakening in the early nineteenth century provided ample alternatives in the religious marketplace. "The crucible of popular theology combined odd mixtures of high and popular culture, of renewed supernaturalism and Enlightenment rationalism, of mystical experiences and biblical literalism, of evangelical and Jeffersonian rhetoric," Nathan Hatch explained.[1] "Free enterprise," Martin Marty stated, "had come to the world of religion."[2] Still, many Americans were suspicious of "extreme" religious upstarts that decried the orthodoxies and religious customs of traditional Christian churches. For a short period after the founding of the Church of Christ (Mormon) in 1830, regional popular opinion about the church was mostly unceremonious. But by the time the fledgling church had established a bursting identity in the early 1830s, the literature turned from curious to suspicious to inflammatory.

The representations of condemnation of JS that follow are obviously a small percentage of what could be depicted but well exhibit the sentiment against him held by contemporary cultural observers. The preponderant resources from the periphery that measured JS are the newspaper and religious periodicals of the period.[3] As one might imagine, given his truth claims and rejection of the religious world around him, JS and his church were not well received. America had been fertile ground since its colonial inception for separatists, outsiders, and religious innovators. With that background, the Mormon appearance, as portrayed in the newspapers, was treated both as a curiosity and just another intrusion on the several variations of mainstream religion, though JS and his followers later gained toxic status.[4]

1. Hatch, *Democratization of American Christianity*, 35.
2. Martin E. Marty, *Pilgrims in Their Own Land: 500 Years of Religion in America* (New York: Penguin Books, 1986), 128.
3. See Dale Broadhurst's "Uncle Dale's Readings in Early Mormon History," mentioned earlier. http://www.sidneyrigdon.com/dbroadhu/artindex.htm#NE. The L. Tom Perry Special Collections at Brigham Young University also has a digital newspaper collection of some nineteenth-century newspapers, though more limited, with facsimiles and transcripts. "19th-Century Mormon Article Newspaper Index," https://contentdm.lib.byu.edu/digital/collection/19CMNI/id/13161/rec/76.
4. See Walter A. Norton's study of newspaper coverage of JS and early Mormonism, "Comparative Images: Mormonism and Contemporary Religions as Seen by Village Newspapermen in Western New York and Northeastern Ohio, 1820–1833" (PhD diss., Brigham Young University, 1991), 243–91.

To the religion editors of the day, JS was a pretension and more, sometimes referred to by them as a false prophet, anti-Christ or a modern "Mohamet" (Muhammed).[5] After newspaper sketches appeared here and there, it took four years and the Mormons' removal to Kirtland, Ohio, to qualify as a threat meriting comprehensive treatment in book form. The best example of diatribe during Mormonism's formative years came from a newspaperman situated just a few miles northeast of Kirtland, Ohio, in the community of Painesville. In 1834, Eber D. Howe, after months of covering the unsettling rise of JS and his church on Ohio's Western Reserve, prepared the most formidable response to Mormonism to that time. It is difficult to overstate the significance then and later of Howe's *Mormonism Unvailed* regarding attitudes generated about the Mormons. The work, intended as exposé, clearly portrayed Howe's denunciation of JS and his family on its first page: "All who became intimate with them [the Smiths] during this period, unite in representing the general character of old Joseph and wife, the parents of the pretended Prophet, as lazy, indolent, ignorant and superstitious."[6] But that was only the beginning.

To substantiate his claims, Howe found an enthusiastic collaborator in erstwhile Mormon Philastus Hurlbut, who supplied Howe with the kind of "evidence" against the Smiths that more than confirmed Howe's contentions. The Hurlbut collection of declarations included views about the Smith's that are consistent and uniformly disparaging. After Hurlbut's baptism into the Church of Christ he became an elder in March 1833. By June he had become entirely estranged from Mormonism, and excommunicated on the grounds of moral infraction. As retribution, Hurlbut traveled the 250 miles from Kirtland to JS's former home near Palmyra, New York, where in November and December 1833 and again in March 1834 he gathered dozens of testimonials and other endorsements that uniformly criticized JS and his family. Howe readily found a place for the interviews in his book. Besides disparaging the character of the Smiths, "money-digging" as a precedent to offset JS's Book of Mormon story, was the primary topic of condemnation: "They [the Smith family] lived, at that time, in Palmyra, about one mile and a half from my residence. A great part of their time was devoted to digging for money," so reported William Stafford.[7] Willard Chase, the Smith's neighbor and the person from whom JS acquired the

5. See Adam Morris, *American Messiahs: False Prophets of a Damned Nation* (New York: Liveright, 2019); J. Spencer Fluhman, "An 'American Mahomet': Joseph Smith, Muhammad, and the Problem of Prophets in Antebellum America," *Journal of Mormon History* 35, no. 3 (Summer 2008): 23–45, which describes JS's categorization by many religionists and others as another imposter to true religion, an attempt by the Christian community to dismiss him as they had the founder of Islam.

6. Howe, *Mormonism Unvailed*, 11.

7. William Stafford, December 8, 1833, in Howe, *Mormonism Unvailed*, 237.

"seerstone" that he used in "translating" the Book of Mormon and his reception of revelations, indicated that the family was "engaged in the money digging business, which they followed until the latter part of the season of 1827."[8] Along with censure for money digging by several who were, curiously, also probably associated with JS in the work, were attendant charges of the misdemeanors of necromancy and magical incantations. Those who knew him also accused JS with other civic foibles: drunkenness, fighting, dishonesty, indolence, and promiscuity. In general, neighbors dismissed the entire Smith family. "Not one of the male members of the Smith family were entitled to any credit, whatsoever. They were lazy, intemperate and worthless men, very much addicted to lying. In this they frequently boast of their skill. Digging for money was their principal employment."[9] The statements gathered by Hurlbut included affirmation by a local judge and a justice of the peace. This feature suggested there was homegrown judicial endorsement of the declarations, though the certifications merely stated that the deponents said they had told the truth. While JS defenders have dismissed the interviews as blatant fabrication, there is sufficient corroboration that several of the themes must be given some credence. However, Hurlbut's demonstrable antagonism toward Mormonism must also be a consideration in the overtones of the statements. And, other credible documentation indicates that the indictments made in the Hurlbut exposé were selective and not representative of all who offered views of the Smiths.[10]

The money-digging dismissals as a counter to the Book of Mormon story never abated during JS's lifetime. John A. Clark, rector of St. Andrews Church in

8. Willard Chase, 1833, in Howe, *Mormonism Unvailed*, 240.

9. Parley Chase, December 2, 1833, in Howe, *Mormonism Unvailed*, 248.

10. Fifty years after the Hurlbut gatherings, William and Edmund Kelley, leaders in the RLDS Church, visited Palmyra, New York, and environs in March 1881 to defuse allegations made at the time by a peeved clergyman determined to find dirt on the Smiths in the area. The Kelleys gathered a number of testimonials that both confirmed some of the Hurlbut charges regarding money digging and Smith family drinking, while at the same time, they discovered affirmations of the Smiths' decency and respectability. These from some of the same families that Hurlbut had previously questioned. Illustrating the objective nature of the Kelley gatherings, Dr. John Stafford said that JS "would do a fair day's work if hired out to a man," though, he said, the Smith's "were poor managers." Stafford, who lived a mile from the Smiths, qualified what he said stating, "They were peaceable among themselves. The old woman had a great deal of faith that their children were going to do something great." And though "Joe was quite illiterate," after the Smiths began to hold school in their home, "he improved greatly." Another interviewee, Thomas Taylor related: "I knew them [the Smiths] very well. They were very nice men, too. The only trouble was they were ahead of the people; and the people, as in every such case turned out to abuse them, because they had the manhood to stand for their own convictions.… I can take you to a great many old settlers here who will substantiate what I say, and if you want to go, just come around to my place across the street there, and I'll go with you." William H. Kelley, "The Hill Cumorah and the Book of Mormon," *Saints' Herald*, June 1, 1881, 167; also reprinted in the *Juvenile Instructor*, October 1, 1882, 301–2.

Philadelphia, in his 1842 travel journal-turned-screed panned the prophet: "Jo Smith, who has since been the chief prophet of the Mormons, and was one of the most prominent ostensible actors in the first scenes of this drama, belonged to a very shiftless family near Palmyra. They lived a sort of vagrant life, and were principally known as *money-diggers*. Jo from a boy appeared dull and utterly destitute of genius."[11] Clark's 1842 assessment suggests the early charges made against JS had stuck. Subsequent scholarly study has confirmed that the family was, indeed, involved in the occupation of treasure seeking, representing a folk subculture common in the Northeast.[12] JS himself, via self-interrogation, disclosed as much in his hypothetical interview in July 1838 as editor of the church's *Elders' Journal*: "Was not Jo Smith a money digger?" to which he drolly answered, "Yes, but it was never a very profitable job to him, as he only got fourteen dollars a month for it."[13] Though his family's involvement in searching for treasure probably engaged them more than JS admitted, he acknowledged the context of his involvement in his 1838/39 history. In October 1825, the history stated that Josiah Stowell hired him and others to find a Spanish silver mine rumored to be somewhere near the Susquehanna River corridor in southern New York and northeastern Pennsylvania. But after "nearly a month without success," JS told Stowell it was futile. "Hence," he stated, "arose the very prevalent story of my having been a money digger."[14]

Religionists of the Day Challenge Joseph Smith

The allegations of deceit and fraud against JS started small, but as the profile of Mormonism enlarged in the America of the 1830s, neither he nor his church could be ignored. And characterizations of the Mormon anomaly were rarely measured. Anti-Mormon sentiment in the nineteenth century exhibited the hostility of the religiously inclined toward the encroachment of JS and his church upon the country's spiritual territory.[15] Precisely coincident to Alexander Campbell's weighty criticism of the Book of Mormon in February 1831, Universalist advocate Dolphus Skinner disqualified Mormonism and the Book of Mormon.

11. John A. Clark, *Gleanings by the Way* (Philadelphia: W. J. and J. K. Simon, 1842), 225.
12. See the entire 1984 fall issue of *BYU Studies* that was devoted to contextualizing JS and his family's participation in the tradition of folk religion, *BYU Studies* 24, no. 4 (Fall 1984): 395–560; Michael Quinn's *Early Mormonism and the Magic World View*, 30–65; and Alan Taylor's "Early Republic's Supernatural Economy," and "Rediscovering the Context of Joseph Smith's Treasure Seeking," *Dialogue* 19, no. 4 (Winter 1986).
13. [No author], *Elders' Journal*, July 1838, 43.
14. Smith, Histories, "History Drafts, 1838–circa 1841," Draft 2, *JSP, H1*:234, 236.
15. David Brion Davis, "Some Themes of Counter-Subversion: An Analysis of Anti-Masonic, Anti-Catholic, and Anti-Mormon Literature," *The Mississippi Valley Historical Review* 47, no. 2 (September 1960): 205–24; J. Spencer Fluhman, *"A Peculiar People": Anti-Mormonism and the Making of Religion in Nineteenth-Century America* (Chapel Hill: University of North Carolina Press, 2012).

Located 120 miles east of Palmyra in Utica, New York, Skinner and his *Evangelical Magazine and Gospel Advocate* portrayed another angle representing the religious tenor in the "West." The *Evangelical Magazine's* February 1831 report from a correspondent in Chagrin [near Kirtland], Ohio, claimed the Mormonites of the area were "*fanatics*" who called "themselves apostles, prophets, &c.," claiming to "perform miracles—call down fire from heaven—impart the Holy Ghost by the laying on of hands, and say that they shall be renovated and live a thousand years." Stipulating JS to be "a man of subtlety and cunning, but of no learning, and as we are informed, much worse than no character," the upstart prophet was nothing more than an "unprincipled, villainous imposter." Sealing the deal, *Evangelical Magazine's* readers were told that the Book of Mormon was a book "filled with blasphemous nonsense, silly stories, pretended prophecies," emphasizing again that JS was a "miserable imposter."[16] To the extent that newspapers and periodicals could influence the public at the time, usually confirming the rumors and gossip of the day, the charge colored, as suggested, everything communicated about JS.

Once JS's "glass-looking" and "money digging" became known as his means of divining the powers of God for gain, rejecting not only the Book of Mormon but also Mormon claims of being the restoration of Christ's ancient church was easy. The allegations of monetary scam and swindle naturally became the premise to describe JS's religious claims of divine intervention. Once JS's Church of Christ took hold, despite the dismissive publicity it received disproportionally from the western regions of the country, JS's character became more of an issue than the easy swipes that were applied to him in Mormonism's infancy. As the fledgling religion spread throughout the American northeast, the regularity of the rebukes increased. Another correspondent of the *Evangelical Magazine* in March 1834, for example, reported that upon attending a gathering in Geneseo, New York, "the doughty Jo. Smith, Jun." showed up. Said to be "about twenty-seven years of age," JS, the observer wrote, "is about six feet in height, neither attenuated nor corpulent. His eyes are rather dull than expressive, hair of a light brown, and his countenance unmarked by any peculiar expression indicative of intense thought or extraordinary intellect." Beyond his visage, "His manner is ungainly, his diction coarse, and his delivery slow and labored," and there was "nothing in his appearance or language to excite much attention, save his presumptuous impiety." Thus, the "impudent ignoramus" offered little to counter prevailing circumstances.[17]

16. "Editorial Correspondence," *Evangelical Magazine and Gospel Advocate*, February 5, 1831, 47. Two months later, A. W. B[enton] paralleled the earlier report in the *Evangelical Magazine* also dismissing JS in his "Mormonites," April 9, 1831, 120. See another February 1831 critique of JS and Mormonism in the *Western Luminary*, February 23, 1831.
17. M. L. F., "Interview with the Mormon Prophet" *Evangelical Magazine and Gospel Advocate*, April 5, 1834.

As the Mormon presence grew, so did their reputation, skewed though it often was. Among religious traditionalists witnessing the expansion of JS's church, explanations of the phenomenon flourished—anything negative to account for its growing presence. In June 1834, Timothy Gunn, a resident of Hartford, Ohio, 140 miles southwest of Kirtland, wrote to a family member in Wendell, Massachusetts, reporting what he said was his "back woods" understanding of the religion. "Wendell had become infested with Mormonites," provoking inquiry from the family member. After taking "some pains to find out the truth respecting them," Gunn determined that, "Elder [Sidney] Rigdon who was formerly a Baptist Minister from New [Y]ork left off preaching and came to Ohio and became a money digger and after many unsuccessful attempts pretended to have a Dream and Said one appeared to him and told him if he would go and dig in a certain place he would find Something more valuable vastly than money." Illustrating the confusion that often reigned in rumors about the Mormons, he claimed that it was Rigdon who "brought forth the Mormon bible" and that it was "the Angel Gabriel [who] came and Snatched away the golden plates."[18] The misinformation had the same effect upon the curious.

JS's early reputation as a scoundrel accompanied him during the Saints' experiences in Ohio and Missouri, actually having gained momentum. He continued to generate controversy and suspicion. By the time Nauvoo rose a decade after Mormonism's founding, despite the significant difficulties during the entirety of the 1830s, JS seemed to have weathered some the public relations crucible. Planted in Nauvoo in 1839, thereafter JS exuded a second wind showing his maturation as prophet among his people. Still, he had become an oddity and object of notoriety from reports of Mormon ingenuity in resurrecting what had to some started to smell like a religious corpse. On the western extensions of American institutions, newspapermen, itinerant preachers, and adventurers interpreted the Saints to their publics who readily reveled in the histrionics.

After ten years at the helm, another critical appraisal of the prophet by a competitor displayed how JS was known at the time. In mid-November 1840, twenty-five-year-old Methodist clergyman Daniel P. Kidder, a western New Yorker, found himself face to face with the Mormon who had created so much chatter as a subterranean religious charlatan. The unplanned connection took place on the riverboat, *Nauvoo*, travelling downstream during Kidder's first journey on the Father of Waters. As the watercraft neared Nauvoo at the "head of the upper rapids," the travelers "laid up for the night." Here Kidder judiciously prepared a multi-hued sketch of the man "who from his notoriety in a variety of ways may deserve here a record of description I took of him at the time." The

18. Timothy Gunn to Levi Benjamin, June 15, 1834, MS 7396, CHL. See also the attribution of Mormonism's origin to Sidney Rigdon in Leonard J. Arrington, "James Gordon Bennett's Report on the 'Mormonites,'" *BYU Studies* 10, no. 3 (Spring 1970): 358–59.

encounter provided Kidder with an engaging diary entry: "He is large, broad shouldered, coarse featured. His dress is clerical quite in fashion, black suit white kerchief & high collar with a fur cap. His temperament—nervolymphatic, excessive perceptive faculties, retreating forehead. Has long light hair, light skin, light blue eyes, large mouth, long teeth several gone & on the whole an excessively sleepy lazy look. His deportment bears every shade between the sanctimonious & the outlandish." Kidder then burrowed into JS's behavior and demeanor. "He is generally familiar & talkative particularly with low company & on low topics. Has a fondness for mingling & cracking jokes with the crew. Lifts at the pole, takes a game of checkers & swigs a 'brandy cocktail' with equal grace. Asks blessing at the table & rails at almost every description of piety under some form. He is a great boaster of humility & kindness but [is] actually pugnacious querulous & abusive in the extreme. Boasts of his good breeding and shows it by snatching a book from a Lady." Undoubtedly hoping for a scandalous exhibition, Kidder was not disappointed: JS "Keeps up a system of espionage on board the boat & undertakes to chastise the passengers for any idle word they may drop respecting him, his doctrines or followers." Moreover, "He is thought to have more than ordinary shrewdness & an intimate knowledge of human nature," possessing "as much braggadocia as any man living." Presciently, he closed, "He is 34 yrs old & probably [has] quite a race yet to run.[19]

Kidder's appraisal of JS conforms to what others had been saying about him for a decade. While it is implausible that Kidder could have gleaned all he declared about him from this sole encounter, JS's reputation clearly provided filler for Kidder's report. JS struck such a chord with Kidder that two years later Kidder expanded his encounter to a full published exposé of JS and the Mormons, determined to eviscerate any plausibility that JS had credibility. "It makes the heart shudder to contemplate the blasphemy [of JS], and the purposed wickedness of such attempts to counterfeit the voice and word of God, for the low and sole purpose of deceiving the ignorant." Conforming akin to every other assault upon JS from the period, Kidder punctuated his declarations: "These pretended revelations, however, were only an introduction to the series of incredible iniquities which, in a similar category, have come down to the present. What man in his senses can, for one moment, entertain the comparison of Mormonism with Christianity?"[20]

Another ministerial visitor to the Mississippi River valley, Benjamin Morris—a clergyman of the American Home Missionary Society advocating Re-

19. Daniel P. Kidder, Diary, 1833–1840, November 13, 1840, vol. 1, Rutgers University, Special Collections, New Brunswick, New Jersey.

20. Daniel P. Kidder, *Mormonism and the Mormons: A Historical View of the Rise and Progress of the Sect Self-Styled Latter-Day Saints* (New York: G. Lane and P. P. Sandford, 1842), 76.

formed theology—dismissed JS in 1841 from Warsaw, Illinois, just downriver from Nauvoo. Besides portraying the Mormons "like the locusts of Egypt" that "consume every green thing in the land," creating a climate where there was "a strong disinclination to live near [them]," he exposed the prophet and his influence over the people: "The power of Smith over his followers is incredible. He has unlimited influence, and his declarations are /as/ the authority and influence of the word of God itself. He is a complete despot, and does as he pleases with his people. Some people consider him a great man; I do not." Like Kidder, Morris also insisted JS to be devious and scheming. "He is not possessed of a single element of greatness, /unless it be/ ~~except his greatness~~ in vice and blasphemy. He is a compound of ignorance, vanity, arrogance coarseness and stupidity and vulgarity. His present ~~potential and~~ unlimited influence had been gained by the force of circumstances, and not by any intrinsic /talents/ ~~powers~~ he possesses. He is only the outside agent of a band of as wicked men, as ever opposed the gospel."[21]

More Than a Curiosity

JS fared no better from the nonreligious world. A correspondent of the *Alexandria Gazette and Virginia Advertiser*, published in Alexandria, Virginia, knowing his mid-Atlantic compatriots would find his report of JS in Nauvoo a curiosity, described the object of his interest on July 11, 1840. The observer's intent as revealed in his report was to unveil the monolithic control JS held over his people. Along with a friend, they "approached his house" to see "him ride up and alight from his beautiful horse." After "handing the bridle to one of his followers in attendance, he waited in front of his gate to receive us." With the visitors in conversation, several Nauvoo leaders then "collected around, apparently anxious to hear the words which fell from his lips." To his followers JS displayed what the visitors expected: "His bearing towards them was like one who had authority; and the deference which they paid him convinced us that his dominion was deeply seated in the empire of their consciences." The correspondent determined that JS's powerful influence derived from "a profound knowledge of human nature" that "evidently taught him that, of all principles, the most omnipotent is the religious principle." JS had figured out that "to govern men of certain classes, it is only necessary to control their religious sentiment."[22] It was too much to expect of JS to have swayed his visitor that he was anything other than a despot.

21. Benjamin F. Morris to Dear Brethren, August 21, 1841, Warsaw, Illinois, quoted in Roger D. Launius, "American Home Missionary Society Ministers and Mormon Nauvoo: Selected Letters," *Western Illinois Regional Studies* 8, no. 1 (Spring 1985): 21. In this particular study, pairs of slash marks, / /, indicate written insertions into the manuscript text.
22. To the Editor of the Alexandria Gazette, "A Glance at the Mormons," *Alexandria Gazette and Virginia Advertiser*, July 11, 1840.

Proximity to Mormon settlements obviously created heightened concerns by the neighbors who had to contend with them. The momentum of public opinion against the Saints blossomed commensurate with the expansion of the Saints' domain and influence. Five years older than JS, Thomas Ford, the Democratic governor of Illinois from 1842–1846, represented the sentiment of Illinoisans at the height of the Saints' tenure in the Prairie State. Americans executing governmental measures of what by 1844 were well-formed mores and institutional protocols simply could not accommodate an independent theocratic organization with apparent territorial aspirations, no matter the latter's professions of government loyalty. Ford, in a substantial portion of his 1854 memoir, emphasized the Saints' intrusion upon his constituents. Written self-defensively, Ford in many ways simply multiplied the criticisms laid at JS once the Mormon became a public figure. Clearly demonstrating his antipathy to JS and the Mormons, who proved the most disruptive factor in his administration, he described the Nauvoo prophet as "the most successful imposter in modern times; a man who, though ignorant and coarse, had some great natural parts which fitted him for temporary success, but which were so obscured and counteracted by the inherent corruption and vices of his nature that he never could succeed in establishing a system of policy which looked to permanent success in the future." Moreover, "His lusts, his love of money and power, always set him to studying present gratification and convenience rather than the remote consequences of his plans." JS could never dispel that reputation, which Ford used in underscoring JS's treachery. "It must not be supposed that the pretended prophet practiced the tricks of a common impostor; that he was a dark and gloomy person with a long beard, a grave and severe aspect, and a reserved and saintly carriage of his person; on the contrary, he was full of levity, even to boyish romping; dressed like a dandy, and at times drank like a sailor and swore like a pirate."[23] Little wonder that JS held such an ignominious profile to mid-nineteenth-century Americans.

Surprisingly, JS also generated a few objective appraisers. With a small delegation of Mormons from Nauvoo, JS marched on Washington, D.C., over the winter of 1839–1840, seeking redress from the government for the Saints' Missouri fiasco. Besides soliciting interest from the U.S. president and petitioning Congress, JS apparently had occasion to speak to the curious willing to listen to him. A small gathering held there the first week of February 1840, allowed him to represent himself. A New York reporter, Matthew L. Davis, attended the meeting, reporting the next day his observations to his wife: "I went last Evening, to hear Joe Smith, the celebrated Mormon, Expound his doctrine." Davis characterized JS as "not an Educated man; but he is a plain, sensible, strong

23. Thomas Ford, *A History of Illinois: From Its Commencement as a State in 1818 to 1847* (1854; repr. Urbana and Chicago: University of Illinois Press, 1995), 249.

minded man. Every thing he says, is said in a manner to leave an impression that he is Sincere. There is no levity—no fanaticism—no want of dignity in his deportment." Indeed, "In his garb there are no peculiarities; his dress being that of a plain, unpretending citizen." Regarding what JS said in his speech that took over two hours, Davis recognized the ring of religious validity: "There was no opinion or belief that he expressed, that was calculated, in the slightest degree, to impair the morals of Society, or in any manner to degrade and brutalize the human species." And, if one would follow his preachments, there was much there that "would soften the asperities of man towards man, and that would tend to make him a more rational being than he is Generally found to be." Throughout, JS "displayed strongly a spirit of Charity and Forbearance," a characteristic that greatly impressed the reporter.[24]

Of all the non-Mormon happenstances with JS, few were more revealing than that of Josiah Quincy and Charles Francis Adams. The Boston Brahmins, with traveling companion William Goforth, apparently had no bone to pick with the Mormons, though they had clearly heard of JS and the Saints before their journey down the Mississippi River in May 1844, just a month before JS was killed. They brought with them a more forbearing perspective regarding Mormonism than their evangelical countrymen, though by no means were they sympathetic to the Saints. Quincy, the fourth Josiah in the line, came from a prestigious, highly educated Boston family. Adams was the grandson and son of former U.S. presidents John and John Quincy Adams. Both had distinguished careers after their visit to Nauvoo. Roughly similar to JS in age, the distant cousins docked in an unplanned visit to Nauvoo at a tenuous time for the city: fear of outsiders, excommunication of dissidents, and JS's vigorous distribution of prophetic direction to the church. The value of their reports of JS are shown by their capture of him in his unvarnished setting.

On May 15, 1844, after the steamer on which they traveled, the *Amaranth*, landed at Nauvoo, Adams, Quincy, and Goforth entered the bustling city—the account of which Adams lengthily depicted in his journal. "At the door of a two-story wooden house with a sign post before it, we stopped and were introduced to the celebrated Joe Smith. A middle-aged man with a shrewd but rather ordinary expression of countenance, unshaved and in clothes neither very choice nor neat. The whole air of the man was that of frank but not coarse vulgarity. He received us civilly and forthwith introduced us into his house." After breakfast and an intimate chat, JS invited the two into "his mother's chamber and showed

24. Matthew L. Davis to Mrs. Matthew L. Davis, February 6, 1840, Washington, D.C., MS 522, CHL. It is not known how the original letter came into possession of the LDS Church. See the background describing the origin of the letter with the text of what JS delivered regarding his beliefs in Smith, Documents, *JSP, D7*:175–79.

us four Egyptian mummies." Explaining to them what was before them, Adams wrote, "The cool impudence of this imposture amused me very much," as he told them about the scrolls being "written by the hand of Abraham." Adams summarized after the visit that there was "a mixture of shrewdness and extravagant self-conceit, of knowledge and ignorance, of wisdom and folly in this whole system of this man that I am somewhat at a loss to find definitions for it."[25]

While Adams proffered a skeptical but not indignant slant toward JS, Quincy explained to his wife by letter the following day being introduced to "a man, in a checked coat, dirty white pantaloons, a beard of some three days growth" known as "General Smith." Noting he was referred to as a "prophet," Quincy penned that while he "had the name but certainly in few respects the look of a prophet," the visitors were invited to join JS at "his mansion," described as "about as dirty as the prophet himself." They clearly caught him in an unprepared state. Their visit to JS in Nauvoo, where they "passed the whole day in his society," proved to Quincy to be "one of the most extraordinary conversations I ever participated in." JS "preached for us, prophesied for us, interpreted hieroglyphics for us, exhibited his mummies and took us to his temple which he is now erecting on a most majestic site of hewn stone." In the end, Quincy admitted being puzzled that "The power he exercises both civilly & religiously is immense, & is a living proof of the insceptibility of human nature to imposition," not exactly a compliment to JS or the Mormons.[26] However, as previously noted, Quincy—in his senior years four decades later—in penning a "series of papers upon former men and things," devoted to JS the last chapter of his 1883 *Figures of the Past* prepared just prior to his death. There he proffered his well-known epitaph for JS, concluding, "such a rare human being is not to be disposed of by pelting his memory with unsavory epithets.... Fanatics and impostors are living and dying every day, and their memory is buried with them; but the wonderful influence which this founder of a religion exerted and still exerts throws him into relief before us, not as a rogue to be criminated, but as a phenomenon to be explained."[27] Quincy's characterization begs consideration that JS possessed an extraordinary persona

25. Henry Adams, "Charles Francis Adams Visits the Mormons in 1844," *Proceedings of the Massachusetts Historical Society* 68 (October 1944–May 1947): 284–86, also published in Boston by the society in 1952.

JS's own journal entry for the day described the visit of Adams, Quincy, and Goforth in two dozen words. *JSP, J3*:251–52.

26. Josiah Quincy to "My very darling wife," May 16, 1844, in Jed Woodworth, "Josiah Quincy's 1844 Visit with Joseph Smith," *BYU Studies* 39, no. 4 (2000): 86–87.

27. Quincy, *Figures of the Past*, 376–77. Lest the reader assume that the Adams/Quincy reports about JS were singularly laudatory, see John J. Hammond's "Re-examining the Adams/Quincy May 1844 Visit to Nauvoo," *John Whitmer Historical Association Journal* 30 (2010): 66–95.

uncharacteristic of the general population, that when freed from the turmoil of his complicated life had appeal to even the most credulous observer.

The views of outsiders, most of whom approached JS with predisposed perspectives, tell us a great deal about how he displayed himself. Though his postures about religion may have been curious and quaint to some, he did not overbear his observers. He did not mask the genuine JS. As one friend asserted, he was "as free from dissimulation [pretending to be more than he was] as any man to be found."[28] His personal deportment refrained from exaggerated sophistication, feigning the polish and refinement of the eastern establishment. Growing up and operating in the more rustic western extension of the country as he did, he may have been naïve to the expectations of his visitors, but the portraits tell us how JS measured up against his own reputation.

The Sentiment of Dissent within Mormonism

The veracity of those just cited are arguably authentic representations of how JS was perceived, and qualify as justifications of their preconceptions or brief, first-blush judgments of the man. However, there is another kind of critic whose opinion helps frame the complicated circumstances in which JS lived. The expressions of former members, showing frustration with their former leader are of a different strain than those who did not know him. Disappointment in JS's prophetic role spurred their dissonance. In contrast to the assessments of outsiders, dissenters were generally more reflective and thoughtful in their evaluations of JS because they were transforming their conceptions of him from that of a true or false/fallen prophet. Having invested their emotional and physical resources over time resulting in spoilage of the faith they once held, their perspectives reveal the extent of their disappointments from optimistic origins. Though categorized as "apostates" by their erstwhile brethren, the reasons they separated from JS and the church are important to the study. Though later reflections of those who left Mormonism, informed by time, are numerous and more extensive than what is given below, the selected contemporary views exhibit attitudes with which JS had to contend as he tried to hold his church together.

Ezra Booth was a thirty-nine-year-old former Methodist minister when he became a Mormon in 1831.[29] After several months in the church, including a missionary journey to Missouri, he became disenchanted and in late summer of 1831 he sent a series of nine letters to the *Ohio Star* in Ravenna, Ohio, explaining

28. John M. Bernhisel to Governor Thomas Ford, June 14, 1844, Nauvoo, Illinois, in Joseph Smith's Office Papers, 1835–1844, Correspondence, 1844, MS 21600, CHL.
29. See the overview of Ezra Booth's life in H. Michael Marquardt, "Ezra Booth on Early Mormonism: A Look at His 1831 Letters," *John Whitmer Historical Association Journal* 28 (2008): 65–87.

and condemning JS and the Church of Christ. The letters written between September and December of the year say much about conditions within the church a year and a half after its organization. Indeed, it is one of the earliest glimpses into the faith, even if by a peeved voice. E. D. Howe recognized the importance of the first-person account of Mormonism from a disgruntled former member and included Booth's letters in his *Mormonism Unvailed* in 1834. Howe also included a letter from Booth to Mormon bishop Edward Partridge on September 20, 1831 (published in the *Ohio Star* on November 24, 1831), challenging Partridge to explain JS:

> Now permit me to inquire, have you not frequently observed in Joseph, a want of that sobriety, prudence and stability, which are some of the most prominent traits in the christian character? Have you not often discovered in him, a spirit of lightness and levity, a temper easily irritated, and a habitual proneness to jesting and joking? Have you not often proven to your satisfaction that he says he knows things to be so by the spirit, when they are not so? You most certainly have. Have you not reason to believe, or at least to suspect, that the revelations which come from him, are something short of infallible, and instead of being the production of divine wisdom, emanate from his own weak mind?[30]

Not only were JS's pretensions and dispositions upsetting to Booth, the potential for his demagoguery proved more insidious: "Some supposed his weakness, nay, his *wickedness*, can form no reasonable objection to his revelations; and 'were he to get another man's wife, and seek to kill her husband, it could be no reason why we should not believe revelations through him, for David did the same.' So Sidney asserted, and many others concurred with him in sentiment."[31] JS clearly disappointed and frightened Booth, who had expected an Old Testament prophet when he joined the faith. Nor could Booth abide the blunt discovery that JS exhibited the traits of common men. After Booth had been "silenced" by the church, he departed JS and the Church of Christ.

Sentiments similar to Booth's were written by Stephen Burnett in April 1838. Burnett, a resident of Orange near Kirtland, Ohio, with others in his family, were early converts to the church. Having at the age of eighteen once accepted appointment as a missionary in January 1832, he broke with Mormonism half a dozen years later. During the unsettled period in Kirtland, heightened by the effect of the country's Panic of 1837, the Kirtland Safety Society—the bank—failed, precipitating great discord because of JS's connection to the institution. It was one thing to exercise patience about religious matters, but the collapse of

30. Ezra Booth to Edward Partridge, September 20, 1831, in Howe, *Mormonism Unvailed*, 203.
31. Ibid.

the already anemic economy and the appearance of chicanery by church leaders proved too much for many members. Beside the bank's failure, dissent about a number of church initiatives gained momentum, with Burnett as a willing agitator. Writing to like-minded Lyman E. Johnson, a newly excommunicated church apostle, Burnett represented the pervasive dissatisfaction with JS among a large contingent of Saints: "My heart is sickened within me when I reflect upon the manner in which we with many of this Church have been led & the losses which we have sustained all by means of two men in whom we placed implicit confidence." It wasn't the religious tenets of Mormonism that frayed the faith of Burnett and others. They centered their antipathy in the leaders. "[T]hat Joseph Smith & Sidney Rigdon are notorious liars I do not hesitate to affirm, & can prove by a cloud of witnesses & this is not all, Joseph has prophecied in a public congregation lies in the name of the Lord & by undue religious influence he has filched the monies of the Church from their pockets and brought them nigh unto destruction, leaving helpless innocence destitute of a comfortable support while he has squandered the hard earnings of these to whom it justly belonged."[32] Burnett represented the feelings of a sizable fraction of men and women, including some once numbered among the leading church councils, who with their families turned away from the faith that had once actuated their lives. And, it was not just in Kirtland in the late 1830s where apostasy riddled the church. Several of the most prominent church leaders in northern Missouri also separated from Mormonism.

Another who separated from the church at the height of the Kirtland and Missouri problems was John Corrill, who in 1831, at the age of thirty-six, became a Mormon after having immigrated to Ohio from Massachusetts. Soon he was ordained a high priest and became counselor to Bishop Edward Partridge. Having spent much of his church experience in Missouri, in the same year of his appointment as church historian in 1838, he became a Missouri state witness against JS and the Saints. Upon the church's expulsion from Missouri, Corrill settled in Illinois, where he was excommunicated in 1839, the year he published his fifty-page *Brief History of the Church*. In his characterization of the Saints, he included his own motives for breaking away from Mormonism, focusing the blame for his angst in JS and the other leaders.

> If Smith, Rigden and others, of the leaders, had managed wisely and prudently, in all things, and manifested truly a Christian spirit, it would have been very difficult to put them down. But their impudence and miscalculations, and manifest desire for power and property, have opened the eyes of many, and did more to destroy them than could possibly have

32. Stephen Burnett to Lyman E. Johnson, April 15, 1838, Orange Township, Geauga Co., Ohio, Letterbook 2, 64–66, Joseph Smith Collection, MS 155, box 2, folder 2, CHL.

> been done otherwise. My opinion is, that if the Church had been let alone by the citizens, they would have divided and subdivided so as to have completely destroyed themselves and their power, as a people, in a short time.[33]

Corrill's distress in the moment negated all he had once believed. "When I retrace our track, and view the doings of the church for six years past, I can see nothing that convinces me that God has been our leader; calculation after calculation has failed, and plan after plan has been overthrown, and our prophet seemed not to know the event till too late." Complaining of the myriad of "trials, difficulties, and temptations, of various kinds," he, like the rest of the church, yearned for relief: "But no deliverance came. The promises failed, and time after time we have been disappointed; and still were commanded, in the most rigid manner, to follow him."[34]

But in the last year of his life, the most consequential critique of JS and his work, precipitating in part his murder, brewed among dissidents. The first week of June 1844 a manifestation of overt rebellion appeared in the form of an opposition newspaper that laid open the swelling discontent roiling just under Nauvoo's surface. Former allies led the charge. They included brothers William and Wilson Law, Francis and Chauncey Higbee, and Robert and Charles Foster, along with Charles Ivins. William Law's defection has drawn the most attention due to his position as one of JS's closest associates, serving as his counselor in the church's First Presidency. The dissenters, according to their testimony, had tried to reform Mormonism from within, but were rebuffed by the prophet, his brother Hyrum, and other leaders. Already having formed an opposition religious organization to JS's Mormonism, their next step was setting up a competing press in the city of the Saints called the *Nauvoo Expositor*. In its first and only issue, besides advocating the conservative stance of ridding Nauvoo of "houses of reveling and dancing, dram-shops [bars and taverns] and theatres," their posting of theological grievances gives insight into the hot topics that had been agitating some church members for months. Professing belief in the "religion of the Latter Day Saints, as originally taught by Joseph Smith," they charged that JS's later "pretentions to righteousness" did not square with what they knew of him. Noting that "many items of doctrine, as now taught, some of which, however, are taught secretly, and denied openly," they "declare[d] them heretical and damnable in their influence." Their objective, they declared, was "to explode the

33. John Corrill, *A Brief History of the Church of Christ of Latter Day Saints, (Commonly Called Mormons)* (St. Louis: self-published, 1839), republished in Smith, Histories, *JSP, H*2:193, 197.
34. Ibid.

vicious principles of Joseph Smith, and those who practice the same abominations and whoredoms; which we verily know are not accordant and consonant with the principles of Jesus Christ and his Apostles." Chief among the "damnable doctrines" were preachments from JS about "a plurality of Gods above the God of this universe;" the "plurality of wives, for time and eternity;" and the "doctrine of unconditional sealing up to eternal life." But the criticism did not stop at doctrine and theology. They also complained about the matter of the "gathering in haste" of the Saints to Nauvoo, and the existence of "secret societies, and combinations" bound by "oaths and obligations," a reference to religious rituals that JS privately instituted among his most trusted associates that were later associated with Mormon temple ceremonies. Lastly, they noted JS's hostility towards government institutions and especially his attempt in Nauvoo to "unite church and state."[35] It is well known that the *Expositor* was destroyed at the instigation of JS and the Nauvoo City Council three days after its June 7 publication, which led to JS's arrest and incarceration in the jail at the county seat, Carthage, Illinois.

The examples above illustrate several of the prominent reasons onetime Mormons became frustrated before rejecting JS. Most who left had accommodated for several years JS's idiosyncrasies and otherworldliness. But crises, of which there were numerous ones in the late 1830s and early 1840s created a significant reckoning for many Saints. During the confusion and trauma, while most stayed tethered, some calculated that JS had failed them in his prophetic role. Having implications for the full scope of their lives in mortality and after, any fervor they once held for him and his church fled in the face of an uncertain future. The imprint they left on JS's church must be understood to appreciate the emotional difficulty that plagued those who followed JS throughout his life.

With an Eye of Faith

But there were, obviously, other points of view. Those who embraced JS's prophetic leadership did so upon a faith that he was, indeed, like unto Moses. And, despite the contemporary charges against the Mormons designating all church members as dupes and lock-step followers, given what is known of those composing the first generation of Mormonism, the claim is not one that is universally defendable. Some, as one might suppose given the nature of a portion of the general population in their religious belief, once in the fold were extreme in their devotions. However, the documentary record exhibiting the writing of early Mormons generally portrays reasonable and thoughtful people following JS, knowing full well that he was merely mortal. As illustrated above, many of them may have been disappointed at one time or another as were their former colleagues-in-arms who departed. But they overlooked the obvious frailties

35. "Preamble," *Nauvoo Expositor*, June 7, 1844, 1, 2.

because his manifestations of powerful persona and religious authenticity far outweighed his weaknesses. And, as many recorded, the persuasions of what they believed to be the Holy Spirit compelled their commitment to him and his promised establishment of Zion.

Many new Mormons went to Kirtland specifically to appraise JS, though not even a small portion of those who answered the missionary's summons to gather wrote about their encounter with him. But enough of them did that their impressions are presently well known. First impressions came by way of anticipation, and while there was fallout among those whose initial taste was unsavory, the conspicuous acceptance of JS by enough individuals to provide momentum for the church indicates an unusual persona. Stephen Post, twenty-five and from New York, met JS in late 1835. "I saw the man [JS]," he wrote, "whom the Lord had chosen to lead the Church out of obscurity[.] he is a tall young man whose face beams with intelligence[.] When I saw and heard him my soul loved him; & truly said I to myself if this is not a man of God where is there one. this truth burst upon my mind that this is the very man even Joseph Smith Jr. whom the Lord hath chosen to bring to pass his act[,] his strange act[,] and bring to pass his work[,] his strange work."[36] To Post, JS fit his expectations. Another to join in 1835, Jonathan Crosby, arrived in Kirtland to size up the man in whom he had hope of a figure to match his anticipations of God's modern activity on the earth. After a genial introduction with others to the prophet, he wrote: "I thought he was a quear man for [a] prophet, at first, he didn't appear exactly as I expected to see a Prophet of God, however, I was not stumbled at all. I found him to be a friendly cheerful pleasant agreeable man. I could not help likeing him."[37]

Surprising to many, no doubt, is William Law's 1837 insight into JS that preceded by seven years his defection from the prophet. Law, four years JS's junior and an Irish immigrant to North America as a boy, presented an exuberant image of the prophet as Law gained a place in Mormonism. First drawn to Mormonism in Upper Canada in 1836, Law had displayed his enterprising disposition there by operating a mill and serving as postmaster. Another local convert, Isaac Russell, befriended Law and introduced him to the faith. Russell in 1837 became one of the small band of Mormon missionaries who crossed the Atlantic to introduce the religion to Great Britain. The men stayed connected while Russell served among the English. Law wrote to him in November 1837, undoubtedly hoping to allay potential fears Russell might have about negative information circulating about the bank crises in Kirtland. With faith and hope,

36. Stephen Post, Journals, ca. December 1835, July 1835–March 1839, v. 1, Stephen Post Papers, MS 1304, CHL.

37. Jonathan Crosby, Life Sketch, quoted in Jessee, "Sources for the Study of Joseph Smith," 13.

despite the collapse of trust many felt toward JS in the midst of the Panic of 1837, Law confirmed to Russell his continuing view that "Bro Joseph is truly a wonderful man[.] he is all we could wish a prophet to be."[38] Upon Russell's return to Kirtland after his mission, he indeed found the church in disarray, undoubtedly disturbing him. Gravitating to the dissenters, he left Kirtland and relocated to northern Missouri where the Saints regrouped. But there Russell's disenchantment grew, manifested by overt actions against JS and other leaders. By spring of 1839, the Twelve Apostles cut Russell from church rolls. But Law did not give up on his friend.

In late 1840, not long before Law became a counselor to JS in the church's First Presidency, he again appealed to Russell: "It is needless for me to express my regret that you remain so long from the Body of the Church, you who have been so very zealous for the cause of Christ." Reminding him of the faith that drew them to the church together, from Nauvoo Law encouraged Russell: "Read the Book of Mormon and you will find that Joseph has not fallen, he has not done his work yet, and if he sins is there no room for repentance, can not God forgive him, and can not we forgive him very often in a day." To underscore his appeal, he stated, "I have carefully watched his movements since I have been here, and I assure you I have found him honest and honourable in all our transactions which have been very considerable[.] I believe he is an honest upright man, and as to his follies let who ever is guiltless throw the first stone at him, I shant do it." Law and others like him reveled in JS's genial temperament and the spiritual matters conveyed by him: "He continues to bring forth the deep mysteries of the Kingdom, and we feast upon them til our souls are made fat, and our hearts rejoice exceedingly. I wish you lived here you would soon change your views of matters and become reconciled."[39] Ultimately, Law's course in the church reveals the path taken by some who eventually could not abide JS's progressive nature and how he attempted to transform the Mormon kingdom. Where he once saw the imprimatur of God upon JS, despite his frailties, personal circumstances changed so dramatically that Law could not in 1844 have heeded the very plea he made to Russell four years earlier. Still, his earlier expressions portray the reflections of many who stayed the course with the prophet.

Among the first English converts immigrating to the United States during the second mission of the Twelve Apostles to Great Britain, William Clayton later influenced Mormonism as few laymen could. A short period of time after Clayton's arrival, JS employed him to be one of his chief scribes and intimates. Born

38. William Law to Isaac Russell, quoted in Lyndon C. Cook, "'Brother Joseph Is Truly a Wonderful Man, He Is All We Could Wish a Prophet to Be': Pre-1844 Letters of William Law," *BYU Studies* 20, no. 2 (Winter 1980): 212.
39. Ibid., 218.

in 1814 in Penwortham, Clayton joined the second company of Saints to leave Liverpool for America, arriving in New York on October 12, 1840. After a month and a half of westward travel via the Erie Canal, Lake Michigan, and overland from Chicago to the Mississippi River, they descended to Nauvoo, where he arrived with his family on November 24. Before a week had passed Clayton wrote to his friend Edward Martin in England, giving his assessment of JS: "We are perfectly satisfied with the appearance of things here and we have abundance of proofs that Joseph Smith Junr is what he pretends to be viz a p[rophet] of the most high God and this is the work of God. I once more bear testimony of the truth of this Gospel in the name of Jesus Christ, it is the work of God and will roll forth to the ends of the earth and the Lord will gather his people." In a continuation of the letter a few days later, he wrote: "Last night a meeting of us was in company with brother Joseph. Our hearts rejoiced to hear him speak of the things of the kingdom. He is an affectionate man and as familiar as any of us. We feel to love him much and so will you."[40]

Two weeks after stepping onto the Nauvoo peninsula, Clayton penned another letter home to friends left behind in England: "We have had the privelege of conversing with Joseph Smith Junr. and we are delighted with his company." Recognizing that those remaining behind in England had concern about the prophet they had chosen to follow, Clayton continued: "We had a privilege of ascertaining in a great measure from whence all the evil reports have arisen and hitherto have every reason to believe him innocent. He is <u>not</u> an idiot, but a man of sound judgment, and possessed of [an] abundance of intelligence and whilst you listen to his conversation you receive intelligence which expands your mind and causes your heart to rejoice.... He seems exceeding well versed in the scriptures, and whilst conversing upon any subject such light and beauty is revealed I never saw before." To qualify JS's outward display, he assured that, "He is very familiar, and delights to instruct the poor saints. I can converse with him just as easy as I can with you, and with regard to being willing to communicate instruction he says 'I receive it freely and I will give it freely.'[41] He is willing to answer any question I have put to him and is pleased when we ask him questions." To dispel any concerns his countrymen might have about the way that JS wore his prophetic mantle, Clayton continued: "He is no friend to iniquity but cuts at it wherever he sees it and it is in vain to attempt to cloke it before him. He has a great measure of the spirit of God, and by this means he is preserved from imposition. He says, 'I am a man of like passions with yourselves,' but truly I wish I was such a man." Summarizing, Clayton expressed his satisfaction at

40. William Clayton to Edward Martin, November 29/December 2, 1840, Nauvoo, Illinois, MS 3682, CHL.

41. A reference to Matt. 10:8.

having made the endeavor to be with the prophet: "If I had come from England purposely to converse with him a few days I should have considered myself well paid for my trouble."[42]

Millen Atwood, a twenty-four-year-old mason from Connecticut, arrived in Nauvoo in May 1841, anticipating the image he had been promised—an Old Testament-like prophet. After arriving on May 21, he wrote, "for the first time in my life did my eyes behold a Prophet of God." Revealing a biblical disposition toward things sacred, he continued, "I washt my body[,] bowd befor the lord in thankfulness for the preservation of my life & the sight I beheld." Two days later "Br. Joseph Smith came up to see us[.] this was the first time I ever shook hands with a prophet[.] he was easy, free & sociable, with all[.] he said that he rejoist to se us being Yankees for said he I was born in the State of Vermont.'" One of those with Atwood was a brother named Robert Pierce. In his initial observation, Pierce, displaying his own skepticism, asked JS directly, "why dont you hold your head up as I do[?]," clearly disappointed in what stood before him. But JS returned the question with one of his own: "Havent you past by a field of wheat when it was ripe & seen some heads stand strait up as your does & others hang down as mine does?" Pierce agreed. "Well sayes Br Joseph the full heads lop[.] the empty or blasted heads with no[t] much in them stand strait up like yours does." Atwood delighted in writing, "Joseph with all presant had a good harty laugh at his expence[.] he comforted our hearts."[43] Atwood's capture portraying his general disposition reflected the side of JS so attractive to many who came to construe him as a prophet.

George Miller, a Virginian born in 1794, converted to Mormonism eight years after relocating to Illinois. He later became one of the principal actors in Nauvoo life, becoming among other things one of the city bishops in 1841. After publication of apostate John C. Bennett's derisive *History of the Saints* in summer 1842, Miller penned a rebuttal letter to Missouri governor Thomas Reynolds who had used Bennett's allegations about the attempted assassination of former governor Lilburn Boggs in May 1842 as a reason to extradite JS to Missouri. Miller's letter to Reynolds contained a plea based upon his experience with JS meant to sway Reynolds's antipathy toward the prophet. Writing from St. Louis on September 4, 1842, Miller entreated the governor: "I have known Joseph Smith intimately for near three & a half years, having been a great portion of that time in his society every day, there being an intimacy between us like that of Brothers, he having frequently unbosomed himself to me, and I unhesitatingly aver, that in every Sense of the terms, a more generous, liberal,

42. William Clayton to "Beloved brethren and sisters," December 10, 1840, MS 5215, CHL.
43. Millen Atwood, May 21, 1841, Reminiscences and Diary, 1842–1844, typescript, 1–3, MS 1809, CHL.

honorable, high toned virtuous man, never existed on the footsool of the great Jehovah, than Joseph Smith."[44]

Like Clayton noted above, twenty-four-year-old John Needham, another Englishman, became one of the hundreds who gathered to Nauvoo in 1843. Besides providing an insightful overview of Nauvoo and the Saints to his countrymen still in Britain, JS became a primary point of his communication. Specifically, Needham's report indicated his surprise and delight that JS did not fit the profile of austerity and asceticism often associated with the religiously pious. While the prophet proved to Needham to be "a great man, a man of principle, a straight forward man," he particularly noted that JS was "no saintish long-faced fellow, but quite the reverse. Indeed some stumble because he is such a straight forward, plain spoken, cheerful man, but that makes me love him the more." And though he was "a stumbling-block to thousands," Needham pled, "I have seen and been in the company of Joseph, and heard him speak several times. I love him, and believe him to be a Prophet of God, and called to do a great work in these last days on the earth."[45] The church organ in England, the *Latter Day Saints' Millennial Star* printed Needham's letter obviously intending to warm potential Mormon émigrés to prospects in Nauvoo and to its principal figure.

George Washington Taggart, who had converted to Mormonism in 1842 in New Hampshire, arrived in Nauvoo the following summer with his extended family. His mother, Susannah, during the first week of September 1843, painfully wrote to her three unbelieving sons who remained behind in Peterborough, to tell them that their father, Washington, and their younger brother Oliver had died the previous week during a particularly precarious period of illness in Nauvoo. A few days later George picked up the pen to finish his mother's letter. To help mollify the news of the death of their father, he tried to persuade them that the family's journey had not been in vain. JS, he told them, was genuine. Describing him as "a young looking Man of His age, which is near 38 years," to Taggart, he was "one of the finest looking men there is in the country." Most important, though, he explained, "He does not pretend to be a man without failings and follies," and "neither is He puffed up with His greatness as manny suppose but on the contrary is familiar with anny decent man." As with so many others who described the prophet, Taggart plainly stated, "He is a Man that you could not help likeing as a man setting a side the religious prejudice which the world has raised against him." JS, he explained, "is ready to talk upon anny subject that anny one wishes, and I asure you it would make you wonder to hear Him talk

44. George Miller to Thomas Reynolds, September 4, 1842, Finding Aid 3.7, 1B/1/, box 2, folder 61, Missouri State Archives, Jefferson City, Missouri, https://www.sos.mo.gov/archives/resources/findingaids/rg003-07.

45. John Needham to Thomas Ward, July 7, 1843, City of Nauvoo, *The Latter-day Saints' Millennial Star*, October 1843, 89.

and see the information which comes out of His mouth and it is not in big words either but that which any one can understand." To underscore Taggart's conclusion, "He is one of the warmest patriots and friends to his country and laws that you ever heard speak on the subject."[46]

A January 1843 letter to a friend from forty-year-old Jonah Randolph Ball sent soon after his own arrival in Nauvoo displayed his initial impressions of the prophet. He represented the pervasively felt connection to JS sensed by most who gathered, giving all for the kingdom. "I calld on the Prophet Joseph," carrying a letter of introduction from the "Presidency at Kirtland, Ohio." Others were with JS when Ball arrived and "we all had a social chat." Describing the prophet, he wrote: "I found Joseph familiar in conversation, easy and unassuming. I found no syconphancy. there is those that came in or went out not even taking their hats or caps off their heads." Soon after his arrival Ball heard JS preach: "He is what the Mormons represent him to be & the stories about him are false[.] & his People <are> No common stock buisness [i.e., holding everything in common] or other ten thousand stories has the least foundation in truth." In earnest he concluded, "this I tell you as the Truth of a Friend & Brother."[47] The expressions represent the persona JS displayed to those who grasped Mormon claims. To them he was not mesmeric or ethereal; his personality was a blend of humanity and spirituality convincing them that he was an approachable man of God.

The individuals noted above arrived in Nauvoo anticipating confirmation of their faith and what they had heard about JS. There were others who arrived at Nauvoo near the same time as Needham, Taggart, and Ball, who did not share their enthusiasm for JS, arriving with other expectations. Charlotte Haven, a single woman of twenty-four from Portsmouth, New Hampshire, who had Mormon cousins in town, emigrated to Nauvoo in early 1843. She wrote several letters to family and friends at home describing what she had observed upon arriving in and after settling in the city. Her particular situation provides both a unique non-Mormon and female glimpse at JS, including what was probably the common take of those not enamored of him. On January 22, 1843, she wrote to "Sister Isa" describing, among other matters in Nauvoo, the Mormon prophet. To Haven, the "very round shouldered" church leader was "a large, stout man, youthful in his appearance, with light complexion and hair, and blue eyes set far back in the head, and expressing great shrewdness, or I should say, cunning. He has a large head and phrenologists would unhesitatingly pronounce it a bad one,

46. George W. Taggart to [his brothers in New Hampshire], September 10, 1843, Albert Taggart Correspondence, 1842–1860, MS 7362, CHL; quoted in Ronald O. Barney, "'A Man That You Could Not Help Likeing': Joseph Smith and Nauvoo Portrayed in a Letter by Susannah and George W. Taggart," *BYU Studies* 40, no. 2 (2001): 171–73.

47. Jonah Randolph Ball to Harvey Howard, January 15, 1843, Nauvoo, Illinois, Jonah R. Ball, Letters, 1842–1843, MS 4393 1, CHL.

for the organs situated in the back part are decidedly the most prominent."[48] His appearance was only the beginning of her disassembly of Nauvoo's preeminent citizen. "I who had expected to be overwhelmed by his eloquence was never more disappointed than when he commenced his discourse by relating all the incidents of his journey [to Springfield]."[49] Put off by JS's demeanor and manner of expression, Hafen continued that his sermon was delivered "in a loud voice, and his language and manner were the coarsest possible. His object seemed to be to amuse and excite laughter in his audience." JS then descended into what Haven determined to be his true character. "He is evidently a great egotist and boaster, for he frequently remarked that at every place he stopped going to and from Springfield people crowded around him, and expressed surprise that he was so 'handsome and good looking.'"[50]

Though Haven found JS pretentious, she described a man of the people who plied his audience with humor, self-deprecation, and teasing exaggeration that endeared him to them. A month later on February 19, in a letter to her mother, Charlotte reinforced her skeptical portrayal of the prophet: "He talked incessantly about himself, what he had done and could do more than other mortals, and remarked that he was 'a giant, physically and mentally.' In fact, he seemed to forget that he was a man." Conceding that she supposed "he has good traits," she acknowledged his reputation of being "very kindhearted, and always ready to give shelter and help to the needy."[51] But JS had made no headway with Charlotte Haven.

Perhaps the most passionate surviving portrait by a devotee of JS came at the end of his life. It was from an insider. With the escalation of discord fulminating in Nauvoo, by the middle of June 1844 JS knew the winds blew against him. Destruction of the opposition *Nauvoo Expositor* on June 10, of which he played a role, precipitated a series of events that threatened any sense of normality among the Saints. Breaking faith with American institutions, though their own press in western Missouri had been destroyed in 1833, crushing the local freedom of the

48. Charlotte Haven to "My Dear Sister Isa," January 22, 1843, in "A Girl's Letters from Nauvoo," *Overland Monthly*, December 1890, 621.

Although it had no relevance to Haven's appraisal, JS had submitted to a phrenologists' evaluation while in Philadelphia in December 1839 and January 1840. See Joseph Smith Collection, MS 155, box 5, folder 19, CHL.

49. Haven, "A Girl's Letters from Nauvoo," 621. JS had recently returned to Nauvoo from a two-week stay in Springfield, Illinois, where in legal proceedings he obtained a writ of habeas corpus from Judge Nathaniel Pope in the Springfield District Court to thwart another attempt at extradition by the state of Missouri. Jeffrey N. Walker, "Invoking Habeas Corpus in Missouri and Illinois," in *Sustaining the Law: Joseph Smith's Legal Encounters*, ed. Gordon A. Madsen, Jeffrey N. Walker, and John W. Welch (Provo, UT: BYU Studies, 2014), 388–96.

50. Haven, "A Girl's Letters from Nauvoo," 621.

51. Ibid., 623.

press exhibited the naiveté held by the Saints in thinking their actions were justified. The *Expositor*'s publishers and their sympathizers used the city council's overt interdiction to actuate their designs to crush JS's and his church's influence. Four days after destruction of the press, apparently recognizing the enormity of the blunder, John M. Bernhisel, a forty-five-year-old New York physician, appealed on June 14 to Illinois governor Thomas Ford's good sense, trying to avert reprisal. Bernhisel, who once presided over the Mormons in New York City and had immigrated to Nauvoo nine months previously, obviously hoped to quell the potential explosion of wills within the county. By letter Bernhisel defended the city council's action, but most important, explained to Ford his perception of JS. Identifying him as the head of the local militia, the Nauvoo Legion, Bernhisel wrote, "Gen. Joseph Smith is naturally a man of strong mental powers, and is possessed of much energy and decision of character, great penetration, and a profound knowledge of human nature." JS was, he explained, "a man of calm judgement, enlarged views, and is eminently distinguished by his love of justice." To those who commonly observed him, "He is kind and obliging, generous and benevolent, sociable and cheerful, and is possessed of a mind of a contemplative & reflective character; he is honest, frank, fearless, and independent."[52]

Given what is known about Bernhisel's subsequent life and sterling service as Utah Territory's representative to Congress in the 1850s and 1860s, his sincerity and directness suggest the conviction of his words. After living in the same home as a boarder with the Smiths for nine months after his arrival in Nauvoo, attempting to allay Ford's fears about JS's disposition, he wrote that it was "in the gentle charities of domestic life, as the tender and affectionate husband & parent, the warm and sympathising friend, that the prominent traits of his character are revealed." Moreover, "his heart is felt to be keenly alive to the kindest and softest emotions of which human nature is susceptible, and I feel assured that his family and friends formed one of the greatest consolations to him." Bernhisel closed his petition appealing to Ford's reason. "It is almost superfluous to add that the numerous rediculous and scandilous reports in circulation respecting him, have not the least foundation in truth."[53] The appeal, apparently never sent, consequently had no effect. Two weeks later JS was dead.

The collective nature of the reports presented above insist that JS and what he represented never was nor ever can be agreed upon by those determined to judge him. The reality of JS's propensity to move the public to take sides suggests that modern students may have difficulty holding in tension the variant views expressed. Still, recognizing the divisive environment he generated is necessary to inform the other aspects of his life that follow in this study.

52. Bernhisel to Ford, June 14, 1844. Though the letter was apparently never sent to Ford, a draft was added to the LDS Church's collection of documents.
53. Ibid.

PART III

Foundational Experiences

CHAPTER 7

Joseph Smith's Declaration

His 1832 History

The entire panorama of JS's life is impossible to understand and represent in total. Given the limitations derived from the fragmented historical record, there are, nevertheless, a number of particularly important manifestations of his initiative that must be considered. This chapter addresses one of the most revealing features of his early ministry: the first attempt to tell his story, his 1832 History. The importance of this evidence of the prophet's maturing progress has generally been subordinated to his later historical productions that more fully portrayed his early experiences. Best illustrated by his 1838/39 History, which became the *History of Joseph Smith*, by the time of its production JS clearly recognized the necessity of publicly exhibiting not only his experiences but also his motivations for what had by that time become more than a religious novelty. JS had become such a presence that not only the public but also the Latter-day Saints gathering to Kirtland and Zion required a background portrayal for their faith. Mormonism at this time was based on events rather than a developed ideology. Those matters had to be explained. Though the 1832 History never came to fruition, as discussed below, the six years between JS's 1832 endeavor and his resolve by the end of the decade to adequately tell his story demonstrate a transition in not only what Mormonism had become but also in how he viewed his prophetic role and how that transition would be best told. Thus, the 1832 History, besides illustrating JS's recognition of the necessity of explaining himself and the events that inaugurated the faith, also became a vehicle in this work to describe events transitioning the faith in its adolescence.

For the two years since its publication, the Book of Mormon had been the center of Mormon gravity. Undoubtedly, every conversation about the upstart religion among outsiders included discussion about the book. During this period the structural foundation of the Church of Christ rose and expanded through design and necessity, mostly unknown to all but those directly involved in the movement. Periodic conferences, men leaving their homes to proselytize, and basic admission rituals generally characterized Mormonism in its formative months. But not until JS determined in 1832 that the growing body of believers required an identification and a means of building community beyond the Book of Mormon did its members assume some of the traits of other more developed religious denominations. While evidence suggests that some early members preferred to remain structureless and free from the trappings of organized religion, early leaders cautiously raised the scaffolding through organizational development and missionizing, even establishing outlying branches of the church where the missionaries had found success. With the establishment of an eight-page monthly, the *Evening and the Morning Star* in Independence, Missouri, in June 1832—a voice for the church—members in both Mormon centers in Kirtland and Zion and elsewhere were woven into an entity not previously possible. But outside the Book of Mormon and the *Evening and the Morning Star*, non-Mormon newspaper and periodical articles and a few pamphlets were the only printed sources that described Mormonism in its first two years of existence. And unsurprisingly the portrayals of the faith in the common press proved unflattering.

The media as it then existed and what it disseminated about Mormonism shaped in many ways the manner in how the religion maneuvered or was portrayed in the existing culture. Newspapers and word-of-mouth in the region east and south of Lake Erie prodded locals to pay attention. One resident of Covert, a village adjacent to Cayuga Lake in New York's Finger Lakes and fifty miles southeast of JS's home, explained in February 1830 to a Connecticut correspondent a few weeks before the Book of Mormon was published, "There is something that has taken place lately that is mysterious to us." Identifying "Joseph" and something about his "gold leaf" Bible, Lucius Fenn stated "there has been considerable of an attention paid to it this winter between these lakes."[1] The Mormon curiosity had already begun to take root even before the church formalized. This chapter proposes the plausibility that the multiplication of newspaper reports and the local promiscuous scuttlebutt—generally derogatory—about JS and his church may have moved the prophet to represent himself on paper for the first time. The necessity of giving his side of the controversy was apparent.[2] The

1. Lucius Fenn to Birdseye Bronson, February 12, 1830, in *Among the Mormons: Historic Accounts by Contemporary Observers*, ed. William Mulder and A. Russell Mortensen (1958; repr. New York: Alfred A. Knopf, 1969), 28.

2. Below are illustrations of the regional press's coverage and characterization of JS prior to the summer of 1832 when his 1832 History was prepared: The "*Golden Bible*," was touted as the "greatest piece of superstition that has ever come within the sphere of our knowledge is one which has for sometime past, and still occupies the attention of a few superstitious and bigoted individuals of this quarter." *Palmyra Freeman*, August 11, 1829; "'Joseph

print coverage and other factors may have combined with other circumstances to move JS to create a narrative account mid-1832 with the prospect of publication. It can only be described as a colossal step for the prophet.

Smith, jr.'—a fellow who, by some hocus pocus," produced "this blasphemous work [the Book of Mormon]." *Rochester Daily Advertiser and Telegraph*, April 2, 1830; "A viler imposition was never practised. It is an evidence of fraud, blasphemy and credulity, shocking to the Christian and moralist." *Rochester Republican*, April 6, 1830; "An ignoramous." *The Gem, of Literature and Science* (Rochester, NY), May 15, 1830; "He pretended that he had been entrusted by God with a golden bible." *The Fredonia Censor*, June 2, 1830; "*spindle shanked* ignoramus Jo Smith." *The Reflector* (Palmyra, NY), June 30, 1830; "Joseph Smith, Jr., a man of subtlety and cunning, but of no learning, and as we are informed, much worse than no character.... The miserable impostor who publishes this book, pretends that the plates were plates of gold containing the record written by Mormon." The Book of Mormon is "one of the most abominable pieces of imposition and blasphemy, that has of late been attempted to be palmed upon the community." *Evangelical Magazine and Gospel Advocate* (Utica, NY), February 5, 1831; Describing JS: "It is passing strange, that in all ages of the world, gross *stupidity* in *an impostor* should be considered among the vulgar, irrefragible proof of his divine mission, and the most bungling piece of legerdemain, will receive from them all the credit of a well attested miracle." *The Reflector*, February 14, 1831; "The age of this modern prophet [JS] is supposed to be about 24 years. In his person he is tall and slender—*thin favored*—having but little expression of countenance, other than that than that of dulness; his mental powers appear to be extremely limited, and from the small opportunity he has had at school, he made little or no proficiency." *The Reflector*, February 1, 1831; "It is well known that Jo Smith never pretended to have any communion with angels, until a long period after the *pretended* finding of his book, and that the juggling of himself or father, went no further than the pretended faculty of seeing wonders in a 'peep stone,' and the occasional interview with the spirit, supposed to have the custody of hidden treasures." *The Reflector*, February 28, 1831 (juggling meant to manipulate, especially in order to achieve a desired and often fraudulent end); "I will take the trouble to make a few remarks on the character of that infamous imposter [JS].... It is reported, and probably true, that he commenced his juggling by stealing and hiding property belonging to his neighbors." *Evangelical Magazine and Gospel Advocate*, April 9, 1831; "Young Joe...was at that period a careless, indolent, idle, and shiftless fellow. He hung round the villages and strolled round the taverns without any end or aim—without any positive defect or as little merit in his character. He was rather a stout able bodied fellow, and might have made a good living.... He was however, the son of a speculative Yankee pedlar, and was brought up to live by his wits." *Episcopal Recorder*, June 18, 1831; "Go where we will we hear little except Mormonism.... There are many who were once respectable and intelligent, who are now following these wretched impostors—these pretended prophets. Joseph Smith Jr. *author* of the new revelation, is now head man in the big family." *Morning Courier*, August 31, 1831; "They believe that their leader is the real Jesus Christ, and that both he and his disciples have infinite powers to work miracles, raise the dead, cleanse lepers—and *they testify that he has cast out many devils*—that the millennium is nigh, and that Philadelphia is the place where Jesus Christ will meet his disciples and followers." *Buffalo Patriot*, September 6, 1831. Most of these items may be found in "Uncle Dale's" [Broadhurst] compilation of newspaper reports related to early Mormonism, see sidneyrigdon.com/dbroadhu/artindex.htm.

Description of the 1832 History

To many modern observers, the background explaining Mormon origins has generally been opportunely packaged in the history JS initiated in 1838/39 that appeared beginning in 1842 as the *History of Joseph Smith*. A half century later B. H. Roberts presented that history as the *History of the Church*. As noted previously, Roberts's edit of JS's *History* created within Mormonism in the twentieth century the components necessary for JS's story to become tradition, even epic, among the Saints. Indeed, its portrayal of his First Vision and the coming forth of the Book of Mormon became canonical in 1880 when its inclusion in the Pearl of Great Price became accepted that year as sacred text by those at the church's October general conference. Thereafter, the 1838/39 account of JS's earliest visionary experiences that composed the *History of the Church* became the official representation of both the First Vision and the coming forth of the Book of Mormon. However, given what is now known about how the 1838/39 history was prepared, present confidence that the history exactly represents JS's thinking and experience has been modified from suppositions of the past. Along with official endorsement by the church in 1880, the more detailed 1838/39 history subordinates, in the thinking of many, the 1832 History as premature, incomplete, or inconsequential as a source to define what happened to JS. Accepting that dismissive premise, however, is a mistake. Overlooking what has come to be known as his earliest history ignores influences on JS that moved him to explain himself for the first time.

As early as 1969, JS scholar Richard L. Anderson recognized the 1832 History to be the "most striking insight into the earliest religious experiences of the Prophet."[3] And because the 1832 History represented JS's initial effort to express his sacred connection to God, its introduction of his First Vision elevates its importance in considering Mormon origins. Marvin Hill, history professor at BYU, stated in 1982 that "Merely on the face of it, the 1832 version [of the First Vision] stands a better chance of being more accurate and unembellished than the 1838[/39] account which was intended as a public statement, streamlined for publication."[4] It is not by chance that JS's story as rendered in the 1832 History serves as Richard Bushman's principal narrative of the First Vision in his masterful 2005 biography of JS, *Rough Stone Rolling*. To Bushman the story is rendered as credible because of its simple, straightforward depiction of events.[5] The

3. Richard L. Anderson, "Circumstantial Confirmation of the First Vision through Reminiscences," *BYU Studies* 9, no. 3 (Spring 1969): 375.

4. Marvin Hill, "The First Vision Controversy: A Critique and Reconciliation," *Dialogue* 15, no. 2 (Summer 1982): 39.

5. Bushman, *Rough Stone Rolling*, 37. A generation earlier, Donna Hill's fine biography of JS, published in 1977, also lead with her discussion about JS's First Vision using the 1832 History. Donna Hill, *Joseph Smith: The First Mormon* (New York: Doubleday, 1977), 47–51.

editors of the Joseph Smith Papers confirm Bushman's emphasis placed upon the portrayal of JS's First Vision, "[T]he circa summer 1832 history provides the most personal, intimate account of JS's early visions available."[6] Thus, in some academic circles in the Joseph Smith Papers-era, the 1832 History account serves not only to illustrate JS's earliest expression of his circumstances but also how he initially conceived of relating his personal experiences with the divine.

Based on circumstantial information—primarily Frederick G. Williams's role as a scribe for JS beginning about February 1832 and other data—Joseph Smith Papers editors date that history to being created "ca. summer 1832."[7] The history, however, abruptly concluded after only six pages, creating many questions about JS's purpose in initiating it. One of the lesser mysteries is whether or not the scribal session with Williams was done in one setting or more, given that there are several breaks in the story suggesting interruptions. The content represents from JS's personal perspective accounts of both the First Vision (in his own handwriting) and the coming forth of the Book of Mormon (dictated to Williams), carrying restoration events to 1829, the year before JS organized his church. Given Williams's identification in the introduction of several significant restoration events postdating the First Vision and Book of Mormon origins, it appears that JS perhaps intended to cover his early experiences to at least the June 1831 Kirtland conference, where he introduced the high priesthood to the church. The abandoned text may well, if completed to that point, have also included other significant institutional events, such as the priesthood restoration through angelic visitations, publication of the Book of Mormon in March 1830, and the organization of the Church of Christ the following month.

It appears that what Williams initially wrote as scribe in 152 words (7.5 percent of the history) was not the dictation of JS,[8] but was probably Williams's own construction to introduce the founding events of Mormonism. Whether JS supplied him with the information or if the wording was based upon common knowledge, is not known. Written in the third person, Williams, however, wrote in such abstruse language that it likely muddled and confused what JS probably hoped to convey. With no explanation, JS then took over and with pen in hand

6. Smith, Histories, "circa summer 1832," *JSP, H1*:10. The complete 1832 History is provided in *JSP, H1*:10–16, and online at http://www.josephsmithpapers.org/paper-summary/history-circa-summer-1832/1, where photographs of the original and a transcription is provided.

7. The editors narrowed the time of the history's production to being "probably…between the 20 July appointment [of Frederick G. Williams as an official clerk of JS] and 22 September 1832." Smith, Histories, "circa summer 1832," *JSP, H1*:7–10. See also Frederick G. Williams, *The Life of Dr. Frederick G. Williams: Counselor to the Prophet Joseph Smith* (Provo, UT: BYU Studies, 2012), 154–56.

8. Percentages total 98.5 percent but are here used as generalizations.

delivered in expressive language the circumstances of his First Vision. His initial 879 words (43 percent) witnessed for the first time the circumstances of his young life that moved him to inquire of God regarding his mortal status. Then, for reasons not known, he stopped writing mid-sentence before continuing his dictation to Williams. Indeed, there may have been a time-lapse in when the narrative was continued. In the following 522 words (25 percent) JS then conveyed to Williams his acquisition of the gold plates by way of the "angel of the Lord," the delay in acquiring them, his marriage to Emma Hale, and the entrance of Martin Harris into the story. Again, without explanation, JS began writing again, this time 109 words (5 percent) describing Harris's "Journy to the Eastern Cittys," explaining that Harris stated the Lord had "shown him [Harris] that he must go to new York City" with copied "c<h>aracters" from the Book of Mormon to present to the "Learned." After JS's brief interlude, Williams again applied his pen and JS apparently continued the dictation to Williams with 367 more words (18 percent). Harris's eastern trip, the loss of the 116 pages of the Book of Mormon text JS had produced, Oliver Cowdery's entrance into the account, and JS's concerns when Emma's father attempted to "turn me out of doors" concluded the history on the sixth page, with space remaining on the page to write. It must also be noted that two singular events found in the 1832 History that appear nowhere else were JS's statements that both Martin Harris and Oliver Cowdery were visited by the "Lord" to confirm their involvement in JS's work.[9] The 1832 History, just over 2,000 words in length, begged for more content but we will likely never know why he cut short his account.[10]

Frederick G. Williams's introductory words, not reflecting at all the first-person portrayal evident in the rest of the document, are indistinct and without context, in contrast to the rest of what JS wrote and dictated. It is also possible that Williams worked from the premise that the events he covered had been previously written, something the Joseph Smith Papers editors also suggest.[11] However, given Williams's vague and cloudy introduction to the narrative, had there been another source upon which the item was based, the present iteration would probably have been written with greater clarity. As it was, Williams described Mormon beginnings in this manner, perhaps giving his own understanding of what happened: "<[F]irstly> he [JS] receiving the testamony from on high," apparently Williams's wording for his representation of JS's early vision. Next, he

9. Smith, Histories, "circa summer 1832," *JSP, H1*:15, 16.

10. Joseph Smith Papers editors suggest, with emphasis upon the 1832 History as being primarily prepared for recordkeeping purposes, that, perhaps, "JS deliberately ended the history where he did, viewing it as part of a larger historical record that would include the work of others assigned as record keepers." Historical Introduction, Histories, "circa summer 1832," *JSP, H1*:5.

11. Historical Introduction, Histories, "circa summer 1832," *JSP, H1*:6.

wrote, "seccondly the ministering of Angels," perhaps a reference to Moroni or to what Warren Parrish, JS's scribe, included in the November 9, 1835, version of JS's First Vision stating that "I saw many angels in this vision."[12] Had this reference referred to Moroni only, it is likely that Williams would have also alluded to the Book of Mormon in the passage. Williams continued: "[T]hirdly the reception of the holy Priesthood by the ministring of—Aangels to administer the letter of the ~~Law~~ <Gospel—> <the Law and commandments as they were given unto him—> and ~~in~~ <the> ordinencs." This puzzling generalization apparently noted the significance of the notions of authority to JS's work, though it is presented without detail or specifics. Then followed, "forthly a confirmation and reception of the high Priesthood after the holy order of the son of the living God[,] power and ordinence from on high to preach the Gospel in the administration and demonstration of the spirit." The "high Priesthood" allusion obviously referred to the innovation in church organization presented the previous year at the early June 1831 conference that included the "reception" of the "high Priesthood" as a priesthood office.

When JS took up the pen to complete Williams's introduction, he continued the third-person introduction summarizing the effect of what had been given him, i.e., "the Kees of the Kingdom of God confered upon him and the continuation of the blessings of God to him." (JS used the concept of "keys" in his revelations over a dozen times prior to the 1832 History, suggesting God had given him dispensation, understanding, and authority to act for him.) JS then broke into the first-person voice to resume and conclude his personal narrative with the vitals of his New England origin by initially noting his birth in "Charon" [Sharon] Vermont on December 23, 1805. Though being raised in the "christian religion," he admitted being "deprived of the bennifit of an education" except in the most rudimentary terms. His large family's "indigent circumstances" placed them in a difficult position after their move to Palmyra, New York. JS then quickly moved to the crux of his narrative—his experiences with the divine. But it is in this sequence that his story has proved controversial, due to its contrast to the more popular 1838/39 rehearsal of Mormon beginnings.

JS's 1832 History is found in the ledger once known in the LDS Church History Library as the Kirtland Letterbook, now identified as Letterbook 1 in the Joseph Smith Papers. Following that six-page history is "ninety-three pages of copied outgoing letters, dated 14 June 1829 through 4 August 1835" associated with JS,[13] which warranted the volume's designation as a letterbook. This volume was one of the accumulated volumes of revelations, letterbooks, minutes, journals, and other papers composing the portable archives kept by JS's scribes

12. Smith, Journals, November 9, 1835, *JSP, J1*:88.
13. Source Note, Smith, Histories, "circa summer 1832," *JSP, H1*:3.

and clerks and eventually carried to the Salt Lake Valley in 1848 by Willard Richards's assistant historian Thomas Bullock.[14] After deposit in what became the LDS Church Historian's Office, precursor to the present LDS Church History Department, the boxes of records were not unpacked until June 7, 1853.[15] Sometime after 1853, perhaps many years later for reasons that are now speculative, the first six pages of the letterbook containing the 1832 History were excised from the volume and filed separately.[16] Given how the church's collection was organized and arranged before its professionalization beginning in the 1970s, it is plausible that the 1832 History was removed from the rest of the letterbook because the copies of letters found in the rest of the book were of a different nature than was the narrative prepared in the initial six pages.[17] However, it does not stretch credulity, to believe that because of the unfamiliar particulars in JS's First Vision described in the 1832 History, addressed below, certain church recordkeepers may have felt compelled to conceal that history.

Questioning the 1832 History's Account of Joseph Smith's First Vision

The literature produced about JS and his First Vision in the past half century is extensive.[18] This is due, in part, to the centrality of JS's First Vision within the corpus of his truth claims. It should be no surprise, then, that the authenticity of

14. Searle, "Willard Richards as Historian," 54.

15. Vogel, *History of Joseph Smith . . . A Source- and Text-Critical Edition*, 1:xvi; Davis Bitton and Leonard J. Arrington, *Mormons and Their Historians* (Salt Lake City: University of Utah Press, 1988), 12–14.

16. Dean C. Jessee, "The Early Accounts of Joseph Smith's First Vision," *BYU Studies* 9, no. 3 (Spring 1969): 277. Joseph Smith Papers editors suggest that the evidence surrounding removal and repair of the excised leafs indicates repairs took place after 1930 and that the narrative was in 1965 still associated with the letterbook, though it was cut from the larger document. Historical Introduction, Smith, Histories, "circa summer 1832," *JSP, H1*:4. See also Stan Larson's attempt to describe the custody and disposition of the 1832 History in "Another Look at Joseph Smith's First Vision," *Dialogue* 47, no. 2 (Summer 2014): 39–43.

17. As the LDS Church Historian's Office grew in the twentieth century, before professional cataloging methods were utilized, materials were organized by classification as "library, manuscript, and written records," facilitated by a "name and subject" file system. To comply with modern conventions of keeping archival collections together to maintain the *sanctity of their original order*, much that had been separated into the "name and subject" files, had to later be redone as department employees recataloged the materials to adhere to modern archival standards. It is possible that given those earlier methods of arrangement, the 1832 History may have been removed from Letterbook 1 for placement in a "subject" file. For former cataloging procedures in the church's historical agency, see Jessee, "Joseph Smith's Chronicler," 112–13; and Jeffery O. Johnson, "The Professionalization of the Archives of the LDS Church and the State of Utah: An Interview with Jeffery O. Johnson," *Mormon Historical Studies* 16, no. 1 (Spring 2015): 200.

18. See the following articles found in *Dialogue* where issues are addressed by the Reverend

the event and how JS related the story has warranted criticism from detractors with extensive rejoinders from defenders. The purpose of this study is not to enter the contentious arena addressing the specifics and credibility of the several accounts, though I contend that their contextual circumstances do not violate reasonable expectations one might hold in multiple transmissions of an event.

There are five renderings of the First Vision that scholars agree were created or commissioned by JS: the 1832 History;[19] the November 9, 1835, entry in JS's journal;[20] the 1838/39 history;[21] the ca. 1841 history;[22] and the 1842 "Church History" known as the Wentworth letter.[23] Other secondhand reports, like

---

Wesley P. Walters and Richard L. Bushman: "Roundtable: The Question of the Palmyra Revival," "New Light on Mormon Origins from the Palmyra Revival," "The First Vision Story Revived," and "A Reply to Dr. Bushman," *Dialogue* 4, no. 1 (Spring 1969): 61–100. Also see the following, listed chronologically: James B. Allen, "The Significance of Joseph Smith's 'First Vision' in Mormon Thought," *Dialogue* 1, no. 3 (Autumn 1966): 29–45; Jessee, "Early Accounts of Joseph Smith's First Vision," 275–94; Anderson, "Circumstantial Confirmation of the First Vision through Reminiscences," 373–404; James B. Allen, "Eight Contemporary Accounts of Joseph Smith's First Vision: What Do We Learn from Them?," *Improvement Era*, April 1970, 4–13; Milton V. Backman Jr., *Joseph Smith's First Vision: The First Vision in Its Historical Context* (Salt Lake City: Deseret Book, 1971); Hill, *Joseph Smith, The First Mormon*, 41–54; Howard, "Joseph Smith's First Vision," 23–30; Lambert and Cracroft, "Literary Form and Historical Understanding," 31–42; Allen, "Emergence of a Fundamental," 43–61; Hill, "The First Vision Controversy," 31–46; Milton V. Backman Jr., "Confirming Witnesses of the First Vision," *Ensign*, January 1986, 32–37; Lawrence Snyder, "Joseph Smith's First Vision: Sacred Narrative and the Problem of History," *Excursus: A Review of Religious Studies* 1, no. 1 (August 1988): 14–19; Richard L. Anderson, "Joseph Smith's Testimony of the First Vision," *Ensign*, April 1996, 10–21; Kent P. Jackson, "The First Vision" in *From Apostasy to Restoration* (Salt Lake City: Deseret Book, 1996), 66–79; Palmer, *An Insider's View of Mormon Origins*, 235–58; Dean C. Jessee, "The Earliest Documented Accounts of Joseph Smith's First Vision," in *Opening the Heavens: Accounts of Divine Manifestations, 1820–1844*, ed. John W. Welch (Provo, UT: Brigham Young University Press and Deseret Book, 2005), 1–33; James B. Allen and John W. Welch, "The Appearance of the Father and the Son to Joseph Smith in 1820," in Welch, *Opening the Heavens*, 35–75; Matthew B. Brown, *A Pillar of Light: The History and Message of the First Vision* (American Fork, UT: Covenant Communications, 2009); Samuel Alonzo Dodge and Steven C. Harper, eds., *Exploring the First Vision* (Provo, UT: Religious Studies Center, Brigham Young University, 2012) (which includes reprints of several early articles about the First Vision as well as new and updated information); Steven C. Harper, *Joseph Smith's First Vision: A Guide to the Historical Accounts* (Salt Lake City: Deseret Book, 2012); and more recently Larson, "Another Look at Joseph Smith's First Vision," 39–43; and Prince, "Joseph Smith's First Vision in Historical Context," 74–94.

19. Smith, Histories, "circa summer 1832," *JSP, H1*:11–13.

20. Smith, Journals, November 9, 1835, *JSP, J1*:87–88.

21. Smith, Histories, "History Drafts, 1838–circa 1841," Draft 2, *JSP, H1*:208–18.

22. Smith, Histories, "History Drafts, 1838–circa 1841," Draft 3, *JSP, H1*:211, 213, 215. The difference between the two accounts expressed here may be another indication of the influence of JS's clerks upon the language of the 1838/39 history.

23. Smith, Histories, "Church History," *JSP, H1*:492, 494.

what was reported to be JS's 1843 interview with David Nye White, editor of the *Pittsburgh Weekly Gazette*, and an entry in Alexander Neibaur's May 1844 journal, add texture to JS's means of characterizing his experiences.[24] However, controversy continues about several issues found within the accounts because there are variances in some of the details of the reports. While there are several differences, three features in particular differ in the 1832 History from the later accounts. First, JS's 1832 reflection provided the background that moved him to call upon God in the first place. But rather than approaching God to inquire about "which of all the sects was right,"[25] as stated in the 1838/39 history, JS's 1832 History indicated he had already determined that none were correct. "At about the age of twelve years," impressed with concern about "the wellfare of my immortal Soul," JS wrote that he began an investigation of the "scriptures" while also observing the "different denominations" operating in the area. From this he concluded, "there was no society or denomination that built upon the gospel of Jesus Christ as recorded in the new testament."[26] Then alluding to the fragmented Christianity he witnessed as a boy, he wrote, "from the age of twelve years to fifteen I pondered many things in my heart concerning the sittuation of the world of mankind" in all of its problems, not the least of which was his own status before God. He wrote that he "felt to mourn for my own sins." After considering "all these things," he "cried unto the Lord for mercy for there was none else to whom I could go and ~~to~~ obtain mercy,"[27] the appeal to heaven that resulted in what is now known as the First Vision.

A second differential of the 1832 History from JS's later histories is dating the founding event of Mormonism. After JS rendered in his own hand what happened to him—"while in <the> attitude of calling upon the Lord a piller of ~~fire~~ light above the brightness of the sun at noon day come down from above and rested upon me"—Williams dated the incident by inserting above the written line and before the words "a piller" that it occurred in JS's "16th year."[28] Williams's emendation identifies JS as being fifteen, putting the First Vision in 1821, which is contrary to the specificity of the later 1838/39 version that placed the event "early in the spring of Eightteen hundred and twenty" when JS would have been but fourteen.[29] It is not known why or when Williams added the phrase. Besides the contrast to the 1838/39 history, Williams's insertion is countered by

24. David Nye White and Alexander Neibaur's reports are reproduced in Jessee, "Earliest Documented Accounts of Joseph Smith's First Vision," in Welch, *Opening the Heavens*, 24–26.

25. Smith, Histories, "History Drafts, 1838–circa 1841," Draft 2, *JSP, H1*:214.

26. Smith, Histories, "circa summer 1832," *JSP, H1*:11–12.

27. Ibid.

28.Ibid., 12.

29. Smith, Histories, "History Drafts, 1838–circa 1841," Draft 2, *JSP, H1*:212.

the report of JS's First Vision found in his journal entry of November 9, 1835, as written by his clerk Warren Parrish where Parrish wrote that JS stated: "I was about 14. years old when I received this first communication,"[30] suggesting it could have been when he was thirteen or as late as when he was fifteen. After James Mulholland's untimely death and the interim appointment of Robert B. Thompson to replace him in preparing the 1838/39 history, JS also commissioned Howard Coray to groom what had already been written of his life for yet another attempt to craft his history. JS supplied him with what Mulholland had already written and other documentation. Consequently, Coray's report describing the First Vision used the identical language of Mulholland's history to date the event, though he prefaced the account with JS stating "I being about 15 years old" at the time of the vision,[31] further confusing the discussion. Lastly, in the March 1842 "Church History" article that became known as the Wentworth letter, the language used to describe the First Vision read, "When about fourteen years of age I began to reflect upon the importance of being prepared for a future state,"[32] which served as the prelude to his First Vision. Here again, the dating of all the accounts appears to have been influenced by the clerks, probably based on JS's own nebulous memory of the sequence of events. This opens an unanswerable question regarding the level of JS's input into creating the chronicle, thus leaving modern readers to speculate about the variables and perhaps other particulars within the several renderings. Many, however, would in remembering the event years later grant to JS the latitude of not being precise in timing the event. For others, it is an issue of his credibility.

The third and most noted contrast between the 1832 History and the subsequent portrayals of JS's First Vision centers in the event itself. As previously noted, while calling upon God, JS wrote in the 1832 story, "a piller of ~~fire~~ light above the brightness of the sun at noon day come down from above and rested upon me and I was filled with the spirit of god." In this inaugural theophany he stated, "the <Lord> opened the heavens upon me and I saw the Lord and he spake unto me saying Joseph <my son> thy sins are forgiven thee."[33] Thus, the controversial issue centers on the statement that the 1832 History limits the appearance of Deity to only "the Lord," i.e., Jesus, when the other four accounts imply there were two personages—God and Jesus—who visited the prophet.

30. Smith, Journals, November 9, 1835, *JSP, J1*:88,

31. Smith, Histories, "History Drafts, 1838–circa 1841," *JSP, H1*:209, 213. The LDS Church first publicized the existence of Coray's draft in 2005, when the Joseph Smith Papers editors received access to the document. See Coray's recollection about his charge from JS in Howard Coray, Reminiscences, undated, MS 8142, CHL. See also Dean C. Jessee, "Howard Coray's Recollections of Joseph Smith," *BYU Studies* 17, no. 3 (Spring 1977): 342–47.

32. Smith, Histories, "Church History," *JSP, H1*:492.

33. Smith, Histories, "circa summer 1832," *JSP, H1*:10–13.

The account of November 9, 1835, for instance, states that "a personage appeard" followed by "another personage."[34] The 1838/39 history simply modified the circumstance to read: "When the light rested upon me I saw two personages (whose brightness and glory defy all description) standing above me in the air."[35] JS's modern detractors have played upon the disparity as one of their primary contentions to refute JS's believability. His subsequent addition and adjustment of detail to his story, one critic insists, demonstrates his deception in 1838/39 by his expansion of that account to bolster his sagging reputation and "to satisfy institutional needs."[36] Though still subordinated to the more popular 1838/39 history later presented by B. H. Roberts as the *History of the Church*, the 1832 History reveals at a significant time JS's own perceptions about his early experiences in a calculated, reasoned display meant to introduce the public to his commission from God. We, then, are left to make sense of what that documentary piece meant at the time, how it fits into the later calendar of historical materials produced by JS, and why he never completed and published the story.

Those who have challenged JS's claims to having seen Deity in or about 1820 have generally skirted a historical analysis of how JS's initial vision was prompted and how it shaped his subsequent experiences, which is the process of historiography. Instead, they have recast the situation into an either/or polemical issue arguing that he invented the experience, thus disqualifying his reliability. The defenders have equally mustered their energies with exceeding zeal. Consequently, the study of JS's early motivations and experiences is so charged with hostility that there is little wonder that the matter cannot be considered in the light of objectivity. In many regards, JS's opponents have won. Except to the believers, JS will always be a questionable character because of the challenge to his primal truth claims. Rather than an appraisal of his circumstances that shaped the language of how he characterized his First Vision in its several iterations—which can be readily ascertained—his audacious and unconventional statements are bent into polar formulations that divert readers from the historical relevance of the First Vision. While scrutinizing the First Vision accounts is entirely fair game, to make the vision the criteria through which JS's trustworthi-

34. Smith, Journals, November 9, 1835, *JSP, J1*:87–88.

35. Smith, Histories, "History Drafts, 1838–circa 1841," *JSP, H1*:214. Most recently, the issue of the 1832 History's mention of only "the Lord" has been discussed by Larson, "Another Look at Joseph Smith's First Vision," 46–54.

36. Palmer, *An Insider's View*, 240, 245. The debate over the particulars of JS's First Vision will undoubtedly continue into the future, with multiple applications of analysis addressing the issues. Popular views of the controversy range on the internet from FairMormon's defense and explanation of JS's declaration about the First Vision (https://www.fairmormon.org/answers/Joseph_Smith%27s_First_Vision), to the criticism of the First Vision from Mormon Research Ministry (http://www.mrm.org/tag/first-vision).

ness is rendered—given the absence of sufficient documentation to adequately surround its telling—renders the critique, as stated by Robert Remini, "polemical and valueless as history."[37]

The First Vision was generally unknown and irrelevant to church members until the early 1840s. This notion may be confusing to modern students who have witnessed emphasis by the LDS Church of the 1838/39 version of the First Vision as published in the *History of the Church*, which informed not only its twentieth-century proselytizing methods but also its curriculum.[38] The 1832 History and JS's journal entry of November 9, 1835, were in his lifetime apparently unknown to all but a handful of his close associates. Even Orson Pratt's *Interesting Account of Several Remarkable Visions*, which first publicized JS's vision in print, primarily circulated only in Scotland.[39] It wasn't until 1842 via the *Times and Seasons* that in JS's "Church History" (the Wentworth letter in March) and his "History of Joseph Smith" (derived from the 1838/39 history in April) the First Vision became part of the public Mormon story. With precedent in Pratt's 1840 pamphlet, the 1842 productions represent how the story transformed from its initial expression reflecting JS's query of God about his soul to an institutional event augmented by the coming forth of the Book of Mormon, restoration of

37. Remini, "Biographical Reflections on the American Joseph Smith," 23.
38. There is dispute about how broadly JS initially disseminated his inaugural experiences. The contemporary documentation demonstrably shows that JS was very selective about those to whom he related his First Vision and other sacred experiences, as will be discussed in Chapter 11. However, it should be noted that some have concluded that JS readily related his First Vision story from the beginning. Mormon apostle John A. Widtsoe argued in 1951 that because of what he said was JS's repeated rehearsal of it, "the story of the First Vision was common knowledge among members of the Church." John A. Widtsoe, *Joseph Smith: Seeker after Truth, Prophet of God* (Salt Lake City: Deseret News Press, 1952), 22–26. More recently, Mark L. McConkie, compiler of a useful and large body of contemporary and noncontemporary recollections and memories about JS, similarly contends that a "pattern" had been formed early indicating JS's "constant retelling of the First Vision." McConkie deduces that conclusion based upon numerous recollections he compiled where JS's contemporaries many years after the fact testify that they heard JS tell his early visionary stories. "The picture," McConkie asserts, "is now much more insistent: Joseph wanted to tell that story, and others wanted to hear it." McConkie, *Remembering Joseph*, 17–18. As stated, the contemporary documentary record, however, does not support such contentions.
39. Orson Pratt, *A[n] Interesting Account of Several Remarkable Visions, and of the Late Discovery of Ancient American Records* (Edinburgh: Ballantyne and Hughes, 1840), reproduced in Smith, Histories, *JSP, H1*:520–46. Orson Hyde published another rehearsal of JS's First Vision in Frankfurt, Germany, two years later. Hyde described his volume as being written based on what "Br. O. Pratt did." Orson Hyde, *ein Ruf aus der Wüste, eine Stimme aus dem Schoose der Erde* (Frankfurt: Im Selbstverlage des Verfassers, 1842). See also Jessee, "Earliest Documented Accounts," 21–23, 33n28, which contains the English translation of Hyde's report of the First Vision.

the priesthoods, and the church's organization.[40] To misunderstand JS's initial intent in relating the personal vision to one with corporate implications reduces the several versions of the story of his acquaintance with Deity to a contrived litmus test for the credibility of Mormonism.

As will be shown, the same influences—bad press and reputation, as well as the need to explain himself—that moved JS to begin preparation of his 1832 History intensified over the years. By 1838, with internal dissent and Mormonism virtually on the run, the urgency to tell his story only deepened. As Donna Hill stated in 1977, "At first he might not have seen the implications which his experience would have for others."[41] The journal account of November 9, 1835, never had exposure and a public purpose. Its primary utility to modern students is to show JS's fuller rehearsal of the event with no other motive than to explain himself to an eccentric visitor. Misappropriating the relevant questions about JS's renderings of his First Vision to polar contentions severely limits reasonable conclusions that fit within what JS was apparently trying to do.

Of interest, even after the several renderings of JS's First Vision were published after 1842, there is no known contemporary evidence that his story was criticized by those in or out of the church as being implausible or that the accounts were contradictory. Had his visionary credibility been of concern to his Missouri and Nauvoo critics, there likely would have been documentation of the dispute.[42] Regarding the criticism he received from modern critics about his First Vision, it is also important to note that JS never enjoyed the luxury of time and distance enjoyed by those like Martin Luther to allow descriptions of

40. JS was told, he wrote in his 1832 History, that the "Lord" told him, "Joseph <my son> thy sins are forgiven thee." Smith, Histories, "ca. summer 1832," *JSP, H1*:13. Similarly, he reported he heard the same message of forgiveness when in his journal entry of November 9, 1835, he related his vision to Robert Matthews: "[A] personage...said unto me thy sins are forgiven thee." Smith, Journals, *JSP, J1*:88. Orson Pratt, also made note of that fact in his 1840 *Interesting Account of Several Remarkable Visions*: "He was informed, that his sins were forgiven." Smith, Histories, *JSP, H1*:523.

41. Hill, *Joseph Smith: The First Mormon*, 52.

42. It is hard to overstate that JS was never able to escape the critical eye of some church members. He was always under review. His less-than-strict personal behavior, for example, is mentioned in charges made concerning his disregard for complying with the church's Word of Wisdom. Smith, Documents, August 19, 1835, Minute Book 1, http://www.josephsmithpapers.org/paper-summary/minute-book-1/1#full-transcript, not printed in *JSP, D4*. In another instance, it was charged that he "extravagantly purchased three suits of cloth[e]s while he was at Washington" the previous winter. Minutes, September 5, 1840, Nauvoo Stake High Council, in John S. Dinger, ed., *The Nauvoo City and High Council Minutes* (Salt Lake City: Signature Books, 2011), 379. Church members even criticized him for reading the dedicatory prayer for the Kirtland House of the Lord instead of delivering it extemporaneously. George A. Smith, "Historical Discourse," November 15, 1864, *JD*, 11:9. The text of the dedicatory prayer is now known as D&C 109.

his seminal experiences space to season. As Fawn Brodie stated, "Joseph Smith dared to found a new religion in the age of printing,"[43] therefore permitting no time for his exploits and pronouncements to mature and cure within the larger culture, cultivating a degree of respectability before being eviscerated by his opponents.

The 1832 History Is First Publicized

Nothing is presently publicly known about anyone's knowledge of the 1832 account in the nineteenth century. In the twentieth century, besides Fawn Brodie's connection to BYU's Wilford Poulson mentioned earlier—who would have had to have seen the 1832 History before 1943—the next earliest available reference thereafter is a remark by Lamar Peterson, who mentioned it in notes taken in a February 1953 interview he had with LDS First Council of Seventy member Levi Edgar Young. A former history professor at the University of Utah, Young apparently told Peterson that after his own pressing inquiry of church leaders to see materials relating to the early history of the church, he was shown a document by Joseph Fielding Smith, then LDS Church historian, that contained a "strange" account of the First Vision. (Whether what he was shown at the time was separated or not from Letterbook 1 is not known.) After seeing the item Young told Peterson, it was then "put back in the vault" and "Remains unused, unknown."[44]

Public disclosure for the first time of JS's 1832 History came in 1965 by way of BYU graduate student Paul Cheesman's master's thesis. It caused a stir among the few academics who were already familiar with the documentary record of early Mormonism.[45] Other believers interested in JS had relied almost exclusively upon Roberts's *History of the Church* to explain the church's origins. Cheesman, an LDS Church Education System employee, cautioned in his thesis that, "Details [about the First Vision] left by Joseph himself…are only sketchy in nature, making a historical analysis of the events highly difficult." And, echoing a conclusion by Hugh Nibley four years earlier, noted JS's sensibility toward exposing his experience: "It is possible that Joseph Smith kept this vision a secret because he felt that communications of this nature were to be treated as sacred and not to be made public."[46] Thereafter the 1832 History became a contested fixture within the Mormon academic community.

43. Brodie, *No Man Knows My History*, vii.
44. See LaMar Peterson's story in Larson, "Another Look at Joseph Smith's First Vision," 41–42; Tanner and Tanner, *Mormonism: Shadow or Reality*, 145. See also Cory Nimer's look at the restrictive procedures regarding access to church-owned documents prevailing in the LDS Church Historian's Office during Joseph Fielding Smith's tenure as church historian: "The Old Guard and Rearguard Actions: Professionalization and the Church Historian's Office," *Journal of Mormon History* 45, no. 1 (January 2019): 110–38.
45. Cheesman, "An Analysis."
46. Cheesman, "An Analysis," 1, 6. See Nibley's statements in Chapter 11.

Further charging the interest of Mormon scholars was the discovery in the 1960s by Dean Jessee of yet another account of the First Vision in the church's collection attributed to JS not previously made public. Though it may be surprising, the content of JS's journals before that time were unknown, even to Mormon academics. While surveying early manuscripts "to identify the handwriting" of JS's clerks, Jessee found the November 9, 1835, entry in JS's journal that described his encounter in Kirtland with a man "who introduced himself as Joshua, a Jewish minister."[47] An itinerant eccentric then circulating through the Western Reserve, Joshua's real name was Robert Matthews, but he also identified himself as the prophet Matthias.[48] JS's scribe at the time, Warren Parrish, summarized the meeting that included JS relating to the unusual visitor that in the midst of "a pillar of fire . . . a personage appeard" to him, followed by "another personage [who] soon appeared," who "said unto me thy sins are forgiven thee." Further, the journal entry stated, "I saw many angels in this vision."[49] Being only familiar at the time with the 1832 History and 1838/39 accounts of JS's initial vision, Jessee said, "When I read it I could hardly believe my eyes. It was different from anything I had seen before."[50] Exposure of the 1832 History and the November 9, 1835, journal account stoked the Mormon historical community and portended what amounted to an explosion of interest and new study into Mormon beginnings.[51]

The previously unknown 1832 History and November 9, 1835, accounts of the First Vision and their variances in detail from the 1838/39 account naturally provoked the critics of Mormonism to charge JS with having a deceptive imagination in recounting his initial vision. This, along with later challenges that his claim of having been driven in his quest by religious revivals in the area prior to 1820, forced Mormon beginnings into being a heated contest between the defenders and detractors.[52] Both sides then mounted concerted contextual

47. Jessee, "Joseph Smith's Chronicler," 121.

48. Paul E. Johnson and Sean Wilentz, *The Kingdom of Matthias: A Story of Sex and Salvation in 19th-Century America* (New York: Oxford University Press, 1994).

49. Smith, Journals, November 9, 1835, *JSP, J1*:88. There is a possibility that the "strange" account of the First Vision mentioned above may have been the entry from JS's November 9, 1835, journal that varies some from the traditional 1838/39 version, though that is unlikely.

50. Jessee, "Joseph Smith's Chronicler," 121.

51. Allen, "Significance of Joseph Smith's 'First Vision,'" 35; Source Notes, Smith, Histories, "History Drafts, 1838–circa 1841," Draft 3, *JSP, H1*:191–92; Historical Introduction, Draft 3, 200. It should be noted that the Coray rendering of the First Vision account in Draft 3 ca. 1841 mentioned above, being derived from the 1838/39 history, was unknown and unavailable to the public before later being transferred by church leaders to the LDS Church History Library in 2005.

52. A summarization of the critics' charges regarding Palmyra revivals is found in Marquardt and Walters, *Inventing Mormonism*, 15–41. Defenders' responses to the issue include

surveys and analysis of Mormon beginnings providing important background for modern conceptions of the foundations of the faith. Thus, soon after Cheesman published his thesis, BYU history professor James B. Allen, a member of Cheesman's thesis committee, issued the first of several significant analyses of what was then the historical community's cumulative understanding regarding the First Vision and the extant record describing the same.[53] Also during this period, Dean Jessee introduced the academic world and other interested parties to the textual transcriptions and descriptions of First Vision accounts then known in his influential 1969 publication, "The Early Accounts of Joseph Smith's First Vision."[54] Scholars and others began inserting other important contextual findings into the renewed discussion of Mormon origins. Allen then prepared in 1970 an important introductory essay for the general Mormon audience regarding First Vision documentation that included the 1832 History.[55] His lineup of the extant First Vision documents in the church's principal periodical, the *Improvement Era*, helped the previously uninformed public to see the implications of what the 1832 History did to the consistency of the unchallenged uniformity of JS portrayals of the great event. The results of the publications just mentioned meant that for the first time the larger community of Mormon history students could see the initial environmental representation from the documentary record concerning JS's First Vision.

The Contextual Setting for the 1832 History

The 1832 History's origin in the summer of 1832 serves three purposes in this work: (1) to serve as a mechanism illustrating perspective concerning the multitude of influences upon JS after two years at the helm of his church, (2) how those influences motivated him at the time, and (3) his intent then to publicly relate his intimate experiences with the divine. Without JS's own articulated motive for creating the narrative, what follows are matters that may have influenced creation of the text. There is, frankly, little in the documentary record that portrays JS's thinking during 1832 other than the eighteen revelations he produced that year, a handful of meetings, four letters he wrote to his wife and W. W. Phelps, and a few other miscellaneous items. While he began keeping a journal

---

D. Michael Quinn, "Joseph Smith's Experience of a Methodist 'Camp-Meeting' in 1820," *Dialogue Paperless*, E-Paper no. 3, expanded version (Definitive), December 20, 2006, http://www.dialoguejournal.com; and Richard Lloyd Anderson, "Joseph Smith's Accuracy on the First Vision Setting: The Pivotal 1818 Palmyra Camp Meeting," in Dodge and Harper, *Exploring the First Vision*, 91–169.

53. Allen, "Significance of Joseph Smith's 'First Vision,'" 29–45; Allen, "Emergence of a Fundamental," 31–42.

54. Jessee, "Early Accounts of Joseph Smith's First Vision," 275–96.

55. Allen, "Eight Contemporary Accounts of Joseph Smith's First Vision," 4–13.

that year, the first entry was not penned until November 27, 1832, leaving the search for meaning to be found in several consequential events early in the year that may have influenced him. They included his ongoing revision of the Bible, then focusing on the New Testament; the January 25, 1832, church conference in Amherst, Ohio, where JS was accepted as president of the high priesthood and a significant dispersal of missionaries occurred; the initial organization of what became the church's First Presidency in March; the personal trauma that month surrounding the deaths of newborn twins followed shortly by his adopted son's death; and the brutal attempt on his life at the end of March when he was tarred and feathered in Hiram, Ohio. And, having to juggle leadership of both Kirtland and Zion, JS in the midst of those difficulties, left for Missouri to implement there the organizational adjustments to church administration exacted earlier in the year. This mix of matters prefaced creation of JS's 1832 History.

The Joseph Smith Papers editors rightly indicate that the 1832 History fits into the larger recordkeeping consciousness established at the church's organization.[56] "Behold there Shall <be> a Record ~~be~~ kept among you,"[57] represented a particular stipulation on April 6, 1830, that provoked later creations of manuscripts and compilations of institutional documents such as revelations, minute books, letterbooks, and other records that portrayed the rise and progress of the church. While there were periods where JS and other church leaders were less than vigilant in chronicling Mormon advances and retreats, surviving records from the period illustrate the seriousness they applied to the organizational injunction. The 1832 History fits into this consciousness.

It has also been suggested that another factor in creating the document could have been Sidney Rigdon's surprising behavior in a July 1832 gathering in Kirtland that may have pushed the prophet to act. Rigdon had been traveling to Missouri with JS since April. A few weeks after Rigdon's return to Kirtland, Reynolds Cahoon, in his own sporadic journal, captured an astonishing assertion by Rigdon that gravely upset the thinking of those who heard his declaration. Rigdon's family had boarded for a time with Cahoon before his return, elevating Cahoon's interest in Rigdon once he arrived in Kirtland.[58] Cahoon, the forty-two-year-old counselor to church bishop Newel K. Whitney, wrote that at a July 6 meeting in Kirtland, Rigdon bellowed before the congregation "that he had a revelation from the Lord & said that the kingdo<m> was taken from <the> Church and left with him."[59] Just four months previously, Rigdon been appointed as counselor to JS in the church's First Presidency. Obviously, the claim frightened those in

56. Smith, Histories, Historical Introduction, "circa summer 1832," *JSP, H1*:6.

57. Smith, Revelations, April 6, 1830, *JSP, R1*:22 [D&C 21:1 (1981)].

58. Richard S. Van Wagoner, *Sidney Rigdon: A Portrait in Religious Excess* (Salt Lake City: Signature Books, 1994), 126.

59. Reynolds Cahoon, Journal, July 6, 1832, MS 1115, CHL.

attendance. Lucy Mack Smith in her memoir described the setting of Rigdon's announcement. After her husband, Joseph Smith Sr., prompted Rigdon to speak before the group, she stated that Rigdon displayed an erratic explosion of emotion. After "pacing back and forth through an aisle" he "replied vehemently" to the congregation that "the keys of the kingdom ~~were~~ <are> rent from the church . . . and you never will have them again untill you build me a new house," which "produced a great excitement" in the people. The very nature of Rigdon's rant that focused on the church not having built a home for him suggests his questionable mental status. All of this occurred in front of Hyrum, JS's brother. Hyrum immediately left to fetch JS from Hiram, Ohio, just over thirty miles south. Mother Smith wrote that her son Hyrum arrived at the John Johnson farm where JS stayed, "laughing" at Rigdon's "frivolous maneuvering," indicating the extreme nature of Rigdon's harangue. JS and Hyrum returned to Kirtland the next afternoon where another meeting had just convened. JS entered the gathering and allayed the fears of the attendees, stating, "I myself hold the Keys of this last dispensation and I forever will hold them in time and in eternity so set your hearts at rest for all is well." He then ordered a council the following day for Rigdon to account for the tirade. His counselor humbly submitted, according to Mother Smith, explaining he was of late suffering from "the most astonishing encounters with the Devil."[60] The admission appeased the council. Given that Rigdon's bluster occurred a hundred days after he had been mangled by a mob in Hiram at the same time JS had been brutalized the last week of March, it is likely that his fitful exhibit was accounted, in part, to his having been dragged by his feet with his head bouncing off the frozen ground as he was mobbed.[61] Thus, the postulation that JS produced his 1832 History as a rejoinder to Rigdon's pathetic appeal probably does not merit consideration as the singular explanation for the production of the history, as the moment quickly passed after JS corrected the situation.

Another of the possible influences swirling around JS in mid-1832 is an argument that his difficult circumstances at the time provoked recollection as a boy of his dismay and confusion regarding his personal salvation that resulted in his First Vision. JS and a small party, upon their return to Kirtland from visiting Zion that spring, had an accident where Newel K. Whitney broke his leg and foot while leaping from a runaway stagecoach. As JS tended to him during his recovery for a month in Greenville, Indiana, JS wrote to his wife Emma on June

60. Anderson, *Lucy's Book*, 561–64; Cahoon, Journal, July 7, 1832. See also Rigdon biographer Richard Van Wagoner's portrayal of the circumstances, including witness Charles C. Rich's reaction to Rigdon's assertions and JS's response, in *Sidney Rigdon*, 126–28.

61. See Van Wagoner's description of Rigdon's mental circumstances, derived from injuries even from his youth, including Rigdon's own description of the assault upon him in his April 6, 1844, Nauvoo general conference sermon, in *Sidney Rigdon*, 114–18.

6, 1832, the first surviving letter of the prophet to his wife. The communication after two months of separation indicated the delay in his return was for him a period of deep reflection upon his past that, it has been argued, may have fueled his inclination to portray his life on paper.[62] The letter is one of the rare windows into JS's interior thinking. Stating to Emma that he found a secluded grove near town where he gave before God "vent to all the feelings of my heart in meaditation and praiyr," he exposed the inner pulses that plagued him. Disclosing what appears at the time to be chronic anxiety about not measuring up to his commission from God, he explained he had rehearsed "past moments of my life" that caused him to "Shed tears of sorrow for my folly in Sufering the adversary of my Soul to have so much power over me as he has <had in times past>."[63] The meditations lowered his spirits, which it has been suggested perhaps paralleled his introspective feelings when he was a fourteen-year-old in New York when he first called upon God. Considering the language in the 1832 History that JS used to explain his apprehensions for relief of his sins, it was posed that JS may have revisited his earliest experiences that served as a stimulus to finally publicly present himself and his motivations by way of a personal account.[64]

Joseph Smith's Consciousness about the Printed Word

Though there is nothing in the historical record that definitively indicates why JS produced his 1832 History, what follows is the proposition that one of the most significant factors for the initiative, an ongoing stimulus, may have been JS's inability to control his environment that stirred unchecked around him. It is unthinkable to believe that how he and his church had been depicted in the press and other settings did not affect him. And words alone did not define what troubled him. His mother, Lucy, noted an attempt on his life as early as the age of fourteen,[65] a preface to numerous other confrontations he faced. JS first displayed his consternation over how he had been depicted among Palmyra villagers and others in the "Preface" to the 1830 Book of Mormon where he lamented the "many false reports [that] have been circulated respecting the following work, and also many unlawful measures taken by evil designing persons to destroy me and also the work."[66] In one of his infrequent public letters delivered in 1835, he

62. Matthew C. Godfrey, "The Second Sacred Grove: The Influence of Greenville, Indiana, on Joseph Smith's 1832 First Vision Account," *Journal of Mormon History* 44, no. 4 (October 2018): 1–18.

63. Smith to Emma Smith, June 6, 1832, *JSP, D*2:249–57.

64. Godfrey, "The Second Sacred Grove," 17, 18.

65. Anderson, *Lucy's Book*, 329. See also Orson Hyde's statement that, "Before he left Palmyra, he was shot at several times, but each time divine providence helped him to escape unharmed. However, on one occasion he was beaten by two men with clubs so violently, that he still bears the scars on his body to this day." Hyde's statement in *ein Ruf aus der Wüste*, as quoted in Jessee, *Papers of Joseph Smith*, 1:425.

66. Joseph Smith, Junior, The Book of Mormon (Palmyra, NY: E. B. Grandin, 1830), [iii].

wrote, "I have been drawn into this course of proceeding, by persecution, that is brought upon us from false rumor, and misrepresentations concerning my sentiments."[67] The torment never left him, as evidenced by a similar expression that opened his 1838/39 history:

> Owing to the many reports which have been put in circulation by evil disposed and designing persons in relation to the rise and progress of the Church of Latter day Saints, all of which have been designed by the authors thereof to militate against its character as a church, and its progress in the world; I have been induced to write this history so as to disabuse the publick mind, and put all enquirers after truth into possession of the facts as they have transpired in relation both to myself and the Church as far as I have such facts in possession.[68]

While the process of JS's consciousness about the dilemma is difficult to conveniently chart, as the layers of criticism leveled at him mounted, a cumulative mindset moved him to act. The 1832 History may have become part of JS's larger stratagem to advance Mormonism in the latter days.

The Book of Mormon's publication in March 1830 immediately put JS and what became his church into America's print culture. He undoubtedly recognized the power and influence of the printed word upon his countrymen. In particular, he certainly understood that the pervasive presence of newspapers swayed the way people thought and acted. Whitney Cross's study of religion in western New York during this period noted that "at least 129 weeklies had commenced in the area before 1820" providing the "primary literary fare for the Burned Over District."[69] As French social critic Alexis de Tocqueville summarized after his investigative tour of America in 1831: "The press wields enormous power in America. It carries the currents of political life into every section of this vast country." The press's pervasive presence took him aback: "The number of periodicals and semi-periodicals in the United States beggars belief." Indeed, "There is hardly a town in the United States without a newspaper."[70] And, as JS well knew at the time, the content of most newspapers almost never gave him or his church a fair shake. Thus, as Tocqueville observed, "When an idea, whether just or unreasonable, takes possession of the American mind, nothing is more difficult than to get rid of it."[71] Still, it appears JS determined to enter the arena, unwilling to concede public opinion about Mormonism to the interests of

67. Joseph Smith "To the Elders of the Church of the Latter Day Saints," in *Latter Day Saints' Messenger and Advocate*, November 1835, 209.
68. Smith, Histories, "History Drafts, 1838–circa 1841," Draft 2, *JSP, H1*:204.
69. Cross, *Burned-Over District*, 102, 103.
70. Alexis de Tocqueville, *Democracy in America*, trans. Arthur Goldhammer (New York: Library of America, 2004), 210, 211, 212.
71. Ibid., 213.

indifferent or hostile editors. While the negative press proved a significant obstacle, it is clear that JS recognized the power of the printed word and that it had a principal role in what he attempted to do.

Evidence indicates that JS's early intention was to deliver Jesus's revelations in print form along with his revision of the Bible, showing his plan to add to the sacred canon. But even with good intentions, complications and resources delayed his ambitions to make better known those features of his prophetic mantle. By the fall of 1831, however, he and church leaders initiated a Literary Firm to shepherd the procedures resulting in the desired publications. (The Literary Firm became part of the church's larger operational business and financial structure called the United Firm.)[72] Regarding printing objectives, it was fortuitous for JS when in June 1831 W. W. Phelps, an experienced newspaperman, became a Mormon. The next month JS appointed him the church's printer. Two months later he commissioned Phelps to purchase a press in Cincinnati and relocate with his family to Zion to establish a church publishing enterprise. Plans soon blossomed to take full advantage of Phelps's press and talents.[73] Thereafter, from 1830–1847—according to Mormon bibliographer Peter Crawley—Phelps, along with Parley P. Pratt, dominated creation of written and published Mormonism.[74]

Church conferences held in the first two weeks of November 1831 enacted measures to materialize JS's designs. At the conference on November 1 at Hiram, Ohio, they formalized the plan to print JS's revelations, ambitiously voting that "ten thousand copies" of the "the Book of commandments" were to be printed, later pared to three thousand.[75] The enterprise fell under the auspices of the new Literary Firm, a function of the church that JS considered "of the greatest importance."[76] By the end of the month, Oliver Cowdery (who also had a printing background) and John Whitmer were on their way from Kirtland to Independence with revelation manuscripts to join Phelps in the publishing enterprise.[77] The move indicates the assertive and confident nature of JS's instincts about the destiny of the Church of Christ, with the prospect that his church no longer needed to operate in the shadows.

The printing strategy had implications for both centers of Mormon gathering. Consequently, provisions were made to prepare buildings to house printing

72. Parkin, "Joseph Smith and the United Firm," 11–12, 31–33,

73. Van Orden, *We'll Sing and We'll Shout*, 51–61; Peter Crawley, *A Descriptive Bibliography of the Mormon Church*, 3 vols. (Provo, UT: Religious Studies Center, Brigham Young University, 1997–2012), 1:33.

74. Crawley, *Descriptive Bibliography of the Mormon Church*, 1:25.

75. Smith, Documents, November 1, 1831, Minute Book 2, *JSP*, *D*2:97; Crawley, *Descriptive Bibliography of the Mormon Church*, 1:38–39.

76. Joseph Smith, Sidney Rigdon, Frederick G. Williams, and Martin Harris to Church Leaders in Jackson County, Missouri, June 25, 1833, *JSP*, *D*3:155.

77. Parkin, "Joseph Smith and the United Firm," 11–12.

establishments in both Independence and Kirtland. JS, while in Zion the summer of 1831, supervised plans to prepare a church headquarters venture there that included not only a temple, but also structures for other church purposes, one of which was a lot for a printing operation.[78] For Kirtland, the revelation JS received on August 2, 1833, specified that part of the plan to crown Kirtland as a center place was not only construction of a House of the Lord, but also held a purpose for a "house for the Presidency" (with administration purposes), besides another building "for the work of the printing of the translation of my Scriptures." What amounted to the design for a headquarters campus in Kirtland included the three buildings, each intended to have a footprint of fifty-five by sixty-five feet.[79] Church leaders modified the original plans and a year after they began to raise the Kirtland House of the Lord, they started work on a two-story building to house both a printing office and a school.[80] Though the printing establishment was destroyed by dissenters during the Kirtland apostasy, a publication function had become a permanent fixture of the faith despite interruptions in JS's plans.

Concurrent with the Phelps/Cowdery/Whitmer work on publishing the revelations, church leaders inserted themselves into the popular mode of communication via religious periodicals. This became the province of Phelps in Missouri. A contemporary press to serve as the voice of Mormonism was a significant step for the church. For the church to be relevant to not only its own adherents but to others as well, a literary profile became important to convey the Mormon message. As Nathan Hatch stated, "religious periodicals had by 1830, become the grand engine of a burgeoning religious culture, the primary means of promotion for, and bond of union within, competing religious groups."[81] Church leaders' intent included establishing a monthly organ with the utilitarian purpose of providing unifying information for church members while also informing their neighbors of the Mormon presence. The first issue of the *Evening and the Morning Star* appeared as a June 1832 publication. Its content clearly illustrated its purpose and pattern: publication of JS's revelations, communication to the laity, essays on the gospel, portrayal of the sectarian world and its calamities, hymns and other items of interest.[82] At the same time in 1832, Phelps also established

78. Ibid., 24. The printing endeavor ended up being housed in the two-story brick home of W. W. Phelps.

79. Smith, Revelations, June 1, 1833, *JSP, R1*:259–60 [D&C 95:11–17 (1981)]; Smith, Revelations, August 2, 1833, *JSP, R1*:246–47 [D&C 94:3–12 (1981), clear text]; Smith, Sidney Rigdon, and Frederick G. Williams to Church Leaders in Jackson County, Missouri, August 6, 1833, *JSP, D3*:228–37.

80. Staker, *Hearken, O Ye People*, 427.

81. Hatch, *Democratization of American Christianity*, 125–26.

82. *Evening and the Morning Star*, June 1832; Van Orden, *We'll Sing and We'll Shout*, 73–79.

a secular newspaper, *The Upper Missouri Advertiser*, designed to promote local and regional interest.[83] Mormonism, now operating in a more progressively urbanized environment, moved to make itself relevant to a broader range of Americans by way of the print culture. Given JS's publishing initiatives and the coincident establishment of a church press, it is entirely plausible that he prepared his 1832 History and its representation of his foundational experiences to parlay his and the church's objectives into public interest via the *Evening and the Morning Star*. He did not lack for reasons to inform audiences both in and out of the church.

Ezra Booth's Letters, Fall 1831

The designs that moved JS and other church leaders to create a literary platform for printing the revelations and publishing a periodical may have also been influenced by the imposing circumstances that faced them daily. Once the Mormons overwhelmed the village of Kirtland, Ohio, in 1831, interior and exterior distractions and interruptions complicated life for community residents. While many advances materialized giving structure to both civic and religious functions within the community, the reality of a religion that had gained its footings remained something for the future. Months before there were imaginations and discussions about a grand temple city in Kirtland, a challenge to JS and his authority appeared in the person of Ezra Booth that showed both the vulnerability and durability of the Mormon prophet. Booth, a thirty-nine-year-old Connecticut native known at the time in northeastern Ohio for his Methodist ministerial background, had transitioned to a fruit grower in Mantua, Ohio, at the time of the Mormon incursion into Portage County. Connected to the Johnson family nearby in Hiram, Booth witnessed JS healing Elsa Johnson, an act so dramatic that it moved him to forsake his religious heritage. He became a Mormon in 1831, adding a significant personality to the faith. Known as "a man of considerable culture and eloquence,"[84] Booth's knowledge and experience set him apart from most Mormons, something in the stripe of Sidney Rigdon's learning. Not only was he one of the first ordained to the church's high priesthood in June 1831, he soon accompanied JS the eighteen hundred miles to Zion (Missouri) and back. With much more experience and polish than JS, on the journey Booth found the twenty-six-year-old prophet wanting in many ways, revealing JS's mortal paraphernalia and shortcomings. Booth's apparent expectations of a larger-than-life biblical-type figure who transcended mortal weaknesses proved too much to accommodate JS in raw form. And, the call to missionary work that subordi-

83. Crawley, *Descriptive Bibliography of the Mormon Church*, 1:32–35.
84. Marquardt, "Ezra Booth on Early Mormonism," 69–70; Staker, *Heaken, O Ye People*, 277.

nated him as a foot soldier from the pastoral position he once held—along with what he perceived to be JS and other Mormon leaders' gentrification—rubbed him wrong. What's more, JS's genial and jovial manner struck him as unbecoming a prophet.[85] He voiced his concerns. By the first week of September 1831, upon his return to Kirtland from Missouri, Booth's dissonance moved church leaders to "silence" him as a preaching elder. But he did not go quietly. Later that month, he initiated what turned out to be a nine-letter assault upon the Church of Christ, the most formidable criticism and public exhibition of Mormonism to that time.[86]

Cast as exposé, Booth's letters to Ira Eddy, a Methodist minister in the Ohio Conference, were printed in Ravenna, Ohio's, *Ohio Star*, forty miles south of Kirtland. The communications as a body proved to be one of the most insightful and damaging collection of documents describing JS and his church. Booth explained that at the outset he "conscientiously believed [JS's religion] to be of God," compelling his conversion from Methodism to Mormonism. The impressions he had upon his conversion to the faith "were deep and powerful, and my feelings were excited to a degree to which I had been a stranger." Within a few months, however, he realized that "Mormonism has in part changed its character, and assumed a different dress, from that under which it made its first appearance on the Western Reserve."[87] He could no longer sustain what enveloped his life. Coupled with the journey to Zion, the fulfillment he contemplated at first became aggravating disappointment.[88]

Clearly written with the intent to dissuade all who might entertain the plausibility of Mormon legitimacy, those in the region took note of Booth's exposé. Though little more than a curiosity to non-Mormons in northeastern Ohio, the letters impacted those who themselves had recently accepted the faith. And the power of the press underscored his complaints. An 1835 recollection of Ambrose Palmer illustrated the turmoil after Booth's letters were published among Mormons to whom Booth once ministered. Writing to Oliver Cowdery, editor of the *Messenger and Advocate* in Kirtland, Ambrose stated that though Booth had helped in 1831 to establish Mormonism "at the 'Bates Corners' in Norton," fifty miles south of Kirtland, church members there were later wounded by what they

85. Staker, *Hearken, O Ye People*, 296, 300.
86. See Mark Staker's sketch of Booth in *Hearken, O Ye People*, 277–87, 304–5; and Marquardt, "Ezra Booth on Early Mormonism," 65–87.
87. Ezra Booth to Rev. Ira Eddy, September 1831, in Howe, *Mormonism Unvailed*, 176, 183.
88. Ezra Booth's nine letters written to Rev. Ira Eddy appeared in Ravenna, Ohio's, *Ohio Star*, October 13, 20, 27; November 3, 10, 17, 24; and two on December 8, 1831. See Mark Staker's description of the letters in *Heaken, O Ye People*, 296–302. The letters, as included in this discussion, were later printed in Howe's *Mormonism Unvailed*, where the impact of Booth's letters reached their greatest influence (175–221).

then read about Booth's refutation of and defection from the gospel. "Not long after, we read Booth's letters as published in the Ohio Star; and although he did not prove that the book of Mormon was not true, yet he gave the whole work such a coloring, or appearance of falsehood, that the public feeling was, that 'mormonism' was overthrown."[89] Booth's censure of the faith, while mostly raising eyebrows in Ohio, moved far beyond the Ohio River Valley. Wesley Perkins, who lived in Lorain County, fifty miles east of Kirtland, sent to family members in Vermont a "paper that Contains A letter written by the Rev. E. Boothe" that "you may survie [survey] them and Sattisfy your Silf."[90] Booth found an effective messenger in the written and printed word.

Though the church mounted no literary reply to Booth at the time, the prophet and his colleagues apparently felt the need to disperse pertinent revelations JS had received to counter Booth's allegations.[91] Booth's attack clearly prompted a December 1, 1831, revelation by JS after most of Booth's letters had been published. JS and Rigdon were told to embark on a mission to "proclaim unto the world in the regions round about & in the Church also, for the space of a season" what amounted to a rebuttal of Booth's charges. The "regions" included nearby "Ravenna [where Booth's letters were published], Shalersville [just southwest of Hiram, Ohio], and other places." The "season" lasted for about a month where they focused on the area where the letters had their initial impact. Specifically pointing to what Booth had done, the intention of the revelation directed JS and Rigdon to "confo[u]nd your enemies; call upon them to meet you, both in publick & in private, & in as much as ye are faithful their shame shall be made manifest."[92] The two church leaders travelled to Ravenna and environs in January 1832, just weeks after publication of Booth's letters the previous fall. There they "did much towards allaying the excited feelings which were growing out of the scandalous letters then being published in the 'Ohio Star,' at Ravenna." Rigdon even challenged Booth to debate.[93] Ambrose Palmer wrote that subsequent to the havoc raised by Booth in Norton, Ohio, "we afterward received preaching from brother R[eynolds]. Cahoon, David Whitmer, and Lyman Johnson, and after that, also by brother Thomas Marsh and others," which somewhat blunted the impact of Booth's defection and declarations.[94]

89. Ambrose Palmer to Oliver Cowdery, January 28, 1835, *Latter Day Saints' Messenger and Advocate*, January 1835, 61–62.

90. Dennis Rowley, "The Ezra Booth Letters," *Dialogue* 16, no. 3 (Autumn 1983): 133–37.

91. Smith, Documents, Historical Introduction, November 1–2, 1831, Minute Book 2, *JSP, D2*:95.

92. Smith, Revelation, December 1, 1831, *JSP: R1*:187 [D&C 71:2, 7 (1981)].

93. "History of Joseph Smith," *Times and Seasons*, July 15, 1844, 576; Historical Introduction, Smith, Revelation, January 10, 1832, *JSP, D2*:155.

94. Palmer to Cowdery, *Messenger and Advocate*, 62. In another instance, Mark Staker suggests that Hyrum Smith and Reynolds Cahoon visited John Johnson family in-laws

Booth's apostasy and criticism reached beyond unsettling fragile Mormon minds. It has been claimed that JS and Sidney Rigdon's significant February 1832 "Vision" of the postmortal world (D&C 76), countering the Christian understanding of heaven and hell, incited an assault upon JS and Rigdon a month later that nearly killed them. Purportedly, the impact on the locals incited them to viciously tar and feather JS and Rigdon after being dragged from their beds on a frozen night at the end of March. Indeed, that may have been one motivation for the violence. But George A. Smith, apostle and church historian in 1864—attempting to educate church members about what he remembered as a young man regarding the attack—related the extreme impact of Booth's claims. He suggested that the assault upon JS at John Johnson's home in Hiram, Ohio, where JS and Rigdon were nearly beaten to death, resulted from the letters Booth wrote. Booth's "nine letters," George Smith said, "culminated in collecting a mob who tarred and feathered Joseph Smith, and inflicted upon his family the loss of one of its number at Hyrum, Portage county, Ohio [the death of JS's adopted son]."[95] Booth's accusations "brought the opposition to the boiling point."[96] Booth's friend and fellow apostate Symonds Ryder with a couple dozen others descended on the Johnson home that cold March night in 1832 and stripped, beat, scratched, smeared, and then poisoned JS. Rigdon did not fare much better. While it may not be directly demonstrable by way of a one to one ratio that Booth's letters provoked JS's 1832 History, overall, it likely was a major factor informing JS of the need to explain himself and his church's designs in light of the numerous allegations made against him.

Others within the geographical orbit of Mormon influence took note of the emerging body of JS's followers in the early months of the faith's existence. Word about the religion moved through the region to the effect that zealous practitioners took note, some determined to expose and excise JS's impertinence and unsettling effect upon the locals. Besides notables such as Alexander Campbell, clerics like Diedrich Willers, a thirty-two-year-old German-born minister of the German Reformed Church, after familiarity with Mormons through the Peter Whitmer family, determined by spreading the word to "nip this work in the bud."[97] David Marks, a Freewill Baptist evangelist, also connected with the Whitmers to find out about JS. After visiting with them, Marks later surveyed a copy of the Book of Mormon, which he wrote, "greatly disappointed" him "in the style and interest of the work." It was a threat that he attempted to scuttle

---

who "may have been influenced by the letters" to allay their fears. Staker, *Hearken, O Ye People*, 339.

95. George A. Smith, Sermon, November 15, 1864, *JD*, 11:4.

96. Bushman, *Rough Stone Rolling*, 177–78.

97. D. Michael Quinn, trans. and ed., "The First Months of Mormonism: A Contemporary View by Rev. Diedrich Willers," *New York History* 54, no. 3 (July 1973): 317–33.

in 1831.[98] Just a few months later, the Whitmers hosted another visitor curious about Mormonism in October 1830—Peter Bauder, another New York preacher who ministered in the area. This time the inquirer actually found JS at the Whitmers. There Bauder, a Christian Primitivist, pried all he could out of the young prophet. Having already determined that JS was one of the "anti-christian" "imposters," Bauder thereafter published a volume where he called the Book of Mormon a "horrid blasphemy" and because JS "could give me no christian experience," condemned him. That is, like others claiming divine commission by way of an extraordinary encounter with heaven, JS failed to convince him he had experienced such an event.[99] (This suggests JS chose not tell Bauder about his First Vision.) Undoubtedly there were numerous others who encountered the upstart religion that exerted such a negative influence in their own circles.[100]

As mentioned, JS clearly took note of what had been said about him from his entrance into the public square. It had to have been a daunting prospect to counter the negativity that had characterized everything that had been previously written about him and his church. Given the significant published impact of Ezra Booth's defection, along with local gossip and other contributing factors, it is reasonable that in 1832 JS recognized the necessity of entering the public arena with his personal story to mollify what he perceived to be public concerns. And while it is not demonstrable that any one, two, or three effects moved JS to sit with Frederick G. Williams to create a narrative, enough surrounding evidence exists to suggest that JS recognized the necessity of publicly explaining himself. That apprehension is something that he addressed more than once during the formative years of Mormonism. Though the 1832 History was never made public in his life, the document and its context hints to us much about the young prophet, his motivations, fears, and determinations. In any case, despite the popularity of JS's later "History of Joseph Smith," which chronicles the summary of his life, his 1832 History serves as an important marker for the time that should not be minimized as his life and history is later measured.

98. David Marks, *The Life of David Marks: To the 26th Year of His Age* (Limerick, ME: Office of the Morning Star, 1831), 340–41.

99. Peter Bauder, *The Kingdom and Gospel of Jesus Christ: Contrasted with That of Anti-Christ* (Canojoharie, NY: A. H. Calhoun, 1834), 36–37. For the expectation of divine intervention to confirm a person's call to the ministry, see Howe, *What Hath God Wrought*, 171, and Tyler, *Freedom's Ferment*, 35.

100. See also the descriptive reports of Nancy Towle and Richard McNemar, which also help portray how people felt about JS and the Mormons at the time. Nancy Towle, *Vicissitudes Illustrated. In the Experience of Nancy Towle, in Europe and America* (Charleston, SC: James L. Burges, 1832), 137–47; Christian Goodwillie, "Shaker Richard McNemar: The Earliest Book of Mormon Reviewer," *Journal of Mormon History* 37, no. 2 (Spring 2011): 138–45.

CHAPTER 8

Order of the Priesthood

Restoration

From Mormonism's beginning, fundamental to the proposition that a restoration of Jesus's gospel was necessary were the words JS wrote in 1832 that he attributed to Jesus in his First Vision. The "world lieth in sin ~~and~~ at this time and none doeth good no not one," Jesus told him. Those who once tended the Christian faith "have turned asside from the gospel and keep not <my> commandments[.] they draw near to me with their lips while their hearts are far from me and mine anger is kindling against the inhabitants of the earth to visit them acording to their ungodliness and to bring to pass that which <hath> been spoken by the mouth of the prophets and Ap[o]stles."[1] Just months before the 1832 History was written, JS obtained a November 1831 revelation, later included as the intended preface to what became the Doctrine and Covenants, explaining the situation requiring a renewal of God's work in the last days.[2] JS stated that Jesus coached him with these words about contemporary religious circumstances: they "have broken mine everlasting Covenant" and "seek not the Lord to establish his righteousness." Instead, "every man walked in his own way & after the ~~imge~~ Image of his own God whose Image is in the likeness of the world & whose substance is that of an Idol which waxeth old & shall perish in Babylon even Babylon the great."[3] The communications confirmed to JS as a youth what he had felt about the status of the world around him: "My intimate acquaintance with those of differant denominations led me to marvel excedingly for I discovered that <they did not ~~adorn~~> ~~instead of~~ adorn~~ing~~ their profession by a holy

1. Smith, Histories, "circa summer 1832," *JSP, H1*:15. The essence of the statement appeared in his 1838/39 history as well, Smith, Histories, "History Drafts, 1838–circa 1841," Draft 2, *JSP, H1*:214.
2. Joseph Smith et al., comps. *Doctrine and Covenants of the Church of the Latter Day Saints: Carefully Selected from the Revelations of God* (Kirtland, OH: F. G. Williams, 1835).
3. Smith, Revelations, November 1, 1831, *JSP, R1*:174–75 [D&C 1:15–16 (1981)].

walk and Godly conversation agreeable to what I found contained in that sacred depository [the Bible]."[4]

JS's rehearsal of his circumstances implied that within the culture he lived, and from his own acquaintance with the Bible, he drew conclusions that nudged him in his mid-teens toward his visit to the stand of trees near his parents' home. That culture, framed not only by the newness of national identity but also the Protestant slant on Christianity, inherently included the concept that the New Testament church had been perverted and that God had withdrawn himself from intervention in the affairs of mankind. This obviously was an anti-Catholic posture. Catholics, from their continuing immigration to America numbered approximately two hundred thousand in 1820 in America when JS was a young man.[5] Their presence provoked derision by evangelicals, Calvinists, Methodists, and others of the day. Anti-Catholic sentiment, centuries old by JS's time, included the difficult to ignore branding of the Roman church and its papal leader as the anti-Christ once decried by New Testament prognosticators. As an inheritor of his surrounding Protestant culture, it is reasonable to assign those feelings to JS, who was religiously groomed in the generalities of his countrymen. Protestants generally held a view arguing that Jesus's church had continued through the ages but that Catholics had taken it away from its original purity. Hence, the need for the Protestant *Reformation*. The apostle Paul's New Testament declarations served as proof texts for later Protestants, warning that what had been established in his time suffered the potential of perversion and destruction. "I know this, that after my departing shall grievous wolves enter in among you, not sparing the flock" (Acts 20:29); and "Let no man deceive you by any means: for that day shall not come, except there come a falling away first" (2 Thess. 2:3–4). Numerous other biblical evidences suggested to nineteenth-century Protestant Americans that Jesus's church waned after the death of the apostles and had left little vestige of what Jesus intended. Justifying their own existence, they usually laid the blame to Catholicism.[6]

The Bible contained apocalyptic texts used by the later Protestant world to justify their validation to separate from the mother church. John's book of Revelation, also termed the Apocalypse, contains passages that later Reformationists insisted be read as condemnations of the remnant Christian church. Though modern scholarship has noted that the book of Revelation "was composed as resistance literature to meet a crisis," i.e., the contemporary "ruthless persecu-

4. Smith, Histories, "circa summer 1832," *JSP, H1*:11.

5. Wood, *Empire of Liberty*, 593. By mid-nineteenth century, Catholics were the largest religious group in America. Marty, *Pilgrims in Their Own Land*, 272.

6. Marty, *Pilgrims in Their Own Land*, 44–47; Garry Wills, *Head and Heart: A History of Christianity in America* (New York: Penguin Books, 2007), 77–78.

tion of the early church by the Roman authorities,"[7] Protestants used the texts for their own purposes. Many took the imagery stated within describing "Babylon the Great," "Mother of Harlots," and "Abominations of the earth" as direct references to Catholics to substantiate their dissent from Rome.[8] The Book of Mormon and revelatory texts produced by JS contained passages that portrayed similar sentiments. Nephi, a principal Book of Mormon figure, stated that hundreds of years before Jesus's birth an angel appeared to him and said: "Thou hast beheld that the Book [Bible] proceeded forth from the mouth of a Jew; and when it proceeded forth from the mouth of a Jew, it contained the plainness of the Gospel of the Lord, of whom the twelve apostles bear record." Following its pristine delivery, the truth went "forth by the hand of the twelve apostles of the Lamb, from the Jews unto the Gentiles." But it then became corrupted by "a great and abominable church, which is the most abominable above all other churches; for behold, they have taken away from the Gospel of the Lamb, many parts which are plain and most precious; and also, many Covenants of the Lord have they taken away." According to the Book of Mormon the dilution of original Christianity was by evil design: "All this have they done, that they might pervert the right ways of the Lord; that they might blind the eyes and harden the hearts of the children of men" (1 Ne. 13:24–27).[9] It became obvious to many, given the sequence described, that Nephi's vision prophetically identified the Roman church as the culprit that perverted the Bible.[10] It is evident that JS embraced the sentiments toward Catholicism held by his Protestant neighbors.

Mormonism in its formative years had little connection with Catholicism, but the prevailing dismissal by Protestants of all things Catholic fed Mormon thinking about how the Roman church figured into what they viewed as the demise of New Testament Christianity. JS represented in January 1833 his thinking about the status of the post-early Christian era by what he wrote to a Rochester, New York, editor—Noah C. Saxton. Stipulating the Mormon view of what had

7. "The Revelation to John," in *The Catholic Study Bible*, ed. Donald Senior et al. (New York: Oxford University Press, 1990), 399.

8. See Rev. 17:1, 5–6, 15, 18, Rev. 18:2–3, 12–13, Rev. 19:2.

9. See also 1 Ne. 13:5–6, 8, 26, 28, 1 Ne. 14:3, 9–13, 15–17, 1 Ne. 22:13–14; 2 Ne. 6:12, 2 Ne. 10:16, 2 Ne. 28:18; D&C 29:21, D&C 88:94.

10. Modern Mormon general authority Bruce R. McConkie explicitly dubbed the Catholic Church the "great and abominable church" in his 1958 *Mormon Doctrine*, though later concerns from his peers pressured him to revise his earlier designation of the Catholics as the "most abominable above all other churches." Bruce R. McConkie, *Mormon Doctrine* (Salt Lake City: Bookcraft, 1958), 108, 129, 135. The book's second edition eliminated specific references to Catholicism and summarized non-Mormon churches as the "Church of the Devil." See McConkie, *Mormon Doctrine*, 2nd ed. (Salt Lake City: Bookcraft, 1966), 137–39.

happened after the death of the ancient apostles, he stated, "we may look at the Christian world and see the apostacy there has been from the Apostolic platform."[11] The apostasy referred to here had echoes of a door slamming shut followed by what many Protestants in the world later described as the "dark ages."[12] Mormons and others, ignorant of the history of the post-New Testament period, followed the Protestant Reformation evidence that Christianity descended into corrupt form requiring the necessity of a godly renewal authorizing his power and particular influence upon those chosen to prepare the world for Jesus's second coming.

JS's followers therefore advanced the concept of a great apostasy into their preachments about Mormonism and its declarations. Sidney Rigdon, for example, informed by his earlier association with the Campbellites, wrote a series titled "The Millenium" from December 1833 to August 1834 in Mormonism's *Evening and the Morning Star*. Rigdon used the apostasy as the catalyst to explain God's work in the last days.[13] Later, in another instance quoted by a correspondent of the *Ohio Free Press*, JS's second-in-command stated "the direct communications with the Almighty, which have been long lost or suspended, in consequence of the general apostacy and the teaching of the false prophets" had been supplanted by the restoration.[14] Other Mormons in the church's formative

11. Joseph Smith to Noah C. Saxton, January 4, 1833, *JSP, D2*:352.

12. Recent Mormon scholarship has attempted to reverse the negative generalization of the "great apostasy" that became a Mormon tradition. See Eric R. Dursteler, "Inheriting the 'Great Apostasy': The Evolution of Latter-day Saint Views on the Middle Ages and the Renaissance," in *Early Christians in Disarray: Contemporary LDS Perspectives on the Christian Apostasy*, ed. Noel B. Reynolds (Provo, UT: Foundation for Ancient Research and Mormon Studies, BYU Press, 2005), 29–65. See also Eric R. Dursteler, "Historical Periodization in the LDS Great Apostasy Narrative," in *Standing Apart: Mormon Historical Consciousness and the Concept of Apostasy*, ed. Miranda Wilcox and John D. Young (New York: Oxford University Press, 2014), 23–54; and Spencer E. Young, "'Complexity and Richness': Reenvisioning the Middle Ages for Mormon Historical Narratives," in Wilcox and Young, *Standing Apart*, 242–64. BYU Professor Charles R. Harrell, gave a general overview of "The Great Apostasy" and how it has been perceived in Mormon history in his *"This is My Doctrine:" The Development of Mormon Theology* (Salt Lake City: Greg Kofford Books, 2011), 31–45.

Despite the revisionistic view about the Middle Ages, other modern LDS commentators and church leaders continue to frame the milieu as a time when God withdrew himself from the affairs of men in the period preceding JS, though the concept is sometimes presented in less pejorative terms. See Jackson, *From Apostasy to Restoration*, 8–56; Tad R. Callister, *The Inevitable Apostasy and the Promised Restoration* (Salt Lake City: Deseret Book, 2006); and Reynolds, *Early Christians in Disarray.*

13. [Sidney Rigdon], "The Millenium," *Evening and the Morning Star*, January 1834, 126–27; February 1834, 131; June 1834, 162; and July 1834, 169.

14. "Latter Day Saints," *Ohio Free Press*, in *Evening and the Morning Star*, May 1836, 315.

period, not surprisingly, reflected similar sentiments.[15] W. W. Phelps upon acquiring designation as the church printer, began his June 1832 publication the *Evening and the Morning Star*, with the avowal "that the most plain parts of the New Testament, have been taken from it by the Mother of Harlots while it was confined in that Church—say, from the year AD 460 to 1400."[16] He used the judgment to justify the necessity of JS revising the King James Bible, then underway.

The universal apostasy became a foundational premise of the Mormons to describe the necessity of God's restorative work in the last days. It became the reasoning behind their assertion that God had to reignite his ancient gospel for modern man. Orson Pratt in his missionary service often used the sequential tact of prefacing the restoration of the gospel by noting the apostasy from "the faith once delivered to the saints, the falling away of the church, the losing of the authority of the priesthood," followed by "the restoration of the church by Ministering of an Angel, Rev. 4th chap."[17] It is demonstrable that in the minds of the Mormons, as it was among their Protestant contemporaries, the perception

15. The church's second periodical, running from October 1834 to November 1837—Kirtland's *Latter Day Saints' Messenger and Advocate*—included in one of its early issues the statement by American reformer Roger Williams describing his recognition that the apostasy had created a situation warranting a renewal of ancient Christianity: "The true church and ministry, had been lost in the Romish apostasy, and could be again restored, only by a special Apostle raised up for that purpose," in "A Summary," *Messenger and Advocate*, April 1835, 103. See also "The Saints of the Last Days," *Messenger and Advocate*, May 1836, 308. Mormon apostle Orson Hyde's "Prophetic Warning" in *Messenger and Advocate*, July 1836, 344, stated: "How plain it is, therefore, that a great apostasy, from the true apostolic order of worship, has taken place."

There remain vestiges of the early Mormon posture. In 1960 church leaders assigned male adults to read T. Edgar Lyon, *Apostasy to Restoration* (Salt Lake City: Deseret Book, 1960), a three-hundred-page volume that chronicled "Christianity in the Graeco-Roman World" to the nineteenth century. For a generalization of early Mormon attitudes toward the "great apostasy," see Richard E. Bennett and Amber J. Seidel, "'A World in Darkness': Early Latter-day Saint Understanding of the Apostasy, 1830–1834," in Reynolds, *Early Christians in Disarray*, 67–99.

16. "Selected," *Evening and the Morning Star*, June 1832, [3].

17. Orson Pratt, *The Orson Pratt Journals*, ed. Elden J. Watson (Salt Lake City: Elden J. Watson, 1975), June 26, 1836, 84–85. See also the Pratt journals for March 1, 1835, 48–49; March 13, 1835, 52; June 2, 1835, 65; August 3, 1835, 68; July 7, 1836, 85–86; July 21, 1836, 87. For other strategies used by early missionaries in their service, see Steven C. Harper, "Missionaries in the American Religious Marketplace: Mormon Proselyting in the 1830s," *Journal of Mormon History* 24, no. 2 (Fall 1998): 1–29.

After the dust settled following JS's death, Pratt advanced at length the significance of "The Universal Apostacy, or the Seventeen Centuries of Darkness." Orson Pratt, *A Series of Pamphlets* (Liverpool: Franklin D. Richards, 1852), 97–112. Also, in his October 31, 1848, "The Kingdom of God," no. 2, part I, 6, Pratt wrote, "Nothing is more certain than that the church of God ceased to exist on the earth when new revelation ceased to be given."

existed that the perversion of Christianity at the hands of the Catholics had interrupted God's plan of redemption. Advancement of the apostasy as the precursor to JS's call from God became a central tenet of Mormonism.[18]

The Consciousness of Authority in Early Mormonism

The premise of having the necessary godly authority to represent heaven had well-known precedence in the New Testament. Jesus's encounter in Matthew 21 with "the chief priests and the elders" where they demanded "By what authority doest thou these things? and who gave thee this authority?" illustrated the relevance of the issue at the time (Matt. 21:23). JS's own consciousness about authorization to act in behalf of God is exhibited in his production of the Book of Mormon where some of the characters had "authority from God," and it was stated that "none had authority to preach" unless they had been commissioned "from God" (Mos. 21:33, 37). It was clear that the component of godly authorization was part of the theology and practice contained in the book. Also understood was that there was an "order" in distribution of that authority (Alma 13:1). Within that "holy order" some of those that acted on God's behalf were recognized by designation of the role they served among the people. Many "were ordained and became high priests of God; and it was on account of their exceeding faith and repentance, and their righteousness before God" (Alma 13:10). Consequently, they "taught with power and authority" (Alma 17:3). A component of implied church organization is also evident within the text; those who held the authority were given "power to baptize" and to "give the Holy Ghost" to believers (3 Ne. 11:21, Moro. 2:2). Also explicit in the Book of Mormon record is the oft-repeated description of the church of God that included notions of God's authority being controlled and administered within the church. It should be no surprise that JS from his work on the Book of Mormon anticipated that the book he produced provided a pattern recognizing the centrality of authority, important for the future he was trying to create.

The word priesthood has been used interchangeably with authority among Mormons for generations. However, it has been well established that the idea of godly authority predated the later representation of priesthood in concept and reference in the early church. Even later Latter-day Saint leaders recognized that the nomenclature about godly power was transitional, as evidenced in Joseph F. Smith's 1889 essay on the "Restoration of the Melchisedec Priesthood." Referencing the June 1831 church conference where the "high priesthood" was established

18. Mormon descriptions of the apostasy are legion in Mormon writings beginning in the nineteenth century. The concept became institutionalized at the beginning of the twentieth century by B. H. Roberts's introduction to his edit of the *History of the Church*, 1:40–94; and James E. Talmage, *The Great Apostasy: Considered in the Light of Scriptural and Secular History* (Salt Lake City: Deseret News, 1909).

in the church, he stated, "until about the time this conference was held, the term *Melchisedec* Priesthood was seldom or never used."[19] Joseph Smith Papers editors explained, "extant records up to June 1831 did not call such authority 'priesthood'; that term—while appearing in both the Book of Mormon and in JS's Bible revision—did not appear in any other contemporary documents until the minutes of a June 1831 conference, which noted that several individuals 'were ordained to the high Priesthood.'"[20]

Research by Mormon scholars in the past generation has also produced an extensive compilation of the historical documentation where priesthood restoration by early Mormons is asserted, specifically referring to JS and Oliver Cowdery's early experiences with divine beings.[21] Perhaps surprisingly, besides reference to the lesser priesthood restoration in his histories—i.e., "Church History" and his 1838/39 history, prepared by his clerks/historians—the prophet's own experiences regarding priesthood restoration are limited to brief references of the event in several revelations, so-called patriarchal blessings, meeting minutes, and conversational reinforcement to church members.[22] And while what JS stated he experienced will always be the focal point regarding Mormon beginnings, it is Oliver's explicit assertions that may best summarize their joint claims given the circumstances of his life and breadth of his witness. One must appreciate Cowdery's centrality to Mormon beginnings and his subsequent journey where he spent as much time out as in the faith.

Though unchurched in 1838 and minimized thereafter in Mormon circles, Oliver maintained to the end of his life his affirmations of what he and JS witnessed with John the Baptist. This, despite there being no advantage to him to

19. Joseph F. Smith, "Restoration of the Melchisedec Priesthood," *Contributor*, June 1889, 311.
20. "Historical Introduction" to "Revelation, 22–23 September 1832 [D&C 84]," *JSP, D*2:290.
21. In June 1988 I prepared, "The Restoration of the Priesthood: Understanding the Role of the Melchizedek and Aaronic Priesthoods in the Early Church in Light of Priesthood Restoration Narratives," upon which much of this chapter is based. The source documentation I provided in that study, identifying the references to priesthood restoration by early Latter-day Saints, was later used by Brian Q. Cannon and the *BYU Studies* Staff in "Priesthood Restoration Documents," *BYU Studies* 35, no. 4 (1995); Brian Cannon et al., "Seventy Contemporaneous Priesthood Restoration Documents," in Welch, *Opening the Heavens*, 215–63. See also Brian Q. Cannon and *BYU Studies* Staff, "Oliver Cowdery and the Restoration of the Priesthood," in *Oliver Cowdery: Scribe, Elder, Witness*, ed. John W. Welch and Larry E. Morris (Provo, UT: Neal A. Maxwell Institute for Religious Scholarship, 2006), 133–53. Other treatments include Steven C. Harper, "Oliver Cowdery as Second Witness of Priesthood Restoration," in *Days Never to Be Forgotten: Oliver Cowdery*, ed. Alexander L. Baugh (Provo, UT: Religious Studies Center, Brigham Young University, 2009), 73–89; and a Joseph Smith Papers compilation, http://www.josephsmithpapers.org/site/priesthood-restoration?p=1&highlight=priesthood%20restoration.
22. Cannon et al., "Seventy Contemporaneous Priesthood Restoration Documents," 233–41.

return to Mormonism when he did. After his father, William Jr., died in Kirtland, Oliver and his wife (the daughter of Peter Whitmer Sr.) separated from Mormonism in 1838, near the same time as did his brother Warren, who had once been JS's scribe. Oliver's in-laws, the influential Whitmers who were still alive, were themselves gone from fellowship near the same time and did not return. This included Book of Mormon witness Hiram Page, whose wife was a Whitmer and sister of Oliver's wife, who also rejected the church in 1838. If anything, their departures were motives for Oliver *not* to reconnect with the religion. Cowdery's return to the faith in 1848, with his attendant declarations within two years of his death confirming his and JS's experience with John the Baptist and Jesus's apostles, do not prove what he and JS said happened to them. But, Cowdery's circumstances and what he stated, as described below, must be appreciated for their evidential value to Mormon claims. Detractors have pointed to Cowdery's dissonance with JS and such things as his attendance while away from the church at Methodist meetings in Tiffin, Ohio, claiming they indicate his wavering nature. There is no credible evidence, however, that he fought against or declaimed his Mormon affiliation or experiences.[23]

Cowdery met JS in early April 1829 at JS's domicile in Harmony, in northeastern Pennsylvania, near the Susquehanna River. Their subsequent work producing text from the gold plates provoked them to inquire of God about the premise of authority as explicitly portrayed in what they had been dictating/writing. Neither JS nor Cowdery committed to paper their May 15, 1829, experience with John the Baptist until several years later.[24] In the October 1834 issue of the *Latter*

23. See, however, Dan Vogel's rejection of Cowdery's witness, where Vogel stated Cowdery's several affirmations of priesthood restoration events are "doubtful and anachronistic," and that Cowdery was prone to "freely expand" and "alter" the documentary record. This pattern, according to Vogel, included his criticism that Cowdery "probably...invented" his collaborative experience with JS in their reception of the priesthood from John the Baptist and Peter, James, and John. This can be explained, Vogel asserted, given Cowdery's "propensity for visions" that fit the definition of "hallucination." Ultimately, Vogel dismissed Cowdery's veracity as a reliable explicator of the truth, insisting "one should not take [Cowdery] too seriously," as "his testimony is suspect." Dan Vogel, "Evolution of Early Mormon Priesthood Narratives," *John Whitmer Historical Association Journal* 34, no. 1 (Spring/Summer 2014): 68, 70–71, 73, 76. Vogel's disqualification of Cowdery conforms to his other rejections of the divine in evaluating JS and Mormon claims. See his Introduction to *Joseph Smith: The Making of a Prophet* (Salt Lake City: Signature Books, 2004).

From a surprising source, see also refutation of later attempts to discredit Cowdery's affirmative witness about Mormon origins from Jerald and Sandra Tanner's "Mormon and Anti-Mormon Forgeries," in *Salt Lake City Messenger*, October 1989. http://www.utlm.org/newsletters/no73.htm. See also Anderson's "Did Oliver Cowdery, One of the Three Special Book of Mormon Witnesses, Express Doubt about His Testimony?"

24. This is undoubtedly one of the reasons that David Whitmer and William McLellin later claimed to have never heard about the priesthood restoration prior to 1834, as described below.

Day Saints' Messenger and Advocate, which Cowdery edited, he stated that while he and JS reviewed Jesus's ministry to the Nephites during their translation of 3 Nephi in the Book of Mormon, they reflected together on the condition of the Christian world at the time. It was, he wrote, "easily to be seen, that amid the great strife and noise concerning religion, none had authority from God to administer the ordinances of the gospel." The situation reflected their consciousness about the apostasy following the death of Jesus's apostles. Following their query, to their surprise and delight, after hearing "the voice of Jesus," "the angel of God came down clothed with glory, and delivered the anxiously looked for message." Dazzled by what they witnessed in the vision, under the angel's "hand" they were given the "priesthood and this authority," providing one of the most basic of the Mormon premises of validity. The Baptist's words tied JS and Oliver's experience to a biblical chain of events to precede Jesus's return: "Upon you my fellow servants, in the name of Messiah I confer this priesthood and this authority, which shall remain upon earth that the sons of Levi may yet offer an offering unto the Lord in righteousness."[25]

Disputes of Priesthood Restoration Claims

Such a claim, confirming though it may be to believers then and now, comparably aroused those critical of JS and Oliver's experiences. Detractors refute the entire contention, insisting that JS and Cowdery invented their stories. Because of Mormon claims about the apostasy and their assertions of heavenly ministrations to JS, critics have turned the study of the history of priesthood restoration and its impact upon Mormonism into an antipodal, binary argument. Because the story was not written down as it happened, and since it is beyond empirical proof, JS and Cowdery's skeptics rest their arguments. Two examples illustrate

25. Cowdery to Phelps, September 7, 1834, in *Messenger and Advocate*, October 1834, 15–16. James Mulholland, as JS's clerk/historian in preparation of JS's "History of Joseph Smith" in 1839, tweaked the angel's language from what Cowdery had written to: "Upon you my fellow servants, in the name of Messiah, I confer the priesthood of Aaron, which holds the keys of the ministering of angels, and of the gospel of repentance, and of baptism by immersion for the remission of sins, and this shall never be taken again from the earth, until the sons of Levi do offer again an offering unto the Lord in righteousness." The alteration suggests, in this particular instance, JS's involvement in the content of his history. Joseph Smith, "History of Joseph Smith," *Times and Seasons*, August 1, 1842, 865, 866; Smith, Histories, "History Drafts, 1838–circa 1841," Draft 2, *JSP, H1*:292. The wording from the "History of Joseph Smith" became part of the Pearl of Great Price in 1851 and was added to the Doctrine and Covenants in 1876 as Section 13. Woodford, "Historical Development of the Doctrine and Covenants," 233–38. See also Mark Staker's treatment of the language of the two renditions of the event and other features for consideration of the lesser priesthood restoration in "'Commissioned of Jesus Christ': Oliver Cowdery and D&C 13," in *You Shall Have My Word: Exploring the Text of the Doctrine and Covenants*, ed. Scott C. Esplin, Richard O. Cowan, and Rachel Cope (Provo, UT: Religious Studies Center, Brigham Young University, 2012), 50–63.

the contention. Mormon detractors Ed Decker, a former Mormon, and Dave Hunt, a Christian apologist, in their 1984 blockbuster critique of Mormonism, *The Godmakers* (with accompanying film in 1983), asserted that "the evidence points to the conclusion that the [priesthood restoration accounts by JS and Cowdery were] fabricated in order to enhance the image of the Mormon Church in the eyes of its critics and to shore up the 'Prophet's' sagging authority in the face of mounting rebellion." Presented without any discussion of the historical context required to properly understand the milieu in which JS and Cowdery worked, *The Godmakers'* claims assert that "had these events actually occurred, they would undoubtedly have been among the first 'proofs' mentioned to prospective converts then as now; and had they been known, it is unthinkable that they wouldn't have been mentioned by *anyone*." Decker and Hunt therefore insist that "one can only conclude that these crucial events for the establishment of the Mormon Church did not in fact ever happen."[26] The critics' arguments suggest that everything before and after the claims of priesthood restoration by JS are the manufacture of a delusional and calculating charlatan determined to prop up himself as a religious despot. Cowdery was his willing dupe. They argue that JS was counterfeit because God would never condescend to such a palpably absurd bestowal of authority. Their arguments contribute to the environment referred to earlier, which shapes the modern discussion about priesthood restoration to an either/or proposition that generally ignores the importance of the event in light of how it affected the restoration thereafter.

Challenges to priesthood restoration claims are not just modern assertions. The debate about JS's spiritual claims was hatched in the decades that followed his death, especially among those who reconsidered their previous affiliation with Mormonism. William E. McLellin, one of the charter members of the Quorum of the Twelve Apostles, left Mormonism in the late 1830s, and subsequently scorned Mormon claims of priesthood restoration. While he affirmed the position that JS had obtained godly authority at one time, he later fought against JS and Oliver Cowdery's foundational claims about obtaining authorization via John the Baptist in 1829. In 1872, McLellin wrote to JS's son Joseph III, then the leader of the RLDS Church: "As to the story of John the Baptist ordaining Joseph and Oliver on the day they were baptized: I never heard of it in the church for years, altho I carefully noticed things that were said. And today I do not believe the story."[27] Another who criticized JS's claims of priesthood restoration was

26. Ed Decker and Dave Hunt, *The Godmakers* (Eugene, OR: Harvest House, 1984), 203–4. This expression mirrored Fawn M. Brodie's earlier conclusion that Joseph Smith invented his claims of divine visitations, see Brodie, *No Man Knows My History*, 25.

27. William E. McLellin to Joseph Smith III, July 1872, Independence, Missouri, in *The William E. McLellin Papers, 1854–1880*, ed. Stan Larson and Samuel J. Passey (Salt Lake City: Signature Books, 2007), 491, 492; see also McLellin's May 24, 1870, letter to D. H. Bays

David Whitmer. Whitmer had been one of JS's most important allies during the church's infancy and, supposedly, someone who might be expected to intimately know the founder's thinking and secrets. Whitmer submitted to an interview regarding the early days of Mormonism in 1885 with Zenos Gurley, an RLDS Church advocate at the time. Whitmer had been estranged from JS and what became the Utah division of Mormonism for almost half a century when he sat with Gurley. Regarding the question of JS's early acquisition of divine authority from heavenly messengers in 1829, the year traditionally accepted by the Mormon faithful, Gurley wrote that Whitmer told him: "I never heard that an angel had ordained Joseph and Oliver to the Aaronic priesthood until the year 1834[,] 5[,] or 6."[28] Both McLellin and Whitmer, who collaborated for several years after their separation from Mormonism, argued, because they had not earlier heard about the event, that JS and Oliver had to have made up the story in the mid-1830s. But as will be explained in Chapter 11, like so many other sacred instances he experienced, JS apparently chose to keep it to himself, as did Cowdery, even from close associates, counter to the logic assumed by Decker and Hunt.

It is also important to note that JS addressed the matter of his restraint in popularizing the story of priesthood restoration. Those cited above who reject

---

where he denied Mormon priesthood claims in *The True Latter Day Saints' Herald*, September 15, 1870, 556. Orson Pratt and Joseph F. Smith also reported visiting McLellin in 1878 whereupon being asked about the priesthood restoration stated he "denounced, in toto, all the revelations in the Doctrine and Covenants, and the idea of the restoration of the priesthood of Melchisedek or of Aaron to man, but believes in the Apostleship which he thinks comprises everything, although he has not faith in the ordination of the first Twelve." "Report of Elders Orson Pratt and Joseph F. Smith," *Latter-day Saints Millennial Star*, December 9, 16, 1878, 769–84, 785–89.

McLellin's perspectives on priesthood once he departed Mormonism are confusing. For example, in 1847–1848 he considered some aspects of JS's priesthood claims to be valid. See McLellin, "James J. Strang, of Voree, Wis.," *Ensign of Liberty of the Church of Christ*, April 1847, 31; McLellin, "Our Principles in Kirtland," *Ensign of the Liberty of the Church of Christ*, March 1848, 67. See also McLellin's January 10, 1861, letter to Joseph III further explaining his views of priesthood in the early church, McLellin, *William E. McLellin Papers*, 440–44. Also complicating McLellin's later stance is the view of Hiram Page who affiliated with him in 1848. One of the eight witnesses of the Book of Mormon (who had also married one of Peter Whitmer Sr.'s daughters), Page left Mormonism in 1838 but later gravitated to McLellin. In a letter on March 4, 1848, he also affirmed: "In the beginning we find the first ordinations were by Peter James and John[.] they ordained Joseph and Oliver; to what priesthood were they ordained; the answer must be to the Holy priesthood on the office of an elder or an apostle which is an additional grace added to the office of an elder[.] these offices Oliver received from those holy messengers before the 6th of april 1830," quoted in Welch, *Opening the Heavens*, 256.

28. Zenos Gurley, "Questions Asked of David Whitmer at His Home in Richmond Ray County Mo, Jan 14 1885," 12–14, MS 4633, CHL; see also David Whitmer, *An Address to All Believers in Christ* (Richmond, MO: self-published, 1887), 64.

priesthood restoration claims, give no credence to the prophet's later explanation, previously mentioned, that "we were forced to keep secret the circumstances of our having been baptized, and having received the priesthood; owing to a spirit of persecution which had already manifested itself in the neighborhood."[29] Given the contentious climate surrounding him, it is not far-fetched to conclude that public censure concerned him and how his intimate sacred experiences were received. He was, by most every measurement, shunned, vilified, and tormented as word of his claims became known, clearly tempering any enthusiasm he might have about exposing himself to public scrutiny. After his initial episodes of rejection, it was several years before JS felt inclined to publicize his acquisition of priestly authority—as perhaps he was planning to do in his 1832 History before he aborted the project.

Oliver Cowdery's Witness

Oliver Cowdery separated from JS and the church in 1838 and remained out of the church for a decade. It is during his dissent and separation from Mormonism—at a time when he could have publicly vented his frustrations at JS and undermined the religion's very foundation of priesthood authority by denying its validity—that Cowdery delivered what was perhaps his most convincing affirmations of what he claimed was his experience with JS. After his disaffection, Cowdery returned to Ohio before moving on to Wisconsin, and in both places, he hung out his lawyer's shingle before reconnecting with the church. JS scholar Scott Faulring portrayed Cowdery's interim circumstances that show, despite Oliver's ire from being maliciously misrepresented by those in Missouri who severed him from Mormonism, he had been open to resolving his differences with the church.[30] Some church leaders had proffered entreaties to him to return during the decade of his absence in the cold. Favorable circumstances, including the exit of some of those who had maligned him in Missouri and Cowdery's proximity to the church in exile in 1848, combined for him to travel to western Iowa to surprise a Mormon conference late that year with his presence.

Knowing about the Mormon exodus westward from Nauvoo, and after the numerous gestures of reconciliation he had received, Cowdery determined to square with his past and rejoin his former cohorts. At Mosquito Creek in western Iowa near Council Bluffs, at an October 1848 church conference for the Saints temporarily settled in the Missouri River valley, the prodigal's eyewitness public declarations about early Mormonism became a phenomenon. Mormon apostle George A. Smith reported the dramatic occurrence to his colleague

29. "History of Joseph Smith" *Times and Seasons*, August 1, 1842, 866; Smith, Histories, "History Drafts, 1838–circa 1841," Draft 2, *JSP, H1*:296. This statement by the prophet concerning persecution is given just after his account of the restoration of the lesser priesthood.
30. Scott H. Faulring, "Return of Oliver Cowdery," in Welch and Morris, *Oliver Cowdery*, 321–62.

Orson Pratt, then in England, who three months later published it to the British Saints: "Oliver Cowdery, who had just arrived from Wisconsin with his family, on being invited, addressed the meeting. He bore testimony in the most positive terms of the truth of the Book of Mormon—the restoration of the priesthood to the earth, and the mission of Joseph Smith as the prophet of the last days." Cowdery "told the people if they wanted to follow the right path, to keep [in] the main channel of the stream—where the body of the Church goes, there is the authority." He further underscored that "this people have the true and holy priesthood; 'for the angel said unto Joseph Smith, jun., in my hearing, that this priesthood shall remain on earth unto the end.' His testimony produced quite a sensation among the gentlemen present who did not belong to the church, and it was gratefully received by all the Saints."[31]

Also in attendance at the conference was Reuben Miller, a thirty-seven-year-old Pennsylvanian who became a Mormon in 1843.[32] Never immersed in Nauvoo Mormonism, he led for a time the Mormon congregation in Norway, Illinois. After JS's death, he met James Jesse Strang in early 1846, drawn to the man who claimed JS had appointed him as his successor. For a brief time, Miller became an ardent advocate for Strang, producing in February 1846 *A Defence of the Claims of James J. Strang to the Authority Now Usurped by the Twelve.*[33] Enamored with Strang, he recruited for the rival of the Twelve Apostles in Nauvoo before joining Strang's colony in southern Wisconsin. But there in proximity to the man, Miller became disillusioned and by midyear separated himself from Strang. He returned to Nauvoo where he embraced the authority of the Twelve Apostles and was rebaptized in the fall of 1846. Determined to rectify his wrong, he recanted his attachment to Strang, publishing in September 1846 before his rebaptism, *James J. Strang, Weighed in the Balance of Truth and Found Wanting.*[34] It is clear from what he wrote that he had resolved that JS had received the priesthood from heavenly emissaries, that JS "was ordained to the Aaronic Priesthood by John the Baptist, and received the keys of the kingdom and of 'the Dispensation of the fullness of times' from Peter, James, and John."[35] Miller's

31. George A. Smith to Orson Pratt, October 20, 1848, Carbonca, Council Bluffs, Iowa, *Latter Day Saints' Millennial Star*, January 1, 1849, 14.
32. For an overview of Miller's life, see Richard Lloyd Anderson, "Reuben Miller, Recorder of Oliver Cowdery's Reaffirmation," *BYU Studies* 8, no. 3 (1968): 277–93.
33. Reuben Miller, *A Defence of the Claims of James J. Strang to the Authority Now Usurped by the Twelve; and Shewing Him to be the True Successor of Joseph Smith, as First President of the High Priesthood* (Burlington, WI: n.p., 1846).
34. Crawley, *Descriptive Bibliography of the Mormon Church*, 1:349–51.
35. Reuben Miller, *James J. Strang, Weighed in the Balance of Truth, and Found Wanting. His Claims as First President of the Melchizedek Priesthood Refuted* (Burlington, WI: n.p., 1846), 12–13. Miller also published another pamphlet against Strang in 1847: *Truth Shall Prevail: A Short Reply to an Article Published in the Voree Herald (Reveille), by J. C. Bennett; and the Willful Falsehoods of J. J. Strang* (Burlington, WI: n.p., 1847).

concern for heavenly authority and how it was restored proved consequential in how he finally settled on Mormon truth claims.

Crossing Iowa in late 1848 to join with the Saints, Reuben Miller arrived at Mosquito Creek on October 15. A week later his journal entry for October 21, 1848, reported Cowdery's testimony to the conference, conveying the same sensation portrayed by George A. Smith to Orson Pratt: "In the early history of this church I stood Identified with her. And [was] one in her Councils." Regarding the Book of Mormon and his role in its production Cowdery stated: "I wrote with my own pen the intire book of Mormon (save a few pages) as it fell from the Lips of the prophet, As he translated <it> by the gift and power of god.... I beheld with my eyes, And handled with my hands the gold plates from which it was translated. I also beheld the Interperters. That book is true. Sidney Rigdon did not write it. Mr Spaulding did not write it. I wrote it myself as it fell from the Lips of the prophet." Cowdery concluded his affirmations declaring, according to Miller: "The channel is here, the priesthood is here. I was present with Joseph when an holy angle [angel] from god came down from heaven and confered, or restored the Aronic priesthood. And said at the same time that it Should remain upon the earth while the earth Stands. I was also present with Joseph when the Melchesideck priesthood was confered by the holy angles of god."[36] Given all that is known about Cowdery at the time, his testimonial, as stated by Miller, about the Book of Mormon and being with JS when "angles" of the Lord appeared to them and conferred upon them the priesthoods cannot be easily dismissed. Cowdery then submitted the following month to baptism by Orson Hyde,[37] whom he had ordained to be one of the original apostles in 1835. While planning to join the Saints in the Salt Lake Valley his health broke. Visiting in Richmond, Missouri, with his Whitmer family members, he died in March 1850.

The reports of George A. Smith and Reuben Miller about Cowdery's confession at the October 1848 conference followed by his rebaptism were the culmination of Cowdery stewing for years about his displacement from the faith, despite his convictions. Two years before the Mosquito Creek conference, Cowdery

36. Reuben Miller, Journal, October 21, 1848, MS 1392, CHL. Two other post-1848 references to Cowdery's affirmations toward the end of his life come from Samuel W. Richards who intersected with Cowdery in the winter of 1848–1849. Cowdery and his wife were stranded during a storm at Richards's home for two weeks, during which time—at Richards's request—on January 13, 1849, Oliver prepared a summary statement regarding restoration events in which he was involved: the coming forth of the Book of Mormon and the priesthood restoration. The account was later published by Richards in Salt Lake City's *Deseret News* on March 22, 1884. Richards also left a written statement on May 21, 1907, where he remembered Cowdery telling him during their winter 1848–1849 visit that "the ministrations of Angels were frequent in restoring Priesthood." Samuel W. Richards, statement, May 21, 1907, MS 3703, CHL.

37. Reuben Miller to Henry Sabey, November 16, 1848, MS 88, CHL.

wrote in March 1846 to Phinehas Young, Brigham's brother, who was Cowdery's brother-in-law and with whom he continued an intimate relationship. The letter's content indicated he had not waned from his earlier assurances. Showing the consistency of his previous declarations, rather than complaining about his dismissal from the church eight years earlier, something Phinehas well knew, Cowdery wrote: "Had you stood in the presence of John ~~and~~ <with> our departed brother Joseph, to receive the Lesser Priesthood and in the presence <of> Peter, to receive the Greater, and looked down through time, and witnessed the effects those two must produce,—you would feel what you have never felt."[38]

Less well known than Cowdery's October 1834 description of John the Baptist appearing to him and JS in 1829 and his 1848 declarations, is his involvement penning a brief narrative found among what came to be known as the initial patriarchal blessings given in the church. Though this account has not been widely disseminated, its credibility is perhaps more telling given the private nature of the expression. The narrative, preceding blessings given by JS to several of his closest associates, is part of what is known as the Patriarchal Blessing Book, found in the Church History Library.[39] Beginning in 1833, JS and his father apparently initiated a practice among the Mormons, undoubtedly based on the biblical patriarch Jacob's fatherly bestowals upon his family.[40] The blessings given by Jacob to his family in Genesis 49 declared the patriarch's and God's specific revelation to the member of his posterity.[41] Rather than patriarchal blessings with which modern Mormons are familiar, as given by local stake patriarchs to individual members, the initial blessing entries in the Patriarchal Blessing Book are familial, those Joseph Smith Sr. gave to his family on December 9, 1834.[42] With the same spirit portrayed by Jacob blessing his posterity in Genesis, Joseph Sr. bestowed heavenly promises on his children and several of their spouses. Oliver Cowdery served as recorder of the blessings. The pertinent matter here involving the Patriarchal Blessing Book concerns a brief narrative prepared by Cowdery that followed his transcription of Joseph Sr.'s blessings to his children and preceded JS's own blessings to his family and others.

38. Oliver Cowdery to Phinehas H. Young, March 23, 1846, MS 2646, CHL. The words "greater" and "higher" were used interchangeably to describe the Melchizedek priesthood.
39. Early Smith blessings associated with the Patriarchal Blessing Book, especially those particular to JS, are well known. See transcriptions found in the Joseph Smith Papers. For a number of reasons, including the sacred nature of patriarchal blessings among Mormons, the Patriarchal Blessing Book and individual patriarchal blessings are not open to research in the Church History Library.
40. See the circumstances and a summary of several December 1833 blessings in Smith, Journals, December 18, 1833, *JSP, J1*:21–24.
41. Gen. 48, 49; John A. Widtsoe, *Evidences and Reconciliations* (1943; repr. Salt Lake City: Bookcraft, 1960), 321–25.
42. Patriarchal Blessing Book, 1833–, CR 500 2, Book 1, CHL.

Oliver's narrative, prepared in September 1835, preceded blessings given by JS to several of his close associates. The narrative provided an important confirmation of Cowdery's 1834 declaration about the lesser priesthood's restoration in the *Messenger and Advocate*.[43] There appears to be no public or institutional motive for inclusion of the priesthood restoration circumstance in the account. While JS and Cowdery translated and transcribed the Book of Mormon in mid-May 1829, the content of the book provoked within them questions about the authority to act for God. Cowdery's narrative stated that he and JS "diligently sought for the right of the fathers, and the authority of the holy priesthood, and the power to admin[ister] in the same." They were, he wrote, "drawn out in mighty prayer to know how we might obtain the blessings of baptism and of the Holy Spirit, according to the order of God." The result: while in "the heavenly vision the angel came down and bestowed upon us this priesthood." That is, the "angel John" appeared to them and ordained them "unto the lesser or Aaronic priesthood...in the town of Harmony, Susquehannah County, Pennsylvania, on Fryday, the 15th day of May, 1829." After the ordination they "repaired to the water, even to the Susquehannah River, and were baptized, he [JS] first ministering unto me and after I to him."[44]

A second and equally consequential statement about JS and Oliver's experience together with John the Baptist also appears in the initial pages of the Patriarchal Blessing Book. In this case, JS personally gave to Cowdery a far-reaching and revealing blessing about his early collaborator. Given on October 2, 1835, as part of the bestowal JS referred to their joint experience when not only did they obtain "by the hand of the angel...the lesser priesthood" but also the greater or higher priesthood "under the hands of th<ose> who had been held in reserve for a long season, even those who rescived it under the hand of the Messiah."[45]

43. The pertinent language about priesthood restoration from this patriarchal blessing was published by Joseph Fielding Smith as early as 1904. Joseph F[ielding]. Smith, "Restoration of the Melchizedek Priesthood," *Improvement Era*, October 1904, 943.

44. Oliver Cowdery narrative, Patriarchal Blessing Book, Book 1, 8–9. The entry concludes: "Oliver Cowdery, clerk and Recorder. Given in Kirtland December 18, 1833, and recorded September 1835." See the explanation by the Joseph Smith Papers editors of the 1833 patriarchal blessings and their expansion/revision in 1835 in "Appendix 5: Blessings to Joseph Smith Sr. and Lucy Mack Smith, Hyrum Smith, Samuel Smith, and William Smith, September 1835," *JSP, D4*:485–94; and "Appendix: Blessings to Don Carlos Smith, Oliver Cowdery, Frederick G. Williams, and Sidney Rigdon, 1–2 October 1835," *JSP, D5*:507–17.

For a description of the plausible site of the Aaronic priesthood restoration, see Mark Lyman Staker, "Where Was the Aaronic Priesthood Restored?: Identifying the Location of John the Baptist's Appearance, May 15, 1829," *Mormon Historical Studies* 12, no. 2 (Fall 2012): 143–59.

45. JS blessing to Oliver Cowdery, October 2, 1835, Patriarchal Blessing Book, 12; Joseph Smith to Oliver Cowdery, October 2, 1835, *JSP, D5*:513–14. Joseph Fielding Smith in 1904,

Again, these references found in the Patriarchal Blessing Book, privately delivered and never meant for distribution or publication, layer more evidence upon the earlier declarations of the men about their experience with John the Baptist.

Primacy of John the Baptist's Priesthood in the Early Church

Mormon priesthood authority and structure appears fixed in the LDS Church today, with the well-defined supremacy of the Melchizedek, or greater, priesthood well known. However, surviving documentation from JS's tenure as church president indicates that church leaders as well as the rank-and-file Saints in the early years viewed the restoration of the Aaronic or lesser priesthood as being at the time *the* essential event in giving the church access to God's legitimizing authority. The strata of power that today includes not only the priesthood of Peter, James, and John, but also that of Moses, Elias, Elijah, and others who conferred their authorities on JS—all fitting under the umbrella of the Melchizedek priesthood—was not systematized during JS's lifetime. In the church's infancy it was the unique visitation of John the Baptist that provided the required power of restoration. Evidence suggests that when Mormon elders and others attempted to explain the religion to inquirers it was the concept of the church having received authority and not the priesthood, per se, that became the burden of their messages.[46] The authority was the authority. The surviving record indicates that church members did not discriminate until much later particulars of the differences between the greater and lesser priesthoods. The contemporary sources, virtually all of church derivation, illustrate that to the early Saints the coming of John the Baptist fulfilled every hope and expectation for authority sufficient to welcome Christ's church and power back to the earth. It is obvious from what has been described above that the prophet and Oliver recognized the coming of Peter, James, and John to be consequential and essential. But the enlarged appreciation of the importance of Jesus's apostles and their role and authority came later. What follows is a sequential rehearsal of the extant sources that illustrate both the understanding of the participators in JS and Cowdery's ordinations and how that information eventually became consumed by church members.

---

suggested this reference to restoration of the higher priesthood may have been the earlier allusion by JS to a follow-up account of the coming of the ancient apostles. Smith, "Restoration of the Melchizedek Priesthood," 943.

46. See, for example, the frequent teaching about priesthood by Orson Pratt in 1833–1835, *Orson Pratt Journals*, June 26, 1833, 19; July 6–7, 18, 1833, 20; August 4, 1833, 22; August 11, 1833, 23; September 1, 1833, 24; December 21, 1833, 28; March 30, 1834, 37; April 5, 1835, 55; William E. McLellin, *The Journals of William E. McLellin: 1831–1836*, ed. Jan Shipps and John W. Welch (Provo, UT: BYU Studies and University of Illinois Press, 1994), 193 (August 4, 1835); Edward Partridge to "Dear Brother," May 26, 1839, Edward Partridge Papers, MS 892, folder 7, CHL.

The month of February 1834 became important for several innovations to church infrastructure, including delivery of general and local protocols of church governance. A Thursday evening, February 12, gathering of priesthood brethren who met at JS's Kirtland home served as another forum for JS to state his experience. Opening the meeting with prayer, the prophet "then rose and said: I shall now endeavour to set forth before this Council, the dignity of the office which has been conferred upon me by the ministering of the Angel of God, by his own voice and by the voice of this Church."[47] While we do not today enjoy an elaboration by JS of exactly what he meant in describing the source of his authority at that moment, it is clear from other documentation that he pointed to the appearance of John the Baptist to him and Oliver Cowdery in May 1829 as their empowerment. Cowdery shared the perception. Just a year later, on the occasion of the blessing of several members of the newly called Twelve Apostles on February 21, 1835, Cowdery, one of those designated to identify the Twelve, gave the new apostles a "Charge." He read to them portions of the revelation received by JS in June 1829 that listed the personal qualities incumbent in their callings, followed by a reminder of the source of their authority: "You have been ordained to the Holy Priesthood, You have received it from those who had their power and Authority from an angel."[48] The statements above given by the only two earthly participants in the restoration of the lesser and greater priesthoods alluded to the fact that their ordination from "the angel" to the lesser priesthood was of singular importance. Were these merely scribal errors or inadvertent substitutions of the singular *angel* for the plural *angels* that referenced Jesus's apostles? Other documents bear out the view that it was not an incidental error in historical recording but a manifestation of the place in the early church of John the Baptist's role, and consequently the priesthood he delivered.[49]

As stated earlier, the seminal importance to JS of the First Vision was generally not known or appreciated among the church members at the time. The Book of Mormon was the material evidence of JS's call. But the feature of restoration that underscored and justified everything as the church grew and developed was the priesthood, God's means of authorizing and ordering the fledgling church. The developmental process understood as priesthood authorization is explained in part by evidence that the importance of the restoration of the

47. Smith, Documents, February 12, 1834, Minute Book 1, *JSP, D3*:429. I propose that "the dignity of the office" of which JS spoke referred to the presidency and leadership of the church. There is little else to fit the situation.

48. Book of Commandments, Chapter 15 (1833); D&C 18 (1981); Smith, Documents, February 21, 1835, Minute Book 1, *JSP, D4*:243.

49. Others have recognized the situation. Richard L. Bushman also stated that in the early years of the church "the question of Melchisedek Priesthood restoration was not of notable importance at that time." Bushman, *Joseph Smith and the Beginnings of Mormonism*, 241n55.

priesthood through "the angel" moved from JS's and Oliver's personal experiences to recognition of its empowering significance for church members by the laity in the mid-1830s. W. W. Phelps, one of the most significant contributors to the corpus of thought in early Mormonism, penned several hymns that were included in the church's first hymnal printed in Kirtland in 1835. Phelps, who after Emma Smith's initial charge to create a hymnal actually took the volume to publication, penned in one of the hymns he contributed a stanza referring to priesthood restoration:

> And an angel surely then,
> For a blessing unto men,
> Brought the priesthood back again,
> In its ancient purity.[50]

The only reference to priesthood restoration in the first hymnal, inclusion of the matter-of-fact assertion that it was "an angel" that returned the priesthood suggests that Phelps affirmed a notion already understood by the Saints.[51]

The same year the hymnal appeared, poet and apostle Parley P. Pratt published in pamphlet form *The Millennium, a Poem*, conveying the same message regarding priesthood restoration. The title of Song III was "The Opening of the Dispensation of the Fulness of Times." It read, in part:

> Again an angel did appear,
> As witnesses do record bear.
> Restored the priesthood, long since lost,
> In truth and power, as at the first;
> Thus commissioned from on high,
> Came forth and did repentance cry.[52]

Once more, the inclusion of the concept of "an angel" being the means of delivery of the priesthood, without subsequent apostolic authority, appears to be implicit in context.

50. Emma Smith, comp., *A Collection of Sacred Hymns for the Church of the Latter Day Saints* (Kirtland, Ohio: F. G. Williams, 1835), 33. This is hymn number 25, "Now We'll Sing with One Accord," in the current LDS hymnal (1985).

51. The same hymn was published as "Hymn 6" three years later in David Rogers's hymnal for the church, *A Collection of Sacred Hymns for the Church of the Latter Day Saints, Selected and Published by David W. Rogers* (New York: C. Vinten, 1838). It should also be noted that this 1838 hymnal acknowledged what by that time was a more expanded understanding of priesthood restoration: "In ancient days men fear'd the Lord, / And by their faith received his word, / Then God bestowed upon the meet, / The Priesthood of Melchizedek" (Hymn 21).

52. Parley P. Pratt, *The Millennium, A Poem: To Which Is Added Hymns and Songs* (Boston: Parley P. Pratt, 1835), 38.

The following year, Stephen Post—who had in 1835 joined with the Latter Day Saints, as they were then known—detailed in his journal the events surrounding the dedication of the Kirtland House of the Lord. He wrote that after JS delivered the dedicatory prayer on March 27, 1836, followed by the administration of the sacramental emblems of bread and wine to those gathered, "Joseph Smith, Jun. testified of the Angel of the Lord [Moroni] appearing unto him to call him to the work of the Lord, & also of being ordained under the hands of the Angel of the covenant [John the Baptist]."[53] On this very important occasion, without mentioning the return of Jesus's apostles, JS noted to the Saints the principal event that authorized performance of his ministerial and administrative duties in the last days. At that time, the authority given by John the Baptist was recognized as the primary mechanism of authorization in the early church. Other documentation of the period, though, indicated that there was anticipation of something more.

At the same time that John the Baptist was acknowledged as the deliverer of primary priesthood authority among church members, recognition of the role of Peter, James, and John in the transmission of priesthood authority gradually became more evident. Several early revelations were revised to be finally included in the 1835 Doctrine and Covenants. One of them, the first segment having been prepared in November 1831, included in its 1835 revision that it was Peter, James, and John who returned to augment the sequence of gospel and priesthood restoration. In particular, the ancient apostles were identified in 1835 as bearing "the keys of your ministry," suggesting additional "keys" not found among what they obtained from John the Baptist.[54] It is impossible to gauge how publication of the revelations and the extent of their consumption by the Saints at that time, including the new dimension of understanding about the role of Peter, James, and John, permeated and affected the church.

If the argument made above is correct, i.e., the lesser priesthood (Aaronic) was sufficient to empower the early church, what are moderns to make of the explicit statement made in Section 3 of the 1835 Doctrine and Covenants (D&C 107), "On Priesthood," that "power and authority of the higher or Melchizedek priesthood, is to hold the keys of all the spiritual blessings of the church?" Moreover, by this authority those ordained were "to have the privilege of receiving the mysteries of the kingdom of heaven—to have the heavens opened unto them—to commune with the general assembly and church of the Firstborn, and to enjoy

53. Stephen Post, Journal, March 27, 1836, Stephen Post Papers, MS 1304, CHL. See also the account of the dedication and surrounding circumstances in Smith, Documents, "Minutes and Prayer of Dedication, 27 March 1835 [D&C 109]," *JSP, D*5:188–209. It should be noted that Post's reference here to the "Angel of the covenant" was also an expression used by others to identify John the Baptist. Orson Hyde to Joseph Smith, June 15, 1841, *Times and Seasons*, October 1, 1841, 552.

54. D&C 50:3 (1835); D&C 27:12 (1981).

the communion and presence of God the Father, and Jesus the Mediator of the new covenant."[55] The lofty bestowal, perhaps inclusive primarily of church leaders, was more ethereal than earthbound and appears to have been given to make a spiritual kingdom of men who had accessible to them the ministrations of Deity. On the other hand, the subsequent clarification in "On Priesthood" that the "power and authority of the lesser, or Aaronic Priesthood, is to hold the keys of the ministering of angels [not necessarily Deity], and to administer in outward ordinances—the letter of the gospel—the baptism of repentance for the remissions of sins, agreeably to the covenants and commandments," perhaps better applied to those at the temporal level who manned the church's utilitarian function.[56]

Modern perspectives of the differences in ranking between the two priesthoods should not be imposed on how early members understood the practicalities of priesthood authority. Present views about the Melchizedek priesthood are derived from the later and expanded understanding of the role and authority acquired from Jesus's chief apostles, described below. Prior to that time, John the Baptist's particular bestowal of authority upon JS and Oliver Cowdery that empowered them to create and run a church remained of singular significance among the Saints.

Evidence illustrating the priority of the lesser priesthood was Orson Pratt's influential 1840 pamphlet published in Edinburgh, Scotland, *Interesting Account of Several Remarkable Visions*. Besides providing the first known report of JS's First Vision in print, the pamphlet explaining Mormon origins also related the coming forth of the Book of Mormon, and the restoration of the priesthood. Though it is assumed Pratt recognized the differentiation between the priesthoods as given in the 1835 Doctrine and Covenants, his emphasis was on John the Baptist's priesthood as the means to empower the church. JS and Cowdery petitioned God, he wrote, because they recognized the absence of the "authority to administer" gospel ordinances such as baptism and were unaware of "how the authority was to be restored." In response to their query, Pratt stated, "a holy angel appeared and stood before them and laid his hands, and ordained them." Perhaps surprising to modern readers, he failed to include anything about Jesus's apostles returning. This, even though the author claimed to have "related the most important facts" about the restoration of the gospel and "of the authority in these days, to administer in the ordinances of the gospel."[57] What he did write, though, represented the essentials understood by the church at the time, focusing upon the initial infusion of godly power to inaugurate the gospel's restoration.

55. D&C 3:9, "On Priesthood," (1835); D&C 107:18–19 (1981).
56. D&C 3:10, "On Priesthood," (1835); D&C 107:20 (1981).
57. Pratt, *Interesting Account of Several Remarkable Visions*, 23, 24.

Other Latter-day Saint leaders held the same view. In June 1841, Orson Hyde, en route to his assigned mission to Jerusalem, wrote from England to JS describing a small book he had written about the restoration of the gospel. The content, he stated, was based on Orson Pratt's *Interesting Account of Several Remarkable Visions.* Returning to Europe from the Holy Land, Hyde in 1842 had his book, "A Cry from the Wilderness, a Voice from the Dust of the Earth" translated into German and published as *ein Ruf aus der Wüste*, in Frankfurt, Germany.[58] Asserting that "God has sent his holy angel directly from heaven with this seal and authority [the priesthood], and conferred it upon men with his own hands," Hyde, like Pratt, identified the power delivered by the "holy angel," neglecting to mention Peter, James, and John's role in priesthood restoration.[59] Other Mormons who wrote about the gospel restoration also confirmed the emphasis upon John the Baptist's priesthood without mention of a subsequent delivery of authority by Jesus's apostles.[60] This awareness of John the Baptist's significance must not be considered to be just a footnote in early Mormon understanding about how the religion came to be.[61] As late as the 1850s two Mormon apostles

58. Crawley, *Descriptive Bibliography of the Mormon Church*, 1:205–8.

59. Hyde to Smith, *Times and Seasons*, 551. Hyde's volume, which he described as "in something the manner that Br. O. Pratt did," prioritized the account of "the angel" restoring the priesthood without any reference to multiple "angels" returning to amplify John the Baptist's purpose. Justus Ernst translation of Hyde, *ein Ruf aus der Wüste* [*A Voice from the Dust*], 31, M230 H994r, CHL.

60. See Lorenzo Snow, *The Only Way to Be Saved…An Explanation of the First Principles of the Doctrine of the Church of Jesus Christ of Latter-day Saints* (London: D. Chalmers, 1841), 11–12 ("an *Angel from God* has visited man in the last days, and restored that which has long been lost, even the priesthood, the keys of the kingdom"); Moses Martin's 1842 booklet *A Treatise on the Fulness of the Everlasting Gospel, Setting forth Its First Principles, Promises and Blessings* (New York: J. W. Harrison, 1842), 54 ("the Angel of God has committed the everlasting gospel, with the Holy Priesthood unto man"); Benjamin Winchester's full-length book in 1843 detailed the ancient biblical priesthood while constructing the setting for the restoration of that priesthood to the earth, which included the passage: "Soon after this Book [of Mormon] was discovered, the Lord sent His angel with the Holy priesthood," *A History of the Priesthood from the Beginning of the World to the Present Time, Written in Defense of the Doctrine and Position of the Church of Jesus Christ of Latter-day Saints* (Philadelphia: Brown, Bicking, and Guilbert, 1843), 147. The same emphasis on the priority of the angel's authorization, with no reference to the higher priesthood being restored by Peter, James, and John appears in nearly a dozen other documents (books, pamphlets, speeches, and missionary diaries) written prior to the death of the Prophet.

61. See JS's emphasis of John the Baptist's purpose in the gospel restoration in Smith, Sermon, March 21, 1841, Martha Jane Coray Notebook, n.d., MS 1998, CHL, though JS also noted that the "keys of ushering into the Kingdom were given to Peter James & Jhon [*sic*]"; *Wilford Woodruff's Journal*, January 27, 1843, 2:213–16; Smith, Journals, January 29, 1843, *JSP*, *J2*:250–53; Franklin D. Richards, [January 29, 1843], Scriptural Items, ca. 1841–1844, MS 4409, CHL; "Mormonism," *Times and Seasons*, May 15, 1843, 200; Smith, Journals, July 23, 1843, *JSP*, *J3*:66–67; Smith, Sermon, March 10, 1844, *Wilford Woodruff's Journal*, 2:359–61.

in describing the restoration of the gospel emphasized John the Baptist's return without mentioning Peter, James, and John.[62] The contrast to present thinking illustrates that modern students must be wary of making anachronistic assumptions about matters of significance to the early Saints.

Helping the Saints to Understand

Despite the church's publication in 1835 of the important declaration regarding church authority titled "On Priesthood" (D&C 107), the detail of the priesthood revelations proved difficult for many to grasp. Confusion clouded member perceptions of what the priesthood meant to the church. Levi Hancock later remembered an incident in January 1832 when he and his missionary companion Lyman Wight "had some conversation on the priesthood and neither of us understood what it was." This, though both had been at the June 1831 conference when dimensions of the priesthoods were explained and expanded. Hancock admitted he "did not understand it and [Wight] could give me no light."[63] It wasn't just the priesthood's restoration that took time to congeal among members, the complexities of authorities and responsibilities within the priesthood also proved perplexing. Progress, though, continued. Five years after Parley Pratt had published his emphasis in 1835 of the "angel's" singular significance to priesthood restoration, he published a book wherein he stressed that JS and Cowdery "received their authority and priesthood, or apostleship, by divine revelation from God—by the voice of God—by the ministering of angels," that is, by the ancient apostles, "and by the Holy Ghost."[64] Parley's clarification evidenced

62. Lorenzo Snow, *The Voice of Joseph, A Brief Account of the Rise, Progress, & Persecutions of the Church of Jesus Christ of Latter-day Saints; with Their Present Position and Prospects in Utah Territory* (Liverpool: S.W. Richards, 1852), 6; Franklin D. Richards, *A Compendium of the Faith and Doctrines of the Church of Jesus Christ of Latter-day Saints* (Liverpool: Orson Pratt, 1857), 222. The latter reference contains much information about the Melchizedek priesthood, but in the book's appendix, the "Chronology of the Most Important Events which have Transpired in the Church of Jesus Christ of Latter-day Saints, from 1820 to 1856," only the priesthood restored by John the Baptist is listed.

63. Levi Ward Hancock, quoted in Matthew C. Godfrey, "A Culmination of Learning: D&C 84 and the Doctrine of the Priesthood," in Esplin, Cowan, and Cope, *You Shall Have My Word*, 171. Hancock died in 1882; his autobiography was assembled later.

64. Parley P. Pratt, *Late Persecution of the Church of Jesus Christ of Latter Day Saints* (New York: J.W. Harrison, 1840), iii. Pratt declared the same regarding "holy angels to reintroduce the pure gospel" in his "Dialogue between a Latter-day Saint and an Enquirer after Truth," *Latter Day Saints' Millennial Star*, January 1842, 131, also published as a pamphlet by Pratt in Manchester, England, in 1842. George J. Adams quoted Parley Pratt in 1840 stating the "authority and priesthood, or apostleship" came in part "by the ministering of angels." George J. Adams, *A Few Plain Facts, Shewing the Folly, Wickedness, and Imposition of the Rev. Timothy R. Matthews; also a Short Sketch of the Rise, Faith, and Doctrine of the Church of Jesus Christ of Latter Day Saints* (Bedford, England: C.B. Merry, 1841), 12. Jedediah M. Grant stated as much in *Collection of Facts Relative to the Course Taken by Elder Sidney Rigdon* (Philadelphia: Brown, Bicking, and Guilbert, 1844), 1.

for some the shift in understanding from John the Baptist's priesthood to Peter, James, and John's authority as the church matured.

Publication of the priesthood revelations associated with the 1835 Doctrine and Covenants, clear though they may be to modern observers based on generations of perspective, failed to portray the operative priesthood to many church members. Even early Mormon leaders did not grasp the scope of what the dual priesthoods held five years after the matter of authority was introduced to the church. Though subsequent revelations elaborated on priesthood function and duty, it was the Twelve Apostles' call in February 1835 that provoked JS to clarify priesthood relationships. To the Twelve he explained, "It is all important that the twelve should understand the power and authority of the priesthoods, for without this knowledge they can do nothing to profit."[65] The necessity moved JS to issue his instruction "On Priesthood" that later appeared as Section 3 in the 1835 Doctrine and Covenants. There he laid out the association of the "Melchizedek and the Aaronic" priesthoods. Later designated as a revelation, the detail of the order "updated the Articles and Covenants and other revelations on church administration" regarding the priesthood.[66] Though the revelations and "Instruction" elaborated on the authorities of the two priesthoods,[67] there remained in many people's thinking ambiguity about priesthood relationships. Elders quorum minutes in late 1836 show that the Kirtland elders requested of Alvah Beman, their president, a discussion about "the two Priesthood[s]," and pressed again a week later for "Pres. Beman [to] request one of the first Presidents [First Presidency] to meet and explain the order of the two Priesthoods."[68] The apostles and missionaries who ministered in Great Britain during the second apostolic mission there had to do the same thing to teach the English Saints about "the nature of the Priesthood & the duties & privliges of the several Offices," just as they did for the American Mormons.[69] Assuming, obviously, they themselves understood the authorities in question.

John Taylor later described the conundrum he encountered while serving as the managing editor of the *Times and Seasons* in Nauvoo.[70] He related that

65. Smith, Documents, February 27, 1835, "Orson Hyde, Record of the Twelve," *JSP, D4*:252.
66. Smith, Documents, between circa March and circa May 4, 1835 [D&C 107], Historical Introduction to "Instruction on Priesthood," *JSP, D4*:311.
67. D&C 3, 82–89 (1835); D&C 107 (1981); D&C 4, 89–95 (1835); D&C 84 (1981). For analysis of the importance of what became D&C 84, see Godfrey, "A Culmination of Learning," 176–78.
68. Lyndon W. Cook and Milton V. Backman Jr., eds., *Kirtland Elders' Quorum Record, 1836–1841* (Provo, UT: Grandin Book, 1985), 19–20 (November 2, 1836). The title found on the minute book reads: "A Record of the first quorum of Elders belonging to the Church of Christ: in Kirtland Geauga Co. Ohio." These minutes are held by the Community of Christ Library-Archives in Independence, Missouri.
69. *Wilford Woodruff's Journal*, June 21, 1840, 1:463.
70. After John Taylor's appointment to assist with publication of the *Times and Seasons*,

when once speaking with JS about the priesthood, its restoration, and keys, the prophet "wished me to write something for him on this subject, but I found it a very difficult thing to do. He had to correct me several times." After JS then instructed him about the "various dispensations and of those holding the keys thereof," Taylor returned to the task. After reviewing what Taylor had written, again JS said, "That is not right." The editor tried once more, only to hear again that "it was not right."[71] While even some church leaders found JS's broad perspective on godly authority difficult to comprehend, it was especially hard for the church's laity. Young Joseph Curtis, a twenty-one-year-old sent from Commerce to preach in north-central Illinois in late 1839, described the difficulty he had in explaining the church position on priesthood. After being rebuffed at one gathering by a man who "advised me to go home and never try to preach again," the following day, November 6, 1839, near Peoria, he met a man "by the name of Calkins" whom he engaged in conversation about the gospel. Though Calkins "treated me well," as Curtis tried to explain church authority he found himself empty: "Not being sufficiently acquainted with the difference of the 2 Priesthoods, he rather got me down."[72] Curtis's confusion illustrates JS's difficulty in informing church members sufficiently about church authority, not to mention other gospel features. The problem of communicating his thoughts to the Saints concerned and plagued JS to the end of his days.[73]

"And I saw another angel fly in the midst of heaven"

Another reason for the dominance of Aaronic priesthood restoration recitals may lie in the importance to the early church of a key biblical passage promising the renewal of the gospel to the earth. On May 12, 1844, just a month and a half before his death, JS preached a sermon lending to the early Saints emphasis of the Aaronic priesthood restoration through John the Baptist. According to Thomas Bullock, one of JS's scribes who recorded minutes of the meeting, the

---

he assumed full proprietorship, a posture occasionally annoying JS. Wilford Woodruff reported that "Brother Joseph once said after He appointed John Taylor the Editor of the paper in Nauvoo that Brother Taylor took every thing & would not let him have anything[.] he said it was his Fish pond and he let John Taylor fish in it, but Joseph Said Brother Taylor will not give me any of the Fish." Wilford Woodruff, March 14, 1860, Historian's Private Journal, 1858, MS 8563, folder 1, CHL.

71. John Taylor, Sermon, December 31, 1876, *JD*, 18:330.

72. Joseph Curtis, Reminiscences and Diary, 1839–1881, November 5–6, 1839, 14, MS 1654, CHL.

73. At a gathering at the unfinished temple in Nauvoo on April 16, 1843, JS stated: "It is my meditati[o]n all the day & more than my meat & drink to know how I shall make the saints of God to comprehe[n]d the visions that roll like <an> overflowing surge; ~~to~~ <before> my ~~vision~~ <mind>. O how I wo[u]ld delight to bring before you things which you never thought of. but poverty. & the cares of the world prevent." Smith, Journals, April 16, 1843, *JSP*, *J*2:360.

prophet emphasized "John the Revelator's" vision in Revelation 14 who "saw an angel flying thro' the midst of heaven, having the everlasting Gospel to preach unto them that dwell on the earth, &c." JS continued, that "Scripture is ready to be fulfilled when great wars, famines, pestilence, great distress, judgements, &c are ready to be poured out on the inhabitants of the Earth." To mitigate the effect, JS stated, "John saw the angel having the holy Priesthood who should preach the everlasting gospel to all nations,—God had an angel, a special messenger, ordained, & prepared for that purpose in the last days."[74] This reference that can only be construed to be John the Baptist's return as being the fulfillment of John the Revelator's prophecy in Revelation 14 opens a heretofore unexplored avenue for understanding the importance of priesthood restoration. The biblical vision reads: "And I saw another angel fly in the midst of heaven, having the everlasting gospel to preach unto them that dwell on the earth, and to every nation, and kindred, and tongue, and people. Saying with a loud voice, Fear God, and give glory to him; for the hour of his judgment is come; and worship him that made heaven and earth, and the sea, and the fountains of water" (Rev. 14:6–7). Present tradition among Mormons is that the prophecy was fulfilled when the angel Moroni returned to the earth entrusting the gold plates to JS, symbolized and memorialized by Moroni's effigy being placed on the top of Mormon temples. However, to most early Saints, Revelation 14:6–7 was generally understood to foretell the coming of John the Baptist.

Apostle David W. Patten, just months before his Missouri death in battle, wrote a letter "To the Saints scattered abroad" that was published in the church organ, the *Elders' Journal* in July 1838. As part of his appeal he quoted Revelation 14:6–7, then added commentary clearly linking the biblical angel to priesthood restoration: "We have learned that this deliverer [angel] must be clothed with the power of all the other dispensations or it could not be called the fullness of times." The "authority" given by the angel, which is "connected with the ordinances, renders the time very desirable to the man of God, and renders him happy, amidst all his trials, and afflictions" because of "this dispensation, as given by the angel of the Lord."[75] In February 1841, Latter-day Saint pamphleteer Benjamin Winchester wrote from Philadelphia in his serialized *Gospel Reflector* about John's prophecy. As a "consequence of the apostacy, the Lord has taken the priesthood or authority from the church; therefore, this angel was to be sent to restore this authority, or commission men to preach the gospel to all nations."[76] In the next issue he wrote, "the Lord sent his holy angel with the holy priest-

74. Smith, Sermon, May 12, 1844, Thomas Bullock, scribe, Joseph Smith Collection, Addresses, MS 155, box 4, folder 6, CHL.

75. David Wyman Patten, "To the Saints Scattered Abroad," *Elders' Journal*, July 1838, 41.

76. Benjamin Winchester, *Gospel Reflector*, February 15, 1841, 89.

hood, which was conferred upon men; thus fulfilling the saying of John: 'I saw another angel fly in the midst of heaven having the everlasting gospel to preach unto them that dwell on the earth,' &c."[77] Others confirmed in their writings that understanding.[78]

Not everyone singularly viewed the connection of priesthood restoration with John's prophecy as did JS. Orson Pratt, for example, besides using Isaiah 29 and Daniel 2, applied Revelation 14:6–7 as a prophetic marker to indicate God's plans for the earth's final purpose. He also apparently associated both priesthood restoration and the angel Moroni's return and delivery of the Book of Mormon plates to JS as fulfillment of John's prophecy in Revelation.[79] Even Oliver Cowdery, when he returned to the church in late 1848 before the Pottawattamie congregation, reflected the shifted thinking about the restoration emphasis. The Book of Mormon, he said, "contains the everlasting gospel, and came in fulfilment of the revelation of John where he says <he seen> an angle ~~shall~~ come with the everlasting gospel to preach to every nation tunge and people."[80] This perspective, like so many other perceptions among church members about how restoration essentials unfolded, was in flux.

Related Aspects of Priesthood Authority in the Early Church

Another angle of early Mormonism regarding priesthood authority that moderns must recognize is that, outside of ordinances, applications of priesthood powers sanctioned today in actions such as healings and other blessings were generally considered by early members as gifts of the spirit or miracles bestowed

77. Winchester, *Gospel Reflector*, March 15, 1841, 177, 183, 187.

78. Charles B. Thompson, *Evidences in Proof of the Book of Mormon, being a Divinely Inspired Record* (Batavia, NY: D. D. Waite, 1841), 144–45; Snow, *Only Way to be Saved*, 11, 12; and Martin, *Treatise on the Fulness of the Everlasting Gospel*, 54. See also Justus Ernst's English translation of Hyde's, *ein Ruf aus der Wüste*, 31.

79. See *Orson Pratt Journals*, March 1, 1835, 48–49; April 1, 1835, 54; April 5, 1835, 55; June 2, 1835, 65; October 17, 1835, 72; April 28, 1836, 78; May 27, 1836, 80–81; June 26, 1836, 84–85; July 7, 1836, 86; July 21, 1836, 87; August 3, 1836, 87–88; August 17, 1836, 88; and October 3, 1837, 93–94.

By the middle of the nineteenth century, church leaders had shifted away from the singular posture once held by members that John the Revelator saw John the Baptist in vision. Instead, the prophecy was interpreted broadly and more encompassing in all aspects of the gospel's restoration. The *Journal of Discourses*, the sermons of LDS Church leaders beginning in 1852 and continuing into the 1880s, contain about fifty-three references to Revelation 14:6–7 alluding to the restoration of the gospel and to the messenger who came as a part of the restoration. Of the fifty-three citations surveyed, forty-four neglect to identify the messenger, four suggest the messenger was Moroni, three associate the angel with the restoration of the priesthood, and two state that the passage has reference to all latter-day messengers.

80. Miller, Journal, October 21, 1848, 14.

upon all believers.[81] Modern perspectives that identify those manifestations of God as the province of priesthood authority were not understood that way by early church members. The Saints in JS's time were reliant upon the precedent of scriptural evidences in the New Testament and Book of Mormon to pattern and validate their procedures and practices. It is demonstrable that ordinances such as healing the sick and rebuking evil spirits that are presently associated with priesthood power were performed during JS's ministry using only the name of Jesus Christ.[82] The present commonly used language in invoking godly power, "by the power of the priesthood," did not appear in the church until the mid-1830s. When the Twelve Apostles were called in February 1835, for instance, no priesthood authorization designated their calls, though it was implicit that their identification as apostles was rooted in apostolic authority previously delivered. Similarly, when some were called to the Seventies Quorum shortly thereafter, neither were they ordained by the power of the priesthood, but "in the name of Jesus Christ."[83] Sanctioning by the "power of the priesthood" first appeared in association with bestowals such as patriarchal and "Zion" blessings.[84] There are numerous surviving accounts of the language used by early Mormons in performing healing ordinances. None of those extant accounts of the healing blessings were verbally empowered by the priesthood, but were, rather, performed in "the name of Jesus Christ." A passage reflecting standard thinking in the church's first decade is illustrated in Samuel D. Tyler's diary of 1838: "Elder [Gardner] S[now] was moved with compassion, he came where I was, & without

81. For example, Ezra Booth noted the expectations of early members for manifestations by way of miracles, quoted in Howe, *Mormonism Unvailed*, 187.

82. See also Jonathan A. Stapley, *The Power of Godliness: Mormon Liturgy and Cosmology* (New York: Oxford University Press, 2018), 82.

83. Smith, Documents, August 17, 1835, Minute Book 1, *JSP, D4*:390.

84. See examples of patriarchal blessings given by Joseph Smith Sr. from 1833–1836 showing the transition from their delivery without authorization, simply stating "Amen," to being given "in the name of Jesus Christ" to "by the authority of the Holy Priesthood" in H. Michael Marquardt, comp., *Early Patriarchal Blessings of the Church of Jesus Christ of Latter-day Saints* (Salt Lake City: Smith-Pettit Foundation, 2007). Though Joseph Sr.'s blessings were usually qualified by being given "in the name of Jesus Christ," Marquardt's work allows the blessings to be tracked by way of the introductory phrase "by the authority of the Holy Priesthood" beginning with Joseph Sr.'s blessing of his brother John on September 26, 1835, 53–54. Clarrisa Smith's blessing the same day also states the same (54), as did Orson Hyde's patriarchal blessing given on December 29, 1835, by "powers of the Holy Priesthood" (59). Beginning in March 1836, Joseph Sr.'s application of priesthood authority to the blessings he gave increased in usage thereafter. See, for example, Marquardt, *Early Patriarchal Blessings*, 66, 69, 74, and 76.

See also the "Zion blessing" of Lorenzo Dow Barnes, January 3, 1836 (recorded on April 24, 1836), given by JS, Sidney Rigdon, and Hyrum Smith, "in the name of Jesus Christ & by the ~~power~~ authority of the High Priesthood." Lorenzo Dow Barnes, Reminiscences and Diaries, 1834–1839, vol. 2, 52, MS 1436, CHL.

my speaking a word, he laid his hands upon my head & meekly entreated our heavenly Father in the name of Jesus Christ that I might be healed & I was healed at that same moment."[85] And a year later, Wilford Woodruff recorded that during the period of malarial sickness when the Saints first settled in Commerce, that "Joseph [Smith] went through the midst of them taking them by the hand & in a loud voice Commanding them in the name of Jesus Christ to arise from their beds & be made whole & they leaped from their beds made whole by the power of God."[86] Calling upon the Lord to heal was at the time considered available to all. Despite the church's male orientation, in the early church gifts of the spirit such as speaking in tongues and healings were the province of the believers, male and female.[87] Wilford Woodruff's wife, Phoebe, who attended to him when he was ill in March 1838, employed the gift. As Woodruff recounted, "I had Prayers & was much better <after my wife laid hands on me and asked the Lord to heal me.>"[88] Incorporating healing as one of the priesthood prerogatives came later as notions of priesthood and authority developed.

During the first decade of Mormonism, the evidence suggests that the priesthood as restored by John the Baptist was sufficient to empower the church and church members in their many manifestations. It is admittedly difficult from the

85. Samuel Tyler, Journal, August 10, 1838, 33, MS 1761, CHL. See also the language of healing attributing the power to Jesus Christ used in Jared Carter, Journal, 1833, 15, 31, 117, MS 1441, CHL; Alfred Cordon, Reminiscence and Journal, MS 9856, CHL, seventeen instances during 1840–1842; *Wilford Woodruff's Journal*, January 16, 1837, 1:121; June 12, 1837, 1:152–53; December 4, 1838, 1:306; Jonathan Dunham, Diaries, November 6, 1837, March 12, 1839, MS 1387, CHL; John Gailey, Reminiscence and Diary, April 1841, October 11, 1841, MS 1089, CHL; Jacob Gates, Journal, April 10, 1836, MS 1501, CHL; Evan M. Greene, Diaries, February 26, 1833, MS 1442, CHL; David Wyman Patten, Journal, MS 603, seven instances during 1832–1834; Stephen Post, Journal, February 13, 1836, March 29, 1837; *Orson Pratt Journals*, June 15, 1833, 16; June 23, 1833, 18; July 4, 1833, 19; September 8, 1833, 25; Levi Richards, Diaries, October 30, 1842, vol. 10, MS 1284, CHL; Willard Richards, Journal, July 16, 1837, MS 1490, CHL; and James Chauncey Snow, Reminiscence, ca. November–December 1834, MS 4452, CHL. Wilford Woodruff also provided the language used to cast out evil spirits: "[I] commanded the devil in the name of JESUS CHRIST to depart out of her," *Wilford Woodruff's Journal*, June 11, 1837, 1:152.

86. *Wilford Woodruff's Journal*, July 22, 1839, 1:347.

87. Dan Vogel and Scott C. Dunn tracked the course of "speaking in tongues" in the early church: "'The Tongue of Angels': Glossolalia among Mormonism's Founders," *Journal of Mormon History* 19, no. 2 (Fall 1993): 1–34. See also Lee Copeland, "Speaking in Tongues in the Restoration Churches" *Dialogue* 24, no. 1 (Spring 1991): 15–21.

88. *Wilford Woodruff's Journal*, March 30, 1838, 1:235. See discussion of the early Mormon conceptions of authority in rites and practice for men and women, and the later restriction of using the gifts of the spirits by women in the nineteenth century in Stapley, *Power of Godliness*, 79–91. See also Linda King Newell, "Gifts of the Spirit: Women's Share," in *Sisters in Spirit: Mormon Women in Historical and Cultural Perspective*, ed. Maureen Ursenbach Beecher and Lavina Fielding Anderson (Urbana, IL: University of Illinois Press, 1987), 111–50.

perspective of the modern world to appreciate the operative empowerment that JS and other leaders obviously employed in advancing the sustaining powers delivered by way of the lesser or Aaronic priesthood restoration. When members referenced the priesthood during most of the 1830s, they inherently spoke of what they understood had been given to JS and Oliver Cowdery by John the Baptist. Though the two had been empowered by Peter, James, and John in the early months of the restoration, modern understanding of the role and powers of the higher priesthood that fuel the church today did not transition until the end of the decade, and then only gradually. As will be shown, it was not until the death of the prophet that in trying to get their footing after the disaster of the assassination that even his closest associates grasped an alternate consciousness of the scope of the authority they held.

CHAPTER 9

Order of the Priesthood

Expansion

In the aftermath of JS's death, significant measures were exacted by Brigham Young and the Quorum of the Twelve Apostles to shore up the sagging spirits of the Latter-day Saints. Though some of JS's initiatives were set aside after he died, soon a number of other strategies that stalled upon the prophet's murder were revitalized. Despite JS's removal, the plan to spread the gospel, stirring since the elders were sent from Kirtland, never abated. Evidence of the renewal was a significant proclamation prepared in April 1845 by Apostle Parley P. Pratt for the world's "Kings," the U.S. "President," the country's "Governors," and "the Rulers and People of all Nations." Undoubtedly written to reaffirm their own perspectives, the "Proclamation" reminded its intended recipients that "the kingdom of God has come," and that it was designed to "fill the whole earth, and shall stand forever." Such confidence was firm, it stated at the outset, because "the great and eternal High Priesthood, after the Order of his Son, even the Apostleship, has been restored; or returned to the earth." Indeed, that authority held "the keys of the kingdom of God" that included the power given to Peter by Jesus, as stated in the New Testament. Consequently, they had authority "to administer in all things pertaining to the ordinances, organization, government and direction of the kingdom of God."[1] The premise, as declared in the proclamation came from the apostles' "authority from on high." Whatever had once been envisioned regarding the destiny of Mormonism, the Twelve Apostles of JS's church into whose hands the kingdom had been delivered had returned to the playing field.

That declarative posture would not have been advanced during the early years of the prophet's life. As will be shown, it took his demise to arouse the Twelve into recognition of what they potentially held. In the early church there

1. *Proclamation of the Twelve Apostles of the Church of Jesus Christ, of Latter-day Saints.* https://contentdm.lib.byu.edu/digital/collection/NCMP1820-1846/id/2818. Peter Crawley argued the April 1845 proclamation had antecedents in JS's revelation of January 19, 1841, see D&C 124 (1981). Crawley, *Descriptive Bibliography of the Mormon Church,* 1:294–96.

was a connection between Jesus's apostles and those who went forth to preach the Mormon gospel. Evidence indicates there was a loose understanding among the early Mormons that there were twelve men to assume the role of apostle in the fledgling church. This perspective appeared early, a few years before the formalization of the Quorum of the Twelve Apostles in 1835.[2] For instance, John Whitmer's priesthood license given to him on June 9, 1830, and signed by JS and Oliver Cowdery, stated he was "an Apostle of Jesus Christ[,] an Elder of this Church of Christ."[3] After his defection, Ezra Booth in his 1831 critique of Mormonism wrote that some of the men professed "to be endowed with the same power as the ancient apostles were," and identified Ziba Peterson as "one of the twelve Apostles."[4] There were even lingering perceptions that David Whitmer had been ordained an apostle in close proximity to the time JS and Oliver Cowdery acquired the designation.[5] Some in the modern LDS Church, from hindsight, have stipulated that JS and Cowdery's designations as apostles in the church's "Articles and Covenants" came by way of their ordinations by Peter, James, and John. However, it is not clear that that view about Jesus's apostles prevailed given the activity of others who were identified as apostles.[6]

Present understanding also incorporates recognition that the lesser and greater priesthood restorations were augmented by subsequent authorities. While they have in the past generally not been packaged with the initial priesthoods as part of priesthood restoration in 1829, the subsequent visions by JS and Oliver Cowdery of Moses, Elias, and Elijah, and other ancient authorities and their bestowal of divine powers also fill the mosaic portraying the church's acquisition of godly authority. Directly related to Elijah's role, JS's 1838/39 history stated that after Moroni had described to him in 1823 the existence of buried gold plates nearby, the angel "commenced quoting the prophecies of the Old testament." Moroni began with passages from Malachi that included a variation of Malachi 4:5: "Behold I will reveal unto you the Priesthood by the hand of

2. Gregory A. Prince, *Power from on High: The Development of Mormon Priesthood* (Salt Lake City: Signature Books, 1995), 7–8, 12–15, 56–58; D. Michael Quinn, *The Mormon Hierarchy: Origins of Power* (Salt Lake City: Signature Books, 1994), 10–14; Godfrey, "A Culmination of Learning," 169.

3. "License for John Whitmer, 9 June 1830," in Smith, Documents, *JSP, D1*:143–44, which also provides context for Whitmer's designation as an apostle.

4. Booth, quoted in Howe, *Mormonism Unvailed*, 180, 208. Peterson was one of the four sent in fall 1830 to deliver the message of the restoration to the Native Americans in the West.

5. Joseph F. Smith in an 1889 article titled "Restoration of the Melchisedec Priesthood," stated that Whitmer's ordination to the "apostleship" came "under the hands of Joseph and Oliver," though he was "not present when they received it under the ministration of the ancient apostles." Smith, *Contributor*, June 1889, 310.

6. Smith, Revelations, April 10, 1830, *JSP, R1*:60.

Elijah the prophet before the coming of the great and dreadful day of the Lord."[7] Nothing more was stated about the meaning of the rendering and Elijah's later role.[8] Consequently, we remain ignorant of how and when some of the features of this expanded view of authority were introduced, though they do exhibit the progressive nature of JS's prophetic understanding and experience.

Some modern church publications that describe the sequential distribution of heavenly power to JS suggest it was an ordered and logical process. The evidence, however, indicates something less certain about the chain and incremental steps of priesthood restoration. Equally unclear is appreciating exactly what the events meant to the recipients as represented in the fragmentary historical record. A contemporary linear course of priesthood development does not exist, especially any produced in detail by JS that specifically address matters of the priesthood he possessed. And, the summary of JS's statements about priesthood restoration must be qualified with the reality that JS rarely wrote about the topic, complicated by the fact that when he did speak about the matter no one captured the scope of what he stated. The exercise in trying to ascertain JS's enlarged thinking, therefore, is difficult. And relying on only extant and fragmentary documentation can contort the effort.

It has been argued that the several instances where JS spoke about Elijah after his Kirtland appearance in 1836 indicate a "phase" of priesthood that "eclipsed" what Peter, James, and John had given to JS and Oliver Cowdery soon after John the Baptist's inauguration of priesthood restoration.[9] That perspective relies on documentation that limits JS's thinking to the post-1836 sermon reports he delivered in Nauvoo in the early 1840s.[10] The importance of that view of Elijah's power to unite the human family is, to be sure, one of the most significant

7. Smith, Histories, "History Drafts, 1838–circa 1841," Draft 2, *JSP, H1*:222, 224. There is the likelihood that the 1838/39 passage may have been informed by Elijah's appearance to JS and Oliver Cowdery in 1836.
8. See Kenneth L. Alford's report of how Christians of the period speculated about the timing of Elijah's promised return. Alford, "'I Will Send You Elijah the Prophet,'" in Esplin, Cowan, and Cope, *You Shall Have My Word*, 43–44.
9. Prince, *Power from on High*, 35–45; Quinn, *Mormon Hierarchy*, 35–36.
10. There is a perplexing feature of the several 1840s sermons where JS spoke of Elijah's *future* coming rather than acknowledging that he had already come on April 3, 1836. There is no explanation for why JS chose to refer to Elijah's impending arrival, especially after having entered the encounter into his journal near the time of the experience. See for example JS's sermons on October 5, 1840, *JSP, D7*:440–41; October 3, 1841, *Times and Seasons*, October 15, 1841, 578; and January 21 and March 10, 1844, where he, according to Wilford Woodruff, elaborated on Elijah's mission: *Wilford Woodruff Journal*, January 21, 1844, 2:341–42; *Wilford Woodruff Journal*, March 10, 1844, 2:359–65. Joseph Fielding wrote that over the winter of 1843, "there was much Preaching through the City[,] much said on the Subject of the Coming or Spirit of Elijah." Joseph Fielding, Journals, 1837–1859, December 1843–March 1859, 22, MS 1567, CHL.

aspects of priesthood restoration. But identifying its "virtually unparalleled importance" ignores the expanding perspective of the Twelve Apostles' authority in the aftermath of their return from the second apostolic mission to England in July 1841.[11] It should also be remembered that Elijah was only one of the trio of ancient prophets who came by vision to JS and Cowdery in the Kirtland House of the Lord. While JS emphasized Elijah's role several times thereafter, there is little comparable in the surviving records about the appearances of Moses and Elias and how their bestowals of authority affected JS and the church.[12] We are mostly left to speculate about what it all meant.

The instruction JS advanced in 1835, "On Priesthood," as Section 3 of the Doctrine and Covenants (now D&C 107), clearly represented the landmark status of the dual priesthoods: "There are in the church, two priesthoods, namely: the Melchizedek, and Aaronic, including the Levitical priesthood." The revelation explained, "Why the first is called the Melchizedek priesthood, is because Melchizedek was such a great high priest: before his day it was called *the holy priesthood, after the order of the Son of God.*" But protecting the too frequent utterance of the "Supreme Being's" name, Melchizedek's appellation became the nomenclature for the priesthood title. To emphasize, the revelation stated, "All other authorities or offices in the church are appendages to this priesthood."[13] Thereafter, JS consistently taught this premise of the priesthood relationships, though, as stated above, evidence indicates members had a difficult time absorbing the nebulous information about priesthood that they were given. A sermon

11. Prince, *Power from on High*, 43.

12. An entry in JS's journal includes the explanation that he received from his father, the church patriarch, a blessing wherein "father anoint[ed] my head, and sealed upon me, the blessings of Moses, to lead Israel in the latter days, even as moses led ~~them~~ <him> in days of old." Smith, Journals, January 12, 1836, *JSP, J1*:167. The January 21 entry, like the September 1830 revelation where JS was told "ye are called to bring to pass the gethering of my Elect," apparently portended Moses's visitation to JS and Oliver Cowdery on April 3, 1836, where he delivered to them the "Keys of the gathering of Israel from the four parts of the Eearth." Smith, Revelations, September 1830, *JSP, R1*:36 [D&C 29:7 (1981)]; and Smith, Journals, April 3, 1836, *JSP, J1*:222.

Elias's purpose, as explained in the visitation on April 3, 1836, was to give to JS and Cowdery "the dispensation of the gospel of Abraham" wherein "in them and their seed all generations after them should be blessed." Smith, Journals, April 3, 1836, *JSP, J1*:22. In a rare identification of who Elias was and what he did, John Taylor, as church president, stated in 1881 that Elias was "'The restorer of all things'—who holds the keys of all dispensations, that in the dispensation of the fullness of times all things may be gathered into one." This is somewhat complicated by recognition that the names of Elijah and Elias are regularly interchanged in discussions about the biblical prophets and what they did. John Taylor, Sermon, August 11, 1881, in Nuttall, *In the President's Office*, 64.

13. Smith, Revelation, Section 3, "On Priesthood" Doctrine and Covenants (1835), 82; D&C 107:105 (1981). See Richard Bushman's appraisal of the "great revelation" and its influence in *Rough Stone Rolling*, 258–60.

JS dictated "On Priesthood" in October 1840 to his scribe Robert B. Thompson—the only time the historical record portrays JS preparing a text meant for delivery—confirmed the revelatory concept prevailing since 1835: "There are two Priesthoods spoken of in the scriptures, viz, the Melchisadeck and the Aaronic or Levitical[.] Altho there are two priesthoods, yet the Melchisadeck priesthood comprehends the Aaronic or Levitical priesthood and is the Grand head, and hold the hig[h]est Authority which pertains to the priesthood." Moreover, that priesthood "is the channel through which all knowledge, doctrine, the plan of salvation and every important ~~matter~~ truth is revealed from heaven."[14] Three months later on January 5, 1841, he further specified: "All priesthood is Melchizedek; but there are different portions or degrees of it. That portion which brought Moses to speak with God face to face was taken away; but that which brought the ministry of angels remained. All the Prophets had the Melchizedek Priesthood and was ordained by God himself."[15] And, in his conference sermon of October 3, 1841, he reminded his listeners that from those prophets there had always "been a chain of authority and power from Adam down to the present time."[16] This perspective remained relevant, but a significant transformation loomed on the horizon regarding the church's authority and perspective on the role of priesthood.

Despite the absence of a calendar identifying JS's sequential understanding and dissemination of that information, there are enough surviving materials to recognize significant advances for the church. From those records, we learn that the course of the Quorum of the Twelve Apostles became the catalyst for the next major advance in priesthood development. When the Twelve and all that they influenced were removed from the American church during their second British Mission initiative in 1839–1841 there was little structural innovation while they were gone. Nevertheless, the perceptible transformation of the Quorum of the Twelve that occurred in England as they converted individuals, families, and even congregations into the composition of church units provided not only experience but confidence for the destiny of the church.[17] The Twelve grew a

14. Smith, Sermon, October 5, 1840, *JSP, D7*:434–35. See Howard Coray's description of the setting where JS dictated the sermon to Robert B. Thompson in Jessee, "Howard Coray's Recollections of Joseph Smith," 344.

15. Smith, Sermon, January 5, 1841, *JSP, D7*:494. This elaborates on the differentiation of the two priesthoods in the 1835 D&C's Section 3 where JS explained the Melchizedek priesthood allowed for "the communion and presence" of Deity, but the Aaronic provided only access to "the ministring of angels." D&C 3:9–10 (1835); D&C 107:19–20 (1981).

16. Smith, Sermon, October 3, 1841, *Times and Seasons*, October 15, 1841, 577.

17. James B. Allen, Ronald K. Esplin, David J. Whittaker, *Men with a Mission: The Quorum of the Twelve Apostles in the British Isles, 1837–1841* (Salt Lake City: Deseret Book, 1992), 309–18; England, *Life and Thought of Orson Pratt*, 71; Quinn, *Mormon Hierarchy: Origins of Power*, 64–67.

church in England providing such strength and momentum that in 1850, three years after the Saints settled in Utah, there were more Latter-day Saints in Great Britain than there were in North America.[18]

Upon the Twelve's return to Nauvoo the summer of 1841, the general pause in expansion while they were gone took a new course. Though in their absence JS had unilaterally introduced the principles of salvation for the dead and was "elected" as the church's "sole Trustee in Trust" for life at the end of January 1841,[19] within six months of the Twelve Apostles' return, the Saints witnessed what proved to be among the most consequential periods of the prophet's tenure. It was a productive, though not well-documented, period. As Dean Jessee explained, once in Nauvoo "the necessity for secrecy and the delegation of his journal keeping [to his clerks], tended to obscure the nature and significance of his work there."[20] But enough survives for moderns to gather, in part, the scope of some of JS's designs.

As if the prophet had been waiting to unload what had been building within him, upon assuming the role in early 1842 as editor of the *Times and Seasons*, the March 1 issue began publication of the Book of Abraham; a project he had been working on since he acquired Egyptian mummies and papyri in 1835. The same issue of the periodical included JS's "Church History," what became known as the Wentworth letter described earlier. "Church History" contained his first personal publication of his foundational experiences. The *Times and Seasons'* following issue, April 1, 1842, then began publication of the exceedingly influential 1838/39 story, the "History of Joseph Smith," which as much as any other indicator overall portrayed the church in perpetuity. Several other innovations clearly associated with priesthood administration, not likely to have been implemented while the Twelve were away, added other significant dimensions to the faith. JS explained his hope, ambition, and excitement at the first of the year. In Willard Richards's hand, JS's journal for January 6, 1842, read that he anticipated the immediate future to be one where God would "restore the ancient <order> of his Kingdom unto his servants & his people." It was "a day in which all things are concurring together to bring about the compl[e]tion of the fullness of the gospel, a fulness of the dispensation of Dispensations even the fulness of Times." He saw the moment as one "to make manifest & set in order in his church those things which have been, and those things, which the ancients prophets and wise men desired to see." What was more, they faced a teeming prospect where "those

18. Richard O. Cowan, "Church Growth in England, 1841–1914," in *Truth Will Prevail: The Rise of the Church of Jesus Christ of Latter-day Saints in the British Isles, 1837–1987*, ed. V. Ben Bloxham, James R. Moss, and Larry C. Porter (Cambridge, England: The Church of Jesus Christ of Latter-day Saints, 1987), 202, 442.

19. JS to Hancock County Recorder, February 2, 1841, Joseph Smith Collection, MS 155, box 4, folder 8, item 2, CHL.

20. Jessee, "Sources for the Study of Joseph Smith," 16.

things begin to be made manifest which have been hid from <before> the foundations of the world & which Jehovah has promised should be made known in his own due time unto his servants to prepare the earth for the return of his glory, even a celestial glory."[21] Consequently, the early months of 1842 were filled with significant advances in priesthood-inspired innovations that changed the course of the faith and understanding of the priesthood at the time.

The Nauvoo Temple, Freemasonry, and the Nauvoo Women's Relief Society

The preface for this advance centered in JS's plan to build to the Lord a temple, following his precedent ambitions to do so in Independence, Kirtland, and Far West. After his disappointing venture to Washington, D.C. over the winter of 1839–1840, upon his return to Nauvoo, JS clearly focused on matters he *could* control and that had undoubtedly been pending in his thinking in the aftermath of the Saints' Missouri debacle. In a July 1840 sermon he noted that it was his intention "to build as great a house as ever Solomen did ~~and~~ if the church will back me up."[22] JS and the First Presidency in October, while the Twelve were still in England, announced to the Saints that "the time has now come when it is necessary to erect a house of prayer, a house of order, a house for the worship of our God; where the ordinances can be attended to agreeably to his divine will, in this region of the country." That was the outward design to accomplish the inward purpose of going "forward and unit[ing] our energies for the upbuilding of the kingdom," including "the Priesthood in their fulness and glory."[23] A call by JS on October 3, 1840, at the church's general conference regarding "the necessity of building the 'House of the Lord'" drew a resolution "that the saints build a house for the worship of God." As the consciousness of church members adjusted to expectations that thereafter "every tenth day be appropriated for the building of said house," another First Presidency proclamation at the beginning of 1841 reminded church members of the attendant necessity of creating a material and civic infrastructure to allow church objectives to go forward.[24] Thus, over the course of the rest of JS's life in Nauvoo, his designs and resources congealed to

21. Smith, Journals, January 6, 1842, *JSP, J2*:26, variances in punctuation removed for clarity. The concept was echoed in his September 6, 1842, epistle to the Saints. "Letter from Joseph Smith," *Times and Seasons*, October 1, 1842, 935.
22. Smith, Sermon, ca. July 19, 1840, *JSP, D7*:340.
23. "To the Saints Scattered Abroad," *Times and Seasons*, October 1840, 178–79. The statement hearkened to the language used by JS in the dedication of the Kirtland House of the Lord. Smith, Journals, March 27, 1836, *JSP, J1*:206. "To the Saints Scattered Abroad" is also found in Smith, Documents, September 1840, *JSP, D7*:409–13.
24. "Minutes of the General Conference of the Church of Jesus Christ of Latter Day Saints, Held in Nauvoo, Hancock County, Ill. Oct., 3rd 1840," *Times and Seasons*, October 1840, 186; "A Proclamation, to the Saints Scattered Abroad," *Times and Seasons*, January 15, 1841, 273–77.

vivify his visions of the Saints' corporeal and spiritual futures symbolized by the temple's construction on the bluff.

Three events in the spring of 1842 provide great insight into how JS designed to implement his visions and objectives for the Saints' future under the umbrella of priesthood development. They illustrate his own amplified understanding of priesthood, even though the full dimension of it was yet to be manifest. Sequentially, the first innovation was introduction of Freemasonry (also referred to as Masonry) into Mormon life. Though Masons professed traditions from antiquity, placing "great store in Old Testament history," modern studies have shown craft practices in the seventeenth century and a formalized origin in London in 1717. While Masons were found in America by the 1730s,[25] we are ignorant of when JS first took sufficient notice of the Masons to weigh their practices and their professions of derivation from the ancient world as something to seriously consider. JS's own brother Hyrum became a Mason in the 1820s, but nothing is known about how Hyrum's connection affected the rest of the family.[26] It was well known that a number of America's "founding fathers' were participating Masons and by the middle of the nineteenth century's first decade there were "between a hundred and a hundred fifty thousand Master Masons" throughout the land.[27] However, there was a period during the 1820s and early 1830s when Masonry lost much of its luster and momentum when one of their dissenting number went missing after publishing an exposé of Freemasonry.[28] A conspiracy resulting in William Morgan's death in 1826 goaded those fearful of Masonic gains to form a political opposition movement, Anti-Masonry, to quell Masonic influence, especially in the environs of western New York. Though Masonry thereafter ebbed from its early prominence, its claims of being from ancient descent proved attractive to numerous Americans, including Mormons.

Freemasonry's connection to the church has merited attention through the years in devotional literature of the Mormons. However, JS's primary intent to incorporate the craft's priesthood antecedents within the faith has generally been ignored to emphasize his embrace of the fraternal aspects of Masonry.[29]

25. Walter A. McDougal, *Freedom Just Around the Corner: A New American History, 1585–1828* (New York: HarperCollins, 2004), 328–29; Wood, *Empire of Liberty*, 51.

26. Homer, *Joseph's Temples*, 79. See also Samuel Morris Brown's view of Masonic influence upon JS in *In Heaven as It Is on Earth: Joseph Smith and the Early Mormon Concept of Death* (New York: Oxford University Press, 2012), 172–91; as well as Brooke, *Refiner's Fire*, 244–53.

27. Homer, *Joseph's Temples*, 38; McDougal, *Freedom Just Around the Corner*, 330–32.

28. Howe, *What Hath God Wrought*, 267–68.

29. LDS Church leader Anthony W. Ivins's *The Relationship of "Mormonism" and Freemasonry* (Salt Lake City: Deseret News Press, 1934), 179, represented JS's utilization of Masonry in this manner: "If ever a man was in need of sympathy and the friendship of good men, that man was Joseph Smith. It was under these circumstances that Joseph Smith

JS's implementation of Freemasonry was not simply a trend that momentarily raised its head and then vanished. There are antecedents from his early translations that included such things as Enochian elaborations, Egyptian cosmology, and ritual purification that had similarities to Masonic tradition.[30] To outsiders, the formalization of the Nauvoo lodge of Masons on March 15, 1842, may have been seen as societal innovation toward community development. Masons were known as stressing "the science, brotherhood, and vision of progress uniquely suited to the founding of a virtuous republic."[31] However, to informed Mormons the fraternal aspects of the association were clearly secondary to the contractual aspects of the craft and its ceremonies that bound initiates to principles and behaviors with biblical overtones. The intersection with Masonry suggests the attraction of JS and other Mormons who believed that Masonry in its antiquarian form possessed the trappings of order within God's ancient work; that is, the priesthood.

Because there is nothing in the historical record for this period that explains *why* JS implemented aspects of the Masonic fraternity into Mormon ideology, including commonalities within Masonic and Mormon rites, nothing definitive about his motivations can be demonstrated. Still, a number of the esoteric secrets of similarity in both organizations by way of signs, tokens, gestures, and other features of ceremonial ritual do exist, as well as generalizations of Mormon thinking about Masonry at the time. Heber C. Kimball, a Master Mason since 1823, reported his view of the craft to Parley P. Pratt in England in June 1842 after organization of the Masonic lodge in Nauvoo in March. This was a month after being initiated by JS on May 4, 1842, into what became known as the Nauvoo endowment. To Pratt he wrote: "Thare is a similarity of preast Hood in masonry. Br Joseph ses [says] masonry was taken from preasthood but has become degenrated. But menny things are perfect."[32] Months later, British convert and immigrant to Nauvoo, Joseph Fielding, gave his layman's impression of Masonry

---

became a member of the Masonic Fraternity." Thirteen years later, historian E. Cecil McGavin tried, first, to show that enemies of the church who charged JS with stealing Masonic rituals for the temple were wrong, and, second, that JS and the Saints became Masons "aware of the fraternal spirit of this organization" that would serve to help them in "making friends with prominent people and thus avoiding bitter persecution." He claimed JS and the Mormons joined the "Masonic fraternity" as a "necessary means to this desired end." E. Cecil McGavin, *Mormonism and Masonry*, rev. ed. (Salt Lake City: Bookcraft, 1956), 12, 13. John A. Widtsoe also attributed Masonry's embrace by JS and the Saints as a mechanism to enhance "the spirit of brotherhood and brotherly love which are the foundations of [the] Masonic fraternity and which characterize Masonic activities." Widtsoe, *Evidences and Reconciliations*, 357–59.

30. Homer, *Joseph's Temples*, 2, 89–178, 199–228.

31. McDougal, *Freedom Just Around the Corner*, 330–31.

32. Kimball to Pratt, June 17, 1842, CHL; Homer, *Joseph's Temples*, 92.

among the Mormons in December 1843: "Many have joind the Masonic Institution[.] this seems to have been a Stepping stone or Preparation for something else, the true origin of Masonry."[33] Later, in November 1858, ever sympathetic to the Masonic brotherhood, Kimball told a body assembled in Salt Lake City: "We have the time [true] Masonary. The Masonary of the day is received from the apostacy which took place in the days of Solomon and David. They have now and then a thing that is correct, but we have the real thing."[34] With biblical precedence from the report of Aaron and his sons' washing and anointing in Exodus 40 and other representations of purification, ceremonial procedures had ample justification. That perspective likely prevailed among Mormon leaders at the time regarding the rites and rituals of Freemasonry being a vestige of God's ancient priesthood. But because of Mormonism's eventual disassociation with Freemasonry toward the end of the Saints' tenure in Nauvoo, its establishment by the church and its leaders in 1842 has generally been misunderstood as being primarily a fraternal exhibit of brotherhood with the objective of promoting loyalty and protection among the brethren. Only in the most recent generation has it been explained that JS and the Saints' intentions of instituting Masonry in the church organization was because of its perceived connection to the biblical patriarchs and their priesthood.[35]

Church chronology presents the stark juxtaposition of the creation by JS of a woman's organization at virtually the same time the Masonic lodge was initiated. On March 17, 1842, two days later, the Female Relief Society of Nauvoo appeared, something quite extraordinary given the patriarchal foundations and function of the faith. Derived earlier in the month from women who had gathered to elevate circumstances in Nauvoo, including their initiative to assist the temple's construction efforts by furnishing clothing accessories to help the laborers, a plan to formally organize a "Lady's Society" was submitted to the prophet. With priesthood ventures then underway, he apparently saw a way to expand the proposal.[36] Ostensibly, the women's design held their purpose to

33. Fielding, Journal, December 1843–March 1859, 22.

34. Stanley B. Kimball, *Heber C. Kimball: Mormon Patriarch and Pioneer* (Urbana: University of Illinois Press, 1981), 83–85; Heber C. Kimball, Sermon, November 13, 1858, Historian's Office History of the Church, 1839–circa 1882, vol. 28, January 1–December 31, 1858, 1085, CR 100 102, CHL.

35. See primarily Homer's, *Joseph's Temples.* It is of note that Brigham Young, according to Wilford Woodruff, laid the death of JS at the hands of a Masonic conspiracy, see *Wilford Woodruff Journal*, August 16, 1860, 5:482. How widely the perception was believed by Mormons is not known. There has been overt hostility in the twentieth century by church leaders to any notion that in Mormon temple ceremonies there was influence from and parallels to the Masonic ritual. See Homer, *Joseph's Temples*, 351–54; Prince, *Leonard Arrington*, 255–59.

36. Jill Mulvay Derr, Janath Russell Cannon, and Maureen Ursenbach Beecher, *Women of Covenant: The Story of Relief Society* (Salt Lake City: Deseret Book, 1992), 26–27.

be "the relief of the poor, the destitute, the widow and the orphan; and for the exercise of all benevolent purposes." The editorial about the organization in the April 1, 1842, *Times and Seasons* indicated that church leaders were confident that "a knowledge of those pure principles of benevolence that flow spontaneously from their humane, and philanthropic bosoms" assured an advance of civilization.[37] But JS also saw a concomitant purpose.

Though it has not until the last generation been formally looked upon as a feature of priesthood dispensation per se, organization of the Nauvoo Relief Society indicates the perception by JS of the symbiotic relationship of men and women, something surprising given women's previous church involvement. Contemporary records do not allow that JS intended that women assume an identical path like the men regarding priesthood authority in the church. There is evidence, however, that dimensions of the priesthood were designed for the females. JS explained to the women on March 31, 1842, their role in harmonizing with the men: "All must act in concert or nothing can be done." Thus, he stated, "the Society should move according to the ancient Priesthood." Further, he said "he was going to make of this Society a kingdom of priests as in Enoch's day—as in Pauls day."[38] That perspective was manifest in the patriarchal blessing given to Leonora Taylor, wife of Apostle John Taylor, by Hyrum Smith on July 23, 1843. Hyrum promised her: "You shall be blest with your Portion of the Priesthood which belongeth unto you," which would be given when she would "be set apart for your anointing & your enduement [endowment.]" This was required for the myriad blessings awaiting her that "you shall possess in Common with your husband."[39] Clearly associated with anticipation of the Nauvoo Temple's purposes, the ceremonies later associated with the temple included women in those aims for which the endowment was administered. Despite the disappointing lack of documentation, the prophet and others, it is evident, recognized women as inherently holding aspects of godly power in concert with the men.[40]

This advance was so significant to JS that it left him at the time with the sense that he had accomplished his purpose. A few weeks after the Nauvoo Relief Society's organization, JS spoke to a gathering of Saints stating: "Some has supposed that Br Joseph could not die but this is a mistake. It is true their has been times when I have had the promise of my life to accomplish such & such things, but having accomplish those things I have not at present any lease of my life & am as liable to die as other men."[41] The events of early 1842 clearly represent JS's

37. "The Ladies Relief Society," *Times and Seasons*, April 1, 1842, 743.

38. Derr et al., *First Fifty Years of Relief Society*, 43.

39. Hyrum Smith, July 23, 1843, Leonora Taylor, Patriarchal Blessing, Patriarchal Blessing Book, 1833–, CR 500 2, Book 3, CHL.

40. See an overview of the period and the several manifestations of authority within the Female Relief Society of Nauvoo in Derr, Cannon, and Beecher, *Women of Covenant*, 23–58.

41. *Wilford Woodruff Journal*, April 9, 1842, 2:168.

ambitious to further enhance the church's organization, practice, and ideology resulting in his feeling of accomplishment at the time. The church's women became a catalyst for advancement of his objectives. At a consequential gathering of the sisters on April 28, 1842, the minutes indicate he "spoke of delivering the keys to this Society and to the church," that "the keys of the kingdom are about to be given to them," enabling them to exercise authority he had previously given to the elders regarding the ability to detect "every thing false." This is the meeting where he symbolically delivered to the women their authoritative mandate: "I now turn the key to you in the name of God and this Society shall rejoice and knowledge and intelligence shall flow down from this time."[42] Evidently the prophet had placed church women into a status that they had not formerly enjoyed with expectations of their unique contributions to the kingdom. Recent scholarship has portrayed in unprecedented volume the importance of women to the nineteenth-century church. Among the expansive representation of JS's designs are other aspects of the Nauvoo Relief Society's reconfiguration of female roles that merit mentioning.

Though there is nothing overtly portrayed in the Nauvoo Relief Society minutes about the matter, enough surrounding evidence exists to suggest that some within the organization had to deliberate the then-secret emergence of plural marriage. Organization of the sisters coincided with the emergence of JS's implementation of polygamy among selected men and women within the church. Discretion about the practice was of utmost importance. With few instances where JS explained his motives and purposes in introducing the practice, some have postulated that the establishment of the Nauvoo Relief Society was a covert means of influencing the church's women to accept his innovative marital designs. Neither records directly associated with the prophet or with women in the Nauvoo Relief Society confirm such a contention. Nevertheless, scholars have drawn upon what survives trying to make sense of the enigmatic connection between what JS tried to do with women in both instances.[43]

Another aspect of the female prerogative addressed in their Relief Society meetings was the matter of their participation in the gifts of the spirit—manifestations of faith with miraculous overtones. As mentioned previously, healing rituals by women—just one of several gifts of the spirit that were later appro-

42. Derr et al., *First Fifty Years of Relief Society*, 56, 57, 59. Regarding the concept of keys and the usage by JS and others see the editors' discussion (57n160).

43. See for example, Devery S. Anderson and Gary James Bergera, eds., *Joseph Smith's Quorum of the Anointed, 1842–1845: A Documentary History* (Salt Lake City: Signature Books, 2005), xi, xxxiii–xxxv; Cheryl Bruno, "Keeping a Secret: Freemasonry, Polygamy, and the Nauvoo Relief Society, 1842–22," *Journal of Mormon History* 39, no. 4 (2013): 158–81; Martha Bradley-Evans, *Glorious in Persecution: Joseph Smith, American Prophet, 1839–1844* (Salt Lake City: Smith-Pettit Foundation, 2016), 279–82.

priated by the men as priesthood derived—was a practice that apparently had circulation among the Saints in the late 1830s and early 1840s. Thus, at the same gathering of the sisterhood mentioned above on April 28, 1842, Eliza R. Snow's minutes describe JS telling them "Respecting the female laying on hands," from their participation in the action "there could be no devil in it if God gave his sanction by healing—that there could be no more sin in any female laying hands on the sick than in wetting the face with water."[44] That is, the effectual evidence of the healing was indication of God's approbation. The emergence of women in JS and other leaders' designs for obtaining the manifestations of the priesthood designed for them is reflected in a statement on May 27, 1842, by Bishop Newel K. Whitney. He told them that it was his view that "In the beginning God created man[,] male and female[,] and bestow'd upon man certain blessings perculiar to a man of God, of which woman partook, so that without the female all things cannot be restor'd to the earth[.] it takes all to restore the Priesthood."[45]

Subsequent circumstances precluded JS's apparent objectives for women to perform their salvific roles in tandem with the male priesthood. Eliza Snow stated on April 20, 1868, "the sudden death of the Prophet, and subsequent expulsion from Nauvoo, blasted all these fond anticipations."[46] However, it is apparent that his intent at the time was to lift the vision of women (and undoubtedly men toward women) to somewhat of a commonality with their male counterparts.[47] The mechanism for that transition, where the gifts of the sisters were to be magnified, apparently were intertwined with his ambitions regarding the temple then being built.

The temple's construction incorporated the preparatory path to culminate the prophetic ambitions of God to prepare his people—all of them—for the day of reckoning. To the female members, JS hinted on April 28, 1842, that a new day had arrived regarding their participation in available blessings, surely connected to the priesthood. He told them, "the time had not been before, that these things could be in their proper order," given that "the church is not organiz'd in its proper order." Neither could the efficacious aspects be understood and performed "until the Temple is completed."[48] The revelation JS obtained in January 1841 included expectations that the Saints replenish the Mormon charter by building a "house" for the Lord to "reveal my <mine> ordinances therein, unto my people," those "things which have been kept hid from before the foundation of the world, things that pertain to the dispensation of the fulness of times." For that purpose, Jesus stated, "I will shew unto my servant Joseph all things

44. Derr et al., *First Fifty Years of Relief Society*, 55.

45. Ibid., 75–76.

46. Ibid., 273.

47. See Stapley, *Power of Godliness*, 79–85.

48. Derr et al., *First Fifty Years of Relief Society*, 54.

pertaining to this house and the priesthood thereof."[49] But with JS's death that promise could not be fulfilled.

While women's benevolent organizations were prevalent in the culture, JS's institutionalization of an official church organization that elevated the status of women in the Church of Jesus Christ of Latter-day Saints was a significant step illustrating his progressive perspectives at the time. By most all accounts women were the men's lesser in American society. They then did not have the franchise to vote; it required generations before that basic right became available to them. Progress had been made at the insistence of women, but it had been agreed to reluctantly by the patriarchal society. Just three years earlier Mississippi was the first state to grant women the right to hold property in their own names, though it required the *permission* of their husbands to do so. Had JS lived and the temple completed in a timely manner, the epitome of the temple with JS's evident plans for women—though laced within the corpus of plural marriage—could have presented a rather different tale about gender relations within the church.

Another incremental and significant move just a few weeks after establishment of a Nauvoo lodge of Masons and the founding of the church's women's organization was the crucial step that came to be known as the Nauvoo endowment. Though the temple was far from complete, priesthood rituals later specific to the temple were secretly distributed by JS to nine men on May 4–5, 1842, in the upper room of his store. In the absence of other sacred space, again using the second floor of his Red Brick Store as he had done in organizing the Masonic Lodge and Women's Relief Society a few weeks earlier, JS called together several trusted associates to deliver to them a covenantal ritual to equip themselves with a sacred personal identity and power to administer in matters of consequence among the Saints.[50] This "endowment" became a significant magnification of the "endowment of power from God on high" that had been first promised to the church elders in 1831. The expression undoubtedly came from Jesus's promise to his own disciples, as found in Luke 24. There he stated that by them "repentance and remission of sins should be preached in his name among all nations," but not before they would "be endued with power from on high" (Luke 24: 47, 49). After the commission to missionaries in June 1831, the concept was instituted again in concert with the dedication of both the Kirtland House of the Lord and the Nauvoo Temple, where the people were given the same promise of divine power to bring about God's purposes.[51]

49. Smith, Revelations, January 19, 1841, *JSP, D7*:518 [D&C 124:40–42 (1981)].

50. Richard E. Bennett, *Temples Rising: A Heritage of Sacrifice* (Salt Lake City: Deseret Book, 2019), 75–83; Anderson and Bergera, *Joseph Smith's Quorum of the Anointed*, 4–7. Though some have assigned those who were endowed early as the "Holy Order," "Anointed Quorum," and "Quorum of the Anointed," the terminology was not evidenced in the earliest notations about those who were initially endowed.

51. Smith, Journals, October 5, 1835, *JSP, J1*:68, where JS told the Twelve Apostles, as they

Though it took another year and a half after the initial delivery of the ordinances to men in Nauvoo, the same ordinances were distributed to select Latter-day Saint women beginning with Emma Smith on September 28, 1843.[52] The ordinance was a significant expansion of the washing and anointing ceremonies in Kirtland, with a number of other symbolic procedures meant to instruct, commit, and enlighten the recipients. The initial procedure involving the nine men predated by three and a half years the general distribution of the ritual blessing to church members in December 1845–February 1846. By this time, the tragic circumstances of Missouri and Illinois mitigated for many Mormons the anticipation of Christ's imminent return that had driven the church at its beginning. Instead, the endowment of power from on high then became the equipment for the Saints' exodus to the West with millennial overtones.

The three enterprises initiated in early 1842 by JS were all priesthood born and represent, as best as can be determined, how the prophet envisioned the expansion of godly purposes through the empowerment he had been given by heavenly messengers.[53] Their importance may have generated greater action and clarity had it not been for one of the prophet's most influential betrayals made manifest over that summer. John C. Bennett, the talented, energetic opportunist whose own charismatic persona seemingly overwhelmed JS once the Saints established themselves on the Mississippi River bank, had pushed his nefarious personal agenda to a level that JS and the Saints could no longer tolerate. Though JS had been warned about Bennett's questionable past soon after the latter's arrival in Nauvoo, JS's disposition apparently allowed the quixotic adventurer to gain his favor and briefly transcend most every other Latter-day Saint in influence as Nauvoo rose on the Hancock County peninsula.

A Massachusetts native just a year older than JS, Bennett soon maneuvered himself to become mayor of Nauvoo, major-general in the Nauvoo Legion, chancellor of the projected University of Nauvoo, a prominent Mason, and assistant president in the church's First Presidency, all stunning demonstrations of prominence. At the same time that JS quietly introduced plural marriage to his close associates, Bennett began to exploit the concept, clandestinely claiming

---

anticipated completion of the Kirtland House of the Lord, to "prepare their hearts in all humility for an endowment ~~from~~ with power from on high." See also JS's instruction to the Twelve Apostles on November 12, 1835, *JSP, J1*:98–99. Regarding the Nauvoo experience, see Smith, Journal, May 4, 1842, *JSP, J2*:53–54; Historian's Office History of the Church, May 4–5, 1842, vol. 3, 1328–29, CR 100 102. See also "Endowment" in the Glossary of *JSP, J3*:481–82.

52. Smith, Journal, September 28, 1843, *JSP, J3*:104. By the end of 1843, eighteen women had obtained their endowment. Anderson and Bergera, *Joseph Smith's Quorum of the Anointed*, xxx.

53. Others have noted the convergence of the three early 1842 initiatives—Freemasonry, Nauvoo Women's Relief Society, and the Nauvoo Temple endowment as part of church development. See Bradley-Evans, *Glorious in Persecution*, 271–85.

to vulnerable women he had license to engage in sexual activity with them. By May 1842 however, at the same time JS began to endow his inner circle with the rituals mentioned above, Bennett's covert deeds became so well known that church leaders had to publicly expose him. Bennett sapped JS's energies and attention and, feeling the disdain of the Mormon public, the former darling of early Nauvoo Mormonism fled Nauvoo with revenge on his mind. Over the summer of 1842 he prepared his own exposé of Mormonism published in August in Boston that gained wide attention. Besides claiming JS had surreptitiously instigated a "Seraglio," or harem in the Mormon stronghold, especially significant was his claim that JS was behind the assassination attempt on former Missouri governor Lilburn W. Boggs on May 6, 1842. That allegation became reason for both Missouri and Illinois to move against JS, severely affecting his liberty thereafter.[54] Whatever designs JS had for the Saints at the year's beginning had been preempted by Bennett, thereafter changing the course of his life and what might have been the further expansion of the prophet's ambitions.

The Rise of the Quorum of the Twelve Apostles and Their Authorities

Coincident to the enlargement of priesthood authority perceptions noted above, growing views about the role and authority of the Twelve Apostles also matured. The perspectives and practical understanding of the Twelve before their mission to England were influenced by their 1835 Doctrine and Covenants designation as the "twelve travelling counsellors [who] are called to be the twelve apostles, or special witnesses of the name of Christ, in all the world." They were, according to the statute, "a quorum equal in authority and power to the three presidents" i.e., the First Presidency previously noted, as well as the "seventy," whose designation followed.[55] Eventually, however, their greater influence flowered, spurred in part by the personalities of those designated as apostles. After the more limited success of the first and then the stunning advance of their second British Mission, the apostles' role solidified into a body second only to JS's in effectual leadership. "As a result of the mission to England, the Quorum of the Twelve Apostles came of age precisely at the time its support and strength were needed most," including the charge to supervise the "business of the church in Nauvoo."[56] That is, JS turned over to the Twelve the temporal administration of the church, such as regulating missionary work and building the temple. It took

54. Bennett, *History of the Saints*, 217–57, 281–87. For an overview of John C. Bennett's life, see Andrew F. Smith, *The Saintly Scoundrel: The Life and Times of Dr. John Cook Bennett* (Urbana: University of Illinois Press, 1997).

55. Smith, Documents, between circa March 1 and circa May 4, 1835 [D&C 107], "Instruction on Priesthood," *JSP, D4*:314.

56. Allen, Esplin, and Whittaker, *Men with a Mission*, 314.

three more years for JS to provide to them the keys he held for spiritual authority and management over the kingdom. The same turmoil created by John C. Bennett and others afflicting JS also hindered the Twelve Apostles after their lengthy absence, negatively absorbing the men's energies and resources. As it turned out, however, their overriding influence as ballast to steady and advance the ship upon their return from Britain promoted the stability that allowed JS and the church to make substantial progress toward the prophet's ends, especially in the purposes of church leadership.

For Mormons, modern perceptions of the primacy of the Melchizedek priesthood and the attendant centrality of the role and authority of the office of apostle are post-martyrdom constructions, as will be shown. However, the prophet was clearly driven by the revelatory process regarding priesthood expansion some time before his death. In seclusion trying to evade extradition to Missouri, continuation of his 1842 initiatives were underscored by his published epistle to the Saints in the *Times and Seasons* issue on October 1, 1842. Written in the first week of September, in a departure from his general pattern of restraint in describing his sacred experiences, he recounted to the church a number of the divine manifestations that he had received that fueled the advances of priesthood to church members. Though notice in the text of the encounters were brusque, he included his communication with Peter, James, and John, explaining that they each declared "their dispensation, their rights, their keys, their honors, their majesty and glory, and the power of their priesthood; giving line upon line, precept upon precept; here a little, and there a little."[57] Other prophetic figures from the past who made themselves known to him were also identified. While withholding contextual particulars of his encounters, it is clear that JS intended that understanding this revelatory progression was central to church members regarding the source of church development and influence. Mormonism was in the process of acquiring dimensions of priestly authority previously only anticipated.

Once it was realized what JS had done to equip his successors, his death served as the catalyst to inaugurate a future pattern for church administration. With three lengthy apostolic administrations in the nineteenth century—1844–1847, 1877–1880, 1887–1889—and a few other interim hiccups, a predictable accession of leadership had been implemented by the end of the century to govern the LDS Church for the future.[58] The apostolic interregnums, as they have been

57. *Times and Seasons*, October 1, 1842, 936. This epistle appeared in the 1844 edition of the D&C and is presently printed as D&C 128 (1981).

58. Reed C. Durham Jr. and Steven H. Heath, *Succession in the Church* (Salt Lake City: Bookcraft, 1970), 1–124. The authors concluded by the end of the Joseph F. Smith administration: "By this time it had become crystal clear that succession in the Presidency worked in a certain predictable—one might almost say, automatic—pattern" (124).

called, while appearing to show tentativeness in church administration, actually portray the consequential understanding grasped by church leaders about the authority held by the Twelve Apostles soon after JS's death. Brigham Young later reflected on the time that soon after JS's death it came to him that JS had provided the means to perpetuate the church and kingdom. In the southern New Hampshire village of Peterborough mid-July 1844, while he and his brethren were in the East advancing both the gospel and JS's candidacy for U.S. president, he received confirmation that JS had been killed. There, in a location that served as a regional center for the church, Young with Orson Pratt were horrified to hear of the prophet's murder. "The first thing which I thought of," Brigham remembered, "was whether Joseph had taken the keys of the kingdom with him from the earth." But sitting together with Pratt, he continued, they "were both learning back on our chairs," when what JS had given to the Twelve actually dawned on him: "Bringing my hand down on my knee, I said the keys of the kingdom are right here with the Church."[59] Though he did not reference then the circumstances of the bestowal upon him and his fellow quorum members, it is clear that something significant had been given to the Twelve, even though JS had apparently not explained to them the full consequence of what he had done. Young published that view a week after the famous August 8, 1844, public display of his contentions versus Sidney Rigdon's successor assertions. Lamenting that the Saints were then "without a prophet," he declared, "but you are not without apostles, who hold the keys of power to seal on earth that which shall be sealed in heaven, and to preside over all the affairs of the church in all the world; being still under the direction of the same God."[60]

The meeting where JS transferred to the Twelve Apostles the "burthen and responsibility of leading this church off from my shoulders on to yours" probably took place toward the end of March 1844. It is not exactly known what the circumstances were when the gathering took place.[61] Several modern commen-

59. "History of Brigham Young," *Latter-Day Saints' Millennial Star*, June 4, 1864, 359.

60. "An Epistle of the Twelve," *Times and Seasons*, August 15, 1844, 618.

61. "Declaration of the 12 Apostles, also called The Last Charge," Brigham Young Collection, Office Files, CR 1234 1, box 74, folder 18, CHL. This is also known as Orson Hyde's "Statement about Quorum of the Twelve, circa Late March 1845," in Joseph Smith Papers, http://www.josephsmithpapers.org/paper-summary/orson-hyde-statement-about-quorum-of-the-twelve-circa-late-march-1845/1. See also Alexander L. Baugh and Richard Neitzel Holzapfel, "'I Roll the Burthen and Responsibility of Leading This Church Off from My Shoulders on to Yours': The 1844/45 Declaration of the Quorum of the Twelve Regarding Apostolic Succession," *BYU Studies* 49, no. 3 (2010): 1–16.

Those who have concluded that JS's "last charge" to the Twelve Apostles was part of the operation of the Council of Fifty include the Joseph Smith Papers editors, who state: "A significant event likely occurred in this meeting, probably in the morning session, about which the minutes are silent." Smith, Administrative Records, Council of Fifty. *JSP, A1*:62.

tators have assigned the event, which came to be known as the Twelve's "Last Charge," to a function of what came to be known as the Council of Fifty. That council, of which JS was the principal figure, was a quasi-religious/political body of about fifty men organized on March 11, 1844, designed to advance Mormonism beyond just denominational status.[62] After years of rejection by American institutions and oppression from their Christian peers, JS and other Nauvoo church leaders formalized a cadre of men, including a few non-Mormons, to pursue measures of protection and future opportunities for Mormonism. While also initiating designs for geographical expansion and prospects of settlement and respite, there was also a millennial component to the organization. The group generally operated in secret, and was mostly unknown to other church members.[63]

Particulars of what transpired in the meeting where the "Last Charge" was given are found only in a March 1845 synopsis of the gathering written by Orson Hyde, one of the Twelve and a member of the Council of Fifty. He stated that they met "in the upper part of the brick building situated upon water Street, commonly known here as 'Joseph's Store.'" Hyde's account, without describing any prefatory background, read that JS met with the Twelve Apostles, along with "many others who were of the quorum of high Priests to which we ourselves belong," suggesting a priesthood-oriented, ecclesiastical purpose for that particular session.[64] For years thereafter, members of the Twelve Apostles in

---

See also Quinn, *Mormon Hierarchy, Origins of Power*, 192–93, 412–13n22; Anderson and Bergera, *Joseph Smith's Quorum of the Anointed*, 71–73; and Rogers, *Council of Fifty*, 33–44. Why there is no record of the transaction between JS and the Twelve Apostles is puzzling, given its importance and later emphasis. The Council of Fifty minutes for the date generally assigned to the transaction, March 26, 1844, give no coverage to the event. It may be that the event occurred on another day. See the entries for the day in the Council of Fifty minutes: Smith, Administrative Records, March 26, 1844, Council of Fifty minutes, *JSP, A1*:63, and a lengthier treatment in 62–73, including discussion about the possible dating of the event in *JSP, A1*:62–63n149. Also see JS's, Wilford Woodruff's, and William Clayton's journals: Smith, Journals, March 26, 1844, *JSP, J3*:208; *Wilford Woodruff Journal*, March 26, 1844, 2:371; and Clayton, March 26, 1844, *Intimate Chronicle*, 128.

62. Smith, Administrative Records, "Volume Introduction," Council of Fifty Minutes, *JSP, A1*:xxiii–xlv.

63. Some members to protect the secrecy of the organization referred to it in veiled terms, such as John D. Lee's reference in his diary to it as the "YTFIF," fifty spelled backwards. John D. Lee, *A Mormon Chronicle: The Diaries of John D. Lee, 1848–1876*, ed. Robert Glass Cleland and Juanita Brooks, 2 vols. (Salt Lake City: University of Utah Press, 1983), 1:80, 88, 98.

64. "Declaration of the 12 Apostles, also called The Last Charge." Hyde apparently prepared the document ca. March 1845 for publication in a pamphlet he designed to dispute Sidney Rigdon's claims to church leadership. It was discussed in a Council of Fifty meeting on March 25, 1845. Because Brigham Young did not endorse its publication, the document remained obscure until the last generation. *JSP, A1*:378–79n592–96.

attendance at the gathering referenced the significant transferal of JS's keys and powers to them at that time.[65] Orson Hyde's reflective meeting summary included that JS stood before the group to explain his intentions, stating that even if his "enemies will kill me," because of all that God had bestowed upon him and the church, "I can go with all pleasure and satisfaction, knowing that my work is done." Indeed, he reminded them "the foundation [has been] laid on which the kingdom of God is to be reared in this dispensation of the fullness of times." Thus, "Upon the shoulders of the Twelve must the responsibility of leading this church hence forth rest until you shall appoint others to succeed you." Under the "hands of Joseph and Hyrum," the latter being the assistant church president, Hyde declared they were then "confirmed by holy anointing" to the apostles' commission.[66]

In the year after JS's death and the Twelve Apostle's assumption of the leadership of the church, Hyde's 1845 report indicated a broadened understanding of how the Twelve had comprehended the particulars of what JS had bestowed upon them. While they had been ordained apostles in the "traveling high council" in 1835, this conveyance was something quite different. Otherwise, Brigham would not have been surprised by the implications of JS's death when he first heard about the assassination. It was coincident to Hyde's report that Parley P. Pratt serving as a missionary in New York published his notable April 6, 1845, *Proclamation of the Twelve Apostles*, declaring the enlarged outline of the Twelve's authority. Clearly, church leaders had been reformulating their perspectives and prerogatives in the aftermath of the prophet's death.

The transition of the Twelve's leadership over the church prior to Brigham Young's appointment as JS's successor as church president, perhaps surprisingly, proved difficult for church leaders.[67] Nevertheless, the premise of their authority was not in dispute. Fortunately, one of the great chroniclers of nineteenth-century Mormonism, Wilford Woodruff, captured Young's own exposition on the transition of authority. Not long after the vanguard of the pioneer Saints arrived in the Salt Lake Valley in 1847, the "Camp of Israel" met near the eastern rim of the Great Basin for Sabbath services on August 15. There Brigham de-

65. See for example, Heber C. Kimball, Sermon, March 23, 1853, quoted in Quinn, *Mormon Hierarchy: Origins of Power*, 194–95; Orson Hyde, Sermon, October 6, 1869, *JD*, 13:80; Wilford Woodruff, Sermon, April 19, 1893, Brian Stuy, ed., *Collected Discourses Delivered by President Wilford Woodruff, His Two Counselors, the Twelve Apostles, and Others*, 5 vols. (Burbank, CA: B. H. S. Publishing, 1987), 3:283; Wilford Woodruff, Sermon, October 4, 1896, Stuy, *Collected Discourses*, 5:188; Wilford Woodruff, Sermon, May 31, 1898, J. Golden Kimball Journals 1883–1887, 1895–1908, vol. 13, 64, MS 1354, CHL.

66. "Declaration of the 12 Apostles, also called The Last Charge."

67. For discussion of the multiple factors in play that delayed reorganization of the First Presidency after JS's death, see Gary James Bergera, *Conflict in the Quorum: Orson Pratt, Brigham Young, Joseph Smith* (Salt Lake City: Signature Books, 2002).

livered important instructions on the priesthood and the manner it then influenced and empowered the church, which reflected how the church would later understand its presiding authority. Among the things he emphasized to those assembled was the premise that: "When Brother Joseph recieved the Priesthood He did not recieve all at once." Rather, "He was A prophet Seer & Revelator before He recieved the fulness of the Priesthood & keys of the kingdom." JS "first recieved the Aronick Priesthood & Keys from under the hands of John the Baptist," but he "then had not power to lay on hands to confirm the Church." Afterward JS "recieved the Patriarchal or Melchisedek Priesthood from under the Hands of Peter James & John who were of the Twelve Apostles & were the Presidency when the other Apostles were Absent." To emphasize the source of their authority, he stated, "From those Apostles Joseph Smith recieved every key power, Blessing, & Privilege of the Highest Authority of the Melchizedek Priesthood ever committed to man on the earth which they held."

After clarifying the reach of that authority, Brigham then explained its implications for those who succeeded JS. Responding to concerns of some church members who "have had fears that we had not power to get revelations since the death of Joseph," and—reinforcing the posture that there was nothing held by JS that was not then possessed by the Twelve Apostles—he insisted, "I want this Church to understand from this day henceforth & forever that an apostle is the Highest office & Authority that there is in the Church & kingdom of God on the earth." From JS's authorization by "Peter James & John," the prophet "gave unto me & my brethren the Twelve all the Priesthood keys Power & Authority which he had. And those are powers which belong to the Apostleship."[68] While the declaration may represent common thinking to modern church members, to those who heard the concept for the first time a transition in governing the church had clearly taken place. The speech clarified that the antecedent particulars of priesthood restoration and development had now been formulated and institutionalized. Obviously, there were numerous later adjustments to priesthood administration during the nineteenth century.[69] But after this time there was no doubt about the hierarchal relationship of the Aaronic to the Melchizedek priesthood nor about the apostolic authority of those who presided over the church.

Complementary evidence of the maturation of the Saints' understanding of the larger role of the Melchizedek priesthood in contrast to the earlier emphasis upon John the Baptist's authority is exhibited in Apostle Orson Pratt's writings. As has been shown, Pratt provided his view about the early and significant

68. *Wilford Woodruff Journal*, August 15, 1847, 3:257.
69. See William G. Hartley, *My Fellow Servants: Essays on the History of the Priesthood* (Provo, UT: BYU Studies, 2010), which contains an overview of the myriad of nineteenth-century administrative priesthood innovations.

events of the restoration in his important 1840 pamphlet, *Interesting Account of Several Remarkable Visions.* There he placed great emphasis on the restoration of the priesthood through the "angel," John the Baptist, with no mention of Peter, James, and John and their subsequent delivery of the greater priesthood. By 1848, however, he delivered what became the institutionalized understanding of the fuller conception of the greater priesthood restoration. In his pamphlet *Divine Authority, or the Question, Was Joseph Smith Sent of God?* he reasoned, "A revelation and restoration to the earth of the *everlasting gospel* through the angel Moroni would be of no benefit to the nations, unless some one should be ordained with authority to preach it and administer its ordinances." Hypothetically eliminating Moroni as one possessing priesthood authority to distribute to JS and Cowdery, he queried, "How then did Mr. Smith obtain the office of an apostle, if Moroni had no authority to ordain him to such office?" Pratt affirmed that "Peter, James, and John came to him [JS] in the capacity of ministering angels, and by the laying on of hands ordained him an apostle, and commanded him to preach, baptize, lay hands for the gift of the Holy Ghost, and administer all other ordinances of the gospel as they themselves did in ancient days."[70] No mention there of John the Baptist's role. Pratt's description of JS's ordination, contrary to his earlier explanations, associated it with the office of apostle, reinforcing the role of the leadership of Brigham Young and the Twelve Apostles.

We remain puzzled today that JS failed to lay out a predictable schematic regarding relationships of priesthood offices and the development of their functions, not to mention a clear path for succession. (It is probably safe to say that at the outset that JS did not believe that planning for a successor was necessary.) Still, within the first generation of Mormonism the tradition of the restoration of the Aaronic or lesser priesthood through John the Baptist had taken a secondary role to the restoration of the Melchizedek or greater priesthood through Peter, James, and John—the apostleship. Had the Saints understood the role of the Melchizedek priesthood in the church's infancy in the manner that it was perceived in the later 1840s it is altogether possible that there would have been much more discussion of its primal importance, including perhaps, something

70. Orson Pratt, *Divine Authority, or the Question, Was Joseph Smith Sent of God?* (Liverpool: R. James, 1848), 4. See also Orson Pratt, "The Question Answered, Was Joseph Smith Sent of God?" *Frontier Guardian*, February 7, 1849; and Pratt, "Evidences of the Book of Mormon and Bible Compared," in *Divine Authenticity of the Book of Mormon*, no. 4 (Liverpool: R. James, 1850), 58, 59, 61, where the discussion of priesthood is based on JS's "History of Joseph Smith" as published in the *Latter-Day Saints' Millennial Star*.

In 1850, fellow apostle John Taylor confronted verbally and in print charges that there was confusion in Mormon minds about the heavenly transmittal of divine authority. See John Taylor, *Three Nights' Public Discussion between the Revds. C.W. Cleeve, James Robertson, and Philip Cater, and John Taylor, of the Church of Jesus Christ of Latter-day Saints* (Liverpool: John Taylor, 1850), 12.

more definitive about how JS and Oliver Cowdery received that authority. As it stands, along with the added dimension of JS and Cowdery's acquisition of the prophetic bestowals associated with the Kirtland House of the Lord as well as other authorities about which JS barely mentioned, the expanded scale of priesthood restoration illustrates the developmental process regarding authority in the church.

Other Considerations Applying to Priesthood Restoration

At the same time that the method of priesthood transfer by way of physical ordination by hands laid on one's head abounded in the church, there also existed an established precedent that apparently recognized the plausibility of priesthood bestowal by way of "voice authorization." The Book of Mormon generally lacks specification about how authority was conveyed among the Nephites, though evidence of godly authority among the people is implicit.[71] There is, though, one explicit instance concerning the later prophet Nephi as described in Helaman 10. Nephi heard the "voice" of the Lord who gave him "power" not only to lead the people, but also the sealing power to bind on earth and in heaven.[72] No hands-on transferal of authority here. JS gave credence to the notion when, in a letter from the Liberty Jail that he sent to real estate speculator Isaac Galland on March 22, 1839, he wrote: "We believe that no man can administer salvation through the gospel, to the souls of men, in the name of Jesus Christ, except he is authorized from God, *by revelation*, or by being ordained by some one whom God hath sent by revelation."[73] The statement distinguished two different means of a man obtaining heavenly authority. That is, God's revelation is also a mechanism to disburse priesthood authority.

Two other instances are important to note regarding the reception of the greater or Melchizedek priesthood authority by heavenly delivery that are not generally discussed in the modern church. The first is found in JS's significant September 6, 1842, epistle to the Saints, D&C 128, which specifically referred to a connection between JS, Oliver, and the three apostles. The language of the reference varied, however, from the procedural description of John the Baptist's appearance to JS and Cowdery given earlier, where he conferred the lesser priesthood upon them by the laying on of hands. Without any context, including the timing of the event, JS stated in the epistle that he and Cowdery heard the "voice of Peter, James, and John, in the wilderness between Harmony, Susquehanna county, and Colesville, Broom county, on the Susquehanna River, declaring themselves as possessing the keys of the kingdom, and of the dispensation of

71. See Mosiah 18:13, 17–18; and Alma 13:1–19.

72. Helaman 10:3, 5–7.

73. Smith to Isaac Galland, March 22, 1839, *Times and Seasons*, February 1840, 54 (emphasis added).

the fulness of times."[74] The second document appeared in James Mulholland's 1839 narrative of JS's life (the 1838/39 history). After the Baptist's appearance where they received the "Aaronick Priesthood, they were told that if they "continued faithful" that they should "also have the Melchisidec Priesthood." After deliberating about this for "some time," and after earnest prayer, while in the "Chamber of Mr Whitmer's house" (Peter Whitmer Sr.'s home in Fayette Township, New York) the "Word of the Lord came unto us, in the Chamber, commanding us, that I should ordain Oliver Cowdery to be an Elder in the Church of Jesus Christ, and that he also should ordain me to the same office."[75]

Modern students are left to ascertain why the simple pattern of the lesser priesthood's bestowal proved more complicated in JS and Cowdery's acquisition of the greater or higher priesthood. It is readily apparent that the single visit and accompanying ordination by the Baptist varied considerably from what JS claimed regarding the seemingly incremental steps of obtaining Peter, James, and John's priesthood. Though there was not a descriptive expression about how they obtained the greater priesthood, as they promised, there is evidence from both JS and Cowdery that a physical transmittal occurred. JS's blessing to Cowdery in October 1835, included the assertion that they obtained "the holy priesthood under the hands of th<ose> who had been held in reserve for a long season, even those who rescived it under the hand of the Messiah," i.e., Peter, James, and John. Along with the implications of Cowdery's declaration in 1848 that, according to Reuben Miller, both priesthoods were "confered by the holy angels of god," the hands-on conveyance of authority that has become Mormon tradition is exhibited.[76]

Critics have made much about the absence of a definitive contemporary description of JS and Cowdery's reception of the greater priesthood.[77] Even sympathetic commentators have given weight to the lack of an explicit reference to the Melchizedek Priesthood restoration narrative by way of a hands-on ordination. As early as 1861, the Reorganized Church of Jesus Christ of Latter Day Saints—a year after Joseph Smith III acceded to be their president—stated in their organ, *The True Latter Day Saints' Herald*, "it has been a prevalent idea among various factions [primarily referencing the LDS Church] that the Melchisedek priesthood, was conferred on Joseph by the laying on of the hands of Peter, James and John, but Joseph's statement [regarding the "voice of Peter, James, and John"

74. Smith, "Letter from Joseph Smith," September 6, 1842, *Times and Seasons*, October 1, 1842, 936.

75. Smith, Histories, "History Drafts, 1838–circa 1841," Draft 1, *JSP, H1*:326.

76. JS blessing to Cowdery, October 2, 1835; Miller, Journal, October 21, 1848.

77. See the criticisms in Chapter 8, as well as Dale Morgan in *Dale Morgan on Early Mormonism*, 392, 393; Brodie, *No Man Knows My History*, 74, 75, 111; LaMar Peterson, *Problems in Mormon Text* (Salt Lake City, UT: n.p., 1957), 11, 12; and Tanner and Tanner, *Mormonism: Shadow or Reality*, 179–83.

in September 1842] shows that this is a false idea."[78] That is, what JS stated was simply the "voice of Peter, James, and John" declaring their authority did not satisfy later claims that they had been physically *ordained* by Jesus's apostles. Furthermore, in the twentieth century, Richard Howard, former church historian of the RLDS Church (Community of Christ), also explained that a Doctrine and Covenants passage in 1835 referring to the role of Jesus's apostles in priesthood restoration lacked confirmation of an objective conferral. Quoting from the 1835 Doctrine and Covenants, Section 50:3,[79] Howard concluded: "From this [passage] one might infer that Peter, James, and John bestowed the Melchizedek priesthood on Joseph and Oliver. Joseph's history, however, mentions no such event—only that he and Oliver were commanded to ordain each other as elders." Given that both JS and Cowdery had written of John the Baptist's ordination, he posited "one might expect to find allusions to their ordination under the hands of Peter, James, and John, if such an event had actually happened." But there was not. He then confirmed RLDS Church historian and apostle Heman C. Smith's statement near the turn of the last century where he asserted it would be "unsafe" to say that "Joseph Smith and Oliver Cowdery were ever ordained literally under the hands of Peter, James, and John." Anyone who made such an assertion, Heman Smith stated, "would have to do so recklessly and without sufficient evidence upon which to base his conclusion."[80] Because the "History of Joseph Smith" was prepared between 1838 and 1856 without including an account of the higher priesthood restoration, something for which modern scholars and others cannot give account, there will always be controversy about the matter.

Addison Everett's Claim

Although it is tangential to the traditional documentary record, in the absence of anything descriptive from JS or Oliver Cowdery regarding the circumstances of the Melchizedek priesthood restoration, a story out of St. George, Utah, in the early 1880s claiming to be a report of JS recounting the event is worth

78. "The Ordination of Joseph the Martyr," *True Latter Day Saints' Herald*, June 1861, 95. See also W. W. Blair's conclusion that: "If Joseph and Oliver had at any time been formally set apart to the Apostleship, directly *under the hands* of Peter, James and John as has been claimed by some, they certainly, one or both of them, would have left some written mention of that fact. No such mention is to be found; and this confirms us in the thought that no such occurrence ever took place." "Restoration of Priesthood, and Offices," *Saints' Herald*, February 15, 1879, 51.

79. "And also with Peter, James, and John, whom I have sent unto you, by whom I have ordained you and confirmed you to be apostles and especial witnesses of my name." D&C 50:12 (1835); D&C 27:12 (1981); D&C 26:3a (RLDS edition, 1911).

80. Richard P. Howard, "Peter, James, and John in Light of the Revision of Sections 7 and 26," *Saints Herald*, May 1, 1982, 28. See also Joseph Smith III, Heman C. Smith, and F. Henry Edwards, eds. and comps., *The History of the Reorganized Church of Jesus Christ of Latter Day Saints*, 6 vols. (Independence, MO: Herald House, 1967), 1:62–65.

visiting. Addison Everett, born in 1805 and a forty-five-year veteran of Mormonism, wrote what appears to be an unprovoked letter in 1882 to Joseph F. Smith, the nephew of JS and son of Hyrum Smith, and at the time a counselor in the LDS Church's First Presidency. Everett claimed to have been an earwitness to JS describing the Melchizedek priesthood restoration. There are several factors that give pause in accepting the story, most prominent being the fact that Everett failed to popularize his experience until nearly forty-years after it was purported to have happened. Because Everett's account has been discussed in other analyses of Melchizedek priesthood restoration, its consideration is here presented.[81]

Three years before he died in 1885, Everett, a New Yorker who had been baptized in 1837, wrote on January 16, 1882, to Joseph F. Smith, perhaps recognizing the void in information about the Melchizedek priesthood restoration, to offer his own testimonial about the event. To qualify his report, he wrote, "I had in My power to Befriend Bro Joseph Just Before he was slain and he has Befrended Me & Visited Me five times Sin[c]e Since His Death & Brother Hiram was with him twice," the last time being in the St. George Temple. Clearly, that otherworldly proviso influenced how his disclosure might be received by later readers. Without explanation for why he wrote at the time, Everett then stated that just before JS and Hyrum Smith went to Carthage, Illinois, in June 1844, he was "passing the Manshion House" in Nauvoo where he saw the prophet and his brother talking to "five or six Brethren in earnest conversation." As Everett overheard the discussion, which would have had to have been lengthy to cover all that Everett said was discussed, he noted several topics in particular. JS reviewed, he wrote, William Law's defection over JS's teachings about "A plurality of Gods," which also included quotation of a few biblical passages; and the approach of a recently returned missionary in the dooryard who informed JS he had recently seen Oliver Cowdery who "Bore a faithful Testimony to the Gospel & to the Book of Mormon." This, according to Everett, provoked JS to elaborate on his collaboration with Cowdery and threats from a mob and a "Prossecuting Atorny" during the work of translation. Everett then claimed that JS related the circumstance where he with Cowdery escaped from a court proceeding as a prelude to restoration of the Melchizedek priesthood. Without identifying the exact timing of the restoration, "A Lawyer By the Name of Reede" represented JS in the court appearance. A local farmer of note with legal experience and twenty years JS's senior, Reed (also identified as Reid in some documentation) was re-

81. Andrus and Andrus, *They Knew the Prophet*, 14–15; Quinn, *Mormon Hierarchy*, 25, 286–87n119, 120; Bushman, *Rough Stone Rolling*, 118.

cruited by the Knight family to be JS's legal advocate in a proceeding against JS in June 1830 in South Bainbridge, New York.[82] JS had been charged with being a "disorderly person," stemming from the stir he made among the locals who knew of his fruitless money-digging activities that they then associated with his translation of the Book of Mormon. The charge was dismissed and he was freed. But because the locals were bent on retribution, Reed had to smuggle him out of town.[83] After wandering "in a dense Forest all Night," Everett reported JS stating that just about when Cowdery gave out, "Br Joseph leaned him against an Oake tree," where Oliver cried out "how long O Lord," followed by "O how Long Br Joseph hav we got to suffer these things." At that moment of despair, "Peter James & John came to us and Ordained ~~to~~ us to the Holy Apostelship and gave <unto> us the Keys of the Disp<e>nsation of the fullness of times." Everett remained unclear about the exact location where the event took place, but wrote, "I heard the Name of the Banks of the Susquehanah river Spoken <of> But where it Was placd I cannot till. No doubt the Oake tree and the field fence was against to the river."[84]

In St. George, Utah, at the time, elderly Saints revived their memories of JS and their early experiences in the church. Attention to Everett's story increased in the telling. Oliver B. Huntington received a February 1881 letter from Everett where Everett related to Huntington what in substance he reported to President Smith about the Melchizedek priesthood restoration the next year. Huntington later packaged Everett's letter in a communication to the church's *Young*

82. Edwin Brown Firmage and Richard Collin Mangrum, *Zion in the Courts: A Legal History of the Church of Jesus Christ of Latter-day Saints, 1830–1900* (Urbana, IL: University of Illinois Press, 1988), 50–51; Bushman, *Rough Stone Rolling*, 116–17; Gordon A. Madsen, Jeffrey N. Walker, and John W. Welch, eds., *Sustaining the Law: Joseph Smith's Legal Encounters* (Provo, UT: BYU Studies, 2014), 91–92, 534. See further information about the date and content of the court event in Dan Vogel, *Early Mormon Documents*, vol. 5 (Salt Lake City: Signature Books, 2003), 434–35; and in "Mormonism," *Morning Star* (Limerick, ME), November 16, 1832.

83. See Reed's report of the incident that he delivered before the Saints in Nauvoo, "Some of the Remarks of John S. Reed, Esq., as Delivered before the State Convention," *Times and Seasons*, June 1, 1844, 549–52. See also JS's portrayal of the circumstance in Smith, Histories, "History Drafts, 1838–circa 1841," Drafts 1–3, *JSP, H1*:398–414, though he mentioned nothing about the events of the Melchizedek Priesthood restoration. See also Lydia Knight's account of her husband, Newel Knight's, lengthy portrayal of the circumstances of the court proceedings in Newel Knight, Autobiography and Journal, ca. 1871, 60–90, MS 19156, CHL, again, mentioning nothing about restoration of the priesthood.

84. Addison Everett to Joseph F. Smith, January 16, 1882, Joseph F. Smith Papers, MS 1325, box 12, folder 15, CHL.

Woman's Journal that they published in November 1890.[85] Another St. George local, Charles Lowell Walker, wrote on October 29, 1882, that at a prayer meeting Everett related the story, similar to the one he wrote to Joseph F. Smith.[86] Though Joseph F. Smith shared the story with other leaders, he ignored Everett's claims in his own 1889 article presented to the church as the "Restoration of the Melchisedec Priesthood."[87] Neither was it used by those of the leaders who were engaged in writing church history at the time, such as George Q. Cannon, also of the First Presidency, and Orson F. Whitney, an assistant church historian. And when Joseph F. Smith's son, Joseph Fielding Smith, addressed the "Restoration of the Melchizedek Priesthood" in the *Improvement Era* in 1904 he did

85. O. B. Huntington, "Words and Incidents of the Prophet Joseph's Life," *Young Woman's Journal*, November 1890, 75–76. Huntington copied Everett's February 17, 1881, letter to him into his diary, a letter that varied some in content from the letter Everett sent to Joseph F. Smith. Oliver B. Huntington, Diary, Book 14, 66–67, MSS 162, L. Tom Perry Special Collections, Brigham Young University.

Huntington circulated other unique incidents from early Mormon history, including what he said was JS's statement that "the moon was inhabited by a race of people, large in stature, averaging six feet, all dressed nearly alike, something like the fashion of the Quakers, and that they lived on an average to near the age of 1000 years," which he said Philo Dibble also heard. O. B. Huntington to A. Milton Musser, November 22, 1879, Amos Milton Musser Collection, 1879–1880, Persecution, MS 1264, CHL. See also Oliver B. Huntington, "The Inhabitants of the Moon," *Young Woman's Journal*, March 1892, 263; and Van Hale, "Mormons and Moonmen," *Sunstone* 7, no. 5 (September/October 1982): 12–17.

86. Charles Lowell Walker, *Diary of Charles Lowell Walker*, ed. A. Karl Larson and Katharine Miles Larson, 2 vols. (Logan, UT: Utah State University Press, 1980), 2:592 (October 29, 1882).

87. Joseph F. Smith, "Restoration of the Melchisedec Priesthood," *Contributor*, June 1889, 307–11 (not to be confused with the article by the same name written by his son Joseph Fielding Smith printed in 1904). "We have not, unfortunately, any account so definite, of the reception by Joseph and Oliver, of the Melchisedec Priesthood as we have of the confirmation of the Aaronic Priesthood" (309).

Apparently, other leaders referenced the information that Everett provided. Apostle Erastus Snow referred to the Melchizedek Priesthood restoration in Logan, Utah, on May 6, 1882. Erastus Snow, Sermon, May 6, 1882, *JD* 23:183; Apostle Franklin D. Richards indicated Joseph F. Smith shared Everett's letter with him on June 15, 1883, Journals, vol. 31, MS 1215, CHL. Assistant church historian B. H. Roberts was also aware of the account. Reviewing the *Latter Day Saints' Millennial Star*, Supplement, 1852, 32–33, while producing his edit of the *History of the Church*, Roberts included in the marginalia of the *Millennial Star* his consideration of Everett's account. On the page that became *History of the Church* 1:97 where JS and Cowdery "travelled all night, except a short time, during which we were forced to rest ourselves under a large tree by the way side, sleeping and watching alternately," Roberts wrote, "was it at this time, i.e., at time of their adventure that Mel. P was restored. See letter of Everett to J. F. S. & Richards' discou[rse]." Roberts Collection, 1883–1933, MS 1278, folder 690.

not mention or even allude to Everett's story, suggesting he did not take seriously the account.[88]

Besides Everett's primary claim, the other angle that he influenced for some is the timing his account suggests for the Melchizedek priesthood restoration. This wrinkle in the timeline of significant early church events comes from Everett's inclusion of lawyer John S. Reed in his story. If, as Everett reported, JS and Oliver's encounter with Peter, James, and John took place in the aftermath of the court affair mentioned, the date of that feature of priesthood restoration took place in late June or the first part of July 1830—*after* JS organized the church in April 1830. This is a significant contrast to what became the traditional Mormon story of the apostles' appearance in the wake of John the Baptist's ordination in 1829.[89]

It should be noted that it does not appear to have been a matter of urgency for church leaders at the time to codify the timing of the restoration of the Melchizedek priesthood in the nineteenth century.[90] Consequently, perceptions about chronology and events varied.[91] George A. Smith, LDS Church historian since the mid-1850s, exhibited the ambiguities about priesthood restoration in 1874 when he replied to a missionary friend who inquired of him about "the time when the Melchisedec Priesthood was given." George A.'s reply portrayed the lack of specificity that prevailed at the time. Not addressing the matter of

88. Joseph F[ielding] Smith, "Restoration of the Melchizedek Priesthood," 938–43. Joseph Fielding Smith, pitted at the time against the RLDS Church and their rival claims, began the article noting that the RLDS Church professed that "this priesthood was not restored by those heavenly messengers [Peter, James, and John], but that it grew out of the Aaronic priesthood." 938.

89. Larry C. Porter, "Dating the Restoration of the Melchizedek Priesthood," *Ensign*, June 1979, 5–10; also Porter, "The Restoration of the Priesthood," *Religious Studies Center Newsletter* 9, no. 3 (May 1995): 1–12.

90. See Robin Jensen's report of church leaders' evident interest to better understand priesthood restoration at the nineteenth-century's conclusion. Jensen, "'Archives of the Better World,'" 268–75.

91. See for example how William I. Appleby characterized the bestowal of priesthood upon JS in his 1844 pamphlet—*A Dissertation on Nebuchadnezzar's Dream*—where he stated, "In the year 1830, *after* the Book was translated and published, the Angel of God according to promise conferred the Holy Priesthood upon Mr. Smith, and gave unto him commandments to Baptize with water in the name of Jesus, and build up the Church of Christ; which accordingly was organized April 6th, A.D. 1830, with six members." William I. Appleby, *A Dissertation on Nebuchadnezzar's Dream* (Philadelphia: Brown, Bicking and Guilbert, 1844), 23 (emphasis added). In Appleby's 1848 autobiography he used the same language, obviously derived from the pamphlet, to state his understanding that the priesthood was given after the Book of Mormon was published. William I. Appleby, Autobiography and Journal, 1848–1856, MS 1401, CHL.

apostolic authority being returned to the earth "before the organization of the church," he wrote "I always understood that the conference of the 6th of June 1831 was the time that Joseph ordained some of the Elders to the higher priesthood of Melchesidic."[92] Undoubtedly, his friend remained perplexed. It took decades for the sequence and particulars of the early events of Mormonism to be systematized.

Lineal Right to the Priesthood

Lastly, there is the matter of priesthood acquisition by lineal right. An often-overlooked aspect of priesthood succession by Mormons today is the fact that JS apparently determined at one time that one of his sons or another family member should succeed him as leader of the kingdom. The issue had currency among the RLDS people, but was of little concern among Mormons after the nineteenth century.[93] The notion had antecedents in the prophetic genealogy portrayed in the biblical record of ancient Israel. Before the prophet's death, there was apparently an assumption among the Mormons that JS would replicate the patriarchal precedent. It followed that JS would live to a ripe old age when he would designate one of his male heirs to succeed him. His premature death moved the matter forward when no one in the church was prepared to instigate a plan that had not been outlined.[94]

Evidence exists of a theoretical framework about lineal rights of priesthood power having been discussed by the prophet at least as early as March 1841: "There was a preistHood Confered upon the sons of Levi throughout the Jeneration of the Jews & he also said they beCome heirs to that pristHood By Linage or Decent,"[95] with implications that the premise remained valid. Not surprisingly, given the biblical example of the ancient patriarchs, the sequence of father-to-son priesthood descent had relevance after JS's death. But due to Joseph III's youth—he was twelve at the time of his father's murder—and other concerns, the issue gained no gravity at the time. As the boy grew older it became an issue

92. George A. Smith to John A. West, June 20, 1874, Historian's Office Letterpress Copybooks, vol. 3, 838, CR 100 38, box 28, folder 4, CHL.

93. The matter would probably have remained irrelevant among Latter-day Saints if the issue had not been raised by Mark Hofmann, famed forger of early Mormon documents. In 1981 Hofmann offered to the LDS Church a January 17, 1844, blessing purported to have been written by JS scribe Thomas Bullock and endorsed by JS that appointed the prophet's son Joseph III as his successor. The document created a stir in the Mormon historical community until the forgery was discovered. Turley, *Victims*, 40–57.

94. See treatments about the situation in Roger D. Launius, *Joseph Smith III: Pragmatic Prophet* (Urbana: University of Illinois Press, 1995), 30–35; and Quinn, *Mormon Hierarchy*, 235–41.

95. Smith, Sermon, March 21, 1841, William Patterson McIntire, Notebook, 1840–1845, 17, MS 1014, CHL.

among those who dissented from Brigham Young's leadership. Illustrating the perception regarding the Smith family's designation as having lineal prerogatives, JS's clerk William Clayton wrote on July 12, 1844, after JS's death, that it was understood that if JS and Hyrum "were taken away," at least in the temporal matters of the church, Samuel H. "would be his successor."[96] Samuel, though, died just a month later, on July 30, 1844, rendering the issue moot. Later, the last living Smith brother, William, claimed his own right to the lineal priesthood after JS's death. But William, who had been one of the apostles and church patriarch before being severed from the church by his former colleagues, managed to only attract a few to his claims.[97] His quixotic and questionable behavior precluded any serious attention by LDS Church leaders regarding his pleas.

Brigham Young apparently had hoped for reconciliation with the Smith family in the aftermath of JS's death but tensions thwarted any efforts to do so. After the church was well established in the West, Young publicly expressed his optimism that someday the Smiths would reconnect to the church. In 1860 he publicly invited JS's "boys" to embrace the LDS Church: "When they make their appearance before this people, full of his [God's] power, there are none but what will say—'Amen! we are ready to receive you.'"[98] When Joseph III assumed leadership of the RLDS Church in 1860, the act probably precluded any reconnection of his family with Utah Mormonism. By 1869 when he sent his younger brothers, Alexander and David Hyrum, to Utah on a proselyting mission they were roundly rebuffed by Mormon leaders. By that time Joseph III had been at the helm of the RLDS Church for almost a decade and there was no mystery about his disdain for the Brighamites.[99] The alternative to apostolic authority from the Smith family thereafter had no relevance to the LDS Church. Even with other contenders like James Jesse Strang, Sidney Rigdon, David Whitmer, and Lyman Wight vying to lead the church, the swell of support for the Twelve

96. Clayton, *An Intimate Chronicle*, 138. The reference concerns the appointment of a "trustee" to be responsible for administering church affairs. See also, Quinn, *Mormon Hierarchy*, 152–54, 213; Irene M. Bates and E. Gary Smith, *Lost Legacy: The Mormon Office of Presiding Patriarch* (Urbana: University of Illinois Press, 2003), 72–73.

97. See William Smith, *A Revelation Given to William Smith, in 1847, on the Apostasy of the Church and the Pruning of the Vineyard of the Lord* (Philadelphia: n.p., 1848), 1; Isaac Sheen's *Melchisedic and Aaronic Herald*, March 1849, 2; *Epistle of the Twelve: Legal Authorities of the Church of Jesus Christ of Latter Day Saints* [William Smith's church] [N.p.: n.p., ca. 1851], 5.

98. Brigham Young, Sermon, June 3, 1860, *JD*, 8:69. It has been argued that, beside Joseph III as JS's oldest son being a viable heir to his father, David Hyrum Smith was determined by JS to have a special status in church leadership in due time. See Quinn, *Mormon Hierarchy*, 231, 238; Launius, *Joseph Smith III*, 225–26.

99. See coverage of the 1869 mission of Joseph III and his brothers—Alexander and David—to Utah in Avery, *From Mission to Madness*, 87–113.

Apostles' leadership moved a sufficient majority of the Saints to accept their declarations of authority by way of their apostleship. Lineal rights to the priesthood had no practical relevance in the church thereafter.[100]

The exercise given above is meant to illustrate the developing transition within the LDS Church of theology, doctrine, and methodology that eventually comprehended priesthood and its restoration. Created by the interspersion of confusion, understanding, and subsequent establishment of norms that fostered patterns of belief and doctrine, Mormon authority after JS was clothed in garb not known during the prophet's lifetime. It emerged in part despite the paltry documentary record representing JS and Cowdery's full explanation of what happened to them in their acquisition of heavenly authority. Cursory expressions about the priesthood from the church's first and second elder, which obscure as much as they reveal, supply modern investigators with only portions of what could be known. Nevertheless, enough survives that it is quite clear that John the Baptist's bestowal of priesthood authority—the lesser/Aaronic priesthood—satisfied to early church members the essentials necessary to both gather and nurture a body of believers. Later the role eventually assumed by the Twelve Apostles by way of the greater or Melchizedek priesthood emerged after JS's demise. As the importance of their authority diffused among the Latter-day Saints, what we now view as priesthood development took root as church leaders formulated what to them was a workable understanding of what the priesthood was and its significance to the emerging kingdom of God.

100. The premise is based upon D&C 22:2 (1835), D&C 68:16 (1981). There it is stated that "literal descendants of Aaron" have "a legal right to the bishopric, if they are the first born among the sons of Aaron," which appeals to the notion of lineal rights within the priesthood. However, the provision has never been implemented within the LDS Church. Later leaders have qualified the designation stipulating that the passage referred to the church's presiding bishop.

CHAPTER 10

Order of the Priesthood

Organization

JS and Oliver Cowdery formed the Church of Christ in April 1830 anticipating Jesus's imminent return as foretold by the New Testament writers. Without precise particulars in preparing for that great event, the collaborators—perhaps counterintuitively—implemented a constitutional foundation for a church that had designs for future perpetuity. With a background of visionary authorization that later provided the bearing walls of the faith, the generalities of the "Articles and Covenants" they created for the church provisioned it with organizational statutes and protocols. Given JS and Cowdery's lack of institutional experience, the platform proved to be one of their great achievements. The traditions of Protestantism widely known at the time of Mormonism's origin presented several models of possible church polity. Those familiar with Christian denominations and their visible liturgy and practice will recognize that Mormonism assumed fundamental aspects of the contemporary religious world into their operations. The King James Version of the Bible, water baptism, ministerial offices, and celebration of the Lord's Last Supper by the early Mormons indicates, with some variations, the embrace by JS and Cowdery of Christian essentials represented in the American landscape.

The religious landscape in America had proven to be a movement in flux. With vague biblical descriptions of a church in the first century, Christians in colonial America had applied the existing evidences of structure to apply polity, principle, and practice to their organizations.[1] With precedent from Europe's Protestant Reformation and their own English dissent from Rome, reformers did not confine themselves to sixteenth-century alternatives to solve the quandary over the perpetuation of Christianity. With establishment in 1534, the Church of England with its attendant political power progressively expected

1. Daniel N. Schowalter, "Church," in *The Oxford Companion to the Bible*, ed. Bruce M. Metzger and Michael D. Coogan (New York: Oxford University Press, 1993), 121–22.

conformity provoking some adherents to rebel. A separatist movement against Anglican dominance drove the dissenters to the North American colonies. Independent and away from British enforcement, a Reformed Christian tradition primarily based on Calvinistic religious perspectives became for many the de facto colonial religion.

A source of stability and unification employed by the Massachusetts Bay Colony nurtured those known thereafter as Puritans. Their Reformed platform used its theological premises to inform both religious and civil government in the colonies.[2] Other attempts to systematize belief among the Protestants took hold in Europe, but the 1647 Westminster Confession commissioned by the Church of England, produced the most detailed of the outlines of belief and practice affecting the American church.[3] Prepared in thirty-three brief chapters of what became the polity of Reformed theology and tradition, the Confession elaborated on matters "Of God, and of the Holy Trinity" and of "Christ the Mediator." Theologically, "God's Eternal Decree" of the "high mystery of predestination" where "some men and angels are predestinated unto everlasting life; and others are foreordained to everlasting death" established believers' perspectives of God's decrees. With the "Fall of Man, of Sin, and the Punishment thereof;" "God's Covenant with Man;" "Free Will," "Justification," "Sanctification," and "Faith," the famous and not so famous divines of the day inculcated the philosophy of life within the elect of God.[4] Regarding baptism, the Confession indicated that it had to be performed by a lawfully called "minister of the Gospel" who administered the ordinance "by pouring, or sprinkling water upon the person" who professed "faith in and obedience unto Christ." Also applicable were the infant children of the "believing parents."[5] The "Westminster Confession would become by far the most influential doctrinal symbol in American Protestant history."[6]

Among the first principles articulated in the Confession was the "authority of the Holy Scripture." It was from the Bible that those who rejected Catholicism and its claims of lineal descent from Jesus's apostles derived their license to create religious bodies of worship. Thus, within the books of the Old and New Testament, the scripture "ought to be believed, and obeyed," and "depends not upon the testimony of any man, or Church; but wholly upon God (who is truth itself) the author thereof: and therefore it is to be received, because it is

2. Edmund S. Morgan, *Visible Saints: The History of a Puritan Idea* (New York: New York University Press, 1963).
3. Ahlstrom, *Religious History of the American People*, 1:118.
4. Westminster Confession, Center for Reformed Theology and Apologetics, http://www.reformed.org/documents/wcf_with_proofs/.
5. Westminster Confession, "Of Baptism," chap. 28.
6. Ahlstrom, *Religious History of the American People*, 1:177.

the Word of God."[7] These elaborated provisions were regulated by appointed "magistrates" through "synods and councils…to set down rules and directions for the better ordering of the public worship of God, and government" of the church. The "synods and councils, ministerially" determined "controversies of faith" and "which decrees and determinations, if consonant to the Word of God, are to be received with reverence and submission; not only for their agreement with the Word, but also for the power whereby they are made, as being an ordinance of God appointed thereunto in His Word."[8] And while the "main body of the Church of England would repudiate the confession…it would remain the basic doctrinal statement of the English and New England Congregationalists."[9] This was in part colonial America's contribution to the pre-Revolutionary religious milieu.

But in the later part of the eighteenth century forward, the Methodists offered alternatives to the strictures of Calvinism that quickly gained traction in both America's rural and urban districts. Francis Asbury, an Englishman born in 1745 who had personal ties to Methodist pioneer John Wesley, immigrated to America in 1771 to evangelize the colonies with the growing Methodist faith. Asbury's success was immediate and with those who embraced Methodism added religious complexity and vitality to the Reformed-satiated religionists of the day. Significantly, they offered an alternative of free-will theology to the determinism of Calvinism. In the last quarter of the eighteenth century, the Methodists had figured out how to move a significant sector of the population to revel in Arminian thought that opposed predestination and strict Calvinism.[10] A vestige of the Protestant Reformation, the principle essential they espoused was the *authority of the scripture*—the Old and New Testaments—that governed everything that fashioned their stance. They had determined, as they codified in 1782, "that the uninterrupted succession of Bishops from the apostles can be proved neither from Scripture nor antiquity,"[11] rejecting Catholic claims of episcopal succession from the Apostle Peter. "The Holy Scripture," they argued, "containeth all things necessary to salvation, so that whatsoever is not read therein, nor may be proved thereby, is not to be required of any man." Moreover, "it should be believed as an Article of Faith, or be thought requisite or necessary to salvation."[12] Therefore,

7. Westminster Confession, "Of the Holy Scripture," chap. 1.
8. Westminster Confession, "Of Synods and Council," chap. 31.
9. Philip Benedict, *Christ's Churches Purely Reformed: A Social History of Calvinism* (New Haven: Yale University Press, 2002), 402.
10. Hatch, *Democratization of American Christianity*, 81–93; Marty, *Pilgrims in Their Own Land*, 170–79; Howe, *What Hath God Wrought*, 176–81.
11. David Sherman, *History of the Revisions of the Discipline of the Methodist Episcopal Church* (New York: Nelson and Phillips, 1874), 100.
12. Ibid., 102.

while "The Church hath power to decree rites or ceremonies, and authority in controversies of faith...it is not lawful for the Church to ordain any thing that is contrary to God's word written."[13]

The outlines and expectations for those who professed to have received God's call to minister were also addressed. As there was no way to glean from the Bible the personalized mark of the Almighty for a particular individual to minister on earth, the collective power of the believers, derived from the authority of the scripture, provided the mechanism. "It is lawful for any man to take upon him the office of public preaching, or ministering the sacraments in the congregation," but it was then necessary that "he be lawfully called and sent to execute the same" by those "who have public authority given unto them in the congregation to call and send ministers into the Lord's vineyard."[14] Methodists determined church governance and ministering by the authority of the scripture for those "called."

It was understood that in church councils those composing the bodies "may err, and sometimes have erred, even in things pertaining unto God. Wherefore things ordained by them as necessary to salvation have neither strength nor authority, unless it may be declared that they be taken out of Holy Scripture."[15] Recognition of the variables that inevitably characterized centralized congregations or far flung outposts also provided encouragement: "It is not necessary that rites and ceremonies should in all places be the same, or exactly alike, for they have been always different, and may be changed according to the diversity of countries, times, and men's manners, so that nothing be ordained against God's word."[16] The enormous success of Wesleyan thought in antebellum America indicates the "Disciplines" worked for the Methodists.

The appeal of Methodism, clearly having made an impression on JS by his own admission, had also drawn interest by others who later became Latter-day Saints.[17] A distinct alternative to the Calvinism of the day, the Methodists were in full bloom in JS's generation. "Before the [Revolutionary] war there were only 4,921 Methodists in America," by 1816 there were "212,000 of them, mostly recent converts."[18] However, despite their strength and several decades of American influence in the nineteenth century's first quarter, the Methodists apparently held little sway upon JS as he matured and the heavenly ministrations of the

13. Ibid., 106.
14. Ibid., 106–7.
15. Ibid., 106.
16. Ibid., 109–10.
17. Smith, Histories, "History Drafts, 1838–circa 1841," Draft 2, *JSP, H1*:210; Bushman, *Rough Stone Rolling*, 69.
18. Marty, *Pilgrims in Their Own Land*, 171.

1820s purged most sympathy he may have held for them, their structure, or other vestiges of Christianity.

Organizational Structure Begins to Unfold

The revelations JS received in the late 1820s plotted a new path for Mormonism, particularly as described in the Book of Mormon. The book's portrayal of the dissemination of religious authority—vague though it was—served as the precedent upon which JS's subsequent revelations outlined a structure for the nascent church. The actuating feature of early Mormonism that ensured its divergence from the rest of Christianity came by way of JS's experiences with Oliver Cowdery during their production of the Book of Mormon in 1829, i.e., the provocation they received from the Nephite text that authority was a necessity requiring divine imprimatur. Though the structure that became Mormonism of the 1830s awaited revelatory direction, there is no mistake that both JS and Cowdery understood that they had been empowered to do something more than replicate the Christianity that surrounded them.

Mormonism developed from a rather different schema regarding church polity and administration. Though there are commonalities with other Christian organizations regarding nomenclature and function, JS's vision of the "ancient order of things" required a substantially diverse construction than what surrounded him.[19] Among many Latter-day Saints, it has long been assumed that JS's encounter with God and Jesus in his First Vision in 1820 fully equipped his thinking and understanding of God and his designs. To make the point of JS's unique circumstances, some have multiplied the summary of what he gleaned from his early experience suggesting he was thereafter comprehensively informed about God's nature and designs. In contrast, LDS Apostle Boyd K. Packer explained in 1996: "Some suppose that the organization was handed to the Prophet Joseph Smith like a set of plans and specifications for a building, with all of the details known at the beginning. But it did not come that way. Rather, it came a piece at a time as the Brethren were ready and as they inquired of God."[20] Scholars of Mormonism have recognized the rollout of belief and understanding: "The LDS belief system was not revealed whole, complete, as it were, in every detail.... Mormonism's theology was introduced incrementally," according to Jan Shipps.[21] That also included the organizational structure of

19. Matthew C. Godfrey, "'Seeking after Monarchal Power and Authority': Joseph Smith and Leadership in the Church of Christ, 1831–1832," *Mormon Historical Studies* 15, nos. 1–2 (Spring/Fall 2012): 16–19.

20. Boyd K. Packer, "The Twelve Apostles," *Ensign*, November 1996, 6.

21. Jan Shipps, *Sojourner in the Promised Land: Forty Years among the Mormons* (Urbana: University of Illinois Press, 2000), 292.

the faith. To misunderstand this process during JS's life promises to not only distort the prophet's growth as a human being but also how he carried out his commission.

By the end of June 1829 when Oliver Cowdery laid down his pen as JS's Book of Mormon amanuensis, several revelations JS had received that influenced the church's emerging configuration had been committed to paper. Starkly countering the notion of a closed canon, the revelations gave specific directions to individuals indicating that the earth then shifted beneath their feet. Two contemporary events underscored the notion. As was discussed earlier, during JS's and Cowdery's translation of the Book of Mormon, on May 15, 1829, John the Baptist delivered to them authority to perform efficacious baptisms. The following month, Oliver obtained what amounted to new revelation about priesthood protocols inspired by what he gleaned from serving as JS's Book of Mormon textual scribe. Scholars have known about Cowdery's revelation for years, though most others have paid little attention to its precedence for JS's "Articles and Covenants." Besides establishing early that Cowdery was at the outset likely a full partner in founding the church, Cowdery's June 1829 divine decree helped shape the inauguration of JS's new religion. JS, soon after the church's organization, obtained a revelation designating him as the only one to receive revelation for the church. But initially, their work together appears to be more of a cooperative venture. Their joint work laid out the likelihood that a Book of Mormon-type gathering of believers could be organized with precedent in the book.[22]

Cowdery's revelation outlined such measures as the mode of baptism: "And now behold these are the words which ye shall say calling them by name saying Having authority given me of Jesus Christ I baptize you in the name of the Father & of the Son & of the Holy Ghost." The revelation also stipulated the protocol of ordination: "Ye shall lay your hands upon them & say In the name of Jesus Christ I ordain you to be a Priest or if he be a Teacher I ordain you to be a Teacher."[23] Besides the procedure for admitting proselytes into the church, the commission to the two also provided for creation of a structure of believers to perpetuate the faith. With foretelling the organization of a church as outlined in JS's "Article and Covenants" that followed, the Cowdery revelation also implied the understanding that JS and Cowdery had acquired power beyond what was given to them by John the Baptist that limited them to perform baptisms.

22. See discussion of the origin of Oliver Cowdery's "Articles of the Church of Christ, June 1829," in *JSP, D1*:368–70.

23. Ibid., 371, not to be confused with the "Articles and Covenants" that became part of the Mormon canon. Cowdery's original document is housed in the CHL as Oliver Cowdery, "Articles of the Church of Christ, 1829," MS 3408; see also Scott H. Faulring, "An Examination of the 1829 'Articles of the Church of Christ' in Relation to Section 20 of the Doctrine and Covenants," in Welch and Morris, eds. *Oliver Cowdery*, 155–93.

The several dozen who gathered on Tuesday, April 6, 1830, at Peter Whitmer Sr.'s farmhouse in Fayette Township, New York, heard delivery of and approved JS's Articles and Covenants that superseded Cowdery's earlier revelation.[24] Still, the text informed the reader that the church's foundation had been "given" to both JS and Oliver.[25] Though the earliest adherents knew it only by handwritten distribution, the charter and bylaws outlining the church organization proved remarkably durable, despite modifications over time. The text first appeared in print on April 19, 1831, in Painesville, Ohio, from a copy that newspaper publisher E. D. Howe had obtained from Martin Harris.[26] It took another year for the church to print the Articles and Covenants in June 1832 as the opening declaration in its *Evening and the Morning Star*. Though its intended publication in the 1833 Book of Commandments came to naught because the church print shop in Independence was destroyed on July 20, 1833, the document had circulated some as evidenced by missionaries copying into their journals the text of the Articles and Covenants as they departed Kirtland for their missions.[27] Finally published in the Doctrine and Covenants in August 1835, the Articles and Covenants held statute status in other revelatory pronouncements from JS.[28]

The Articles and Covenants boldly stipulated several extraordinary elements of anticipatory expectation for JS and Cowdery. Both had been "called of God & ordained an Apostle of Jesus Christ."[29] Particulars about the purposes of God and the role of Jesus as redeemer, including affirmations about Protestant priorities regarding "grace," "justification," and "sanctification," portrayed fundamentals of church theology at the outset. Other essential components of the religion were presented "so that all things may be done in order."[30] After baptism, members should expect of themselves "that there may be works & faith agreeable to the Holy scriptures walking in holyness before the Lord."[31] Duties of the several initial church offices of apostle, elder, priests, teachers, and deacons were announced, though, as the Joseph Smith Papers editors state, the Articles and Covenants "did not explicitly associate these offices with the priesthood."[32] The

24. Smith, Revelations, April 10, 1830, *JSP, R1*:60–68 [D&C 20]. Note the date affixed to the revelatory text being April 10 versus the date of the church's organization on April 6.
25. Smith, Revelations, April 10, 1830, *JSP, R1*:60 [D&C 20:2–3 (1981)].
26. "The Mormon Creed," *Telegraph* (Painesville, OH), April 19, 1831.
27. Book of Commandments (1833), Chapter 24, 47–55; "Book of Commandments," *JSP, R2*:59–67. See Zebedee Coltrin's missionary diary that includes at the beginning the Articles and Covenants. Zebedee Coltrin, Diaries, 1832–1834, MS 1443, CHL.
28. Smith, Revelations, October 1830, *JSP, R1*:49 [D&C 33:14 (1981)]; Smith, Revelations, February 9, 1831, *JSP, R1*:77 [D&C 42:13 (1981)].
29. Smith, Revelations, April 10, 1830, *JSP, R1*:60 [D&C 20:2–3 (1981)].
30. Smith, Revelations, April 10, 1830, *JSP, R1*:65 [D&C 20:68 (1981)].
31. Smith, Revelations, April 10, 1830, *JSP, R1*:65–66 [D&C 20:69 (1981)].
32. Introduction to Smith, Revelations, September 22–23, 1832, *JSP, D2*:290 [D&C 84 (1981)].

language the offices were to use in administering the ordinances of the church—regular gatherings in "conference," authorization through "certificate" and "license," and the finality of those "expelled from the church"—were all found in the document. An outline that sustained the church throughout JS's life had been instituted. Order became high priority. Upon the church's removal from New York to Ohio, another revelation JS received reflected the consciousness of doing things uniformly: "I say unto you that it shall not be given to anyone to go forth to preach my Gospel or to build up my Church except he be ordained by someone who has authority and it is known to the Church that he has authority and has been regularly ordained by the heads of the Church."[33] The injunction illustrated the caution applied to expanding the church to ensure that general and local affairs were handled expeditiously.

Mormon sentiment regarding godly authority held that there had been "no legal administrator, neither had been for fourteen hundred years, until God had called them to the office."[34] The premise thereafter became standard understanding of church members and its missionaries regarding the anticipated renewal of biblical power. Ezra Booth, for example, reported Mormon consciousness in October 1831 that what they did had divine authorization; their baptisms, he stated, were "prefaced with—'having authority given me of Jesus Christ.'"[35] Authority held within the church therefore became one of the most important features of Mormonism to justify the place of JS in the Christian world. Periodic ordinations of men to the priesthood offices of elder, priest, teacher, and deacon were common in the church's first year. But the June 1831 conference held in the Kirtland area added another dimension of priesthood illustrating that the church had turned another corner.

The reader will remember that those in early Mormonism not only planned for the imminent Second Coming of Jesus, they also expected extraordinary manifestations from heaven to prepare for the event. They saw the church as the primary catalyst to actuate the biblical prophecies unfolding before them. Consistent with the incremental roll out of events such as reception of authority first from John the Baptist and then from Peter, James, and John, they awaited continuing enablement to vivify the church. Revelations obtained by JS in January and February 1831 laid out further augmentation, though much of what JS had obtained from Jesus was distributed by word of mouth as the revelations were not yet published. As male followers learned, the expectation had a collective

33. Smith, Revelations, February 9, 1831, *JSP, R1*:76–77 [D&C 42:11 (1981), clear text].
34. Oliver Cowdery, interview with Josiah Jones, ca. November 1830 (but written in 1831) in Kirtland, Ohio, "History of the Mormonites," *Evangelist*, June 1, 1841, 134–35.
35. Ezra Booth to Ira Eddy, October 20, 1831, *Ohio Star* (Ravenna, OH), quoted in E.D. Howe, *Mormonism Unvailed*, 180. This predates insertion of notions of "by the power of the priesthood" that emerged later in the church, as previously described.

component that came by way of a conference gathering of priesthood holders in June 1831. The highly anticipated meeting running from June 3–6 drew sixty-two elders, priests, and teachers from the surrounding area to Kirtland.[36] First they foresaw an extraordinary dispensation of power to the faithful: "You shall be endowed with power from on high,"[37] and "that inasmuch as they are faithful and exercise faith in me I will pour out my spirit upon them in the day that they assemble themselves together."[38]

Second came the addition of a new feature of the church's authority: the higher priesthood. Those familiar with the manner in which the modern church discusses priesthood may misunderstand the developmental stage of this priesthood innovation. Among the first items of business conducted at the June 1831 conference were the ordinations of five men "to the high Priesthood under the hand of br. Joseph Smith jr." Modern jargon classifies those ordained as being made "high priests" in the church's Melchizedek priesthood (though that designation came later). But to members at the time, the notion of "high Priesthood" may have initially suggested a classification elevated above the priesthood offices of elder, priest, teacher, and deacon.[39] The paucity of description of just what JS meant in introducing the new designation likely helped create the apparent confusion that followed the action. The extant record allows us only glimpses at what the new position held for the church at the time. At a meeting two weeks after the conference those ordained to the "Highpriesthood" were simply listed on the same conference roster with the "Elders," "Priests," "Teachers," and "Deacons," suggesting the designation was understood as another priesthood office rather than another dimension of authority.[40] However, the next winter, at a "General Conference" held in Zion, some attending were classified as "Elders... who were ordained to the H. P. H. [high priesthood]," and "Elders who were not ordained to the H. P. H.,"[41] indicating that some understood the high priesthood to be an added dimension to the priesthood offices then existing. Later the concept was understood simply to be an additional priesthood office in the greater or Melchizedek priesthood.

JS instituted a third component of the "high priesthood" several months later at a conference on October 25, 1831. The innovation suggested a priesthood component that tied apostolic authority as expressed in Jesus's bestowal of a sealing

36. See overview and texts from the conference in *JSP, D1*:317–32.
37. Smith, Revelations, January 2, 1831, *JSP, R1*:58 [D&C 38:32 (1981)].
38. Smith, Revelations, February 1831, *JSP, R1*:88–89 [D&C 44:2 (1981), clear text].
39. See discussion regarding the relationship of the "higher priesthood," "Melchizedek Priesthood," and the office of "high priest" in Smith, Documents, Historical Introduction, circa June 3–4, 1831, Minute Book 2, *JSP, D1*:320–21.
40. Smith, Documents, October 25–26, 1831, Minute Book 2, *JSP, D2*:80.
41. Smith, Documents, Oliver Cowdery to Joseph Smith, January 28, 1832, *JSP, D2*:165.

function upon Peter to the restoration. The text in Matthew stated: "I will give unto thee the keys of the kingdom of heaven: and whatsoever though shalt bind on earth shall be bound in heaven: and whatsoever thou shalt loose on earth shall be loosed in heaven" (Matt. 16:19). At the Orange, Ohio, conference on October 25, JS—according to minutes kept by Oliver Cowdery—told the men in attendance "that the order of the Highpriesthood is that they have power given them to seal up the Saints unto eternal life." There may have been a millenarian component to the promise, but nothing survives to describe how the measure was meant to alter the effectual course of a Mormon's life. The promise, likely referencing similar notions in the Bible where the faithful were "sealed in the Lamb's Book of Life,"[42] may also have been included in the concept. Thus, some missionaries dispersed thereafter sometimes sealed up entire Mormon congregations to eternal life during their missionary travels.[43] Though the practice soon lost its urgency, five years later JS formulated a modified notion of the function of sealing after he and Oliver witnessed the heavenly visitation and conferral of authority connected with the dedication of the Kirtland House of the Lord in April 1836. There, as described earlier, JS stated, "Elijah, the Prophet" appeared to them and gave them yet other keys to seal and bind on earth and in heaven.[44] Another manifestation of the concept, somewhat coincident to the Kirtland Temple dedication, is Joseph Smith Sr.'s use of the phrase "I seal thee up unto eternal life" in the patriarchal blessings he gave to members in 1835–1836.[45]

The conference at Orange, Ohio, on October 25, 1831, also demonstrated that inherent within priesthood offices was the understanding among members that there existed a hierarchy in distribution and the functions of authority. Priesthood holders—those of the high priesthood, elders, priests, teachers, and deacons who attended the conference—received instruction from JS about progression within the structure when he stated "that those who had been previously

42. Smith, Documents, October 25, 1831, Minute Book 2, *JSP, D2*:82, 85 [Rev. 3:5, 13:8, 17:8, 20:12, 21:27].

43. Showing the extension of God's promises, the church elders were told on November 1, 1831, to "preach the gospel to every creature," baptizing them with the expectation that those who believed would "be blessed with signs," that they would "know the signs of the times," and that "power" would be given "to seal them up unto Eternal life." The elders accordingly responded. The same day—in another articulation of revelation—JS stated that regarding divine authority given to the church, it provided them power "to seal both on earth and in heaven." Smith, Revelations, November 1, 1831, *JSP, R1*: 153–54, 173–76 [D&C 68:8–12, 1:8 (1981)]. Consequently, missionary Orson Pratt on August 26 and September 8, 1833, before leaving New Hampshire for Kirtland, "sealed up the Church to eternal life," *Orson Pratt Journals*, 24–25. See also Reynolds Cahoon, mid-November 1831, Diary, MS 1115, CHL; Prince, *Power from on High*, 162–63; and Godfrey, "A Culmination of Learning," 172.

44. Smith, Journals, April 3, 1836, *JSP, J1*:222.

45. See Marquardt, *Early Patriarchal Blessings of the Church of Jesus Christ of Latter-day Saints.*

ordained Priests would be ordained Elders, & the others would be ordained Priests."[46] One's priesthood rank inevitably impacted how the men viewed each other. Considering man's nature to achieve and receive notice, it is significant that there was not more discord over the matter than there was among the brethren. An elders quorum meeting in Kirtland in July 1838 illustrated how some viewed the sequence of positions within the structure. With the proposal that several be ordained to the Melchizedek priesthood, one brother complained about their "Ordination on the Account of thair not passing through the Lessor Priesthood," which he "concidered proper and necesery." The comment provoked a motion to seek the counsel of church leaders to resolve the matter.[47] It should be no surprise that over time men began to associate priesthood office with status in the church. To the women's Relief Society, JS spoke on April 28, 1842, of the "disposition of man, to consider the lower offices in the church dishonorable and to look with jealous eyes upon the standing of others." He lamented the "nonsense of the human heart, for a person to be aspiring to other stations than appointed of God."[48] While rarely provoking overt rebellion, the sensitivity about priesthood grade within the church for some remained an issue for generations.

Effectuating the Priesthood Structure

The rudimentary distribution of authority represented above with its several facets not common in modern Mormon priesthood practice indicates in part the developmental nature of the priesthood offices and their function in the church's first years. It also shows the departure from informality that some within the early church anticipated when they first joined.[49] Layering the church with offices, designations, and functions took some away from the early hope that Mormonism would simply operate as a gathering of believers with the Book of Mormon in hand and the portal of baptism to confirm their adherence as they awaited the second return of Jesus. That sentiment lost currency as JS's revelations multiplied.

As one might suppose, once Kirtland received designation as the gathering place, church members at the outset practiced their faith within what proved to be a local arrangement. At the same time Kirtland grew, the Independence,

46. Smith, Documents, October 25, 1831, Minute Book 2, *JSP, D2*:86.

47. *Kirtland Elders' Quorum Record*, July 15, 1838, 46–47.

48. Derr et al., *First Fifty Years of Relief Society*, 54. See also Brigham Young's words given on February 16, 1847, describing the condition of jealousy over church position in the early church: John D. Lee, *Journals of John D. Lee: 1846–47 and 1859*, ed. Charles Kelly (Salt Lake City: University of Utah Press, 1984), 77–78.

49. See David Whitmer's explanation of how JS corrupted the original intent of the restoration by the addition of priesthood offices, hierarchy, and other "errors." Whitmer, *An Address to All Believers in Christ*, 28, 33–35, 42, 45–48.

Missouri, satellite designated as Zion also required administrative direction. Though Zion also had centralized characteristics, congregations in the region also formed. Each had a presiding authority with others in the congregation falling under operational provisions of the Articles and Covenants. As the church grew, the fledgling branches in both the East and West required regular nurturing. Oliver Cowdery, for instance, at a small October 1831 conference in Hiram, Ohio, "made a move that this conference take into consideration the propriety of appointing six Elders to visit the several branches of this church setting them in order."[50] Consequently, "As the Church expanded and became more geographically diverse," according to JS scholar Matthew Godfrey, "Smith implemented a more formal administrative structure in the Church," though "some of his followers—many of whom had been schooled in religions with more democratic structures—did not readily accept such control."[51] The move indicated that growing congregations of the church that formed away from the hubs of Kirtland and Independence required attention to be kept within the orbit of Mormon protocols.

Within the outline of conventions explained in the Articles and Covenants, JS then had to instruct both the early believers and the new initiates in the generalities and subtleties of his perspectives. He planned for opportunities "so that the members might understand the ancient manner of conducting meetings as they were led by the Holy Ghost," considering "that this was not perfectly known by many of the Elders of this Church."[52] The appeal to biblical antecedents, augmented with implications that JS had received revelation about ecclesiastical structure, proved to be his method of furnishing the church with strategy and structure. The gesture illustrated his confidence that the inspiration of the Holy Spirit would congeal the minds and hearts of church members into unity and singular purpose. Though there were times when JS expected conformity, the premise also represented his style of administration by allowing expressions of individuality in church affairs rather than dogmatic insistence upon conformity to rigid outlines of performance. The early principle established soon after the church's organization stating that "all things shall be done by common consent in the Church"[53] established a consciousness dispelling the notion of a dictatorial and despotic hierarchy. That is, proposals for adjustments and changes were raised before the members for approval before implementation, in theory spontaneously moving the church toward what JS presented to them. This provided the foundation for the later operations of conferences, councils, and quorums,

50. Smith, Documents, October 11, 1831, Minute Book 2, *JSP, D*2:75.

51. Godfrey, "'Seeking after Monarchal Power and Authority,'" 31.

52. Smith, Documents, October 11, 1831, Minute Book 2, *JSP, D*2:75.

53. Smith, Revelations, July 1830, *JSP, R*1:32 [D&C 26:2 (1981)]. See also D&C 28:13, 104:71, 72, 85 (1981).

supported by a prevailing sentiment toward conformity for most that shaped their church participation.

Modern students of Mormonism attempting to understand this period when the church was under construction will find in the surviving documentary record a complex, and sometimes confusing, implementation of priesthood provisions in both Kirtland and Independence.[54] To make sense of priesthood development during this period, some have provided plausible explanations for the process.[55] However, JS's thinking about the development does not exist other than what is conveyed in the revelations and occasional brief statements he made as captured in meeting minutes held during the period. Reflections on priesthood development that later appeared in the "History of Joseph Smith" benefit from hindsight in conveying how the constituent parts came together early to provide the structure that survived JS. Incremental insertions of provisions for behavior and practice for the lay priesthood reveal what turned out at the time to be a decided expansion and distribution of authority, duty, and expectation.

It should not be hard to grasp that in establishing an effectual faith for those who gravitated to JS's declarations, his youth, inexperience, and personality affected how his message was received. This was especially so among several adherents who upon their conversions undoubtedly looked upon their attachment to Mormonism as providential and an opportunity to display their own gifts. As temperaments emerged, some showed proclivity toward leadership and others toward discipleship, the followers. The faith's revelatory foundations stipulated a structural organization that portended interpersonal relationships that were not always predictable or positive. After all, the converts' previous religious experiences that prepared them for JS's religion were packed with accumulated attitudes and determinations that were not wiped clean by their baptisms. During a meeting held on December 5, 1834, Oliver Cowdery gave his view of new

54. See Matthew C. Godfrey's overview of the early development of priesthood understanding in "A Culmination of Learning," 167–81. An example of the difficulty to grasp priesthood relationships at the time is found in the matter of Francis Gladden Bishop's ordination from seventy to high priest in April 1840 where, in the midst of confusion, quorum leaders had to clarify relationships between the elders, seventies, and high priests. See "Conference Minutes," for the April 6, 1840, general conference in Nauvoo, *Times and Seasons*, April 1840, 92. See also the puzzling priesthood nomenclature applied to several "Temples to be built" for priesthood purposes on the City Plat of Zion for June 24, 1833: "Sacred Apostolic repository for the use of the Bishops," the "house of the Lord for the presidency of the high priesthood after the order of Aron," and the "house of the Lord... for the ~~priesthood~~ high priesthood after the order of Aron." Plat of the City of Zion, *JSP, D*3:129.

55. See for example, Prince, *Power from on High*; Gregory A. Prince, "Mormon Priesthood Organization," in Givens and Barlow, *Oxford Handbook of Mormonism*, 167–81; and Quinn, *Mormon Hierarchy*, 1–77.

initiates into the church. Though they embraced the gospel with "eagerness," some "were unwilling to forego their former opinions and notions relative to church government, and the rules and habits proper for good order, harmony, peace, and beauty of a people destined, with the protecting care of the Lord, to be an ensample and light of the world."[56] Still, evidence suggests that many early converts exhibited the richness of their own maturation as Christians wherein they readily delivered their devotions to the young prophet and the restored gospel he offered. Mormonism in its infancy provided little applied configuration, something that undoubtedly proved inviting to some who attached themselves to the faith to exhibit what God had already done for them. Among the most interesting features of early Mormonism and how the organizational structure emerged is how those men who became the visible additions to the developing hierarchy responded to JS and his growing accumulation of revelations around which the faith was formed.

Those familiar with Mormon beginnings are aware of the significant effort it took for JS to corral those around him who had applied their own perspectives to their new prerogatives.[57] Some were familiar with other methods of organizational structure and means of addressing functional matters. Despite the revelations JS received and what they indicated to be the will of God, JS's lack of experience at administrative leadership made for inconsistencies and lack of clarity in some of what members had to consider. As a result, men who had participated in other organizations, when assigned duties in the developing church, apparently applied their own understanding to relevant matters of the moment. Naturally, there was discord; some even challenging JS's primacy as God's specific leader of the people. Capable men like Sidney Rigdon and Edward Partridge when called upon to fill their important ecclesiastical roles exhibited tendencies contrary to how JS viewed circumstances. Consequently, JS obtained divine instruction meant to settle ambiguities about his singular role. Even Oliver Cowdery who had shared so much with him and had been the recipient of divine instruction acknowledged by JS, challenged a number of matters he advanced. Thus, a September 1830 revelation prepared for Oliver specified: "No one shall be appointed to Receive commandments & Revelations in this Church excepting my Servent Joseph for he Receiveth them even as Moses & thou shalt be obedient unto the things which I shall give unto him."[58] There were growing pains, to be sure. But an organizational structure came together reliant on the early revelations that uniquely characterized Mormonism.

Highlights that illustrate how JS's plans were enacted are useful to see the

56. "Account of Meetings, Revelation, and Blessings, 5–6 December 1834," *JSP, D4*:197.
57. See Godfrey, "'Seeking after Monarchal Power and Authority,'" 18–30.
58. Smith, Revelations, [September 1830], *JSP, R1*:41 [D&C 28:2 (1981)].

outlines of church development. For the first year and a half, though the specificities of the Articles and Covenants suggest immediate operational implementation, only a loose provision of administration by the first and second elder actually existed. Offices with duties established at the outset and augmented by the inclusion of the office of high priest one year later were still in blueprint stage. The call of Edward Partridge in February 1831 to be the church's bishop had to have awakened members to something more than theoretical discussion. It reflected JS's perceptions regarding the need to imprint the growing church with a functional outline. That he designed the role of bishop to address the church's temporal affairs clearly illustrated to members that something more than congregational assembly described their church.[59] It proved a major step in church administration.

Later in the year, JS dictated a weighty revelation that not only showed his thinking but also the promptings that moved him in bricking the framework delivered by way of the Articles and Covenants. The November 11, 1831, instruction included plans for leadership and administration of each of the offices mentioned in the Articles and Covenants. Provided to assist in managing "the Church Laws respecting Church business," the "Lord of Hosts" revealed that "there must needs be presiding elders to preside over those who are of the office of an elder."[60] Hence came Orson Pratt's appointment as president of the elders at the January 25, 1832, conference in Amherst, Ohio.[61] This occurred four years before establishment of an elders quorum. Similarly, provisions for men to preside over the priests, teachers, deacons, and high priests in each of their duties were stipulated. The fact that most of the revelatory direction of this sort apparently remained mostly unknown to church members allowed JS to roll out the impressions he received without being pressured by those privy to the direction to immediately implement them.

In March 1832 JS instituted by revelation another incremental addition to the corpus of the religion by putting into place a formal presiding leadership—something more concrete than a first and second elder. Mormonism had acquired the trappings of an institution. A three-person "presidency of the high Priest Hood" represented what came to be known as the church's First Presidency: the triumvirate of JS, Jesse Gause, and Sidney Rigdon.[62] A year later at an "assembly of the high Priests," JS "ordained" Rigdon and Frederick G. Williams, who had replaced Gause after he had drifted, "by the Laying on of the hands to be equal

59. Smith, Revelations, February 4, 1831, *JSP, R1*:74–75 [D&C 41:9–12 (1981)].

60. Smith, Revelations, November 11, 1831, *JSP, R1*:168 [D&C 107:60 (1981)].

61. *Orson Pratt Journals*, January 25, 1832, 11; Historical Introduction, Smith, Revelation, January 25, 1832, *JSP, D2*:157–58.

62. Smith, Revelations, March 15, 1832, *JSP, R1*:199–200 [D&C 81:1–2 (1981)].

with him [JS] in holding the Keys of the Kingdom and also to the Presidency of the high Priest hood."[63] Besides demonstrating again JS's determination to allocate authority and influence, the enactment also added a continuing formality to church leadership. Bishops Edward Partridge and Newel K. Whitney had been appointed the previous year to help regulate the growing numbers and to mitigate the poverty of church members in a design to mark most every feature of the community. Thus, "a definite centralization of power in Joseph Smith and a select group of elders had occurred in 1831 and 1832."[64] The moves occurred at the same time that for the men a Mormon form of a "priesthood of all believers" permeated the laity of the church.[65] The church progressed thereafter beyond survival to establish protocols that eventually took root by way of the egalitarian distribution of the priesthood.

As church members worked to implement the revelatory injunctions JS received regarding the roles and duties of members, a dimension of democratic distribution of church government rose in the church. Underlain with the notions of "common consent" of the governed, JS further distributed decision-making authority to male groups within the church. Though circumstances occasionally provoked what appeared to be instances of autocracy, once priesthood structure took shape he chose to include others in significant decisions affecting the religion.[66] He insisted, to be sure, on his followers adhering to the revelatory pronouncements he delivered to the church. But the confidence he placed in priesthood bodies in whom he trusted, given their exhibition of allegiance to the church, indicated realization that extending authority and responsibility contributed to the collective good of all.

Conferences and Councils

Joseph Smith Papers scholar Joseph F. Darowski has shown how JS implemented "conferences and councils" to handle matters covering the broad range of administrative obligations that appeared as the church grew.[67] With members

63. Smith, Documents, March 18, 1833, Minute Book 1, *JSP, D3*:42.
64. Godfrey, "'Seeking after Monarchal Power and Authority,'" 30.
65. Martin Luther taught that Paul showed "that all Christians are priests," and advanced the idea, "we, who have been baptized, are all uniformly priests in virtue of that very fact." This was later dubbed the "priesthood of all believers" as widely accepted in Protestant circles. John Dillenberger, ed., *Martin Luther: Selections from His Writings* (New York: Anchor Books, 1962), 33, 345.
66. For instances of charges against JS for dictatorial rule, see Godfrey, "'Seeking after Monarchal Power,'" 29.
67. Joseph F. Darowski, "Seeking after the Ancient Order: Conferences and Councils in the Early Church Governance, 1830–1834," in *A Firm Foundation: Church Organization and Administration*, ed. David J. Whittaker and Arnold K. Garr (Salt Lake City: Religious Studies Center, Brigham Young University, and Deseret Book, 2011), 97–113. See also "Church Presidencies and Councils," in Smith, Journals, *JSP, J1*:452–54.

accepting JS as the organizational head of all that was done in the church, they also recognized what he had given them as a form of autonomy. For instance, as early as November 1831 church disciplinary matters were initially considered by revelation to be handled by "a confrenc of high priests."[68] More and more, church conferences/councils were called upon to render not only decisions for the church but even to jointly with JS access the will of the Lord, i.e., receive collective revelation. For something as seemingly mundane as determining the immediate future of one of the members, rather than laying the decision solely at JS's stoop, a "councel of high Priests" determined the "will of the Lord respe[c]ting" Solomon Humphrey. After the council listened to Humphrey's circumstances and needs, they determined that Humphrey "should devote himself entirely to the work of the ministry."[69] With JS as one of the council, the procedure shows what he tried to do in distributing decision-making to his cohorts. But some high priest and elder councils determined much weightier matters.

On March 23, 1833, such a "councel" gathered in Kirtland to determine a plan to secure the land upon which the Kirtland House of the Lord would later be built.[70] JS ensured it not to be his unilateral decision. Councils of high priests and elders in both Kirtland and Zion met as groups and occasionally together during 1833 and into early 1834 to counsel regarding matters consequential or not, including disciplinary cases. Bishop's councils and courts fell under jurisdiction of Bishops Partridge in Zion and Whitney in Kirtland. There were also extensions of priesthood groups designed to achieve order in the kingdom as it continued to grow. As one might expect, territorial disputes occasionally arose between the priesthood groups. Obviously addressing contention that had arisen in Zion, a high priest council in August 1833 "Resolve[d] that no High priest Elder or Priest shall ordain any priest Elder or High priest in the land of Zion without the consent of a Conference of Highpriests."[71] Eventually, the men of the church collaborated to buttress the outline of organization JS established, understanding that adjustments and constrictions were imposed as circumstances required.

Kirtland High Council

JS formalized the council pattern previously employed in the church on Wednesday, February 12, 1834, when the "high Priests and Elders of the Church in Kirtland" met in council at his home. There JS told them, "I have never set before any council in all the order in which a Council ought to be conducted,

68. Smith, Revelations, November 1, 1831, *JSP, R1*:154 [D&C 68: 15 (1981)]. As priesthood structure expanded, the language of the revelation was later changed to assign the duty from the "confrenc of high priests" to the "first presidency of the chich [church]" (154).

69. Smith, Documents, December 5, 1832, Minute Book 1, *JSP, D2*:323.

70. Smith, Documents, March 23, 1833, Minute Book 1, *JSP, D3*:47–48.

71. Smith, Documents, August 28, 1833, Minute Book 2, http://www.josephsmithpapers.org/paper-summary/minute-book-2/1#full-transcript.

which, perhaps has deprived the Councils of some, or many blessings."[72] This, he explained, was not his own idea. He told the men "he would show the order of Councils in ancient days...as shown him by vision."[73] Clearly JS had resolved his thinking and inspirations with a plan to outline how administrative circumstances were to be handled in the future. Five days later a "Conference of High Priests" met, again at JS's home, where they "proceeded to organize the Presidents Church Council."[74] As shown by Darowski, who analyzed the methodology engaged to govern the church in its early years, the "Presidents Church Council" during the Kirtland period served as "the high council of the Church at Kirtland [and] also the high council of the Church itself when functioning as the president's Church court or council."[75] The *revised* minutes and content of the February 17 meeting were of such consequence that they were included in the compilation of revelations then being arranged. Published as Section 5 of the 1835 Doctrine and Covenants (D&C 102), the purpose of the "high council" was explained as "settleing important difficulties which ~~may~~ <might> arise in the church, which ~~cannot~~ <could not> be settled by the Church, or the bishop's council to the satisfaction of the parties."[76]

Known thereafter as the Kirtland high council, twelve men composed the body led by a three-man presidency: the "presidency of the high priesthood," i.e., the church's First Presidency. Though the initial minutes of the February 17, 1834, meeting stated that "The President [i.e., JS] could also transact business alone,"[77] his intention was to implement a distribution of decision-making into the growing church. He noted that in his day the Apostle Peter "was the president of the Council" and "held the Keys of the Kingdom of God," though in his absence "his Counsellors Could transact business."[78] The procedure set a pattern. Primary among the Kirtland high council's duties was the requirement to ensure that the "law of Heaven" prevailed in their transactions and difficulties, most applicable in matters that were ecclesiastically oriented. In all, the hope was that deliberations would be handled with fairness and equity. After all had been appointed and instructed over several days, JS stated, likely with much relief, "the Council was organized according to the ancient order, and also according to the mind of the Lord."[79] Rather than create under his purview

72. Smith, Documents, February 12, 1834, Minute Book 1, *JSP, D*3:429.
73. Smith, Documents, February 17, 1834, Minute Book 1, *JSP, D*3:437.
74. Ibid., 436.
75. Darowski, "Seeking after the Ancient Order," 109.
76. Smith, Documents, Revised Minutes, February 18–19, 1834, Minute Book 1, *JSP, D*3:440 [D&C 5:96 (1835); D&C 102:2 (1981)].
77. Smith, Documents, February 17, 1834, Minute Book 1, *JSP, D*3:437.
78. Ibid.
79. Smith, Documents, February 19, 1834, Minute Book 1, *JSP, D*3:446.

a greater concentration of authority and control as the church expanded, what JS called the "ancient order" provided a systematic outline with distribution of authority for the conduct of church entities to handle the growing membership.

To illustrate the necessity of organizing official protocols to handle church difficulties, just six months later a formidable circumstance warranted jurisdiction by a priesthood council. In what would have naturally fallen under the responsibility of the Kirtland high council, the fact that the plaintiff in the matter happened to be a member of that council may have been one of the reasons "a number of high priests and elders of the church of the Latter-Day Saints" (not necessarily of the council) met together to hear the complaint. On August 11, 1834, Massachusetts native Sylvester Smith (no relation to JS, hereafter SSmith), charged JS "with criminal conduct during his journey to and from Missouri this Spring & Summer,"[80] not a trivial accusation. During the extended Zion's Camp venture earlier in the year, SSmith claimed JS had violated the integrity of his office, including misuse of church funds.[81] Though not a judicial proceeding, the council gathered to hear SSmith's grievance.

The charges created quite a stir in the town, nothing like it having previously transpired. Newel K. Whitney, the Kirtland bishop, presided over the meeting. The council immediately called upon JS to give his side of the dispute. The prophet explained that the "causes" of the fracture between him and SSmith came from the "jealousies of brother Sylvester and others." JS's straightforward explanation of the circumstances likely unnerved SSmith, moving him to waiver from his allegations. He then made "a partial confession for his previous conduct, asking forgiveness for accusing brother Joseph publicly." The "Assembly" then met as a council to discuss the charges, ultimately siding with JS's defense of himself. Given the negative effect of SSmith's charges followed by his reversal, one of the council proposed a form of public humiliation for SSmith, stating "that it was his opinion the plaster ought to be as large as the wound," recommending SSmith's confession be "published abroad." The moderator, Whitney, then proceeded "after a few remarks, to give a decision according, to a motion previously made, (viz.) that an article be published in the Evening & the morning Star." The council intended that church members knew that "the church in Kirtland had investigated the conduct of brother Joseph Smith Junr. while journeying to the West and returning, and that we find that he has acted in every respect in ~~the~~ an honorable and proper Manner, with all monies and other properties entrusted to his charge."[82]

80. Smith, Documents, August 11, 1834, Minute Book 1, *JSP, D4*:99.

81. See Smith, Documents, Historical Introduction, August 11, 1834, Minute Book 1, *JSP, D4*:97–99.

82. Smith, Documents, August 11, 1834, Minute Book 1, *JSP, D4*:100–1.

But SSmith backstepped after his admission and would not let the matter rest. Two weeks later he "objected against abiding by the decision of the former council, and proceeded to Justify himself in his former conduct." The reconvened council determined to "rebuke" him for his remonstrance, disqualifying him to "act further in his office in the Church."[83] Still, Smith continued to press his original complaint. The council listened over several gatherings to extended testimony. On August 29 they ruled again that if SSmith would acknowledge his error in accusing JS he would be accepted back into fellowship, to which SSmith agreed. But his submission proved short lived. The measures taken against him continued to fester. It took until September 24, after weeks of unrest, for the council to finally render a decision that SSmith be removed from his position as a Kirtland high councilor, though he could retain his office as a high priest, to which SSmith acquiesced as well.[84] Though SSmith later left the church in 1838, in October 1834 after all he had said over the previous two months, he wrote an endorsement of the prophet for publication claiming that despite his disagreements with JS, the prophet was above reproach during the Zion's Camp episode.[85] The procedure illustrates the lengthy measures and forbearance church leaders employed to accommodate complaints, even against JS, to bring order to the kingdom. Resolutions to such matters encouraged church leaders that the application of administration by council could keep the church apace with its growth and challenges.

Missouri High Council

At the same time that Kirtland continued growing as a center of gathering, the Mormons in Missouri tried to regroup after their expulsion from Jackson County at the end of 1833. To invigorate the remnants of the Missouri faithful, even in the aftermath of the disappointment of Zion's Camp meant to recover their Missouri lands, JS formed an ecclesiastical organization in Clay County, north of the Missouri River where they had relocated. Parallel to what he had done in Kirtland earlier in the year, JS organized there on July 3, 1834, "a general Council of High Priests" to do exactly what he had done for the Kirtland Mormons earlier in the year.[86] Structured and purposed like their Kirtland counter-

83. Smith, Documents, August 23, 1834, Minute Book 1, *JSP, D4*:109.

84. Smith, Documents, September 24, 1834, Minute Book 1, *JSP, D4*:174. Sylvester Smith was thereafter appointed a president of the First Quorum of the Seventy when they were first called in February 1835, suggesting that confidence in him had been restored at the time. Smith, Documents, Historical Introduction, February 28–March 1, 1835, Minute Book 1, *JSP, D4*:255.

85. Sylvester Smith to Oliver Cowdery, October 28, 1834, *Latter Day Saints' Messenger and Advocate*, October 1834, 10–11.

86. Smith, Documents, July 3, 1834, Minute Book 2, *JSP, D4*:90.

parts, twelve men in Missouri were appointed to compose a high council with David Whitmer, W.W. Phelps, and Whitmer's brother John as counsellors to preside over the twelve. (The three were dissimilar to the presidency that led the Kirtland council, who were also the "presidency of the high priesthood"—the First Presidency.) Enacting the council method of local governance illustrated JS's confidence in the Kirtland model and those committed to build the church and serve its people. Wilford Woodruff, then staying in Missouri, witnessed the formation of the Missouri high council. "I attended the Meeting at Lyman Wights," he wrote, "at which time Joseph Smith the Prophet Organized the High Council. Joseph was Clothed with the power of God." Portraying his earnest intentions, even at the time he needed the support of those he placed in charge, JS, according to Woodruff, "Chastised David Whitmore & others for unfaithfulnes. Said their hearts were not set upon the building up the Kingdom of God as they should be." Still, he installed David Whitmer to "Preside over the Land of Zion" with W.W. Phelps and John Whitmer as counselors.[87] Members sometimes required thick skins to bear JS's reproof but most understood his intentions when pushing church objectives.

A significant insight into JS's thinking came from the call and installation of the presidency and high council of Zion. Following the high council's installation five months earlier in Kirtland, creation of the two administrative bodies—imbued with the instructional apparatus to conduct church affairs even in JS's absence—left the prophet with what appears to have been an incremental accomplishment that to him once appeared illusive. Despite the traumatic expulsion of the Mormons from Jackson County three and a half years after organization of the church, the means to perpetuate the church at a general and local level, evidenced in both Ohio and Missouri, had been established. To another "council of High Priests" at Lyman Wight's home in Clay County, Missouri, on July 7, 1834, JS told those assembled "if he should now be taken away that he had accomplished the great work which the Lord had laid before him, and that which he had desired of the Lord." He had then "done his duty in organizing the High Council, through which Council the will of the Lord might be known on all important occasions in the building up of Zion, and establishing truth in the earth."[88]

The issues attended to as found in the minutes for the high councils in both Kirtland and Clay County, Missouri, indicate Mormonism's ground level effect upon church members. The councils were required to rule on matters of fellowship, church discipline, and propriety regarding church objectives. They demonstrated to church members a predictability of how to adjudicate the

87. *Wilford Woodruff Journal*, July 1834, 1:13.
88. Smith, Documents, ca. July 7, 1834, Minute Book 2, *JSP, D4*:93.

inevitable conflicts arising wherever the Saints were located. However, there were inevitable irregularities in how situations were handled in the explosive circumstances among the Saints in Missouri during their turbulent tenure there. This included the discipline that eventually removed Oliver Cowdery from the church.[89] A couple of lesser examples tasked to the Missouri high council illustrate the range of concerns brought before the body. John Whitmer's extensive minutes from a meeting on July 31, 1834, cover a case where one member stated that another brother had visited the Colesville Branch, originally of New York, then one of the westernmost church units in Clay County on the north side of the Missouri River. The elder in visiting the Colesville Saints had encouraged church members there regarding their use of the gifts of the spirit, specifically speaking in tongues. The practice was generally out of vogue at the time. What's more, the brother in question did an "underhanded" and "clandestine" maneuver in ordaining a man to the "office of high priest; insisting that he had obtained a witness from the Lord for the same," again a break from protocol. Witnesses were called to testify before the high council regarding the charges, one stating he personally had challenged the errant brother to refrain from encouraging members of the Hulet Branch, near Colesville, in their use of the gifts of the spirit contrary to what was then being taught in the church. After a great deal of testimony and discussion over two days the brother charged with the misdemeanor admitted his mistake. That was not, however, the end of it. Also informed that his ordination of the man to be a high priest was "illegal therefore not acknowledged by us to be of God," making it "void and good for nothing," he was stripped of his licenses as an elder and high priest leaving him as a "private member in this Church."[90]

Later in August 1834, another brother appeared before the council to answer a complaint that he taught that "all disease in this Church is of the Devil and that medicine administered to the sick is of the Devil, for the sick in the Church ought to live by faith." The elder acknowledged he had taught the "doctrine" and "believed it to be correct." After discussion, president of the council David Whitmer rendered a decision: "It is not lawful to teach the Church that all disease is of the devil. But if there is any that has this faith let him have it to himself." Furthermore, those that condemn the use of "roots and herbs administered to the sick, and all wholesome vegitables which God has ordained for the use of

89. Smith, Documents, April 12, 1838, Minute Book 2, *JSP, D6*:83–94; Larry E. Morris, "'The Private Character of the Man That Bore That Testimony': Oliver Cowdery and His Critics," 282–84, in Welch and Morris eds., *Oliver Cowdery: Scribe, Elder, Witness*; Hales, *Joseph Smith's Polygamy*, 1:133–36, 142.

90. Minutes, July 31–August 1, 1834, Minute Book 2, http://www.josephsmithpapers.org/paper-summary/minute-book-2/1#full-transcript.

man," teaching that "these things are of Satan," were in error; "such teachings is not of God."[91] These exhibits of the range of matters considered of consequence by some church members portray how the Latter-day Saints struggled to understand the complexities confronting them in their embrace and practice of their religion.

The intricacies addressed by the two high councils fulfilled JS's expectations that upon delivering the authority and responsibility for governing the church in local jurisdictions they were equipped to operate without his immediate influence. The Zion high council functioned as if they had been empowered to govern all church business in their surroundings, taking charge of the actions of the council that met regularly. Matters of consequence were addressed as they arose in the community. The council, for example, dispatched Orson and Parley Pratt with John Corrill and Simeon Carter on July 31, 1834, to "visit the church throughout the county and hold public meetings" to ensure that to the degree possible members were kept informed about church enactments and operations.[92] To the extent feasible, JS had established agencies that held authority and autonomy in administration of the church's local matters.

The order within the priesthood gained dimensions that ensured a hierarchical structure providing boundaries and guidelines that benefitted the church thereafter. The minutes of priesthood gatherings in both Kirtland and northern Missouri (Minute books 1 and 2 in the Joseph Smith Papers) prove to be a significant body of records that portray the sequential expansion of JS's thinking and method of governance. Particulars demonstrate the attention to all matters relevant to the growing church that resulted in the institutionalization of many of the measures JS obtained through his revelatory facility. However, the arrangement—sometimes tightly applied—likely contributed to defections in both Kirtland and Independence. The dissent, though, did little to alter the continuing advance of Mormonism.

The Twelve Apostles and the Seventy

JS's vision of priesthood organization led in 1835 to two other substantial additions to the structure. The first was the insertion of a formalized apostolic body into the Mormon story. Introducing the premise of modern-day apostles was a bold notion. The "office of apostle did not exist in other churches in the United States."[93] As previously stated, JS and Oliver Cowdery had been identified as apostles at the church's founding, though it held an equation with the office

91. Minutes, August 21, 1834, Minute Book 2, http://www.josephsmithpapers.org/paper-summary/minute-book-2/1#full-transcript.

92. *Orson Pratt Journals*, July 31, 1834, 43.

93. Smith, Documents, Introduction, February 14–15, 1835, Minute Book 1, *JSP, D4*:219.

of elder at the time.[94] The concept that twelve apostles were to be part of the restoration of the primitive church appeared early, though the term apostle may have been applied as a function rather than position in its early usage. John Whitmer at the June 9, 1830, church conference, for example, received a ministerial license "signifying & proveing that he is an Apostle of Jesus Christ an Elder of this Church of Christ."[95] Evidence exists indicating that from the outset, JS actuated a search for twelve men to fill the apostolic role in his attempt to replicate the New Testament pattern.[96] Such a measure should not be surprising. But early enthusiasm for identification of Mormon elders as apostles appears to have faded by the mid-1830s.

Evidence shows that in June 1829 that twelve disciples were to be part of JS's reinvigoration of early Christianity. Subsequently, Oliver Cowdery and David Whitmer were assigned to "search out the twelve."[97] The appointment of Cowdery and Whitmer in 1829 to the task of selecting the Twelve Apostles found Martin Harris out of sorts with JS and the church at the time. Otherwise, Harris would likely have been included in the assignment.[98] To some early members who knew about the revelation, the prospect of having modern apostles confirmed their eagerness to see JS's plan unfold. The delay in actuating the call of apostles to be part of the church is not surprising when seen in the light of his incremental understanding of establishing a church. The vision JS had to move the church from governing by conferences and councils to implementing the specificities associated with the organization of the high councils in Kirtland and Zion in 1834 was a major milestone in the pattern. But clearly more remained to be enacted.

The discouraging ordeal of Zion's Camp mid-1834 to recover the property and lands in Jackson County, Missouri, ripped from them the previous year, frustrated church leaders and members in many ways. Yet as so many have said since, the venture provided a crucible that thereafter marked many of the participants as loyal and refined, providing a cadre of men who could be trusted after proving themselves in their disappointment. Determined not to forget their sacrifice, JS called a February 8, 1835, gathering in Kirtland. Already a revelation JS received on June 22, 1834, recognized what they had done and delivered to them a promise: "I have prepared a blessing and an endowment for them."[99]

94. See Smith, Revelations, April 10, 1830, *JSP, R1*:60; Oliver Cowdery, Revelation, June 1829, *JSP, D1*:370–71.

95. "License for John Whitmer," June 9, 1830, *JSP, D1*:144.

96. Prince, *Power from on High*, 12–15.

97. June 1829, Book of Commandments, 15:42 (1833), no manuscript for the revelation survives; D&C 18:37 (1981).

98. See B. H. Roberts's explanation in the *History of the Church*, 2:186–87n; Smith, Documents, Introduction, February 14–15, 1835, Minute Book 1, *JSP, D4*:221.

99. Smith, Revelations, June 22, 1834, *JSP, R1*:285 [D&C 105:18 (1981)]. See Alexander L.

The collection of devotees on February 8 served as the catalyst from which most of the future apostles and seventies were called. Later that week, on February 14, a priesthood gathering assembled where the "first business of the meeting was for the three witnesses of the Book of Mormon, to pray each one and then proceed to choose twelve men from the church as Apostles to go to all nations, kindred toungs and people."[100] The "record of the transactions of the twelve apostles," later prepared by Orson Hyde and William E. McLellin to chronicle their work, stated that those in the proceedings were moved "by the spirit of prophecy and revelation to choose and set apart from among all the elders of the church the following persons to fill that high and responsible station." Then followed in the record the names of Thomas B. Marsh, David W. Patten, Brigham Young, Heber C. Kimball, Orson Hyde, William E. McLellin, Parley P. Pratt, Luke Johnson, William Smith, Orson Pratt, John F. Boynton, and Lyman E. Johnson.[101] After their call, the twelve men were blessed individually, some on February 14, 15, 21, and 26, by Cowdery, Whitmer, and Harris.[102] The language of Orson Pratt's blessing represents the intentions of the blessings: "You are chosen, and set apart to be ordained to this Apostleship and this ministry. You shall go forth and preach the gospel and do a mighty work. You shall be sustained. The Holy spirit shall enlighten thy mind. Thou shalt travel from nation to nation. The Lord God shall preserve thee and return thee safe, with songs of everlasting joy upon thy head."[103] In contrast to the previous year's call of the "high council" in Kirtland where they were stipulated to be a "standing council for the church," later in the year when the Doctrine and Covenants was first published, the "twelve" were called as a "travelling, presiding high council," though they were designated to operate "under the direction of the presidency of the church."[104] The call of the Twelve Apostles, though not viewed at the time

---

Baugh, "Parting the Veil: Joseph Smith's Seventy-Six Documented Visionary Experiences," in Welch, *Opening the Heavens*, 291.

100. Smith, Documents, February 14, 1835, Minute Book 1, *JSP, D3*:227–28.

101. See transcriptions of text of the Quorum of the Twelve Record, February–August 1835, CR 2 178, CHL, in *JSP, D4*:233–34, 249–52, 287–89, 293–95, 306–8; Ronald K. Esplin and Sharon E. Nielsen, "'The Record of the Twelve, 1835': The Quorum of the Twelve Apostles' Call and 1835 Mission," *BYU Studies Quarterly* 51, no. 1 (2012): 21.

102. See Smith, Documents, February 14, 15, 21, 1835, Minute Book 1, *JSP, D4*:229–33, 239–47. For an overview of the calls of the Twelve and seventy, see Richard E. Turley Jr., "The Calling of the Twelve Apostles and the Seventy in 1835," in *Joseph: Exploring the Life and Ministry of the Prophet*, ed. Susan Easton Black and Andrew C. Skinner (Salt Lake City: Deseret Book, 2005), 230–42.

103. Smith, Documents, February 21, 1835, Minute Book 1, *JSP, D3*:242.

104. D&C 5:2 (1835); D&C 3:12 (1835); D&C 102:3, 107:33 (1981). See discussion of the circumstances of JS's explanation to the Twelve Apostles about this matter in Smith, Documents, between circa March 1 and circa May 4, 1835 [D&C 107], Historical Introduction to "Instruction on Priesthood," *JSP, D4*:308–12.

with the gravity later attached to their place in the hierarchy of the church as described in Chapter 9, further underscored a growing and developing church with future global implications.[105]

A consequential "Charge" to the Twelve Apostles by Oliver Cowdery, indicated that the role of the three witnesses extended beyond just designation of the apostles. Cowdery's commission outlined high expectations for the men just called. In the spirit of the apostles of old, he enjoined them to prepare themselves as witnesses of God and the Book of Mormon "to all nations." The sober call urged them to: "Be prepared at all times to make a sacrafice of your lives, should God require them in the advancement and building up of his cause." Indeed, Oliver told them to "prepare your minds to bid a long farewell to Kirtland, even till the great day come," i.e., Jesus's Second Coming. But they would not proceed unadorned. They were not to "go to other nations" until they received their "endowment." This referred to the promised godly endowment to be given upon completion of the Kirtland House of the Lord. Being "endowed with power from on high" would equip them with "that wisdom, that intelligence and that power which characterized the ancient Saints and now ~~characterized~~ characterizes the inhabitants of the upper world."[106]

The second organizational advance in 1835 was the call of the seventy. Two weeks after the formation of the Twelve Apostles as a church unit, seventy other men were called to fulfill another purpose. Also drawn from the Zion's Camp veterans, forty-three persons at first were named with the intent of filling the group to the number seventy with others soon following.[107] Like the inclusion of the Twelve Apostle's call appearing in the first edition of the Doctrine and Covenants, Section 3 defined and called the seventy to "preach the gospel, and to be special witnesses unto the Gentiles in all the world."[108] Also like the Twelve, those called received blessings specific to each of them. Furthermore, they were "to act in the name of the Lord, under the direction of the twelve, or the travelling high council, in building up the church and regulating all the affairs of the same, in all nations."[109]

From their blessings given at the time of their calls we may ascertain in part how the role of the seventy was viewed at the time. Three blessings contain language suggesting perceptions at the time about the office of seventy: "We

105. See Ronald K. Esplin, *The Emergence of Brigham Young and the Twelve to Mormon Leadership* (Provo, UT: Joseph Fielding Smith Institute for Latter-day Saint History and BYU Studies, 2006), 189–92.

106. Smith, Documents, February 21, 1835, Minute Book 1, *JSP, D*4:242–47.

107. For a portrayal of the surrounding events by one who was called to be one of the second seventy, see Stephen Post, Journal, February 1835.

108. D&C 3:11 (1835); D&C 107:25 (1981).

109. D&C 3:11–12 (1835); D&C 107:34 (1981).

ordain you an Elder and one of the Seventy,"[110] and to another "set apart by prophecy to the apostleship of the first Seventy."[111] Yet another wrote of his ordination, that the language stipulated, "I lay my hands upon thy head to ordain thee a high priest of the 70. in the name of Jesus."[112] Thereafter, as understood by nineteenth-century church leaders, men of that status were often referred to as one of the seventy elders or "seventy apostles."[113] Seven men among the group were appointed presidents to supervise the men's operations.

The premise for the seventy came, like the call of the Twelve, from the New Testament: Luke 10, though a precedent also appeared in Numbers 11 as well. The Lukan account contained language stating Jesus called "other seventy" and "sent them two and two before his face into every city and place, whither he himself would come" (Luke 10:1).[114] A missionary portfolio clearly awaited those called by church leaders on February 28, 1835. The plan held for subsequent quorums of seventy to be called. With the initial quorum of seventy being filled by May 1835, others were appointed to the second quorum as early as August 1835.[115] By 1837 three quorums had been appointed.[116] Clearly, JS's vision of spreading the gospel had moved to another dimension. By the end of the church's tenure in Nauvoo in 1846, there were nearly three dozen quorums of seventy with 80 percent of priesthood holders in Nauvoo being seventies.[117] The mission to call the world to repentance anticipating Jesus's return, a priority initiative for the church, drew from Mormonism some of its best men.

For months before the Doctrine and Covenants was published in September 1835, JS had been refining his vision(s) on church organization. Dozens of divine manifestations dictated by him to scribes since his immersion in the Book of Mormon filled the pages of the two manuscript volumes used to chronicle his interactions with Jesus. And none of the revelations were more consequential than

110. Blessing of Burr Riggs, March 1, 1835, *JSP, D4*:276.

111. Cyrus Smalling ordination, June 30, 1835, *JSP, D4*:351.

112. Stephen Post, Journal, February 13, 1835.

113. Wilford Woodruff, December 21, 1856, *JD*, 4:147; October 8, 1875, *JD*, 18:126; November 1, 1891, Stuy, *Collected Discourses*, 2:284; Brigham Young, May 21, 1877, *Deseret News*, in *The Essential Brigham Young* (Salt Lake City: Signature Books, 1992), 231, 235; Hartley, *My Fellow Servants*, 376–78.

114. Some Bible translators of the Greek New Testament used the figure of "seventy-two" instead of "seventy" to describe those sent "two by two" ahead of Jesus to prepare the people. See for example, Alfred Marshall, *The Interlinear KJV-NIV: Parallel New Testament in Greek and English* (Grand Rapids, MI: Zondervan, 1975), 204–5.

115. Smith, Documents, August 17, 1835, Minute Book 1, *JSP, D4*:391.

116. Lyndon W. Cook, *A Tentative Inquiry into the Office of Seventy, 1835–1845* (Provo, UT: Grandin Book, 2009), 8, 53–61.

117. Milton V. Backman Jr., "'The Keys are Right Here': Succession in the Presidency," in *Lion of the Lord: Essays on the Service of Brigham Young*, ed. Susan Easton Black and Larry C. Porter (Salt Lake City: Deseret Book, 1995), 121.

what JS presented as the Lord's directives regarding the church's priestly structure. The prophet prepared between March and early May 1835 an important text ("On Priesthood") that became D&C 3 (1835), i.e., D&C 107 (1981), which included a word defining the grouping of priesthood offices: quorum.[118] The quorum identified thereafter constituted bodies of priesthood holders among the Mormons. New revelatory information built upon an important November 11, 1831, revelation to become "On Priesthood."[119] Mentioned previously, it explained to members for the first time in print the relationship between the church's "two priesthoods," Aaronic and Melchizedek, and how men in the priesthood offices identified therein were to function. Within the text appeared clarifications of duty and responsibility for Melchizedek priesthood holders—high priests and elders. Among other matters, those holding the Melchizedek priesthood received the charge to administer in "spiritual things,"[120] with the Aaronic priesthood, defined as an "appendage to the greater, or Melchizedek Priesthood" having the "power in administering outward ordinances."[121]

Language from "On Priesthood" in the 1835 Doctrine and Covenants included what has subsequently been confusing for some trying to understand relationships in the priesthood revelation obtained by JS. The First Presidency, identified in the revelation as the "three presiding high priests" and "presidency of the church" also constituted a "quorum." After them, the Twelve Apostles were formed in "a quorum equal in authority and power to the three presidents, previously mentioned [the First Presidency]." Moreover, the seventy were then told that they too formed "a quorum equal in authority to that of the twelve especial witnesses or apostles, just named." The Kirtland and Zion high councils were also identified as quorums "equal in authority, and in the affairs of the church,

118. Smith, Documents, between circa March 1 and circa May 4, 1835 [D&C 107], "Instruction on Priesthood," *JSP, D4*:314–15. While the first references to a quorum refer to priesthood designations, church leaders also later applied the concept to those who received the Nauvoo Temple endowment, who were referred to as the "Quorum of the Anointed." See Anderson and Bergera, *Joseph Smith's Quorum of the Anointed.*
119. Section 3 of the 1835 D&C began with the new text prepared for the document ("On Priesthood") followed by the November 11, 1831, revelation and other material apparently added as the final revelation was augmented and composed. See Revelation Book 1, *JSP, R1*:168–71, to see the language that became verses 31–44 in Section 3 (1835) and verses 59–100 in Section 107 (1981). See also the emendations that rendered the final text in Woodford, "Historical Development of the Doctrine and Covenants," 1398–1432.
120. D&C, 3:5 (1835); D&C 107:10 (1981).
121. D&C, 3:10 (1835); D&C 107:14 (1981). JS's unfolding instructions indicated early that the principal office of the "Greater Priesthood" was that of "High Priests," supplemented by "Appendages" composed of "Bishops" and "Elders." In the "Lesser Priesthood" the principle office was that of "Priests," with appendages of "Teachers" and "Deacons." See the schematic and explanation in "Organization Charts" in *JSP, D2*:481.

in all their decisions, to the quorum of the presidency, or to the travelling high council."[122] The probable confusion for modern readers is evident, though perhaps it was better understood by members when the text was first published than it is today. A number of modern Mormon commentaries defer to Hyrum M. Smith and Janne M. Sjodahl's 1923 explanation of the possible intent: "There can never be two or three quorums of equal authority at the same time, therefore in the revelation where it reads that the Twelve Apostles form a quorum equal in authority with the First Presidency and that the Seventies form a quorum equal in authority with the Twelve, it should be understood that this condition of equality could prevail only when the ranking quorum is no longer in existence, through death or otherwise."[123] While this may be the most plausible explanation of the dilemma, the ambiguous language of the revelation has not been clarified by church leaders.

Assistant President and Patriarch

Two more additions to the leadership structure in the first week of December 1834, neither applicable in today's church, filled roles reflecting the developing organization. Discussions among leaders at this stage apparently moved JS to insert Oliver Cowdery as the church's assistant president, with his father, Joseph Smith Sr., as church patriarch. An entry for December 6, 1834, in JS's 1834–1836 history, illustrates sentiments at the time: there was "a lengthy conversation held upon the subject of introducing a more refined order into the Church."[124] When the First Presidency was initially organized in Kirtland in March 1832, JS apparently intended that Oliver Cowdery be a part of the presidency. Because Cowdery, JS's primary collaborator at the outset, had been given duties in Missouri and perhaps for other considerations, he "was not previously ordained <to the Presidency.>" The plan stipulated "by the angel while in company with President Smith, at the time they recievd the office of the lesser priesthood" included Cowdery's placement in the church's highest assembly. The historical documentation recording the event on December 5, 1834, indicated that the First Presidency gathered in Kirtland "for the purpose of ordaining" Cowdery "to the office of assistant President of the High and Holy Priesthood" in the church. As such he was "to officiate in the absence of the President [JS]," followed in line by Sidney Rigdon and Frederick G. Williams, the other member of the presidency

122. D&C 3:11–12 (1835); D&C 107:24, 26, 36 (1981).

123. Smith and Sjodahl, *The Doctrine and Covenants*, 700. Though not fully addressing the confusion of the revelatory language, see also Michael Quinn's expansive portrayal of the fallout regarding church leadership after JS's death, bearing on the inert effect of the revelation. Quinn, "Mormon Succession Crisis," 187–233.

124. Smith, Histories, December 6, 1834, "History, 1834–1836," *JSP, H1*:37.

who had replaced Jesse Gause.[125] The following day, "On further reflection," the history indicated that in concert with Cowdery's ordination, Hyrum Smith and Joseph Smith Sen. were also appointed "to the office of Presidency of the high priesthood."[126] John Smith, Joseph Sr.'s brother and uncle to JS and Hyrum, was also later added to the number of assistant councilors in September 1837.[127] The actions illustrate JS's dissemination of authority and church expansion that warranted adjustments in the organizational structure, though he left no explanation of why he made the adjustments.

In concert with Joseph Smith Sr.'s appointment as assistant president, he may also have been formalized as church patriarch the same day, December 6, 1834. Though Joseph Sr. had given blessings previously, they probably reflected the biblical vestiges of family bestowals after the manner of Jacob's pronouncements in Genesis 49. Given JS's sensibilities about biblical restoration serving as antecedents for features of his church, it should not be surprising that a patriarchal-type office would be included in the construction of church administration. The notion of fatherly blessings was augmented by the reality that many church members did not have fathers who were church members, precluding them from receiving such blessings. Here the church patriarch could satisfy the need given the circumstantial demand.

There is little concrete support upon which modern investigators may depend for understanding JS's thinking or motivations about the patriarchal role. Evidence from what was later called the Patriarchal Blessing Book housed in the LDS Church History Library, however, indicates the seriousness by which prophetic blessings were given in the early church. Not only were they delivered, they were recorded by Oliver Cowdery. That initial volume, prepared in 1835, contains apparent revisions of blessings initially delivered in 1833 and the blessings given thereafter. The revisions that were made, without explanation, contribute to modern confusion about the origin of the blessings and when Joseph Sr. was first appointed.[128] His appointment on December 6, 1834, as church

125. Smith, Histories, "History, 1834–1836," *JSP, H1*:32, 34. It has been argued that the documentation providing justification for Cowdery's installation as assistant president then and not earlier was created by Cowdery himself. Comparable information from JS or others does not exist to add understanding of the move at the time. See also Brian Hales's analysis of the delay in inserting Cowdery into the church presidency. Brian C. Hales, "'Guilty of Such Folly?': Accusations of Adultery and Polygamy Against Oliver Cowdery," *Mormon Historical Studies* 9, no. 2 (Fall 2008): 19–28.

126. Smith, Histories, "History, 1834–1836," *JSP, H1*:37–38.

127. Smith, Documents, September 3, 1837, Minute Book 1, *JSP, D5*:422.

128. See Michael Quinn's summarization of the difficulty in understanding from the surviving documentation the patriarchal office, the blessings, their timing, and how they figured into Mormon belief and practice at the time. Quinn, *Mormon Hierarchy*, 46–57. See also

patriarch seems to better fit the administrative adjustments that were made in church leadership at that time than Cowdery's claim that the office originated in December 1833. Just three days after the December 6 conferral, Joseph Sr. gave blessings to his children, including spouses, befitting the new appointment.[129]

Further Refinement and Completion of the Organization

With the presiding quorums having been established, preparations for completion of the Kirtland House of the Lord pulled church leaders together to effectuate more systematic methods of conducting church business. Several meetings in the middle of January 1836 produced satisfying results, proving the church had moved toward JS's objectives. At the conclusion of a gathering on January 13, JS stated: "This has been one of the best days that I ever spent, there has been an entire unison of feeling expressed in all our proceedings this day, and the Spirit of the God of Israel has rested upon us in mighty power."[130] Two days later, January 15, what was called a "grand council," "organized the authorities of the church agreeably to their respective offices in the same." The meeting in the "council room in the Chapel" of the almost completed Kirtland House of the Lord, established protocols and decorum for church administrative undertakings that included "rules and regulations to govern the house of the Lord in Kirtland."[131] Perpetuating a pattern established by a Kirtland "General Assembly" where the several priesthood bodies were polled in August 1835 regarding acceptance of the Doctrine and Covenants, the process was designed to elicit consensus within the church.[132] After the proposed rules were read at the January 15 meeting, the "presidency" of the high council (the First Presidency) "passed" the measure by "unanimous voice." Then the "high council" itself also simultaneously passed the rules, followed by the "twelve" who did the same, as did the "Seventy." Then the bishoprics of both Kirtland and Zion voted in "favour" of the rules. After the expressed consensus, the proposal received acceptance "as a law to govern the house of the Lord in this place." The respectful, patient discussions resulting in uniform acquiescence obviously pleased JS. From the "deliberations" he then

---

Irene Bates and Gary Smith's study of the church office of patriarch that counters Quinn's position, stating Joseph Sr. was installed as church patriarch in December 1833. Bates and Smith, *Lost Legacy*, 33–42. See also Marquardt, *Early Patriarchal Blessings*, ix.

129. Patriarchal Blessing Book, 1–8. Following those blessings as given on December 9, 1834, Oliver Cowdery—serving as clerk—wrote a brief narrative that included: "Joseph Smith, sen. was ordained a president and patriarch, under the hands of his son Joseph, myself, Sidney Rigdon, and Frederick G. Williams, presidents of the church," 8.

130. Smith, Journals, January 13, 1836, *JSP, J1*:151.

131. Smith, Journals, January 15, 1836, *JSP, J1*:153.

132. Smith, Documents, August 17, 1835, Minute Book 1, *JSP, D4*:382–96; D&C, "General Assembly," August 17, 1835, 255–57 (1835).

articulated the value of handling church business in this predictable manner: "Each speak in his turn, and in his place, and in his time and season, that their may be perfect order in all things."[133] The brethren witnessed how the church had come together.

It also appears that the January 15, 1836, meeting was the first time that quorums of the church were officially incorporated as functioning entities into the church structure. The high priests, for instance, approved the prophet's talented younger brother Don Carlos, age nineteen, to be their "president to preside" over the "high priesthood." Sixty-year-old Alvah Beman (sometimes Beaman), through the same process, became "President of the Elders in Kirtland." Oliver Cowdery's father, William Jr., at age seventy, became "president over the priests of the Aaronic priesthood in Kirtland." Oliver Olney, age thirty-nine, became the second choice to "preside over the teachers in Kirtland," replacing George Johnson who had served as president pro tem since the teachers organized in late 1834. Ira Bond's appointment at age thirty-seven to preside "over the deacons in Kirtland" followed.[134] Thereafter, there was precedence that the church had arrived at a status of functional organization that could move an entire people toward a singular objective.[135]

Obviously, there remained a great deal of work for the quorums to grasp where they fit and how they operated once they were activated. Previously, an important May 2, 1835, gathering of "the Presidency, the Twelve a part of the Seventy, and some other Elders of the church" met "in order to consult the affairs of the church." JS laid before the quorums their disparate prerogatives. Besides being ranked by age, the Twelve Apostles learned they had "no right to go into Zion or any of its stakes and there undertake to regulate the affairs thereof where there is a standing High Council." Instead, they were "to go abroad and regulate all matters relative to the different branches of the Church." But their "business" had to be accomplished "by the voice of the Church." Yet "when the twelve pass a decision in the name of the church," it stood. The "standing high council" (the Kirtland high council), had domestic duties, with no "authority to go into the Churches abroad and regulate the matters thereof, for this belongs to the Twelve." The seventy were told that if their growing labors "in the vineyard" required additional manpower, the "seven presidents of the first seventy" had the authority "to call and ordain other Seventy and send them forth to labor...until

133. Smith, Journals, January 15, 1836, *JSP, J1*:154. W. W. Phelps wrote his wife Sally referencing the "Grand Council," and explained it was "one of the most interesting meetings I ever saw." The following day he "sat in counsel with the presidency to draft rules for the Lord's house." Adding to the excitement, the following day another "Grand Council" was held, "much more interesting than the first." William Wines Phelps, Letters, 1835–1841, 109, MS 8711, CHL.

134. Smith, Documents, January 15, 1836, Minute Book 1, *JSP, D5*:147.

135. "Communicated," *Evening and the Morning Star*, May 1834, 160, see also 152.

if need be they set a part apart seven times Seventy, even until there shall be one hundred & forty and four thousand." They were also precluded from infringing on the duties assigned to the Twelve unless they were asked by that body to assist in the work. Yet, if the need arose beyond their capabilities, the "twelve and the Seventy" were empowered "by virtue of their offices to call upon the Church to assist them."[136] The work had to be done.

From modern perspectives, the structure rings of bureaucratic obligation and demand. Besides the lines of priesthood responsibility being defined, provisions were made to limit priesthood officers from imposing themselves upon congregational church units. "No individual has a right to go into any church and ordain any minister for the Church, unless it is by the Voice of the Church." And to prevent officiousness, protecting the autonomous nature of local congregations, "No Elder has a right to go into any branch of the church and appoint meetings or regulate the Church without the consent or advic[e] of the presiding Elder of said branch."[137] The outline was designed not only to engineer the work, but also to draw lines to prevent hard feelings that would inevitably rise in the practical application of church practice.

Establishment of the Kirtland House of the Lord culminated three years of the church and its members' energies and resources. JS was on the verge of his greatest triumph to date. The temple's interior design accentuated the priesthood structure that he had been trying to institute. The lower court possessed three tiers of ascending pulpits at both the west and east ends, the Melchizedek priesthood officers designated to sit on the west pulpits and the Aaronic priesthood leaders on the east. The dedicatory services began on March 27, 1836, with the congregation filling the seats in the court between the pulpits. Expectations were high that something extraordinary awaited them upon the temple's completion and dedication. After preliminary matters, JS "made a short address" where he "called upon the several quorums and all the congregation of saints to acknowledge," i.e., approve, the leaders of the church. He presented them by their positions: the First Presidency, the Twelve Apostles, the seventies, the high councils of both Kirtland and Zion, and the presidencies of the elders, priests, teachers, and deacons. All were unanimously accepted.[138]

Three days after the dedication, "According to appointment," yet another step in both the sacral ordinances of the church and its organization transpired. JS's journal for March 30, 1836, recorded that "the presidency, the 12, the seventies, the high ~~councils~~ councils, the Bishops and their entire quorums, the Elders, and all the official members in this stake of Zion amounting to about 300

136. Smith, Documents, May 2, 1835, Minute Book 1, *JSP, D4*:299–306.

137. Ibid., 302.

138. The events of the first day of dedication, including the ceremonial installation of priesthood officers, is covered in JS's journal. Smith, Journals, March 27, 1836, *JSP, J1*:200–11.

met in the temple of the Lord to attend to the ordinance of washing of feet." The ritual, coupled with attendant promises of obtaining the "endowment of power from on high," followed the extensive preparatory work associated with accentuation of the priesthood quorums. Completion of the House of the Lord and its ceremonies tied to the endowment moved JS's realization of his vision of church organization that drove him over the previous two years. After the "washing of feet" and further explaining priesthood duties to the quorums, he stood before the church members where he proclaimed that he had finally "completed the~~ir~~ organization of the church" after having "passed through all the necessary ceremonies." The lengthy preparations were then in place and "they now were at liberty after obtaining their lisences to go forth and build up the kingdom of God."[139] With the superstructure in place, for the first time the church solemnized and fixed the priesthood's future order. Now fully organized, church operations henceforth generally reflected JS's pattern established spring of 1836.

The Early Function of Priesthood Quorums

A portrayal of how priesthood quorums functioned after their organization is warranted. Outside of church centers of gathering, missionaries served to regulate the church and apply the generalities of church discipline to emerging congregations.[140] But the intentions for priesthood quorums are best illustrated where members concentrated. The administrative records kept that show JS's function as prophet, including Minute Books 1 (the Kirtland Council Minutes) and 2 (the "The Conference Minutes, and Record Book, of Christ's Church of Latter Day Saints," commonly referred to as the "Far West Record") in the Joseph Smith Papers, serve as the primary means by which we appraise the early church organization. In contrast, the records kept by the Twelve Apostles and the seventy illuminates only aspects of how they perceived their assignments. The minutes of the teachers and elders quorums, organized in 1834 and 1836 respectively, provide perspectives on the primary undertakings of those groups. Organizational procedures for the high priests, priests, and deacons, if they were ever created in written form, do not survive. Church offices later associated with the priesthood were an initial fixture of JS's church, though elders, far more numerous than the others at the outset, were the primary priesthood operatives going forward.

Early portrayals from JS's revelations and subsequent minutes pertaining to the teachers and elders quorums reveal how the men who filled the roles of their respective groups handled their chartered purpose. Though presently the office of teacher is subordinated to all priesthood offices save the deacons, its functionary role in the mid-1830s was designed, apparently, as one of great

139. Smith, Journals, March 30, 1836, *JSP, J1*:215.
140. Harper, "Missionaries in the American Religious Marketplace," 17.

consequence. Modern readers must remember that present Aaronic priesthood offices were held in the early church by adults.[141] Thus, a teacher's duty required in the church's Articles and Covenants that they "watch over the church always and be with them and strengthen them and see that there is no iniquity in the church, no evil speaking, and see that the church meets together often and also see that all the members do their duty."[142] Particulars that described institution of the teachers quorum in Kirtland are unknown at present, though the church's teachers apparently organized in late 1834. Evidence from quorum minutes indicate the teachers applied the same criteria of behavior expected of members of previous conferences and councils. It is likely they met for the first time in November 1834 and monthly thereafter. The minutes show that the group, small as it was—seven attended the first meeting, though in 1835 the Doctrine and Covenants stipulated that twenty-four were designed to compose the quorum—attempted to enact their charter as expressed above in the church's Articles and Covenants.

Teachers quorum minutes indicate the men, who generally paired up to attend to their duties, took seriously the charge to police their quorum and other church members. Indeed, the substance of their initial meetings were of that sort. On Christmas Day 1834, the teachers quorum met in what they called a "conference" to consider those "making use of tobacco," an infraction of the church's health code—the Word of Wisdom—delivered by JS the previous year. The quorum resolved on June 4, 1836, to revisit the issue and to identify those who "will not keep the word of wisdom and report them at the next meeting." On January 31, 1835, they considered a dispute between two members about a "pair of stears [steers]." The next month when thirteen attended, they assigned one of their number to work with "the Elders" quorum to handle a problem between a man and his wife. A March 28 gathering resulted in one brother being assigned to "labor" with a member charged with "lying or extortion." Two others

141. The offices of elders, priests, teachers, and deacons identified in the church's Articles and Covenants inaugurating the religion in April 1830 were designed to be manned by adults. At present the priesthood is divided into those who hold the lesser or Aaronic Priesthood (males younger than eighteen years of age) and those who hold the higher or Melchizedek Priesthood (usually those older than eighteen). But in the early church, the formidable duties assigned in the revelations to deacons, teachers, and priests at the outset, were meant to be performed by mature adults. Not until the church relocated to Utah did experiments in ordaining young men to the office of deacon occur, as per current tradition. By the end of Brigham Young's administration, it became recognized throughout the church the benefits of training young men for adult responsibilities. Designating the young men as priesthood holders inserted them into the lesser priesthood roles of deacons, teachers, and priests with their own list of duties different than the challenging responsibilities given to their adult counterparts in the church's early days. See Hartley, *My Fellow Servants*, 50–56.

142. Smith, Revelations, April 10, 1830, *JSP, R1*:64 [D&C 20:53–59 (1981), clear text].

accepted the assignment to "laber" with a husband and wife in the church at the same time a quorum member was requested to take a deacon with him and find out why one of their members "does not attend with us." After another meeting in August 1835, they apparently did not meet again until the spring of 1836. A May 19, 1836, gathering proved to be a training session in "the articles and covenants" of the church, followed by their last meeting in Kirtland, June 4. The group did not gather again until March 1838 in Far West, Missouri.

It is clear in the reconstitution of the teachers quorum in Far West that their purposes and demands did not change, having the same prospects about church members' adherence to church standards that they held in Kirtland. The earlier expectations for observance of priesthood protocols were evident: "We will not hold any one in our quorum in fellowship who will not observe the word of wisdom in as mutch as our circumstances will admit of." The following month the minutes reported a decision by the group, it being motioned and carried, "that we will not hold any member in our quorum in fellowship who will not <settle his own difficulties in the church> [and] show him self approved in all things."[143] With the quorums' charge to keep church members in line, it was not always easy for those called to minister nor was it for those to whom they ministered.

The Elders Quorum

The January 15, 1836, council mentioned above also initiated an elders quorum in Kirtland fourteen months after the teachers quorum organized. Different from the policing mandate for the teachers, the elders quorum apparently "concerned itself solely with ordinations and problems of its members" that numbered over "three hundred male members."[144] Given that the seventy who were called had explicit designation as church emissaries, the elders apparently assumed ministerial duties among their own, preparing the brethren for further responsibility. As it turned out, the elders soon witnessed attrition as the seventies quorums grew. The lesser priesthood ranks were then tapped to replenish the elders quorum.

Following institution of the elders quorum on January 15, 1836, the men gathered for the first time ten days later, though the minutes do not identify the numbers that attended. With members of the First Presidency minus JS in attendance, quorum president Alvah Beman, one of the church's older men, chose

143. Teachers Quorum Minutes, December 1834–December 1845, MS 3428, CHL, see especially December 25, 1834, January 31, 1835, February 28, 1835, June 27, 1835, May 19, 1836, June 4, 1836, March 31, 1838, April 26, 1838. Though this record is identified in the CHL catalog by its modern designation as the "Teachers Quorum Minutes," the word quorum was not used when the book was created. Rather the group identified themselves as a "conference" until May 9, 1841, when the minutes state they were a "quorum of Teachers," consistent with how priesthood groups were known by that time.
144. *Kirtland Elders' Quorum Record*, x, xi.

two counselors who were fully supported by those gathered. Their purpose was to prepare "themselves for the holy anointing," specifically the ordinance of "purification," or symbolic cleansing, anticipated in completion of the Kirtland House of the Lord.[145] Three days later, in a worshipful gathering where "the Lord poured out his spirit, and some spake with tongues and prophecied,"[146] twenty-four elders obtained their anointings. In the following weeks many more followed in the process equipping them to receive their endowment of power during dedicatory services. At first, rather than meeting monthly like the teachers, the elders gathered weekly, sometimes several times a week, given the gravity of their preparations. Even after the temple's dedication they often met several times a month. Minutes evidence they occasionally approved licenses for members, prayed for each other, gave testimonials, shared their experiences, and satisfied requests from members who asked that hands be laid on them for the restoration of health. Public confession of misdeeds demonstrated the ambition to not only heal wounds but to create an environment of conciliation among the brethren. One elder, for example, confessed "he was saucy" to another member, expressing contrition that he had injured the feelings of the man and further explained "that he pretended to know more than he did and did not know half as mutch as he thought he did."[147]

Much teaching and training took place. JS attended occasionally to teach, lift, and reprove. As suggested, preparation for their upcoming experience in the temple became a reason to meet. As with most other features of JS's life, only portions of what he said during his infrequent visits were captured in a way that gives modern students the substance of what he tried to convey to his brethren. At a gathering on March 29, 1837, he urged that the "Elders who were Not anointed must be anointed" in preparation for another solemn assembly to be held for those who were not in Kirtland for the House of the Lord's dedication the previous year. There he warned that "unless the church acts in ~~perfect~~ greater union than they had for the winter past it Should be Scourged untill they Should feel it four fold to that of the dispersion of Zion,"[148] an ominous prediction given the trauma after being expelled from Jackson County, Missouri. JS's intentions, when described, illustrate his incessant ambition to refine those who had embraced Mormonism with the prospect that they would become the elders of modern-day Israel.

Where the teachers were charged with keeping order in the church at large, discipline became an internal function within the elders quorum meetings, as it was for the other quorums. In March 1836 the elders met to consider charges

145. Ibid., January 25, 1836, 3.
146. Ibid., January 28, 1836, 4.
147. Ibid., May 21, 1841, 56.
148. Ibid., March 29, 1837, 26. See also the minutes for April 5, 1837, 29.

brought by one brother against a young brother who didn't match expectations of proper behavior. Two others testified they saw the young man at the school house "jumping and behaved himself in an unchristian like manner, and was reproved by them." They considered the accusation to be serious enough that the quorum voted to withdraw the "hand of fellowship from him" and referred the case up to the high council.[149] In another instance, an elder accused one of the quorum members of "stealing" and his wife of "tatling lying & mischief," and that it could be proven. The quorum then examined "witnesses which testified in favor" of the accused. The decision of the quorum was for the accuser to confess to the accused and "make the plaster as broad as the sore."[150] In February 1837 they appointed a "Vigilence Committee" of three to scrutinize quorum members' behavior,[151] but it appears the actions were more ministerial than punitive. It is clear that the wide range of matters confronting the elders quorum reflected many of the everyday ups and downs facing the community of believers. But the atmosphere of persistent inspection proved discomfiting to many.

It took JS six years to organize the superstructure of the church, though it functioned at different levels of effectiveness while under construction. Once the blueprint had been created, it is not surprising that despite the remarkable success of organizing the brethren, JS had difficulty in transferring his vision of priesthood order to those who had been organized. Such structure for the laity was conceptually new to most of the men. What turned out to be an important gathering of priesthood quorums called the first week of February 1836 to meet in the nearly finished Kirtland House of the Lord illustrates the circumstances. The quorums separated into separate rooms with JS sequentially appearing before each of them. "I laboured with each of these quorems for some time to bring to the order which God had shown to me." His journal reported that he "went from room to room repeatedly & charged each separately—assuring them that it was according to the mind of God." However, "notwithstanding all my labour—while I was in the east room with the Bishops quorems I f[e]lt by the spirit that something was wrong in the quorem of Elders in the west room."[152] He then adjourned to where the elders met. Besides "reprimand[ing] us for our evil deeds which was the cause of our darkness," minutes of the elders quorum meeting included that JS "prophesied saying this night the key is turned to the nations; and the angel John is about commencing his mission to prophesy before kings, and rule[r]s, nations tongues and people."[153] The statement represented a significant

149. Ibid., March 11, 1836, 10.

150. Ibid., April 14, 1838, 42.

151. Ibid., February 17, 1837, 38.

152. Smith, Journals, February 6, 1836, *JSP, J1*:180–82.

153. *Kirtland Elders' Quorum Record*, February 6, 1836, 6–7. There is nothing in JS's journal about this consequential statement or reports from any other entities to describe the

assertion. But some did not give it much attention, with enough taking it lightly that it caused "the spirit of the Lord to withdraw."[154] Keeping the brethren in step proved to be a perpetual struggle.

The momentous three-year ambition to build a House of the Lord to empower and vivify church members and to pull the priesthood brethren together included the coincident placement of formalized means to govern the church according to JS's recurring visions of priesthood purpose and organization. After the useful preparatory experiment with conferences and councils, exhibiting a distribution of authority and responsibility to others as the church grew and developed, the rise of quorums within the church put into place the formerly nebulous notions of an institution first articulated at the church's organization in 1830. It is probably safe to state that most church members were ignorant of what JS and his administrative colleagues were doing as they built the framework of the church's organization. Publication of the 1835 Doctrine and Covenants, with its opening declarations about priesthood, was clearly intended to inform members of the revelatory imprimatur that empowered the church. Still, evidence suggests that educating the Saints about priesthood and its role and function became an ongoing duty and necessity for leaders.[155]

Mormon Worship

Perhaps surprisingly, given all of the innovations in structure JS introduced to the church, there is little from him that defined protocols of how the Mormons were to publicly worship. An August 7, 1831, revelation JS received in Missouri provided general instructions applying to "how to keep the Sabbath and how to fast and pray and what it was etc. etc." But other than to enjoin the church to "go to the house of prayer and offer up thy Sacraments upon my holy day" and complementary matters regarding one's attitude about keeping sacred the Sabbath day on Sunday, there was nothing of procedural direction. Indeed, the revelation closed with Jesus stating, "trouble me no more concerning this matter."[156] The Articles and Covenants' sacramental obligations of "meet[ing] together oft to partake of bread and wine," which included kneeling "with the Church," became central to Mormon worship at the outset.[157] But sacral practice associated with

---

implications of what this meant. The report, as produced by JS's scribes in his "History of the Church" for the date, indicates JS met in the temple with the several quorums separately "to bring them the order which God has shown to me." His visit with the elders produced the expression above. See also Historian's Office History of the Church, February 6, 1836, vol. 2, Book B1, 702, September 1, 1834–November 2, 1838, CR 100 102.

154. Smith, Journals, February 6, 1836, *JSP, J1*:181.

155. See, for example, the communication to John Burk by JS et al., on June 1–2, 1835, *JSP, D4*:326–33.

156. Smith, Revelations, August 7, 1831, *JSP, R1*:130–32 [D&C 59 (1981), clear text].

157. Smith, Revelations, April 10, 1830, *JSP, R1*:66–67 [D&C 20:76–79 (1981)].

other Christian churches and words like Eucharist, liturgy, homily, missal, and lection eluded JS's interest in replicating, though the practices found parallel expressions with other terminology in Mormonism. The supplemental features of the modern organization, i.e., the auxiliary functions of the church, appeared to satisfy church necessities as warranted.

The division of Great Salt Lake City into nineteen Mormon wards soon after the Saints arrival, with the attendant construction of meetinghouses may suggest to moderns that the Utah experience mirrored the church during the prophet's lifetime. However, in Mormonism's formative years, gatherings of Saints to worship were primarily limited to homes, barns, schoolhouses, and in the Kirtland House of the Lord, during and after construction. There sacramental services were held, composed of sermons delivered and the emblems of the last supper reenacted. JS's home also served as the setting for many worship and instructional services, and once the print shop behind the temple in Kirtland was operational, it along with the school house also provided meeting space for the Mormons. Members appear to have been content with such meeting arrangements even though many came from organizations that had formalized their worship with meetinghouses. The mainstream churches as well as "outsiders" like the Quakers and Shakers built structures with pulpits and pews to deliver their messages of salvation. Mormons, however, handled community worship as their circumstances allowed and never built meetinghouses per se during JS's lifetime.

Once the Saints established themselves in Nauvoo, the makeup of the city in the 1840s allowed for gatherings to be held in numerous sites without constructing chapels for religious purposes. For example, when the "Young Gentlemen and Ladies Relief Society of Nauvoo"—an organization for teenagers, not to be confused with the Nauvoo Women's Relief Society organized on March 17, 1842—were called to meet together in early 1843, as their numbers grew they met first in a home, then in a school room, then JS's home, followed by a move to the "lodge-room over President Smith's store."[158] The Nauvoo Temple, under construction since 1841, provided a meeting site for public worship as the rooms were finished. Charlotte Haven, who had resided in the city for several weeks wrote home to her mother in New Hampshire giving her impressions of the gatherings to hear JS: "I know, dear Mother, you would be highly amused were you now to look from our parlor window at the crowd of people that are passing from their devotions in the Temple. As that edifice has neither roof nor floor, preaching is held there only on pleasant Sundays. Then planks are laid loosely over the joists and some boards are placed for seats, but not half enough to ac-

158. "A Short Sketch of the Rise of the Young Gentlemen and Ladies Relief Society of Nauvoo," *Times and Seasons*, April 1, 1843, 154–55.

commodate the people; so men, women, and children, take with them chairs, benches, stools, etc."[159]

But it was outside gatherings at the "temple stand" just west of the temple and in other nearby outdoor groves where most general worship in Nauvoo transpired in accommodating weather. The temple stand served as a primary venue for JS teaching the people. One correspondent to the *Boston Bee*, characterizing his experience in Nauvoo, described the manner of Mormon services at the time: "The Mormons have not yet completed their great Temple, and have no commodious place of worship, but the apostles and elders preach in private houses on the Sabbath, and at other times, though I seldom attend these latter meetings; but when the weather will admit, they meet in the grove, or on the rough floor of the basement of the Temple, and then the prophet frequently preaches."[160] There was no urgency among church leaders to erect a commodious church meetinghouse.

The Priesthood and Nauvoo's Wards and Quorums

As one might suppose, once the Saints relocated to Commerce/Nauvoo and acquired a semblance of permanence to which they had not been accustomed, the established priesthood protocols and functions expanded and assumed new dimensions. Modern observers might find it confusing, as William G. Hartley stated, to discover in examining church and priesthood formalities that the Saints' manner of doing things in Nauvoo was comparable to entering "a foreign country." Indeed, the current Mormon "understanding of stakes, wards, and quorums" serve to help administer church purposes today, but if assumed to replicate Nauvoo conventions will only "confuse the study of Nauvoo's priesthood work."[161] The priesthood precedents that emerged in Kirtland and Missouri transitioned to a new era of church administration with intricacies that stretch modern understanding.

For the first time, in Commerce JS and church leaders created local congregations called "wards," subordinate within the church's diocesan-type stakes. (Branch was the designation for most outlying congregations where numbers were thin.) Once JS settled upon Commerce, Illinois, as his center of orbit in 1839, that fall the Saints gathered there for a "general Conference," October 5–9. There the prophet created a stake (later known as the Nauvoo Stake) as an ecclesiastical unit, with a stake president. Three bishops were appointed to lead the city's upper, middle, and lower congregational wards. Twelve men constituted

159. Haven, "A Girl's Letters from Nauvoo," 622.

160. "From the *Boston Daily Bee*," Letter to the Editor [*Times and Seasons*], March 24, 1843, reprinted in the *Times and Seasons*, May 15, 1843, 200.

161. Hartley, *My Fellow Servants*, 362.

the high council like the ones in Kirtland and Zion. To establish a church organization for those on the Iowa side of the Mississippi River immediately opposite Commerce, a "branch of the Church" was also created, though it functioned more like a stake. JS's uncle John became president. And, like Commerce, the Iowa unit also had a high council.[162] The earlier templates for church organization had become predictable, though information about the discussions relating to how the patterns for local and outlying church jurisdictions were conceived do not survive, if they were ever created. In any case, leaders reached for and instituted functionalities to better serve church purposes. Sometimes those early patterns do not match the structure familiar to moderns. As Hartley stated, "We find, for example, a stake being formed within a branch, high priests serving as deacons, four types of bishops, wards with presidents, and branches with bishops."[163] The pattern of church organization known to adherents after the nineteenth century took decades to standardize.

The Commerce/Nauvoo advances were layered on the Kirtland model of church development where structure and quorums were initiated. The Saints' incremental progress established not only civic and economic footings in Nauvoo, but spring of 1841 also proved significant for church organizational arrangement in the growing city. Built upon the precedents of priesthood quorum development in Ohio, on March 21, 1841, "The Lesser Priesthood was Organized in [the] City of Nauvoo" by the city's bishops. Samuel Rolfe was appointed "President of Priests Quorum," Elisha Everett filled the role as "President of Teachers," and Phineas R. Bird became "Prest. Of Deacons," each man choosing two counselors.[164] Remembering their practical application of lesser priesthood duties in Ohio and Missouri, the reinvigoration evidenced what JS had earlier instituted regarding church structure and polity. Two weeks later, what was to become among the most celebratory events within Mormonism up to that point, brought together the energy, momentum, and enthusiasm that had been building as the Saints recovered from their Missouri disaster.

With immigration underway by the British and American Mormons and expanding Latter-day Saint communities in the region, the much-anticipated annual general conference of April 6–9, 1841, unfolded. The church had been organized for eleven years. There JS recognized the importance of accentuating what had been the faith's remarkable revival of the previous two years. As if Mormonism operated in a new era, the Illinois legislature had granted the city an organizational charter, a militia—the Nauvoo Legion—a university, an agricultural and manufacturing association, and a "Nauvoo House Association." At the con-

162. "Proceedings of the General Conference, Held at Commerce, Hancock County, Illinois, on Saturday the 5th day of October, 1839," *Times and Seasons*, December 1839, 30–31.
163. Hartley, *My Fellow Servants*, 355.
164. Organization of Lesser Priesthood, circa 1845, CR 100 396, CHL.

ference the Legion presented a dramatic mustering with church military complements from Iowa. Confidence soared as city residents were entertained and delighted. Besides the sermons and instruction, solemnities also included final placement of the cornerstones of the temple overlooking the Mississippi. Public baptisms for both the living and dead portrayed the vitality of the religion. At the conference, JS and his counselors—the First Presidency—were presented to each of the priesthood quorums for approval. The procedure, according to JS, was designed to elicit from the men "a majority in each quorum." The presidents of each group queried their members to confirm member sentiments. According to the report, the presidency were "unanimously accepted" by the church's priesthood quorums. The proceedings of the conference symbolized the renewal of Mormonism.[165]

JS's church evidenced sustainability due to the framework of ecclesiastical and priesthood development designed to accommodate the many functions of church government. The hierarchal structure differed from much of normative Christianity. With a critical eye, Charlotte Haven, the New Englander mentioned earlier who had family in the church, after a few weeks in Nauvoo in early 1843 offered her view of church administration and those who filled the rolls: "The church called the Latter-Day Saints of Jesus Christ is governed by a high priest, a council of thirty, twelve elders or apostles, teachers, deacons, and a bishop for each ward of the city." Haven also assumed that other than JS, the church's additional officers "are appointed annually by revelation to Joseph Smith, the prophet, patriarch, and high priest."[166] Haven's appraisal of leadership structure, absent any understanding of what Mormonism had been in the previous decade and despite errors in perception, indicates the religion had taken a denominational form that had to Mormons become routine.

Within Nauvoo, priesthood holders and quorums were marshalled into modified arrangements that determined how they should work in concert with one another. The few surviving records in the LDS Church's holdings showing priesthood activity in Nauvoo help outline what the church did as Mormonism matured into a sustainable organization. The lesser priesthood, for example, was called upon to survey the community for its first ecclesiastical census in 1842, giving an important portrait of Nauvoo Mormonism at the time.[167] Later Nauvoo

165. "Celebration of the Anniversary of the Church," *Times and Seasons*, April 15, 1841, 375–77; in the same issue, see also "Laying the Corner Stone of the Temple," 380–83; "Report of the First Presidency," 384–86; and "Minutes of the General Conference of the Church of Jesus Christ of Latter Day Saints," 386–88. See also documentary coverage of the week's events in *JSP, D8*:98–118; Clayton, *Manchester Mormons*, 206–11; Glen M. Leonard, *Nauvoo: A Place of Peace, A People of Promise* (Salt Lake City: Deseret Book and Brigham Young University Press, 2002), 233–35.
166. Haven, "A Girl's Letters from Nauvoo," 627.
167. Nauvoo Stake Ward Census, 1842, LR 3102 27, CHL.

records for the Nauvoo priests quorum (which illustrate practicality in operation by also including teachers and deacons) and the high priests of Nauvoo's 5th and 9th wards survive, portraying—in part—what church leaders tried to do to service member and church needs.[168] Change became inevitable along with church demographics. With the regular influx of immigrants, between 10 and 20 percent of Nauvoo's population were British immigrants and, in 1843, one resident claimed it seemed like a third of the city was English.[169] By August 1842 the three wards had become ten, just increasing the complexities and interrelatedness of priesthood entities to city and other church strategies. Minutes of the Nauvoo Stake high council, illustrating church management within the city, and the Nauvoo City Council, reflecting the legal and operational accoutrements of the city, reveal development of a theocratic enterprise that portended at the time later implementations of the administrative range of JS's religion in the last half of the nineteenth century.[170]

The realities of cooperative human interaction in accomplishing church purposes was something that needed constant attention. As Nauvoo grew and became the place of gathering for most Saints, a remnant remained in Kirtland with the House of the Lord reminding them of what Mormonism had once been. Without the ability to personally nurture the fold and knowing of friction in the community, JS wrote to one of the Kirtland leaders reiterating the ultimate intention of the gospel's design: "In order to conduct the affairs of the kingdom in righteousness it is all important, that the most perfect harmony kind feeling, good understanding and confidence should exist in the hearts of all the brethren. [A]nd that true Charity—love one towards another, should characterize all their proceedings." Having previously experienced himself what confronted the Kirtland brethren, he continued: "If there are any uncharitable feelings, any lack of confidence, then pride and arrogancy and envy will soon be manifested and confusion must inevitably prevail and the Authorities of the Church set at nought."[171] The church's success to that point—despite the many setbacks—exhibited JS's sensibilities that the Christian charities and virtues had to be the basis of the religion's existence. Enough of the Latter-day Saints embraced the premise that threats directed at church unity did not flourish to the point of enervating JS's endeavors. Nevertheless, discordant personalities and other cir-

168. Nauvoo Stake Priests Quorum Minutes, January–June 1845, LR 3102 21; Nauvoo 5th Ward High Priests Minutes, December 1844–April 1845, LR 3278 21; Nauvoo 9th Ward High Priests Minutes, November 1844–February 1845, LR 3501 21, CHL. See also the record that describes the "Presiding Bishopric Bishop's Quorum" in Nauvoo, "A Record of the Quorum of the Lesser Priesthood," CR 4 122, CHL.

169. Leonard, *Nauvoo*, 184; Haven, "A Girl's Letters from Nauvoo," 619.

170. Minutes of the two organizations are held in the CHL. For transcriptions, see Dinger, *Nauvoo City and High Council Minutes*.

171. Smith to Oliver Granger, ca July 22–28, 1840, *JSP, D7*:362.

cumstances prevailed in Kirtland that scuttled hopes of a continuing Mormon presence there.

Once in Nauvoo, along with the theological configurations underlying the purpose of it all, what JS had established provided the basis of sustainability that exceeded his own persona. The church he formalized when he was a twenty-four-year-old displays remarkable attachment to its nineteenth-century precedents. Though there have been, to be sure, significant modifications of the structure since the 1830s, the modern church still relies on many of the foundational markers exhibited in JS's revelations and innovations. The surviving historical record, incomplete as it is, provides ample evidence of JS's ingenuity and ambition to generate through the premises of priesthood authority something much more than just an outline of what an ecclesiastical organization might become. The exercise above recounts the complex, evolving, and protracted discharge of plans to accommodate the birth and development of a people who viewed themselves as the restoration of primitive Christianity. With the support and influence of others, JS had created a church.

PART IV

Joseph Smith as a Man and Prophet

CHAPTER 11

Underlying the Personality of Joseph Smith

Its Influence on His History

JS's personality may be the most important objective of discovery in the pursuit of who he was and what he did.[1] As will be shown, grasping the center and boundaries of that personality, however, is difficult to ascertain because of several idiosyncratic dispositions of the prophet. As Dean Jessee explained, while JS "produced a sizeable collection of papers," they did not necessarily actually reveal his "thoughts and personality." That is, "the lack of personal writing, the wide use of clerks taking dictation or even being assigned to write for him, and the editorial reworking of reports of what he did and said" provide virtually a secondhand portrayal of the man.[2] JS's authentic profile therefore has been rendered through a lens that has been influenced more by what others thought of him than of what he explained about himself.

Jessee's work disclosed the limited and filtered influence of JS on his own papers. It turns out, Jessee wrote, that from the outset JS had difficulty in transferring his thoughts to paper.[3] In this light, JS's use of clerks and scribes is critical as we attempt to pry open the past to understand his motives and behavior. "A complicated life and feelings of literary inadequacy explain this dependence" on his scribes, Jessee explained. Quoting from JS's own letters, Jesse wrote that JS "lamented his 'lack of fluency in address,' his 'imperfections of...writings' and his 'inability' to convey his ideas in writing. Communication seemed to him to present an insurmountable barrier. He wrote of the almost 'totel darkness of

1. An earlier version of this chapter appeared as Ronald O. Barney, "Joseph Smith and the Conspicuous Scarcity of Early Mormon Documentation," in Ashurst-McGee, Jensen, and Howcroft, *Foundational Texts of Mormonism*, 373–401.
2. Jessee, *Personal Writings of Joseph Smith*, 2.
3. This posture contradicts the revelations that he produced, including the Book of Mormon. Where he apparently had ready capacity to dictate the spiritual impressions he obtained, he proved hesitant in addressing other matters that faced him.

paper pen and ink and a crooked broken scattered and imperfect language.'"[4] Thus, besides his instincts for keeping much of his spiritual life to himself, which are discussed below, he inherently felt inadequate to express what he could about his experiences. Not understanding this important feature of JS's personality could significantly distort one's expectations for clarity from the documentary record he left behind and how it described his life.

Jessee was the first to systematically bore into that record, culling subtleties that forced all thereafter to rethink how the most oft-used sources had influenced previous interpretations of JS and his work. Regarding his journals covering the years of 1832 to 1844—not to be confused with the "History of Joseph Smith" and the *History of the Church* noted above—Jessee wrote, as noted earlier: "Of the 1,587 manuscript pages comprising the Smith journal, 31 contain holograph writing, where he is known to have put his own thoughts on the paper. Another 250 were evidently dictated to scribes."[5] His scribes composed the rest. Clearly, JS's journals did not qualify as the intimate expressions traditionally affixed to them. JS's sermons also posed a problem. The extant notes of the sermons are vital documents for understanding his thinking in his maturity. They were in his last years the primary means of delivering his revelations to the church. But what was captured is nothing near a complete record. Only a small percentage of his preachments were chronicled.[6] Modern students of JS must recognize how these factors influence what can and cannot be said about the prophet.

The scarcity of written copies of JS's sermons and the compilation of his life late in his career ("History of Joseph Smith") point to a larger issue, one that Dean Jessee's meticulous work helped subsequent scholars to appreciate. Despite the extensive work of JS's clerks/historians, there are voids in the record. Some documentation that one might think would be central to his ministry is conspicuously absent. Only by reviewing what survives, while asking at the same time why he never revealed his innermost thinking or produced essential descriptions of several of his most significant experiences, can we see how his personality tempered what we can know about him. As stated previously by David McCullough on why he declined to biograph the thirty-second American president: "There are many reasons why I didn't do Franklin...but one is that Franklin Roosevelt never put his heart on paper. He never expressed what he really felt or really thought about anything, on paper."[7] JS, as it turned out, proved

4. Jessee, *Personal Writings of Joseph Smith*, 2–3. Jessee quoted from Joseph Smith to Emma Smith, June 6, 1832; Joseph Smith to W.W. Phelps, November 27, 1832; Joseph Smith to Moses Nickerson, November 19, 1833; and Joseph Smith to Emma Smith, March 21, 1839, all found in *Personal Writings of Joseph Smith*, 265, 269, 325, 449.
5. Jessee, *Papers of Joseph Smith*, 2:xxii–xxiii.
6. Jessee, "Priceless Words and Fallible Memories," 23.
7. McCullough, in Zinsser, *Extraordinary Lives*, 35–36.

similarly reluctant to expose his innermost thoughts and feelings, though there are indications that he once considered the strategy in chronicling his life.[8]

This chapter considers three aspects of JS's distinctive leadership style as manifestations of his personality that formed and fostered what became The Church of Jesus Christ of Latter-day Saints and its history. The three traits of JS's peculiar personal character illustrated below are rooted in the acknowledgment of a recognized dearth of significant documentation—the kind of historical record that, had such material been created, would likely have rendered a rather different perspective on Mormon beginnings than presently exists. Contrary to what one might expect or have come to believe: (1) JS largely kept to himself the sacred experiences that shaped his personality and validity as a religious leader; (2) JS often chose not to insert himself into church dialogue when one might think he would be most inclined to do so; and (3) JS appears to have little to no interest in having his numerous sermons captured and distributed, which besides giving inspiration and encouragement to church members, also became in his last years his principal medium for delivering his revelations to the church.

When considered together, these matters are perplexing. It makes sense that he restrained himself in describing his sacred experiences; there are numerous scriptural precedents for such sensitivity. But what was he thinking that caused him to behave so counterintuitively to one whose commission was to reveal and elaborate Jesus's designs for the latter-day world? What, for instance, caused him to retreat from an aggressive literary influence when he had the necessary apparatus and forum to do so? What moved him to dismiss the necessity of capturing and then distributing the sermons he delivered to the Saints? Thus far, no logical or demonstrable explanations have been advanced. We are left to piece together hints from the fragments found in the documentary record to give some meaning to what is now unexplainable.

It may be most likely that his early experiences fashioned his attitude. JS himself later reflected upon the response he received when he first explained his initial vision of Deity to one he thought might lend a sympathetic ear. The Methodist minister he told within a few days of his experience "treated my communication not only lightly but with great contempt." As word spread, he recounted, it "excited a great deal of prejudice against me."[9] Richard Bushman speculated that, indeed, "he may have held back for fear of ridicule." But Bushman also

8. JS's expressions written in the first days of the journal exhibit, at least at the beginning, some attention to his feelings: "Oh may God grant that I may be directed in all my thaughts[.] Oh bless thy Servent Amen"; "my mind is calm and serene for which I thank the Lord"; and "Oh Lord deliver ~~out~~ thy servent out of temtations and fill his heart with wisdom and understanding." Smith, Journals, November 27, 28, and December 4, 1832, *JSP, J1*:9, 11.

9. Smith, Histories, "History Drafts, 1838–circa 1841," Draft 2, *JSP, H1*:216.

posited that in JS's early years it "may have been the natural reticence of a teenage boy keeping his own counsel."[10] Bushman's observation identifies a significant feature of JS's personality that helps explain why he did not disseminate information about himself—especially his sacred experiences.

The evidence or lack thereof regarding the foundational events of JS's church have been used by polemicists in attempts to *prove or disprove* his claims. These milestone events include his first vision of Deity, probably in 1820; his encounters with the angelic messenger of the golden plates, later identified as the Book of Mormon prophet Moroni, 1823–1827; and the bestowals of divine authority upon JS and his associate Oliver Cowdery by John the Baptist and by the apostles Peter, James, and John. The adversarial contentions center on whether JS had the experiences he later described or if he invented them. Setting aside the issue of whether he really experienced the things he claimed to have had, one can still ask *when and why* he started telling the stories that were only later committed to paper. The intent here is to illustrate for the reader how JS's personality influenced the records upon which we judge his life and his work.

Sacred Experience and Sense of Privacy

The paramount event of Mormonism—even though it was not heralded as such during most of JS's lifetime—is what is known today as his First Vision. As explained earlier, while he did not relate specifics at the time, JS later claimed that he had seen in or around 1820 the resurrected and glorified Jesus Christ and God, the Eternal Father, though he did not characterize the "personages" at the time. He first implied the event when in 1830 he prepared the Articles and Covenants of the church.[11] But the trackable paper trail describing this vision did not begin until the summer of 1832—postdating the event by twelve years—stoking the polarized contests about the validity of his story. Twelve years is a long time to conceal such an important moment.

Writing of JS's vision, Fawn M. Brodie—whose skeptical portrait of JS credited him little—postulated that "the awesome vision he described in later years was probably the elaboration of some half-remembered dream stimulated by the early revival excitement and reinforced by the rich folklore of visions circulating in his neighborhood." Indeed, she claimed, "it may have been sheer invention, created some time after 1830 when the need arose for a magnificent tradition."[12] Those determined to discredit JS and his First Vision recognize that doing so not only disembowels the prophet's veracity, it also questions the legitimacy of Mormonism itself. The critics primarily focus on varying particulars in the several rehearsals of the event attributed to JS to negate the event as nothing more

10. Bushman, *Rough Stone Rolling*, 40.
11. "Articles and Covenants, circa April 1830 [D&C 20]," *JSP, D1*:121, and note 49.
12. Brodie, *No Man Knows My History*, 25.

than his calculating ploy. Critical investigation of what JS claimed, obviously, is entirely warranted. But understanding his ongoing circumstances illustrates that the demands by his critics for a boilerplate witness from JS is unrealistic. Other claimants to divine intervention have not been so easily dismissed. In the early years of the sixteenth century, for example, Martin Luther, who was unsettled for years about "the luxury, avarice, ignorance, and greed" of the Catholic clergy, with pointed criticism of the "chicanery of that warrior-pope Julius II,"[13] claimed a transformational time when he finally "understood the nature of grace."[14] The event provided the impetus for him to act. Occurring, as scholars claim, sometime between 1513 and 1519, the event later famously known as his "tower experience" led him "to a fresh understanding of the Gospel." Though Luther's later references to the incident "underwent extensive transformation," which include contradictions to his timing of the "experience," Luther has not been decertified as an honest man, nor have the uncertainties been used to explain away the Protestant reformation.[15] JS has never enjoyed such deference.

A number of explanations have been advanced by believers to justify JS's delay in telling his story. As stated previously, JS indicated in the case of his reception with Oliver Cowdery of the priesthood in May 1829, that the hostile social environment at the time prohibited telling the marvelous story: "We were forced to keep secret the circumstances of our having been baptized, and having received this priesthood; owing to a spirit of persecution which had already manifested itself in the neighborhood."[16] The contextual evidence confirms the validity of the assertion. As word spread regarding JS's claims of accessing the divine, he received not only cold rejoinders but, over time, physical abuse. That same documentation also demands that fear of persecution was not the only reason for JS's reticence to reveal his experiences with the sacred.[17]

It is implausible in the minds of some that JS, if he actually experienced the divine visitations he professed, did not run up Stafford Road to Palmyra's Main Street to declare the phenomenon or at least to rush home to put his experience

13. Roland H. Bainton, *Here I Stand: A Life of Martin Luther* (New York: Pierce and Smith, 1950; Nashville: Abingdon Press, 1978), 55. Citations refer to the 1978 edition.

14. Eric Metaxas, *Martin Luther: The Man Who Rediscovered God and Changed the World* (New York: Penguin Books, 2017), 95–97; Lyndal Roper, *Martin Luther: Renegade and Prophet* (New York: Random House, 2017), 86.

15. Dillenberger, *Martin Luther: Selections from His Writings*, xvii. See also Marty, *Martin Luther: A Life* (New York: Penguin Books, 2008), 37; and Roper, *Martin Luther*, 86–88.

16. "History of Joseph Smith," *Times and Seasons*, August 1, 1842, 866; Smith, Histories, "History Drafts, 1838–circa 1841," Draft 2, *JSP, H1*:296.

17. Others have argued as much, but have addressed only Joseph Smith's reluctance to discuss his First Vision. See Hugh Nibley, "Censoring Joseph Smith's Story, Part 1," *Improvement Era*, July 1961, 522; Allen, "Significance of Joseph Smith's 'First Vision,'" 34; Hill, *Joseph Smith: The First Mormon*, 52–53; Bushman, *Joseph Smith and the Beginnings of Mormonism*, 58.

to paper so that all would know of God's recent activity on earth. The evidence for the first years of his prophetic career indicates, however, that JS instinctively kept quiet regarding many features of his ministry. The record shows that he apparently looked upon the events as demanding restraint on his part in divulging the sacral nature of what he had experienced. Hugh Nibley sensed in 1961 JS's instinctual inclinations. Undoubtedly reflecting on Brodie's earlier insinuations regarding the absence of JS's contemporaneous disclosure of his experiences, Nibley wrote: "One may ask, why should Joseph Smith have waited so long to tell his story officially. From his own explanation [the 1838/39 account of the First Vision that was published in 1842 in the *Times and Seasons*][18] it is apparent that he would not have told it publicly at all had he not been 'induced' to do so by all the scandal stories that were circulating." Nibley in 1961 did not benefit from the texts of JS's First Vision that came to light thereafter (described above) that shed greater light on JS's motives in telling his story. Yet, his conclusion exactly fit JS's disposition.[19]

This posture is difficult for contemporary observers to understand, as for much of the twentieth century Mormon missionaries used the LDS Church's codified First Vision story among their initial testimonials regarding JS and the restoration of Jesus's gospel. This is in contrast to the first cadre of Mormon missionaries who, by design, simply proclaimed "the first principles and ordinances of the gospel" underscored by the material evidence of the Book of Mormon. Though JS apparently considered in 1832 the public disclosure of his experience with Deity, because he thereafter refrained from doing so until the early 1840s the pervasive story today may have been known to but a limited number of early Mormons in the church's first decade. Indeed, as previously stated, the first description of the vision did not appear in print until 1840 when Orson Pratt published the story in Scotland as a missionary tract.[20] Proclamation of the gospel's restoration during the first decade of Mormonism did not include

18. Joseph Smith, "History of Joseph Smith," *Times and Seasons*, April 1, 1842, 748.

19. Hugh Nibley, "Censoring Joseph Smith's Story, Conclusion," *Improvement Era*, November 1961, 813. Others, such as James B. Allen, have also surmised that the sacred nature of Joseph Smith's experiences may have precluded his public disclosure of them. Allen, "Emergence of a Fundamental," 46.

20. Pratt, *Interesting Account of Several Remarkable Visions*, also published as "Orson Pratt, *A[n] Interesting Account of Several Remarkable Visions*, 1840," in Smith, Histories, *JSP, H1*:517–46. From the late 1960s to the 1980s several scholarly defenders of Joseph Smith, including Dean Jessee, published treatments of the scope of Joseph Smith's rehearsals of the First Vision in order to disarm claims of critics, such as Wesley P. Walters and Jerald and Sandra Tanner, who contended that Joseph Smith fabricated accounts of his divine authorization. Others who published important affirmative clarifications of Joseph Smith's theophanies, besides Jessee, include James B. Allen, Milton V. Backman, and Richard L. Anderson, all BYU professors.

the First Vision. Thus, the assertion that JS resisted dissemination of his holiest personal experiences may at present be received with surprise by believers and unbelievers alike.

A Pattern of Reticence

The "present state of the evidence" that Nibley drew upon suggests that JS was sensitive to incurring the displeasure of Deity by divulging his heavenly or spiritual encounters. Smith generally followed that pattern regarding the protection of sacred matters for the remainder of his tenure as prophet. For instance, minutes of a gathering on October 25, 1831, of church elders in Orange, Ohio, thirteen miles southwest of Kirtland, portray JS's refusal to discuss his personal manifestations of God even among his closest associates. Present at the meeting were most of JS's most trusted colleagues, including Oliver Cowdery and several others who were Book of Mormon witnesses and future members of the church's First Presidency and Quorum of the Twelve Apostles. Yet when his brother, Hyrum, proposed to JS that he relate to the small gathering "the information of the coming forth of the Book of Mormon" that all present "might know for themselves," JS declined, asserting "it was not intended to tell the world all the particulars of the coming forth of the book of Mormon." Indeed, he continued, "it was not expedient for him to relate these things."[21] If there was ever an optimum moment for him to share and confirm such an important matter with his closest associates, this was such a time. Yet he refused. Cowdery, who had shared with JS a number of the most supernal experiences of Mormonism's founding and who took the minutes of the October 25 meeting, could have offered firsthand validation as, indeed, could have the others who reported having seen the golden plates. Still, JS resisted.[22]

It should not be surprising that many of the things JS taught were done so in private settings, particularly to the Twelve Apostles. To Parley P. Pratt who remained behind in England after the apostles' second mission, Heber C. Kimball,

21. Smith, Documents, October 25–26, 1831, Minute Book 2, *JSP, D2*:84.

22. Except that the Book of Mormon came by way of "the power of God," JS never explained "how" he translated the Book of Mormon, though he was reported to describe the circumstantial context of the "coming forth of the Book of Mormon" in numerous settings. See John W. Welch, "The Miraculous Translation of the Book of Mormon," in *Opening the Heavens: Accounts of Divine Manifestations, 1820–1844* (Provo, UT: Brigham Young University Press and Deseret Book, 2005), 77–213. Cowdery, while describing features of the coming forth of the Book of Mormon to W. W. Phelps, also remained silent regarding the divine manifestations that he experienced incident to his initial association with JS. Oliver Cowdery to W. W. Phelps, September 7, 1834, *Messenger and Advocate*, October 1834, 15–16; see also JS's reference to Oliver keeping his own counsel in Smith, Histories, "History Drafts, 1838–circa 1841," *JSP, H1*:284. This may or may not have concerned Jesus's appearance to Cowdery described in Smith, Histories, "circa summer 1832, History," *JSP, H1*:16.

wrote in June 1842 to describe JS's favorable circumstances at the time: "Brother Joseph feels as well as I Ever see[n] him." Perhaps one of the explanations for JS's temporary opportune status was that "he has got a Small company that he feels safe in thare ha[n]ds. And that is not all, he can open his bosom to[o] and feel him Self safe." To JS's intimates, Kimball explained, he delivered "some pressious things... on the preasthood that would caus your Soul to rejoice." But reflecting JS's sensibilities about what he had taught, Kimball told Pratt that "I can not give them to you on paper fore they are not to be riten."[23] Two years later, JS stated to a gathering of the Twelve Apostles, Bishop George Miller, and the Nauvoo Temple committee, after discussing important matters pertinent to their assignments: "Can this council keep what I say [and] not make it Public? all held up their hands."[24] Controlling how what he said to his intimates was dispersed was important to him.

Many students of JS today lament the prophet's instincts of reluctance about publicizing the intervention of the divine in his life. As stated, some of the tendencies were likely inborn and others learned. JS shared his concerns about revealing sacred matters with those he believed would honor the same. To a November 1835 gathering of several members of the newly appointed Quorum of the Twelve Apostles, he warned: "Let us be faithful and silent brethren, <and> if God gives you a manifestation, Keep it to yourself."[25] JS placed the apostles at the head of the church's missionary force, and sent them into the field to lead the effort, but they were instructed not to witness of all they knew. Thus, in his own case, rather than publicly bellowing his private communications with heaven—as would seem a reasonable course of action for a person trying to convince others of God's new revelation—JS kept his own counsel and expected those in his inner circle to do the same.[26] There were occasions, however, where

23. Heber C. Kimball to Parley P. Pratt, June 17, 1842, Parley P. Pratt Collection, Correspondence, 1842, MS 897, CHL.

24. Smith, March 10, 1844, quoted in Jessee, "Sources for the Study of Joseph Smith," 17; also in Smith, Journals, March 10, 1844, *JSP, J3*:200–1.

25. Smith, Journals, November 12, 1835, *JSP, J1*:98.

26. JS, while he later felt constrained to give particulars of the founding events of Mormonism, remained sensitive to the principle of keeping sacred things sacred. In an 1841 sermon he said: "The reason we do not have the secrets of the Lord revealed unto us is because we do not keep them but reveal them. We do not keep our own secrets but reveal our difficulties to the world even to our enemies. Then how would we keep the secrets of the Lord?" He told them he could "keep a secret till dooms day." *Wilford Woodruff's Journal*, November 19, 1841, 2:143. Showing that JS's teachings had taken root, JS's brother Hyrum later publicly instructed: "Therefore beware what you teach! for the mysteries of God are not given to all men; and unto those to whom they are given they are placed under restrictions to impart only such as God will command them; and the residue is to be kept in a faithful breast, otherwise he will be brought under condemnation. By this God will prove his faithful servants, who will be called and numbered with the chosen." Hyrum Smith to "the brethren of the Church of Jesus Christ of Latterday Saints," in *Times and Seasons*, March 15, 1844, 474.

JS encouraged disclosure of heavenly manifestations determined by the sanctity of the setting. At a gathering of priesthood quorums on February 6, 1836, in the Kirtland House of the Lord, which had been rising for three years, JS invited that "if any obtain a prophecy or vision ~~not~~ to rise & speak that all may be edified & rejoice together."[27] This instance, though, undoubtedly dictated by the circumstance, was unusual and uncharacteristic of JS's instinctual protocols.

Just two months later, on April 3, 1836, amidst the spiritual fervor erupting in the small but growing village of Kirtland during the dedicatory rites of the Mormon temple, JS and Oliver Cowdery claimed to witness yet another series of phenomenal visions. In contrast to his other experiences with the divine, in this case, at or near the time of the event, JS dictated the vision's substance to his scribe at the time—Warren Cowdery, Oliver's brother. The text (well known to modern Mormon followers given its publication in the D&C as Section 110), consisted of the announcement that not only had Jesus of Nazareth appeared to JS and Oliver, but also the Old Testament figures of Moses, Elias, and Elijah. JS claimed that those three ancient personalities provided him and Cowdery with divine authority empowering them with religious capacity previously unavailable.[28] Despite JS committing to his journal what he and Cowdery experienced, he did not at the time or later use the visionary experience to add weight and gravity to his position. While the experience is recorded in his private journal, no contemporary evidence exists that he overtly publicized the marvelous encounter, though several individuals at the time indicated they heard that something extraordinary had occurred in the Kirtland House of the Lord.[29] Also,

---

It should be noted that upon the introduction of plural marriage in Nauvoo, secrecy became a fundamental expectation of JS in the environment surrounding the limited number of those who participated, a partial justification being antecedents from the Masonic tradition. As has been suggested, one ulterior purpose of the Nauvoo Women's Relief Society may have been to protect and keep secret JS's initiation of the practice. Homer, *Joseph's Temples*, 181–83, 197–202.

27. Smith, Journals, February 6, 1836, *JSP, J1*:181.

28. Smith, Journals, April 3, 1836, *JSP, J1*:219–22.

29. At least some aspects of the visions were also known to W. W. Phelps, who was part of JS's inner circle. In a letter to his wife, Sally, on April 3, 1836, Phelps stated that after the "curtains were dropt in the after noon," there was "a manifestation of the Lord to Br. Joseph and Oliver, by which they warned that the great & terrible day of the Lord as mentioned by Malichi was near, even at the doors." William W. Phelps to Sally Phelps, April 3, 1836, Kirtland, Ohio, William W. Phelps Papers, VMSS 810, L. Tom Perry Special Collections, Brigham Young University, Provo, Utah. See also Lucius Pomeroy Parsons to "Dear Sister," April 10, 1836, cited in Vogel, "Evolution of Early Mormon Priesthood Narratives," 79.

Reuben Miller, who did not become a Mormon until 1843, published a pamphlet indicating that by that time there was some understanding of the events of April 3, 1836, and their consequential addition to Mormonism. Miller, *James J. Strang*, 12–13. JS obtained "restoring power of the Melchisedek Priesthood from Elias, and the sealing and binding powers of the same from Elijah."

there is no extant record indicating that JS or Oliver ever publicly referred to the event thereafter.[30] When Willard Richards and his associates later used his journals to draft his 1838/39 history, they included the April 3, 1836, journal account to relate the Kirtland House of the Lord's story in the "History of Joseph Smith." It may be that the majority of the church and the world first became aware of the account when it appeared in the serialization of JS's history in the *Deseret News* on November 6, 1852.[31] Unless one recognizes JS's idiosyncratic disposition to conceal aspects of his personal experience with heaven, the absence of the event from his litany of visionary claims, despite a contemporary private record of the incident, is contradictory and enigmatic.

A Private Personality

Was JS's careful clutch of religious experiences learned or instinctual? Donald L. Enders, one of the leading scholars of this generation on JS and his family, has argued that there was an instinctual component to his behavior. Contrary to modern sentimental portrayals of young JS running home from the nearby grove where he witnessed his initial vision to tell his mother of the phenomenon, Enders stated that JS did not immediately share his remarkable experiences with his family. While others have overlooked that JS actually held back his story from his mother, Enders cited a later December 1842 redaction to what became the codified First Vision story, penned by JS's scribe Willard Richards. Returning from the grove, Mother Smith noticed her son's unusual countenance, and asked him "what the matter was?" Instead of pouring out his heart, JS replied "never mind[,] all is well—I am well enough—off," simply telling his mother, "I have learned for myself that Presbyterianism is not True."[32] He did not explain what happened to him! Certainly his mother never claimed to have heard such a declaration even though she had an opportune circumstance to do so while writing her own biographical portrait of her son.[33]

This exchange after the First Vision is only the first instance exhibiting JS's reticent inclinations. One of the most well known of all Mormon foundational

30. Indeed, in several sermons JS delivered toward the end of his life, he spoke of the promised coming of Elijah as if it was still in the future. See his message of March 10, 1844, in *Wilford Woodruff Journal*, 2:365.

31. Smith, "Life of Joseph Smith," *Deseret News*, November 6, 1852. The account was later canonized in 1880 as "Joseph Smith—History" in *The Pearl of Great Price*, one of the standard works of the Church of Jesus Christ of Latter-day Saints, and added to the 1876 edition of the Doctrine and Covenants.

32. Jessee, *Papers of Joseph Smith*, 1:273; Smith, Histories, "History Drafts, 1838–circa 1841," *JSP, H1*:215n51.

33. When Lucy Mack Smith wrote about her son's First Vision in her autobiography, rather than including her personal observation of learning about the vision, she quoted the "History of Joseph Smith" entry from the *Times and Seasons*, April 1, 1842, 748.

stories is JS's claim that an angel named Moroni appeared to him in September 1823 to reveal the location of the gold plates from which he later translated the Book of Mormon. A feature of JS's account of the story again reveals his instinctual behavior. As referred to previously, in JS's journal entry of November 9, 1835, wherein he related some of his remarkable experiences to Robert Matthews, it is clear that JS initially kept the events of a most remarkable night from his father. After recounting to Matthews the well-known story of Moroni's appearance to him three times in one night in September 1823, Warren Parrish, JS's scribe who captured the prophet's story, wrote, "after the vision had all passed, I found that it was nearly day-light." Later that day, as the male family members labored in a nearby field, JS exposed his physical weakness from little or no sleep the previous night. His father, noticing that he was not his usual self, asked whether or not JS was ill. He replied that he "had but little strength." So, as he explained, his father told him to "go to the house." One might think that this would have been a good time to tell his father of the phenomenal visions that had consumed the night. Instead, as JS recounted it, "I started [home] and went part way and was finally deprived ~~deprived~~ of my strength and fell, but how long I remained I do not know." It was during this incapacitation that "the Angel came to me again and commanded me to go and tell my Father, what I had seen and heard." It is reasonable to ask, "Why did the youth of seventeen initially refrain from telling his father of the previous night's visitations?" Enders noted that according to Lucy Mack Smith, "he was afraid his father would not believe him."[34] Yet after JS reported what he had witnessed, the elder Joseph Smith "wept and told me that it was a vision from God [and] to attend to it."[35] This event, near the beginning of his prophetic journey, indicated that his instinct for silence on spiritual matters found expression early, prompted in part by fear of ridicule, even from his family.

While concern about how his experiences would be viewed significantly influenced him, another weighty attribute influencing JS precluded dissemination of much of what he experienced. This one was not innate, but likely learned from the sacred texts. JS may have been familiar with the New Testament instances where Jesus refrained from revealing sacred occurrences and his works to strangers and often cautioned those upon whom he worked his mysterious powers to "tell no one."[36] And as JS, while still a young man, translated the Book of Mormon, he may have taken note when the text declared: "It is given unto

34. Anderson, *Lucy's Book*, 340.

35. Smith, Journals, November 9, 1835, *JSP, J1*:89. JS, in the history he initiated in 1838/39, also recounted the circumstances of having to have been told by the angel to tell his father what happened. Smith, Histories, "History Drafts, 1838–circa 1841," Draft 2, *JSP, H1*:230, 232. See also Lucy Mack Smith's account of the event in Anderson, *Lucy's Book*, 339–40.

36. See, for example, Matt. 8:4, 9:30, and especially 17:9.

many to know the mysteries of God nevertheless they are laid under a strict command that they shall not impart only according to the portion of his word which he doth grant unto the children of men."[37] That is, those having access to God's manifestations must keep them to themselves unless God told them otherwise. The religious protocol to keep sacred things close to the vest likely appealed to JS's instinctual feelings about what had happened to him.[38]

A Dearth of Documentation

Because of a dearth of contemporary information describing JS's early life, it is impossible to define the full scope of his religious experiences, and how or whether or not he related them. One telling indicator is found in the epistle to his followers that he had published on October 1, 1842, in the church's periodical, the *Times and Seasons*. He usually did not write to the Saints in this manner, but the summer of 1842 found him taking great care to avoid capture by Missouri authorities trying to extradite him for his purported role in the attempted assassination of former governor Lilburn Boggs. Writing from seclusion on September 6, 1842, JS turned to theology, stating to his followers that in order for a complete restoration of the ancient religious world to the earth, including God's authority to perform efficacious religious ordinances such as baptism, "a whole, and complete, and perfect union, and welding together of dispensations, and keys, and powers, and glories should take place, and be revealed from the days of Adam even to the present time."[39] Thus, to restore both ancient Israel and primitive Christianity in a modern "dispensation of the fulness of times," the very players who staged God's work in biblical times were required to return to earth to deliver to JS all of the power and authority they themselves possessed during their mortal sojourns. The prophet's September 6 epistle not only fleetingly mentioned revelations from Jesus "at sundry times, and in divers places," but also announced that "divers angels" from "Adam, down to the present time" had manifested themselves to him.[40] He identified several of them by name, including Adam, Gabriel, and Raphael, a figure from the biblical Apocrypha.[41]

37. Smith, Revelations, "Book of Mormon," *JSP, R3*: Part 1, 415 [Alma 12:9].
38. Subsequent revelatory instruction given to Joseph Smith, later codified into Mormon scripture, emphasized the importance of discreet care with divine manifestations: summer 1828 [D&C 10:35]; April 1829 [D&C 6:12]; March 1830 [D&C 19:21; Moses 1:42, 4:32]; June 22, 1834 [D&C 105:23].
39. "Letter from Joseph Smith," September 6, 1842, *Times and Seasons*, October 1, 1842, 935. This epistle was later inserted into the Doctrine and Covenants in 1876 as Section 128.
40. The language, "sundry times and divers places" is an expression apparently well known from the Westminster Confession in its declaration about the "Holy Scripture." Westminster Confession, chap. 1.
41. Ibid., 936; Tobit 3:17, 5:1–12:22.

JS confirmed his generalization of numerous visits from divine beings in his Wentworth letter. He revealed that besides receiving the ministrations of Moroni, he had "received

Though this brief expression about the biblical figures' appearances to JS was made public in the *Times and Seasons,* the details and content of these extraordinary spiritual experiences are nowhere to be found in JS's writings or sermons.

Publicity

Another unusual factor of JS's personal style had to do with the manner in which he popularized his own role as leader of the fledgling church. In the most recent generation JS has been "diagnosed" with numerous psychological disorders by those attempting to explain his unusual charisma, psyche, and influence over his followers.[42] These diagnoses include megalomania, symptoms of which are an insatiable quest for notoriety, power, and influence. But, if pervasive power was JS's design, such a person would undoubtedly manipulate and influence circumstances to elevate his visibility and status over his disciples to ensure his persona to be an object of veneration. One of the primary arguments against JS being a psychological misfit is the fact that he rejected the option to insert himself into the public square by literary means, even among his own people, when it was his prerogative and advantage to do so.

Many of JS's contemporaries calculated their ministries to instruct, educate, and otherwise influence their followers through the printed word. Ellen G. White, the central figure of Seventh-day Adventism's founding in the middle of the nineteenth century, published five thousand periodical articles and forty books—along with penning tens of thousands of manuscript pages—much of which was explained to be inspired revelatory material.[43] Another of JS's contemporaries, Alexander Campbell, began a literary career that coincided with his ministry. He edited *The Christian Baptist* from 1823 to 1830, then published the *Millennial Harbinger* through the rest of his life to 1866. During the 1830s, at the same time his rival JS envisioned the expansion of his own church, each monthly issue of Campbell's magazine contained forty-eight pages, with Campbell himself contributing between ten and fourteen articles per number, a remarkable literary output.

The Mormons also had denominational publications, but in contrast to the examples of White and Campbell, JS was only tangentially involved. Their first periodical was the *Evening and the Morning Star,* first published in June 1832 in Independence, Missouri. By this time there were over a thousand followers of

many visits from the angels of God unfolding the majesty, and glory of the events that should transpire in the last days." Joseph Smith, "Church History," *Times and Seasons,* March 1, 1842, 707, also reproduced in Smith, Histories, "Church History," *JSP, H1*:495.

42. See Bergera, "Joseph Smith and the Hazards of Charismatic Leadership;" Morain, *Sword of Laban*; and Anderson, *Inside the Mind of Joseph Smith.*

43. Ahlstrom, *Religious History of the American People,* 1:581; Marty, *Pilgrims in Their Own Land,* 323; Ellen G. White Writings, http://www.whiteestate.org/cdrom/cdrom.asp#research.

JS, primarily located in two regions of the country, the old Western Reserve of Ohio and the western border of Missouri. Published by W.W. Phelps in Independence, the *Star*, offered eight pages per issue, rallying the Mormons with new revelations received by JS, as well as other information of religious and secular interest. Once the Mormons were forced northward from Independence in July 1833, and the press destroyed, the locus of the periodical moved to Kirtland where it continued publication until September 1834. During this nearly two-and-one-half-year period, in immediate proximity to JS, one might expect regular installments from the prophet to his people providing instructive guidance to further his designs and ultimately endear him to them personally. JS never employed such a strategic move. Indeed, besides the implicit understanding that the revelations printed therein came from JS, his name appeared in the periodical during its entire run only about two dozen times, usually identified as being in attendance at a conference meeting. Only once did he appear as a signatory; his critique of Alexander Campbell's attacks upon him and the Book of Mormon in the *Star's* final issue.[44]

This is not the behavior one might expect to see from a man whose ambition was to conquer the minds and hearts of even a small portion of the less-populated sector of America. And while his literary presence increased somewhat in subsequent church periodicals—the *Messenger and Advocate*, the *Elders' Journal*, and the *Times and Seasons*—it, too, was infrequent. This was even the case when he served as the official editor of the last two organs (the *Elders' Journal* and the *Times and Seasons*).[45] It is demonstrable, for example, that two of the major essays in the latter publication traditionally attributed to him were actually written by John Taylor, managing editor of the periodical.[46] It is possible that JS took

44. Joseph Smith to "Dear Brother," September 24, 1834, *Evening and the Morning Star*, September 1834, 192.

45. JS edited the *Elders' Journal* from October 1837 to August 1838 and edited the *Times and Seasons* from February 1842 to October 1842.

46. Two pamphlets published by Joseph Hyrum Parry in the mid-1880s brought to light John Taylor's authorship of two articles published in the *Times and Seasons* that had been credited to JS. Richard L. Anderson discovered the disparity, noting that Parry published in 1884 a pamphlet titled *Items of Church History, The Government of God, and The Gift of the Holy Ghost, Articles Written by the Prophet Joseph Smith* (Salt Lake City: Jos. Hyrum Parry, 1884). Parry had assigned authorship of the *Times and Seasons* articles to JS. In 1886, however, Parry revised *Items of Church History*, perhaps due to John Taylor's influence who was church president at the time, by assigning Taylor as author of the articles—"Government of God" and "Gift of the Holy Ghost." A printed note of errata included in the 1886 reprint stated: "The articles in this Pamphlet titled, 'The Gift of the Holy Ghost' and 'The Government of God,' though appearing in 'The History of Joseph Smith' were not written by the Prophet himself, but by President John Taylor, who at that time had charge of the 'Times and Seasons,' though the Prophet Joseph was the editor." Parry, *Items of Church History, the Government of God and the Gift of the Holy Ghost, Articles Written by the Prophet Joseph Smith and President John Taylor* (Salt Lake City: Jos. Hyrum Parry, 1886), 31.

up the pen himself from time to time to author other materials, though there were other talented men available to assist in the endeavor.[47] But other than his direct involvement in February and March 1842 when he became editor of the *Times and Seasons*, JS's influence was primarily hands-off.

Another example of JS's detachment from literary interplay during his ministry is production of the "Lectures on Faith" that appeared as the first of two parts constituting the first edition of the 1835 Doctrine and Covenants. As the constituent components of the volume were assembled, the "Lectures," which derived from the classroom-type setting in the Kirtland School of the Elders, became the "Doctrine" that prefaced the revelations—the "Covenants." Here JS could have asserted his influence over the text. And until the last part of the twentieth century, most commentators on JS and his teachings attributed the "Lectures" to JS's production. However, modern literary scholarship and analyses of the lectures assign the production to Sidney Rigdon, while acknowledging that JS undoubtedly contributed to the project.[48] The seven lectures (prepared as a catechism) comprised about 28 percent of the text, with JS's revelations containing about 72 percent of the material.[49]

Not everyone was familiar with Parry's revision, however. Interestingly, Joseph Fielding Smith in his 1938 *Teachings of the Prophet Joseph Smith*, attributed the "Government of God" and "Gift of the Holy Ghost" essays to Joseph Smith. For the essay on "The Government of God" Apostle Smith stated, "An Editorial by the Prophet on the Failure of Man-made Government and the Right of God to Rule" (248); for "The Gift of the Holy Ghost" his attribution stated "An Editorial in the 'Times and Seasons,' by the Prophet" (242).

47. W. W. Phelps often performed the ghostwriter role in writing such things as JS's *General Smith's Appeal to the Green Mountain Boys* (Nauvoo, IL: Taylor and Woodruff, 1843), in https://www.josephsmithpapers.org/paper-summary/general-joseph-smiths-appeal-to-the-green-mountain-boys-december-1843/1; and *General Smith's Views of the Powers and Policy of the Government of the United States* (Nauvoo, IL: John Taylor, 1844), in https://www.josephsmithpapers.org/transcript/general-smiths-views-of-the-powers-and-policy-of-the-government-of-the-united-states-7-february-1844?print=true. See also Van Orden, *We'll Sing and We'll Shout*, 325–44.

48. See Elinore H. Partridge, "Characteristics of Joseph Smith's Style and Notes on the Authorship of the Lectures on Faith." Task Papers in LDS History 14 (Salt Lake City: History Division, Historical Department, Church of Jesus Christ of Latter-day Saints, 1976); Alan J. Phipps, "The Lectures on Faith: An Authorship Study" (master's thesis, Brigham Young University, 1977); Noel B. Reynolds, "The Case for Sidney Rigdon as Author of the Lectures on Faith," *Journal of Mormon History* 32, no. 3 (Fall 2005): 1–41. See also the analysis of the Joseph Smith Papers editors allowing that "JS was apparently involved." "Appendix 1, First Theological Lecture on Faith, circa January–May 1835," *JSP, D4*:458–59.

49. Those who have insisted that JS authored the "Lectures" have generally deflected in one way or another the lecture's incompatible statements with what JS later taught, which are well known. A prominent example, is the pronouncement in "Lecture Fifth" of the character of the godhead. The "Father," it states, is "a personage of spirit, glory and power," the "Son" a "personage of tabernacle, made, or fashioned like unto man," with the "Holy Spirit" being the "mind" of God." "Lecture Fifth, of Faith," D&C (1835), 53. It is possible that JS may have concurred at the time in how the Godhead was defined in 1835.

The primary factor laying the lectures to someone other than JS, however, is the very nature of the production. Had the seventy-four pages of the lectures been written by JS it would have been one of the most extensive and declarative announcements of his ministry, entirely uncharacteristic of his prophetic style. Throughout his life, as stated above, he felt that writing and producing his thoughts on paper was outside his aptitude and generally deferred to his scribes and clerks/historians to write for him.[50] He did not produce texts after the manner and scale of the "Lectures." JS's province was the production of sacred records through "translation" and revelation, and later his impromptu delivery of sermons.

Sermon Record

By the time JS appeared as part of America's religious demographic, among the educated clergy the skill and method of delivering a sermon had become something of an art form.[51] The Mormons, including JS, did not ignore this means of communication that had become standard in the young country's religious structures. Again, it was Dean Jessee who first identified for readers the scope of JS's sermonizing. Jessee pointed out that private and institutional reports of 250 of JS's sermons survive. He postulated that if JS delivered a statistically comparable number of sermons prior to his ministry in Nauvoo, he may have delivered as many as 450 over the course of his career. To our disappointment, mentions or accounts of what he said exist for only about 20 percent of what he likely delivered, and none of them are verbatim reports.[52] It remains surprising that a man who calculated to create a religious environment of uniform polity and belief never commissioned his clerks to capture his language so that his instructions and teachings could be communicated in the print media for his followers and others. In contrast to many of his religious contemporaries, he delivered, but never later disseminated, what he preached to his followers.

Like his discomfort in expressing himself on paper, JS also discounted his verbal abilities in conveying his thoughts and emotions. Clearly his insecurity

50. Besides several others who served as scribes for JS, see also the arguments made that W.W. Phelps was a primary ghostwriter for JS in Michael Hicks, "Joseph Smith, W.W. Phelps, and the Poetic Paraphrase of 'The Vision,'" *Journal of Mormon History* 20, no. 2 (Fall 1994); Samuel Brown, "The Translator and the Ghostwriter: Joseph Smith and William Phelps," *Journal of Mormon History*, 34, no. 1 (Winter 2008): 26–62; and Van Orden, *We'll Sing and We'll Shout*, 325–44.

51. Phyllis M. Jones and Nicholas R. Jones, eds., *Salvation in New England: Selections from the Sermons of the First Preachers* (Austin: University of Texas Press, 1977), 3–24; Jon Butler, *Awash in a Sea of Faith: Christianizing the American People* (Cambridge, MA: Harvard University Press, 1990), 57, 172–74. See also the analysis of JS's sermonizing in Smith, "Joseph Smith's Sermons and the Early Mormon Documentary Record," in Ashurst-McGee, Jensen, and Howcroft, *Foundational Texts of Mormonism*.

52. Jessee, "Priceless Words and Fallible Memories," 23.

with verbal and written English affected his style as a prophet. "I cannot find words to express myself," he confessed to a congregation in April 1843. "I am not learned." He then lamented, "O that I had the the language of the archangel to express my feeling once to my frends. but I never expect to."[53] Despite this plague of insecurity in articulation, the sermon became in the last years of his life one of the most important means of his communication and delivery of divine communication to the Latter-day Saints.

In April 1843, at the same time JS explained to his followers that he had trouble expressing himself, Nauvoo acquired another immigrant from England, part of an incessant immigration cycle of British Saints arriving in America during the early 1840s. This one, however, happened to be the first convert to Mormonism in England, baptized at the beginning of the initial apostolic mission to Great Britain in 1837. Thirty-year-old George D. Watt was an educated man who knew the specialized skill of shorthand (phonography), which he learned in Scotland in 1842 while serving as a missionary after his conversion.[54] When Watt immigrated to Nauvoo he apparently arranged with JS to lecture about and teach shorthand to Nauvoo residents in the assembly room on the second level of JS's store. A promotional advertisement in Nauvoo's newspaper, *The Wasp*, promised to introduce the new and superior system of Pitman shorthand to the Saints: "This system, which, from its simplicity, is remarkably easy of attainment and pleasing in practice, is so true and perfect a method of writing, that any word in *any* language, names, of persons and places, the precise pronunciation of a person, &c. can be expressed by it with perfect ease and precision; be read at any distance of time without the possibility of mistake, and with a greater ease than longhand—it is, therefore, admirably adapted for every species of composition."[55] To underscore its utility over existing practice, the notice in Nauvoo's newspaper stated that an apt comparison between the phonographic Pitman and longhand note-taking was the advance of "railway locomotives" over "stage coaches."[56]

Observers today know about JS's Nauvoo sermons because persons in the audience captured in notes the substance (and periodic quotations) of what he said, always of an abbreviated nature. Often only a short paragraph represented the content of a lengthy speech. Occasionally, especially when the delivery was covered by one of JS's clerks—like William Clayton, Willard Richards,

53. Smith, Journal, April 16, 1843, *JSP, J*2:361.
54. Ronald G. Watt, *The Mormon Passage of George D. Watt: First British Convert, Scribe in Zion* (Logan, UT: Utah State University Press, 2009), 33, 45. The same year that Watt became a Mormon, his countryman Isaac Pitman introduced a modified shorthand method, "a forty-sound alphabet system," that would eventually replace the prevailing technique known as Taylor shorthand.
55. Advertisement, *The Wasp*, April 26, 1843.
56. Ibid.

or Thomas Bullock—or by Apostle Wilford Woodruff, a more detailed and comprehensive report was produced, though it too represented only a small fraction of what he had delivered. Given those circumstances, one would think that Watt's arrival in Nauvoo might be looked upon by JS as a godsend; finally, someone could capture precisely his words for publication, distribution, or even archival purposes. It did not happen. Despite his proximity to Watt, JS apparently never engaged the services of the man who taught those skills above his Red Brick store, though he delivered over fifty sermons in and around Nauvoo after Watt's arrival.

The absence of George D. Watt in JS's stable of clerks raises questions about what JS hoped to accomplish by way of his sermonizing: they were not, with very few exceptions, recorded, published, or read. The New England clergy had earlier mastered the Sabbath sermon, a medium of communication apparently not shared by ministers in other regions of the young country.[57] Perhaps JS, on the geographical fringe of society, did not see the necessity or utility of preserving his messages to the Saints. But, given the status of revelatory imprint that obviously characterized JS's Nauvoo sermons, this hardly seems likely. That JS ignored what Watt could do for him remains a significant puzzle regarding JS's ministry and his prophetic style. Six months after JS's death, at the encouragement of Apostle Willard Richards—JS's primary clerk/historian at the end of his life—Watt started in January 1845 to record speeches and other communications. At the church's April 1845 general conference, Watt began his career capturing sermons of church leaders. Brigham Young then assigned him to the trio of Nauvoo scribes that included Willard Richards and Thomas Bullock, who became influential in preserving that period of Mormonism. Thereafter Watt's shorthand skills were used in meetings of church leaders, with his transcriptions of some of their public speeches appearing in the *Times and Seasons*.[58] But he never scribed for JS.

In contrast to the lack of attention JS showed to preserving his sermons, he went to some trouble to have his early revelations recorded, compiled, and published. The Doctrine and Covenants, the volume where his revelations were published, contained the theology, doctrines, polity, and protocols that thereafter governed the church. There was both a practical and an archival purpose

57. Butler, *Awash in a Sea of Faith*, 172.

58. Watt, *Mormon Passage of George D. Watt*, 49–50. Watt later performed one of the most significant endeavors of capturing nineteenth-century Mormonism by initiating what became the twenty-six-volume compilation titled the *Journal of Discourses*, which, early on, were his transcriptions in Pitman shorthand of church leader sermons. Subsequent scribes carried the endeavor to completion in the 1880s.

in the revelations' publication. But after their initial printing in 1835, the output of "thus saith the Lord"–type revelations that characterized many of his earlier codified texts precipitously declined. While he added before his death eight "revelations" to the Doctrine and Covenants in 1844, during the Nauvoo period JS's revelations to the church were dispersed primarily by way of his sermons (though a few were distributed by way of epistle).[59] Yet even after the sermons had taken on this crucial revelatory role he made no effort to have their language or content precisely captured for contemporary or future use.[60]

This is not to suggest that JS was not sanguine about what he said and how his words were received by the listener. Numerous followers declared that he spoke with compelling power. (Others, usually skeptical visitors, picked at his lack of polish and erudition.) JS regarded his speaking opportunities with much gravity. He cared about how his words were received but was apparently content to have the extent of his inspired words internalized by the hearer. He said on Sunday, August 6, 1843, that "eve[r]y word that procedeeth from the mouth of Jehovah has such an influenc[e] over the hum[a]n mind[,] the logical mind. that it is convince[i]ng without <othr> testimo[n]y. faith cometh by hearing."[61] The expression, referencing Romans 10:17, suggests that JS's primary ambition was to reveal the word of God resulting in the increase of faith for the hearer. Besides what appears to be a calculated determination not to have his words prepared for later dissemination, it was also apparently rare for him to review the notes of his sermons written by Willard Richards, his secretary and clerk/historian.[62] Not only did JS refrain from having his words secured by phonographic transcription, he also never spoke from a prepared text.[63]

59. See Joseph Smith, "Tidings," *Times and Seasons*, September 15, 1842, 919–20 [D&C 127]; "Letter from Joseph Smith," September 6, 1842, *Times and Seasons*, October 1, 1842 [D&C 128].
60. The texts of most of Joseph Smith's sermons included in the "History of Joseph Smith" were inserted after his death by the initial compilers of his history, in some cases from reports recorded in their own journals.
61. Smith, Journal, August 6, 1843, *JSP, J3*:73.
62. Smith, Journal, April 17, 1843, *JSP, J2*:363. The review concerned JS's sermon on death and the resurrection delivered the previous day, April 16, 1843.
63. A note from one of JS's clerks, Howard Coray, described one circumstance where JS dictated a text included for delivery in preparation for the October 1840 general conference. Peculiarly, JS did not deliver the sermon, leaving that duty to the clerk who took the dictation, Robert B. Thompson. But other than this unusual instance, no known preliminary sermon text is known to exist. Howard Coray, Autobiographical Sketches, n.d., Howard Coray Papers, ca. 1840–1941, MS 2043, CHL; "Minutes of the General Conference of the Church of Jesus Christ of Latter Day Saints, Held in Nauvoo, Hancock County, Ill.," October 5, 1840, *Times and Seasons*, October 1840, 187.

Some, though not all, of his speaking ventures in Nauvoo may have attracted as many as several thousand people.[64] As there was never a meetinghouse in Nauvoo for regular worship, though the unfinished temple sometimes served as a preaching venue, JS's primary Nauvoo sermons were given outdoors. The "temple stand" just west of the edifice then under construction became a popular preaching site for JS. Occasionally a few paragraphs of what he said would appear in the church periodical, the *Times and Seasons*. The local newspaper, *The Wasp*, later renamed *The Nauvoo Neighbor*, was another outlet for themes of his preaching. However, other than the scriptural texts he produced, he was satisfied with being a verbal rather than a literary prophet. Indeed, when Brigham Young and the Twelve returned to Nauvoo from their second apostolic mission to Great Britain, Young wrote to the Saints who remained in England to say that if they wanted to access JS's teachings, they would have to relocate to Nauvoo. Serving as a lure for the British Mormons to emigrate, he explained that JS's "instructions to us, are as the voice of the Lord, and whose admonitions we ever regard as true and faithful, and worthy the confidence of all who profess the Gospel of Jesus Christ." But, he noted, those who wished to hear the prophet's voice, to obtain his words, could only do so if they were present to listen to "those teachings which can be had only at this place."[65] With convenient outlets such as the *Times and Seasons* and *The Wasp* in Nauvoo, and even the church's British periodical, the *Latter-day Saints' Millennial Star*, it is curious that JS chose for his sermons to benefit only those who heard them in person.

There are no satisfactory modern explications of the reasons for JS's behavior resulting in his neglect to write, chronicle, produce, record, or disseminate much of the material we would expect from a religious leader. It remained for his followers to digest and then circulate what could be gleaned from his teachings through a few like Parley P. Pratt, who was very influential in disseminating JS's instructions.[66] The revelations, JS's scribe-written journals and histories, cur-

64. Wilford Woodruff calculated the size of JS's audience several times, though no precise measurements were taken. See Woodruff's report of JS's speech on July 3, 1842, where about "six thousand persons assembled," *Wilford Woodruff Journal*, 2:181; his June 30, 1843, presentation before "about seven or eight thousand," *Wilford Woodruff Journal*, 2:255; a few days later on July 4, 1843, JS spoke to "near 13,000" who had congregated, *Wilford Woodruff Journal*, 2:256; "six or eight thousand saints" gathered on March 7, 1844, to hear him, *Wilford Woodruff Journal*, 2:353; and for his "King Follett" discourse on April 7, 1844, Woodruff stated that "about twenty thousand souls assembled together," *Wilford Woodruff Journal*, 2:378, a figure that is likely exaggerated given Nauvoo's population of several thousand less at the time.

65. Brigham Young et al., "An Epistle of the Twelve, To the Church of Jesus Christ of Latter Day Saints, in its various Branches and Conferences in Europe," *Times and Seasons*, April 1, 1842, 738.

66. Crawley, *Descriptive Bibliography of the Mormon Church*, 26.

sory references to his involvement in meetings, the abbreviated sermons, and how he has otherwise been characterized by a disappointingly small number of his followers shape what we think of the prophet today. From that relatively small database, many have been confident that JS not only could be but has been known. The totality of the record and what we now know about his life, however, indicates we ought to be more cautious in our final determinations than confining him to outlines created in the past.

CHAPTER 12

Underlying the Character of Joseph Smith

"Great men always wear the imprints of the times and circumstances which call their talents into action; but history is sure to preserve the name of any man who has had the strength and genius to stamp his own character on the people over whose destinies he presided." So said Francis Grund, an immigrant German noble who came to America in the 1830s, dubbing his appraisal as the *Aristocracy in America.*[1] Playing off Alexis De Tocqueville's noted *Democracy in America* of 1835, Grund's spin touted peculiarities of his adopted country provoking his reference to the man whose impress on the United States had most recently altered the identity of the country: Andrew Jackson. It was a time already marked by heroes and their creation, a spillover from the country's founding generation that recognized the notion of glorious triumphs and larger-than-life figures: "A society cannot maintain its social cohesion unless a decisive majority of its members hold in common a number of guiding ideas and ideals. One of the necessary social ideals is a symbolic hero to embody, in a personal form, the recognized goal of the society's endeavors."[2] The country heralded great men; women came much later. Parson Weems (Mason Locke Weems), a Maryland clergyman and later a Virginia bookman, began a series of heroic portraits of notable Americans at the beginning of the nineteenth century that included George Washington, Benjamin Franklin, and William Penn. By the time of Grund's description of Jackson over a half-dozen biographies of Thomas Jefferson had appeared. Perhaps it was the yearning for transcendent personalities to justify the innate hope that some mortals actually had within them the imprimatur of greatness. Humans have always yearned for others of their species, in reality or mythology,

1. Francis J. Grund, *Aristocracy in America: From the Sketch-Book of a German Nobleman* (New York: Harper and Brothers, 1959), 260, first published in 1839 in London in two volumes.
2. Arnold Toynbee, *An Historian's Approach to Religion* (London: Oxford University Press, 1956), 220.

to rise above the mundane to exhibit the extraordinary, even the divine.[3] But consequent to the dream was a level of scrutiny that sorted the applicants for distinctiveness by high expectations. It was into this setting that JS entered with his claims about the divine. It could not have been easy for him.

The tall order for JS to rise to the anticipations matching his contentions put a target on his back from the outset. As mentioned previously, the incomplete historical record complicates the quest to conveniently ascertain the footprint that he actually filled. Deriving the inner JS is even more complicated and difficult. But there will be no chance, I assert, for success in this endeavor without acknowledging the preternatural character of what shaped his life. To confine him to empirical explanations only punctures the primary component that must be included in the study of the man. To investigate a religious figure, the student must at least consider the prospect of the reality of the person's experience with God, whether or not its truth is accepted by the reader. Martin Luther's biographer, Martin Marty, explained: "Biographers of controversial, spiritually profound figures regularly receive warning that in a changed world, often described as secular, publics cannot identity with or find relevant [personalities] that reflect remote times and places."[4] How can the significance of the religious influences specific to the subject, especially one from the historical past, be explained to a secularly satiated community?

Perhaps the most relevant questions presently asked about JS focus on his character, posed to question or authenticate his prophetic posture and to justify his relevance to the modern world. This work, though, is not a treatment of whether or not JS subscribed to the "Scout Law," simply examining whether he was "brave, clean, and reverent?"[5] Rather this chapter considers several of the important features of his life regarding how he conducted himself and identifies a number of the significant characteristics of his personality and character. This prospect also requires examination of his behavioral traits. He had, for example, tendencies to overstatement, fears about how he would be perceived, impatience with those who professed allegiance but who were reluctant followers, pugilistic inclinations, and distain for all criticism; all of which are mannerisms shared by many others in the population. At the same time, he displayed notable compassion and understanding, sensibilities toward the needs of the unfortunate, and a general willingness to entertain those with whom he did not agree. He "wanted

3. Joseph Campbell, *The Hero with a Thousand Faces* (Princeton, NJ: Princeton University Press, 1973).
4. Marty, *Martin Luther*, xiii.
5. See Richard Bushman's insightful portrayal of JS's manner and deportment in Richard Lyman Bushman, "Was Joseph Smith a Gentleman? The Standard for Refinement in Utah," in *Nearly Everything Imaginable: The Everyday Life of Utah's Mormon Pioneers*, ed. Ronald W. Walker and Doris R. Dant (Provo, UT: Brigham Young University Press, 1999), 27–43.

good feelings...harmony and uplift."[6] He could have handled some things better and was willing to change his stance when required. His routine disclaimer admitting his mortal liabilities indicated he understood his limitations despite his efforts to refine himself: "I do not, nor never have, pretended to be any other than a man 'subject to passion,' and liable, without the assisting grace of the Savior, to deviate from that perfect path in which all men are commanded to walk!"[7] This chapter attempts to portray features of his character in light of how he saw himself and conveyed his persona to his fellow Saints and others.

JS was sensitive to how he appeared to his contemporaries. Congeniality pervaded exhibits of his natural disposition toward joviality and good will that served him well. He knew, for the most part, what his followers thought of him. While his instincts for amiable association generally characterized his conduct, he recognized the need for gravity when required. Sometimes he had to show a more austere side to ensure that he was taken seriously. In the heat of a council's deliberation in May 1843 regarding the fellowship of an errant member—after listening to others who offered their contrary views, including his brother Hyrum who argued for mercy—he offered "a little Council if we saw fit to except it." He stated that the brother in question should be silenced and lose his ministerial license and "if he would not do that let him go out of the Church." Finding suitable solutions to the myriad of challenges he faced forced him into uncomfortable circumstances. He had to be judicious in all that he did, even exposing his parental impatience with those who tested him: "The Saints need not think because I am familiar with them & am playful & Cheerful that I am ignorant of what is going on."[8]

Some gave or give him no room for having attributes of normalcy. He was, they argue, treacherous by nature. His duplicity included susceptibility to religious fraud. There is, according to one of his biographers, "evidence of conscious misdirection" in all that he did.[9] He also, it has been claimed, qualified as phantasmic: "Smith may have been a victim of his own delusions, that he truly believed that he was receiving revelations when, in fact, they originated in his subconscious."[10] Another prefaced his characterization of JS by stating, "Modern society seems almost to expect eventual deceit from its public figures" and JS only confirmed the charge: "In the shadows and contours of Joseph Smith's wonder-filled life lie similar contradictions."[11] The general intent of the detractors is characterized in the strategy to plant in the reader's mind the possibility,

6. Bushman, *Rough Stone Rolling*, 181.

7. Joseph Smith, *Latter Day Saints' Messenger and Advocate*, December 1834, 40.

8. *Wilford Woodruff Journal*, May 27, 1843, 2:236.

9. Vogel, *Making of a Prophet*, xi.

10. Ibid., x.

11. Richard S. Van Wagoner, *Natural Born Seer: Joseph Smith, American Prophet, 1805–1830* (Salt Lake City: Smith-Pettit Foundation, 2016), xii–xiii.

even plausibility, that all that he did was rooted in dishonesty and deception given the vacancy of real connections to heaven.

How does one determine JS's core character and if what he professed was genuine? As evidenced by the variance in motives of his appraisers, it is impossible to measure and weigh the surviving evidence of his life to arrive at consensus. But there are features of his life that appear discernible. Religious historian Laurie Maffly-Kipp argued that he could not simply be dismissed because he flouted the culture that groomed him. She contended that evidence from JS's historical record has to drive any modern determination of who he was. Her criteria for measurement, sincerity: "Did he mean what he said? Did he feel religious inside? Did his outer actions match his inner state?"[12] Questions to be asked upon which his followers would agree. The insinuations, Maffly-Kipp implies, were that he was what he represented himself to be. John L. Brooke, who assigned JS's thinking to "the sectarian tradition of the Radical Reformation," also expressed his willingness to "accept the personal sincerity of Joseph Smith's prophetic claim."[13] Those measurements can only be determined through scrutinizing the full range of the historical documentation, not just those who lionize him or prop him up as a swindler. The checkered scope of the surviving evidence is broad enough that the conceivability of ferreting from the record exhibits of his character, for good or ill, is possible.

Generalizations were shown earlier of how some have tried to place JS subject to psychological structures purporting to explain his alleged pathological roots. These include propositions that his diseased psyche rendered him prone to "megalomaniacal fantasies, including paranoid delusions" (in part to explain his visions) derived from his psychosomatic afflictions. Other allegations include the charge that JS suffered at times from a tenuous grasp on reality.[14] The premises of the accusations have been prepared, apparently, to dually diminish JS's character and the legitimacy of the church he founded. Specific charges of JS's abnormality and contaminated persona are: (1) "his use of military imagery," (2) "his defiance of state laws," (3) "his manipulation of the political process," (4) "his control of the financial affairs of the church and its members," (5) "the creation of the Council of Fifty," (6) "his ordination as king," (7) "his campaign for the presidency of the United States," (8) "failed prophecy," (9) "his abrogation of established church judicial procedures," (10) "his failure to specify an apparent successor," (11) "his practice of plural marriage," and (12) "the destruction of the *Nauvoo Expositor*," all of which were claimed to reflect "what may

12. Laurie F. Maffly-Kipp, "Tracking the Sincere Believer: 'Authentic' Religion and the Enduring Legacy of Joseph Smith Jr.," in *Joseph Smith Jr.: Reappraisals after Two Centuries*, ed. Reid L. Neilson and Terryl L. Givens (New York: Oxford University Press, 2009), 179.
13. Brooke, *Refiner's Fire*, xiv.
14. Bergera, "Joseph Smith," 239.

be either maladaptive responses to Joseph's environment or possible evidence of a growing sense of self-importance and personal omnipotence."[15] His own words are used to condemn him, "no man ever did such a work as I," and "when I have proved that I am right and get all the world subdued under me, I think I shall deserve something."[16] These circumstances require explanation. But in all cases, judgments about his character are subjectively based on the flavoring one applies to the documentary record.

Critics have lined up statements that show not only JS's vulnerabilities and exhibitions of hyperbole, but also the prophet's extreme thinking about himself. The premises are proposed apparently believing the judgments should disqualify JS as a credible human being. Though a number of the compromising examples are accurate, in their isolation from the majority of the documentation, JS is rendered basically and fatally flawed. JS, human that he was, did, indeed, shed the governor of discretion occasionally and exhibited himself as domineering, using offensive vernacular to diminish his foes, and other imprudent expressions. But recognizing that the bulk of what was purported to represent JS's thinking and expressions were prepared by his clerks/historians, Dean Jessee warned those who read the *History of the Church* that they needed to acknowledge the influence of JS's scribes on his journals and history. Readers trying to understand JS, he wrote, "may obtain impressions of boasting and egotism, or coarseness and ill-humor, when in effect these traits may not have been characteristic of Joseph Smith's personality at all, but of those who wrote the History under his direction or in his absence."[17] The latter statement does not entirely exonerate him from the exhibits of humanness that may sound offensive and extreme, even to a Mormon ear. But, as previously stated, the personalities of those who prepared his record, examples of which are below, must be considered in evaluating what survives:

> "I wish ~~all~~ the lawyer who says we have no powers in Nauvoo may be choked to death with his own words[.] dont employ ~~my~~ Lawye[r]s for their knowledge for I know more than they all."[18]

> "I combat the errors of ages; I meet the violence of mobs; I cope with illegal proceedings from executive authority; I cut the Gordian knot of powers; and I solve mathematical problems of Universities: WITH TRUTH, *diamond truth, and God is my 'right hand man.'*"[19]

15. Ibid., 242.
16. Ibid., 241.
17. Jessee, "Reliability of Joseph Smith's History," 39.
18. Smith, Journal, June 30, 1843, *JSP, J3*:44.
19. Joseph Smith to James Arlington Bennet, November 13, 1843, Nauvoo, Illinois, *Times and Seasons*, November 1, 1843, 375.

> "God made Aaron to be the mouth piece for the Children of Israel, and he will make me be God to you in his stead, and the Elders to be the mouth for me; and if you don't like it you must lump it."[20]

> "I know more [about God] than all the world put tog[ethe]r."[21]

> "If they want a beardless boy to whip all the world, I will get on the top of a mountain and crow like a rooster: I shall always beat them.... I have more to boast of than ever any man had[.] I am the only man that has ever been able to keep a whole <church> together since the days of Adam—a <large> majority of the whole have stood by me: <neither> Paul, John, Peter nor Jesus ever did it. I boast that no man ever did such a work as me—the followers of Jesus ran away from him, the Latter Day Saints never ran away from me yet."[22]

When isolated from the larger scale of weight and measurement that must be applied to the study of JS, the language expressed above may diminish for modern readers traditional attributions of JS's rise above the corruption of mortality. His critics insist that the handful of statements above *are* the indicators of who he was. The instances displayed are certainly a component of his character, but as Jessee warned, the surviving language undoubtedly include scribal influences. Still, the student must determine how the tendencies fit within the larger corpus of what we know about the prophet.

The force of modern criticisms of JS and his work are such that it is generally impossible for many to describe what may have been his strategies by way of any other means than defensive responses. It turns out that no matter how the evidence is amassed, JS, by the nature of what he declared, fell into explanation by binary arguments. Nonpolemical public figures, few though they may be, often enjoy definition in settings where their virtues and vices are not used as either pharmaceuticals to enhance or surgical tools to disembowel. As suggested, the historical record is necessary to authenticate JS's dispositions and idiosyncrasies regarding how he conducted his life. Understandably, what survives as history, while far from complete, shows JS in the conflicted environment in which he lived.

The prophetic station he declared and aspired to obviously inflated his circumstances and view of himself. Still, whether or not it was a conscious decision,

20. Joseph Smith, Sermon, April 8, 1844, 2, Thomas Bullock, scribe, Joseph Smith Collection, Addresses, MS 155, box 4, folder 6, item 3, CHL. William Clayton reported his language in this regard to be: "He will make me to be God in your stead & they [the elders] be mouth for me." Smith, Sermon, April 8, 1844, 2, William Clayton, scribe, General Church Minutes, 1839–1877, CR 100 318, box 1, folder 19, item 3, CHL.
21. Smith, Sermon, April 7, 1844, Thomas Bullock, scribe, CR 100 318, CHL.
22. Smith, Sermon, May 26, 1844, 1–2, Joseph Smith Collection, Addresses, MS 155, box 4, folder 6, item 5, CHL.

from the start JS generally represented himself as a man of the people. Though there are evidences of hubris from time to time, consistently throughout his life he insisted to be nothing more than an earthly sojourner trying to do the best he could. He obviously took note of the Book of Mormon's King Benjamin whose disclaimer to his people conveyed his own limitations: "I have not commanded you to come up hither, that ye should fear me, or that ye should think that I, of myself, am more than a mortal man; but I am like as yourselves, subject to all manner of infirmities in body and mind" (Mosiah 2:10–11). Believers hold JS with great reverence given all that he accomplished and what he revealed as a prophet. Thus, apportioning him to *mere mortal* status may appear disrespectful, even blasphemous. However, recognition of the ambiguities about JS's range of behavior found in the records presents a far more realistic portrait of the prophet than one characterized by simple dualistic interpretations. As essayist Sydney J. Harris stated, "Holding the polarities in tension means finding the optimum point at which they work together best; and this is not necessarily in the middle."[23] The notion is a fair description of how the student of JS must work to judge how the surviving evidences are used to ascertain a fitting profile.

Joseph's Rehearsal of His Beginnings

In the effort to understand how JS saw himself, illustrated by how he portrayed his life in the several instances where he disclosed his personal background, his attempts to explain his story and how the heavens overwhelmed his life are informative. The two primary efforts JS personally undertook to relate his story—the aborted 1832 History and his 1838/39 narrative that became the "History of Joseph Smith"—illustrate that he paid no attention to representing his origins as anything other than common. "I was born in the year of our Lord one thousand eight hundred and five, on the twenty-third day of December, in the town of Sharon, Windsor county, state of Vermont."[24] That's it. Nothing more was written in the two histories about the incidences of his youth, even though the opportunity was large to insert the remarkable and miraculous from his birth. Similarly, his mother Lucy Mack Smith, in her biographical portrayal of JS produced in the months after his death, opened her narrative about her son stating: "I shall say nothing respecting him until he arrived at the age of fourteen. However, in this I am aware that some of my readers will be disappointed, for I suppose, from questions which are frequently asked me, that it is thought by some that I shall be likely to tell many very remarkable incidents which attended his childhood;

23. Sydney J. Harris, *The Authentic Person: Dealing with Dilemma* (Niles, IL: Argus Communications, 1972), 41.

24. Smith, Histories, "History Drafts, 1838–circa 1841," Draft 2, *JSP, H1*:204. The later interpolation in that history describing his leg operation in Lebanon, New Hampshire, was added in December 1842 by his scribe Willard Richards (205n37).

but, as nothing occurred during his early life, except those trivial circumstances which are common to that state of human existence, I pass them in silence."[25] When taken in consideration of what JS became, the admission is remarkable.

To emphasize his self-perception in light of his origins and status, JS explained to church members in 1834 that he recognized his own condition and his inevitable weaknesses. Coincident to publication of Painesville, Ohio, newspaperman E. D. Howe's vituperative 1834 critique of Mormonism and JS—*Mormonism Unvailed*—JS prepared for publication in the church's *Latter Day Saints' Messenger and Advocate*, a rejoinder and his own disclaimer to transcendence. The array of speculation about the boy's origins by 1834 classified him as everything but trustworthy and sound, as evidenced in the numerous testimonials about him found in Howe's book. JS's appeal for reason about his circumstances came far too late to erase what had become indelible in the minds of his generation. Still, he ventured into the public arena to explain his persona. As a boy growing up in Vermont and then New York, he stated, "as is common to most, or all youths, I fell into many vices and follies." Demanding, though, that his "accusers" had falsely claimed him "guilty of gross and outrageous violations of the peace and good order of the community," he stated: "I have not, neither can it be sustained, in truth, been guilty of wronging or injuring any man or society of men; and those imperfections to which I allude, and for which I have often had occasion to lament, were a light, and too often, vain mind, exhibiting a foolish and trifling conversation."[26]

Admitting to being a child of folly, he insisted about the absence in his life of anything scandalous and mean spirited to soil his character. He was embarrassed, he said, to admit his "former uncircumspect walk, and unchaste conversation: and more particularly, as I often acted in violation of those holy precepts which I knew came from God." Despite the confession, he added "that (I do not, nor never have, pretended to be any other than a man 'subject to passion,' and liable, without the assisting grace of the Savior, to deviate from that perfect path in which all men are commanded to walk!)"[27] JS's stark acknowledgment of his shortcomings must be considered in any appraisal reliant upon the historical record. The intent is clear: to represent himself as he saw himself, nothing more than an ordinary mortal who shared with the rest of humanity their limitations. To overlook JS's disclosures or to misuse his objective in relating them, casts his miscues in strawman terms that skew his natural character. Because he was always under inspection, moments of foolishness inevitably appear in the records. What follows is an argument, however, that JS's general bearing reflected his dominant instincts about his status and inclusion in the mass of humanity.

25. Anderson, *Lucy's Book*, 329; Smith, *Biographical Sketches of Joseph Smith*, 73.
26. Joseph Smith, *Latter Day Saints' Messenger and Advocate*, December 1834, 40.
27. Ibid.

"I was nothing but a man"

After the explicit and public confession in the church organ illustrated above, it perhaps follows that he may have thought his admission would undermine his quest for adulation, if, as his detractors claim, that was his ambition. Not only did he *not* retract or modify the statement, he piled on similar disclosures. In a November 6, 1835, entry in his journal his scribe reported him diminishing any expectations of heavenly aura about him: "I was this morning introduced to a man from the east, after hearing my name he ~~replied~~ remarked that I was nothing but a man; indicating by this expression that he had supposed that a person, <to> whom the Lord should see fit to reveal his will, must be something more than a man." Always aware of being subject to inspection, JS reckoned, "he seems to have forgotton the saying that fell from the lips of St. James that Elias was a man of like passions unto us, yet he had such power with God that He in answer to his prayer, shut the heavens that they gave no rain for the space of three years and six months, and again in answer to his prayer the heavens gave forth rain and the earth brought forth fruit"[28] (Js. 5:17–18). A week later he explained to the Twelve Apostles, as captured by his scribe: "I am determined to do all that I can to up-hold you, although I may do many things <invertaintly> [inadvertently] that are not right in the sight of God."[29] This self-characterization appeared regularly throughout his life. To the Nauvoo Relief Society in August 1842, he admitted: "Altho' I do wrong, I do not the wrongs that I am charg'd with doing—the wrong that I do is thro' the frailty of human nature like other men. No man lives without fault."[30] And in a sermon delivered on May 21, 1843, he is reported to have said, "<many think a prophet must be a gret deal better than any body else.—>" Plying irony he continued with likely a smile on his face: "Suppose I would condesc[e]nd. yes I will <call it.> condesce[n]d, to be a great deal better than any of you. I would be raised to the highe[s]t heaven, and who should I have to accompany me." He then affirmed, "I dont want you to think I am very righteous. for I am not very righteous."[31] It is clear that he wanted to impress upon the Saints that he did not consider himself but of the same substance as were they.

JS's efforts to disabuse the church of him believing himself to be watertight in his mortal sojourn became widely known among the Saints. Church members had come to know and understand that JS made no pretensions to human omnipotence. Samuel H. Davis—a Mormon watcher and editor of the *Peoria (IL) Register and North-Western Gazetteer*, located a hundred miles due east of

28. Smith, Journals, November 6, 1835, *JSP, J1*:85.
29. Smith, Journals, November 12, 1835, *JSP, J1*:97.
30. Derr et al., *First Fifty Years of Relief Society*, 93.
31. Smith, Journal, May 21, 1843, *JSP, J3*:20. See also Smith, Sermon, July 23, 1843, *JSP, J3*:66.

Nauvoo—wrote in the April 17, 1840, issue of his paper that Mormons in Nauvoo held JS to be supreme. Besides believing JS to be "infallible," Davis stated, "they implicitly obey his directions, and are prepared to follow wherever he shall point the way."[32] The following week, however, Davis published a rejoinder from a church member to his characterization of JS and the Saints. Davis's newspaper was "incorrect" the Mormon correspondent stated, "in saying that the members of this society regard Joseph Smith as infallible. On the contrary they consider him subject to the passions and imperfections common to all men—infirmities which were shared by the ancient prophets and apostles."[33] A follower in Nauvoo in March 1843, explained to Boston readers where Mormonism had then taken root, what JS represented himself to be at the time: "He said he did not profess to be a *very good man*, but acknowledged himself a sinner like other men, or as all men are, imperfect; and it is necessary for all men to grow into the stature of manhood in the gospel."[34] Matthew L. Davis, the New York journalist referred to earlier, writing to his wife after listening to JS's public speech while the latter was in Washington, D.C. wrote: "<Towards> the close of his address, he remarked, that he had been represented, as pretending to be a Saviour, a worker of miracles, &c, all this was false. He made no such pretensions. He was but a man, he said—a plain untutored <man>; seeking what he should do to be saved. He performed no miracles. He did not pretend to possess any such power."[35]

JS knowingly opened himself to criticism by further impressing upon the church the manner in which the revelations he received identified his fallible status. The honest expressions wherein he indicted himself cannot be brushed aside as inconsequential, perhaps partially informed by his admonitions from God. The reproof and admonitions found in the revelatory texts continued throughout his ministry. What appears to be the first revelation, outside the Book of Mormon, that JS received from Jesus in mid-1828 included the expression: "And behold how oft you [JS] have transgressed the commandments and the Laws of God and have gone on in the Persuasions of men.... behold thou art Joseph and thou wast chosen to do the work of the Lord but because of transgression if thou art not aware thou wilt fall."[36] Some months later, another censure from the Lord: "And now I command my servant Joseph to repent, and walk more uprightly before me, and yield to the persuasions of men no more."[37]

32. Samuel H. Davis, *Peoria (IL) Register and North-Western Gazetteer*, April 17, 1840.
33. Ibid., April 24, 1840.
34. "Mormonism," *Boston Bee*, March 24, 1843, reported in *Times and Seasons*, May 15, 1843, 199–200.
35. Davis to Davis, February 6, 1840.
36. Smith, Revelations, July 1828, *JSP, R1*:10 [Book of Commandments, 2:3–4 (1833); D&C 30:3–4 (1835); Doctrine and Covenants 3:6, 9 (1981), clear text].
37. Joseph Smith, Book of Commandments 4:7 (1833); D&C 32:4 (1835); D&C 5:21 (1981).

Within months of the church's organization, he heard: "Thou are not excusable in Thy transgressions."[38] At a November 1831 conference of elders in Hiram, Ohio, the revelation JS obtained included this reminder to those gathered: "Your eyes have been upon my Servent Joseph <Smith Jr—> & his language you have known, & his imperfections you have known."[39] Again in May 1833 to JS, the inspired text stated, "<you> Joseph you have not kept the commandments and must needs stand rebuked before the lord."[40] The expressions tell us two things: he did not try to embroider his image to gain power and influence, a major claim of his antagonists, and he ensured that church members would recognize that the heavenly rejoinders properly represented his actual status before the people.

He routinely exposed his recognition of his own mortal shortcomings to disarm any who might entertain the idea that he saw himself as operating beyond the boundaries of the human experience. He ensured that new arrivals to Commerce/Nauvoo perceived the premise. British convert William Clayton wrote home to England to friends and family after his arrival in Commerce (Nauvoo) in late 1840, "Joseph says, that when he is out preaching he always tells the people not to come here for examples, but to set them and to copy from the Savior who is our pattern."[41] The missionaries who dispersed from church centers raised the level of expectation that an extraordinary figure had founded the faith. JS, to blunt disappointment after all that the missionaries had declared, delivered to a group of immigrants in the fall of 1842 yet another admission of his feeble condition. Meeting at his store "a number of brethren and sisters...who had arrived this morning from the neighborhood of New York," he told them he "was but a man, and they must not expect me to be perfect; if they expected perfection from me, I should expect it from them; but if they would bear with my infirmities and the infirmities of the brethren, I would likewise bear with their infirmities."[42] For those who accepted his repudiations of superiority, it added to their understanding of not only their current leader but also the biblical models from the ancient world.

A now-famous expression that appeared in JS's journal in February 1843 has been oft-used through the years by friends and foes alike to qualify the prophet's range of heavenly influence. The statement reflected his sensibility to the capacity of his prophetic role, with undertones about those of that stripe who pre-

38. Smith, Revelations, July 1830, *JSP, R1*:30 [Book of Commandments 25:3 (1833); D&C 9:1 (1835); D&C 24:2 (1981)].
39. Smith, Revelations, November 2, 1831, *JSP, R1*:156 [D&C 25:2 (1835); D&C 67:5 (1981)].
40. Smith, Revelations, May 6, 1833, *JSP, R1*:391 [D&C 82:8 (1835); D&C 93:47 (1981)]. See also these other examples of JS exhibiting his weaknesses as included in the revelatory texts: D&C 1:17–19, 24; 6:19; 10:2, 37; 20:5; 29:3; 35:17–18; 64:5, 7; 90:1, 6, 17–18; 111:1; 124:1; 128:18; and 132:45 (1981).
41. Clayton to "Beloved brethren and sisters," December 10, 1840.
42. Smith, Journal, October 29, 1842, *JSP, J2*:164.

ceded him in the ancient world. To Nauvoo immigrants from Michigan, Willard Richards reported JS stating to them, "'A Prophet is not always a Prophet' only when he is acting as such."[43] JS's intention, it is apparent, was to dispel any preconceived perceptions that the newcomers to Nauvoo might have about the Mormon prophet's claims to divine assistance and the limits of his reach. But it also portrayed what he had learned about himself and how he navigated in the world.

Joseph Smith's Intellect

The disclosures indicated above demonstrably show his insistence that his followers recognize his limitations. The absence of lists of accomplishment reflecting his genuine modesty have sometimes created the notion that he was of common intellect and restricted spiritual prowess, merely a marionette of the Almighty. A great deal of disproportionate emphasis about his commonness was derived from a statement made by his widowed wife, not long before her death in 1879. It has colored most subsequent descriptions of her husband's brainpower. In Emma Smith Bidamon's last days she responded to a query from her son Joseph III, leader of the RLDS Church, about his father. Stated to make the point that producing the Book of Mormon was beyond JS's abilities, Emma's general characterization has served to reveal in some people's thinking JS's mental limitations. Published in the RLDS Church's organ, the *Saints Herald*, the report stated: "Joseph Smith could neither write nor dictate a coherent and well-worded letter; let alone dictating a book like the Book of Mormon.... It would have been improbable that a learned man could do this; and, for one so ignorant and unlearned as he was, it was simply impossible."[44] A few years later, assistant LDS Church historian Andrew Jenson, who went on to become one of the most important agents for the preservation of Mormon history and culture in the last decades of the nineteenth and first half of the twentieth century, also reflected JS's intellectual boundaries. Instead of lauding JS's cognitive gifts, Jenson stated in 1888: "The advantages which Joseph had for acquiring scientific knowledge were thus exceedingly small, being limited to a slight acquaintance with two or three of the common branches of learning. He could read without difficulty and write a very imperfect hand; and he also had a very limited understanding of the elementary rules of arithmetic." He emphasized, "These were the highest and only attainments; while the rest of those branches so universally taught in the common schools throughout the United States were entirely unknown to him."[45] The reflections of Emma Smith and Jenson were presented with the hope that, despite his inherent limitations, observers who appreciated

43. Smith, Journal, February 8, 1843, *JSP, J*2:256.
44. Emma Smith, "Last Testimony of Sister Smith," *Saints' Herald*, October 1, 1879, 290.
45. Jenson, "Joseph Smith, The Prophet," 353.

the remarkable scope of what JS produced would recognize the hand of God in his life, particularly in producing the Book of Mormon. But perhaps because JS rarely wrote and philosophized, he has generally been excluded as one who exhibited virtuosity in what he thought. Instead, by some he was granted little but a general knowhow in managing the process of Mormonism.

The first generation of Saints knew the disparity between JS's human exhibit and unrealistic expectations of surpassing mortal limitations. Still, he delivered by way of his divine pronouncements a sustainable church and standards for his adherents to live by that satisfied the expectations his followers laid to the role of a modern prophet. To those who recognized what unfolded before them, JS's accomplishment thereafter fixed their admiration, especially in the realm of access to God and his purposes. A skeptical visitor to Nauvoo in April 1842 related in print a conversation he had with a Nauvoo resident where, after stating he believed JS to be an imposter, the Latter-day Saint made what to the inquirer was a surprising admission. JS "might be as bad as he was reported to be," the Mormon stated, "but that his prophecies would not thereby be proved false. He might be a swindler, a liar, a drunkard, a swearer, and still be a true prophet. David was a murderer and an adulterer, and yet was a true prophet." Moreover, JS's defender stated, "Smith might be as infamous as David was, and even deny his own revelations, and turn away from his religion, and go to hell; but this would not affect the revelations which God had given him." Indeed, "the truth of Mormonism did not depend on the character of Smith or of any other man."[46] Brigham Young said as much in 1860. Granting JS's weaknesses and displays of humanness, Young affirmed that "though Joseph Smith should steal horses every day, or gamble every night, or deny his Savior from the crowing of the cock in the morning until sunset in the evening, I know that the doctrine he preaches is the power of God to my salvation, if I live it."[47] To separate from JS the credential he earned through the revelations he delivered and their practicality in informing and influencing the lives of his adherents is to ignore the energizing power of early Mormonism to his followers, even in their extremely difficult circumstances.

Opposition and Destiny

There were two prevailing influences that underscore JS's life, which must be given account in all considerations of his thinking and behavior. All that is discussed below about his personality and conduct passes through the channels of destiny and opposition he created when first articulating his claims. In part these dominating motivations help explain how he responded to the world he

46. Caswall, *City of the Mormons*, 46–47.
47. Brigham Young, *Deseret News*, April 4, 1860; also published in *JD*, 8:16.

confronted. It should go without saying that the two influences mentioned do not explain all that provoked him. But they do serve as the primary backdrop behind how he played out his life. This contention is drawn from compelling evidences of those dual influences. Insertion of opposition and destiny as factors that influenced his subsequent responses informs most other matters that he acted upon.

Though JS had experienced opposition his entire career, his seemingly nonchalant expression to Nauvoo church members reminded them of the recurrent imposition of persecution that afflicted him: "As for the perils which I am called to pass through, they seem but a small thing to me, as the envy and wrath of man have been my common lot all the days of my life."[48] Two years later, at the end of his life, in the midst of perhaps the most intense countermotion from errant church members he had experienced, JS tried to reassure the faithful in a sermon on Sunday, May 26, 1844, that he did not crumble under the accusations made against him: "I am right here on the spot <where> I intend to stay." He had "been in perils…oftener than anyone in this generation." Even "as Paul boasted," he said, "I have suffered more than Paul did." Indeed, "I should be like a fish out of water, if I were out of persecution." The tense climate was necessary, he said "to keep me humble." Undoubtedly smiling, he admitted, "I am not nearly so humble as if I was not persecuted."[49] This was no exaggeration; during the entire course of his life once he became a public figure, he never experienced tranquility except in brief respite from time to time. And he did not blush from warning those who joined with him that they, too, would likely be subjects of similar oppression. On a Thursday afternoon, April 7, 1842, in a speech at the church's general conference, JS stated that one of his objectives in the sermon "was to choose young men, and ordain them, and send them out to preach that they may have an opportunity of proving themselves, and of enduring the tarring and feathering and such things as those of us who have gone before them, have had to endure."[50] Persecution came with the territory.

While antagonism characterized feelings toward JS from the outside world, the obstruction he felt from within the church was a threat of greater consequence. Beginning in Kirtland within a handful of years after the church's founding and then reignited in Missouri and Nauvoo, internal dissent crippled every initiative advanced by the prophet. He could never be sure how what he taught was consumed, whether it ingratiated his hearers or sent them reeling. He had to contend with the naysayers even among those once trusted with

48. Joseph Smith, "Tidings," *Times and Seasons*, September 15, 1842, 919; D&C 127: 2 (1981).
49. Smith, Sermon, May 26, 1844, 1, Joseph Smith Collection, Addresses, MS 155, box 4, folder 6, item 5, CHL.
50. Smith, Sermon, April 7, 1842, *Times and Seasons*, April 15, 1842, 761.

his confidence. So vivid were the fractures that some thought it might be the church's undoing. Though there were incessant entreaties to the malcontents, once it became apparent that reconciliation for many of the mutineers was unlikely, the winnowing became routine and expected. The dividing issues were many. But they were summed up as the spirit of apostasy. Brigham Young later laid the cause of Mormon struggles to the Mormon flank: "What has produced your persecutions and sorrow? What has been the starting point of all your afflictions? They began with apostates in your midst; these disaffected Spirits caused others to come in, worse than they, who would run out and bring in all the devils they possibly could."[51] JS's cousin and later church historian, George A. Smith, reflected in 1864 that Kirtland was a "time that tried men's souls; for a man that would stand up in the streets and say he was Joseph's friend, could not get a greater compliment than being called a lick skillet. Joseph had few friends."[52] The defection, George A. stated, included some "among the leading Elders of the Church, in Kirtland the High Council, one of the members of the first Presidency, some of the seven Presidents of the seventies, and a great many others [who] were so darkened that they went astray in every direction."[53] Mormon settlements in northern Missouri and on the Mississippi peninsula of Nauvoo witnessed revival of the contention born in Kirtland that never abated.

The surviving documentary record shows JS driven by what he believed to be his appointment from Jesus, and the consequent antagonism stemming from it. As he later explained, he knew from the outset his course to be unique and unusual. Over time he concluded, "It seems as though the adversary was aware at a very early period of my life that I was destined to prove a disturber & annoyer of his kingdom, or else why should the powers of Darkness combine against me. why the oppressin & persecution that arose against me, almost in my infancy."[54] After his initial commission from Deity, subsequent encounters reinforced his initial perceptions about his role. He later said that one of those theophanies provided his lifelong charter: "God had a work for me to do, and that my <name> should be had for good and evil among all nations kindreds and tongues, or that it should be both good and evil spoken of among all people."[55]

51. Brigham Young, Sermon, March 27, 1853, *JD*, 1:82.

52. George A. Smith, Sermon, November 15, 1864, *JD*, 11:11. Oliver Huntington, later describing the cycle of apostasy in Kirtland and recrimination against the faithful, wrote that "The real Mormons were designated by the appellations of Lick skillets, and every Lick skillet had to suffer." Oliver B. Huntington, "History of Oliver Boardman Huntington," Diary 2, 1845–1846, 15, MSS 162, L. Tom Perry Special Collections, Brigham Young University, Provo, Utah.

53. Smith, *JD*, 11:11.

54. Smith, History, December 2, 1842, Willard Richards scribe, Historian's Office History of the Church, vol. 1, Book A1, Note B, 132–33, CR 100 102.

55. Smith, Histories, "History Drafts, 1838–circa 1841," Draft 2, *JSP, H1*:222.

That dispensation from God fueled and shaped his thinking and attitude thereafter. In a Sunday sermon in late August 1843, he declared, "I bear record this morning that all the combined powers of ea[r]th & hell shall not over come this ~~by~~ boy." In the same speech, he acknowledged the incongruity of his mortal weaknesses in light of what he had been called to do, stating "If I have sinned I have sinned outwardly," but not in the performance of his appointment.[56] That commission impelled him and his work to the end of his life, "I calculate to be one of the Instruments of setting up the Kingdom of Daniel, by the word of the Lord, and I intend to lay a <foundation that will> revolutionize the whole world."[57] He never flagged from the call.

His initial rebuff after his First Vision by the local clergyman undoubtedly unnerved him, as he stated in his 1838/39 narrative. Thereafter, retrospectively, JS frequently referred to the resistance he sensed; not only the preponderant negativity filling the early published reports about Mormonism, but also the personal accounts of his followers that confirm his perceptions. Naturally to him and his supporters, that environment fostered concessions that the resistance they felt was due to the mortal war waged between good and evil. Thus, citing the rejection of Jesus by his enemies, the Mormons assumed that the brand of persecution that characterized their faith actually confirmed their perceptions of being God's people. It affected their motivations and every strategy they employed in what they believed to be their divine commission. America's uncultivated interior, which served as the predecessor of Mormon attempts to urbanize their domain, initially allowed for space to grow a church in a setting of tranquility. However, not only civilization but also American Christianity caught up with them. Mormon faith claims and objectives, as well as the character of the people, were incessantly subject to criticism. Thus, everything about JS's life once he became an adult played out in the fighting pit.

Joseph Smith's Facility for Leadership

The success of JS can be measured in part by the manner in which his followers reacted to him and his unique personality. Even those with demonstrable devotion had to make decisions about how much of what he taught they could embrace. Initially the primary image of church leadership was JS, and to a lesser degree, Oliver Cowdery, though at first Cowdery saw himself in a larger light. A hierarchy did not exist in the first years of Mormonism, so the collection of families who accepted the restoration message could readily manage their devotion and how they perceived JS fit his new role as a prophet. The cluster of believers who had gathered around Manchester, Fayette, and Colesville, New

56. Smith, Journal and Sermon, notes by Willard Richards, August 27, 1843, *JSP, J*2:85.
57. Smith, Sermon, May 12, 1844, Joseph Smith Collection, Addresses, MS 155, box 4, folder 6, CHL.

York, soon established sustainable faith communities, however small, where commonality of belief and purpose led to reinforcement of their commitment as they watched others do the same. The readymade gathering spot on the Western Reserve of Ohio that followed, somewhat handed to them by the happenstance of the missionary initiative to Native Americans on the Missouri River in late 1830, did not require grubbing the land to carve a spot in the wilderness to survive. A community soon blossomed. During the transition, the singular leadership of JS could be accommodated due to the nascent, unstructured nature of new promises and a fresh way of thinking that emerged from the New Testament template that echoed through the woods. The trappings of organization did not appear until it became apparent to both JS and his followers that a revelatory outline for a religious monarch was not part of JS's inspiration and thinking. There was a populist feel to early Mormonism, even as eventually church offices and functions were instituted.

Management became an issue once the church assumed formalized status in Ohio. With a bishop and counselors designated in early 1831, JS organized the following year what later became known as the First Presidency, with him as president and counselors. As the church and its configuration expanded, personalities and how they influenced the church became an increasingly consuming issue. Many of the revelations that JS received contained admonition and instruction to temper and encourage the personalities who, for the most part, readily complied with what JS expressed to them through his declarations. But the reality of the human condition became evident, in many cases stalling or mitigating those directives. Even among his chief lieutenants, steadfastness and predictability could not always be banked upon. No matter the time or the situation, behind every decision JS made he had to wonder how church members would respond. Many who could be depended upon or championed his objectives in one setting, could and did turn on him in others. Despite the incredible advance of Mormonism in its formative years, lukewarm is a word that described a portion of church members in circumstances that directly affected them. Still, overcoming doubt and caution became a characteristic of many who had grasped JS's claims, who then translated their hope into mortar that helped stabilize the structure. Often in the early period, circumstances tested their commitment. It was an astonishing expectation for the men who embraced Mormonism to kiss their families goodbye, and with another who had done the same thing, leave whatever stability they may have established to carry the religion's declarative message to wherever they were sent.

How church members responded to JS's prophetic leadership had a profound and lasting effect upon the manner in which he conducted his life and his church. He could not have anticipated how he would deliver to his followers what Jesus had given him or how his idiosyncrasies would affect those he admonished. The documents show his exultation when the less committed stepped up to exhibit the kind of discipleship he advanced. However, in exhibitions of disappointment he spared no feelings when rebuking the lethargic in the consequent revelations issued. Though it is difficult to quantify for numerous reasons, JS's success in balancing the many variables confronting his ministry, including failures, stands out because the basic components he enacted congealed into something that had predictable trappings. While Brigham Young must be credited with institutionalizing many features of JS's preachments and revelations, what JS produced before his death requires note because of its durability.

Generosity of Spirit

It appears that JS's initial instinct in dealing with people was to credit them as honorable. He generously accommodated those who appeared sincere and especially persons who seemed amenable to instruction and guidance. But acceptance of his counsel was always a line of demarcation for those in whose trust JS invested. "Joseph did not like to be crossed."[58] To his Twelve Apostles—associates who he most wanted to comply with his leadership—on January 16, 1836, he admitted, "I have sometimes spoken to[o] harsh from the impulse of the moment and inasmuch as I have wounded your feelings brethren I ask your forgiveness, for I love you and will hold you up with all my heart in righteousness before the Lord, and before all men."[59] JS, given the weight he carried—perhaps self-imposed—demonstrated in this example that he was not immune from minimizing others as he tried to rally his followers to his objectives.

It always cheered him when he saw people respond affirmatively. However, if he accepted one who manifested the trappings of devotion, should they fall from grace, like most others who lead people, he refrained from coddling the recalcitrant ones. The complexity of his life precluded specific attention to every person who crossed him. Nevertheless, there are prominent examples of his acceptance of apology and repentance that reveal his inclinations to recover the wanderer, even those who calculated to do him wrong. Harvey Whitlock became a Mormon in 1831 and was one of the first to be ordained a high priest that June. He with others suffered the sting of expulsion in late 1833 when vigilantes ran the Church of Christ out of Jackson County, Missouri. Later, however, he lost his way and dropped out. After his defection, mortified, he wrote to JS on September 28, 1835, to "umbosom my feelings, and unravil the secrets of my heart." Full of remorse for "the abyss into which I have fallen," he admitted at length to "crimes of the deepest dye," confessing "my hands are swift to do iniquity, and my feet are fast running in the paths of vice and folly." He prostrated himself

58. Bushman, *Rough Stone Rolling*, 249.
59. Smith, Journals, January 16, 1836, *JSP*, *J1*:158–59.

before JS. On November 16, 1835, JS warmly replied: "I have recieved your letter of the 28th Sept. 1835, and I have read it twice, and it gave me sensations that are better imagined than described; let it suffice, that I say the very flood-gates of my heart were broken up: I could not refrain from weeping, I thank God, that it has entered into your heart, to try to return to the Lord, and to his people."[60]

A few months later on April 1, 1836, amidst JS's intense preparations for the dedication of the Kirtland House of the Lord, he had his scribe include this entry into his journal: "Among the number [who visited me] was Leeman Copley, who testified against me in a suit I brought against Doctor P[hilastus]. Hurlbut for threatening my life." Copley "confessed that he bore a fals testimony against me, in that suit but verily thought at the time that he was right[.] but on calling to mind ~~all~~ all the circumstances connected ~~the~~ with the things that transpired at that time he was convinced that he was wrong, and humbly confessed it and asked my forgiveness, which was readily granted."[61]

Peter Burnett saw JS for the first time in Far West, Missouri, during the summer of 1838. Just beginning his legal career, Burnett became one of JS's attorneys during the period when JS unsuccessfully tried to fend off Missouri's intent to arrest and jail him. Burnett remembered in his memoir when upon his entry to Far West he, "found there John McDaniel, a young merchant of Liberty. John was wild, imprudent, and fond of frolics."[62] McDaniel had previously "openly ridiculed Smith's pretensions to the gift of prophecy, and his remarks had been reported to the prophet." Apparently believing what he had said was of no consequence, the following day McDaniel and Burnett together "went to hear Smith preach." But after sermons by two of the brethren, JS then took the podium "full of the most intense excitement." He spared no censure. "He boldly denounced McDaniel in the most severe terms, saying, in substance, that no man should come to Far West and openly vilify and slander him, and that, if his brethren would not protect him, he would protect himself." Burnett, startled, wrote that he had "not heard of the remarks of McDaniel, and was wholly taken by surprise." He turned to McDaniel, who sat next to him "and he was as pale as a corpse, but did not stir or open his lips." Having dismissed JS by reputation and supposing that what he said about JS did not matter, when the service concluded, "McDaniel requested me to go with him to see Smith, and we did so." McDaniel apologized, JS accepted, and "the matter there terminated."[63]

60. Smith, Journals, November 16, 1835, containing letters from Harvey Whitlock to Joseph Smith, September 28, 1835, and Joseph Smith to Harvey Whitlock, November 16, 1835, *JSP, J1*:101–4.

61. Smith, Journals, April 1, 1836, *JSP, J1*:101–4.

62. Peter H. Burnett, *Recollections and Opinions of an Old Pioneer* (New York: D. Appleton, 1880), 56–57. Burnett, a Democrat, later immigrated to the west coast and became a judge of the provisional Oregon Supreme Court in 1845–1846. He then moved to California where he became the state's first elected governor in late 1849.

63. Ibid. McDaniel had been engaged to a young Mormon woman, Eliza Kingsley, begin-

Loyalty among those allegiant to JS became the measurement most prized to the prophet. "As the years went by, and one stalwart after another deserted him," according to Richard Bushman, "Joseph came to value loyalty above every other virtue."[64] Thus, defection became anathema, especially in times of strain. Consequently, JS's absolution for betrayal became all the more significant. Perhaps the most well-known example of JS's inclination to forgive is the case of W. W. Phelps. Besides being the church-appointed printer, Phelps became one of JS's inner circle in the church's early years and a principal in the establishment of the church in Zion. But by spring 1838, Phelps had cashiered Mormonism, with church action taken against him for defying counsel and defalcation in March 1838. Caught up in the flurry of confusion during the peak of Mormon troubles in Missouri, Phelps found himself testifying against JS before Missouri judge Austin A. King in Richmond mid-November 1838. Phelps's bitterness at the time, prompting his witness against JS, contributed to JS's incarceration over the coming winter, literally placing his life in peril. Fleeing Missouri, Phelps moved his family to Ohio in 1839. There he unexpectedly came in contact with Mormon apostles Orson Hyde and John E. Page who persuaded him to reconsider his defection. Weeks later at the end of June 1840, shamed, Phelps wrote JS in Nauvoo from Dayton, Ohio: "I am alive and with the help of God I mean to live still. I am as the prodigal Son, though I never doubt or disbelieve the fulness of the Gospel. I have been greatly abased and humbled.... I have seen the folly of my way and I tremble at the gulf I have passed.... I know my situation, you know it, and God knows it, and I want to be saved if my friends will help me.... I have done wrong and I am sorry. The beam is my own eye."[65]

A month later after reading Phelps's letter, JS returned the favor. "I must say that it is with no ordinary feelings I endeavor to write a few lines to you.... I am rejoiced at the priviledge granted me. You may in some measure realise what my

---

ning about 1838. However, after McDaniel broke the arrangement, she was crestfallen and died a broken woman. McDaniel then ventured to Santa Fe, New Mexico, looking for his fortune. With a gang of cohorts staking out the Santa Fe Trail between Independence and Santa Fe, in 1843 they mobbed Antonio José Chávez, a descendant of one of New Mexico's most notable families, and his small entourage. They stole Chávez's gold and goods and murdered him before fleeing to Missouri. Killing the New Mexican who descended from one of the founders of New Mexico exacerbated what were already borderland tensions between the territory and Mexico. McDaniel and his brother were eventually taken into custody, though several of the marauders got away. Taken to St. Louis for trial, the McDaniels were tried, convicted, and hanged there in 1845. Lyman Omer Littlefield, *Reminiscences of Latter-day Saints* (Logan, UT: Utah Journal, 1888), 82–83; Ralph Emerson Twitchell, *Leading Facts of New Mexico History*, 2 vols. (Cedar Rapids, IA: Torch Press, 1911–1912), 2:83–84. See also Marc Simmons, *Murder on the Santa Fe Trail: An International Incident, 1843* (El Paso: Texas Western Press, 1987).

64. Bushman, *Rough Stone Rolling*, 170.

65. William W. Phelps to Joseph Smith, June 29, 1840, Dayton, Ohio, Joseph Smith Collection, Letterbook 2, 155, MS 155, CHL.

feelings, as well as Elder [Sidney] Rigdon's & Bro Hyrum [Smith]'s were when we read your letter, truly our hearts were melted into tenderness and compassion when we asscertained your resolves &c." JS then explained that, "It is true, that we have suffered much in consequence of your behavior—the cup of gall already full enough for mortals to drink, was indeed filled to overflowing when you turned against us: one with whom we had oft taken sweet council together, and enjoyed many refreshing seasons from the Lord." Nevertheless, Phelps's former friend stated, "Believing your confession to be real and your repentance genuine, I shall be happy once again to give you the right hand of fellowship, and rejoice over the returning prodigal." The letter closed with, "Come on dear Brother since the war is past, For friends at first are friends again at last."[66]

Tolerance, Compassion, and Religious Freedom

It is asserted by detractors that JS in his delusions focused his energies toward establishing a theocratic-political empire with himself at the pinnacle, meant to dominate and subordinate all who were not of his stripe. This was an especially prevalent charge by the critical contingent in the nineteenth century. Without question, in the context of the spread of the restored gospel throughout the world to prepare for the anticipated return of Jesus to the earth, there were worldwide implications within Mormonism. "[B]y the time of the organization of the Council of Fifty [March 1844], Joseph Smith and others saw them as referring to the literal kingdom of God on earth," according to Joseph Smith Papers editors.[67] The notion of Christ and his agents assuming the preeminent positions of governance associated with his Second Advent were derived by JS from both biblical and modern revelations.

However, had material world domination—as many assert—been his nefarious intent, his efforts to ensure that his people warranty the rights of their countrymen to follow their own religious inclinations appears non sequitur. Like his contemporary Daniel Webster, the noted Massachusetts senator and orator, he believed, "All, all, proclaim that Christianity, general, tolerant Christianity, Christianity independent of sects and parties, that Christianity to which the sword and fagot are unknown, general tolerant Christianity, is the law of the land."[68] At a meeting of the Council of Fifty on April 11, 1844, restricted to only those who were members of the group, JS expressly wished it to be known and recorded that there were men of that body "who were not members of the church of Jesus Christ of Latter Day Saints, neither profess any creed or religious sentiment whatever." It was, he stated, their prerogative to then "act upon

66. Joseph Smith to William W. Phelps, July 22, 1840, Nauvoo, Illinois, Joseph Smith Collection, Letterbook 2, 157–58, CHL.
67. Smith, Administrative Records, Volume Introduction, Council of Fifty Minutes, *JSP, A1*:xxviii–xxix.
68. Irving H. Bartlett, *Daniel Webster* (New York: W. W. Norton, 1978), 171.

the broad and liberal principal that all men have equal rights, and ought to be respected, and that every man has a privilege in this organization of choosing for himself voluntarily his God, and what he pleases for his religion."[69] It is the case that as the Mormons recoiled at the uniform abridgement of their constitutional guarantees, they took measures to assert their legal rights. JS, himself, believed there were "two or three things lacking in the constitution of the United States" concerning protecting "rights" and the "principles of liberty." He stated in the Council of Fifty's April 11 meeting that if a "President or Governor" fails to protect their "subjects" and "enforce those principles," he ought to "lose his head," i.e., "he ought to be put away from office."[70] When JS's disposition to protect the religious liberty of all is understood, his conclusion to mount a campaign desiring the presidency of the United States to further his personal designs loses its taint of theocratic imposition. As the Saints finally assembled the constituent parts of their society into something operational after their arrival in Nauvoo, Illinois, JS, as a city councilman, introduced a city ordinance clearing any murkiness about his devices. A Nauvoo council meeting held on March 1, 1841, acted upon his proposal to ensure the rights of "religious Societies." The application, the report reads, was read three times before being passed, suggesting modification of the language but also indicating the final consensus of the city council in accepting JS's intentions. Presented as "An Ordinance in relation to religious societies," section 1 read: "Be it ordained by the City Council of the City of Nauvoo, That the Catholics, Presbyterians, Methodists, Baptists, Latter-Day Saints, Quakers, Episcopalians, Universalists, Unitarians, Mohammedans, and all other religious sects, and denominations whatever, shall have free toleration, and equal privileges, in this city." Putting teeth into the declaration, the act also provided that "should any person be guilty of ridiculing, abusing, or otherwise depreciating, another, in consequence of his religion, or of disturbing, or interrupting, any religious meeting, within the limits of this city, he shall on conviction thereof before the Mayor, or Municipal Court, be considered a disturber of the public peace, and fined in any sum not exceeding five hundred dollars, or imprisoned not exceeding six months, or both, at the discretion of said Mayor or Court."[71] Threats of a fine and jail time to discourage religious bigotry of any sort underscored the gravity of JS's intent. When the forces of opposition grew to the proportion that the church and JS himself were threatened, he naturally took measures to protect himself and the church the same as would anyone else under the circumstances. But there is no mistake that he envisioned religious liberty as one of the foundational premises derived from American institutions.

69. Smith, Administrative Records, April 11, 1844, Council of Fifty Minutes, *JSP, A1*:97.
70. Ibid., 101.
71. "An Ordinance in Relation to Religious Societies," *Times and Seasons*, March 1, 1841, 336–7.

A stranger in Pittsburgh in early 1842 who had been influenced by Mormon missionary/apostle John E. Page deliberated his religious future by inquiring by mail of JS "to know through you the laws and regulations of your church—what is required of its members." In short, he asked, "what is required to constitute good membership?" Having just taken over as editor of the church's Nauvoo organ, the *Times and Seasons*, JS included in the issue of March 15, 1842, his reply to Richard Savary. While specifically addressing Savary's query about any imposed financial obligation to the church upon its members, JS also illustrated his sentiments about the status of the non-Mormon world:

> Respecting how much a man of property shall give annually, we have no special instructions to give; he is to feed the hungry, to clothe the naked, to provide for the widow, to dry up the tear of the orphan, to comfort the afflicted, whether in this church, or in any other church, or in no church at all, wherever he find them, to believe and obey all that God has revealed, does reveal, or will reveal, to do good unto all men, to be a member in good standing in the Church of Jesus Christ of Latter-Day Saints.[72]

Savary became a Mormon.

JS's insistence that the Latter-day Saints as a people embrace the sentiment, is summarized in a July 1843 sermon when he revealed his inclinations: "If we would s[e]cure & cultivate the love of others we must love others. even our enemies—as well as friends." Surely smiling when he said it, "why is it this babler [speaking of himself] gains so many followers. & retains them?'" Because, he said, "I possess the principle of love, All I can offer the world [is] a good heart & a good hand." To underscore his liberality, he followed, "Mormons can testify whether I am willing to lay down my life for a Mormon." And "If it has been demonstrated that I ~~am~~ have been willing to die for a mormon I am bold to declare <befo[r]e heaven> that I <am> just as ready to die for a presbytiran. a baptist or any other denomination." For, he declared, "It is a love of libe[r]ty which inspires my soul. civil and religious libert[y]—were diffused into my soul by my grandfathers. while they dandled me on their knees."[73] Later in the year in another Sunday sermon, he repeated the attitude, "It is one of the first principles of my life, & one that I have cultivated from my childhood. Having been taught it of my father. to allow eve[r]y one the libe[r]ty of conscience."[74] His declarations, direct and consistent, clearly represented his core belief, especially in light of how he and his church had been excluded from qualification for such consideration.

72. Editor, *Times and Seasons*, March 15, 1842, 731–32.
73. Smith, Sermon, July 9, 1843, *JSP, J*3:55.
74. Smith, Sermon, October 15, 1843, *JSP, J*3:113. See also a similar expression in *Wilford Woodruff Journal*, April 7, 1844, 2:383.

"The frailty of human nature"

JS's temperament toward assuming the social level of his followers, ensuring that they recognized his awareness that he was a man with feet of clay like themselves and that he understood them and calculated his life to enrich theirs, undoubtedly went far to underscore his relationships with others. The full span of his idiosyncrasies is impossible to define, even if a comprehensive historical record were available. But there are in JS's life heavily weighted symptoms of his commonness given how they show up throughout his life. Those then and now who expected that he should surpass the shortcomings inherent within the human family were and are disappointed as they became and become aware that JS does not fit the unrealistic model of mortal preeminence.

One of the compromising symptoms that followed him throughout life was his disposition to physically confront those who countered him. Known for his raw exhibitions of strength and athleticism,[75] the gift apparently augmented his instinct to both protect himself and to inflict justice. He knew and conceded his weakness, sometimes apologizing and other times justifying his behavior. An incident is instructive from June 1835, where JS's brother-in-law Calvin Stoddard, who had been involved in the movement since its beginning, challenged him in a "controversy about water" that ended in a scrap. The dispute pushed Stoddard to file a complaint in the local Court of Common Pleas accusing JS of assault and battery. Stoddard's complaint charged that after a verbal exchange, "Smith then came up and struck him on the forehead with his flat hand." The impact of "the blow knocked him down" followed by JS repeating "the blow four or five times, very hard [that] made him blind." However, in the proceedings, JS's mother, the mother-in-law of Stoddard, and JS's brother William, also a brother-in-law of Stoddard, testified before the court that precipitating the encounter, Stoddard came "cursing and swearing" claiming he would "whip him, and drew his cane upon Joseph." JS, they said, then "struck Stoddard with a flat hand," knocking him down, followed by JS popping him a couple more times. Another who witnessed the confrontation stated that "Stoddard struck at Smith first, and raised his cane in a threatening attitude." After the testimony, the court ruled that JS had acted in "self-defence" and "the "accused was then acquitted," though it probably did not help the accuser that he failed to appear before the court.[76] A report of reconciliation would have been a satisfying coda to the affair, but the scuffle may

75. Alexander L. Baugh, "Joseph Smith's Athletic Nature," in *Joseph Smith: The Prophet, The Man*, ed. Susan Easton Black and Charles D. Tate Jr. (Provo, UT: Religious Studies Center, Brigham Young University, 1993), 137–150.

76. *Painesville (OH) Telegraph*, June 26, 1835. See also the Historical Introduction to "Letter to Church Brethren, June 15, 1835," in *JSP, D4*:347–49; and Gordon A. Madsen, "Tabulating the Impact of Litigation on the Kirtland Economy," in Madsen, Walker, and Welch, *Sustaining the Law*, 228–29.

have contributed to Stoddard's estrangement from the religion before his death the following year. Just six months after the Stoddard scrape, JS's well-known physical clash with his brother William also raised the eyebrows of those who witnessed the tussle.[77]

The prophet had a reputation, and he knew it. While presiding in the Nauvoo Mayor's Court in February 1843, it became known to him that "2 boys were seen fighting in the street. by Mills tavern." When JS saw what was going on, he "ran over immediately & caught one of the boys (who had began ~~the~~ to fight with clubs) & stopped him. & then, the other." JS then "gave the bystander[r]s a lecture for not interfering in such cases.— & retur[ned] to Court." He then declared, likely to the amusement of the onlookers, "No body is allowed to fight in this city but me."[78] Six months later in August 1843, bad blood between JS and Walter Bagby, a Carthage, Illinois, tax collector, reached the pitch where, after an insult from Bagby, JS "siezd him by the throat to choke him off."[79] William Clayton, who apparently witnessed the exchange, wrote that Bagby grabbed "a stone to through [throw] at which J. was so enraged that he followed him & struck him two or three times." Daniel H. Wells, then a non-Mormon official in Nauvoo, stemmed the skirmish, followed by JS telling Wells "to assess the fine and he was willing to pay it."[80] JS never tried to cover up his weakness and inclination to confront his foes, feeling justified given his circumstances.

Those familiar with JS's situation and personality conceded justification for his behavior. His nephew Joseph F. Smith, son of Hyrum, related a circumstance late in life where as a young boy he witnessed an event that vividly remained with him thereafter. To a congregation gathered in Salt Lake City's Sixteenth Ward on the anniversary of JS's birth in 1894, the younger Joseph, then a member of the church's First Presidency, stated: "I will tell you a little circumstance that I saw myself and you would think it very inappropriate of a Prophet." One day at the end of March 1843, he and his cousin, JS's son Alexander Smith, were "amusing" themselves playing marbles in front of his uncle's home on the Nauvoo flat. He said, "The fence ran along within six or eight feet of the door of the Mansion, and we were playing at the gate just outside the stone steps, when all of a sudden

77. Smith, Journal, October 29 and December 16, 1835, *JSP, J1*:77–79, 124. See also Bushman, *Rough Stone Rolling*, 294–303.

78. Smith, Journal, February 20, 1843, *JSP, J2*:268. The month previously, JS at a New Year's gathering had bragged about previously whipping two men, one a Baptist minister, who confronted him. Smith, Journal, January 1, 1843, *JSP, J2*:209. See Luke Johnson's report that may have included the Baptist minister mentioned, where, after being insulted by the minister, JS "boxed his ears with both hands" before he "kicked him into the street." "Autobiography and History of Luke Johnson," *Millennial Star*, January 7, 1865, 5–7.

79. Smith, Journal, August 13, 1843, *JSP, J3*:78.

80. Ibid., 78n359. See also county official Jacob B. Backenstos's deposition stating that "Joseph Smith committed an assault on the body of one Walter Bagby by striking him." Helen Bourne Fleming Collection, 1836–1963, MS 9670, folder 13, CHL.

the door flew open and I looked, and there came a great, big man right off the end of Joseph Smith's foot, and he lit on the sidewalk just by the gate." Astonished, he remarked, "I wondered what in the world was the matter." Later he learned that the man, who had once been a church official and insider, "was there insulting the Prophet, and abusing him in his own house." JS, he said, had apparently had enough of the harangue, "so he opened his door and invited him out." But when the man "did not go as quickly as the Prophet wanted him to go... he gave him the assistance of his boot, and helped him out." Defending his uncle in front of an audience composed mostly of people who did not personally know JS, and perhaps to better portray in context the unrelenting opposition imposed upon him, Joseph F. presented the stark realization that JS had booted a man out of his home. "Well, now, some biased man would say: 'Why, would a prophet of God do such a thing as that!' Some would be shocked beyond measure to think that the man who beheld the face of God and the face of His son Jesus Christ... should be seen to kick a man out of his house that was abusing him." But after describing the litany of abuses piled on the prophet, he said, "There was never a moment of his life that he was free from such things as these, being hounded, and abused, and insulted by wicked men." Known for having a temper of his own as a young man, Joseph F. concluded that JS would have been "less a man if he had not kicked [the man] out of his house on that day."[81]

There are numerous other instances where JS submitted to his inclinations to physically settle matters given the cumulative effect of persecution and insult, much to the consternation of observers. One, however, took comfort in JS's admission of his tendencies to fight. Allen J. Stout, a policeman in Nauvoo, later admitted: "[H]e once went to the Prophet with a confession of a weakness of his own that he feared might unfit him for the position he held. It was that of [a] fiery temper and [being] quick to the fight. He said he had that very day threshed a man." JS's reply: "In his own youth he had to learn to fight much against his own will, for his parents had taught their children that quarreling and fighting are sins that are beastly, and whenever he had laid his hand in anger on a fellow creature it gave him sorrow and a feeling of shame."[82] JS's impulsive temperament to physically confront opponents, something of which he was not proud, followed him throughout his life.

81. Joseph F. Smith, Sermon, December 23, 1894, *Salt Lake Herald*, January 12, 1895, 210–11. Corroborating evidence places the date of the event as March 28, 1843. See Historian's Office History of the Church, March 28, 1843, vol. 11, 150, CR 100 102.

82. Lafayette C. Lee, Notebook, n.d., MS 964, CHL. See another instance where JS confronted or defended his disposition to fight as reported by George A. Smith, June 20, 1855, Deseret Theological Institute Records, MS 14939, folder 1 (typescript MS 2737, box 89, folder 2), CHL. See also JS's statement in an interview where he addressed his actions on behalf of the Nauvoo City Council when he "had occasion to knock a man down more than once." Smith, Interview, November 3, 1841, *JSP, D8*:348–49.

Joseph Smith's Greatest Challenge

Perhaps the most universal and persistent historical conundrum that has confronted JS's followers since his ministry is his and Mormonism's embrace of plural marriage. While it may not be considered a character trait, a case can be made that how he handled the matter reflected his thinking, uncertainties, and disposition. The great difficulty is that the scarcity of sources describing how he coped with what he did do not allow us clarity or essential insight about what he thought or how he handled the incongruities that faced him. That JS refused to reveal his thinking is undoubtedly one of the primary reasons that the LDS Church has not officially, until recently, addressed JS's behavior and motives.[83] In part to show good faith in confronting its controversial past, the church provided a considerable discussion of JS and plural marriage in its "Gospel Topic" productions in 2014.[84] Others in scholarly works have tried to piece together the shards of documentation to present a plausible analysis of what they think JS tried to do after first entertaining the concept in the early 1830s while he revised the Bible.[85] More recently, physician Brian C. Hales, after years of research has presented the broadest portrayal to date of JS's marital practice and intentions for the Saints.[86] But Mormons can never explain JS's initiation of plural marriage to a level of understanding and justification that will relieve him of the taint of

83. Historians of the RLDS Church, before it became the Community of Christ in 2000, dealt with their own difficulty resulting from the absence of documentation from JS regarding plural marriage. Reliance upon Emma Smith's denials of her husband's involvement in polygamy forced, for several generations, their posture that JS was free from the marital irregularity. The Community of Christ now recognizes the evidence of JS's plural marriages, though they do not consider the practice to have been divinely inspired. See Scherer, *Journey of a People*, 398–409.

84. https://www.lds.org/topics/plural-marriage-in-the-church-of-jesus-christ-of-latter-day-saints?lang=eng.

85. A number of explanatory monographs about JS and polygamy have been written in the past two generations rehearsing the problems of trying to implement among the Saints what he perceived to be the ancient biblical order of marriage. The most important analyses regarding the practice in Nauvoo, by date of publication, are Kimball Young, *Isn't One Wife Enough: The Story of Mormon Polygamy* (New York: Henry Holt, 1954); Stanley S. Ivins, "Notes on Mormon Polygamy," *Western Humanities Review* 10, no. 3 (Summer 1956); Danel W. Bachman, "A Study of the Mormon Practice of Plural Marriage before the Death of Joseph Smith" (master's thesis, Purdue University, 1975); Lawrence Foster, *Religion and Sexuality: The Shakers, the Mormons, and the Oneida Community* (Urbana, IL: University of Illinois Press, 1984); Richard S. Van Wagoner, *Mormon Polygamy: A History* (Salt Lake City: Signature Books, 1989); Todd Compton, *In Sacred Loneliness: The Plural Wives of Joseph Smith* (Salt Lake City: Signature Books, 1997); Kathryn M. Daynes, *More Wives than One: Transformation of the Mormon Marriage System, 1840–1910* (Urbana, IL: University of Illinois Press, 2001); B. Carmon Hardy, *Doing the Works of Abraham: Mormon Polygamy, Its Origin, Practice, and Demise* (Norman, OK: Arthur H. Clark, 2007); George D. Smith, *Nauvoo Polygamy: "...But We Called It Celestial Marriage"* (Salt Lake City: Signature Books, 2008).

86. Hales, *Joseph Smith's Polygamy*.

abridging the monogamy of western culture to follow what his critics assert was his libidinous instincts.

The topic's significance is multidimensional. Of first importance for the student to understand, there is almost nothing from JS during his involvement with polygyny and polyandry that describes how he first grasped the concept and what its implications were thereafter in his life. However, from his connections to Fanny Alger and Lucinda Pendleton Morgan Harris in the later 1830s to his Nauvoo marriages beginning in 1841, the secondary literature reliant upon the fragmentary documentary record amply supports the generalities of what occurred. With the other overviews, the Hales study includes not only the instigation of the practice but also provides for some the possible theological backdrop for what JS conceived as its purpose. But despite the scholarly appraisals—criticisms and justification alike—JS's practice of plural marriage will undoubtedly never have consensus of interpretation or understanding. And though the Mormons themselves are among the most vociferous advocates of one man/one woman matrimonial arrangements today, the taint of the past forever follows them because of the sixty years of its practice by the LDS Church.

One of the reasons for today's attitudes is the matter of how JS handled the existence of the premise. JS never publicly addressed the circumstances other than to deny and deflect his involvement in polygamy. The attempt to divert the issue on his part is a major fissure to his image by moderns. No surprise then that detractors have used his deception about what he had done to discredit the entirety of his work. "One cannot ignore Smith's capacity to deceive. One of the clearest evidences of this is his repeated public denial during the early 1840s of his own and others' plural marriages."[87] Two instances illustrate the point. The October 1, 1842, issue of the *Times and Seasons*, of which JS was the nominal editor, publicly denied charges made earlier in the year by John C. Bennett that an underground "secret wife system" clandestinely operated in Nauvoo at JS's instigation. The rebuttal editorial used the statement "On Marriage" that appeared in the 1835 Doctrine and Covenants to show that Mormons countenanced only monogamous unions. A dozen high profile men of the community along with nineteen women of a similar stripe, a number of whom certainly had knowledge of JS's teaching about plural marriage, stipulated the veracity of the editorial. They endorsed the premise of the falsity of Bennett's allegations, stating that Bennett himself had foisted the "spiritual wife system" upon unwitting women.[88]

87. Vogel, *Joseph Smith*, ix.

88. "On Marriage," *Times and Seasons*, October 1, 1842, 939–40. There is the possibility that church denials of Bennett's twisted "spiritual wifery" may have been justified in the minds of those whose names were appended to the editorial. While at least several of them certainly knew of JS's teachings about plural marriage, they believed that Bennett's chicanery was altogether different than what JS was teaching. See Hales, *Joseph Smith's Polygamy*, 2:189–92, who described the phenomenon.

Another noted incident was in a sermon on May 26, 1844, where JS is reported to have said, "What a thing it is for a man to be accused of committing adultery, and having seven wives, when I can only find one."[89] Early members recognized the inconsistency in what JS and others represented at the time. One Nauvoo resident explained to her parents in the East that her new husband related that when he first got wind of polygamy and other doctrinal novelties it "tried his faith very much." Already having had a run-in with some leaders about his criticism in Missouri of "Daniteism,"[90] he then later heard JS's brother Hyrum explain JS's teachings about plural marriage, which after consideration he accepted. "But a few weeks before the murder [of JS and Hyrum] Hyrum denied that he and Joseph had the revelation concerning it but said that it referred to ancient times; and it was published [so] in the [Nauvoo] *Neighbor*."[91] The man's wife asked him how he could reconcile the contradiction. Knowing their tenuous circumstances in Nauvoo at the time, the husband told her that Hyrum probably said what he did to reduce the "excitement,"[92] a view likely held by others. From hindsight it is clear and not surprising why JS and others denied their involvement with

89. Smith, Sermon, May 26, 1844, Joseph Smith Collection, Addresses, MS 155, box 4, folder 6, item 5, CHL.

90. Known as the Danites, the quasi-official body of men established as a defense of Latter-day Saints in northern Missouri later assumed in the minds of some Mormons a marauding character with retribution as their intent. JS had been involved initially. See Leland H. Gentry and Todd M. Compton, *Fire and Sword: A History of the Latter-day Saints in Northern Missouri, 1836–1839* (Salt Lake City: Greg Kofford Books, 2011), 221–266; Alexander L. Baugh, *A Call to Arms: The 1838 Mormon Defense of Northern Missouri* (Provo, UT: Joseph Fielding Smith Institute of Latter-day Saint History and BYU Studies, 2000), 33–46; Quinn, *Mormon Hierarchy*, 92–103; and Bushman, *Rough Stone Rolling*, 349–55.

91. The reference to an item of denial of polygamy from Hyrum Smith appearing in the *Nauvoo Neighbor* may be an instance of Scott misremembering the timing and venue of Hyrum's refutation. An "Affidavit of Hyrum Smith" had appeared in the *Times and Seasons* on August 1, 1842, that contained a denial of JS ever teaching that "fornication and adultery was right, or poligamy or any such practices." "Affidavit of Hyrum Smith," *Times and Seasons*, August 1, 1842, 870–71. The timing, however, predated Hyrum's knowledge of JS's involvement in the practice. Several weeks before Hyrum was killed, he was associated with a related matter reported in the *Nauvoo Neighbor*. "On February 26, 1844, a man named Orsamus F. Bostwick was brought before the mayor's court in Nauvoo and fined for slander. Bostwick had claimed that Hyrum Smith had spiritual wives and that many women in Nauvoo were involved with 'spiritual wifery,' promiscuity, and prostitution." However, there was no denial by Hyrum of polygamy reported in this circumstance. See the "Voice of Innocence," published on March 20, 1844, in the *Nauvoo Neighbor*, quoted in Derr et al., *First Fifty Years of Relief Society*, 151.

92. Sarah Hall Scott to "My Dear Father and Mother," July 22, 1844, quoted in George R. Partridge, ed., "The Death of a Mormon Dictator: Letters of Massachusetts Mormons, 1843–1848," *New England Quarterly* 9, no. 4 (December 1936): 598; and Isaac Scott to "Dear Brother," March 11, 1845, quoted in Partridge, "The Death of a Mormon Dictator," 606.

plural marriage within Kirtland, Far West, and Nauvoo's highly volatile circumstances.[93] While rumors stirred first in Kirtland and then Nauvoo for several years, it is reasonable to say that when word of the practice from former insiders became public in early June 1844, it added fuel to the atmosphere that led to JS's death at month's end. Modern observers will inevitably misapprehend JS's plural marriage conundrum because of not only the absence of his own explanation of the practice, the distance of time, and the foreignness of the innovation, but also the pattern of decades of condemnation thereafter that ensured he and his intentions would never be understood.

Besides the issue of plural marriage, defenders and detractors of JS describe him and his character from very different perspectives regarding the myriad of features that portray his life. The nature of the surviving historical record, with all of its uncertainties, guarantee that absolutist determinations from those who write about him will never quell the controversy that the prophet brought to the religious landscape. Yet, if taken as a whole, there is enough that remains as demonstrable markers to show the man on a stage where moderns can see him, how he negotiated his own circumstances, and how it affected the world around him. Nevertheless, the limitations imposed by the incomplete historical record will always, along with the biases of those who contend about him, ensure he and his character will remain objects of vigorous debate in the future.

93. See for example, Hales, *Joseph Smith's Polygamy*, 1:173–77, 2:189–92.

CHAPTER 13

Underlying What Joseph Smith Thought and Taught

It should be evident that the surviving body of materials that can be directly tied to JS has shaped our present understanding of the breadth of his thinking. At the same time, what we know about how JS did things has also informed us that there may be portions of what passed through his mind that never found expression in the written word. We are left to extrapolate from the extant record what he thought and what motivated him. Those documents, as noted, are his own limited writings, the scriptural texts he produced, the sermons he delivered (derived from the notes of his hearers), what others said they heard from and about him, and the histories he initiated produced by his clerks/historians. The common characteristic in all the records is evidence of JS's complete immersion in a world where the supernatural formed the stage upon which he performed. He operated in a dimension reflecting the Book of Mormon statement that "to some it is given to know the mysteries of God" (Alma 12:9). JS's life shows the ubiquitous display of his acceptance of the premise that a spiritual reality operated parallel with the tangible, empirical existence that moved most humans. Those who embraced Mormonism, whether naturally inclined toward that disposition or instinctually more earthbound, found in JS reinforcement in their hope that the biblical premise describing the relationship of God and man was plausible. Thus, in appraising the remnants of the Mormon past, JS students employing the tools of historiography must accommodate the proposition that JS and many of his contemporaries operated in what to them was a compelling, nonphysical realm.

What follows are several elaborations on significant themes taught by JS that reflect his thinking and teaching about God and man that give insight into how he viewed his divine commission, his church, its people, and the rest of the human family.[1] In considering these matters, readers must recognize the importance of placing JS's thinking and teachings within the context in which they were created. Appreciating his intentions and the milieu in which he delivered the philosophy and principles he believed requires allowance for his unique perspectives and manner of portraying the will of God. As Richard Bushman has explained, JS "made the transcendent literal and the mundane heavenly," and that "mixing of the mystical with the plain was pure Joseph Smith."[2] The importance of the historical record to understand the milieu influencing JS's thinking and teaching requires suspension of systematic models that demand adherence to formulaic constructions of religious perspectives. We are severely limited in our appraisals due to the scarcity of what is arguably, and perhaps surprisingly, a significant portion of what he said and taught. As implied in Chapter 11, it is likely that we will remain ignorant of many of the essentials that he emphasized to his followers, as well as hints of much more that he considered than we have previously supposed. Despite the significant efforts made by those who have investigated and tried to categorize the range of JS's teachings, it still must be conceded that searching for his prophetic distinctiveness is difficult for even the spiritually inclined of today who attempt to grasp the unusual arena in which he operated.

Joseph Smith's Understanding of the Status of Mankind

What follows are several prominent matters reflecting what appears to be JS's thoughts to the degree that what survives of his expressions can be comprehended. Without question he embraced the biblical declarations of God's attention to mankind as found in the Pentateuch, the Jewish Torah traditionally known as the first five books of Moses. The author(s) of Genesis laid out the primary fundamentals of God's special creation: "Let us make man in our image, after our likeness.... So God created man in his own image, in the image of God created he him; male and female created he them" (Gen. 1:26–27). The story became for Mormon believers even more their own as they read that the Pentateuch was found on the brass plates obtained by Nephi in Jerusalem where he, too, understood that "Adam and Eve...were our first parents" (1 Ne. 5:11). The

1. The breadth of the volumes describing JS's teachings cannot be summarized in a chapter. Ehat and Cook's substantive and scholarly *Words of Joseph Smith*, though dated and limited to only the Nauvoo period, remains the most important exhibition of JS's teachings. Others like Larry Dahl and Donald Cannon's *Encyclopedia of Joseph Smith's Teachings* summarize many of his teachings by topic. Another useful volume that shows JS's teachings and their relevance in their larger historical context is Harrell, "*This is My Doctrine.*"
2. Bushman, *Rough Stone Rolling*, 477, 478.

Book of Mormon also gave purpose to the creation, explaining that the mortality of mankind was a "state of probation," and that all of the race was lost "because of the transgression of their parents" (2 Ne. 2:21). But Adam wittingly submitted to the process of the fall "that men might be" (2 Ne. 2:25), thereby enabling God's plan for his children's mortality to unfold.

From the revelations he produced, JS further explained the ratio of God to his mortal offspring. In his revision of the Bible he stated that after Moses "beheld the world and the ends thereof, and all the children of men" that it became apparent "that man is nothing, which thing I never had supposed" (Moses 1:8, 10). Still, given the criteria placed upon mankind to make the most of their earth life, tempered by the numerous obstacles and vicissitudes to which they were subjected, Jehovah told Moses that his "work" and "glory" was ultimately "to bring to pass the immortality and eternal life of man" (Moses 1:39). The crux of the plan was that Jesus's later role, after being collaborator with the Father in creation of the earth and populating it with God's children, was, by design, to "redeem the children of men from the fall" (2 Ne. 2:26). The primary feature of the redemption laid upon God's children was their option to choose whether or not to follow God's plan. The binary alternative was, according to what JS learned, the choice to embrace the Almighty or to ignore or fight against his design by following Satan, the devil, whose determination it was to thwart the Father's work and glory. With that understanding, Lehi in the Book of Mormon (and consequently JS) became aware that God's children "have become free forever, knowing good from evil; to act for themselves and not to be acted upon, save it be by the punishment of the law at the great and last day." That condition of mortality included provision that "men are free according to the flesh; and all things are given them which are expedient unto man. And they are free to choose liberty and eternal life, through the great Mediator of all men, or to choose captivity and death" (2 Ne. 2:26–27).

The role of Jesus to orchestrate the plan for those who populated the earth that JS advanced included Jesus's role as Moses's God (Jehovah) and Peter's Savior (Christ). The sacred texts JS produced emphasized Jesus's status as the redeemer of mankind with the premise that he was foreordained in the premortal world to save God's earthly children before preparing the way for their eternal journey. The characterization of Jesus in JS's "Articles and Covenants," for instance, explicitly summarizes Jesus's redemptive role. But, perhaps surprisingly, outside JS's abundant explications of Jesus and his redeeming task as mankind's savior found in the Book of Mormon and his other revelations, the extant documentary record contains relatively little of JS's explications about Jesus. There is the possibility that he addressed the matter of Jesus's redemption to a greater extent than what survives. As it is, the most famous statement about

Jesus that can be tied directly to JS is his declarative affirmation about Christ in the July 1838 issue of the *Elders' Journal*, of which he was editor. As referred to earlier, in what appears to be a response to the mischaracterization of Mormons, JS posed to himself twenty questions about him and his church that he then answered. Reciting several issues he supposed were held by the outside world, some with his wry humor, he proffered, "What are the fundamental principles of your religion." "Answer. The fundamental principles of our religion is the testimony of the apostles and prophets concerning Jesus Christ, that he died, was buried, and rose again the third day, and ascended up into heaven." Everything else, he wrote, "are only appendages to these, which pertains to our religion."[3] The premise fit the revelations he advanced as divine inspiration. The practical effect of Jesus's merciful intervention for God's children was his promise that "all your losses will be made up to you in the resurrecti[o]n provi[d]ed you continue faithful." JS confirmed the notion by asserting "by the vision of the almighty I have seen it."[4]

The grand design, according to JS, was recognition that all of the Almighty's sons and daughters composed the human family. While establishing the reality of the proposition as being important in all mortal human interactions, there was also a consequence in failing to recognize the connections between those living and their forebears. To ignore that feature of God's purposes crippled in his mind one of its most essential justifications, "that the earth will be smitten with a curse, unless there is a welding link of some kind or other, between the fathers and the children." JS's teaching about that "link"—the "sealing and binding power"—expanded mankind's obligations and opportunities regarding the "principles in relation to the dead and the living; that cannot be lightly passed over." He stated it was of such consequence that it determined the eternal status of mankind, for "their salvation is necessary and essential to our salvation."[5]

Besides his implementation of rituals and ordinances to vivify the concept, he also expanded the vision of mortal opportunity by implementing what he saw as the biblical scheme of the ancient prophets and their priesthood designed to shape the order by which humans could return to God. The premise held that, according to Mormon historian Gordon Irving, Heavenly Father "had joined Adam and Eve for eternity as husband and wife and placed them at the head of the human family." Consequently, "their children were natural 'heirs of the priesthood' and were 'born in the covenant' and recognized by God as legitimate members of his family and legal heirs to his kingdom." The result, if

3. [No author], *Elders' Journal*, 43–44.
4. Smith, Journal, April 16, 1843, *JSP, J*2:360.
5. Joseph Smith, "Letter from Joseph Smith," September 6, 1842, *Times and Seasons*, October 1, 1842, 935.

properly understood, tied "the chain of families stretching back to Adam, who was linked to God." Those not directly connected to the familial lines, "could be 'grafted' into the patriarchal order, thus becoming 'legal heirs,' and acquiring the 'fathers in the priesthood' necessary to link each one to the chain of families built up in the days of the patriarchs." The far-reaching implication came to be known as "The Law of Adoption." Thus, Irving stated, "the 'family of God' became more than a metaphor."[6] The trajectory of JS's religion had sharply diverged from the offerings of the Christian community.

"I teach them correct principles and they govern themselves"

Thereafter, JS taught a religion that at once had the trappings of orthodoxy and conformity while at the same time recognizing the intuitions and freedom of spirit necessary to actuate the latent dispositions and initiatives within his followers. His perception of God's design in the purposes of mortality for the human family included a feature widely heralded thereafter in Mormonism as "agency," an individual's option to choose his or her own destiny. Rather than man's predetermined assignment of eternal salvation or damnation taught in Calvinism, JS's earliest expression by way of the Book of Mormon included that, "men are free according to the flesh" (2 Ne. 2:27). That is, it was upon individuals to determine by their yearning and devotion their eternal status rather than God's predestined fate. The premise was manifest in other revelations that established man's individuality. Not only did God endow mankind with capacity, he also imbued them with an expectation to exercise their singular independence by the unfettered aptitude to make choices.

Central to the overall construction of what became Mormon doctrine was the understanding that a premortal condition preceded earth life.[7] With numerous accommodations to the prospect of an eternity that preceded earth life found in biblical and Mormon revelatory texts, JS first overtly articulated the scenery behind God's organization of the earth and his purposes in doing so in his productions of the books of Moses and Abraham, which he initiated in 1830

6. Gordon Irving, "The Law of Adoption: One Phase of the Development of the Mormon Concept of Salvation, 1830–1900," *BYU Studies* 14, no. 3 (1974): 294. Also see Samuel M. Brown and Jonathan A. Stapley's portrayal of how the premise of "adoption" operated and developed in Mormon theology in the nineteenth century. Brown, "Early Mormon Adoption Theology and the Mechanics of Salvation," and Stapley, "Adoptive Sealing Ritual in Mormonism," in *Journal of Mormon History* 37, no. 3 (Summer 2011): 3–52, 53–118, respectively. Brigham Young later explained his own perceptions derived from JS of how the principle that he called the law of adoption affected his family, which by then had incorporated plural marriage. Lee, *Journals of John D. Lee, 1846–47 & 1859*, February 17, 1847, 83.

7. For descriptions of Mormon conceptions of the premortal existence, see Harrell, "*This is My Doctrine*," 199–226; Givens, *When Souls Had Wings*, 212–20.

and 1835, respectively. The spirit state before creation of the earth, where spirits had an intellect that allowed them to exercise the agency with which they were endowed, formed the theological foundation upon which the Mormon conception of man's everlasting journey was established. JS, it was reported, related to the Saints in January 1841: "The first step in the salvation of men is the laws of eternal and self-existent principles. Spirits are eternal. At the first organization in heaven we were all present and saw the Savior chosen and appointed, and the plan of salvation made and we sanctioned it."[8] The story of that premortal existence included the description in JS's Book of Abraham's twist of what the Bible called the "war in heaven" (Rev. 12:7). That setting, where premortals were presented with choices regarding their eternal destiny, provided the options of compliance to divine commands or full agency to resist with the risk of faltering (Moses 1:1–4; Abr. 3:22–28). According to the theology, agency as a divine strategy prevailed and humans were conceived with the opportunity to choose the course of their lives. Coercion was anathema to the principle.

With that backdrop, JS's articulation of one of Mormonism's most vivifying premises is best shown in the remembrances of two of his close associates. "Some years ago, in Nauvoo," John Taylor, one of JS's apostles and ghostwriters, began, "a gentleman in my hearing, a member of the Legislature, asked Joseph Smith how it was that he was enabled to govern so many people, and to preserve such perfect order; remarking at the same time that it was impossible for them to do it anywhere else." Circumstances suggest that the "gentleman" was Stephen A. Douglas, then an influential judge in Illinois who became a U.S. Senator and later opponent of Abraham Lincoln as the Democratic candidate in the 1860 election. Taylor's report described what may have been a meeting on January 1, 1843, in Springfield, Illinois. Stating that after the question by the "gentleman," JS explained that "it was very easy to do that," replying "I teach them correct principles, and they govern themselves." Howard Coray, another of JS's scribes and also apparently an eyewitness to the exchange, related the situation and stated that he heard JS say, "I simply teach them the truth, and they govern themselves."[9] JS articulated via revelation on August 1, 1831, the license for church members to pursue their personal dispositions toward living the religion: "It is not meet that I [Jesus] should command in all things, for he that is compelled in all things, the same is a slothful and not a wise servant.... Men should be anxiously engaged in a good cause and do many things of their own free will and bring to pass much righteousness, for the power is in them, wherein they

8. Smith, Sermon, January 5, 1841, *JSP, D7*:494–95.

9. John Taylor, "The Organization of the Church" (from the *Etoile du Deseret*), *Latter-Day Saints' Millennial Star*, November 15, 1851, 339; Coray, Autobiographical sketches.

are agents unto themselves."[10] That is, individuals were given a realm in which to operate where they were endowed with power to function on their own initiative. The principle of human agency became one of the most well-known concepts that JS infused into Mormon doctrine and theology.

In JS's delivery of God's plan, the overlay of the schematic for humans was simple in its conception. But as everyone knows, earth life is complex with the effects of economics, politics, nationality, race, gender, religion, and nature and nurture, rendering compliance to God's divine purposes—as found in the sacred texts—complicated. JS appealed to his followers' sensibilities based upon Christian ideals and the revelations he received from Jesus. To be sure, his teachings were presented in generalities that represented his understanding, derived since his youth, regarding the purposes of God to temper the complexity of life by adhering to Christian principles. While JS served as editor of Nauvoo's *Times and Seasons*, John Taylor—the de factor editor of the periodical—represented what likely reflected JS's thinking as well. "[W]hile one portion of the human race is judging and condemning the other without mercy, the great parent of the universe looks upon the whole of the human family with a fatherly care and paternal regard; he views them as his offspring; and without any of those contracted feelings that influence the children of men, causes '*his sun* to rise on the evil and on the good; and sends *his* rain on the just and on the unjust.'" Then followed the assurance that the father of heaven and earth administered justice evenhandedly among his children: "If human laws award to each man his deserts, and punish all delinquents, according to their several crimes; surely the Lord will not be more cruel than man, for he is a wise legislator, and his laws are more equitable, his enactments more just, and his decisions more perfect than those of man; and as man judges his fellow man by law, and punishes him according to the penalty of the law; so does the God of heaven judge 'according to the deeds done in the body.'"[11] In another essay published by JS as *Times and Seasons* editor, with the same author attribution as the previous essay, the Mormon view about man's mortality and connection to God was described: "As God governed Abraham, Isaac and Jacob, as families, and the children of Israel as a nation, so we, as a church, must be under his guidance if we are prospered, preserved, and sustained. Our only confidence can be in God, our only wisdom obtained from him; and he alone must be our protector and safeguard, spiritually and temporally, or we fall."[12]

10. Smith, Revelations, August 1, 1831, *JSP, R1*:126 [D&C 58:26–28 (1981), clear text].
11. While Joseph Smith served as editor of the journal, John Taylor handled the composition of much editorial content, and may have actually written, "Baptism for the Dead," from which this excerpt is taken. Still, it is likely that the expressions also represented JS's thinking. Editor, "Baptism for the Dead," *Times and Seasons*, April 15, 1842, 759, 760 (emphasis in original).
12. Editor, "The Government of God," *Times and Seasons*, July 15, 1842, 857.

Joseph Smith's God

To better appreciate the understanding held by JS of the God of Abraham, Isaac, and Jacob, who was Jehovah of the Old Testament and Book of Mormon, and Jesus, the revealer of his modern revelations, consideration about how he perceived and characterized Deity is relevant. The Book of Mormon and JS's revelations are replete with declarations of God's love for his children and the mercy he extended to them. The texts influenced the manner in which JS not only carried out what he believed to be the will of God, but also reflected how God looked upon not only him but the entire range of humanity. In JS's April 7, 1844, theological elaboration later called the King Follett discourse, Thomas Bullock's insightful but limited notes of the speech indicate that a primary theme of the sermon was the character of God. "There are very few who understand rightly the char[acter] of God," JS explained. "I want to ask this cong[regation]: every man wom[an] & child to ans[we]r the question in their own heart[,] what kind of a being is God[?] I ag[ai]n rep[ea]t the quest[io]n, what kind of a being is God[?]" The query prepped the vast congregation for JS's emphatic declaration: "God himself who sits enthroned in yonder Heavens is a man like unto one of yourselves who holds this world in its orbit & upholds all things by his power[.] if you were to see him today you wo[ul]d see him [as] a man for Adam was a man like in fashion & image like unto him."[13] He had said as much in other settings, but this articulation aroused not only the contemporary Saints but also their descendants for generations.

Coupled with that articulation about God, JS also inserted an attendant aspect about the divine that it is clear he also believed. It is not known the extent of his perceptions and how they affected him overall, but it is evident it was central to his thinking. He said to the April 1844 gathering, "I am going to tell you the des[ign]s of God to the human race & why he interferes with the affairs of man."[14] From all appearances, JS accepted the biblical God: full of mercy, but as evident from scriptural writ *only* to those who abided his primacy and majesty. JS appeared, as will be shown, to accept the dichotomous portrayals of God within the scriptures, i.e., the righteous to be blessed, the wicked to be destroyed; though JS was generally disposed to emphasize the merciful manifestations of God.

The "Evil One"

Also found within JS's revelations was inclusion of a place in his presentation of God's plan for God's adversary and foil, Satan. The explicit portrayal of the existence and influence of Satan in JS's revelations indicates in his theological construction the devil's role as God's nemesis. Questions remain about where JS

13. Smith, Sermon, April 7, 1844, Thomas Bullock, scribe, CR 100 318.
14. Ibid.

derived his perceptions about the contrast between God and his purposes and his adversary's designs. Most modern biblical scholarship recognizes that the concept of a rival to God does not exist in the Old Testament until the "third/second centuries BCE" (before the Common Era, or A. D.), where "a character who is the archenemy of Yahweh and humankind" became a presence.[15] However, Mormons, largely due to their temple ritual drama, generally subscribe to the notion that Satan from the outset influenced mankind's mortal journey. That figure embodied all evil, as its attributes developed in the minds of those who subscribed to holy writ, and was known by a variety of designations and manifestations. Thus, Isaiah's statement in chapter 14:12–15 where he laments Lucifer's fate: "How art thou fallen from heaven, O Lucifer, son of the morning,"[16] corroborates their theology. The personification of evil in the sacred texts fit, as JS represented in Moses 4:1–21 and Abraham 3:22–28, into God's overall plan to test the human family for loyalty to him. However, this can be confusing to modern students as in the Old Testament, within the writings of the early prophets, there is "no evil force or influence such as Satan operating in opposition to God." The primitive biblical texts advance the premise that God was the "source of both good and evil."[17] Indeed, as some scholars have advanced, there is "a Hebrew word that is translated as 'Satan' in the Jewish Bible, but the word is not meant as the name of a personality or person. To give this Satan too much agency would be to diminish the power of the one and only God, according to ancient Judaism."[18] Thereafter, a transition to accommodate a specific character for the "evil one" preceded creation of the New Testament texts. Though conceptual development is obscure, the gospel writers began to depict Satan "as an evil, sinister being who tempts mortals to sin" (1 Thess. 2:18; Matt. 4:1–11), realized as Satan being depicted "as a specific person who is both a liar and archenemy of God" in the book of Revelation.[19]

When JS began his prophetic ministry, the revelations he produced represented the New Testament perspectives by containing explicit reference to God's enemy as Satan and the devil: seventy-two verses in the Book of Mormon, fifty-seven in the Doctrine and Covenants, and twenty-nine instances in the Book of Moses. Moreover, the notion of evil as the foil of God's goodness is mentioned in ten dozen verses in the Book of Mormon, twenty-five in the Doctrine and

15. Hector Ignacio Avalos, "Satan," in Metzger and Coogan, *Oxford Companion to the Bible*, 679.

16. JS's modern revelations contain only two references to Lucifer: 2 Ne. 24:12 and D&C 76:26.

17. Harrell, *"This is My Doctrine,"* 194. See Ex. 4:11, 7:2–3; Deut. 32:39; Isa. 45:5–7, 63:17, for example.

18. Jon M. Sweeney, *Inventing Hell: Dante, the Bible, and Eternal Torment* (New York: Jericho Books, 2014), 21.

19. Harrell, *"This is My Doctrine,"* 196.

Covenants, seven in the Book of Moses, and four times in the Book of Abraham. JS's letters and sermons referenced Satan and his designs dozens of times. As he narrated his life, in the minimal way that he did, the opposition JS experienced from his youth was attributed to Satan and his plan to thwart God's work. JS's binary view of the primal powers influencing the world since mankind's origin are unmistakable in his understanding of how they affected God's children. The claims of Mormonism thereafter circle the proposition that there is a God in heaven, that his son was Jesus Christ, and that they are personally involved in earthly affairs. Their sovereignty, however, cannot be appreciated without the presence of Satan and his objectives in the divine timeline.

The Duality of God's Dealings with His Children

An ongoing debate about the interest of God in shaping his children's devotions to him is derived from the biblical record. God's mercies, compassion, forgiveness, love, and understanding exhibited in the Bible have provoked libraries of commentary. There is the other emotion of God that many choose not to address.[20] Jehovah (or Yahweh) is characterized in a portion of the Old Testament with human-type passions that include exhibitions of anger, wrath, vengeance, and antipathy toward the enemies of Israel, who are another population of God's children. Portrayal of the Hebrew God of retribution toward his enemies (disobedient children) began in the Pentateuch.[21] Following the Pentateuch, the "Warrior God" revealed in Joshua, Judges, and 1 and 2 Samuel created a lasting image of the Almighty among the Israelites, attributing their acquisition of the Promised Land to Jehovah's logistical and ruthless intervention. God went before the enemies of the Hebrews in the book of Joshua and laid waste any vestige of the Canaanites, Amorites, Hittites, Perizzites, Jebusites, and Hivites. However, many moderns steeped in Christian traditions are put off by this image of God, focusing rather on the merciful Jesus who they say taught of the necessity of loving one's enemies that "stands in sharp contrast to the command of the Old Testament God to take up arms."[22] Some argue that the Hebraic portrayal of God paralleled the perceptions of other ancient cultures regarding their own deities. "Many of the gods cultivated by ancient cultures were militant figures believed to fight for—and, on occasion, *against*—their own devotees. Religion in the Bible is no different." Jehovah (Yahweh), the Hebrew God, "is a god of battles, rejoicing in warlike activities and praised for military achievements—hence the reference to the 'Book of the Wars of Yahweh' in Numbers 21:14."[23]

20. Grant Underwood describes the contrast as "Apocalyptic Dualism," *The Millenarian World of Early Mormonism* (Urbana: University of Illinois Press, 1999), 42–57.
21. See Deut. 29, for example.
22. Senior et al., *The Catholic Study Bible*, RG 122.
23. Robert P. Carroll, "War," in *What the Bible Really Says*, ed. Morton Smith and R. Joseph Hoffman (New York: HarperCollins, 1993), 155–56.

Thus: "Many readers of Joshua (and other OT books) are deeply troubled by the role that warfare plays in this account of God's dealings with his people. Not a few relieve their ethical scruples by ascribing the author's perspective to a pre-Christian (and sub-Christian) stage of moral development that the Christian, in light of Christ's teaching, must repudiate and transcend."[24] It should be noted, as biblical scholar Bart Ehrman stated: "The God of vengeance is found not only in the Old Testament, as some Christians have tried to claim. Even the New Testament God is a God of judgment and wrath, as any reader of the book of Revelation knows."[25] (A careful reading of portions of the Gospels also illustrates the negative fate Jesus warned against for those who did not conform to God's teachings.) It is plausible that the rendering of the militant and vengeful characteristics of Jehovah was how the biblical Hebrews and Christians understood and justified what happened among them, including the notion of God's preoccupation with their destiny. Thus, as some Bible commentators argue, the book of Joshua is a reflective attribution of the Hebrews to God for the triumphs over the Canaanites, the narrative of which was not written until several hundred years after the events described occurred.[26]

JS never expressly explained his thinking about the controversy, but from the texts he produced we can ascertain some notion of how the stories affected his thinking. For example, in his early work revising the Old Testament, he made a slight adjustment to the King James Version text of Joshua 11:20 that provides insight into how he viewed the Lord's attributes of emotion. The story of Joshua and Israel's entry into the land of promise is well known and boldly presents Jehovah's command to obliterate the Canaanites. The KJV renders Joshua 11:20 as, "For it was of the Lord to harden their hearts, that they should come against Israel in battle that he might destroy them utterly, and that they might have no favour, but that he might destroy them, as the Lord commanded Moses." JS, however, altered that perception in his biblical revision. He changed verse 20 in Joshua 11 assigning culpability for the Canaanites destruction to their own devices: "For it was of the Lord to distroy them utterly, because they [the Canaanites] heardened there hearts, that they should come against Israel~~,~~ in battle; that they might <ha>ve no favor, that they might destroy them <in> battle,

24. *The N[ew] I[nternational] V[ersion] Study Bible* (Grand Rapids, MI: Zondervan, 1985), 369.

25. Bart D. Ehrman, *Jesus, Interrupted: Revealing the Hidden Contradictions in the Bible (and Why We Don't Know About Them)* (New York: HarperOne, 2009), 11. Even Jesus's parables have condemnatory implications. See for example, Matt. 12, 13.

26. Gene M. Tucker, "The Book of Joshua," in Metzger and Coogan, *Oxford Companion to the Bible*, 386; Harvey Cox, *How to Read the Bible* (New York: HarperOne, 2015), 66, 76–77.

as the lord commanded Moses."[27] That is, they deserved it, rather than Jehovah manipulating them to fight against Israel to bring about their destruction.[28]

In another instance, in early December 1830, JS altered the KJV rendering of a passage to remove from God an attribute that had and has been assumed among many Bible readers; a sentiment repeated several times in the Bible. In Genesis 6:6–7 the KJV reads that "it repented the Lord that he had made man on the earth, and it grieved him at his heart."[29] As in the passage above, JS assigned in his revision the attitude to Noah, not to the Lord: "And it repented Noah and his heart was pained that the Lord had made man on the earth and it greived him at the heart."[30] Here JS rejected the Hebrew portrayal of Jehovah's personality and replaced it with his own perception of the Lord's emotive nature.[31]

Despite the modifications to the biblical text, given what JS produced in the Book of Mormon and the revelations of the Doctrine and Covenants, he apparently incorporated the dual nature of God. His revelation of November 3, 1831, known as the "appendix" to the Doctrine and Covenants (D&C 133), at once exhibits both the merciful and the vengeful God. About the wicked, Jehovah/Jesus told JS, "I have trampled them in my fury and I did tread upon them in mine anger and their blood have I sprinkled upon my garments and stained all my raiment for this was the day of venge[a]nc[e] which was in my heart," followed by noting "the loving kindness of their Lord and all that he hath bestowed upon them according to his goo[d]ness and according to his loving kindness forever and ever[.]"[32]

The binary perspective JS held about God's attitude toward his favored and despised children apparently held throughout his life, though, as will be shown, his own genial and optimistic sentiment suggests he naturally leaned toward God's kindly disposition toward the human family. While God's mercies

27. Scott H. Faulring, Kent P. Jackson, and Robert J. Matthews, eds., *Joseph Smith's New Translation of the Bible: Original Manuscripts* (Provo, UT: Religious Studies Center, Brigham Young University, 2004), 71 (Old Testament Manuscript 2, Josh. 11:20).
28. See Robert J. Matthews's report of JS's adjustments in this regard to the Old Testament text about "the nature of God" in his *"A Plainer Translation": Joseph Smith's Translation of the Bible, A History and Commentary* (Provo, UT: Brigham Young University Press, 1985), 309–14. The other instances of JS exculpating Jehovah as the one hardening the hearts of the enemies of Israel identified by Matthews are: Ex. 4:21, Ex. 7: 3, 13, Ex. 9:12, Ex. 10: 1, 20, 27, and Ex. 11:10.
29. Other modern translations of the Bible, instead of "repented," use the expressions "was sorry" and "regretted."
30. Faulring, Jackson, and Matthews, *Joseph Smith's New Translation of the Bible*, 111–12 (Old Testament Manuscript 1, Gen. 6:6).
31. JS similarly adjusted the biblical passages of Ex. 32:14; 1 Sam. 15:11; 2 Sam. 15:11; Psalms 135:14; Jer. 18:8, 10, Jer. 26: 3, 13, 19, Jer. 42:10; Amos 7:3, 6; and Jonah 3:10.
32. Smith, Revelations, November 3, 1831, *JSP, R1*:302–3 [D&C 133:51–53 (1981)].

and positive intervention are well known in the Mormon scriptures, there are also plentiful representations from JS's sacred texts that exhibit not only God's manipulation of earthly circumstances, but also his dismissal and rejection of those who did not line up in righteousness. Regarding those who the Book of Mormon identifies as wicked, rebellious, and unrighteous, there is no ambiguity about God's disgust with that division of his children. Just over 5 percent of the Book of Mormon, 346 verses of 6,633, exhibit passages illustrating God's wrath, anger, cursing, judgments, condemnation, and maneuvering of circumstances regarding the imminent fate and eternal destiny of the unrighteousness. God's methods of retribution include fire, famine, earthquakes, thunder and lightning, utter destruction, affliction by all manner of diseases, and death as punishment on earth, and damnation in eternity for their rebellion.

It is clear from the Book of Mormon text that JS perceived attributes of the vengeance and retribution found in the biblical God as a major factor in understanding what the book taught about God and his relationship to his errant children. The rendering, for instance, of God's obliteration of the wicked in 3 Nephi 9 is far more devastating and comprehensive than even Joshua's conquest of Canaan. There is no mystery in Nephi's expression in 1 Nephi 17 that while "the Lord esteemeth all flesh in one; he that is righteous is favored of God." For "he raiseth up a righteous nation, and destroyeth the nations of the wicked. And he leadeth away the righteous into precious lands, and the wicked he destroyeth, and curseth the land unto them for their sakes." But for those who keep the commandments, "he loveth those who will have him to be their God" (1 Ne. 17: 35, 37–38, 40). A few other examples also make the point.

> "I will curse them even with a sore curse" (1 Ne. 2:23).
>
> "I will afflict thy seed by the hand of the Gentiles" (2 Ne. 10:18).
>
> "I will visit the people in mine anger; yea, and I will not turn my fierce anger away" (Alma 8:29).
>
> "The sword of vengeance hangeth over you; and the time soon cometh that he avengeth the blood of the saints upon you, for he will not suffer their cries any longer" (Morm. 8:41).

Furthermore, the revelations JS received that appeared in the Doctrine and Covenants reflect the same proportional viewpoint of God's allegiance to the righteous and his condemnation of the wicked. Of the 3,649 verses found in the Doctrine and Covenants (1981), 206 contain references to the retributive, vengeful God who controlled earthly affairs, or 5.6 percent of the text. As clearly as it was stated in the Book of Mormon, JS's subsequent revelations also portray his understanding of God's disposition toward the two sectors of his children. Three examples from the Doctrine and Covenants amply illustrate the sentiments.

> "For a desolating scourge shall go forth among the inhabitants of the earth, and shall continue to be poured out from time to time, if they repent not, until the earth is empty, and the inhabitants thereof are consumed away and utterly destroyed by the brightness of my coming. Behold, I tell you these things, even as I also told the people of the destruction of Jerusalem; and my word shall be verified at this time as it hath hitherto been verified" (D&C 5:19–20).

> "For the hour is nigh and the day soon at hand when the earth is ripe; and all the proud and they that do wickedly shall be as stubble; and I will burn them up" (D&C 29:6).

> "Desolation shall come upon this generation as a thief in the night, and this people shall be destroyed and scattered among all nations" (D&C 45:19).

Together, of the 10,282 verses in the Book of Mormon and the Doctrine and Covenants, 552, or 5.3 percent of the verses, contain expressions of the Lord's condemnation of those of his children who reject him or fight against the righteous, punctuated by their eternal condemnation if they did not repent. The evidence suggests that JS subscribed to the premise.

However, as shown throughout JS's life, the stark judgments illustrated within the Bible and the modern revelations were tempered by his instinctual disposition to credit humans with more than binary judgments. While JS occasionally used condemnatory rhetoric himself, his behavior exhibiting kind-heartedness, forbearance, and tolerance toward others indicate he adhered to an inner compass that hearkened to an understanding of circumstances that coincided with the scripturally merciful Jesus.[33] Did JS ever fall short in his own behavior? Obviously, he did. But as Brigham Young reflected his view before the Saints on JS in September 1859: while JS "was constituted like other men, and would have required years and years longer in the flesh to become a Moses in all things," given the brief period that he lived, "he was as good a man as ever lived in the flesh, Jesus excepted."[34] JS's followers widely shared the perception.

33. As stated, there are instances in the New Testament where Jesus is reported to have exhibited the characteristics of the Old Testament God of vengeance. See, for example, Matt. 10:11–15, where he condemned those who would not listen to his disciples: "It shall be more tolerable for the land of Sodom and Gomorrah in the day of judgment than for that city" (15). See also Luke 10:11–12.

34. Brigham Young, Sermon, September 1, 1859, *JD*, 7:243.

JS championed the admonitions of Jesus regarding attitudes toward the reluctant. Those listening to him deliver his dedicatory prayer for the Kirtland House of the Lord on March 27, 1836, heard him state: "We know that thou hast spoken by the mouth of thy prophets, terrible things concerning the wicked, in the last days, that thou wilt pour out thy judgments, without measure." But he also affirmed, "we delight not in the destruction of our fellow men; their souls are precious before thee."[35] And on January 20, 1843, he instructed Orson Hyde that "when he spoke in the name of the Lord, it should prove true, but do not cu[r]se the people."[36] He clearly understood the emphasis explained in the scriptures for adherence to the higher road, the expectations of Jesus that far outweighed insistence that God was always on anxious watch against those who violated his laws. Brigham Young later related, "Joseph said, many and many a time, to us, 'Never be anxious for the Lord to pour out his judgments upon the nation.'"[37]

Enlarging upon the interventions of the Lord upon his children on the earth, JS taught that life's challenges, including what are now referred to as "acts of God," were not designed just to punish the wicked. In the late summer of 1839, JS spoke to a gathering assembled at his own home "concerning [the] uselessness of preaching to the world about great judgments," but instead stated, likely from experience, that the better way was "to preach the simple gospel." Continuing the theme about calamities, end times, and the "vengeance" of God upon "the proud and all that do wickedly," he dismissed the notion that the righteous should escape the fate of all mortals who fall "prey to disease to pestilence ~~&c and yet~~ &c by reason of the weakness of the flesh." Misfortunes and tragedies would come, he emphasized, and "it is an unhallowed principle to say that such and such have transgressed because they have been preyed upon by disease or death for all flesh is subject to death." Therefore, those who judged others due to the afflictions borne ought to be careful: "'Judge not' lest ye be judged."[38]

Literal Approach to the Scriptures

The faith of the Latter-day Saints was and is generally described by others in homogenous terms in their attitudes and behavior. They were, however, as with most other religious bodies of that time and today, composed of not only different economic and domestic backgrounds but also of a variable range of be-

35. "Kirtland, Ohio, March 27th, 1836," *Latter Day Saints' Messenger and Advocate*, March 1836, 279; D&C 109: 43 (1981).
36. Smith, Journals, January 20, 1843, *JSP, J2*:247.
37. Brigham Young, Sermon, May 15, 1865, *JD* 11:107.
38. Smith, Journal, September 29, 1839, *JSP, J1*:352–53.

liefs. Still, as is so often applied to minority groups, they were lumped together and roundly condemned. Jacksonville (Illinois) College professor Jonathan B. Turner in 1842 classified Mormonism as a religious upstart, no different than other imposter movements through the years that also flaunted their singularity. "They are all perfectly sure that their dogmas, and those of their teachers, are true," Turner belittled, "for they have the witness of the Spirit to their truth in their own souls." Though critical in intent, Turner also captured an aspect of common belief among the Saints regarding their disposition toward sacred texts. "They profess a literal interpretation of so much scripture as is needful to their several schemes."[39] To outsiders, Mormons "pretend to read and believe the Bible literally,"[40] not a surprising conclusion given how Mormons attempted to replicate the biblical past.

Not only did the Mormons believe the Bible, as Mormon scholar Grant Underwood stated, "the Saints out-Bibled the biblicists."[41] A primary theme against Mormonism in its formative years stemmed from their belief in the Book of Mormon, assumed by their critics to be a replacement for the Christian Bible. The notion did not reflect actual circumstances. Mormons thrived in the atmosphere of the biblical aura that saturated their dialogue and justified their premises for validity. But Jonathan Turner was right about how they generally interpreted the Bible. The probability of literalistic interpretations of the biblical record tended to materialize as a means of establishing precedent, authority, and conformity. By modern standards, the trend fits a strain of fundamentalism that characterizes development in aspects of most religious systems.[42] As it turned out, according to Gordon Irving, to Mormons: "The Bible was to be understood literally. For Mormons of the 1830s the literal view of the scriptures involved several accepted assumptions: the meaning of the various books was both clear and consistent, historical accounts were accurate and factual, biblical prophecies were to be fulfilled exactly as written, and many parts of the Bible were of direct application to modern times."[43] Another consequence of the theological

39. Jonathan B. Turner, *Mormonism in All Ages: Or the Rise, Progress, and Causes of Mormonism, with the Biography of Its Author and Founder, Joseph Smith, Junior* (New York: Platt and Peters, 1842), 102.
40. Haven, "A Girl's Letters from Nauvoo," 627.
41. Underwood, *The Millenarian World of Early Mormonism*, 58.
42. Modern Mormons are assigned the classification of "fundamentalists" in Martin E. Marty and R. Scott Appleby, eds., *Fundamentalisms Observed* (Chicago: University of Chicago Press, 1994), 4. See also the characterization of early fundamentalist thinking in Gordon Irving, "The Mormons and the Bible in the 1830s," *BYU Studies* 13, no. 4 (Summer 1973): 477.
43. Irving, "Mormons and the Bible," 476.

progression were declarations from the believers regarding the infallibility of the sacred records that established the movement, i.e., biblical inerrancy.[44] Oliver Cowdery, for example, certainly held that posture. The "sacred and important promises" made in the Bible, he wrote, were delivered not to be perceived "figuratively" or in a manner to require "*spiritualizing*," but rather were prepared "as conspicuously plain, and are meant to be understood according to their *literal* reading, as those passages which teach us of the creation of the world, and of the decree of its Maker to bring its inhabitants to judgment."[45] Designation of these attributes of early Mormons, however, did not necessarily reflect the scope of how JS perceived the revealed texts.[46]

The disclaimers invoked by JS upon the scriptural texts became well known. While he made declarative statements that rang with literalistic tone, his later insertion of qualifications that tempered the absolutist inclinations of some toward the scriptures have become creedal in Mormonism. "We believe the bible to be the word of God as far as it is translated correctly,"[47] he confirmed in March 1842.[48] "Joseph Smith's expanding theological understanding at any given time dictated which biblical conceptions or events he took literally and which he understood less literally, not literally at all, or even as uninspired," argued Philip L. Barlow, Mormon scholar of American religion. It is important, he continued, "to distinguish how Smith said or thought he understood the Bible from how he used it in practice. For example, the kinds of changes he made in his biblical revision reveal that he found the KJV frequently *unclear*, contradictory, and erroneous. He often interpreted scripture metaphorically." Yet, JS conveyed in the revelations he produced and the things he taught the clear sense that what God had revealed reflected actual circumstances. "[Joseph Smith] was a biblical literalist not because he was incapable of figurative understanding but because he believed the stories of the Bible were history rather than legend." Consequently, it is "essential to recognize the enduring literalistic dimension of his mind. That is, although the Prophet acknowledged metaphorical interpretation

44. Ibid., 477.

45. Oliver Cowdery to W. W. Phelps, n.d., *Latter Day Saints' Messenger and Advocate*, February 1835, 78 (emphasis in original). See also Underwood, *Millenarian World of Mormonism*, 58–66.

46. An exercise of JS deconstructing part of the book of Revelation can be found in his April 8, 1843, sermon found in Joseph Smith Collection, MS 155, box 4, folder 5, item 1, CHL.

47. Smith, "Church History," *Times and Seasons*, March 1, 1842, 709. For the background of the development and construction of the "Articles of Faith," see David J. Whittaker, "The 'Articles of Faith' in Early Mormon Literature and Thought," in *New Views of Mormon History: Essays in Honor of Leonard J. Arrington*, ed. Davis Bitton and Maureen Ursenbach Beecher (Salt Lake City: University of Utah Press, 1987), 63–92.

48. Smith, "Church History," *Times and Seasons*, March 1, 1842, 709.

and even biblical error, for him, the major events told in the Bible corresponded with external reality."[49]

Dimensions of Joseph Smith's Views of Doctrine

JS is famous for embroidering the glories of heaven while tempering the finality of eternal damnation as taught by the Christian world. His multilevel view of the postmortal world that came by way of his 1832 "Vision," illustrating the categorization of eternal assignments, shaped Mormon thinking thereafter. Known today as Doctrine and Covenants, Section 76, the February 1832 revelation promised greater hope for those conflicted with the binary definitions of heaven and hell. The "Vision" offered a general description of what awaited human beings after their mortal journey: glories designed for the faithful and a more comprehensive definition of the evil-doer's fate than previously understood. The premise taught by JS was a significant departure from the prospects of the eternal path of mankind as taught by the Christian world. While JS's definition of the "three degrees of glory" found in the vision dominate discussion about his new view of the afterlife, much found in his revelatory text focuses on perdition: over 20 percent of the verses. That section of the revelation defined the fate of those whose spiritual crime was not only denial of Jesus Christ as redeemer, but also their fight against him and his work on earth: "They are they who are the sons of perdition of whom I say that it had been better for them ~~to have never~~ never <to have> been born for they are vessels of wrath doomed to suffer the wrath of God with the Devel and his angels through~~out~~ eternity concerning whom I have said there is no forgiveness ~~for them~~ in this world nor in the world to come." They came to that circumstance "having denied the holy ~~ghost~~ <Spirit> after having received it and having denied the only begoten son of the fathe[r] ~~crucifying~~ <haveing crucified> him unto themselves and put~~ting~~ him to an open shame[.]"[50] The doctrine indicated that many of the concepts JS learned early in his ministry generally carried through the length of his prophetic tenure, though, as will be shown in Chapter 14, further revelation modified his thinking.[51] Clearly, these were expressions of JS's belief in the warnings

49. Philip L. Barlow, *Mormons and the Bible: The Place of the Latter-day Saints in American Religion*, 2nd ed. (New York: Oxford University Press, 2013), 34, 35–36 (emphasis in original).

50. Smith, Revelations, February 16, 1832, *JSP, R1*:318 [D&C 76:32–38 (1981)].

51. See Wilford Woodruff and Thomas Bullock's reports of JS's King Follett sermon where he articulated at the end of his life again the premise of "sons of perdition," even assigning the fate to those "apostates" who fought against him and the Saints at the time. *Wilford Woodruff Journal*, April 7, 1844, 2:386–87, and Smith, Sermon, April 7, 1844, Bullock, scribe, CR 100 318.

explicit in the scriptural texts, old and new, about the edicts of the Almighty and how they applied to his children who took no heed to the declarations of prophetic figures. To JS, the ultimate of heavenly glory, and its several dimensions, and eternal damnation were not figurative; they were to be understood literally.

The Pelatiah Brown Incident before the Nauvoo High Council

Another incident portraying JS's perceptions about his religion and the manner in which he must be understood comes from a sermon he delivered at a church conference held in Nauvoo, Illinois, on April 8, 1843. Speaking to the congregation gathered on the floor of the Nauvoo Temple then under construction, he related that one of the older Saints, Pelatiah Brown, had come to him chagrined that the Nauvoo high council had reprimanded the latter at their March 19 session for "teaching false doctrine."[52] JS, well into his tenure as church president, took the opportunity at the conference to explain to the Saints his attitude toward doctrine and belief. Brown had just been called on a mission to establish a branch of the church in JS's boyhood home, Palmyra, New York. But prior to his departure the high council called him before their body to censure him for teaching errant doctrines regarding the beasts spoken of in the book of Revelation. To disarm the matter JS explained to the congregation: "I never thought it was right to call up a man and try him because he erred in doctrine, it looks too much like Methodism and not like Latter day Saintism. Methodists have creeds which a man must believe or be kicked out of their church. I want the liberty of believing as I please, it feels so good not to be tramelled." What's more, "It dont prove that a man is not a good man, because he errs in doctrine."[53] After deconstructing the portion of Revelation that discussed the beast(s) in the first dozen chapters, he called to Brown in the audience and said, "dont say any thing about the beast, but preach those things the Lord has told you to preach about, repentance and baptism for the remission of sins."[54] Overall JS took liberties regarding interpretation of scripture that only he claimed. And despite his authoritative pronouncements regarding God's insistence about proper understanding of the sacred texts in numerous other settings, what he taught to the April 8, 1843, conference attendees portrayed his concern about dogma and its potentially divisive effects.

52. John S. Dinger, ed., *The Nauvoo City and High Council Minutes* (Salt Lake City: Signature Books, 2011), 455.

53. Smith, Sermon, April 8, 1843, William Clayton, scribe, Joseph Smith Collection, MS 155, box 4, folder 5, item 1, CHL. To the Council of Fifty, on April 11, 1844, JS stated, "A man's religious opinions should never be called in question." Smith, April 11, 1844, Minutes, Council of Fifty, *JSP, A1*:100.

54. Smith, Sermon, April 8, 1843, William Clayton, scribe.

Man's Obligations to Others: The Christian Virtues

At the end of JS's life, the Mormon vitriol against the Missourians for what they had done to him and to the Saints in the 1830s was known among Latter-day Saints everywhere in both word and print. Multiple petitions to the Missouri government and to Washington for redress had gone ignored. Etched deep into the consciousness of all who suffered during the time, the ordeal became emblematic of the evil designs of men toward them. Few among the Mormons had suffered more than JS. And no one had condemned more roundly the egregious treatment imposed by Missouri upon the Saints as did the prophet. Still, he inclined toward reconciliation and forgiveness in the tragedy's aftermath. At a particularly poignant time when opposition mounted against him in early 1844, he appealed to church members to temper their judgment upon those who had oppressed them. "One of the most pleasing scenes that can transpire on earth, is, when a sin has been committed by one person against another, to *forgive that sin*: and then, according to the sublime and perfect pattern of the Savior, pray to our Father in heaven, *to forgive also*." Continuing, he stated, "the real peace makers of a western world, will go forth, good Samaritan like, and pour in the oil and the wine, till all that can be healed, are made whole; and after repentance, they shall be forgiven; for verily the scriptures say: 'Joy shall be in heaven over one sinner that repents, more than over ninety and nine just persons that need no repentance.'"[55] JS applied his understanding of Jesus's religion and its demanding call to forgive and resolve human affronts to the end of his life.

JS's instincts toward human relationships were shown in not only concerns about how church members got along, he also insisted that biblical standards for fraternal exchange among his followers were acquired and practiced. The New Testament model for engaging the human family never escaped his attention. As captured by Wilford Woodruff, JS taught the Saints on the Iowa side of the Mississippi River opposite Commerce (Nauvoo) on July 2, 1839: "Ever keep in exercise the principles of mercy & be ready to forgive our brother on the first intimations of repentance & asking forgiveness & should we even forgive our brother or our enemy before they ask it our heavenly father would be equally as merciful unto us, & also we ought to be willing to repent of & confess all of our own sins & keep nothing back."[56] Another who noted JS's teachings that July day, his clerk James Mulholland, also wrote of JS's counsel about pride. He "addresst them, and gave much instruction calculated to ~~if~~ guard them against selfsufficiency, selfrighteousness & selfimportance, touching upon many subjects of importance & value to all who wish to walk humbly before the Lord, but

55. Smith, March 8, 1844, "A Friendly Hint to Missouri," *Times and Seasons*, March 15, 1844, 473–74 (emphasis in original).
56. Smith, Sermon, July 2, 1839, *JSP, D6*:519.

especialy teaching them to observe charity, wisdom & fellow feeling with Love, one towards another in all things & under all circumstances."[57]

To the Nauvoo Women's Relief Society that he and they initiated in March 1842, JS, while recognizing the natural disposition of women to accentuate the virtues and charities of life, reminded them that same year that they "should be arm'd with mercy notwithstanding the iniquity among us."[58] Two weeks later a case study presented itself. In minutes kept by Eliza R. Snow, he addressed the women stating, "he was going to preach mercy." To make his point, he said, "Supposing that Jesus Christ and angels should object to us on frivolous things, what would become of us? We must be merciful and overlook small things." Specifically referring a woman among them whose reputation was in question, he continued, "It grieves me that there is no fuller fellowship—if one member suffer all feel it." It is "by union of feeling we obtain pow'r with God. Christ said he came to call sinners to repentance and save them." For this "Christ was condemn'd by the righteous jews because he took sinners into his society," though he noted, Jesus "took them <up>on the principle that they repented of their sins." He explained, "It is the object of this Society to reform persons, not to take those that are corrupt, but if they repent we are bound to take them and by kindness sanctify and cleanse from all unrighteousness, by our influence in watching over them." Turning to the woman who had been censured by the other sisters, he said, "In the name of the Lord I now make you free." Returning to the congregation he continued: "Nothing is so much calculated to lead people to forsake sin as to take them by the hand and watch over them with tenderness. When persons manifest the least kindness and love to me, O what pow'r it has over my mind, while the opposite course has a tendency to harrow up all the harsh feelings and depress the human mind." After more counsel of the same vein he closed, "Sisters of this Society, shall there be strife among you? I will not have it—you must repent and get the love of God. Away with self-righteousness."[59]

An Attempt to Educate the Church

One of the more revealing insights into JS's ambition to educate early church members in the central doctrines and principles of Christianity has been described by JS scholar Robin Jensen. The initiative "would have out-scaled any other theological project during Joseph Smith's life."[60] From what has been viewed by many as cryptic notations on and within the earliest collection of manuscript volumes containing church records, there is evidence JS and his

57. Smith, Journal, July 2, 1839, *JSP, J1*:344–45.
58. Derr et al., *First Fifty Years of Relief Society*, 69.
59. Ibid., 78–79.
60. Robin Scott Jensen, "Ignored and Unknown Clues of Early Mormon Record Keeping," in Turley Jr. and Harper, *Preserving the History of the Latter-day Saints*, 147.

closest associates intended to create a platform to study and disseminate doctrine and theology. While the prophet "did not develop anything like a systematic theology,"[61] it is clear he intended that Mormons would have a theological understanding of things in heaven and on earth. The basis of the study appears to have been JS's revelations and his revision of the KJV.[62] Foundational church records, such as what were later known as the "Book of Commandments and Revelations," "Kirtland Revelation Book," JS's "Letter Books," and the "Kirtland Council Minute Book," all now found within the Joseph Smith Papers project, had topics affixed to the covers of the volumes apparently indicating the original intent of the volumes as the means to inculcate the gospel within church members.

On July 17, 1833, Frederick G. Williams noted that on that day he "commenced classifying the different Subjects of the Scriptures and reviewing the same."[63] As Jensen explained, the "summer of 1833 was an important time in the development of Mormon scripture," as "two weeks before the date of the statement above, Joseph Smith and Frederick G. Williams finished the revision of the Bible."[64] In establishing the project, Jensen stated, the words "Repentance" and "Sabbath Day" appear on the binding that became JS's 1835–1836 journal. "Faith" was penned on the exterior of the "Egyptian Alphabet." And "Second Coming of Christ" and "Gift of the Holy Ghost" were found on the Kirtland Elders' Quorum Minute Book before it became a minute book. "Upon opening the books... it becomes apparent that the first page of each volume is related to the words on the cover."[65] The plan appeared ambitious. "Incredibly, as many as ten volumes full of scriptural citations from Joseph Smith's Bible revision were attempted as a major scribal project as early as 1833." With "two topics per ledger volume, a total of about twenty topics may have been used."[66] Jensen argued the system illustrates "a dramatic shift in medium and represented a profound change in how record keeping was viewed."[67] It is not clear what derailed the original intent as a "collection of gospel topics," but the volumes were eventually repurposed with content specific to the ledgers, such as JS's 1835–1836 journal.[68] The telltale evidence on the covers of the manuscript volumes illustrates his intent to inculcate Jesus's Christianity as a course of study.

61. Blake T. Ostler, *Exploring Mormon Thought: The Attributes of God* (Salt Lake City: Greg Kofford Books, 2001), 74.
62. Jensen, "Ignored and Unknown Clues," 151, 153.
63. Ibid., 151.
64. Ibid.
65. Ibid., 148–49.
66. Ibid., 153.
67. Ibid., 147, 138.
68. Ibid., 154.

The Periphery of Joseph Smith Teachings

The teachings of JS that have provided the basis for not only the foundational core of Latter-day Saint thought but also extended the futurity of Mormonism are well known. They have been distributed widely in any number of ways in the twentieth century. But what of the things that he stated that are out of the mainstream? JS taught, according to reliable documentation, things that eventually were dropped from the corpus of what today are considered the truths he delivered to the Saints. Central to understanding the scope of JS's ministry is that there were features of his thinking that were later rejected or ignored by subsequent leaders as either incorrect, misunderstood, or irrelevant.[69] These matters have almost always been disregarded by the faithful, some believed to be either just more anti-Mormon propaganda or produced by members believed to have been sorely mistaken. One compiler of JS material, not a church history scholar, who did not accept reports of questionable or unfamiliar teachings of JS stated, "Some things [regarding his teachings] I have deliberately excluded, such as those accounts which we know to be historically inaccurate, false, or maliciously prejudicial."[70] Two examples of controversial material are included to illustrate the point.

JS, always calculating how the prophecies and pronouncements of ancient scripture were to be fulfilled in his time—besides relying on the impressions he felt regarding practical Christianity—explored his culture for elements that augmented his thinking and appreciation for God's work in the latter days. An oft-discussed matter that he apparently embraced was the location and later discovery of the "Lost Ten Tribes," said to have dispersed after they were conquered by Assyria in 721 BCE.[71] Among the Mormons, the *scattering* of the ten tribes of Israel was the antecedent for the *gathering* of Israel in the last days, which has been identified to be among the most significant theological features of the faith.[72] Awaiting their recovery by the Lord, JS is said to have stated, according to

69. For a description of the revision by later church leaders of some of what their predecessors taught, see Thomas G. Alexander, "The Reconstruction of Mormon Doctrine: From Joseph Smith to Progressive Theology," *Sunstone* 5, no. 4 (July–August 1980): 24–33.
70. McConkie, *Remembering Joseph*, x.
71. Two of the most noted contemporary volumes addressing the matter were Elias Boudinot, a Cherokee Indian leader, in *A Star in the West; or, A Humble Attempt to Discover the Long Lost Ten Tribes of Israel Preparatory to the Return to Their Beloved City, Jerusalem* (Trenton, NJ: D. Fenton, S. Hutchinson, and J. Dunham, 1816); and Ethan Smith's *View of the Hebrews; of the Tribes of Israel in America* (Poultney, VT: Smith and Shute, 1825). For treatment of how *View of the Hebrews* has been used in the Mormon context, see Charles D. Tate Jr.'s introduction to the reprint of Ethan Smith's *View* in 1996—*View of the Hebrews: 1825, 2nd Edition* (Provo, UT: Religious Studies Center, Brigham Young University, 1996).
72. See Latter-day Saint perspectives based upon teachings of church leaders in Daniel H. Ludlow, *A Companion to Your Study of the Old Testament* (Salt Lake City: Deseret Book, 1981), 41–46.

Brigham Young, "that the Ten Tribes were on a Portion of Land separated from this Earth."[73] Bathsheba Smith, general president of the LDS Church's Relief Society, said she heard JS say, "Peradventure, the Ten Tribes were not on this globe, but a portion of this earth had cleaved off with them and went flying into space, and when the time comes when the 'earth reels to and fro like a drunken man and the stars from heaven fall,' it would join on again."[74] While the circumstances of JS making such statements are not known, others also claimed to have heard him describe the temporary location of the ten tribes, adding that they were in a hollow in the North Pole or that Jesus's apostle John was among them preparing for their delivery.[75] The teachings have not been advocated by the modern church.

A theme addressed with regularity in JS's ministry was the resurrection of the dead, the glorious result of Jesus's ultimate sacrifice in God's plan to redeem his earthly children. JS obtained in part the broad perspective of the importance of the resurrection and the doctrine of physical/spiritual restoration from the revelation he received in 1829 within the Book of Mormon. While acknowledging to his son Corianton, the Book of Mormon prophet Alma reviewed particulars regarding the resurrection, "there are many mysteries which are kept" by God regarding how Christ brought "to pass the resurrection of the dead" (Alma 40:2, 3). JS thereafter affirmed the promise, though he applied an angle to God's promises likely unfamiliar to modern church members. Wilford Woodruff captured JS stating on March 20, 1842: "All men will come from the grave as they lie down, whether old or young. Their will not be added unto ther stature one cubit neither taken from it[,] All being raised by the power of God having the spirit of God in their bodies & not Blood. Children will be enthroned in the presence of God & the Lamb with bodies of the same stature that were on earth."[76] JS reiterated the statement in an important sermon on May 12, 1844, meant to comfort the hearts of mourning parents in the loss of their children. According to notes taken by Thomas Bullock, in emphasizing the promises regarding the postmortal world, JS reminded parents in the gathering, "in order for you to receive your children to yourself, you must have a promise, some ordinance some blessing <in order to assend above principalities>...they must rise just as they died." That is, beloved children who die in their youth retain the physical dimensions characterizing them when they died; they would not physically grow

73. *Wilford Woodruff Journal*, September 8, 1867, 6:363.

74. Bathsheba W. Smith, "Recollections of the Prophet Joseph Smith," *The Juvenile Instructor*, June 1, 1892, 344.

75. Todd M. Compton, *A Frontier Life: Jacob Hamblin, Explorer and Indian Missionary* (Salt Lake City: University of Utah Press, 2013), 13; Benjamin F. Johnson, *My Life's Review* (Independence, MO: Zion's Printing and Publishing, 1947), 93; and Oliver B. Huntington Diary, Book 14, 62–63, MSS 162.

76. *Wilford Woodruff Journal*, March 20, 1842, 2:163.

in the resurrection. Nevertheless, he continued, "we can there hail our lovely infants with the same glory, the same loveliness in the celestial glory where they all enjoy alike." Furthermore, though "they differ in stature, in size—the same glorious spirit gives them the likeness of glory and bloom." To emphasize the declaration, in the next breath JS declared: "When did I ever teach any thing wrong from this stand? when was I ever confounded?...I never told you I was perfect—but there is no error in the revelations which I have taught."[77] Besides the bold declaration of his revelatory facility, it appears his view on the status of children in the resurrection prevailed beyond his life.

Despite the pronouncement, supported in other statements made by JS, later followers were confused by what appeared to be his articulation of the doctrine.[78] Brigham Young spoke more than once upon the confusion. Explaining the circumstance of JS's position upon the resurrection of children, according to Wilford Woodruff, Young said on January 31, 1861: "The question has often been asked how is it with little Children? Will they grow or not after death? Joseph once said they would, & then He said they would not," though he said JS "never had any revelation upon the subject." Young's perspective suggesting that JS's statement was made of his own accord and not by revelation, qualified his own view of the teaching: "I have no doctrin to give upon the subject."[79] Several years later, again according to Woodruff, President Young said, "He had also herd Joseph say that Children would not Grow after death & at another time that they would grow & he hardly knew how to reconcile it."[80] There the ambiguity rested for a generation. However, a few months before his death in November 1918, LDS Church president Joseph F. Smith related the instance in 1854 when he met with his aunt Agnes Coolbrith Smith, wife of JS's brother Don Carlos Smith, who related that upon the death of one of her children JS told her: "You will have the joy, pleasure, and satisfaction of nurturing this child, after its resurrection, until it reaches the full stature of its spirit."[81] To at least Joseph F. Smith, the problem was resolved, as was, accordingly, the church thereafter. The process illustrates how those who followed had to deal with some of what JS taught.

JS entertained the boundaries of thought and conduct established by God and expected of mankind. It influenced his practical application of revelatory injunctions and shaped his hope and understanding of the eternities. And

77. Smith, Sermon, May 12, 1844, Joseph Smith Collection, Addresses, MS 155, box 4, folder 6, CHL.

78. See discussion of JS's teaching in Ehat and Cook, *Words of Joseph Smith*, 136n22.

79. *Wilford Woodruff Journal*, January 31, 1861, 5:554.

80. Ibid., September 8, 1867, 6:363.

81. Joseph F. Smith, "Status of Children in the Resurrection," *Improvement Era*, May 1918, 571.

though he never involved himself in theological debates as advanced by the philosophers and theologians of the day regarding the nature of God and man, he assumed the role of declarer and was consistent throughout his life in his perceptions of the Almighty and mankind's special creation and earthly purpose. Fundamentals of what he thought and taught survive even today. They are best understood by moderns presented in the context they were delivered.

CHAPTER 14

A Course of Revelation

Line upon Line, Precept upon Precept

JS's declaration that he had been appointed by the Almighty to inaugurate the preparatory events preceding Jesus's second return, set him apart within the American religious landscape. Not only was it impossible for his religious competitors to entertain his assertions, even among the Mormons there was variance in perceptions and compliance. To a collection of elders in Norton, Ohio, fifty miles south of Kirtland, JS described in April 1834 his lament that what he taught was not more readily understood and accepted by church members: "It is very difficult for us to communicate to the churches all that God has revealed to us, in consequence of tradition." This was because "we are differently situated from any other people that ever existed upon this earth: Consequently those former revelations cannot be suited to our condition, because they were given to other people who were before us."[1] Negotiating the contrast between the ancient texts, which underscored his adherents' understanding of God's plan for his children with the layers of new revelation he produced, limited JS in his prophetic role by his own admission. To Brigham Young in Kirtland, JS said, "if I was to reveal to this people what the Lord has revealed to me, there is not a man or woman would stay with me."[2] Heber C. Kimball later quoted the prophet telling a congregation, "would to God I could tell you what I know! but you would call it blasphemy, and there are men on this stand who would want to take my life."[3] Thus, it is reasonable to conclude that there were many things that JS thought and believed during his prophetic tenure that he never delivered to the Saints.

There is little collective data from early adherents of the LDS Church regarding their perceptions about prophetic revelation in the first generation. But

1. Smith, Documents, April 21, 1834, Minute Book 1, *JSP, D4*:15.
2. Brigham Young, Sermon, May 25, 1862, *JD*, 9:294.
3. Orson F. Whitney, *Life of Heber C. Kimball* (Salt Lake City: Bookcraft, 1973), 322, first published in 1888.

within settings of Mormonism where the church established itself, the leaders and people, even with their disparate backgrounds, helped create a cohesive collection of believers on the extended reaches of American civilization. There were limitations obviously. It is probable that one of the reasons the Zion experiment in western Missouri fractured, besides non-Mormon resistance, was the absence of a center of gravity in the person of JS for most of the Saints' tenure there. The Mormon identity with JS as the religion's principal personality is explained by the faithful's acceptance of him and his revelations to influence their lives. Despite the hazards inherent in countering the national ethos, Mormonism penetrated its adherents to the degree that—in spite of the formidable climate of opposition—they progressively acquired the wherewithal to ensure their survival. While perhaps only the Mormons themselves appreciated the scope of their accomplishment, by most any measurement JS and his revelations in his time created a sustained subculture with the necessaries for perpetuation.

One of the significant factors influencing the twentieth-century silent and baby boomer generations' perceptions of what a prophet was in the ancient world, especially among the Mormons, arguably came from Cecil B. DeMille's mid-1950s portrayal of the prophetic figure of Moses in the blockbuster movie, *The Ten Commandments*. Depiction of God's thunderous voice and fiery stylus left no mystery to the audience about how God captured the attention of his designated appointee. It was then up to the chosen one to deliver the message with courage and without restraint. That creative model, however, likely distorts what the evidence suggests was the manner in which JS received direction from God to benefit the fledgling Mormon constituency. Even though there are few examples to illustrate the range of what happened to him and how he enacted his revelatory experiences, the evidence about one significant tenet of the faith portrays his progressive grasp of divine inspiration. This particular illustration defines what JS characterized to be the means by which much of what he delivered to the Saints was conceived: the "line upon line, precept upon precept; here a little, and there a little" method of formulating doctrinal and procedural standards.[4] Developmental Mormon peculiarities such as the evolution of the "word of wisdom" given by JS "not by commandment or constraint" to the tenet later being imposed as a matter of fellowship have been explained by others.[5] But

4. Joseph Smith, "Letter from Joseph Smith," September 6, 1842, *Times and Seasons*, October 1, 1842, 936; D&C 128:21 (1981).
5. See Paul H. Peterson, "An Historical Analysis of the Word of Wisdom" (master's thesis, Brigham Young University, 1972); Thomas G. Alexander, "The Word of Wisdom: From Principle to Requirement," *Dialogue* 14, no. 3 (Autumn 1981): 78–88; Lester E. Bush Jr., "The Word of Wisdom in Early Nineteenth-Century Perspective," *Dialogue* 14, no. 3 (Autumn 1981): 46–65; and Paul H. Peterson and Ronald W. Walker, "Brigham Young's Word of Wisdom Legacy" *BYU Studies* 42, no. 3 (2003): 29–64.

perhaps the best demonstrable textual landmark of JS's prophetic role exhibiting the incremental development of the revelatory chain is his periodic direction regarding the premise of the vicarious salvation of the dead by proxy ordinances.

Melding the Ancient and Modern World

One of the more significant surviving expressions about connections of the living to the dead from JS was one he received during a particularly conflicted time. In September 1842, while secluded from the public to avoid extradition to Missouri and apparently with time to think and contemplate, he prepared a letter for the church that included somewhat of a summary understanding of what he had gained through his ministry.[6] The September 6 epistle, published the following month in the church's *Times and Seasons*, included JS's pronouncement that it was "necessary in the ushering in of the dispensation of the fulness of times; which dispensation is now beginning to usher in, that a whole, and complete, and perfect union, and welding together of dispensations, and keys, and powers, and glories should take place, and be revealed, from the days of Adam even to the present time." But that was not enough, and here he identified his own role. Through divine intervention, he implied he implemented "those things which never have been revealed from the foundation of the world, but have been kept hid from the wise and prudent." Then identifying the ancient prophetic figures who had appeared to and ministered to him, he generalized their role and purpose. He received from "each one their dispensation, their rights, their keys, their honors, their majesty and glory, and the power of their priesthood."[7] Therein he presented himself as one in a line of the biblically great to perpetuate God's mortal plan with the reception of the keys of eternal salvation for the modern world.

One of the most fertile periods of JS's prophetic life, as previously noted, was during the time when he amended the biblical text. The inspired revision he undertook from 1830–1833 likely triggered numerous queries of the Lord by the

6. Andrew H. Hedges, "'They Pursue Me without Cause': Joseph Smith in Hiding and D&C 127, 128," *Religious Educator* 16, no. 1 (2015): 42–59.

7. Smith, "Letter from Joseph Smith," September 6, 1842, *Times and Seasons*, October 1, 1842. LDS Church historian Orson Pratt, by assignment of Brigham Young, prepared a revision and expansion of the D&C published in 1876. Pratt then selected and inserted twenty-six texts under the classification of revelations into the D&C. These included the September 6, 1842, epistle as Section 128. See the historical background and deconstruction of textual formation and emendation of D&C 128 found in Woodford, "Historical Development of the Doctrine and Covenants," 1669–1700; and Richard E. Turley Jr. and William W. Slaughter, *How We Got the Doctrine and Covenants* (Salt Lake City: Deseret Book, 2012), 81–89.

prophet for clarification and understanding in emending the ancient scripture. Even though the "angel of the Lord" emphatically told the Book of Mormon prophet Nephi that "many plain and precious things [were] taken away from the book [the Bible]" by the "great and abominable church,"[8] it is clear that most of the biblical language as rendered in the KJV was left intact. For example, when JS came to the foundational passage regarding entrance into God's kingdom—John 3:5—he deleted in the reworked text only the word "of" from the KJV. He let the concept stand, i.e. "except a man be born of water and the spirit, he cannot enter into the kingdom of God." A review of JS's teachings on the matter shows that he embraced the premise at face value.

During his period of biblical revision Joseph received the significant revelation previously mentioned, "The Vision," a pronouncement that challenged what then was the Christian world's conception of heaven and hell. The directive received in February 1832, known today as Doctrine and Covenants Section 76, built on the apostle Paul's expressions about the resurrection in 1 Corinthians 15:40–42, and in 2 Corinthians 12:2, where Paul implied variations in the resurrection rewards, including the notion of a "third heaven." With JS's later pronouncement that there were "many Kingdoms" in the postmortal world,[9] the progressive revelations he obtained retained the biblical baptismal premise in John 3:5 as imperative. A September 22–23, 1832, revelation about the priesthood emphasized: "They who beleiveth not on your words and are not baptized in water in my name for the remission of there sins that they may receive the holy ghost shall be damned and shall not come into my fathers kingdom where my father and I am."[10] It appeared, then, that the issue of baptism was settled. However, as the Kirtland House of the Lord rose, upon inquiring of the Lord as to the status of his deceased, unbaptized brother Alvin, JS received direction that modified the previous stipulation. In January 1836, while preparing the Saints for the promised heavenly outpouring associated with the solemn assembly attached to the temple's dedication in late March 1836, JS received divine directive that altered his understanding of the salvation landscape. "The heavens were opened upon us and I beheld the celestial kingdom of God, and the glory thereof," he dictated to his scribe. In the vision he explained, "I saw father Adam, and Abraham and Michael and my father and mother, my brother Alvin [Smith] that has long since slept, and marvled how it was that he had obtained ~~this~~ an inheritance <in> ~~this~~ <that> kingdom." It puzzled him, he explained, that Alvin was in the celestial realm given that he "had departed this life, before the Lord <had> set

8. 1 Ne. 13:28, also v. 26, 29, 32, 34.
9. Smith, Revelations, December 27, 1832, *JSP, R1*:228 [D&C 88:37 (1981)].
10. Smith, Revelations, September 22–23, 1832, *JSP, R1*:348–49 [D&C 84: 37 (1981)].

his hand to gather Israel <the second time> and had not been baptized for the remission of sins."[11] The quandary resulted in a communication with concepts of salvation that JS had not previously entertained: "Thus ~~said~~ came the voice <of the Lord un>to me saying all who have died with[out] a knowledge of this gospel, who would have received it, if they had been permited to tarry, shall be heirs of the celestial kingdom, for I the Lord <will> judge all men according to their works according to the desires of their hearts."[12] Though the wicked were still culpable for their deeds as per JS's other declarations, the prophet reframed salvation into something that accommodated the vast numbers of those who had or would never hear the gospel in mortality but who theoretically would otherwise have embraced it. To JS the outlook of eternity had been transformed.

It cannot be demonstrated that JS in 1836 had formulated at that time the vehicle to implement God's plan for the salvation of the dead. It is clear, however, that his confidence and understanding regarding the postmortal plan of God for his children increasingly expanded. After the Mormons relocated themselves in the northern Missouri county of Caldwell and established the community of Far West, the church revived their Kirtland periodical—the *Elders' Journal* initiated in October 1837 that had supplanted the earlier *Messenger and Advocate*. The Kirtland tumult that forced the Saints to relocate to Missouri postponed publication of the third issue until July 1838 in Far West. As mentioned earlier, with JS as the editor, the July installment contained twenty responses to questions JS had posed in the November 1837 issue in Kirtland. Clearly meant as a public relations maneuver, the questions and answers were designed to address issues that had arisen about the Mormons. The sixteenth of the twenty questions read: "If the Mormon doctrine is true what has become of all those who have died since the days of the apostles?" JS's response indicated that the *hereafter* offered options missed in mortality, something he had not previously articulated in print: "All those who have not had an opportunity of hearing the gospel, and being administered to by an inspired man in the flesh, must have it hereafter, before they can be finally judged."[13] While JS may have entertained the idea for some time, this statement was another step beyond the previous revelations he had

11. Smith, Journal, January 21, 1836, *JSP, J1*:167–68 [D&C 137:5–6 (1981)]. When the LDS Church added the text of JS's January 21, 1836, vision to the D&C in 1981, the phrase in the journal that included JS seeing "father Adam, and Abraham and Michael," was redacted to eliminate the name of Michael, given that Adam and Michael are known in Mormon theology as the same person, Michael being the premortal Adam. This suggests that JS's perceptions about those in the eternal world had not yet congealed or that his clerk at the time, Warren Parrish, misunderstood what he stated.

12. Smith, Journal, January 21, 1836, *JSP, J1*:167–68. It is not known how quickly and widely the information he received was made known given the absence of subsequent references to the principle.

13. [No author], *Elders' Journal*, July 1838, 43.

received. The July 1838 reply included implications from 1 Peter in the New Testament where Peter stated, "For this cause was the gospel preached also to them that are dead, that they might be judged according to men in the flesh" (1 Pet. 4:6). JS's thinking by this time suggested that the notion of postmortal chances to satisfy biblical expectations regarding salvation had expanded, though still accommodating the foundational John 3:5 injunction.

The winter of 1838–1839 that JS spent in the dank stone jail in Liberty, Missouri, served as the culmination of another Mormon crucible after displacement from both Ohio and Missouri. The defection of several of his closest associates and the uncertainties facing his people driven from Missouri undoubtedly forced grave concerns as well as great resolve during his four-month imprisonment. The conditions could have broken him. But from them he apparently reconsidered all that he had initiated. Outraged by his incarceration and the plight of the Saints run out of Missouri, within months he mounted his well-known 1839–1840 campaign to the nation's capital to appeal the injustices to the executive and legislative branches of the federal government. Nothing was gained from the venture other than his renewed determination. At the same time that he strategized about how to ameliorate the disaster that had been thrust upon his people, he also introduced a theological concept that proved to be one of the most dominant themes of the last five years of his life.

It is too much to say that JS in 1840 calculated an incremental delivery of the principles of salvation for the dead that had firmed in his mind over the previous months. Still, he set the stage for understanding the innovation at the church's spring conference in Nauvoo that year. Having emphasized the previous year the necessary integration of God's plans for recovery of his children using the biblical line, "they without us ~~could~~ <cannot> be made perfect,"[14] he then used the same language to justify his introduction of proxy ordinances for the dead. His April 8, 1840, conference sermon reiterated, as captured by editors of the *Times and Seasons*, the biblical essential of baptism for entrance into the kingdom of God (John 3:5). He then illustrated the doctrine and concepts of salvation "with a very beautiful and striking figure, and throwing a flood of light on the subjects which were brought up to review."[15] The mortal fundamental emphasized throughout his ministry regarding entrance into God's rest had not diminished despite the expanded information about the requirement he had acquired. By summer's end, in a time of sickness and death in Nauvoo, he had formulated how he would introduce the teaching in a manner that included those who passed away before the restoration of the gospel. Evidence indicates he had already been ruminating upon the matter.

14. Smith, Sermon, n.d. [before 1840], Willard Richards, Pocket Companion, circa 1840, MS 1490, box 2, folder 6, CHL.
15. "Conference Minutes," April 8, 1840, *Times and Seasons*, April 1840, 94.

In what has to be considered one of the most significant revelatory announcements he ever made, he not only shaped how church members would thereafter consider the terrestrial requirements of religious ordinances, he also opened what had been a closed ceiling for some regarding God's eternal plan for all of his children. The idea countered the Calvinistic premise that lingered in much of Christian thought that salvation and damnation were static. He took the occasion of Mormon stalwart Seymour Brunson's funeral on August 15, 1840, to shake up Latter-day Saint thinking about the eternal destinies of their forebears. While we do not have a contemporary report of what he said on that occasion, we know from subsequent sources that he introduced to the Saints an enlightening perspective on what was likely an underlying concern about those who had family members who died, some having not accepted the gospel.[16] George A. Smith, while later serving as LDS Church historian, stated that in his unsuccessful search for a contemporary record of the sermon he found, among other documentation, that the Saints were "astonished" at what they heard.[17] JS expounded the phrase from 1 Corinthians 15:29, stating: "Else what shall they do which are baptized for the dead, if the dead rise not at all? why are they then baptized for the dead." The notion had generally been overlooked by the Christian world, though some had tried to accommodate the concept that explicitly appeared in Paul's writings.[18] JS's grasp of the belief of God's intention to offer salvation and its attendant requirements to the whole of humanity, thereafter underscored the theological and cosmic perspectives he pronounced.

Less than two months after JS's initial announcement of the concept to church members, he began unfolding components of his thinking to the church. The epistle he and the church presidency sent "To the Saints Scattered Abroad," as published in the October issue of the *Times and Seasons*, also coincided with the report of the church's October 1840 general conference. The report indicated JS "spoke of the necessity of building a 'House of the Lord' in this place," which he had determined would facilitate the newly articulated doctrine. "Whereupon it was resolved, that the saints build a house for the worship of God." Like the

16. See Ryan G. Tobler's significant elaboration of the circumstances that may have moved JS to address the concept of baptism for the dead in August 1840 and the subsequent implementation of the doctrine and practice among the Saints. "'Saviors on Mount Zion': Mormon Sacramentalism, Mortality, and the Baptism for the Dead," *Journal of Mormon History* 39, no. 4 (Fall 2013): 182–238.

17. George A. Smith to "Editor of the news," n.d., George A. Smith Papers.

18. See Elias Boudinot, *The Second Advent, or Coming of the Messiah in Glory* (Trenton, NJ: O. Fenton and S. Hutchinson, 1815), in Grunder, *Mormon Parallels*, no. 65 (269); and Jacob[?] Gass and Johan Peter Miller, *Chronicon Ephratense: A History of the Community of Seventh Day Baptists at Ephrata, Lancaster County, Penn'a, by "Lamech and Agrippa"* (Lancaster, PA: S.H. Zahm, 1889), also in Grunder, *Mormon Parallels*, no. 158 (601). See also documentation of other nineteenth-century discussions about baptism for the dead via 1 Cor. 15:29 by the Christian world in Tobler, "Saviors on Mount Zion," 187–88.

Kirtland House of the Lord precedent, what became the Nauvoo Temple held the promise of being a catalyst to empower the Saints through ordinances to perform their latter-day purposes. The following day, October 4, after introducing the premise for a temple there, JS then bore down on what would become one of its constituent parts, delivering "a discourse on the subject of baptism for the dead, which was listened to with considerable interest, by the vast multitude assembled."[19] Temples, or at least temple plans, were central to JS's concept of Zion and the expansion of empowerment to God's people, having been part of the kingdom from the outset: first Jackson County, then Kirtland and Far West, and now Nauvoo. With the revelatory backdrop of 1842, as described in Chapter 9, JS's matured ambitions for church members appeared to materialize in the promises associated with the Nauvoo Temple.

It is worth noting that all of JS's instruction about baptism for the dead and the construction of Nauvoo's temple had been disseminated to the Saints in the absence of the Quorum of the Twelve Apostles. Most of the Twelve were in England at this time, having left for Great Britain in 1839, initiating the second apostolic mission. It is not known to what extent the Twelve Apostles previously knew of what had stirred JS's thinking about salvation for the dead beyond the few disclosures previously mentioned. Given what he wrote to them on December 15, 1840, however, the concept of baptism for the dead was apparently something new to them. Two months after the October conference where he elaborated to the Saints his conviction about the importance of vicarious baptisms, JS wrote to Brigham Young and the Twelve in England. "I presume the doctrine of 'Baptizm for the dead' has ere this reached your ears, and may have raised some inquiries in your mind respecting the same." Noting that the apostle Paul's letter to the Corinthians indicated the New Testament saints incorporated the practice, he stated that now the modern Saints "have the priviledge of being baptized for those of their relatives who are dead, who they feel to believe would have embraced the gospel if they had been priviledged with hearing it, and who have received the gospel in the spirit through the instrumentality of those who may have been commissioned to preach to them while in the prison." JS trusted they would "see its consistancy, and reasonableness," and how it "enlarged" Jesus's gospel.[20] While the Twelve ministered in England, the first baptisms for the dead were performed, likely in the Mississippi River, beginning the month after the Brunson funeral sermon.

19. "To the Saints Scattered Abroad," and "Minutes of the General Conference of the Church of Jesus Christ of Latter Day Saints," October 3–4, 1840, *Times and Seasons*, October 1840, 178–79, 186.

20. Joseph Smith, "Letter to Quorum of the Twelve, 15 December 1840," *JSP, D7*:469–70. Of interest, when an "Extract" of JS's letter to the Twelve Apostles was published in the *Times and Seasons* in January 1841, the paragraph about "baptism for the dead" was not included for publication. The decision to omit in print the teaching about baptism for the dead suggests concern at the time of how the principle would be received by the larger public.

Regrettably, while it appears most Saints readily accepted the concept of baptism for the dead, little was done to capture on paper the significance of the innovative addition to Latter-day Saint theology and practice. Indeed, Brigham Young later stated that while JS had received a revelation on the matter, he apparently failed to record it, and no scribal report was prepared of what he said at the Brunson funeral.[21] LDS Church historian George A. Smith, later lamented:

> In tracing the history of the church I find the Records almost Intirely Destitute of any ~~thing~~ thing correct or Reliable, concerning the Doctrine & administration of the ordinances of babtism for the Dead. I have not only Searched all the Records at my command of a Public nature, but have Saught among Private Journals & from oral statements of various Individuals to make myself acquainted with the history of the Introduction of this Doctrine to the Church, & of the administration[n] of Its ordainances During the Lifetime of the Prophet from the Records kept by James Sloan the church Recorder & Register of Babtisms for the dead[.][22]

What the church had at the time was an unlined volume of just over a hundred pages indicating that some baptisms were recorded beginning on October 21, 1840, suggesting that the baptisms performed prior to that date were not recorded.[23] The record shows something less than a systematic strategy in recording the vicarious work performed.

A few months after introducing the doctrinal concept of baptism for the dead to the Saints, the Saints began the ritual in haphazard fashion. Then the prophet, undoubtedly after stewing about the implications of the principle, obtained further impressions from the Lord that warranted a written revelation; this time applying an official imprimatur formalizing the ordinance. Though the premise for a temple in Nauvoo had been discussed previously, the January 19, 1841, revelation to JS comprised several topics addressing expectations of the Saints. The primary themes specified attention to the necessity of building two edifices: "A house to ~~mine~~ my name" (a temple), that included within it "a baptismal font" for baptisms for the dead, as well as another structure, a "house for

21. Brigham Young, February 10, 1845, Seventies Record, Book B, 1844–1847, 66, CR 3 51, CHL.

22. George A. Smith to "Editor of the [Deseret] news," n.d., George A. Smith Papers. A reminiscence of Simon Baker recounts what he remembered of JS's sermon at the Brunson funeral. Historical Department Journal History of the Church of Jesus Christ of Latter-day Saints, 1830–2008, CR 100 137, August 15, 1840, CHL.

23. "Nauvoo Baptisms for the Dead in the Mississippi River," Family History Library, Salt Lake City, Utah. https://www.familysearch.org/library/books/records/item/386499-nauvoo-baptisms-for-the-dead-in-the-mississippi-river?viewer=1&offset=0#page=1&viewer=picture&o=info&n=0&q=.

boarding" (a hotel), both of which represented a significant spiritual and civic advance within Mormonism.[24] It was slow going, but the months of anticipation materialized.

In the previous year or so, anxious Saints had completed vicarious ordinances for nearly seven thousand deceased family members along with friends and a number of noted American figures such as "Gen George Washington."[25] Many of the transactions were performed, as had baptisms of individuals at the time of their entry into the church, without being recorded. But as the practice became institutionalized, greater care was applied to ensure the activities were given the gravity they warranted. The October 1841 general conference served as the setting to adjust how the vicarious ordinance was being performed among church members. There JS spoke several times "on the doctrine of Baptism for the Dead," declaring it as the only way that men can appear as saviors on Mount Zion. The premise "was listened to with intense interest by the large assembly." But on the conference's third day, JS concluded the morning session with the abrupt statement, "There shall be no more baptisms for the dead, until the ordinance can be attended to in the font of the Lord's House."[26] Resources and energies were then marshaled and on November 8 Brigham Young dedicated the newly constructed wooden baptismal font in the basement of the unfinished temple. Once baptisms were confined to the temple, there were expectations of financial commitment through tithes to access the opportunity to save one's dead.[27]

A pause in JS's public life allowed him an unusual period of time in sequester to contemplate matters that required his attention. Having been put on guard after circulation of charges of his instigation of Lilburn Boggs's attempted assassination, he stepped out of public life knowing he was a wanted man. Coupled with unfinished business to corral the Mormon leader after he fled Missouri jurisdiction in April 1839, he became their public enemy. In collaboration with the state of Illinois, Missouri officials engineered the process to arrest and extradite him to answer for his alleged crimes. Early in August 1842 two deputized authorities from Missouri and Illinois caught up with and arrested JS. The warrant mispresented facts about the charges, specifically that JS had personally initiated

24. Smith, Revelation, January 19, 1841, *JSP, D7*:516–17 [D&C 124: 27, 29, 56 (1981)]. The bulk of the revelation was published in the *Times and Seasons*, June 1, 1841, 424–29.
25. Haven, "A Girl's Letters from Nauvoo," 630; M. Guy Bishop, "'What Has Become of Our Fathers?' Baptism for the Dead at Nauvoo," *Dialogue* 23, no. 2 (Summer 1990): 89; Susan Easton Black and Harvey Bischoff Black, comps., *Annotated Record of Baptism for the Dead, 1840–1845*, 7 vols. (Provo, UT: Brigham Young University Press, 2002), 1:v.
26. Smith, Sermon, October 3, 1841, "Minutes of a Conference of This Church of Jesus Christ of Latter Day Saints," *Times and Seasons*, October 15, 1841, 578.
27. Bishop, "'What Has Become of Our Fathers?,'" 93.

the assault on Boggs as an "accessory before the fact to an assault with intent to kill" Boggs.[28] Though there was ample proof that JS was in Nauvoo during the attack, that underlying fact did not prevent the attempts of government officials to bring him to their justice. Freed in the short term by counter measures, JS then spent most of the next two months hiding, believing that both states were in league to lay the assassination attempt at his door.

Yearning to connect with the Saints during his seclusion, on September 1, 1842, he "wrote" a letter to the church that included a portion about baptism for the dead illustrating the importance to him at the time of the doctrine and practice. William Clayton, JS's clerk and aide, distributed the unusual communiqué to the Saints as JS stayed low to avoid the clutch of Missouri law. The directive, besides addressing the urgency of building the Nauvoo Temple, included another element of the practice, adding further institutional attachment to the ordinance. With the imprimatur of "thus saith the Lord" to his words, the statement emphasized: "When any of you are baptised for your dead, let there be a Recorder; and let him be eye witness of your baptisms; let him hear with his ears, that he may testify of a truth, said the Lord." The directive insisted that the "records be had in order" for preservation and "remembrance from generation to generation,"[29] illustrating how the practice formalized.

Indicating the press of the matter upon his mind even while under duress, and still determined to elude capture by Missouri and Illinois, several days later JS dictated a letter on September 6, 1842, expanding on the September 1 epistle. Baptism for the dead, he wrote, "seems to occupy my mind, and press itself upon my feelings the strongest, since I have been pursued by my enemies." Continuing, he stated, "I have had a few additional views in relation to this matter, which I now certify." The ordinances, he said, had to be verified in records kept by clerks in each ward so "the general church recorder can enter the record on the general church book." Particulars of the work was important, he declared, "to answer the will of God."[30] Both September 1842 letters were then printed in the church's *Times and Seasons* within weeks, establishing once more among church members JS's insistence on the importance of the doctrine and practice of salvation for the dead through ordinances of the gospel.

28. "Persecution," *Times and Seasons*, August 15, 1842, 888.

29. Joseph Smith, "Tidings," September 1, 1842, *Times and Seasons*, September 15, 1842, 919–20; D&C 127:5–7, 9 (1981). The letter was added to the new 1844 edition of the D&C prepared just prior to the death of JS. Smith, Revelation, September 1, 1842, *JSP, R*2:678–80 [D&C 105 (1844)].

30. Joseph Smith, Letter, September 6 [7], 1842, *Times and Seasons*, October 1, 1842, 934; D&C 128: 1–5 (1981). Like the September 1, 1842, letter to the Saints from JS, the September 6, 1842, epistle was added to the D&C in 1844 and then in Orson Pratt's 1876 revision of the book at Brigham Young's charge.

While some of JS's teachings on salvation for the dead were later codified in the 1844 Doctrine and Covenants revision, a primary vehicle for his dissemination of God's revelations toward the end of his life came via his sermons. In his last months, he tried to explain to the Saints the breadth of what he had envisioned. His expansive expressions of revelation during the April 1844 general conference are noted for their elaboration of several doctrinal/theological/cosmological features he had formerly introduced. It is evident that he had been contemplating the notions for some time. He stepped up to share these ideas with the people at a time when serious internal complications of disaffection confronted him. He responded with an outpouring of information reemphasizing some of what he had taught before, as well as never before delivered revelation.[31] Besides his famous April 7, 1844, King Follett funeral discourse, he revealed via sermons on March 10, April 8, May 12, May 26, and June 16, important doctrinal declarations summarizing his thinking. His clarification of his followers' role in the salvation of their deceased ancestors was used as a primary theme to update them on an enlarging scope of their responsibility and opportunity.

Two sermons he gave during the church's April 1844 general conference are remembered as being particularly pointed regarding salvation for the dead. Willard Richards, who kept JS's journal at the time, reported him stating: "We are looked upon by God as though we were in Eternity—the greate[s]t responibity resting upon us is to look after our dead.—they without us cann[o]t be made perfct,"[32] referencing a theme he had been preaching for at least five years. From the rudimentary premise of baptism for the dead in August 1840, the following day of the conference he significantly expanded the vicarious work's range. As William Clayton reported, JS stated, "when we want to save our dead we go through all the ordinan[c]es same as for ourself from bap[tism] to ordination & end[owmen]^{t}.... there must be a particular spot for the sal[vation]. of our dead."[33] Thus, not only baptisms, but also all other sacred Mormon ordinances required living proxies to enable the dead in the eternities. Wilford Woodruff's notes of the April 8 sermon included his understanding that "when the place is prepared you must go through all the ordinances of the house of the Lord so that you who have any dead friends must go through all the ordinances for them the same as for yourselves." The temple was the "place ordained for the redeeming of the dead."[34] The following month JS returned to his then persistent refrain regarding the Saints' obligation to substitute for their deceased relatives to receive the full range of salvific mortal ordinances associated with the Mormon

31. See *Wilford Woodruff Journal*, March 7, 1844, 2:354–55.
32. Smith, Sermon, April 7, 1844, Willard Richards, scribe, *JSP, J*3:220.
33. Smith, Sermon, April 8, 1844, William Clayton, scribe.
34. *Wilford Woodruff Journal*, April 8, 1844, 2:388.

temple. It "is not only necessary," he stated, "that you should be baptized for your dead, but you will have to go thro' all the ordinances for them, same as you have gone through, to save yourselves."[35] The adaptation of sacred ritual within the temple, though only partially implemented in Nauvoo, marked a significant milestone within Mormonism. When seen in this light, it is clear that the biblically inspired baptisms, washings, and anointings associated with the Mormon tenure in Kirtland were initiatory in the very sense of the word.

Brigham Young's summary a few months after JS's death regarding the progressive course of the prophet's revelations shows Young's understanding of the incremental expansion of JS's revelatory experience. In the incomplete Nauvoo Temple on a Monday evening in February 1845, Brigham explained to the seventies, that upon returning from England in 1841, JS told him about baptism for the dead. Brigham emphasized that "the particulars connected with the ordinance" were not "revealed at the time the Revelation was first given." Soon, more "Revelation was given commanding him to appoint a clerk and witness that it might be as it was written, that out of the mouth of two or three witnesses every word or order should be established and written. Furthermore, he stated, "Neither was it revealed to Br Jos at that time, who would be the proper Persons to be baptized for and in behalf of the dead, nor where & when this servis should be attended too." Young concluded the rehearsal stating, "Br Jos laid a foundation for a great work, even a greater [one] than any other man in this generation; but let <me> tell, he did not have every thing revealed to him pertaining to Carring [carrying] out the work of the Lord—nether was it nessary."[36] A few weeks later on April 6, 1845, Brigham conveyed in public what he had told the seventies previously, though he added another angle: "When the doctrine of baptism for the dead was first given, this church was in its infancy, and was not capable of receiving all the knowledge of God in its highest degree."[37] But as JS grew and developed, so also did the scope of his prophetic vision.

Bathsheba Wilson Smith, wife of JS's cousin George A. Smith and later general president of the LDS Church's Relief Society organization, suggested that the Saints were not aware of the extent of the information JS had obtained about the premise of salvation for the dead. She later reported in the church's *Woman's Exponent*, "The last words she had heard the Prophet say were, that he wanted to preach a sermon on baptism for the dead for he had received a revelation on that subject, but he never had the opportunity to preach again."[38] We derive from

35. Smith, Sermon, May 12, 1844, Thomas Bullock, scribe, Joseph Smith Collection, Addresses, MS 155, box 4, folder 6, CHL.

36. Young, February 10, 1845, Seventies Record, Book B, 1844–1847, 66.

37. Brigham Young, "Speech," April 6, 1845, City of Joseph [Nauvoo], *Times and Seasons*, July 1, 1845, 954.

38. Bathsheba W. Smith, July 20, 1906, "Relief Society Reports," *Women's Exponent*, September 1906, 18.

this recollection that JS had acquired yet further inspiration regarding baptism for the dead that he took with him to the grave.

In Young's speech on April 6, 1845, he underscored that the step-by-step process of divine direction illustrated in JS's revelations was the method by which God would continue to inform the church: "Joseph in his life time did not receive everything connected with the doctrine of redemption, but he has left the key with those who understand how to obtain and teach to this great people all that is necessary for their salvation and exaltation in the celestial kingdom of our God."[39] Young implied that JS's successors had been sufficiently endowed with direction and understanding that they were equipped to carry on the revelatory procedures for the Saints then and later. The incremental acquisition of direction about salvation for the dead may not typify how other concepts were impressed upon JS's mind. Some notions like the "first principles and ordinances of the gospel," i.e., faith, repentance, baptism, and the gift of the Holy Ghost, remained constant throughout JS's ministry. But he transformed other significant matters such as marital practice, Mormon cosmology, priesthood order, and the eternal destiny of mankind over time.

Revelations and Joseph Smith's Religion

The nature of JS's revelations has proven to be a significant tool for both believers and nonbelievers to assemble their views of the prophet. Latter-day Saints have generally believed the source of JS's divine pronouncements came from Jesus Christ. His revelations state as much: "Hearken ~~ye~~ & listen to the voice of him who is from all eternity to all eternity the great I am even Jesus Christ th[e] light & the life of the world."[40] For many it was accepted that the words were literal expressions of Jesus's voice and language. Besides the revelations of great magnitude, it did not matter to the faithful that some prophetic statements were mundane or seemingly inconsequential for the church at large. Others, however, did not share such acceptance. One early twentieth-century historian of Illinois sneered that, "Mormonism substituted a religion of revelation to Joseph Smith by a God who could announce the names of the trustees of the Nauvoo House and prescribe that his servant Joseph Smith and his seed should forever receive free board there," as well as "revelations commanding that this man should tarry here and that man should go there, revelations admonishing, reproving, and praising his followers by name."[41] The Saints, however, were not put off by the commonness of some of what JS advanced as revelation. Significant matters, such as the framework for church administration via the "Articles and Covenants

39. Young, "Speech," *Times and Seasons*, July 1, 1845, 955.
40. Smith, Revelations, January 5, 1831, *JSP, R1*:68 [D&C 39: 1–2 (1981)].
41. Theodore Calvin Pease, *The Frontier State, 1818–1848* (1918; repr. Urbana: University of Illinois Press, 1987), 341.

of the Church of Christ,"[42] or the designation of Independence, Missouri, as the "city of Zion,"[43] were complemented by the range of divine direction reflecting their view of God as a personal, empathetic being preoccupied with their welfare. Others fit their image of God as a proactive, involved personage whose concern could be also shown in commonplace issues that affected church members. Perhaps JS's pronouncements may have been easier to comprehend for some had they been labeled as A revelations (the extremely consequential ones), B revelations (the strategic ones), C revelations (the personal ones to adherents that may or may not be classed A or B), or D revelations (the more everyday ones meant "to keep his followers in order").[44] Instead, there is no calculator to discriminate and sort the gravity of the divinely inspired words.

The manner in which JS presented the revelations he received, often introduced with the wording "thus saith the Lord," justified his expectation of how they would be received by church members. As the divine expressions circulated, first by handwritten copies and later by the printed word, evidence indicates the adherents took seriously the attribution JS gave to them as representing Jesus's mind and will. How the concept was viewed through the years, though, has varied. Orson Whitney, for example, wrote in 1905—the centennial year of JS's birth—about the nature of the text produced by JS in his revelations: "We come face to face with his literary style, as stamped upon the word of God of which he was the original revelator. Here are no translations, such as the Book of Mormon and the Book of Abraham; here is no revision, such as the 'Inspired Translation;' but revelation, immediate and direct, constituting him the sole human oracle of the divine utterance."[45] Another of the church apostles, John A. Widtsoe in 1951 explained his understanding of JS's contributions to the revelations at the time: "Except in revelations copied from spoken words of celestial messengers, the language of the revelations is almost wholly the language of Joseph Smith, made forceful and eloquent by the exaltation of inspiration. God gives the ideas; the Prophet expresses them as best he can."[46] Thus, understanding of the precise meaning of "the word of the Lord" remains subject to the eye of the beholder.[47]

Though Latter-day Saints remain the primary enthusiasts of JS's capacity, some outside of Mormonism have sensed the power of his revelations. Harold

42. "The Articles and Covenants of the Church of Christ," *Evening and the Morning Star*, June 1832, [1]; D&C 20 (1981).

43. Smith, Revelations, July 20, 1831, *JSP, R1*:122 [D&C 57: 2–3 (1981)].

44. Pease, *Frontier State*, 341.

45. Orson F. Whitney, "Joseph Smith in Literature," *Improvement Era*, December 1905, 142.

46. Widtsoe, *Joseph Smith*, 262. See also John A. Widtsoe, *The Message of the Doctrine and Covenants* (Salt Lake City: Bookcraft, 1969), 9.

47. Smith, Revelations, August 30, 1831, *JSP, R1*:139 [D&C 63:1 (1981)].

Bloom, for instance, prefaced his 1994 volume *The Western Canon* with a pointed characterization of JS's prophetic facility. Defining the leading voices contributing to Western culture—such as Shakespeare, Goethe, Freud, Dickenson—Bloom next identified the three principal "shocks" that kickstarted that culture: Moses, Jesus, and Mohammed. This then followed: "Perhaps some day, well on in the twenty-first century when Mormonism has become the dominant religion of at least the American West, those who come after us will experience a fourth such shock when they encounter the daring of the authentic American prophet Joseph Smith in his definitive visions, *The Pearl of Great Price* and *Doctrine and Covenants*."[48] Even Fawn Brodie, who dismissed JS's legitimacy as an authentic designee of God, acknowledged, "At times he appropriated the lyrical style of the Bible so expertly that the instrument sounded under his touch with astonishing brilliancy and purity of tone."[49]

Though the Book of Mormon is the artifact by which he is most often appraised, and upon which many outside the faith attribute the basis of Mormonism, it is arguable that JS's subsequent revelations were equally influential in how he built and shaped his people. His revelations (and later his sermons) may be the most relevant means to measure his prophetic aura. He dared to speak the "word of the Lord." And though he often displayed the physiognomy of an extraordinary man, his normality and acquaintance with the struggles of life precluded him from transcending his circumstances. Still, he exhibited throughout his adulthood his identity as a prophet of God. And though he may not fit the model for moderns of a Moses-like figure created by Hollywood, the revelations he produced and how their content characterizes the outward expressions of his self-identity as a prophet, remain among the most important measurements to apply to his brief life.

48. Harold Bloom, *The Western Canon: The Books and School of the Ages* (New York: Harcourt Brace, 1994), 6 (emphasis in original).
49. Brodie, *No Man Knows My History*, 93.

CHAPTER 15

Prophet, Seer, and Revelator

Within a generation of America's independence from the *old world* a swell of emotion and religious engagement typified the *new world* aspirations of its constituents. The permutation of post-Revolutionary War Christianity into transformative manifestations that paralleled the political commotion that had erupted in North America split and divided, and split and divided again, the veneer of the country's religion. The "Second Great Awakening" triggered a surge of religious emotion across the countryside and made religious orators and itinerant preachers famous in the land. "Christendom had probably not witnessed a comparable period of religious upheaval since the [sixteenth-century] Reformation—and never such an explosion of entrepreneurial energy," asserted Nathan Hatch.[1] Men—and women—of vision, charismatic and spiritual power, along with yearnings for destinies shown by their heroic defense of "Christ crucified," or some variation of that objective, pricked the curiosity of their countrymen with vigor and relentless evangelical innovation. Individuals whose names, many now forgotten, were undoubtedly known to early Mormons—Timothy Dwight, Nathaniel William Taylor, Bennet Tyler, Asahel Nettleton, Lyman Beecher, Charles Grandison Finney, and Mother Ann Lee, to name a few—and cast American religion into configurations never before imagined.

JS's bold and naïve entrance into the arena of the religious luminaries, with his declarations about God and Jesus to post-Revolutionary America, had little chance of acceptance. Nevertheless, with visions and self-perception that at least in his own mind set him apart from the limited world he saw about him, what he witnessed, felt, and heard left him with no recourse but to respond to the impulses that moved him. Because he preferred to keep his thinking to himself, we know little except generalizations about how he negotiated his circumstances at

1. Hatch, *Democratization of American Christianity*, 225–26.

the time. He did explain, however, the imprint upon his mind left by his childhood nurturing in biblical belief that undoubtedly marked his thinking about God's ancient work and its foretold implications for his world. His own professions of profound interest in ascertaining heavenly approbation resulting in his early visions, given all that transpired thereafter, suggests his unyielding determination to follow what he claimed was his commission from the Almighty. Whether or not he initially saw himself in prophetic terms is impossible to determine. But we extrapolate from his later narratives that he soon saw himself as far more than a local figure. He had designs because of what he experienced, adolescent though they initially appear to be, to actually trigger the restoration of Jesus's gospel in preparation for the Lord's Second Advent.

Widespread familiarity of biblical text by early nineteenth-century Americans, despite the equally prevalent variation in belief and practice, presented common notions of heroic Judeo-Christian personalities portrayed in the Bible. From the sacred texts, the voices of men like Ezekiel, Jeremiah, Amos, Hosea, Peter, and Paul became regular models to emulate. A prophet, as one 1830 Bible dictionary defined the term, besides being one who foretold "what is yet to come," was "a person inspired and appointed by God to reveal his will, to warn of approaching judgments, to explain obscure passages of Scripture, or to make known the truths of the Bible, and urge men to obedience."[2] But stereotypes of what the attributes were that made such a man in those days were probably created from perceptions that they and their miracles exceeded human norms. The *Oxford Companion to the Bible* concedes today that there is no universally accepted or "comprehensive definition of an Israelite prophet," but that along with their larger-than-life reputations those of this designation in biblical tradition usually "manifested great diversity of character and function."[3] "The word in Hebrew for a prophet is *nābî'*, understood to mean 'called.'" It is the recognition that men on earth could be the emissaries of the Almighty. But being a "prophet was not an office or profession like judge or priest. A person from any occupation could come to be prophet. The prophet Ezekiel was a priest; the prophet Amos was a cowboy." To the Israelites, those called by God had to "perform a special task with regard to the people."[4] The Americans who tried to mimic the biblical world readily appreciated the role of ancient prophets.

As Christianity became a fixture of life in North America, some religious figures provoked comparisons to heroic Hebrew antecedents among those who hearkened to their enthusiasm. When Francis Asbury emigrated from England

2. Howard Malcom, *A Dictionary of Important Names, Objects, and Terms, Found in the Holy Scriptures. Intended Principally for Youth* (Boston: Lincoln and Edmands, 1830), 177, quoted in Grunder, *Mormon Parallels*, no. 232.
3. Metzger and Coogan, "Prophets," *Oxford Companion to the Bible*, 621.
4. Richard Elliot Friedman, *Who Wrote the Bible?* (New York: Summit Books, 1987), 36.

to North America in the 1770s with John Wesley's Methodism in his valise, he was so successful that he eventually acquired the standing of being the founder of Wesleyan belief in what became the United States. Asbury's fervent, ambitious model of Methodism, became noted as something beyond effective preaching. The appellations of "apostle" and "prophet" were applied to him representing the remarkable work that he did revitalizing the work of his biblical predecessors.[5] Numerous religious enthusiasts thereafter paralleled Asbury's vision of Christianizing the New World.

With eager and receptive prospects spreading from the seaboard cites into America's interior, the opportunity to fashion a unique contribution to God's work took root. The early American republic proved a fertile time for religious regeneration and the lustrous characters it produced. With diverse manifestations of the spirit and claims to extraordinary dispensations from God, normative religion had expanded far beyond Calvinist Congregationalism. Options for both leaders and followers enlarged the forecast of a renewal of primitive Christianity, though many of the novelties were short lived. A volatile and impatient clientele loomed as a field ready to harvest.

As implied above, a number of the religious personalities in the post-Revolutionary period were thought of as prophetic-type figures. While some named above are known today for their durable impact upon American religious history, others like lesser-known Isaac Bullard (leader of "the Pilgrims" in Vermont beginning in 1817), provoked attention in their time because of their odd and charismatic claims of God's prophetic imprimatur.[6] JS, thrown into the mix, immediately became suspect. He conveniently fit, according to a Vermont newspaper in 1831, into the same fraudulent niche Bullard had recently occupied. "Our readers will recollect a similar delusion which raged some ten years ago in the case of the 'Pilgrims.' Their Prophet—Old Isaac [Bullard], as he was called—came from Canada with a few, and encamped in Woodstock [Vermont]." The "Pilgrims's" nonsense, the report declared, outraged "not Christianity only but humanity, by their absurd opinions and absurder practice—by taking the assertions of their infatuated leader for divine revelation." Bullard and his followers had "induced many decent people who should have known better to join them, under the empty promise of being led to the holy land." It was not unreasonable for many then to assign "resemblances between the Pilgrims and Mormonites in manners and pretensions." Indeed, the Vermont Chronicle asserted, "we should think Old Isaac had re-appeared in the person of Joe Smith, and was intending

5. Ezra Squier Tipple, *Francis Asbury: The Prophet of the Long Road* (New York: Methodist Book Concern, 1916), 14, 23, 32, 45, 60, 77, 161, 181, 182, 259, 280, 327.
6. F. Gerald Ham, "The Prophet and the Mummyjums: Isaac Bullard and the Vermont Pilgrims of 1817," *Wisconsin Magazine of History* 56, no. 4 (Summer 1973): 290–99.

to make another speculation."[7] The representation shows the chilly reception that confronted JS in his time. Not just anyone could make assertions of God's special attention and expect an audience and, if they really possessed the gifts, a following that matured into something that transcended their own personality.

Mormons today have been prone from hindsight to argue that America with its Judeo-Christian values, coupled with the guarantees of political freedom and religious liberty at the beginning of the nineteenth century, created a climate favorably conducive to JS and the emergence of his religion. No one at the time except JS and his followers believed such a notion, given the pitiful situation of the faith. Still, he declared that he was not just a preacher or even a clergyman but something more. Upon the organization of the church he informed those who embraced the "restored gospel" that Jesus had designated him God's adjunct on earth.[8] Over time the revelations he received identified him as "a Seer, a revelator, a translator, & a prophet, having all the gifts of God, which he bestoweth upon the head of the chu[r]ch." As one might imagine, there were few notions more off putting to Americans than that someone like JS had the audacity to proclaim that he had been appointed by the Almighty to be "like unto Moses."[9] But JS never shied from the premise, despite the indignation his impudence created among Americans.

Those who became Mormons had been nurtured in the biblical models of prophetic authority and definition. The appeal that a man among them had been designated by God as the modern extension of his sacred work in the ancient world, filled a latent hope among some of the people. A modern prophet called by God, of the biblical stripe, therefore became a principal proclamation of Mormon adherents and their missionaries who presented their message within the biblical context. The nineteenth-century understanding of the prophetic role accommodated, for some at least, the possibility that God could again speak from heaven; there was enough in the New Testament about end times and Jesus's fulfilment of the biblical saga portending something spectacular, with attendant warnings about imposters. Americans had become accustomed to read about them in the media of the day. Some lasted longer than others. When the youthful JS climbed to the soapbox to assert his appointment there is little wonder that he immediately became in the minds of most Americans just another claimant to the favor of the biblical God who by that time had settled into a configuration proposed by Protestant America. But in JS, the offering included new scripture on a scale unfamiliar to seekers.

7. "The Mormon Delusion," *Vermont Chronicle*, June 24, 1831. See also Grunder, *Mormon Parallels*, no. 11.
8. Smith, Revelations, April 6, 1830, *JSP, R1*:22 [D&C 21:1 (1981)].
9. Smith, Revelations, November 11, 1831, *JSP, R1*:171 [D&C 107:92 (1981)].

The Circumstances of Joseph's Sacred Texts

The means of revelation consumed JS once he stepped into his role. What he did beginning in 1828 via the books of Mormon, Moses, Abraham, and the Doctrine and Covenants were remarkable literary productions derived from someone like him. While his detractors are reluctant to concede the phenomenon, stripped from polemics the texts have been difficult to explain coming from the Vermont farm boy. The significance of the Book of Mormon as representative of his revelations cannot be overstated, despite formidable criticism of its authenticity as a historical record by the curious and detractors alike. Overlooking the Book of Mormon's emphatic objective to declare and define Jesus's messianic performance as savior and redeemer, with the lesser objectives of reasserting God's primacy in mankind's affairs, misses the book's most remarkable illustration of JS's prophetic role. Others see as much. "The Book of Mormon should rank among the great achievements of American literature," stated Pulitzer Prize-winning historian Daniel Walker Howe, "but it has never been accorded the status it deserves, since Mormons deny Joseph Smith's authorship, and non-Mormons, dismissing the work as a fraud, have been more likely to ridicule than read it."[10] Similarly, Gordon Wood, while not affirming the scriptural nature of the book as would the Mormons, asserted, "The Book of Mormon is an extraordinary work of popular imagination and one of the greatest documents in American cultural history."[11] And as mentioned previously, Wayne Hudson, the non-Mormon scholar of religion in Australia, classified the book as a reflection of JS being "a genuine prophet" in terms of who he was and what he produced, in particular the Book of Mormon. Further, Hudson waved off those "who reduce Joseph's prophethood to automatic writing, religious genius, or folk occultism," also stating that those who attempt "to reduce the Book of Mormon to Joseph's own biography are absurdly insensitive to the greatness and range of the book."[12]

Yet, despite such acknowledgments, the Book of Mormon continues to be used by opponents to disqualify JS, as to discredit him and the book compromises Mormon foundational claims. Nevertheless, the postulations advanced to explain away the book and its implications of JS as a determined fraud have never surpassed the circumstances of his production of a six hundred-page book in sixty days, via dictation of a clean text with but few exhibits of cross outs, erasures, insertions, redactions, etc., evident in the transcription.[13] The contextual

10. Howe, *What Hath God Wrought*, 314.

11. Wood, "Evangelical America and Early Mormonism," 381.

12. Hudson, "Prophethood of Joseph Smith," 201, 202, 206.

13. See for example, Royal Skousen's "Critical Text of the Book of Mormon Project." Volume 1, *The Original Manuscript of the Book of Mormon* was published in 2001; volume 2, *The Printer's Manuscript of the Book of Mormon* in two parts also appeared in 2001; volume 3, *The History of the Text of the Book of Mormon* in two parts was published in 2016;

circumstances of what JS and Oliver Cowdery did between April 7 and the end of June 1829 demand, in explaining how they could do such a thing, much more than anyone has presented to date. Cowdery's own corroboration of the process remains among the formidable marks of the extraordinary collaboration. The magnitude and implications of the book—manifest by selected internal and external evidences—are used by both defenders and detractors to buttress their arguments.[14] In the end, the book—no matter how JS created it—exhibits the astonishing artifact that illustrates the centrality of JS's occupation of deriving from heaven the divine will in creation of religious literature. Whether his claims match how the texts are viewed is generally determined by the attitude of the readers in approaching JS's prophetic claims.

JS's claims of revelatory facility have also provoked speculation about his purported insight into the origins of Jewish, early Christian, and Western traditions that fueled his religion-making thinking. A revelation he received in May 1833 added a dimension of cosmic construction to Mormonism that proved within a few years after its reception to be a central component of the undergirding Mormon premise that explained not only the postmortal potential of the human family but also its eternal origins. JS stated that Jesus told him that not only was he, Jesus, "in the beginning with the father," but JS, as well as the rest of mankind, "were also in the beginning with the Father." Summarized by the declaration, "Man was also in the beginning with God" and that "Intelligence, or the light of truth, was not created or made,"[15] fixed JS's explanation of God's plans for his children in infinite terms. Most often used by Mormons to explain the spiritual nursery of sorts that preceded earth life, notions of a premortal existence gave gravity to concepts of freewill and eternal purpose that at the time generally separated Mormons from most of their Christian counterparts. Another revelation JS obtained a few years later confirmed the premise. The ancient patriarch Abraham was alleged to have written a significant clarification about man's premortal existence: "Now the Lord had shewn unto me, Abraham,

---

and the second edition of his six-part *Analysis of Textual Variants of the Book of Mormon* was published in 2017 (Provo, UT: FARMS, Brigham Young University, 2001–2017).

14. See for example, affirmative studies by Noel B. Reynolds, ed., *Book of Mormon Authorship Revised* (Provo, UT: Foundation for Ancient Research and Mormon Studies, 1997); Terryl L. Givens, *By the Hand of Mormon: The American Scripture that Launched a New World Religion* (New York: Oxford University Press, 2002); Grant Hardy, *Understanding the Book of Mormon: A Reader's Guide* (New York: Oxford University Press, 2010). Other scholarly studies of a different perspective include Brent Lee Metcalfe, ed., *New Approaches to the Book of Mormon: Explorations in Critical Methodology* (Salt Lake City: Signature Books, 1993); Vogel, *Joseph Smith*, 130–465; Palmer, *An Insider's View*, 39–133; and Simon G. Southerton, *Losing a Lost Tribe: Native Americans, DNA, and the Mormon Church* (Salt Lake City: Signature Books, 2004).

15. Smith, Revelations, May 6, 1833, *JSP, R1*:255–56 [D&C 93:21, 23, 29 (1981)].

the intelligences that were organized before the world was; and among all these there were many of the noble and great ones" (Abr. 3:22–23).[16] Followed by JS's conceptual portrayals of the idea, the resulting doctrinal absorption by the Saints of the premise thereafter significantly influenced Mormon theology and cosmology.[17] Mormon scholar Terryl Givens presented a comprehensive overview of how the conception of premortal existence was a widely held proposition that could be found in Semitic, Greek/Roman, and post-first-century expressions that helped form Western thought. But "Unlike many paradigms that have succumbed to philosophical or scientific critique, preexistence was not really vanquished in a contest of ideas." However, continuing discussion about preexistence in Christian thought apparently fell the "victim of collateral damage" and became a "casualty of the theological and political battles that rages throughout the early Christian world."[18] Thus, when JS built the thinking into the corpus of Mormon thought, he "appears to be one of the few Christian thinkers to develop notions of preexistence" not dependent on classical expressions of the concept. JS's "unique" presentation of the factor of premortal life, "unlike virtually all other versions," "did not arise out of Smith's engagement with any particular moral, theological, or philosophical dilemma."[19]

A few other scholars have attempted to consign JS's unique religious construction and thinking to antiquity, something more than modern coincidental expression. John L. Brooke, a Tufts University history professor stated, "Joseph Smith's cosmology becomes comprehensible only when it is placed in a setting broader than that of antebellum America." Though he conceded his premise to be "theological *conjuncture*," Brooke attributed JS's elaborations, rather than being rooted in early American thinking, to the "extreme perfectionism forged in the Radical Reformation from the fusion of Christianity with the ancient occult hermetic philosophy."[20] That is, JS's exposure to folk belief, which included acceptance of magic, alchemy, and other theological esoterica at the beginning of the nineteenth century, was derived from two centuries of philosophy that had survived on the religious underground in Europe and colonial America. Though Brooke's conclusions have been openly challenged by Mormon scholars such as Richard Bushman who stated that "to informed Latter-day Saint readers

16. Joseph Smith, "The Book of Abraham," *Times and Seasons*, March 15, 1842, 720.

17. See Mormon apostle Orson Pratt's early elaboration on "The Pre-existence of Man," serialized in his *The Seer*, February–September 1853, 17–24, 37–41, 49–57, 65–72, 81–89, 97–104, 113–121.

18. Givens, *When Souls Had Wings*, 322.

19. Ibid., 216–17.

20. Brooke, *Refiner's Fire*, xiv, xvi.

who know Mormonism well, the book crumbles to dust," because Brooke "forces connections with hermetic philosophy that simply cannot be shown to exist,"[21] it nevertheless indicates entertainment of the idea that JS's religious world and thinking was much larger than simply attributing it to the phenomena of the "burned-over district."

Besides JS's periodically intense study of the Bible in the three years following the publication of the Book of Mormon and the subsequent foray into what became known as the Book of Abraham, he also apparently showed, in one scholar's thinking, a proclivity to the first-century Christian church not previously attributed to him. Aziz Suryal Atiya, born in Egypt in 1898 and his country's first Fulbright scholar in 1951, after a distinguished career in other settings became professor of Languages and History at the University of Utah in 1959. Dr. Atiya gained a reputation as a world-recognized scholar of the Coptic faith—one of the earliest surviving sects of Christianity—highlighted by his instigation of and appointment as editor-in-chief of the eight-volume *Coptic Encyclopedia* published by Macmillan (1991). With that background and through a number of coincidental circumstances, Atiya became familiar with JS and thereafter fit the Mormon prophet into a late manifestation of the early Coptic world.

Atiya is known for accidentally discovering in the 1960s at the New York Metropolitan Museum what became known as the Joseph Smith Papyri now associated with the LDS Church's Book of Abraham. He later helped negotiate the transfer of the papyri from the museum to the LDS Church. Though he did not credit the documents as actually representing the literal writings of Abraham, his subsequent relationship with church leaders allowed him to share with them mutual interest in ancient texts and his perception of Mormon connections to the Coptic world. To one LDS Church leader he said, "'I could read some of the gnostic [Coptic] articles...as if I were reading L.D.S. theological institutions.' Yet the men who wrote such articles know nothing about Mormonism and are not Mormons."[22] While he had "a lot of doubts about a lot of things in Mormonism," what he had gathered about JS provoked his curiosity about the sources from which he obtained his information, including JS's apparent uncanny perceptions of first-century Christian thinking. Atiya posed: "How Joseph Smith knew all this, I don't know." JS, he said, was "very erudite, more [so] than Mormons think." Given his own background in the Coptic milieu,

21. Bushman, *Believing History*, 280. See other critiques of Brooke noted in Bushman, "A Joseph Smith for the Twenty-First Century," *BYU Studies* 40, no. 3 (2001): 170–71n28.
22. Aziz S. Atiya, interview, August 12, 1985, 46–47, interviewed by Everett L. Cooley, Everett L. Cooley Oral History Project no. 42, University of Utah Marriott Library, Manuscripts Division, Salt Lake City, Utah.

he was baffled, he said, that JS "knew more of the Copts than the Copts themselves." But "Where he got his information, I don't know."[23] He later conceded, "Mormons claim Joseph Smith received [his insight] from God; I say he received it from the Copts.... Mormonism is derived from Coptology."[24] Like Brooke's claim, Atiya did not supply the reader with a compelling documentary argument. But Atiya's appraisal suggests something beyond JS just feeding off his immediate circumstances.

Joseph Smith and His Revelations

It can be argued that the seminal years of Mormonism best represent what JS may have settled into as a prophet. Without question, he saw himself as the means of God's delivery to the world of his mind and will in the final stretch of the earth's life. Inherent in that message was the call to righteousness. It is evident that even in all of his interruptions, diversions, and hiccups, the attempt to create a righteous people stands as the constant throughout his ministry. He saw himself as a prophetic figure in the style of a Hebrew patriarch delivering God's thinking to mankind. To overlook that basic premise leads to misconstruing JS's purposeful intentions.

The nature of JS's business that formed once a church was established, demanded something of him that he had likely not contemplated at the beginning. After the church's organization and subsequent duties complicated his life, he sporadically maintained his stylistic presentation of divine instructions and confirmations. Despite the effort necessary to produce revelatory script, involving both his and a scribes' attention in their otherwise nonliterary environment, the "words" of the Lord became paramount to capture and disseminate, irregular as it was at times. The July 1833 interdiction by Independence, Missouri, vigilantes of the revelations compiled to that date, must have overwhelmed him, perhaps something akin to his loss of the 116 pages five years earlier. He recovered from the loss, and when the Doctrine and Covenants—his accumulated revelations—appeared in Kirtland two years later it confirmed to him the Lord's solid promises, if not his own pluck. His abilities as translator and revelator served as confirmation as few other evidences did that he had the approbation of God. Already he may have contemplated translation of the sealed portion of the gold plates. Thus, coincident to publication of the revelations in 1835 his emotions must have soared when the Egyptian artifacts he acquired that year portended more text.

23. Aziz S. Atiya, interview, manuscript of Aziz S. Atiya biography, 545, excerpt copy in possession of the author.
24. Ibid., 530.

From the documentary fragments of the time, modern students are left to assume that, according to JS, his translation of the Book of Mormon first came by way of his use of the translating tools, i.e., the Urim and Thummim in 1828, augmented by use of the seer stone in a hat in 1829.[25] However, definitive understanding about the methodology JS applied in producing the manuscript with Oliver Cowdery is anything but clear. Despite all of the significant analyses applied to date to explain how JS came up with the words he dictated to Cowdery, the possibilities of explanation remain optional, likely depending on one's attitude toward JS or the organizations he fostered.[26] Similarly, the means by which the texts of his revision of the Bible, the Book of Abraham, and the serial revelations he received are unknown to all but him, though much investigation has been applied through the years attempting to elucidate what he did.[27]

A Seer

The extant fragments of information from early Mormonism that provide us with somewhat of a profile of how JS understood this role are found in the prophetic texts he produced. While JS kept no record of his biblical study, there is no mistaking his interest with the Bible. Later reflections suggest he had familiarity with the Old and New Testament, though his interest was generally not analytical but interpretative. It did not escape him that Jesus, as represented in the book of John, confronted the Jews of his time declaring, "Your father Abraham rejoiced to see my day: and he saw it, and was glad" (John 8:56). He perhaps understood the passage to represent a "vision" experienced by Abraham,

25. Michael Hubbard MacKay and Nicholas J. Frederick, *Joseph Smith's Seer Stones* (Provo, UT: Brigham Young University, Religious Studies Center and Deseret Book, 2016).
26. Mormon scholarship in the past two generation regarding the Book of Mormon and its translation, understandably, is vast in number and breadth of analysis. See, for example, Richard Van Wagoner and Steven C. Walker, "Joseph Smith: 'The Gift of Seeing,'" *Dialogue* 15, no. 2 (Summer 1982): 48–68; and recent works by Royal Skousen, *Book of Mormon Critical Text Project*, http://criticaltext.byustudies.byu.edu/; Givens, *By the Hand of Mormon*; Hardy, *Understanding the Book of Mormon*; Brant A. Gardner, *The Gift and Power Translating the Book of Mormon* (Salt Lake City: Greg Kofford Books, 2013); and Michael Hubbard MacKay and Gerrit J. Dirkmaat, *From Darkness unto Light: Joseph Smith's Translation and Publication of the Book of Mormon* (Salt Lake City: Brigham Young University, Religious Studies Center and Deseret Book, 2015).
27. Regarding textual analysis of JS's revision of the Bible, including the Book of Moses, see Matthews, *"A Plainer Translation"*; and Faulring, Jackson, and Matthews, *Joseph Smith's New Translation of the Bible.* For the Book of Abraham, see the recent works of Robert K. Ritner, *The Joseph Smith Egyptian Papyri: A Complete Edition* (Salt Lake City: Signature Books, 2013); and Joseph Smith Papers, *JSP, R4*. For the Doctrine and Covenants, see Woodford, "Historical Development of the Doctrine and Covenants"; and Joseph Smith Papers, *JSP, D1–7*.

wherein he saw things that are otherwise unobservable to other humans. This was a feature that characterized biblical prophets as understood by the traditional Christian world that surrounded him.[28] It is not clear when JS acquired or understood his propensity to see as per Abraham's vision, but while he produced the Book of Mormon text, several of the figures he described during his translation had the distinction of exhibiting the faculty Jesus represented Abraham to possess. JS understood, from his own experiences, that Abraham and the Book of Mormon characters he would describe were "seers," those who could see beyond the realm of normal mortal consciousness.[29]

In the Book of Mormon's book of Mosiah, the text distinguishes the scope of a prophetic seer. While the language indicates that a seer is also a revelator and a prophet, the Book of Mormon figure Ammon gave definition that helps also to classify how JS viewed himself. A "seer can know of things which are past, and also of things which are to come," Ammon stated, even "shall secret things be made manifest, and hidden things shall come to light." Further, "things which are not known shall be made known" by the seer (Mosiah 8:15–18). Rather than expand upon this type of figure throughout the Book of Mormon, the text is mostly silent about seers thereafter until in the last produced portion of the Book of Mormon where the protagonist Nephi provided greater clarity about what might be expected from one of those godly characters. Under the influence of "the spirit," Nephi lamented the deplorable status of Jerusalem's inhabitants because of their bad behavior. His view of the Israelites at the time was not unlike that of the prophetic seers before him. Jehovah, Nephi stated, "surely did show unto the prophets of old all things concerning them," i.e., those in Jerusalem (1 Ne. 19:21). What did those "prophets of old" see? Nephi wanted his readers to understand that through a visionary state he saw the fate of Jerusalem. What was required for the prophets to "see" these things? There is no textual explanation, but the book's language clearly denotes something visionary, observing something beyond or outside of the normal range of human experience. Later in Nephi's text, JS dictated that Joseph, of biblical Egyptian fame, "truly saw our day" (2 Ne. 3:5). According to the Book of Mormon text, Nephi viewed the era when a "seer shall the Lord my God raise up... a choice seer" to Nephi's descen-

28. John L. McKenzie, *Dictionary of the Bible* (New York: Macmillan, 1965), 694–99.

29. See the application of seeric attributes to JS in Steven C. Walker, "Seer," in *Encyclopedia of Mormonism*, 4 vols., ed. Daniel H. Ludlow (New York: Macmillan, 1992), 3:1292–93. Latter-day Saint tradition in the twentieth century identified those with access to extraordinary godly information as both prophets and seers. See Orson F. Whitney, "What Joseph Beheld," in *Cowley & Whitney on Doctrine*, comp., Forace Green (Salt Lake City: Bookcraft, 1963), 233–41; Sidney B. Sperry, *The Voice of Israel's Prophets: A Latter-day Saint Interpretation of the Major and Minor Prophets of the Old Testament* (Salt Lake City: Deseret Book, 1952), 4–8.

dants, in particular, because the "seer" would be of the same lineage (2 Ne. 3:6, 7, 11). It did not escape JS that the language of the translation he dictated identified himself as that "seer." Thus, from the text most often associated with JS's claims, he drew fundamentals of his future role.

Lucy Mack Smith, mother of JS and his biographer, described to her readers the result of her son's access to things unseen by the general run of humanity. After JS's connection to Moroni and surrounding events, Mother Smith explained the effect of his unusual experience as he explained what he had *seen* regarding the context of what he was doing. As the family would gather she related, in the passage well known among Mormons: "In the course of our evening conversations Joseph would give us some of the most ammusing recitals which could be imagined[.] he would describe the ancient inhabitants of this continent their dress thier maner of traveling the animals which they rode The cities that were built by them the structure of their buildings with every particular of their mode of warfare their religious worship—as particularly as though he had spent his life with them."[30] Mormons have long applied the attributes of seeric figures in the past to JS and his abilities to see things unavailable to others.

The biblical record, both the Old and New Testaments, establishes for the reader precedent from which to consider JS and his own experiences. Accordingly, among the greatest challenges facing investigators of JS is the attempt to measure and understand his experiences with the spiritual world. Were they of his own making or did he materially experience or intuit what he asserted? While many have tried to dissect JS's cursory accounts of his extraordinary experiences, attempting to prove or disprove the claims, the authenticity of the events are matters of acceptance or not of the divine. For instance, language from his 1832 History, partially repeated in the "History of Joseph Smith," opens with JS's background that prompted him in the first place to call upon "the Lord." When he finally mustered the determination to verbally call upon God, as a result, "a piller of ~~fire~~ light above the brightness of the sun at noon day come down from above and rested upon me and I was filled with the spirit of god and the <Lord> opened the heavens upon me and I saw the Lord." He did not clarify as to whether the theophany was a physical one (though he "saw" the light and the Lord) or one played out in his mind or inner resources.[31] In another instance, on January 21, 1836, he received a further heavenly directive, "whether in the body or out I cannot tell,"[32] language similar to that used by the apostle Paul in one of his "visions and revelations" as recorded in 2 Corinthians 12:1–3. Another phrase from the 1832 History giving insight in how JS defined his experiences is

30. Lucy Mack Smith's 1844–45 memoir, quoted in Anderson, *Lucy's Book*, 345.
31. Smith, Histories, "circa summer 1832," *JSP, H1*:12–13.
32. Smith, Journal, January 21, 1836, *JSP, J1*:167.

found in his description of his visitation from Moroni: "I supposed it had been a dreem of [or] Vision but when I considred I knew that it was not."[33] During his revision of the Bible in December 1830, known as the "Book of Moses," JS attributed to the biblical figure Enoch an experience described this way, "I saw the Lord; & he stood before my face, & he talked with me, even as a man talketh, one with another, face to face."[34] It should not be surprising that some view this as a parallel application to what he himself may have experienced.

Two other visionary incidents also provide insight into JS's perspective, distinguishing between alternative manifestations that he said he experienced. In one instance, the account of what he called in February 1832 his "Vision" of postmortal glory,[35] one shared with Sidney Rigdon, a subtle distinction about what they experienced became known. The "Vision" affirmed Jesus's revelatory procedure to influence the recipient, "by my spirit will I enlighten them and by my power will I make known unto them the secrets of my will yea even those things which eye has not seen nor ear heard nor yet entered into the heart of man." Then, prefacing the unleash of heavenly inspiration to him and his associate Rigdon regarding the postmortal judgment, JS stated that by, "the power of the spirit our eyes were opened and our understandings were enlarged so as to see and understand the things of God." Further, he characterized his ocular and verbal exchange with Jesus, who he said, "we saw and with whom we conversed in the heavenly vision."[36] Four years later JS witnessed a vision with similar characteristics. In the April 3, 1836, visitations of Jesus to JS and Oliver Cowdery—followed by the biblical prophets Moses, Elias, and Elijah—JS's scribe, Cowdery's brother Warren, described what he heard from JS who dictated the vision. "The vail was taken from their minds and eyes of their understandings were opened." They "saw the Lord standing upon the breast work of the pulpit before them," details of which included a small platform of "pure gold" bearing the glory of Jesus's stature. JS then exclaimed to Warren Cowdery that Jesus's eyes were "as a flame of fire," his head of hair "was like pure snow; his countenance being "above the brightness of the sun," and he had a voice that was "the sound of the rushing of great waters." The subsequent arrivals of Moses, Elias, and Elijah, however, were simply described as "appearances."[37] A comprehendible under-

33. Smith, Histories, "circa summer 1832," *JSP, H1*:14.

34. Faulring, Jackson, and Matthews, *Joseph Smith's New Translation of the Bible*, 615 (Old Testament Manuscript 2, Moses 7:4).

35. "The Vision" was the first entry in what was once referred to in the CHL as the "Kirtland Revelation Book," and now in the *Joseph Smith Papers* as Revelation Book 2, *JSP, R1*:314–26; and was first published as "A Vision" in the *Evening and the Morning Star*, July 1832, [10].

36. Smith, Revelations, February 16, 1832, *JSP, R1*:315–16 [D&C 76:10, 12, 14 (1981)].

37. Smith, Journal, April 3, 1836, *JSP, J1*:219–20. Added to the LDS canon in 1876 (D&C

standing of what constituted the visionary experience, however, is still not clear to the layman.

Another insight into how JS viewed his celestial moments is his preface to his revision of Genesis, part of his larger work of biblical emendation. In the portrayal of Moses's own other-worldly meeting with God, JS included Moses's statement that, "mine eyes ~~mine own eyes~~ <have beheld God> but not mine <natural> eyes <but my spiritual>, for mine <natural> eyes could not have beheld for I should have withered & died in his presence But his glory was upon me & I beheld his face for I was transfigered before him."[38] The reference to transfiguration may have parallels with the Matthew 17 event wherein Jesus was transfigured upon the mount in front of his chief apostles (Matt. 17:1–9). Of the experience, though, the New Testament is silent on the nature of the event. Beyond these attendant features of JS's visionary episodes, we simply cannot know what processes were involved with how JS witnessed the divine callers who altered his life: God, Jesus Christ, Moroni, John the Baptist, Peter, James, and John, and numerous other past figures.

The matters described above are presented to indicate somewhat the range of what the historical record states that JS perceived was his province with the seeric dispensation given him. His assumption of the role of prophet, as stated in the early revelations he received, provided him with opportunities to exhibit his prescience and charisma, while at the same time wedging him away from those he undoubtedly hoped would respond to the message of the restoration.

Oliver Cowdery's Portrait of a/the Prophet in Early Mormonism

After destruction of the *Evening and the Morning Star* in Independence in July 1833, the church's publishing establishment moved to Kirtland, along with a number of the refugee Saints. There Oliver Cowdery replaced W. W. Phelps as the church's printer and soon a new monthly, the *Latter Day Saints' Messenger and Advocate*, provided both continuity and confirmation of the Mormon ambition to build the kingdom of God. Cowdery's role as editor of the *Messenger and Advocate* also gave him, from his unique perspective, opportunity to provide to the church and others interested in things Mormon significant new details

110), it was written by Warren Cowdery in the first rather than the third person. As it turns out, the proximity of chronicling the event to the actual vision is unparalleled in JS's life. There is no equivalent transcendent event where the account immediately abuts the incident, which adds to the credibility of the occurrence. The event is further discussed in Chapter 11.

38. Faulring, Jackson, and Matthews, *Joseph Smith's New Translation of the Bible*, 84 (Old Testament Manuscript 2, Moses 1:11).

about the church's founding, growth, and development. The fact that the 1832 History never made it past the letterbook in which it was written may have influenced Cowdery's intent to inform Mormons about what he and JS thought were the faith's essentials. One significant issue soon addressed by Cowdery was the prophetic role assumed at the time by JS. Cowdery's essay proved to be one of the more significant insights about how he and JS viewed their identities and missions. A number of external and internal criticisms directed at and about JS had circulated in the aftermath of the Mormon failure in Missouri. Besides the power of rumor and innuendo, the day's print culture also proffered censure of JS and Mormon designs. Besides numerous newspaper editorials and articles, Alexander Campbell's *Delusions* (1831/1832), Ezra Booth's published letters (1831), and E. D. Howe's *Mormonism Unvailed* (1834) reached the hands of many invested in the local surges of Mormonism. Campbell, Booth, and Howe's criticisms, and others of a similar bent, were sophisticated and substantive and undoubtedly had an impact on those within and outside the church. Called into question by those critics who emotively pierced the thinking of numerous Mormons, the church had offered nothing in the nature of a defense. However, beginning with the October 1834 publication of the *Messenger and Advocate*, Cowdery—in collaboration with JS—began publishing a series of his letters to his predecessor W. W. Phelps, clearly intended to initiate understanding among the Saints about the faith's founding. Cowdery could say things about Mormonism's origins that no one else, other than JS, could provide.

Cowdery's eight letters to Phelps printed in the *Messenger and Advocate* after October 1834 not only helped set church memory about several important matters but also thereafter provoked the manner in which that memory and the church's history would be distributed. Understanding of the seminal events of Mormonism at the time was a vague story that had been disseminated only by word of mouth. But in the second letter, published in November 1834, Cowdery detoured from his stated purpose of telling the Mormon story and assumed the role of explicator of JS's prophetic role. Howe's invective against JS, *Mormonism Unvailed*, had just been published a few miles northeast of Kirtland. Cowdery reminded his readers of their commonly held perceptions about God's intervention with the human family through appointed and anointed ones in antiquity. Noting that godly men of old were "looked upon as men of perfection, holiness, purity, and goodness, far in advance of any since," he reminded his readers that it seemed to have been forgotten that those figures "were men of infirmities and subject to all the feelings, passions, and imperfections common to other men."[39] Equating JS's humanness, which was apparent to all, with the celebrated

39. Oliver Cowdery to W. W. Phelps, n.d., *Latter Day Saints' Messenger and Advocate*, November 1834, 27–32.

biblical sages and prophets, Cowdery's intent was clearly to disarm those who expected too much from JS. "When looking over the sacred scriptures," he continued, "we seem to forget that they were given through men of imperfections, and subject to passions. It is a general belief that the ancient prophets were perfect—that no stain, or blemish ever appeared upon their characters while on earth." Likewise, even the New Testament believers recognized the limitations of their Old Testament heroes: "James said that Elias was a man subject to like passions as themselves." It was a mistake then and now to look "upon the ancient prophets as a race of beings superior to any in those days; and in order to be constituted a prophet of God, a man must be perfect in every respect."[40] Despite the extraordinary factors constituting his persona, juxtaposing the biblical model with JS was necessary to allay those who came to Mormonism expecting a human enshrouded in the divine. The role and characteristics of both ancient and the Saints' modern prophet, it was intended to be understood, were not that different.

Perceptions of How God Worked with His Prophets

Part of the mystery of JS's life must be considered in light of how he viewed himself as the Lord's anointed. Generations of tradition presently shape for modern followers' interpretation of how JS carried out the will of God. In this understanding, the temptation is great to rely on earlier, even primitive, constructions of man's relationship to deity. If graphed, the picture would show vertical alignment. That is, God identifies a man—though the Bible also allows for some women to fit the description of prophetess[41]—and then begins communication with him as his delegate to the people. The Hebrew Bible created the epitome. The example of Moses throughout the Pentateuch exhibits and helps solidify this architype for the Judeo-Christian world. There are allowances in the scriptural texts for more than one of the "anointed" ones at a time, something Mormons quickly recognize in the circumstances of Lehi, a Book of Mormon prophet and contemporary of the biblical Jeremiah. But in both the biblical and Book of Mormon model, the theoretical graph showing the relationship between God and man places God at the top of the vertical line with a descending arrow from the Almighty to the man. There are numerous examples from the scriptural texts showing this perpendicular method of communication between God and man. The theoretical image shows no oligarchy, no committee, no collective sharing direct communication with God. A prophet is a prophet because he is the *one* selected and appointed by God to the role.

40. Ibid., 31–32.

41. R.N. Whybray, "Prophets," in Metzger and Coogan, *Oxford Companion to the Bible*, 620; Michael Coogan, *God and Sex: What the Bible Really Says* (New York: Twelve, 2010), 43–46.

And in JS's case, several of the early revelations given to him pointed out that *he* was the one among his peers who merited the designation. The archetype was not unfamiliar to them because of the biblical precedent. A September 1830 revelation, dictated just five months after the organization of his church, explicitly differentiated JS from all others who may have had claims to God's singular attention, "no one shall be appointed to Receive commandments & Revelations in this Church excepting my Servent Joseph for he Receiveth them even as Moses."[42] A February 1831 revelation declared as much in light of unexpected and challenging spiritual phenomenon that arose among a few members in Kirtland: "there is none other appointed unto you to receive commandments & Revelations."[43] The biblical pattern of Moses's encounters with Jehovah became the predictable form thereafter for JS among those who had gravitated to his claims. But in addition to the traditional template of Jehovah-to-prophet communication, which fits the classical vertical configuration, there is another picture that may help us to a greater degree understand the broader implication of JS's prophetic mantle and how he viewed his commission from God.

The Inspiration of a Prophet: Prophetic Prerogative

Richard Bushman posed a fundamental question about the scope of JS's prophetic role: Were JS's "ideas to be attributed to him or to God?" The question suggests an either/or dichotomy that has prevailed since his emergence as a public figure in the nineteenth century. The default response from many of JS's opponents is that he fashioned the entirety of what became Mormonism in his pathological mind, where megalomania, epilepsy, paranoia, or calculated fraud precluded acceptance of him as a biblical-style prophet. Bushman wisely reminded his readers of such limited scope: "To insist that Smith devised every revelation himself—obscures the very quality that made the Prophet powerful. To get inside the movement, we have to think of Smith as the early Mormons thought of him and as he thought of himself—as a revelator."[44] Mormon perspectives on the premise, however, vary. Apostle Orson Pratt, for example, stated in December 1872, that "Joseph the Prophet in writing the Doctrine & ~~Revelation~~ Covenants, received the ideas from God, ~~as~~ but clothed those ideas with such words as came to his mind."[45] Orson F. Whitney, then assistant church historian but within months appointed to the church's Quorum of the Twelve Apostles, asserted in December 1905 that while most Latter-day Saints likely

42. Smith, Revelations, September 1830, *JSP, R1*:41 [D&C 28:2 (1981)].

43. Smith, Revelations, February 1831, *JSP, R1*:84 [D&C 43:3 (1981)].

44. Bushman, *Rough Stone Rolling*, xxi.

45. Orson Pratt, December 9, 1872, School of the Prophets Salt Lake City Records, 1872–1874, CR 390 7, CHL.

considered JS's revelations as "God's utterances, and therefore, not the words or works of Joseph Smith," that scenario was likely faulty in its limitations regarding God's work with his prophet. Whitney may have replied to Bushman's query about the source of JS's inspiration in this manner: "I answer that they are God's and Joseph's combined. The Prophet was not a mere machine, a mere speaking trumpet, in the process of receiving and giving the word of God. He still had his agency, and was an intelligent, self-acting being, though the inspired instrument and mouthpiece of Deity. The word of God that came to him was independent of him, and yet his mind was the mold in which it was formed; his vocabulary the earthly vehicle of expression." Indeed, that "which is divinely begotten may have human conception and delivery." JS's revelations, he concluded, were "divine in origin and in utterance, though they are revelations of Jesus Christ, spiritually, yet in the letter they bear the impress of Joseph Smith, and are the product of his genius, just as much as the inspired writings of Isaiah, Jeremiah, and Ezekiel, are the literary creations of those ancient seers."[46] If Whitney was correct, JS's occupation as a prophet assumes a much larger dimension than just spokesman.

In the spring of 1829, as JS dictated and Oliver Cowdery scribed what became the text of the Book of Mormon, a passage from what was later designated the book of Helaman undoubtedly caught JS's attention. The "voice" of the Lord came to Nephi III comforting him with the recognition that he had in "unwearingness" devoted himself to delivering the word of the Lord while seeking his "will" and keeping his "commandments." Due to his faithfulness, Nephi gained privilege with a unique dispensation of power whereby "all things shall be done unto thee according to thy word for thou shalt not ask that which is contrary to my will." This implies a disciple so familiar with the will of God that there was no need to second guess Jehovah. The Lord told Nephi, "ye shall have power over this people & shall smite the earth with famine & with pestilence & destruction according to the wickedness of this people." Moreover, he was told, "I give unto you power that whatsoever ye shall Seal on earth shall be Se<a>led in Heaven & whatsoever ye shall loose on earth shall be loosed in Heaven & thus shall ye have power among this <people>."[47]

As Nephi exercised this unusual privilege of authority among the Nephites, the record reported he manipulated the environment by invoking a famine to punish the people. And, as the editor, Moroni, then summarized, "& so it was done according to the words of Nephi."[48] It cannot be overlooked that Nephi apparently did not revoke the famine himself but instead pled with the Lord to temper the effects of the punishment, "wilt thou turn away thine anger," and

46. Whitney, "Joseph Smith in Literature," 142.
47. Smith, Revelations, "Book of Mormon," *JSP, R3*: Part 2, 183 [Hel. 10:4–7].
48. Ibid., 185 [Hel. 11:5].

"wilt thou hearken unto me & cause that it may be done according to my words." In other words, *please confirm what I have done.* The Lord sanctioned Nephi's words by "send[ing] forth rain upon the face of the earth."[49] The effect was that Nephi was subsequently known as "having great power & authority given unto him from God."[50] The symbiosis of God's will and Nephi's compliance illustrates an important component of how JS viewed his own role.

Commenting on Helaman 10's portrayal of God's bestowal of prerogative upon Nephi, BYU religion professors Joseph Fielding McConkie and Robert L. Millet in 1991 stated; "So complete is the trust that God has in Nephi, so perfect is the assurance that he would not do or say anything contrary to the divine will, that Nephi is granted the promise that all that he asks, all that he says, and all that he does in the name of the Lord will be honored. What Nephi prays for he will get, because his hands are clean and his heart pure."[51] McConkie and Millet confirm application of the premise in several modern and ancient revelations:

> "he that asketh in the spirit asketh according to the will of God wherefore it is done even as he asketh."[52]
>
> "& if ye are purified & cleansed from all sin ye shall ask whatsoever you will in the name of Jesus & it shall be done but know this it shall be given you what you shall ask."[53]
>
> "& it came to pass that after I had prayed & laboured with all diligence the Lord said unto me I will grant unto thee according to thy desires because of thy faith."[54]

Early in JS's ministry he obtained a revelation as part of his revision of the Bible regarding the apostle Paul's epistle found in 1 Corinthians 7:14. Paul's text addressed familial and religious obligations among the Jews provoking this commentary from JS: "For this cause the apostle [Paul] wrote unto the church giving unto them a commandment not of the Lord but of himself."[55] Here JS suggested that an authorized servant of the Lord, Paul in this case, acted for God by way of his own intuition. This concept is imbedded in a significant revelation JS received a year after the Church of Christ was organized (May 9, 1831), where he was reminded that "he [JS] is possessor of all things for all things are subject

49. Ibid., [Hel. 11:12–13].
50. Ibid., 187 [Hel. 11:18].
51. Joseph Fielding McConkie and Robert L. Millet, *Doctrinal Commentary on the Book of Mormon*, 4 vols. (Salt Lake City: Bookcraft, 1991), 3:385–86.
52. Smith, Revelations, circa March 8, 1831, *JSP, R1*:100 [D&C 46:30 (1981), clear text].
53. Smith, Revelations, May 9, 1831, *JSP, R1*:108 [D&C 50:29–30 (1981)].
54. Smith, Revelations, *JSP, R3*: Part 1, 239 [Enos 1:12].
55. Smith, Revelations, circa December 1830, *JSP, R1*:443 [D&C 74:5 (1981)].

unto him both in Heaven & on the Earth." Furthermore, the passage concludes "The spirits shall be subject unto you [JS]."[56] Having conducted his ministry for over a decade, nowhere is this component of power and authority to act with prophetic prerogative more clearly implied than in JS's September 6, 1842, epistle to the Saints. In this particular example, JS's reference to the power to "bind" and "seal" concerns the matter of salvation for the dead. But the premise exceeds this instance. "It may seem to some to be a very bold doctrine that we talk of," referring to the "power which records, or binds on earth, and binds in heaven: nevertheless, in all ages of the world, whenever the Lord has given a dispensation of the priesthood to any man by actual revelation, or any set of men, this power has always been given. Hence whatsoever those men did in authority, in the name of the Lord, and did it truly and faithfully...it became a law on earth and in heaven, and could not be annulled, according to the decrees of the great Jehovah."[57] The language indicates that JS understood that the power to bind on earth and in heaven, had been given to him to affect God's purposes on the earth. The notion also included the necessity of confirmation by the Lord, according to the instincts he felt within and the inspiration impressed upon him from without. Nevertheless, JS believed he had been given, because of his righteous intent, license to enact what he felt was necessary to advance God's kingdom.

The language of the revelation given to him a year later on July 12, 1843, reinforced to him what he had learned about the broad arena in which he functioned. JS's inclusion of the verbiage below to explain the prophetic authority he exercised in his now famous revelation concerning the "principle and doctrine" of the biblical prophets' marital arrangements is a reminder that he believed he acted with authorization. Upon inquiring of the Lord about the biblical patriarchs' "having many wives and concubines,"[58] JS learned in summary: "I gave unto <thee>, my Servant Joseph, an appointment" to "restore all things: Ask what ye will, and it shall be given unto you, according to my word." Moreover, he said that the Lord told him, "I have conferred upon you the keys and power of the Priesthood, wherein I restore all things." Therefore, "whatsoever you seal on earth shall be sealed in heaven; and whatsoever you bind on earth, in my name, and by my word, saith the Lord, it shall be eternally bound in the heavens." Likely referencing the opposition that had already arisen from those who knew about JS's polygamy, the revelation continued: "Whatsoever you give on earth, and to whomsoever you give any one on earth, by my word, and according to my

56. Smith, Revelations, May 9, 1831, *JSP, R1*:107–8 [D&C 50:27, 29–30 (1981)].
57. Smith, "Letter from Joseph Smith," September 6, 1842, *Times and Seasons*, October 1, 1842, 934–35.
58. Smith, Revelation, July 12, 1843, 1, Revelations Collection, MS 4583, box 1, folder 75, item 1, CHL, available online in digital form accessed from the CHL catalog; D&C 132:45–48 (1981). This revelation did not become part of the D&C until 1876.

law, it shall be visited with blessings and not cursings, and with my power, saith the Lord, and shall be without condemnation on earth & in heaven."[59]

While license to act independently of God was not part of the injunction, collaboration between them appeared anticipated and expected. Daniel Tyler, who became a Mormon in 1833, described an event that would have occurred in late 1835 that he said left a lasting impression upon him. As JS lamented to the Saints his sadness in having "so much trouble in the house of his friends," the prophet also said, "The Lord once told me that if at any time I got into deep trouble and could see no way out of it, if I would prophesy in His name, he would fulfill my words."[60] JS presented the sentiment to church members March 10, 1844: "The Lord once told me that what I asked for I should have."[61] Certainly, JS's self-perception of his role and what he had been given by God was extraordinary. And enough of that identity was conveyed to his faithful followers who fully embraced him that they had confidence that they truly did have a Moses among them.

JS filled the role of prophet in a way not only ensuring that his church could survive, but, based on the historical record, he also supplied it with the fuel to empower adherents with the adornment of Christianity. As Richard Bushman concluded, "Perhaps his signal trait was trust in his own inspiration" to bring about God's purposes.[62] While JS obviously felt most comfortable in his role as a revelator, best shown in the revelations he produced in the first years of his ministry, the other and more difficult function he assumed as leader of a people suggests an extraordinary ability to inspire and move others. Both contemporary and modern observers recognized the trait. The non-Mormon in Lewiston, Illinois, who wrote about JS two weeks after his death, concluded, "notwithstanding [his negative reputation] he was a remarkable man, and has left the impress of his genius upon the age in which he lived; he has carved out for himself a title to a page in the history of his country, and his name will be remembered, for good or for evil, when the names of half the ephemeral Statesmen of the age will be forgotten."[63] Recognition of JS as fitting the description of latter-day prophet is, obviously, a subjective one. The polarity about the proposition previously described indicates no chance of reconciliation to a universally accepted perspective. But it is important to understand to the degree possible the manner in which JS saw himself. It explains much about what he did.

59. Ibid.

60. Daniel Tyler, "Recollections of the Prophet Joseph Smith," *Juvenile Instructor*, February 15, 1892, 127–28.

61. *Wilford Woodruff Journal*, March 10, 1844, 2:365.

62. Bushman, *Rough Stone Rolling*, 561.

63. H. M., "Joe Smith, the Mormon Prophet," *New York Tribune*, July 20, 1844.

Epilogue

There is no illusion held that this volume resolves what has been the ubiquitous and recurrent conflict about JS once he advanced his name and his life as being God's singular prophetic voice of early nineteenth-century America. Looking at the macro level of the range of humanity today and their perceptions of the role of religion in the culture, the claims are preposterous, except to the several million people who have embraced Mormonism to one degree or another. Those dismissing JS today—many who were once a part of the faith—roll out lengthy examples of the confusions, failures, incongruities, inconsistencies, irregularities, and irreconcilable assertions of JS and his associates regarding the posture that God designated him to be one "like unto Moses." Little wonder that since their inception Mormons have found all that they advance critically scrutinized.

At the micro level, which this study purports to be, JS was confined to his own culture in America as it developed. Though his designs were ambitious and ultimately global, in many ways he could not supersede the thirty-eight years defining his antebellum life. However, seen through the full scope of the surviving documentary record associated with Mormon beginnings, his obscure emergence as someone consequential on the American religious scene remains a matter of growing interest. Heretofore sculpted and justified by whatever arrangement or negation of the sources that are used to define him, how he is portrayed—the biases, predispositions, intentions, and passions—is determined through the lens of his interpreters. As has been emphasized throughout this work, the documentary record and its inherent limitations demands much more than the binary offerings that have characterized so much of what has been written about him.

As with all other modern constructions of the past, had there been a complete contemporary rendering of what was possible to be chronicled at the time, this and all other portrayals of JS would undoubtedly have a different outline.

But what has survived, due primarily to the devotion of those committed to ensure that not only JS but also his teachings and legacy were remembered, offers some semblance of who JS was and what he tried to do. The intent of this work is to illustrate in both rudimentary and complex form that modern investigators must consider in their studies the panoramic scope of JS as represented in the historical record, incomplete that it may be.

The information age, with its seemingly unlimited offering of voices, has in the twenty-first century upset many Mormon traditionalists raised on ineffectual curriculum about its past and traditions that have given short shrift to the demands of cultural and historical integrity. As noted, however, the LDS Church has recently recognized the need to expand understanding and attention to matters that at one time were easier to overlook and dismiss. With publication of the Joseph Smith Papers and the attendant contributions of the complementary historical work accomplished in the immediate past, opportunities to appraise Mormon beginnings from the full range of surviving documentation has never been more available. JS and his life, consequently, remains fertile ground for discovery. The prophet's contemporary world, arguably, demands greater attention than just fodder for proving or disproving his veracity. There is evidence from both defenders and detractors that Mormon historiography is moving forward to the advantage of those invested in JS. And it must be understood that from this new era of JS study there will always remain affirmation, criticism, and ambiguity. It remains for the reader to answer for themselves the question posed by the Philadelphia editor in May 1861: "Have we not had a prophet among us?"

Select Bibliography

Printed Items

Adams, George J. *A Few Plain Facts, Shewing the Folly, Wickedness, and Imposition of the Rev. Timothy R. Matthews; also a Short Sketch of the Rise, Faith, and Doctrine of the Church of Jesus Christ of Latter Day Saints.* Bedford, England: C. B. Merry, 1841.

Adams, Henry. "Charles Francis Adams Visits the Mormons in 1844." *Proceedings of the Massachusetts Historical Society* 68 (October 1944–May 1947); 267–300.

Ahlstrom, Sydney E. *A Religious History of the American People.* 2 vols. Garden City, NY: Image Books, 1975.

Alexander, Thomas G. "The Reconstruction of Mormon Doctrine: From Joseph Smith to Progressive Theology." *Sunstone* 5, no. 4 (July–August 1980): 24–33.

———. Review of Gary Topping, *Leonard J. Arrington: A Historian's Life. BYU Studies* 48, no. 3 (2009): 164–65.

———. "The Word of Wisdom: From Principle to Requirement." *Dialogue* 14, no. 3 (Autumn 1981: 78–88).

Alford, Kenneth L. "I Will Send You Elijah the Prophet." In *You Shall Have My Word: Exploring the Text of the Doctrine and Covenants,* edited by Scott C. Esplin, Richard O. Cowan, and Rachel Cope, 34–49. Provo, UT: Religious Studies Center, Brigham Young University, 2012.

Allen, James B. "Eight Contemporary Accounts of Joseph Smith's First Vision: What Do We Learn from Them?" *Improvement Era,* April 1970.

———. "Emergence of a Fundamental: The Expanding Role of Joseph Smith's First Vision in Mormon Religious Thought." *Journal of Mormon History* 7 (1980): 43–61.

———. Review of Gregory A. Prince, *Leonard Arrington and the Writing of Mormon History. BYU Studies Quarterly* 57, no. 2 (2018): 176–84.

———. "The Significance of Joseph Smith's 'First Vision' in Mormon Thought." *Dialogue* 1, no. 3 (Autumn 1966): 29–45.

———. "William Clayton and the Records of Church History." In *Preserving the History of the Latter-day Saints,* edited by Richard E. Turley Jr. and Steven C. Harper, 83–114. Provo, UT: Religious Studies Center, Brigham Young University, 2010.

Allen, James B., Ronald K. Esplin, and David J. Whittaker. *Men with a Mission: The Quorum of the Twelve Apostles in the British Isles, 1837–1841.* Salt Lake City: Deseret Book, 1992.

Allen, James B., and John W. Welch. "The Appearance of the Father and the Son to Joseph Smith in 1820." In *Opening the Heavens: Accounts of Divine Manifestations, 1820–1844,* edited by John W. Welch, 35–75. Provo, UT: Brigham Young University Press and Deseret Book, 2005.

Anderson, Devery S., and Gary James Bergera, eds. *Joseph Smith's Quorum of the Anointed, 1842–1845: A Documentary History.* Salt Lake City: Signature Books, 2005.

Anderson, Lavina Fielding, ed. *Lucy's Book: A Critical Edition of Lucy Mack Smith's Family Memoir.* Salt Lake City: Signature Books, 2001.

Anderson, Richard L. "Circumstantial Confirmation of the First Vision through Reminiscences." *BYU Studies* 9, no. 3 (Spring 1969): 373–404.

———. "Did Oliver Cowdery, One of the Three Special Book of Mormon Witnesses, Express Doubt about His Testimony?" *Ensign*, April 1987.

———. "Joseph Smith's Accuracy on the First Vision Setting: The Pivotal 1818 Palmyra Camp Meeting." In *Exploring the First Vision*, edited by Samuel Alonzo Dodge and Steven C. Harper, 91–169. Provo, UT: Religious Studies Center, Brigham Young University, 2012.

———. "Joseph Smith's Testimony of the First Vision." *Ensign*, April 1996.

———. "Reuben Miller, Recorder of Oliver Cowdery's Reaffirmation." *BYU Studies* 8, no. 3 (Spring 1968): 277–93.

Anderson, Robert D. *Inside the Mind of Joseph Smith: Psychobiography and the Book of Mormon.* Salt Lake City: Signature Books, 1999.

Andrus, Hyrum, and Helen Mae Andrus, comps. *They Knew the Prophet.* Salt Lake City: Bookcraft, 1974.

Appleby, William I. *A Dissertation on Nebuchadnezzar's Dream.* Philadelphia: Brown, Bicking and Guilbert, 1844.

Arrington, Leonard J. *Adventures of a Church Historian.* Urbana, IL: University of Illinois Press, 1998.

———. *Confessions of a Mormon Historian: The Diaries of Leonard J. Arrington, 1971–1999.* Edited by Gary James Bergera. Salt Lake City: Signature Books, 2018.

———. "An Economic Interpretation of the 'Word of Wisdom.'" *BYU Studies* 1, no. 1 (Winter 1959): 37–49.

———. "James Gordon Bennett's Report on the 'Mormonites.'" *BYU Studies* 10, no. 3 (Spring 1970): 353–64.

Ashurst-McGee, Mark, Robin Scott Jensen, and Sharalyn D. Howcroft, eds. *Foundational Texts of Mormonism: Examining Major Early Sources.* New York: Oxford University Press, 2018.

Avery, Valeen Tippetts. *From Mission to Madness: Last Son of the Mormon Prophet.* Urbana: University of Illinois Press, 1998.

Bachman, Danel W. "A Study of the Mormon Practice of Plural Marriage before the Death of Joseph Smith." Master's thesis, Purdue University, 1975.

Backman, Milton V., Jr. "Confirming Witnesses of the First Vision." *Ensign*, January 1986.

———. *Joseph Smith's First Vision: Confirming Evidence and Contemporary Accounts.* 2nd ed. Salt Lake City: Bookcraft, 1980.

———. "'The Keys are Right Here': Succession in the Presidency." In *Lion of the Lord: Essays on the Service of Brigham Young*, edited by Susan Easton Black and Larry C. Porter, 107–27. Salt Lake City: Deseret Book, 1995.

Barlow, Philip L. *Mormons and the Bible: The Place of the Latter-day Saints in American Religion.* 2nd ed. New York: Oxford University Press, 2013.

Barney, Ronald O. "Joseph Smith and the Conspicuous Scarcity of Early Mormon Documentation." In *Foundational Texts of Mormonism: Examining Major Early Sources*, edited by Mark Ashurst-McGee, Robin Scott Jensen, and Sharalyn D. Howcroft, 373–401. New York: Oxford University Press, 2018.

———. "'A Man That You Could Not Help Likeing': Joseph Smith and Nauvoo Portrayed in a Letter by Susannah and George W. Taggart." *BYU Studies* 40, no. 2 (2001): 165–79.

———. "The Restoration of the Priesthood: Understanding the Role of the Melchizedek and Aaronic Priesthoods in the Early Church in Light of Priesthood Restoration Narratives." Unpublished manuscript, June 15, 1988.

———. "'There is the Greatest Excitement in This Country That I Ever Beheld': Mormonism's New England Ministry of the Forgotten Eli P. Maginn." *Mormon Historical Studies* 15 no. 2 (Fall 2014): 157–272.

Bates, Irene M., and E. Gary Smith. *Lost Legacy: The Mormon Office of Presiding Patriarch.* Urbana: University of Illinois Press, 2003.

Bauder, Peter. *The Kingdom and Gospel of Jesus Christ: Contrasted with That of Anti-Christ. A Brief Review of Some of the Most Interesting Circumstances, Which Have Transpired since the Institution of the Gospel of Christ, from the Days of the Apostles.* Canojoharie, NY: A. H. Calhoun, 1834.

Baugh, Alexander L. *A Call to Arms: The 1838 Mormon Defense of Northern Missouri.* Provo, UT: Joseph Fielding Smith Institute of Latter-day Saint History and BYU Studies, 2000.

———, ed. *Days Never to Be Forgotten: Oliver Cowdery.* Provo, UT: Religious Studies Center, Brigham Young University, 2009.

———. "Joseph Smith's Athletic Nature." In *Joseph Smith: The Prophet, The Man,* edited by Susan Easton Black and Charles D. Tate Jr., 137–150. Provo, UT: Religious Studies Center, Brigham Young University, 1993.

———. "Parting the Veil: Joseph Smith's Seventy-Six Documented Visionary Experiences." In *Opening the Heavens: Accounts of Divine Manifestations, 1820–1844,* edited by John W. Welch, 264–326. Provo, UT: Brigham Young University Press and Deseret Book, 2005.

Baugh, Alexander L., and Richard Neitzel Holzapfel. "'I Roll the Burthen and Responsibility of Leading This Church Off from My Shoulders on to Yours': The 1844/45 Declaration of the Quorum of the Twelve Regarding Apostolic Succession." *BYU Studies* 49, no. 3 (2010): 1–16.

Beecher, Maureen Ursenbach, and Lavina Fielding Anderson eds. *Sisters in Spirit: Mormon Women in Historical and Cultural Perspective.* Urbana, IL: University of Illinois Press, 1987.

Bennett, John C. *The History of the Saints: Or, an Exposé of Joe Smith and Mormonism.* 3rd ed. Urbana, IL: University of Illinois Press, 2000. First published 1842 by Leland and Whiting (New York).

Bennett, Richard E., and Amber J. Seidel. "'A World in Darkness': Early Latter-day Saint Understanding of the Apostasy, 1830–1834." In *Early Christians in Disarray: Contemporary LDS Perspectives on the Christian Apostasy,* edited by Noel B. Reynolds, 67–99. Provo, UT: Foundation for Ancient Research and Mormon Studies, Brigham Young University Press, 2005.

Benton, A. W. "Mormonites." *Evangelical Magazine & Gospel Advocate,* April 9, 1831.

Bergera, Gary James. *Conflict in the Quorum: Orson Pratt, Brigham Young, Joseph Smith.* Salt Lake City: Signature Books, 2002.

———. "Joseph Smith and the Hazards of Charismatic Leadership." In *The Prophet Puzzle: Interpretive Essays on Joseph Smith,* edited by Bryan Waterman, 239–57. Salt Lake City: Signature Books, 1999.

Bible. King James Version.

Bishop, M. Guy. "'What Has Become of Our Fathers?' Baptism for the Dead at Nauvoo." *Dialogue* 23, no. 2 (Summer 1990): 85–97.

Bitton, Davis. *Images of the Prophet Joseph Smith.* Salt Lake City: Aspen Books, 1996.

———. "Ten Years in Camelot: A Personal Memoir." *Dialogue* 16, no 3 (Autumn 1983): 9–19.

Bitton, Davis, and Leonard J. Arrington. *Mormons and Their Historians.* Salt Lake City: University of Utah Press, 1988.

Bitton, Davis, and Maureen Ursenbach Beecher. *New Views of Mormon History: Essays in Honor of Leonard J. Arrington.* Salt Lake City: University of Utah Press, 1987.

Black, Susan Easton, and Andrew C. Skinner, eds. *Joseph: Exploring the Life and Ministry of the Prophet.* Salt Lake City: Deseret Book, 2005.

Black, Susan Easton, and Charles D. Tate Jr., eds. *Joseph Smith: The Prophet, The Man.* Provo, UT: Religious Studies Center, Brigham Young University, 1993.

Black, Susan Easton, and Harvey Bischoff Black, comps. *Annotated Record of Baptism for the Dead, 1840–1845.* 7 vols. Provo, UT: Brigham Young University Press, 2002.

Black, Susan Easton, and Larry C. Porter, eds. *Lion of the Lord: Essays on the Service of Brigham Young.* Salt Lake City: Deseret Book, 1995.

Bloom, Harold. *The American Religion: The Emergence of the Post-Christian Nation.* New York: Simon and Schuster, 1992.

Bloxham, V. Ben, James R. Moss, and Larry C. Porter, eds. *Truth Will Prevail: The Rise of the Church of Jesus Christ of Latter-day Saints in the British Isles, 1837–1987.* Cambridge, England: The Church of Jesus Christ of Latter-day Saints, 1987.

Bradley, Don, and Mark Ashurst-McGee. "Joseph Smith and the Kinderhook Plates." In *A Reason for Faith: Navigating LDS Doctrine & Church History*, edited by Laura Harris Hales, 93–115. Provo, UT: Religious Studies Center, Brigham Young University; Salt Lake City: Deseret Book, 2016.

Bringhurst, Newell G. *Fawn McKay Brodie: A Biographer's Life.* Norman: University of Oklahoma Press, 1999.

———. *Reconsidering No Man Knows My History.* Logan, UT: Utah State University Press, 1996.

Brodie, Fawn M. "Fawn McKay Brodie: An Oral History Interview." *Dialogue* 14, no. 2 (Summer 1981): 99–116.

———. *No Man Knows My History: The Life of Joseph Smith.* 2nd ed. New York: Alfred A. Knopf, 1975. First published in 1945.

Brooke, John L. *The Refiner's Fire: The Making of Mormon Cosmology, 1644–1844.* Cambridge: Cambridge University Press, 1994.

Brown, Matthew B. *A Pillar of Light: The History and Message of the First Vision.* American Fork, UT: Covenant Communications, 2009.

Brown, Samuel M. "Early Mormon Adoption Theology and the Mechanics of Salvation." *Journal of Mormon History* 37, no. 3 (Summer 2011): 3–52.

———. *In Heaven as It Is on Earth: Joseph Smith and the Early Mormon Concept of Death.* New York: Oxford University Press, 2012.

———. "The Translator and the Ghostwriter: Joseph Smith and William Phelps." *Journal of Mormon History* 34, no. 1 (Winter 2008): 26–62.

Burton, Alma P., comp. *The Discourses of Joseph Smith.* Salt Lake City: Deseret Book, 1967.

Bush, Lester E., Jr. "The Word of Wisdom in Early Nineteenth-Century Perspective." *Dialogue* 14, no. 3 (Autumn 1981): 46–65.

Bushman, Richard Lyman. *Believing History: Latter-day Saint Essays.* Edited by Reid L. Neilson and Jed Woodworth. New York: Columbia University Press, 2007.

———. *Joseph Smith and the Beginnings of Mormonism.* Urbana, IL: University of Illinois Press, 1984.

———. "A Joseph Smith for the Twenty-First Century." *BYU Studies* 40, no. 3 (2001): 155–71.

———. *Joseph Smith: Rough Stone Rolling; A Cultural Biography of Mormonism's Founder.* New York: Alfred A. Knopf, 2005.

———. "Joseph Smith's Many Histories." In *The Worlds of Joseph Smith: A Bicentennial Conference at the Library of Congress*, edited by John W. Welch, 3–20. Provo, UT: Brigham Young University Press, 2006.

———. "The Visionary World of Joseph Smith." *BYU Studies* 37 no. 1 (1997–1998): 183–204.

———. "Was Joseph Smith a Gentleman? The Standard for Refinement in Utah." In

Nearly Everything Imaginable: The Everyday Life of Utah's Mormon Pioneers, edited by Ronald W. Walker and Doris R. Dant, 27–43. Provo, UT: Brigham Young University Press, 1999.

Callister, Tad R. *The Inevitable Apostasy and the Promised Restoration.* Salt Lake City: Deseret Book, 2006.

Campbell, Alexander. "Delusions." *Millennial Harbinger*, February 7, 1831.

———. *Delusions, An Analysis of the Book of Mormon; With an Examination of Its Internal and External Evidences, and a Refutation of Its Pretences to Divine Authority.* Boston: Benjamin H. Greene, 1832.

Cannon, Brian Q., and *BYU Studies* Staff. "Oliver Cowdery and the Restoration of the Priesthood." In *Oliver Cowdery: Scribe, Elder, Witness*, edited by John W. Welch and Larry E. Morris, 133–53. Provo, UT: Neal A. Maxwell Institute for Religious Scholarship, 2006.

———. "Priesthood Restoration Documents." *BYU Studies* 35, no. 4 (1995): 162–207.

Cannon, Donald Q. "Angus M. Cannon and David Whitmer: A Comment on History and Historical Method." *BYU Studies* 20, no. 3 (Spring 1980): 297–99.

Cannon, George Q. *The Life of Joseph Smith, the Prophet.* Salt Lake City: Juvenile Instructor Office, 1888.

Cannon, Jeffrey G. "The Image as Text and Context in Early Mormon History." In *Foundational Texts of Mormonism: Examining Major Early Sources*, edited by Mark Ashurst-McGee, Robin Scott Jensen, and Sharalyn D. Howcroft, 336–350. New York: Oxford University Press, 2018.

Caswall, Henry. *The City of the Mormons; Or, Three Days at Nauvoo, in 1842.* London: J. G. F. and J. Rivington, 1842.

Cheesman, Paul R. "An Analysis of the Accounts Relating Joseph Smith's Early Visions." Master's thesis, Brigham Young University, 1965.

Clark, John A. *Gleanings by the Way.* Philadelphia: W. J. and J. K. Simon, 1842.

Clayton, William. *An Intimate Chronicle: The Journals of William Clayton.* Edited by George D. Smith. Salt Lake City: Signature Books, 1995.

———. *Manchester Mormons: The Journal of William Clayton, 1840–1842.* Edited by James B. Allen and Thomas G. Alexander. Santa Barbara, CA, and Salt Lake City: Peregrine Smith, 1974.

Cohen, Charles L. "No Man Knows My Psychology: Fawn Brodie, Joseph Smith, and Psychoanalysis." *BYU Studies* 44, no. 1 (2005): 55–78.

Compton, Todd M. *A Frontier Life: Jacob Hamblin, Explorer and Indian Missionary.* Salt Lake City: University of Utah Press, 2013.

———. *In Sacred Loneliness: The Plural Wives of Joseph Smith.* Salt Lake City: Signature Books, 1997.

Cook, Lyndon C. "'Brother Joseph Is Truly a Wonderful Man, He Is All We Could Wish a Prophet to Be': Pre-1844 Letters of William Law." *BYU Studies* 20, no. 2 (Winter 1980): 207–18.

———. *A Tentative Inquiry into the Office of Seventy, 1835–1845.* Provo, UT: Grandin Book, 2009.

Cook, Lyndon W. C., and Milton V. Backman Jr., eds. *Kirtland Elders' Quorum Record, 1836–1841.* Provo, UT: Grandin Book, 1985.

Copeland, Lee. "Speaking in Tongues in the Restoration Churches." *Dialogue* 24, no. 1 (Spring 1991): 15–21.

Corrill, John. *A Brief History of the Church of Christ of Latter Day Saints, (Commonly Called Mormons).* St. Louis: self-published, 1839.

Cowan, Richard O. "Church Growth in England, 1841–1914." In *Truth Will Prevail: The Rise of the Church of Jesus Christ of Latter-day Saints in the British Isles, 1837–1987*, edited by V. Ben Bloxham, James R. Moss, and Larry C. Porter, 199–235. Cambridge, England: The Church of Jesus Christ of Latter-day Saints, 1987.

Cowdery, Oliver. *Defense in a Rehearsal of My Grounds for Separating Myself from the Latter Day Saints.* Norton, OH: Pressley's Job Office, 1839.

Crawley, Peter. *A Descriptive Bibliography of the Mormon Church.* 3 vols. Provo, UT: Religious Studies Center, Brigham Young University, 1997–2012.

Cross, Whitney R. *The Burned-Over District: The Social and Intellectual History of Enthusiastic Religion in Western New York, 1800–1850.* Ithaca, NY: Cornell University Press, 1982.

Dahl, Larry E., and Donald Q. Cannon, eds. *Encyclopedia of Joseph Smith's Teachings.* Salt Lake City: Deseret Book, 1997.

Darowski, Joseph F. "Seeking after the Ancient Order: Conferences and Councils in the Early Church Governance, 1830–1834." In *A Firm Foundation: Church Organization and Administration*, edited by David J. Whittaker and Arnold K. Garr, 97–113. Salt Lake City: Religious Studies Center, Brigham Young University, and Deseret Book, 2011.

Davis, David Brion. "Some Themes of Counter-Subversion: An Analysis of Anti-Masonic, Anti-Catholic, and Anti-Mormon Literature." *The Mississippi Valley Historical Review* 47, no. 2 (September 1960): 205–24.

Daynes, Kathryn M. *More Wives than One: Transformation of the Mormon Marriage System, 1840–1910.* Urbana, IL: University of Illinois Press, 2001.

Decker, Ed, and Dave Hunt. *The Godmakers.* Eugene, OR: Harvest House, 1984.

DePillis, Mario S. "The Quest for Religious Authority and the Rise of Mormonism." *Dialogue* 1, no. 1 (Spring 1966): 68–88.

Derr, Jill Mulvay, Janath Russell Cannon, and Maureen Ursenbach Beecher. *Women of Covenant: The Story of Relief Society.* Salt Lake City: Deseret Book, 1992.

Derr, Jill Mulvay, Carol Cornwall Madsen, Kate Holbrook, and Matthew J. Grow, eds. *The First Fifty Years of Relief Society: Key Documents in Latter-day Saint Women's History.* Salt Lake City: Church Historian's Press, 2016.

Dinger, John S., ed. *The Nauvoo City and High Council Minutes.* Salt Lake City: Signature Books, 2011.

Dirkmaat, Gerrit, and LaJean Purcell Carruth. "The Prophets Have Spoken, but What Did They Say." *BYU Studies Quarterly* 54, no. 4 (2015): 25–118.

Dodge, Samuel Alonzo, and Steven C. Harper, eds. *Exploring the First Vision.* Provo, UT: Religious Studies Center, Brigham Young University, 2012.

Durham, Reed C., Jr., and Steven H. Heath. *Succession in the Church.* Salt Lake City: Bookcraft, 1970.

Dursteler, Eric R. "Historical Periodization in the LDS Great Apostasy Narrative." In *Standing Apart: Mormon Historical Consciousness and the Concept of Apostasy*, edited by Miranda Wilcox and John D. Young, 23–54. New York: Oxford University Press, 2014.

———. "Inheriting the 'Great Apostasy': The Evolution of Latter-day Saint Views on the Middle Ages and the Renaissance." In *Early Christians in Disarray: Contemporary LDS Perspectives on the Christian Apostasy*, edited by Noel B. Reynolds, 29–65. Provo, UT: Foundation for Ancient Research and Mormon Studies, Brigham Young University Press, 2005.

Ehat, Andrew F., and Lyndon W. Cook, eds. *Words of Joseph Smith: The Contemporary Accounts of the Nauvoo Discourses of the Prophet Joseph.* Provo, UT: Religious Studies Center, Brigham Young University, 1980.

Elders' Journal of the Church of Latter Day Saints. October 1837–August 1838.

England, Breck. *The Life and Thought of Orson Pratt.* Salt Lake City: University of Utah Press, 1985.

Ensign of The Church of Jesus Christ of Latter-day Saints, 1971–.

Epistle of the Twelve: Legal Authorities of the Church of Jesus Christ of Latter Day Saints. [William Smith's church]. [N.p.: n.p., ca. 1851].

Esplin, Ronald K. *The Emergence of Brigham Young and the Twelve to Mormon Leadership.* Provo, UT: Joseph Fielding Smith Institute for Latter-day Saint History and BYU Studies, 2006.

Esplin, Scott C., Richard O. Cowan, and Rachel Cope, eds. *You Shall Have My Word: Exploring the Text of the Doctrine and Covenants.* Provo, UT: Religious Studies Center, Brigham Young University, 2012.

Esplin, Ronald K., and Sharon E. Nielsen. "'The Record of the Twelve, 1835': The Quorum of the Twelve Apostles' Call and 1835 Mission." *BYU Studies Quarterly* 51, no. 1 (2012): 4–52.

The Essential Brigham Young. Salt Lake City: Signature Books, 1992.

The Essential Joseph Smith. Salt Lake City: Signature Books, 1995.

Evans, John Henry. "Genius or Seer?" *Improvement Era*, December 1905.

———. *Joseph Smith: An American Prophet.* New York: Macmillan, 1933.

Evening and the Morning Star. June 1832–September 1834.

F., M. L. "Interview with the Mormon Prophet." *Evangelical Magazine and Gospel Advocate*, 5 April 1834.

Faulring, Scott H. "An Examination of the 1829 'Articles of the Church of Christ' in Relation to Section 20 of the Doctrine and Covenants." In *Oliver Cowdery: Scribe, Elder, Witness*, edited by John W. Welch and Larry E. Morris, 155–93. Provo, UT: Neal A. Maxwell Institute for Religious Scholarship, 2006.

———. "Return of Oliver Cowdery." In *Oliver Cowdery: Scribe, Elder, Witness*, edited by John W. Welch and Larry E. Morris, 321–62. Provo, UT: Neal A. Maxwell Institute for Religious Scholarship, 2006.

Faulring, Scott H., Kent P. Jackson, and Robert J. Matthews, eds. *Joseph Smith's New Translation of the Bible: Original Manuscripts.* Provo, UT: Religious Studies Center, Brigham Young University, 2004.

Firmage, Edwin Brown, and Richard Collin Mangrum. *Zion in the Courts: A Legal History of the Church of Jesus Christ of Latter-day Saints, 1830–1900.* Urbana, IL: University of Illinois Press, 1988.

Fluhman, J. Spencer. "An 'American Mahomet': Joseph Smith, Muhammad, and the Problem of Prophets in Antebellum America." *Journal of Mormon History* 35, no. 3 (Summer 2008): 23–45.

———. *"A Peculiar People": Anti-Mormonism and the Making of Religion in Nineteenth-Century America.* Chapel Hill: University of North Carolina Press, 2012.

Fluhman, J. Spencer, Kathleen Flake, and Jed Woodworth, eds. *To Be Learned is Good: Essays on Faith and Scholarship in Honor of Richard Lyman Bushman.* Provo, UT: Neal A. Maxwell Institute for Religious Scholarship, Brigham Young University, 2017.

Ford, Thomas. *A History of Illinois: From Its Commencement as a State in 1818 to 1847.* Urbana and Chicago: University of Illinois Press, 1995.

Foster, Lawrence. *Religion and Sexuality: The Shakers, the Mormons, and the Oneida Community.* Urbana, IL: University of Illinois Press, 1984.

Gamma. "The Mormon Prophet." *Christian Reflector*, January 2, 1845.

Gardner, Brant A. *The Gift and Power Translating the Book of Mormon.* Salt Lake City: Greg Kofford Books, 2013.

Garr, Arnold K. "Which Are the Most Important Mormon Books." *BYU Studies* 43, no. 3 (2002): 35–47.

Gentry, Leland H., and Todd M. Compton. *Fire and Sword: A History of the Latter-day Saints in Northern Missouri, 1836–1839*. Salt Lake City: Greg Kofford Books, 2011.

Givens, Terryl L. *By the Hand of Mormon: The American Scripture that Launched a New World Religion*. New York: Oxford University Press, 2002.

———. *When Souls Had Wings: Pre-Mortal Existence in Western Thought*. New York: Oxford University Press, 2010.

Givens, Terryl L., and Philip L. Barlow, eds. *The Oxford Handbook of Mormonism*. New York: Oxford University Press, 2015.

Godfrey, Kenneth W. "A Note on the Nauvoo Library and Literary Society." *BYU Studies* 14, no. 3 (Spring 1974): 386–89.

Godfrey, Matthew C. "A Culmination of Learning: D&C 84 and the Doctrine of the Priesthood." In *You Shall Have My Word: Exploring the Text of the Doctrine and Covenants*, edited by Scott C. Esplin, Richard O. Cowan, and Rachel Cope, 167–81. Provo, UT: Religious Studies Center, Brigham Young University, 2012.

———. "The Second Sacred Grove: The Influence of Greenville, Indiana, on Joseph Smith's 1832 First Vision Account." *Journal of Mormon History* 44, no. 4 (October 2018): 1–18.

———. "'Seeking after Monarchal Power and Authority': Joseph Smith and Leadership in the Church of Christ, 1831–1832." *Mormon Historical Studies* 15, nos. 1–2 (Spring/Fall 2012): 15–37.

———. "'We Believe the Hand of the Lord Is in It': Memories of Divine Intervention in the Zion's Camp Expedition." *BYU Studies Quarterly* 56, no. 4 (2017): 99–132.

Goodwillie, Christian. "Shaker Richard McNemar: The Earliest Book of Mormon Reviewer." *Journal of Mormon History* 37, no. 2 (Spring 2011): 138–45.

Grant, Jedediah M. *Collection of Facts Relative to the Course Taken by Elder Sidney Rigdon*. Philadelphia: Brown, Bicking, and Guilbert, 1844.

Griffiths, Casey Paul. "The Chicago Experiment": Finding the Voice and Charting the Course of Religious Education in the Church." *BYU Studies* 49, no. 4 (2010): 91–130.

Groesbeck, C. Jess. "The Smiths and Their Dreams and Visions: A Psycho-Historical Study of the First Mormon Family." *Sunstone* 12 (March 1988): 22–29.

Grow, Matthew J. "The Role of the Church History Department in Mormon Scholarship: A Reflection on the Leonard J. Arrington Era and the Present." In *To Be Learned is Good: Essays on Faith and Scholarship in Honor of Richard Lyman Bushman*, edited by J. Spencer Fluhman, Kathleen Flake, and Jed Woodworth, 167–78. Provo, UT: Neal A. Maxwell Institute for Religious Scholarship, Brigham Young University, 2017.

Grunder, Rick. *Mormon Parallels: A Bibliographic Source*. 2nd ed. LaFayette, NY: Rick Grunder Books, 2014. CD.

Hale, Van. "Mormons and Moonmen." *Sunstone* 7, no. 5 (September/October 1982): 12–17.

Hales, Brian C. "'Guilty of Such Folly?': Accusations of Adultery and Polygamy Against Oliver Cowdery." *Mormon Historical Studies* 9, no. 2 (Fall 2008): 19–28.

———. *Joseph Smith's Polygamy: History and Theology*. 3 vols. Salt Lake City: Greg Kofford Books, 2013.

Hales, Laura Harris, ed. *A Reason for Faith: Navigating LDS Doctrine & Church History*. Provo, UT: Religious Studies Center, Brigham Young University; Salt Lake City: Deseret Book, 2016.

Hammond, John J. "Re-examining the Adams/Quincy May 1844 Visit to Nauvoo." *John Whitmer Historical Association Journal* 30 (2010): 66–95.

Hardy, B. Carmon. *Doing the Works of Abraham: Mormon Polygamy, Its Origin, Practice, and Demise.* Norman, OK: Arthur H. Clark, 2007.

Hardy, Grant. *Understanding the Book of Mormon: A Reader's Guide.* New York: Oxford University Press, 2010.

Harper, Steven C. *Joseph Smith's First Vision: A Guide to the Historical Accounts.* Salt Lake City: Deseret Book, 2012.

———. "Missionaries in the American Religious Marketplace: Mormon Proselyting in the 1830s." *Journal of Mormon History* 24, no. 2 (Fall 1998): 1–29.

———. "Oliver Cowdery as Second Witness of Priesthood Restoration." In *Days Never to Be Forgotten: Oliver Cowdery,* edited by Alexander L. Baugh, 73–89. Provo, UT: Religious Studies Center, Brigham Young University, 2009.

Harrell, Charles R. *"This is My Doctrine:" The Development of Mormon Theology.* Salt Lake City: Greg Kofford Books, 2011.

Hartley, William G. *My Fellow Servants: Essays on the History of the Priesthood.* Provo, UT: BYU Studies, 2010.

Hatch, Ephraim. *Joseph Smith Portraits: A Search for the Prophet's Likeness.* Provo, UT: Religious Studies Center, Brigham Young University, 1998.

Hatch, Nathan O. *The Democratization of American Christianity.* New Haven: Yale University Press, 1990.

Hauglid, Brian M. "The Book of Abraham and Translating the Sacred." *BYU Religious Education* (Winter 2017): 12–15.

Haven, Charlotte. "A Girl's Letters from Nauvoo." *Overland Monthly,* December 1890, 616–38.

Hedges, Andrew H. "'They Pursue Me without Cause': Joseph Smith in Hiding and D&C 127, 128." *Religious Educator* 16, no. 1 (2015): 42–59.

Hicks, Michael. "Joseph Smith, W. W. Phelps, and the Poetic Paraphrase of 'The Vision.'" *Journal of Mormon History* 20, no. 2 (Fall 1994): 63–84.

Hill, Donna. *Joseph Smith: The First Mormon.* New York: Doubleday, 1977.

Hill, Marvin S. "Brodie Revisited: A Reappraisal." *Dialogue* 7, no. 4 (Winter 1972): 72–85.

———. "The First Vision Controversy: A Critique and Reconciliation." *Dialogue* 15 no. 2 (Summer 1982): 35–53.

———. "Foreword." In *The Essential Joseph Smith.* Salt Lake City: Signature Books, 1995.

———. "Secular or Sectarian History? A Critique of *No Man Knows My History.*" *Church History* 43, no. 1 (March 1974): 78–96.

The Holy Scriptures, Inspired Version, by Joseph Smith, A New Corrected Edition. Independence, MO: Herald Publishing House, 1973.

Homer, Michael W. *Joseph's Temples: The Dynamic Relationship between Freemasonry and Mormonism.* Salt Lake City: University of Utah Press, 2014.

Howard, Richard P. "Joseph Smith's First Vision: The RLDS Tradition." *Journal of Mormon History* 7 (1980): 23–30.

———. "Peter, James, and John in Light of the Revision of Sections 7 and 26." *Saints Herald,* May 1, 1982.

Howcroft, Sharalyn D. "A Textual and Archival Reexamination of Lucy Mack Smith's History." In *Foundational Texts of Mormonism: Examining Major Early Sources,* edited by Mark Ashurst-McGee, Robin Scott Jensen, and Sharalyn D. Howcroft, 298–335. New York: Oxford University Press, 2018.

Howe, Daniel Walker. *What Hath God Wrought: The Transformation of America, 1815–1848.* New York: Oxford University Press, 2007.

Howe, Eber D. *Mormonism Unvailed: Or, A Faithful Account of that Singular Imposition and Delusion, From Its Rise to the Present Time.* Painesville, OH: self-published, 1834.

Hudson, Wayne. "The Prophethood of Joseph Smith." In *Joseph Smith Jr.: Reappraisals after Two Centuries*, edited by Reid L. Neilson and Terryl L. Givens, 201–8. New York: Oxford University Press, 2009.

Huntington, Oliver B. "The Inhabitants of the Moon." *Young Woman's Journal*, March 1892.

———. "Words and Incidents of the Prophet Joseph's Life." *Young Woman's Journal*, November 1890.

Hyde, Orson. *Ein Ruf aus der Wüste, eine Stimme aus dem Schoose der Erde.* Frankfurt: Im Selbstverlage des Verfassers, 1842.

Irving, Gordon. "The Law of Adoption: One Phase of the Development of the Mormon Concept of Salvation, 1830–1900." *BYU Studies* 14, no. 3 (Spring 1974): 291–314.

———. "The Mormons and the Bible in the 1830s." *BYU Studies* 13, no. 4 (Summer 1973): 473–88.

Ivins, Anthony W. *The Relationship of "Mormonism" and Freemasonry.* Salt Lake City: Deseret News Press, 1934.

Ivins, Stanley S. "Notes on Mormon Polygamy." *Western Humanities Review* 10, no. 3 (Summer 1956): 229–39.

Jackson, Joseph H. *A Narrative of the Adventures and Experience of Joseph H. Jackson in Nauvoo, Disclosing the Depths of Mormon Villainy.* Warsaw, IL: n.p., August 1844.

Jackson, Kent P. *From Apostasy to Restoration.* Salt Lake City: Deseret Book, 1996.

Jensen, Robin Scott. "'Archives of the Better World': The Nineteenth-Century Historian's Office and Mormonism's Archival Flexibility." PhD diss., University of Utah, 2019.

———. "Ignored and Unknown Clues of Early Mormon Record Keeping." In *Preserving the History of the Latter-day Saints*, edited by Richard E. Turley Jr. and Steven C. Harper, 135–64. Provo, UT: Religious Studies Center, Brigham Young University, 2010.

———. "Joseph Smith's Chronicler: An Interview with Dean C. Jessee." *Mormon Historical Studies* 13, no. 1–2 (Spring/Fall 2012): 98–124.

———. "Postscript to Dean C. Jessee's Reprint of 'The Reliability of Joseph Smith's History.'" *Journal of Mormon History* 43, no. 4 (October 2017): 33–36.

Jenson, Andrew. "Joseph Smith, the Prophet." *The Historical Record* 7, nos. 1–3 (January 1888): 353–576.

Jessee, Dean C. "The Earliest Documented Accounts of Joseph Smith's First Vision." In *Opening the Heavens: Accounts of Divine Manifestations, 1820–1844*, edited by John W. Welch, 1–33. Provo, UT: Brigham Young University Press and Deseret Book, 2005.

———. "The Early Accounts of Joseph Smith's First Vision." *BYU Studies* 9, no. 3 (Spring 1969): 275–94.

———. "Howard Coray's Recollections of Joseph Smith." *BYU Studies* 17, no. 3 (Spring 1977): 341–47.

———, ed. *The Papers of Joseph Smith: Autobiographical and Historical Writings, Volume 1.* Salt Lake City: Deseret Book, 1989.

———, ed. *Personal Writings of Joseph Smith.* Revised edition. Salt Lake City: Deseret Book, 2002.

———. "Priceless Words and Fallible Memories: Joseph Smith as Seen in the Effort to Preserve His Discourses." *BYU Studies* 31, no. 2 (Spring 1991): 19–40.

———. "The Reliability of Joseph Smith's History." *Journal of Mormon History* 3 (1976): 23–46.

———. "Sources for the Study of Joseph Smith." In *Mormon Americana: A Guide to Sources and Collections in the United States*, edited by David J. Whittaker, 7–28. Provo, UT: BYU Studies, 1995.

———. "The Writing of Joseph Smith's History." *BYU Studies* 11, no. 4 (Summer 1971): 439–74.

Johnson, Benjamin F. *My Life's Review.* Independence, MO: Zion's Printing and Publishing, 1947.

Johnson, Janiece, and Jennifer Reeder. *The Witness of Women: Firsthand Experiences and Testimonies from the Restoration.* Salt Lake City: Deseret Book, 2017.

Johnson, Jeffery O. "The Professionalization of the Archives of the LDS Church and the State of Utah: An Interview with Jeffery O. Johnson." *Mormon Historical Studies* 16, no. 1 (Spring 2015): 180–224.

Johnson, Paul E., and Sean Wilentz. *The Kingdom of Matthias: A Story of Sex and Salvation in 19th-Century America.* New York: Oxford University Press, 1994.

Jones, Christopher C. "The Complete Record of the Nauvoo Library and Literary Institute." *Mormon Historical Studies* 10, no. 1 (Spring 2009): 180–204.

———. "The Power and Form of Godliness: Methodist Conversion Narratives and Joseph Smith's First Vision." *Journal of Mormon History* 37, no. 2 (Spring 2011): 88–114.

Jones, Edward T. "The Theology of Thomas Dick and Its Possible Relation to Joseph Smith." Master's thesis, Brigham Young University, 1969.

Jorgensen, Lynne Watkins. "The Mantle of the Prophet Joseph Passes to Brother Brigham: A Collective Spiritual Witness." *BYU Studies* 36, no. 4 (1996–97): 125–204.

Journal of Discourses. 26 vols. Liverpool and London: LDS Booksellers Depot, 1855–1886.

Juvenile Instructor. 1866–1929.

Kelley, William H. "The Hill Cumorah and the Book of Mormon." *Saints' Herald*, June 1, 1881.

Kidder, Daniel P. *Mormonism and the Mormons: A Historical View of the Rise and Progress of the Sect Self-Styled Latter-Day Saints.* New York: G. Lane and P. P. Sandford, 1842.

Kimball, Stanley B. *Heber C. Kimball: Mormon Patriarch and Pioneer.* Urbana: University of Illinois Press, 1981.

Kirkham, Francis W. *A New Witness for Christ in America: The Book of Mormon.* Independence, MO: Zion's Printing and Publishing, 1942.

Lambert, Neal E., and Richard H. Cracroft. "Literary Form and Historical Understanding: Joseph's First Vision." *Journal of Mormon History* 7 (1980): 31–42.

Larson, Stan. "Another Look at Joseph Smith's First Vision." *Dialogue* 47, no. 2 (Summer 2014): 39–43.

———. "The Historicity of the Matthean Sermon on the Mount in 3 Nephi." In *New Approaches to the Book of Mormon*, edited by Brent Lee Metcalfe, 115–63. Salt Lake City: Signature Books, 1993.

Latter Day Saints' Messenger and Advocate. October 1834–September 1837.

Latter-day Saints' Millennial Star. May 1840–December 1970.

Launius, Roger D. "American Home Missionary Society Ministers and Mormon Nauvoo: Selected Letters." *Western Illinois Regional Studies* 8, no. 1 (Spring 1985): 16–45.

———. "Is Joseph Smith Relevant to the Community of Christ." *Dialogue* 39, no. 4 (Winter 2006): 58–67.

———. *Joseph Smith III: Pragmatic Prophet.* Urbana: University of Illinois Press, 1995.

Lee, John D. *Journals of John D. Lee: 1846–47 and 1859.* Edited by Charles Kelly. Salt Lake City: University of Utah Press, 1984.

———. *A Mormon Chronicle: The Diaries of John D. Lee, 1848–1876.* Edited by Robert Glass Cleland and Juanita Brooks. 2 vols. Salt Lake City: University of Utah Press, 1983.

Leonard, Glen M. *Nauvoo: A Place of Peace, A People of Promise.* Salt Lake City: Deseret Book and Brigham Young University Press, 2002.

Littlefield, Lyman Omer. *Reminiscences of Latter-day Saints.* Logan, UT: Utah Journal, 1888.

Ludlow, Daniel H., ed. *Encyclopedia of Mormonism.* 4 vols. New York: Macmillan, 1992.

Lyon, T. Edgar. *Apostasy to Restoration.* Salt Lake City: Deseret Book, 1960.

MacKay, Michael Hubbard. *Sacred Space: Exploring the Birthplace of Mormonism.* Provo, UT: Religious Studies Center, Brigham Young University, 2016.

MacKay, Michael Hubbard, and Gerrit J. Dirkmaat. *From Darkness unto Light: Joseph Smith's Translation and Publication of the Book of Mormon.* Salt Lake City: Brigham Young University, Religious Studies Center and Deseret Book, 2015.

MacKay, Michael Hubbard, and Nicholas J. Frederick. *Joseph Smith's Seer Stones.* Provo, UT: Brigham Young University, Religious Studies Center and Deseret Book, 2016.

Madsen, Gordon S., Jeffrey N. Walker, and John W. Welch, eds. *Sustaining the Law: Joseph Smith's Legal Encounters.* Provo, UT: Brigham Young University Press, 2014.

Madsen, Truman G. *Joseph Smith, the Prophet.* Salt Lake City: Bookcraft, 1993.

Maffly-Kipp, Laurie F. "Tracking the Sincere Believer: 'Authentic' Religion and the Enduring Legacy of Joseph Smith Jr." In *Joseph Smith Jr.: Reappraisals after Two Centuries,* edited by Reid L. Neilson and Terryl L. Givens, 175–88. New York: Oxford University Press, 2009.

Marks, David. *The Life of David Marks: To the 26th Year of His Age.* Limerick, ME: Office of the Morning Star, 1831.

Marquardt, H. Michael, comp. *Early Patriarchal Blessings of the Church of Jesus Christ of Latter-day Saints.* Salt Lake City: Smith-Pettit Foundation, 2007.

———. "Ezra Booth on Early Mormonism: A Look at His 1831 Letters." *John Whitmer Historical Association Journal* 28 (2008): 65–87.

———, trans. *Joseph Smith's 1832–34 Diary: Also Joseph Smith's 1832 Account of His Early Life.* Salt Lake City: Modern Microfilm, 1979.

———, trans. *Joseph Smith's 1835–36 Diary.* Salt Lake City: Modern Microfilm, 1979.

———, trans. *Joseph Smith's 1838–39 Diaries.* Salt Lake City: Modern Microfilm, 1982.

Marquardt, H. Michael, and Wesley P. Walters, *Inventing Mormonism: Tradition and the Historical Record.* Salt Lake City: Smith Research Associates, 1994.

Martin, Moses. *A Treatise on the Fulness of the Everlasting Gospel, Setting forth Its First Principles, Promises and Blessings.* New York: J. W. Harrison, 1842.

Matthews, Robert J. *"A Plainer Translation": Joseph Smith's Translation of the Bible, A History and Commentary.* Provo, UT: Brigham Young University Press, 1985.

McConkie, Bruce R. *Mormon Doctrine.* Salt Lake City: Bookcraft, 1958 and 1966.

McConkie, Joseph Fielding, and Robert L. Millet. *Doctrinal Commentary on the Book of Mormon.* 4 vols. Salt Lake City: Bookcraft, 1991.

McConkie, Mark L. *Remembering Joseph: Personal Recollections of Those Who Knew the Prophet Joseph Smith.* Salt Lake City: Deseret Book, 2003.

McGavin, E. Cecil. *Mormonism and Masonry.* Salt Lake City: Bookcraft, 1956.

McLellin, William E. "James J. Strang, of Voree, Wis." *Ensign of Liberty of the Church of Christ,* April 1847.

———. *The Journals of William E. McLellin: 1831–1836.* Edited by Jan Shipps and John W. Welch. Provo, UT: BYU Studies and University of Illinois Press, 1994.

———. *The William E. McLellin Papers, 1854–1880.* Edited by Stan Larson and Samuel J. Passey. Salt Lake City: Signature Books, 2007.

Metcalfe, Brent Lee, ed. *New Approaches to the Book of Mormon: Explorations in Critical Methodology.* Salt Lake City: Signature Books, 1993.

Miller, Reuben. *A Defence of the Claims of James J. Strang to the Authority Now Usurped by the Twelve; and Shewing Him to be the True Successor of Joseph Smith, as First President of the High Priesthood.* Burlington, WI: n.p., 1846.

———. *James J. Strang, Weighed in the Balance of Truth, and Found Wanting. His Claims as First President of the Melchizedek Priesthood Refuted.* Burlington, WI: n.p., 1846.

———. *Truth Shall Prevail: A Short Reply to an Article Published in the Voree Herald (Reveille), by J. C. Bennett; and the Willful Falsehoods of J. J. Strang.* Burlington, WI: n.p., 1847.

Millet, Robert L. *Precept upon Precept: Joseph Smith and the Restoration of Doctrine.* Salt Lake City: Deseret Book, 2016.

Morain, William D. *The Sword of Laban: Joseph Smith, Jr. and the Dissociated Mind.* Washington: American Psychiatric Press, 1998.

Morgan, Dale. *Dale Morgan on Early Mormonism: Correspondence & a New History.* Edited by John Philip Walker. Salt Lake City: Signature Books, 1986.

Morris, Larry E. "'The Private Character of the Man That Bore That Testimony': Oliver Cowdery and His Critics." In *Oliver Cowdery: Scribe, Elder, Witness*, edited by John W. Welch and Larry E. Morris, 281–319. Provo, UT: Neal A. Maxwell Institute for Religious Scholarship, 2006.

Mulder, William, and A. Russell Mortensen, eds. *Among the Mormons: Historic Accounts by Contemporary Observers.* New York: Alfred A. Knopf, 1969.

Neilson, Reid L., and Terryl L. Givens, eds. *Joseph Smith Jr.: Reappraisals after Two Centuries.* New York: Oxford University Press, 2009.

Neilson, Reid L., and Ronald W. Walker, eds. *Reflections of a Mormon Historian: Leonard J. Arrington on the New Mormon History.* Norman, OK: Arthur H. Clark, 2006.

Newell, Linda King. "Gifts of the Spirit: Women's Share." In *Sisters in Spirit: Mormon Women in Historical and Cultural Perspective*, edited by Maureen Ursenbach Beecher and Lavina Fielding Anderson, 111–50. Urbana, IL: University of Illinois Press, 1987.

Nibley, Hugh. "Censoring Joseph Smith's Story, Part 1." *Improvement Era*, July 1961.

———. "Censoring Joseph Smith's Story, Conclusion." *Improvement Era*, November 1961.

Nimer, Cory. "The Old Guard and Rearguard Actions: Professionalization and the Church Historian's Office." *Journal of Mormon History* 45, no. 1 (January 2019): 110–38.

Norton, Walter A. "Comparative Images: Mormonism and Contemporary Religions as Seen by Village Newspapermen in Western New York and Northeastern Ohio, 1820–1833." PhD diss., Brigham Young University, 1991.

Nuttall, L. John. *In the President's Office: The Diaries of L. John Nuttall, 1879–1892.* Edited by Jedediah S. Rogers. Salt Lake City: Signature Books, Smith-Pettit Foundation, 2007.

"The Ordination of Joseph the Martyr." *True Latter Day Saints' Herald*, June 1861.

Ostler, Blake T. *Exploring Mormon Thought: The Attributes of God.* Salt Lake City: Greg Kofford Books, 2001.

Owens, Lance S. "Joseph Smith: America's Hermetic Prophet." In *The Prophet Puzzle: Interpretive Essays on Joseph Smith*, edited by Bryan Waterman, 155–71. Salt Lake City: Signature Books, 1999.

Packer, Boyd K. "The Twelve Apostles." *Ensign*, November 1996.

Packer, Cameron J. "Cumorah's Cave." *Journal of Book of Mormon Studies* 13, nos. 1–2 (2004): 50–57.

Palmer, Grant H. *An Insider's View of Mormon Origins.* Salt Lake City: Signature Books, 2002.

Parkin, Max H. "Joseph Smith and the United Firm: The Growth and Decline of the Church's First Master Plan of Business and Finance, Ohio and Missouri, 1832–1834." *BYU Studies* 46, no. 3 (2007): 5–66.

Parry, Joseph Hyrum. *Items of Church History, The Government of God, and The Gift of the Holy Ghost, Articles Written by the Prophet Joseph Smith.* Salt Lake City: Jos. Hyrum Parry, 1884, rev ed. 1886.

Partridge, Elinore H. "Characteristics of Joseph Smith's Style and Notes on the Authorship of the Lectures on Faith." Task Papers in LDS History 14. Salt Lake City: History Division, Historical Department, Church of Jesus Christ of Latter-day Saints, 1976.

Partridge, George R., ed. "The Death of a Mormon Dictator: Letters of Massachusetts Mormons, 1843–1848." *New England Quarterly* 9, no. 4 (December 1936): 583–617.

Patten, David Wyman. "To the Saints Scattered Abroad." *Elders' Journal,* July 1838.

Paul, Robert. "Joseph Smith and the Manchester (New York) Library." *BYU Studies* 22, no. 3 (Summer 1982): 333–56.

Penrod, Don L. "Edwin Rushton as the Source of the White Horse Prophecy." *BYU Studies* 49, no. 3 (2010): 75–131.

Peterson, LaMar. *Problems in Mormon Text.* Salt Lake City, UT: n.p., 1957.

Peterson, Paul H. "An Historical Analysis of the Word of Wisdom." Master's thesis, Brigham Young University, 1972.

Peterson, Paul H., and Ronald W. Walker. "Brigham Young's Word of Wisdom Legacy." *BYU Studies* 42, no. 3 (2003): 29–64.

Phipps, Alan J. "The Lectures on Faith: An Authorship Study." Master's thesis, Brigham Young University, 1977.

Porter, Larry C. "The Restoration of the Priesthood." *Religious Studies Center Newsletter* 9, no. 3 (May 1995): 1–12.

Pratt, Orson. *Divine Authenticity of the Book of Mormon.* Liverpool: R. James, 1850–1851.

———. *Divine Authority, or the Question, Was Joseph Smith Sent of God?* Liverpool: R. James, 1848.

———. *A[n] Interesting Account of Several Remarkable Visions, and of the Late Discovery of Ancient American Records.* Edinburgh: Ballantyne and Hughes, 1840.

———. *The Orson Pratt Journals.* Edited by Elden J. Watson. Salt Lake City: Elden J. Watson, 1975.

———. "The Pre-existence of Man." *Seer,* February–September 1853.

———. "The Question Answered, Was Joseph Smith Sent of God?" *Frontier Guardian,* February 7, 1849.

———. *Reply to a Pamphlet Printed at Glasgow, with the "Approbation of Clergymen of Different Denominations."* Liverpool: R. James, 1849.

———. *A Series of Pamphlets.* Liverpool: Franklin D. Richards, 1852.

Pratt, Parley P. *Late Persecution of the Church of Jesus Christ of Latter Day Saints.* New York: J. W. Harrison, 1840.

———. *Letter to Queen Victoria.* Manchester, England: n.p., 1841.

———. *The Millennium, A Poem: To Which Is Added Hymns and Songs.* Boston: Parley P. Pratt, 1835.

———. *Mormonism Unveiled: Zion's Watchman Unmasked, and its Editor, Mr. L. R. Sunderland Exposed.* New York: O. Pratt and E. Fordham, 1838.

———. *Proclamation to the People of the Coasts and Islands of the Pacific; of Every Nation, Kindred, and Tongue by an Apostle of Jesus Christ.* [Sydney, New South Wales]: C. W. Wandell, [1851].

Prince, Gregory A. "Joseph Smith's First Vision in Historical Context: How a Historical

Narrative Became Theological." *Journal of Mormon History* 41, no. 4 (October 2015): 74–94.

———. *Leonard Arrington and the Writing of Mormon History.* Salt Lake City: University of Utah Press, and Tanner Trust Fund, 2016.

———. "Mormon Priesthood and Organization." In *The Oxford Handbook of Mormonism*, edited by Terryl Givens and Philip L. Barlow, 167–81. New York: Oxford University Press, 2015.

———. *Power from on High: The Development of Mormon Priesthood.* Salt Lake City: Signature Books, 1995.

Quinn, D. Michael. *Early Mormonism and the Magic World View.* 2nd ed. Salt Lake City: Signature Books, 1998.

———, trans. and ed. "The First Months of Mormonism: A Contemporary View by Rev. Diedrich Willers." *New York History* 54, no. 3 (July 1973): 317–33.

———. "Joseph Smith's Experience of a Methodist 'Camp-Meeting' in 1820." *Dialogue Paperless*, E-Paper no. 3, expanded version (Definitive), December 20, 2006.

———. *The Mormon Hierarchy: Origins of Power.* Salt Lake City: Signature Books, 1994.

———. "The Mormon Succession Crisis of 1844." *BYU Studies* 16, no. 2 (Winter 1976): 187–233.

———, ed. *The New Mormon History.* Salt Lake City: Signature Books, 1992.

Reeder, Jennifer, and Kate Holbrook, eds. *At the Pulpit: 185 Years of Discourses by Latter-day Saint Women.* Salt Lake City: Church Historian's Press, 2017.

Remini, Robert V. "Biographical Reflections on the American Joseph Smith." In *The Worlds of Joseph Smith: A Bicentennial Conference at the Library of Congress*, edited by John Welch, 21–30. Provo, UT: Brigham Young University Press, 2006.

———. *Joseph Smith.* New York: Viking Penguin, 2002.

Reynolds, Noel B., ed. *Book of Mormon Authorship Revised.* Provo, UT: Foundation for Ancient Research and Mormon Studies, 1997.

———. "The Case for Sidney Rigdon as Author of the Lectures on Faith." *Journal of Mormon History* 32, no. 3 (Fall 2005): 1–41.

———, ed. *Early Christians in Disarray: Contemporary LDS Perspectives on the Christian Apostasy.* Provo, UT: Foundation for Ancient Research and Mormon Studies, Brigham Young University Press, 2005.

Ricks, Stephen D., Donald W. Parry, and Andrew H. Hedges, eds. *The Disciple as Witness: Essays on Latter-day Saint History and Doctrine in Honor of Richard Lloyd Anderson.* Provo, UT: Foundation for Ancient Research and Mormon Studies, 2000.

Riess, Jana. *The Next Mormons: How Millennials are Changing the LDS Church.* New York: Oxford University Press, 2019.

Riley, I. Woodbridge. *The Founder of Mormonism: A Psychological Study of Joseph Smith, Jr.* London: William Heinemann, 1903.

Ritner, Robert K. *The Joseph Smith Egyptian Papyri: A Complete Edition.* Salt Lake City: Signature Books, 2013.

Roberts, B. H. *A Comprehensive History of the Church of Jesus Christ of Latter-day Saints, Century I.* 6 vols. Provo, UT: Brigham Young University Press, 1965.

Rogers, Jedediah S., ed. *The Council of Fifty: A Documentary History.* Salt Lake City: Signature Books, 2014.

Rowley, Dennis. "The Ezra Booth Letters." *Dialogue* 16, no. 3 (Autumn 1983): 133–37.

Saints: The Story of the Church of Jesus Christ in the Latter Days, Volume 1; The Standard of Truth, 1815–1846. Salt Lake City: The Church of Jesus Christ of Latter-day Saints, 2018.

Scherer, Mark A. *The Journey of a People: The Era of Restoration, 1820–1844*. Independence, MO: Community of Christ, Seminary Press, 2013.

Searle, Howard C. "Willard Richards as Historian." *BYU Studies* 31, no. 2 (Spring 1991): 41–62.

Sheen, Isaac. *Melchisedic and Aaronic Herald*, March 1849.

Sherlock, Richard. "Faith and History: The Snell Controversy." *Dialogue* 12, no. 1 (Spring 1979): 27–42.

Shipps, Jan. *Mormonism: The Story of a New Religious Tradition*. Urbana: University of Illinois Press, 1985.

———. "The Prophet Puzzle: Suggestions Leading toward a More Comprehensive Interpretation of Joseph Smith." *Journal of Mormon History* 1 (1974): 3–20.

———. *Sojourner in the Promised Land: Forty Years among the Mormons*. Urbana: University of Illinois Press, 2000.

Sillitoe, Linda, and Allen Roberts. *Salamander: The Story of the Mormon Forgery Murders*. 2nd ed. Salt Lake City: Signature Books, 1989.

Smith, Andrew F. *The Saintly Scoundrel: The Life and Times of Dr. John Cook Bennett*. Urbana: University of Illinois Press, 1997.

Smith, Emma, comp. *A Collection of Sacred Hymns for the Church of the Latter Day Saints*. Kirtland, Ohio: F. G. Williams, 1835.

———. "Last Testimony of Sister Smith." *Saints' Herald*, October 1, 1879.

Smith, Ethan. *View of the Hebrews; of the Tribes of Israel in America*. Poultney, VT: Smith and Shute, 1825.

Smith, George D. *Nauvoo Polygamy: "... But We Called It Celestial Marriage."* Salt Lake City: Signature Books, 2008.

Smith, Hyrum M., and Janne M. Sjodahl. *The Doctrine and Covenants, Containing Revelations Given to Joseph Smith, Jr., the Prophet*. Salt Lake City: Deseret Book, 1973.

Smith, Joseph. *A Book of Commandments for the Government of the Church of Christ*. Zion [Independence, MO]: W. W. Phelps, 1833.

———. *Book of Mormon*. Palmyra, NY: E. B. Grandin, 1830.

———. *The Doctrine and Covenants of The Church of Jesus Christ of Latter-day Saints, Containing Revelations Given to Joseph Smith, the Prophet*. Salt Lake City: The Church of Jesus Christ of Latter-day Saints, 1981.

———. *Doctrine and Covenants of the Church of the Latter Day Saints: Carefully Selected from the Revelations of God*. Kirtland, OH: F. G. Williams, 1835.

———. *History of the Church of Jesus Christ of Latter-day Saints, Period I. History of Joseph Smith, the Prophet, by Himself*. Edited by Brigham H. Roberts. 2nd ed. rev. 7 vols. Salt Lake City: The Church of Jesus Christ of Latter-day Saints, 1932–1951.

Smith, Joseph, III, Heman C. Smith, and F. Henry Edwards, eds. and comps. *The History of the Reorganized Church of Jesus Christ of Latter Day Saints*. 6 vols. Independence, MO: Herald House, 1967.

Smith, Joseph F. "Restoration of the Melchisedec Priesthood." *Contributor*, June 1889.

———. "Shall We Record Testimony." *Improvement Era*, March 1898.

———. "Status of Children in the Resurrection." *Improvement Era*, May 1918.

Smith, Joseph F[ielding]. "Restoration of the Melchizedek Priesthood." *Improvement Era*, October 1904.

Smith, Lucy. *Biographical Sketches of Joseph Smith the Prophet and His Progenitors for Many Generations*. Liverpool: S. W. Richards, 1853.

Smith, William. *A Revelation Given to William Smith, in 1847, on the Apostasy of the Church and the Pruning of the Vineyard of the Lord*. Philadelphia: n.p., 1848.

———. *William Smith on Mormonism.* Lamoni, IA: Herald Steam Book and Job Office, 1883.

Smith, William V. "Joseph Smith's Sermons and the Early Mormon Documentary Record." In *Foundational Texts of Mormonism: Examining Major Early Sources,* edited by Mark Ashurst-McGee, Robin Scott Jensen, and Sharalyn D. Howcroft, 190–230. New York: Oxford University Press, 2018.

Snow, Lorenzo. *The Only Way to Be Saved…An Explanation of the First Principles of the Doctrine of the Church of Jesus Christ of Latter-day Saints.* London: D. Chalmers, 1841.

———. *The Voice of Joseph, A Brief Account of the Rise, Progress, & Persecutions of the Church of Jesus Christ of Latter-day Saints; with Their Present Position and Prospects in Utah Territory.* Liverpool: S. W. Richards, 1852.

Snyder, Lawrence. "Joseph Smith's First Vision: Sacred Narrative and the Problem of History." *Excursus: A Review of Religious Studies* 1, no. 1 (August 1988): 14–19.

Southerton, Simon G. *Losing a Lost Tribe: Native Americans, DNA, and the Mormon Church.* Salt Lake City: Signature Books, 2004.

Sperry, Sidney B. *Doctrine and Covenants Compendium.* Salt Lake City: Bookcraft, 1965.

———. *The Voice of Israel's Prophets: A Latter-day Saint Interpretation of the Major and Minor Prophets of the Old Testament.* Salt Lake City: Deseret Book, 1952.

Staker, Mark L. "'Commissioned of Jesus Christ': Oliver Cowdery and D&C 13." In *You Shall Have My Word: Exploring the Text of the Doctrine and Covenants,* edited by Scott C. Esplin, Richard O. Cowan, and Rachel Cope, 50–63. Provo, UT: Religious Studies Center, Brigham Young University, 2012.

———. *Hearken, O Ye People: The Historical Setting of Joseph Smith's Ohio Revelations.* Salt Lake City: Greg Kofford Books, 2009.

———. "Where Was the Aaronic Priesthood Restored?: Identifying the Location of John the Baptist's Appearance, May 15, 1829." *Mormon Historical Studies* 12, no. 2 (Fall 2012): 143–59.

Stapley, Jonathan A. "Adoptive Sealing Ritual in Mormonism." *Journal of Mormon History* 37, no. 3 (Summer 2011): 53–118.

———. *The Power of Godliness: Mormon Liturgy and Cosmology.* New York: Oxford University Press, 2018.

Stuy, Brian., ed. *Collected Discourses Delivered by President Wilford Woodruff, His Two Counselors, the Twelve Apostles, and Others.* 5 vols. Burbank, CA: B. H. S. Publishing, 1987.

Swensen, Russel B. "Mormons at the University of Chicago Divinity School: A Personal Reminiscence." *Dialogue* 7, no. 2 (Summer 1972): 37–47.

Talmage, James E. *The Great Apostasy: Considered in the Light of Scriptural and Secular History.* Salt Lake City: Deseret News, 1909.

Talmage, Jeremy. "Forging a Dream: The Fabrication of Mosiah Hancock's Premortal Vision." *Mormon Historical Studies* 18, no. 2 (Fall 2017): 71–91.

Tamez, Jared. Review of S. Michael Tracy, *Millions Shall Know Brother Joseph Again: The Joseph Smith Photograph. Journal of Mormon History* 35, no. 3 (Summer 2009): 249–55.

Tanner, Jerald and Sandra. *Mormonism: Shadow or Reality.* 4th ed. Salt Lake City: Utah Lighthouse Ministry, 1982.

Taylor, Alan. "The Early Republic's Supernatural Economy: Treasure Seeking in the American Northeast, 1780–1830." *American Quarterly* 38, no. 1 (Spring 1986): 6–34.

———. "Rediscovering the Context of Joseph Smith's Treasure Seeking." *Dialogue* 19, no. 4 (Winter 1986): 18–28.

Taylor, John. *Three Nights' Public Discussion between the Revds. C. W. Cleeve, James Robertson, and Philip Cater, and John Taylor, of the Church of Jesus Christ of Latter-day Saints.* Liverpool: John Taylor, 1850.

Teachings of Presidents of the Church, Joseph Smith. Salt Lake City: The Church of Jesus Christ of Latter-day Saints, 2007.

Thompson, Charles B. *Evidences in Proof of the Book of Mormon, being a Divinely Inspired Record.* Batavia, NY: D. D. Waite, 1841.

Times and Seasons. November 1839–February 1846.

Tobler, Ryan G. "'Saviors on Mount Zion': Mormon Sacramentalism, Mortality, and the Baptism for the Dead." *Journal of Mormon History* 39, no. 4 (Fall 2013): 182–238.

Topping, Gary. *Leonard J. Arrington: A Historian's Life.* Norman, OK: Arthur H. Clark, 2008.

Tracy, Shannon M. *In Search of Joseph.* Orem, UT: KenningHouse, 1995.

———. *Millions Shall Know Brother Joseph Again: The Joseph Smith Photograph.* Salt Lake City: Eborn Publishing, 2008.

Tullidge, Edward W. *Life of Joseph the Prophet.* New York: Tullidge and Crandall, 1878.

Turley, Richard E., Jr. "The Calling of the Twelve Apostles and the Seventy in 1835." In *Joseph: Exploring the Life and Ministry of the Prophet,* edited by Susan Easton Black and Andrew C. Skinner, 230–42. Salt Lake City: Deseret Book, 2005.

———. *Victims: The LDS Church and the Mark Hofmann Case.* Urbana, IL: University of Illinois Press, 1992.

Turley, Richard E., Jr., and Steven C. Harper, eds. *Preserving the History of the Latter-day Saints.* Provo, UT: Religious Studies Center, Brigham Young University, 2010.

Turley, Richard E., Jr., Janiece L. Johnson, and LaJean Purcell Carruth, eds. *Mountain Meadows Massacre: Collected Legal Papers.* 2 vols. Norman: University of Oklahoma Press, 2017.

Turley, Richard E., Jr., and William W. Slaughter. *How We Got the Doctrine and Covenants.* Salt Lake City: Deseret Book, 2012.

Turner, Jonathan B. *Mormonism in All Ages: Or the Rise, Progress, and Causes of Mormonism, with the Biography of Its Author and Founder, Joseph Smith, Junior.* New York: Platt and Peters, 1842.

Tyler, Alice Felt. *Freedom's Ferment: Phases of American Social History from the Colonial Period to the Outbreak of the Civil War.* New York: Harper Torchbooks, 1962.

Tyler, Daniel. "Recollections of the Prophet Joseph Smith." *Juvenile Instructor,* February 15, 1892.

Underwood, Grant. "Attempting to Situate Joseph Smith." In *The Worlds of Joseph Smith: A Bicentennial Conference at the Library of Congress,* edited by John W. Welch, 41–52. Provo, UT: Brigham Young University Press, 2006.

———. *The Millenarian World of Early Mormonism.* Urbana: University of Illinois Press, 1999.

Van Orden, Bruce. *We'll Sing and We'll Shout: The Life and Times of W. W. Phelps.* Provo, UT: Religious Studies Center, Brigham Young University, 2018.

Van Wagoner, Richard S. "The Making of a Mormon Myth: The 1844 Transfiguration of Brigham Young." *Dialogue* 28 no. 4 (Winter 1995): 159–82.

———. *Mormon Polygamy: A History.* Salt Lake City: Signature Books, 1989.

———. *Natural Born Seer: Joseph Smith, American Prophet, 1805–1830.* Salt Lake City: Smith-Pettit Foundation, 2016.

———. *Sidney Rigdon: A Portrait in Religious Excess.* Salt Lake City: Signature Books, 1994.

Van Wagoner, Richard S., and Steven C. Walker. "Joseph Smith: 'The Gift of Seeing.'" *Dialogue* 15, no. 2 (Summer 1982): 48–68.

Vogel, Dan. *Early Mormon Documents.* 5 vols. Salt Lake City: Signature Books, 1996–2003.

———. "Evolution of Early Mormon Priesthood Narratives." *John Whitmer Historical Association Journal* 34, no. 1 (Spring/Summer 2014): 58–80.

———, ed. *History of Joseph Smith and the Church of Jesus Christ of Latter-day Saints: A Source- and Text-Critical Edition.* 8 vols. Salt Lake City: Smith-Pettit Foundation, 2015.

———. *Indian Origins and the Book of Mormon.* Salt Lake City: Signature Books, 1986.

———. *Joseph Smith: The Making of a Prophet.* Salt Lake City: Signature Books, 2004.

———. *Religious Seekers and the Advent of Mormonism.* Salt Lake City: Signature Books, 1988.

Vogel, Dan, and Scott C. Dunn. "'The Tongue of Angels': Glossolalia among Mormonism's Founders." *Journal of Mormon History* 19, no. 2 (Fall 1993): 1–34.

Walker, Charles Lowell. *Diary of Charles Lowell Walker.* Edited by A. Karl Larson and Katharine Miles Larson. 2 vols. Logan, UT: Utah State University Press, 1980.

Walker, Jeffrey N. "Invoking Habeas Corpus in Missouri and Illinois." In *Sustaining the Law: Joseph Smith's Legal Encounters,* edited by Gordon S. Madsen, Jeffrey N. Walker, and John W. Welch, 388–96. Provo, UT: Brigham Young University Press, 2014.

Walker, Ronald W., and Doris R. Dant, eds. *Nearly Everything Imaginable: The Everyday Life of Utah's Mormon Pioneers.* Provo, UT: Brigham Young University Press, 1999.

Walker, Ronald W., Richard E. Turley Jr., and Glen M. Leonard. *Massacre at Mountain Meadows: An American Tragedy.* New York: Oxford University Press, 2008.

Walker, Ronald W., David J. Whittaker, and James B. Allen. *Mormon History.* Urbana: University of Illinois Press, 2001.

Walker, Steven C. "Seer." In *Encyclopedia of Mormonism,* edited by Daniel H. Ludlow, 1292–93. New York: Macmillan, 1992.

Walters, Wesley P., and Richard L. Bushman. "Roundtable: The Question of the Palmyra Revival." *Dialogue* 4, no. 1 (Spring 1969): 61–81.

Waterman, Bryan, ed. *The Prophet Puzzle: Interpretive Essays on Joseph Smith.* Salt Lake City: Signature Books, 1999.

Watson, Elden J. "The 'Prognostication' of Asa Wild." *BYU Studies* 37, no. 3 (1997–98): 223–30.

Watt, Ronald G. *The Mormon Passage of George D. Watt: First British Convert, Scribe in Zion.* Logan, UT: Utah State University Press, 2009.

Welch, John W. "The Miraculous Translation of the Book of Mormon." In *Opening the Heavens: Accounts of Divine Manifestations, 1820–1844,* 77–213. Provo, UT: Brigham Young University Press and Deseret Book, 2005.

———, ed. *Opening the Heavens: Accounts of Divine Manifestations, 1820–1844.* Provo, UT: Brigham Young University Press and Deseret Book, 2005.

———, ed. *The Worlds of Joseph Smith: A Bicentennial Conference at the Library of Congress.* Provo, UT: Brigham Young University Press, 2006.

Welch, John W., and Larry E. Morris, eds. *Oliver Cowdery: Scribe, Elder, Witness.* Provo, UT: Neal A. Maxwell Institute for Religious Scholarship, 2006.

Whitmer, David. *An Address to All Believers in Christ.* Richmond, MO: self-published, 1887.

Whitney, Orson F. "Joseph Smith in Literature." *Improvement Era,* December 1905.

———. *Life of Heber C. Kimball.* Salt Lake City: Bookcraft, 1973. First published in 1888.

Whittaker, David J. "The 'Articles of Faith' in Early Mormon Literature and Thought." In *New Views of Mormon History: Essays in Honor of Leonard J. Arrington,* edited by

Davis Bitton and Maureen Ursenbach Beecher, 63–92. Salt Lake City: University of Utah Press, 1987.

——, ed. *Mormon Americana: A Guide to Sources and Collections in the United States.* Provo, UT: BYU Studies, 1995.

Whittaker, David J., and Arnold K. Garr, eds. *A Firm Foundation: Church Organization and Administration.* Salt Lake City: Religious Studies Center, Brigham Young University, and Deseret Book, 2011.

Widtsoe, John A. *Evidences and Reconciliations.* Salt Lake City: Bookcraft, 1960.

——. *Joseph Smith: Seeker after Truth, Prophet of God.* Salt Lake City: Deseret News Press, 1952.

——. *The Message of the Doctrine and Covenants.* Salt Lake City: Bookcraft, 1969.

Widtsoe, John A., and Leah D. Widtsoe. *The Word of Wisdom: A Modern Interpretation.* [Salt Lake City]: Deseret News Press, 1938.

Wilcox, Miranda, and John D. Young, eds. *Standing Apart: Mormon Historical Consciousness and the Concept of Apostasy.* New York: Oxford University Press, 2014.

Williams, Frederick G. *The Life of Dr. Frederick G. Williams: Counselor to the Prophet Joseph Smith.* Provo, UT: BYU Studies, 2012.

Winchester, Benjamin. *Gospel Reflector*, February 15 and March 15, 1841.

——. *A History of the Priesthood from the Beginning of the World to the Present Time, Written in Defense of the Doctrine and Position of the Church of Jesus Christ of Latter-day Saints.* Philadelphia: Brown, Bicking, and Guilbert, 1843.

Wood, Gordon S. "Evangelical America and Early Mormonism." *New York History* 61, no. 4 (October 1980): 358–86.

Woodford, Robert J. "The Historical Development of the Doctrine and Covenants." PhD Dissertation, Brigham Young University, 1974.

Woodruff, Wilford. *Wilford Woodruff's Journal, 1833–1898. Typescript.* Transcribed and edited by Scott G. Kenney. 9 vols. Salt Lake City: Signature Books, 1983–1985.

Woodworth, Jed. "Josiah Quincy's 1844 Visit with Joseph Smith." *BYU Studies* 39, no. 4 (2000): 71–87.

Young, Kimball. *Isn't One Wife Enough: The Story of Mormon Polygamy.* New York: Henry Holt, 1954.

Young, Spencer E. "'Complexity and Richness': Reenvisioning the Middle Ages for Mormon Historical Narratives." In *Standing Apart: Mormon Historical Consciousness and the Concept of Apostasy*, edited by Miranda Wilcox and John D. Young, 242–64. New York: Oxford University Press, 2014.

Young Woman's Journal, October 1889–October 1929.

Zinsser, William, ed. *Extraordinary Lives: The Art and Craft of American Biography.* Boston: Houghton Mifflin, 1986.

Joseph Smith Papers Project

Grow, Matthew J., Ronald K. Esplin, Mark Ashurst-McGee, Gerrit J. Dirkmaat, and Jeffrey D. Mahas, eds. *Council of Fifty, Minutes, March 1844–January 1846.* Vol. 1 of the Administrative Records series of *The Joseph Smith Papers*, edited by Ronald K. Esplin, Matthew J. Grow, and Matthew C. Godfrey. Salt Lake City: Church Historian's Press, 2016.

MacKay, Michael Hubbard, Gerrit J. Dirkmaat, Grant Underwood, Robert J. Woodford, and William G. Hartley, eds. *Documents, Volume 1: July 1828–June 1831.* Vol. 1 of the Documents series of *The Joseph Smith Papers*, edited by Dean C. Jessee, Ronald K. Esplin, Richard Lyman Bushman, and Matthew J. Grow. Salt Lake City: Church Historian's Press, 2013.

Godfrey, Matthew C., Mark Ashurst-McGee, Grant Underwood, Robert J. Woodford, and William G. Hartley, eds. *Documents, Volume 2: July 1831–January 1833*. Vol. 2 of the Documents series of *The Joseph Smith Papers*, edited by Dean C. Jessee, Ronald K. Esplin, Richard Lyman Bushman, and Matthew J. Grow. Salt Lake City: Church Historian's Press, 2013.

Dirkmaat, Gerrit J., Brent M. Rogers, Grant Underwood, Robert J. Woodford, and William G. Hartley, eds. *Documents, Volume 3: February 1833–March 1834*. Vol. 3 of the Documents series of *The Joseph Smith Papers*, edited by Ronald K. Esplin and Matthew J. Grow. Salt Lake City: Church Historian's Press, 2014.

Godfrey, Matthew C., Brenden W. Rensink, Alex D. Smith, Max H Parkin, and Alexander L. Baugh, eds. *Documents, Volume 4: April 1834–September 1835*. Vol. 4 of the Documents series of *The Joseph Smith Papers*, edited by Ronald K. Esplin and Matthew J. Grow. Salt Lake City: Church Historian's Press, 2016.

Rogers, Brent M., Elizabeth A. Kuehn, Christian K. Heimburger, Max H Parkin, Alexander L. Baugh, and Steven C. Harper, eds. *Documents, Volume 5: October 1835–January 1838*. Vol. 5 of the Documents Series of *The Joseph Smith Papers*, edited by Ronald K. Esplin, Matthew J. Grow, and Matthew C. Godfrey. Salt Lake City: Church Historian's Press, 2017.

Ashurst-McGee, Mark, David W. Grua, Elizabeth A. Kuehn, Alexander L. Baugh, and Brenden W. Rensink, eds. *Documents, Volume 6: February 1838–August 1839*. Vol. 6 of the Documents series of *The Joseph Smith Papers*, edited by Ronald K. Esplin, Matthew J. Grow, and Matthew C. Godfrey. Salt Lake City: Church Historian's Press, 2017.

Godfrey, Matthew C., Spencer W. McBride, Alex D. Smith, and Christopher James Blythe, eds. *Documents, Volume 7: September 1839–January* 1841. Vol. 7 of the Documents series of *The Joseph Smith Papers*, edited by Ronald K. Esplin, Matthew J. Grow, and Matthew C. Godfrey. Salt Lake City: Church Historian's Press, 2018.

Davidson, Karen Lynn, David J. Whittaker, Mark Ashurst-McGee, and Richard L. Jensen, eds. *Histories, Volume 1: Joseph Smith Histories, 1832–1844*. Vol. 1 of the Histories series of *The Joseph Smith Papers*, edited by Dean C. Jessee, Ronald K. Esplin, and Richard Lyman Bushman. Salt Lake City: Church Historian's Press, 2012.

Davidson, Karen Lynn, Richard L. Jensen, and David J. Whittaker, eds. *Histories, Volume 2: Assigned Historical Writings, 1831–1847*. Vol. 2 of the Histories series of *The Joseph Smith Papers*, edited by Dean C. Jessee, Ronald K. Esplin, and Richard Lyman Bushman. Salt Lake City: Church Historian's Press, 2012.

Jessee, Dean C., Mark Ashurst-McGee, and Richard L. Jensen, eds. *Journals, Volume 1: 1832–1839*. Vol. 1 of the Journals series of *The Joseph Smith Papers*, edited by Dean C. Jessee, Ronald K. Esplin, and Richard Lyman Bushman, Salt Lake City: Church Historian's Press, 2008.

Hedges, Andrew H., Alex D. Smith, and Richard Lloyd Anderson, eds. *Journals, Volume 2: December 1841–April 1843*. Vol. 2 of the Journals series of *The Joseph Smith Papers*, edited by Dean C. Jessee, Ronald K. Esplin, and Richard Lyman Bushman, Salt Lake City: Church Historian's Press, 2011.

Hedges, Andrew H., Alex D. Smith, and Brent M. Rogers, eds. *Journals, Volume 3: May 1843–June 1844*. Vol. 3 of the Journals series of *The Joseph Smith Papers*, edited by Ronald K. Esplin and Matthew J. Grow. Salt Lake City: Church Historian's Press, 2015.

Jensen, Robin Scott, Robert J. Woodford, and Steven C. Harper, eds. *Revelations and Translations, Volume 1: Manuscript Revelation Books*. Facsimile edition. Vol. 1 of the Revelations and Translations series of *The Joseph Smith Papers*, edited by Dean C. Jessee, Ronald K. Esplin, and Richard Lyman Bushman. Salt Lake City: Church Historian's Press, 2009.

Jensen, Robin Scott, Richard E. Turley Jr., and Riley M. Lorimer, eds. *Revelations and Translations, Volume 2: Published Revelations.* Vol. 2 of the Revelations and Translations series of *The Joseph Smith Papers,* edited by Dean C. Jessee, Ronald K. Esplin, and Richard Lyman Bushman. Salt Lake City: Church Historian's Press, 2011.

Skousen, Royal, and Robin Scott Jensen, eds. *Revelations and Translations, Volume 3, Part 1: Printer's Manuscript of the Book of Mormon, 1 Nephi–Alma 35.* Facsimile edition. Part 1 of vol. 3 of the Revelations and Translations series of *The Joseph Smith Papers,* edited by Ronald K. Esplin and Matthew J. Grow. Salt Lake City: Church Historian's Press, 2015.

Skousen, Royal, and Robin Scott Jensen, eds. *Revelations and Translations, Volume 3, Part 2: Printer's Manuscript of the Book of Mormon, Alma 36–Moroni 10.* Facsimile edition. Part 2 of vol. 3 of the Revelations and Translations series of *The Joseph Smith Papers,* edited by Ronald K. Esplin and Matthew J. Grow. Salt Lake City: Church Historian's Press, 2015.

Jensen, Robin Scott, and Brian M. Hauglid, eds. *Revelations and Translations, Volume 4: Book of Abraham and Related Manuscripts.* Facsimile edition. Vol. 4 of the Revelations and Translations series of *The Joseph Smith Papers,* edited by Ronald K. Esplin, Matthew J. Grow, Matthew C. Godfrey, and R. Eric Smith. Salt Lake City: Church Historian's Press, 2018.

Newspapers

Alexandria Gazette and Virginia Advertiser.
Buffalo Patriot.
The Gem, of Literature and Science (Rochester, NY).
Deseret News (Salt Lake City, UT).
The Fredonia Censor (Fredonia, NY).
Kansas City Journal.
Liberal Advocate (Rochester, NY).
Morning Courier New York Enquirer, for the Country.
Morning Star (Limerick, ME).
New York Tribune.
Omaha Herald.
Palmyra Freeman (Palmyra, NY).
Peoria Register and North-Western Gazetteer (Peoria, IL).
Philadelphia Sunday Mercury.
The Reflector (Palmyra, NY).
Rochester Daily Advertiser and Telegraph.
Rochester Republican.
The Salt Lake Herald.
Salt Lake Tribune.
The Telegraph (Painesville, OH).
Warsaw Signal (Warsaw, IL).
The Wasp (Nauvoo, IL).
Vermont Chronicle.

Manuscripts

Affidavits about Celestial Marriage, 1869–1915. MS 3423. CHL.

Appleby, William I. Autobiography and Journal, 1848–1856. MS 1401. CHL.

Atiya, Aziz S. Interview. Manuscript of Aziz S. Atiya biography. Excerpt in possession of author.

———. Interview. Everett L. Cooley Oral History Project, no. 42. University of Utah Marriott Library, Manuscripts Division, Salt Lake City, Utah.
Atwood, Millen. Reminiscences and Diary, 1842–1844. MS 1809. CHL.
Ball, Jonah R. Letters, 1842–1843. MS 4393 1. CHL.
Burgess, James. Journal 1841–1848. MS 1858, CHL.
Cahoon, Reynolds. Diary. MS 1115. CHL.
Carter, Jared. Journal. MS 1441. CHL.
Church Historian's Office, History of the Church, 1839–ca. 1882. CR 100 102. CHL.
Clayton, William. Letter, December 10, 1840. MS 5215. CHL.
———. Letter, November 29/December 2, 1840. MS 3682. CHL.
Coltrin, Zebedee. Diaries, 1832–1834. MS 1443. CHL.
Coray, Howard. Autobiographical Sketches, n.d. Howard Coray Papers, ca. 1840–1941. MS 2043. CHL.
———. Reminiscences, undated. MS 8142. CHL.
Cordon, Alfred. Reminiscence and Journal. MS 9856. CHL.
Cowdery, Oliver. Letter, March 23, 1846. MS 2646. CHL.
Curtis, Joseph. Reminiscences and Diary, 1839–1881. MS 1654. CHL.
Davis, Matthew L. Letter, February 6, 1840. MS 522. CHL.
Dunham, Jonathan. Diaries. MS 1387. CHL.
Fleming, Helen Bourne. Helen Bourne Fleming Collection, 1836–1963. MS 9670. CHL.
Gailey, John. Reminiscence and Diary. MS 1089. CHL.
Greene, Evan M. Diaries. MS 1442. CHL.
Gunn, Timothy. Letter, June 15, 1834. MS 7396. CHL.
Gurley, Zenos. "Questions Asked of David Whitmer." MS 4633. CHL.
Historian's Office. History of the Church, 1839–circa 1882. CR 100 102. CHL.
———. Letterpress Copybooks, 1854–1879, 1885–1886. CR 100 38. CHL.
Huntington, Oliver B. Diaries, 1843–1932. MSS 162. L. Tom Perry Special Collections, Brigham Young University, Provo, Utah.
Hyde, Orson. *ein Ruf aus der Wüste*. Translated by Justus Ernst. M230 H994r. CHL.
Kidder, Daniel P. Diary, 1833–1840. Special Collections, Rutgers University, New Brunswick, New Jersey.
Knight, Newel. Autobiography and Journal, ca. 1871. MS 19156. CHL.
Lee, Lafayette C. Notebook. MS 964. CHL.
McIntire, William Patterson. Notebook, 1840–1845. MS 1014. CHL.
Miller, George to Thomas Reynolds, September 4, 1842. Missouri State Archives, Jefferson City, Missouri.
Miller, Reuben. Journal. MS 1392. CHL.
———. Letter to Henry Sabey, November 16, 1848. MS 88. CHL.
Musser, Amos Milton. Amos Milton Musser Collection, 1879–1880. MS 1264. CHL.
Nauvoo 5th Ward High Priests Minutes, December 1844–April 1845. LR 3278 21. CHL.
Nauvoo 9th Ward High Priests Minutes, November 1844–February 1845. LR 3501 21. CHL.
Nauvoo Stake Priests Quorum Minutes, January–June 1845. LR 3102 21. CHL.
Nauvoo Stake Ward Census, 1842. LR 3102 27. CHL.
Partridge, Edward. Edward Partridge Papers. MS 892. CHL.
Phelps, William W. William W. Phelps Papers. VMSS 810. L. Tom Perry Special Collections, Brigham Young University, Provo, Utah.
Plural Marriage Affidavits, circa 1870. MS 2673. CHL.
Post, Stephen. Journals. Steven Post Papers. MS 1304. CHL.
Pratt, Orson. Historian's Office Correspondence Files, 1856–1926. CR 100 394. CHL.
Pratt, Parley P. Collection. Correspondence, 1842–1845. MS 897. CHL.

Presiding Bishopric Bishop's Quorum Minutes, 1841–1851: "A Record of the Quorum of the Lesser Priesthood." CR 4 122. CHL.
Revelations Collection. MS 4583. CHL.
Richards, Franklin D. Journals. MS 1215. CHL.
———. Scriptural items, ca. 1841–1844. MS 4409. CHL.
Richards, Levi. Diary. MS 1284. CHL.
Richards, Samuel W. Statement. MS 3703. CHL.
Richards, Willard. Journal. MS 1490. CHL.
———. Pocket Companion, circa 1840. MS 1490. CHL.
Roberts, Brigham H. B. H. Roberts Collection, 1883–1933. MS 1278. CHL.
School of the Prophets. Salt Lake City Records, 1872–1874. CR 390 7. CHL.
Seventies Record. Book B, 1844–1847. CR 3 51. CHL.
Smith, George A. Deseret Theological Institute Records. MS 14939. CHL.
———. 1834–1877. MS 1322. CHL.
Smith, Joseph. Joseph Smith Collection. MS 155. CHL.
———. Joseph Smith's Office Papers, 1835–1844. MS 21600. CHL.
Smith, Joseph F. Joseph F. Smith Papers. MS 1325. CHL.
Snow, James Chauncey. Reminiscence, ca. November–December 1834. MS 4452. CHL.
Taggart, Richmond. Letter. MS 9864. CHL.
Teachers Quorum Minutes, December 1834–December 1845. MS 3428. CHL.
Tyler, Samuel. Journal. MS 1761. CHL.
Young, Brigham. Brigham Young Collection, Office Files. CR 1234 1. CHL.

Websites

"19th Century Mormon Article Newspaper Index." L. Tom Perry Special Collections, Brigham Young University. https://contentdm.lib.byu.edu/digital/collection/19CMNI/id/13161/rec/76.
The "Book of Conference A." Also known as the Kirtland Council Minute Book and as "Minute Book 1" in the Joseph Smith Papers, Administrative Records. http://www.josephsmithpapers.org/paper-summary/minute-book-1/1#full-transcript.
Broadhurst, Dale. "Uncle Dale's Readings in Early Mormon History." http://www.sidneyrigdon.com/dbroadhu/artindex.htm#NE; https://www.google.com/#q=uncle+dale%27s+old+mormon+articles.
"The Conference Minutes, and Record Book, of Christ's Church of Latter Day Saints." Also known as the "Far West Record" and "Minute Book 2" in the Joseph Smith Papers, Administrative Records. https://www.josephsmithpapers.org/paper-summary/minute-book-2/1#full-transcript.
"Church Buys Printer's Manuscript of Book of Mormon from Community of Christ," September 20, 2017. https://www.lds.org/church/news/church-buys-printers-manuscript-of-book-of-mormon-from-community-of-christ?lang=eng.
The Church of Jesus Christ of Latter-day Saints, Gospel Topics. https://www.lds.org/topics.
Community of Christ, Library and Archives. https://www.cofchrist.org/about-the-library.
First Vision, FairMormon. https://www.fairmormon.org/answers/Joseph_Smith%27s_First_Vision.
First Vision, Mormon Research Ministry. http://www.mrm.org/tag/first-vision.
Joseph Smith Papers. http://www.josephsmithpapers.org/
L. Tom Perry Special Collections, Brigham Young University. https://lib.byu.edu/special-collections/; https://lib.byu.edu/collections/?q=tag:digital.

Lucy Mack Smith, History, 1845, Joseph Smith Papers. https://www.josephsmithpapers.org/paper-summary/lucy-mack-smith-history-1845/354.

"Nauvoo Baptisms for the Dead in the Mississippi River," Family History Library, Salt Lake City, Utah. https://www.familysearch.org/library/books/records/item/386499-nauvoo-baptisms-for-the-dead-in-the-mississippi river?viewer=1&offset=0#page=1&viewer=picture&o=info&n=0&q=

"Plural Marriage in The Church of Jesus Christ of Latter-day Saints." https://www.lds.org/topics/plural-marriage-in-the-church-of-jesus-christ-of-latter-day-saints?lang=eng.

"Priesthood Restoration." http://www.josephsmithpapers.org/site/priesthood-restoration?p=1&highlight=priesthood%20restoration.

Proclamation of the Twelve Apostles of the Church of Jesus Christ, of Latter-day Saints. https://contentdm.lib.byu.edu/digital/collection/NCMP1820-1846/id/2818.

Skousen, Royal. *Book of Mormon Critical Text Project.* http://criticaltext.byustudies.byu.edu/.

"Special Report: Mormonism Besieged by the Modern Age." https://www.reuters.com/article/us-mormonchurch/special-report-mormonism-besieged-by-the-modern-age-idUSTRE80T1CM20120131.

Tanner, Jerald and Sandra. "Mormon and Anti-Mormon Forgeries." *Salt Lake City Messenger*, October 1989. http://www.utlm.org/newsletters/no73.htm.

Watson, Elden J. "Joseph Smith's First Vision: A Harmony," 1983. http://eldenwatson.net/harmony.htm,

Weber, Curtis G. "Skulls and Crossed Bones?: A Forensic Study of the Remains of Hyrum and Joseph Smith." http://mormonhistoricsites.org/wp-content/uploads/2013/04/Skulls-and-Crossed-Bones-A-Forensic-Study-of-the-Remains-of-Hyrum-and-Joseph-Smith.pdf.

Index

A

Aaronic (lesser) priesthood, 177, 181; designed for adults in early church, 256–57; 257n141; in Nauvoo, 264, 265

Adams, Charles Francis, on JS, 115–16

Allen, James B., 19n7, 42n26, 54, 149

Anderson, Richard L., 136

Apostasy from New Testament Christianity, 162, 163–64, 165; recent Mormon interpretations of, 164n12

Apostleship: importance of, 190–213, 229; JS and Oliver Cowdery as apostles, 192, 229

Arrington, Leonard J., 18–21, 19n7, 101n45

"Articles and Covenants," JS and Oliver Cowdery's, 192, 228–29, 234, 237, 257, 261, 361–62

Asbury, Francis, 365–66

Ashurst-McGee, Mark, 41–42

Atiya, Aziz Suryal, 371; on JS, 371–72

Assistant President of the Church, 251

Atwood, Millen, 125

B

Ball, Jonah Randolph, 127

Barlow, Philip L., 338–39

Barstow, George, 73n21

Bauder, Peter, 160

Beman, Alvah, Elders' Quorum president, 184

Bennett, John C., 58, 20506, 207; claimed JS tried to assassinate Lilburn W. Boggs, 206

Bergera, Gary James, 37

Bernhisel, John M., 128–29.

Berry, Wendell, 12

Bitton, Davis, 19n7; on faith, 43–44

Bloom, Harold, 13, 34; on JS, 362–63

Boggs, Lilburn W., 125, 206, 357–58

Book of Abraham, 26, 41

Book of Commandments (Mormon scripture), 154, 229

Book of Mormon (Mormon scripture), 26, 133, 134, 136, 145, 153, 160, 178, 181, 248, 276, 363, 368; accounts of origin of, 5, 137, 138, 181; anti-Catholic sentiment in, 163; authority in, 166; church in, 166; influence on JS, 281–82; influence on organization of the church, 227–28; JS's translation of, 277, 373; manuscript(s) of, 18, 18n4, 368; publication of, 5

Booth, Ezra: influence on JS, 156–60; on JS, 117–18, 156–57

Boynton, John F., and call to Twelve Apostles, 247

Bradley, Don, 41–42

Branches, church, 5, 134, 234, 254, 263, 264

Brief History of the Church (Corrill), 119

Brigham Young University, L. Tom Perry Special Collections, 28

Brodie, Fawn M. *See No Man Knows My History*

Brooke, John L., 97, 295, 370–71

Brown, Pelatiah, 340

Bullard, Isaac ("Pilgrim"), comparison to JS, 366–67

Bullock, Thomas, JS clerk/historian, 78, 140, 185

Burnett, Peter H., attorney for JS, 310

Burnett, Stephen, on JS, 118–19

Bushman, Richard Lyman, 11, 20, 67, 90; on JS, 273–74, 293–94, 293n5, 309, 311, 323, 380, 384; on claim that JS deriving his thinking from hermetic philosophy, 370–71; on speculation in writing history, 59–60, 100

C
Cahoon, Reynolds, 150, 158
Campbell, Alexander, 58, 159; appraisal of JS and Book of Mormon, 95, 95n22, 109; and Disciples of Christ, 94–96, 95n22; writings, 283–84
Carruth, LaJean Purcell, and Pitman shorthand, 30
Catholicism, 162, 223, 225, 275; bias against, 162–63, 163n10; early Mormon attitude toward, 163; JS's likely view of, 162, 163; 166
Caswell, Henry, 42n26
Chase, Daryl, 17
Cheesman, Paul R., 147
Church Historian's Press (LDS), 21
"Church History" (Wentworth letter), in *Times and Seasons*, 73n21; also updated in Rupp's *He Pasa Ekklesia* as "Latter Day Saints," 74
Church of Christ (1830), 5, 73–74, 133, 137, 146. *See also* Church of Jesus Christ of Latter-day Saints
Church of Jesus Christ of Latter-day Saints (LDS), 5, 204; claims of mismanagement of its history, 9–10, 23, 31, 52, 63, 386; culture and influence of, 9–10, 48; description of members, 32; early criticism of, 156–57; Gospel Topics, 30; organization at Fayette, New York, 5, 73–74, 229; persecution of, 5; providing access to its history, 26–27, 44, 47, 386; restructure of in Kirtland, January 1836, 253; scholars' cooperation with RLDS scholars, 24–25; succession in leadership, 208–13. *See also* Church of Christ (1830)
Clayton, William, 41; on JS, 123–25, 221, 302
Clerks/historians/scribes, JS's: influence on JS's history, 2, 6, 7, 8, 9, 40, 52, 67–68, 69–79, 74–75, 139–40, 167, 196, 272; influence on characterization of JS, 271; influence on JS's revelations, 70
Common consent, 234, 237, 254, 255
Community of Christ (formerly Reorganized Church of Jesus Christ of Latter Day Saints, RLDS), 20, 21; cooperation with LDS scholars, 24–25; emphasis on Jesus Christ, 20–21; on higher priesthood restoration, 214–15; temple, 20; views on Joseph Smith, 21n14.
Conferences, 230, 234, 238–39; June 1830 (Fayette, NY), 246; June 1831 (Kirtland, OH), 89, 137, 139, 166–67, 183, 220, 230–31; October 1831 (Orange, OH), 231–33, 277; October 1831 (Hiram, OH), 234; November 1831 (Hiram, OH), 70, 154; January 1832 (Independence, MO), 231; January 1832 (Amherst, OH), 89, 150, 237; January 1832, (Independence, MO), 231; October 1839 (Commerce, IL), 263; April 1840 (Nauvoo, IL), 353; October 1840 (Nauvoo, IL), 197, 354; April 1841 (Nauvoo, IL), 264–65; October 1841 (Nauvoo, IL), 195, 357; April 1844 (Nauvoo, IL), 359; October 1848 (Pottawattamie County, IA), 172–75; October 1880 (Salt Lake City, UT), 136
Copley, Leman, 310
Coray, Howard, 78, 143
Corrill, John, 119–20
Council of Fifty, 28–29, 312, 313
Councils, 234, 238
Cowdery, Oliver, 138, 154, 157, 167–69, 172, 177, 234, 235–36, 275, 277, 307, 373; as an apostle, 192, 229, 245; as editor of *Messenger and Advocate*, 168–69, 377–79; Assistant President to JS, 251; charged to "search out the twelve," 246; "Charge" to the Twelve Apostles, 248; claims that history was forgotten, 65; critics of, 168, 168n23, 170; excommunication of, 244; forgeries of Cowdery statements, 168n23; letters on early history to W. W. Phelps, 378–79; on JS's early visions, 75; on biblical literalism, 338; on priesthood restoration, 71, 167, 169, 172–77, 178, 187; organization of the church, 5, 223, 227; portrayal of a prophet (JS), 377–79; rebaptized, 174; revelation (1829), "Articles of the Church of Christ," 228; "second elder," 237; visions with JS, 172–77, 192, 194, 279–80
Cowdery, Warren, 168, 279, 376

Crawley, Peter, 154
Crosby, Jonathan, on JS, 122
Critics of JS, 24–25, 33, 35, 48, 91, 98, 109–11, 385; "apostates," 117–21; E. D. Howe, 107

D
Darowski, Joseph F., on conferences and councils, 238–40
Davis, Matthew L., journalist on JS, 114–15, 301
Davis, Samuel H., 300–301
Decker, Ed. (critic of priesthood restoration), 170
Defenders of JS, 3, 34–35, 38, 44, 47, 48, 62, 83, 91, 108, 141, 144, 148
DePillis, Mario (Catholic scholar of Mormonism), 90–91
Deseret News, 7; review of Bushman, *Rough Stone Rolling*, 48; "History (Life) of Joseph Smith" in, 77
Doctrine and Covenants (Mormon scripture), 26, 161, 249, 363, 372; manuscript revelations, 18; means of distributing JS's revelations, 359
documentary (historical) record: importance of understanding, 12–13, 19, 33, 34, 35, 36, 39–40, 41, 44, 45, 48, 52–53, 59, 60, 87, 105, 133, 177, 193, 267, 272, 273, 297, 385–86; incomplete, about JS, 273, 282–83, 293, 322–23, 386; judging the credibility of, 56–59, 63–64

E
"Early Account of Joseph Smith's First Vision" (Jessee), 149
Ehrman, Bart D., 68, 332
ein Ruf aus der Wűste (A Cry from the Wilderness, Hyde), 182
Elders' Journal (1837–1838, periodical), 186, 352; JS as editor of, 284, 352
Elias, 177, 192; appearance in Kirtland House of the Lord, 279–80
Elijah, 177, 192–94, 193n10, 300; appearance in Kirtland House of the Lord, 279–80; sealing power, 232
Ellis, Joseph J., on presentism, 55; on cultural influence, 98
Empiricism, primacy of, in culture, 43
Enders, Donald L., 280, 281
"Endowment of power from on high," 199, 201, 204–5, 248, 256
Epicurus, regarding empiricism, 42
Esplin, Ronald K., 17, 21
Evans, John Henry, 36; on JS, 96
Evans, Richard L., on truth, 44
Evening and the Morning Star (1832–1834, periodical), 134, 155–56, 164, 165, 229, 283–84
Everett, Addison, on priesthood restoration, 215–20

F
Faith and reason, 43
Faith, in study of JS, 42–44
Faulring, Scott H., 172
Female Relief Society of Nauvoo, 29, 29n34, 233; JS delivered keys to, 202; JS to, 342; organization of, 200; and the priesthood, 201–4; plural marriage, 202; gifts of the spirit, 202–3.
Fielding, Joseph, on similarities of Masonry and priesthood, 199–200
First Fifty Years of Relief Society (Derr, et al.), 29
First Presidency, 150, 237, 250
First principles and ordinances, 276
First Vision, JS's, 4–5, 9, 38, 136, 162, 273, 274; 1832 account of, 4–5, 136, 137, 138, 139, 375–76; 1838/39 account of, 141, 145; ca. 1841 history of, 141; "Church History" (Wentworth letter), 141, 145; bibliography of, 140n18; Community of Christ perspective on, 21n14; criticism of, 275–76; challenges to, 144, 146; first printed statement of, by Orson Pratt, 181, 276; JS's reluctance to tell, 276–77, 280; November 1835 account, 141, 146, 148; second-hand accounts of, 141–42, 145, 145n39; understanding of by early members, 145, 178
Ford, Thomas (governor of Illinois and critic of JS), 114
Forgeries, 11, 63–64, 63n39
Freemasonry, 97, 198–200, 204; and anti-Masonry movement, 198; claims of ancient origin, 198–99; commonalities with Mormonism, 199; equation

of priesthood with Masonry, 198–200; William Morgan's exposé of and subsequent murder, 198

G

Gause, Jesse, 237, 252
Givens, Terryl L., on JS's notions of man's premortal existence, 97, 370
Gottschalk, Louis: on memory as history, 67; methodology of history, 50, 54–57
Greek psalter, JS and, 42n26
Groesbeck, C. Jess, psychobiography of JS, 62
Grunder, Rick, explained JS's milieu, 91–92. See also *Mormon Parallels*
Gurley, Zenos, 171

H

Hancock, Levi, on understanding priesthood, 183
Harris, Martin, 138, 229, 246
Harris, Sydney J., 298, on historians, 59
Hartley, William G.: on priesthood in early church, 256–57, 264; on wards in Nauvoo, 263n161
Hatch, Nathan O., on America's religious climate, 89, 99, 106, 155, 364
Hauglid, Brian M., on Book of Abraham, 41
Haven, Charlotte, on JS, 127–28, 262; on LDS church, 265
Healings and other gifts of the spirit in the name of Jesus Christ (not by priesthood), 187–89, 189n85
Higbee, Chauncey, 120
Higbee, Francis, 120
Hill Cumorah, cave in, 57–58, 58n21
Hill, Marvin S., 34n6, 136
Historian's Office (LDS), 18, 140
History: bias in written, 63, 67, 78; nineteenth-century perspective on, 65; speculation in written, 59, 60–62; twentieth-century perspective on, 65
History Division, Historical Department, (LDS), 18, 21
Historian's Office. *See* History (Historical) Department (LDS)
Historical method (historiography), 50–64.
History (Historical) Department (LDS): 17–18, 21, 29n35; catalog, 30; transcription of Pitman shorthand initiative, 29–30
"History of Joseph Smith" (also "Life of Joseph Smith," 1842–1858, also represented as 1838/39 history). *See* Roberts, Brigham Henry (B. H.), *History of the Church of Jesus Christ of Latter-day Saints*
History of the Church of Jesus Christ of Latter-day Saints (1902–1912). *See* Roberts, Brigham Henry (B. H.), *History of the Church of Jesus Christ of Latter-day Saints*
History of the Saints (Bennett), 125, 206
Hofmann, Mark, 11, 63–64
Homer, Michael W., 97, 200, 200n35
Howard, Richard P., 214–15
Howe, Daniel Walker, 99, 368
Howe, E. D., 58, 299
Hudson, Wayne, 94n21, 368
Hurlbut, Philastus, 107, 310
Hume, David, 43
Hunt, Dave (critic of priesthood restoration), 170
Huntington, Oliver B., 217, 218n85
Hyde, Orson, 182: call to Twelve Apostles, 247; described Twelve Apostles receiving JS's "Last Charge," 209–10

I

Improvement Era (1897–1970, periodical), 149
Independence, Missouri (Zion), 20, 155, 233–34
Information age, 9, 22, 40–41, 44, 48–49, 52, 79
Interesting Account of Several Remarkable Visions (O. Pratt), 145, 181
Irving, Gordon I.: law of adoption, 325–26; on Mormon view of Bible, 337

J

Jackson, Joseph H., on JS, 58–59
James, William, on faith, 43
Jensen, Marlin K., 10n18
Jensen, Robin Scott, 19n10; on JS initiative on religious education of Saints, 342–43; on JS's clerks, 71

Jenson, Andrew, on JS, 303
Jessee, Dean C., 6n9; 8, 19, 19n10, 21, 26, 52, 76–77, 140n17, 148, 149, 196; appraisal of JS's personality, 271–72; influence of clerk/historians on JS's history, 296; on B. H. Roberts's influence on *History of the Church*, 77–78; scholarship about JS, 272
Jesus Christ, 2, 307; appearance in JS's First Vision, 142–47; appearance in Kirtland House of the Lord, 279–80; as redeemer, 181, 229; endowment by, 24, 204, 248; in the Book of Mormon, 169; "in the name of," 124, 188–89, 190, 213, 228, 230; JS on, 324–25, 376; revelations to JS, 2, 5, 90, 104, 142, 154, 161, 203–4, 230, 249, 261, 361; psychoanalyzed, 60–61; Second Coming of, 2, 164, 169, 223, 230, 233, 248, 249, 348, 365; "tell no one" per his miracles, 281; voice of, in lesser priesthood restoration, 169
Johnson, Elsa, healing, 156
Johnson, Jeffery O., 17, 140n17
Johnson, John (Hiram, Ohio), 159
Johnson, Luke, call to Twelve Apostles, 247
Johnson, Lyman, 119, 158; call to Twelve Apostles, 247
John the Baptist: as fulfillment of Rev. 14:6–7, 185–87; primacy of his priesthood, 177–90; JS on, 182n61
Jorgensen, Lynn Watkins, refuting claims against Brigham Young's "transfiguration," 81
Joseph Smith and the Beginnings of Mormonism (Bushman), 20
Joseph Smith Collection, History Department (LDS), 17–18, 18n3
Joseph Smith Institute for Latter-day Saint History (BYU), 21, 26
Joseph Smith Papers (2008–), 3, 21, 26, 30, 31, 46, 139, 343, 386; Council of Fifty minutes, 28–29; editors of, 136–37, 138, 140n16, 150, 167, 312; Minute books 1 and 2 (Kirtland Council and Far West Record), 245, 256; website, 22
Joseph Smith: Rough Stone Rolling (Bushman), 20, 136
Joseph Smith, the First Mormon (Hill), 136n5, 146
Journal of Mormon History, 24

K

Kidder, Daniel P., critic of JS, 111–12
Kimball, Heber C., 277–78; call to Twelve Apostles, 247; on cave in Hill Cumorah, 57–58; on Masonry, 199, 200;
Kinderhook plates, JS on, 41
Kirtland apostasy, 155
Kirtland High Council, 239–40, 241–42, 243, 250, 254; duties of, in D&C 102, 240, 243; "Presidents Council," 240
Kirtland House of the Lord (temple), 155, 180, 239, 253, 255, 261, 360; dedication of, 255–56, 351; endowment, 204–5; JS and Oliver Cowdery's vision in, 279–80, 376; washing feet in, 256
Kirtland, Ohio, 155; printing office, 155

L

Latter Day Saints Messenger and Advocate (1834–1837, periodical), 71, 71n13, 157, 168–69
Latter Day Saints' Millennial Star (1840–1970, periodical), 7, 126; "History of Joseph Smith" in, 77
Law, William, 120; on JS, 122–23
Law, Wilson, 120
"Lectures on Faith" (Rigdon), 285–86
Literary Firm, 154
Luther, Martin, 88, 146, 238n56, 275

M

Madsen, Truman, on JS, 36–37
Maffly-Kipp, Laurie, 295
Marks, David, on early Mormonism, 159
Marquardt, H. Michael, 74n26, 148n52, 188n84
Marsden, George A., on Jonathan Edwards, 37
Marsh, Thomas, 158; call to Twelve Apostles, 247
Martin, Edward, 124
Marty, Martin E., 293; on religion in the early American republic, 106
Matthews, Robert ("Joshua the Jewish minister"), 148

McLellin, William E.: call to Twelve Apostles, 247; criticized priesthood restoration, 170–71, 170n27
McCullough, David, on writing biography, 52–53; 272–73
McDaniel, John, 310
McKay, David O., 23
Media, on JS, 133–35, 134n2, 146
Melchizedek (greater/higher) priesthood, 139, 177, 180–81, 207, 231
Memory as history, 65–83
Methodists, 225–27, 365–66; appeal of to JS, 226
Miller, George, on JS, 125–26
Miller, Reuben, on Oliver Cowdery's testimony on priesthood restoration, 173–74, 214
Millet, Robert L., 22, 382
Missouri (Zion) High Council, 242–43, 250
Mormon historiography, rise of, 23–24
Mormon Parallels (Grunder), 93–94, 103, 103n50
Mormonism Unvailed (Howe), 107, 118, 378
Mormon History Association (1965), 24; conferences, 24–25
Mormon underground, 24
Moroni, 192, 274; appearance to JS, 180, 281; as fulfillment of Rev. 14:6–7, 186–87, 187n79; Moroni/Nephi as Book of Mormon messenger, 72
Moses, 177, 192, 349; appearance in Kirtland House of the Lord, 279–80
Mountain Meadows Massacre, 28
Mulholland, James, JS's clerk/historian, 71–75, 78

N

Nagle, Paul C., on writing biography, 47
Nauvoo Expositor (1844, periodical), 120–21, 128–29
Nauvoo Legion, 129
Nauvoo House, 356–57
Nauvoo, Illinois, 6, 264–66
Nauvoo Relief Society. *See* Female Relief Society of Nauvoo
Nauvoo Temple, 197–98, 203–4, 355, 356, 358, 359–60; ceremonies (including endowment), 121, 199, 201, 204; importance of, 203
Needham, John, on JS, 126
New Mormon history, 23–24
New Witness for Christ in America (Kirkham), 10
Nibley, Hugh, 147, 276, 277
No Man Knows My History: The Life of Joseph Smith (Brodie), 10, 22–23; 23n18, 91, 147, 274, 363; critiques of, 22n17

O

Owens, Lance, 37

P

Packer, Boyd K., on JS, 227
Page, Hiram, 168, 170n27
Palmer, Ambrose, on effect of Ezra Booth, 157–58
Papers of Joseph Smith (Jessee), 19, 26, 40
Parrish, Warren, 148, 281
Partridge, Edward, 118, 119; as first bishop, 237, 238, 239
Patten, David W.: call to Twelve Apostles, 247; on priesthood restoration, 186;
Pearl of Great Price (Mormon scripture), 136, 363
Perkins, Wesley, on effect of Ezra Booth, 158
Personal Writings of Joseph Smith (Jessee), 19
Peter, James, and John's priesthood (Melchizedek), 177, 180–84, 191, 207, 211, 213–15, 230
Peterson, Lamar, on 1832 history, 147
Peterson, Ziba, 192
Phelps, W. W., 40, 149, 165, 311–12; as historian/ghostwriter for JS, 75–76, 78; as church printer, 154, 155–56; as editor of *Evening and the Morning Star*, 284; in presidency in Missouri (Zion), 243; on priesthood restoration, 179; probable clerk/historian who wrote "Church History" (Wentworth letter), 74
Phrenology, JS and, 127
Pierce, Robert, 125
Polemics in study of JS and Mormonism, 6, 24, 25, 34–37, 38, 47–48, 58–59,

62–63, 83, 105, 144, 146, 170, 274, 295, 297, 375, 380, 386
Polygamy, JS's, 318–19; angel with sword threatening JS, 81, 81n57; and Female Relief Society, 202, 204, JS on, 318–21
Post, Stephen, on JS, 122, 180
Poulson, M. Wilford, 23, 147
Pratt, Orson: on authority of Twelve Apostles vs. John the Baptist, 211–12; call to Twelve Apostles, 247; first elders' president, 237; first to publish JS's First Vision, 276; on JS's clerks, 72–73; missionary preachment of, 165, 165n17; view on Rev. 14:6–7, 187
Pratt, Parley P., 154, 245, 290; call to Twelve Apostles, 247; on priesthood restoration, 179, 183
Presentism (opposite of historical sense), 53–56.
Priesthood (authority), 166, 167, 192, 231, 250; early members' lack of understanding of, 183–85; gifts of the spirits vs. priesthood authority, 187–89; greater/higher priesthood (Melchizedek), 139, 177, 180–81, 207, 231; lesser priesthood (Aaronic), 177; lineal right of Smith family to, 220–22; primacy of lesser priesthood (Aaronic), 177–83, 182n60, 185; stratified offices, 233; transition from primacy of lesser to greater/higher, 206–13, 222
Priesthood offices and quorums, function of, 160; bishops, 237, 238, 239; deacons, 229, 230, 231, 254, 256; elders', 229, 230, 231, 237, 254, 256, 257–58; high priests, 231, 232, 239, 254, 256; priests, 229, 230, 231, 254, 256; teachers, 229, 230, 231, 254, 256–57, 258
Priesthood restoration, 137, 139, 145–46, 166, 274; Addison Everett's claims about, 215–20; Rev. 14:6–7 and, 165, 185–87, 187n78; dispute of claims concerning, 169–72; greater/higher (Melchizedek), 177, 212–14; lesser (Aaronic), 71, 167; JS's witness to, 171–72, 176; Oliver Cowdery's witness to, 169, 169n25, 172–77; voice authorization, 213, 214
Proclamation of the Twelve Apostles (P. Pratt), 191, 210
Prophets, seer, and revelator, 364–84
Protestant Reformation, 162, 164, 165
Psychohistory (psychobiography), 60–62

Q

Quincy, Josiah, on JS, 38, 115–17
Quinn, D. Michael, 148n52, 251n123, 252n128; on folk religion and magic world view, 97–98

R

Ravenna, Ohio, 157, 158
Red Brick Store, JS's, 204
Reformed (Calvinist) theology, 88, 223, 354
Relief Society. *See* Female Relief Society of Nauvoo
Religion in early American republic, 87–90, 94–100, 106, 223–25, 364–66
Remini, Robert V., on intentions of those who write about JS, 63, 145
Reorganized Church of Jesus Christ of Latter Day Saints (RLDS). *See* Community of Christ (2000)
"Restoration of the Melchisedec Priesthood" (J. F. Smith), 166, 192
Reynolds, John, on JS, 38
Reynolds, Thomas, 125
Richards, Willard, as JS's clerk/historian, 76, 196, 303, 359; influence upon JS's history, 76–77, 78
Rigdon, Sidney, 6, 7, 111, 118, 119, 158, 159, 164, 376; claims of leadership, 150–51; in First Presidency, 237, 251, "Lectures on Faith," 285–86
Riley, I. Woodbridge, and the psychobiography of JS, 61
Rhodes, Richard, on presentism, 54–55
Roberts, Brigham Henry (B. H.), *History of the Church of Jesus Christ of Latter-day Saints* (1902–1912), 6–9, 6n9, 7n10, 8n13, 27n28, 44–47, 62, 67, 69–79, 136, 147, 235, 298; on faulty recollections, 80; JS's influence on creation of, 6, 8, 69, 77–78. *See also* Joseph Smith, 1838/39 history
Robinson, George, 6

Russell, Isaac, 122–23
Ryder, Symonds, 159

S

Saints: The Story of the Church of Jesus Christ of Latter-day Saints (LDS), 30
Salvation for the dead, 196
Savary, Richard, 314
Schweitzer, Albert, on psychobiography of Jesus, 60–61
Searle, Howard C., on clerks/historians' influence on JS's history, 78, 79; on Willard Richards's writing JS's history, 76
Second Coming (Jesus's). *See* Jesus Christ
Second Great Awakening, 87–89, 99, 106, 364
Selected Collections from the Archives of the Church of Jesus Christ of Latter-day Saints (Turley), 26–27
Sesquicentennial history (LDS), 20, 20n11
Seventy, 206, 248–48, 250, 254–55; early equation with apostleship, 249; missionary portfolio, 249; quorums, 249
Shaw, George Bernard, on discerning viewpoints of documentation, 58
Shipps, Jan, the "Prophet Puzzle," 13, 51–52
Signature Books, JS's journals, 25
Skinner, Dolphus, critic of JS, 110
Smith, Bathsheba Wilson, on JS and baptism for the dead, 360–61
Smith, Emma Hale, 40, 138, 149; characterized JS, 303; first hymnal, 179; received Nauvoo endowment, 205
Smith family, speculation of biological disease in, 61
Smith, George A., 33, 159, 306; memory as history, 65; on JS's history, 77, 78; on Oliver Cowdery's witness of priesthood restoration, 172–74; on sources for JS's salvation of the dead, 354, 356
Smith, Hyrum, 277; Assistant President to JS, 252; attendance at Moor's Charity School, 4; church patriarch, blessings, 201; death of, 6; Mason, 198
Smith, John (JS's uncle), Assistant President to JS, 252
Smith Jr., Joseph: and Bible (KJV), 4n7, 332–33, 338, 348, 351; appearance of biblical angels to, 282–83; appointment from Jesus Christ, 96, 273; as apostle, 192, 229, 245; as prophet, seer, and revelator, 368–84; birth, 4, 139, 298; blessing to Oliver Cowdery about priesthood restoration, 176; Bible revision by, 332–33; 350–51, 376, 377; boastful hyperbole of, 296–98; Book of Abraham production by, 41, 372; Book of Mormon translation by, 10, 277, 303; charged with attempt to assassinate Lilburn W. Boggs, 125, 206, 357; chose not to reveal his inner self, 271–86, 322, 364; "Church History" (Wentworth letter), 73–74, 73n21; Civil War prophecy, 1–3, 102; claims of biological/mental disease, 61, 283, 295–96; claim of having keys to the kingdom, 139, 151; compared to Mohammed, 107, 107n5; congeniality, 294; correspondence of, 152–53, 271–72, 355; could not reveal all he had been given, 12, 348; criticisms of JS's family, 108–9; cultural influences upon, 93–100, 103–4, 103n50; death of, 6, 201; descriptions (including criticisms) of, 32–33, 36–37, 38, 92, 94, 95, 108–29, 134n2, 146n42, 156–57, 160, 283, 294–97, 312; disposition to fight, 315–17; editor of *Elders' Journal* and *Times and Seasons*, 77, 284; encounter with Robert Matthews, 281; epistles, 207, 350, 354, 358, 383; family, 150; "first elder," 237; forgiver, 309–12; generosity of spirit, 309–312, 312–14; hesitation/inability to convey thoughts on paper, 271–72, 283–85; humanness of (including admissions of), 36, 41, 47, 118–21, 123, 124, 146n42, 156, 296–304, 309, 315–17, 378–79; in First Presidency, 150; influence on his history, 78; influence of print culture on, 152–60, 378; initiated Nauvoo endowment, 204; intellect, 303–4; judicious, 294; Kinderhook plates, 41; lack of pretention, 294; "line upon line" method of revelation, 349–61; loyalty, valued by, 311; memory as history, 66–67; mission to Washing-

ton, D.C., 38, 114–15, 353; on agency of man, 326–28; on biblical inerrancy and literalness, 336–39; on Christian virtues, 341–42; on doctrine, 340; on his role as prophet, 350, 367, 374–75; on Jesus Christ, 324–25, 331, 369, 373, 376; on man's premortal existence, 369–70; "On Priesthood" (1835), 183–85, 194, 206, 250, 261; "On Priesthood" (1840), 195; on priesthood organization, 227–61; on priesthood restoration, 167, 171–72, 176, 177, 178, 185–87; on "the Vision" (D&C 76), 339–40, 351, 376; opposition from within church, 305–7; organized Church of Christ, April 6, 1830, 5; persecution of, 5, 6, 150, 152–53, 273, 275, 304, 349, 358; personality, 12–13, 271–91, 293–94; photographs of, possible, 33–34, 34n5; polygamy, 81, 318–21; on polygamy, including denial of, 318–21, 320n91; 383; periphery of, teachings (lost ten tribes and resurrection of children), 344–46; portrayal of retributive God, 333–36; president of the high priesthood, 150, 237; and prophetic prerogative, 380–84; record keeping, 150; religious background, 4–5, 87, 139; religious freedom, 312–14; religious innovation, 90–91, 96, 100–101; reticence to reveal visions, 274–82; revelations, 154, 158, 159, 161, 230, 236, 237, 249, 333, 351, 354, 356, 361–62, 372; revision of the Bible, 150, 332–33; salvation of the dead (including baptism for the dead), 350–61, 383; and seerstones, 10, 108, 373; sermons, 67–68, 68n7, 271, 272, 273, 286–90, 353, 354, 359, as means of relating his revelations, 359; shot at, 152, 152n54; 159; sincerity, 295; spiritual nature of, 293, 322; succession to, 212; tar and feathered, 150, 159, 305; treasure seeking/money-digging/magic, 10, 23, 93, 97–98, 107–11, 370; "Trustee-in-Trust," 196; view of postmortal world, 339; views on relationship of God and man, 323–36; view of Satan/Devil, 329–31; vision, with Oliver Cowdery, in Kirtland House of the Lord (D&C 110), 279–80, 376; vision of "ancient order of things," 227, 234, 240, 241, 245; word of wisdom, 101–2, 349; Zion's Camp, 156. *See also* First Vision

Smith, Joseph, journals (1832–1844), 17, 25–26, 40, 52, 148, 149, 196; quantification of, 272

Smith, Joseph, 1832 history: 6, 23, 25, 67, 100, 133–60, 161, 298; contents of 1832 history, 136–39; 142–44; first publicized, 147; what may have influenced creation of, 149–60

Smith, Joseph, 1838/39 history, 6, 7, 67, 100, 109, 133, 136, 139, 144, 145, 146, 153, 160, 167, 192, 196, 235, 272, 279–80, 298

Smith, Joseph, "Church History" (Wentworth letter, 1842), 73–74, 73n21, 167, 196

Smith, Joseph F.: on the scarcity of evidence of JS's polygamy, 82; on JS, 316–17; on JS and resurrection of children, 346; on those advancing JS recollections, 79–80; reaction to Addison Everett's claims of priesthood restoration, 218–19; solicited testimonies of JS's plural wives, 82–83

Smith, Joseph Fielding, 147

Smith Sr., Joseph, 150, 281; Assistant President to JS, 252; church patriarch, 252–53; family, 4, 20, 88

Smith, Lucy Mack, 4, 151, 152, 280; biography of JS, 45, 45n35, 298–99; on JS's seeric abilities, 375

Smith, Sylvester, charges against JS, 241–42

Smith, William, call to Twelve Apostles, 247

Snow, Gardner, on healing in the name of Jesus Christ, 188–89

Sperry, Sidney B., on word of wisdom, 101n45

Stout, Allen J., on JS, 317

T

Taggart. George W., on JS, 126–27

Tanner, Jerald and Sandra, 25, 26, 55n14, 79n47

Taylor, Alan, on folk religion, 97–98

Taylor, John, explanation of JS's being commanded to practice polygamy, 82;

JS on, as general editor of *Times and Seasons*, 184n70, 284–85, 284n45, 328; on JS, 327; on difficulty of understanding JS's teaching on priesthood, 184–85; writing for JS, 328
Taylor, Leonora, patriarchal blessing, 201
Teachings of Presidents of the Church: Joseph Smith (LDS), 27
Teachings of the Prophet Joseph Smith (J. F. Smith, Jr.), 8n13
Ten Commandments (DeMille), model of a prophet, 349
Times and Seasons (1839–1846, periodical), 7, 71n13, 72, 196; dispute of church organization site, 73–74; "History of Joseph Smith" in, 77; John Taylor as managing editor of, 184–85, 284–85; JS as editor, 196.
Thompson, Robert B, JS clerk, 75, 78
Truth, Richard L. Evans on, 44
Turley, Richard E. Jr., 26–27; per Mountain Meadows Massacre, 28
Turner, Jonathan B., on JS and Mormons, 337
Twelve Apostles, Quorum of, 191–92, 195–96, 197, 206–13, 245–48, 250, 254; call of, 247–48; given keys of the kingdom by JS in March 1844, 207–10; missions to Great Britain, 355; Oliver Cowdery's "Charge" to, 248; supervised church business, 206
Tyler, Alice Felt, 99
Tyler, Samuel D., on healing in the name of Jesus Christ, 188–89

U

Underwood, Grant, 90n11, 337
United Firm, 154
Upper Missouri Advertiser (1832–183?, newspaper), 156
Urban, G. R., on credibility of the historical record, 56

V

Van Wagoner, Richard, on Mormon mythmaking, 79n47, 80–81
Vogel, Dan, 7n10, 7n12; criticized Oliver Cowdery, 168n23; on "History of Joseph Smith"/*History of the Church*, 77, 79; on JS, 319; on JS's influence on his history, 78, 97

W

Wards, in Nauvoo, 262–63; in Salt Lake City, 262
Wentworth letter. *See* Joseph Smith, "Church History"
Westminster Confession (Church of England), 224–25
White, Ellen G., writings, 283
Whitmer, David, 158; as apostle, 192; charged to "search out the twelve," 246; criticized priesthood restoration account, 171; president of church in Missouri, 243, 244
Whitmer, John, 154; as apostle, 246; history, 6; priesthood license, 192, 246; in church presidency in Missouri, 243
Whitmer, Peter, Sr., family, 159–60, 168
Whitlock, Harvey, 309–10
Whitney, Newel K., 203, bishop, 238, 239, 241
Whitney, Orson F., on JS, 362
Widtsoe, John A., on JS, 145n38, 362
Willers, Diedrich, 159
Williams, Frederick G., and 1832 history, 137, 160; in First Presidency, 237, 251; on JS's scriptural education initiative, 343
Wills, Gary, on presentism, 56
Wilson, Douglas L., on memory, 68
Winchester, Benjamin, on priesthood restoration, 186–87
Women, Mormon, 29, 29n34; and the priesthood, 200–204. *See also* Female Relief Society of Nauvoo
Wood, Gordon S., on America's founding fathers, 88; on cultural influence, 98, 99; on presentism, 55, 56; religious climate in America, 89
Woodruff, Wilford, JS healing in the name of Jesus Christ, 190; on JS's history, 77, 78
Word of wisdom. *See* Joseph Smith, word of wisdom; Brigham Young, on word of wisdom
Wright, N. T., on faith, 42

Y

Young, Brigham, 290; blamed Masons for JS's death, 200n35; call to Twelve Apostles, 247; dedicated Nauvoo Temple baptismal font, 357; on apostates, 306; on authority of the Twelve Apostles, 210–11; on cave in Hill Cumorah, 57–58; on JS, 36, 304; on JS's teaching about resurrection of children, 346; on JS's salvation for the dead, 360; reviewed JS's history, 77; statement about authority to organize church, 74; on word of wisdom, 101–2, 101n45

Young, Levi Edgar, 147

Young, Phinehas H., 174–75

Z

Zinsser, William: on biography, 44; on speculation in writing history, 59

Zion's Camp, 156, 241–42; "a blessing and endowment" for, veterans, 246–47